MORE SONGWRITERS ON SONGWRITING

MORE SONGWRITERS ON SONGWRITING

WITHDRAWN

PAUL ZOLLO

Da Capo Press

Designed by Jack Lenzo

Set in Berkeley Oldstyle by Perseus Books

Cataloging-in-Publication data for this book is available from the Library of Congress.
First Da Capo Press edition 2016
ISBN: 978-0-306-81799-1
ISBN: 978-0-306-82244-5 (e-book)

Published by Da Capo Press, an imprint of Perseus Books, LLC, a subsidiary of Hachette Book Group, Inc.
www.dacapopress.com

Da Capo Press books are available at special discounts for bulk purchases in the U.S. by corporations, institutions, and other organizations. For more information, please contact the Special Markets Department at Perseus Books, 2300 Chestnut Street, Suite 200, Philadelphia, PA 19103, or call (800) 810-4145, ext. 5000, or e-mail special.markets@perseusbooks.com.

10 9 8 7 6 5 4 3 2 1

Credits

The bulk of the interviews collected here were originally conducted for various magazine stories and in those stories were often edited down from the original conversation. Those conversations have been restored in full here. The following interviews were originally conducted for *Song-Talk* magazine, the journal of the National Academy of Songwriters: Gene Clark, John Stewart, John Sebastian, Paul Williams, Bryan Ferry, Daryl Hall, Michael Smith, Difford and Tilbrook, and Peter, Paul and Mary. Interviews originally conducted for *Performing Songwriter* magazine are Randy Newman, Aimee Mann, Rickie Lee Jones, Joan Armatrading, Brian Wilson, and Bernie Taupin. Interviews originally conducted for *American Songwriter* magazine are James Taylor, Richard Sherman, Leiber and Stoller, Dave Stewart, Loretta Lynn, Sheldon Harnick, John Prine, Elvis Costello, Rickie Lee Jones, Randy Newman, Patti Smith, Chrissie Hynde, Alice Cooper, Jorge Calderon, Brian Wilson, Paul Simon, Ringo Starr, Richard Thompson, Matisyahu, and Stephen Stills. The interviews with Jeff Barry and Joe Henry were conducted live on the web series *Songwriters on Songwriting Live* at the Songwriting School of Los Angeles. The interview with Sia was conducted for the program of the 2015 Grammy Awards. The interviews with Herbie Hancock, Rob Zombie, Donald Fagen, and Joe Jackson were conducted for this book. The interview with Marjorie Guthrie has never previously been published.

The following photos were taken by Paul Zollo: Aimee Mann, Alice Cooper, Brian Wilson, Darryl Hall, Dave Stewart, Herbie Hancock, James Taylor, Jeff Barry, Leiber & Stoller, Joe Henry, John Prine, Jorge Calderon, Kris Kristofferson, Matisyahu, Michael Smith, Patti Smith, Paul Simon, Paul Williams, Randy Newman, Richard Thompson, Richard Sherman, Rickie Lee Jones, Ringo Starr, Rob Zombie, Sia, and Stephen Stills. They are used by permission of Paul Zollo Photography, Los Angeles.

The following photos were taken by the great Henry Diltz: Donald Fagen, Gene Clark, John Sebastian, John Stewart, Joan Armatrading, and

"All songwriters are links in a chain."

—Pete Seeger

"The writing of a song is a triumph of the human spirit."

—Van Dyke Parks

Dedicated to my father, Burt Zollo,
to my son, Joshua Zollo,
and to all songwriters everywhere.

Table of Contents

Acknowledgments

Special thanks go to Ben Schafer and Da Capo Press, who not only have kept the first volume of this journey alive, *Songwriters on Songwriting*, but they also turned it into a textbook for colleges that teach songwriting. Without them, this second volume would never have been conceived or executed, and my gratitude for this privilege is boundless. Thank you for your patience, faith, and support always.

Also great thanks extended forever to my father, Burt Zollo, for teaching me about the beauty of words, of books, and of song. And heartfelt forever thanks to Pete Seeger for your wisdom and ongoing inspiration. To Else Blangsted for your love, good advice, humor, and talking to your boys in heaven for me over these years. To Van Dyke Parks for your introductions to greatness and ongoing brilliance. To my son, Joshua Zollo, for being my beamish boy forever, I love you, and to my wife, Leslie, for your faith in me. Thanks to my mom, Lois Zollo, for being the best mom ever. To my sister Peggy Miller and brother Peter Zollo for your love. To my many dear friends for your love and energy through these long days and for understanding me and caring about that understanding, especially Tomas Ulrich, Michael Hughes, Earl Grey, Jeff Gold and Holly Gold, Sandy Ross and Lee Hirsch, Amy Linton, Paula McMath, Jilly Freeman, Michelle Williams, Tom Bowden, Michael Wisniewski, Susan Downs, Henry Diltz, Neil Rosengarden, Andy Kurtzman and Anne Kurtzman, Lisa Dubell, Smokey Miles, Andy Kenyon, Lisa Johnson, Sarah Kramer, Dan Kirkpatrick, Scott Docherty, Deborah Presley Brando, Katie Presley, Edoardo Tancredi, and Billy Salisbury. To Kathy West for your great transcribing, without which this volume would never be complete. To my agent, Anthony Mattero, for believing in me. To my brother in song Darryl Purpose for writing so many beautiful songs with me and for your generosity. To *American Songwriter* magazine for employing me for so long and for honoring the art of songwriting every day. To Rob Seals and the Songwriting School of Los Angeles for building a temple to song and for giving me a beautiful place within it, a home for our web series *Songwriters on Songwriting Live,* with so much love and joy. To Steve Goodman for my first songwriting lesson. To Paul Simon and Bob Dylan for teaching me how to write songs. To Artie Garfunkel for your beautiful harmony, in song and in life. To Rickie Lee Jones for your timeless spirit. To Zippy for everything.

And to the memory of two gentle dear friends and beautiful songwriters, D. Whitney Quinn and P. F. Sloan, for your lives in song. I wish I had more time with both of you.

And to all songwriters everywhere for writing songs. Don't ever stop.

Introduction

"It really is a living spirit being born."

—Rickie Lee Jones

"It's living art, captured for all time."

—P. F. Sloan

My first memory is of a song. A song spinning in infinity. A bright red 45 single of a song about farm animals, replete with their individual sounds. Pretty delightful stuff. Over and over—I couldn't get enough of it.

Skip ahead a few years to another single spinning, another eternal 45. I'm in a little room at the very far end of a vast old apartment on Aldine Avenue in Chicago, the home of my Aunt Shirley and Uncle Miles. Dusty sunlight streamed in from the window above almost horizontally, the sun making its early winter descent. I was on the floor with a little electric record player, an ancient small boxy machine that played no LPs, only 45s. In its middle was a black cylinder on which records neatly slid. One side, one song. It was pure and right, and it was the center of my universe, 1966.

I was seven. Up on the bookshelf over the bed was the book *Frankenstein*, tucked in between other nonthreatening titles. But my proximity to it was mildly terrifying. Trying not to look in that direction, I directed my attention instead to what mattered most. The *song*.

Music trumped everything, even being all alone in a giant apartment with volumes about monsters just overhead. I had one record and one only, but it was enough: Simon & Garfunkel, "Homeward Bound." (On the B-side was "Leaves That Are Green.")

It enthralled me. It was both human and electric, chords shifting from major to minor, simple drums spelling out the folk-rock groove, all

1

crested by two voices in harmony, singing words that to me were the essence of beauty. It was a bit beyond my grasp, this tale of playing music abroad and yearning for home—not only had I never been out of the country at this point, I had never even been away from my happy home in the kingdom of Illinois.

But the idea of the narrator being both a "poet and a one-man band" made perfect sense, as I knew—even then—that this same man writing the song was also making the music. And that promise, of a musician performing the thing he creates himself, and the boundless bounty of expression that spelled, shone to me like a bright star.

The song spoke to me, and spoke to some place deep in me, and expansive. Even the rhymes thrilled me. I always loved the beautiful completion rhymes bring to an idea, and the whole song started with, "Sitting in a railway station / Got a ticket for my destination." That made me happy. It still does. A couplet for the ages.

It was a true wonder to behold. This entire world, seamlessly fusing so many disparate components: melody, harmony, groove, finger-picked guitar, drums, rhymed verse, romance, and more! All of those delicious ingredients wed together into an organic whole, this swift passage of time. A universe in under 3 minutes (2:42 to be exact). And one I could freely enter and lose myself within. It was a genuine and timeless joy, and at my fingertips.

It was the most moving experience of my life to that point. Not only was I all alone to absorb this transformative musical elixir; I could control my intake, playing it over and over, injecting it directly into my heart and mind, as I still do to this day with songs.

I even toyed with vari-speed. The B-side of this single, "Leaves That Are Green," started with a honky-tonk piano, the sound of which, when sped up faster to 78 rpm instead of 45, sounded delightfully manic. But it was a controlled and musical mania, and it belonged to me. It was my secret passion, and I loved it. There was no inclination whatsoever to share this with any of the other humans. It was self-discovery in solitude, the dynamic that aligns perfectly with songwriting: this intimate and individual connection with the musical muse.

It launched my journey as a songwriter, setting me on the path I've been on ever since. There was no profession that to me seemed more thrilling or important, with the notable exception of astronaut, but not so much to walk on the moon—which seemed cold and lonely to me—but for the weightlessness. The idea of flying appealed to me, as it does to most earthbound creatures. But I decided I could fly farther and for a full lifetime by writing songs.

I wrote my first one the summer that man landed on the moon, 1969. I was ten. Prior to then I'd been writing abstract, free-verse poems—mostly nonsensical—just playing with words, really. Then I wrote my own lyrics for Simon's "The Sound of Silence." Mine was called "The Look of Absence." (Which I told him about years later. He smiled and said, "Hey, that sounds like one of mine." Indeed. Evidently, the idea of masking my influences had yet to occur to me.) Yet it was a great education for me: although my lyrics made little sense, I was learning the first stages of songwriting: merging words and music. Making them fit. All the rhymes were in the right place, the phrasing was right, and even syllabic stress—something some modern songwriters neglect—was perfect.

And it's there that songs live, in this delicate yet dynamic union of disparate elements. Music—abstract and emotional—and language—intellectual and specific. It's the "crucial balance," as Simon put it, at the heart of songwriting, the marriage of words and music. It is the one constant through all these interviews, all the styles, years, generations. All united in the same mission, ultimately: combining words and music.

My first true song, words and music, was written on my beloved acoustic Silvertone guitar and called "Time Changes the Scene." Even then, at ten, my main theme was how quickly time passes. I was feeling nostalgic for the good old days, I guess, back when I was seven.

But even then I recognized with awe the unique power of song and the way ideas expressed in song, underscored and actualized by music, were received in a way far more powerful than mere words.

I also received with awe this understanding that while being carried down the river of life, with time and everyday chaos infiltrating every moment, one could create something immaculately conceived and ordered. Something that would exist outside of time and be durable so as to never "fall apart on the street like a cheap watch," to quote Van Dyke Parks.

That was the goal. Not to create good songs. But great ones. As Patti Smith explains in her interview in this volume, the whole difference between poetry and songwriting to her was that a songwriter writes a song not for an elite group of song enthusiasts but for the world. The entire *world*! That's a big target audience. And designed to work not just for now or next season but for the ages. To write a song people want to hear and to play and to sing across generations. It's a lofty goal, to put it lightly, and it says a lot about songwriters—all songwriters—that one would even attempt something so bold. It takes a certain kind of *chutzpah*—Yiddish for crazy courage. That is where songwriters live, after all, on the edge of courage and crazy. It's creative chutzpah, the audacity of making art.

I started writing songs, as do almost all songwriters, not unlike somebody who has never driven before getting behind the wheel. I really had no clue about any of it—the words or the music—so I did it blindly, with love and faith guiding. Though my inaugural song began in G, it ended in E—a whole other key. Ending a melody where it begins—the return to tonic, as it's known—is a fundamental concept, common to most of the music we hear, regardless of genre or generation. But this is how all songwriters learn to write songs. This is the journey of discovery, and though all of our journeys are distinct, they are connected.

I learned by studying and learning to play—as I still do to this day—songs I loved. To get inside their architecture, to learn the components that add up to that effect.

Because there's a whole lot to learn when learning to write songs. It's why almost all the great songwriters interviewed here and in the first volume admitted to years spent writing bad songs before they wrote good ones. (With the exceptional exceptions of Laura Nyro, Janis Ian, and John Prine, all of whom, remarkably, began with masterpieces.) It's because writing a song, any song, is not unlike painting a cubist painting. Songs encompass many elements at once, and it's in the seamless fusion of those elements that greatness is achieved. But in each of these pursuits—the creation of music and lyrics—is a whole world to discover. Music is a universe unto itself, with melody, rhythm, and harmony. Lyrics, as well, encompass a complex realm of considerations, combining language both poetic and colloquial, weaving together metaphor, symbology, storytelling, and more in rhymed verses. Add to those aspects the mastery of song structure itself—the precise architecture of verse, chorus, bridge and other song forms—into which the words and the music take their place.

And despite the impact of songwriters such as Dylan and Lennon and McCartney, who forever expanded the potential of the popular song, the song form itself was never exploded and replaced. Dylan, The Beatles, Simon, and the rest showed great respect for the song—and within its narrow confines created miracles. And it is in that accomplishment—creating something eternal and unlimited within a restricted form—that the full and true phenomenon of the song is realized. That, as Krishnamurti said, "limitations create possibility." That within this tiny room, this narrow space, this fast passage of time, a songwriter can create something boundless.

Once I started writing songs, I never stopped. To this day nothing is as compelling, exciting, or fulfilling.

I played my dad my songs always. He was a writer himself, the author of three books, and was a tough critic. But a consistent one. His chief word was "trite." Meaning he'd heard it before. Meaning *everyone* had heard it before. It had been done. So my mission became to write *anything* he didn't find trite. To discover new content in songs and new ways of transmitting it. Ultimately I did get there.

I also played one of my songs for my junior high music teacher, Camille Bertagnolli, a sparkling piano-playing teacher with an infectious passion for music and teaching. She led the Glee Club, as it was known, a choir of boys and girls singing songs in simple harmony.

I wasn't really sure, however, if she'd have any interest in hearing a song I wrote. After all, the songs she taught our class were famous ones by legendary songwriters such as the Gershwins or modern standards like "Fire and Rain," written by James Taylor. All songs that astonished me for their beauty.

But she did want to hear my song. She asked me to play it then and there in her big musical office, and she listened intently, as if it mattered. Because it did matter, as she taught me. She let me know in no uncertain terms that writing songs *mattered*. Her words changed my life. I was already committed to this thing. But because of her, I became reverent in my devotion. "For the rest of your life," she said, "you will always be rich. Because you have music in you."

The song I played her was called "Picnic Island." She loved it. Though the words added up to some sort of sense, the music was well conceived, a mostly major-key verse set against a minor-key chorus. Not only did she praise its structure, she immediately did what I always do now: she figured out what the chords were. She even informed me that a chord I was playing in a funny position and didn't recognize was simply C major. (She was right.) That night she notated the song, wrote out the music and lyrics, so she could teach it to the class.

This was an honor for which I was unprepared. The whole class—all those voices—were going to all sing my song? And at the same time? It seemed like an impossible dream. But the very next day of class she passed out the dittoed pages with my song in purple ink and my name on it as the writer—right where names like James Taylor and Gershwin had been—and announced, "This is *very* special. One of our own students, Paul Zollo, has written a song, and we are going to learn it."

It was the first time in my life I had felt tears of joy. I didn't shed any, as I recall, but I was so moved by the emotion of hearing my song elevated to this great place that I welled up with a feeling I'd never known before that. It was an honor and a thrill unparalleled in my life up to then. I remember the sound of hearing my song sung by our entire choir. It was stunning. This little creation, born on my humble guitar strings, now sung—with spirit—by the whole bunch. Sure, she changed the groove somewhat so it had more of a musical theater bounce than I intended. But I could live with that. The song was in the world now, and what happened was out of my control. I felt what can best be termed as parental pride.

As if she hadn't done enough to transform my life forever, Mrs. Bertagnolli included this song in our holiday concert. My song. Both my parents—even my father, who was never around during the workday—was there. He even taped it on a cassette, a tape I still have and cherish. It was momentous. I knew then that there could not possibly be anything in life more fulfilling than being a songwriter. And I've never really wavered from that idea.

I also had a great guitar teacher named Judd Sager who was seventeen when we started, which to eleven-year-old me seemed very grown up. He had long and hip hair and a mustache, could play guitar and sing beautifully, and was one of the coolest people I had ever met up to that point, like if some cool fusion of George Harrison and David Crosby walked into my home. At first he taught both my brother Peter and myself, but my brother had other talents, and music became my province alone.

Like Mrs. Bertagnolli, Judd was excited that I wrote my own songs and was using guitar—almost from the moment I started playing—as a songwriting tool. Knowing well that a songwriter's vocabulary consists of the chords he knows that support melodies—and being inspired and excited by brilliant chordal usage by our mutual heroes that the time, such as Lennon and McCartney especially and George Harrison and Paul Simon—he taught me new chords every week.

These were golden for me, each one. I was so hungry and happy to get new information on this, already clearly my life mission, each was received like a gift, knowing each added new synapses in my musical brain that would forever expand my understanding of music. But he did more than teach me new chords; he insisted I write a new song every week using these chords. Which was a brilliant exercise that enriched me both as a guitarist and songwriter. When a chord was in my own song, I found, I learned how to play it! Even the hard ones, like F major, which, as every guitarist knows, is the first really tough chord to play. So my guitar chops quickly expanded. But so did my harmonic vocabulary, the tool bag from which I compose my songs.

I grew up in the beautiful Chicago suburb of Wilmette, just north of the city. At that time Chicago was home to a great and thriving folk music scene with wonderful clubs like the Earl of Old Town that featured local legends Steve Goodman, Bob Gibson, John Prine (see page 434), Michael Smith (see page 462), and others. It also had the great *Midnight Special* radio show on our classical station, WFMT, which, on Saturday nights only, swapped Mozart, Beethoven, and the rest for our heroes Pete and Woody and those heroes coming in their wake. That show, which remains the Chicago equivalent of Carnegie Hall for singer-songwriters, is still on the air.

It was the weekly open mic nights at Steve Goodman's own club, Somebody Else's Troubles on Lincoln Avenue, or the Spot by Northwestern University that I learned how to perform. (It was also at the Spot where I learned to handle hecklers, who were frequent there, drunk on beer and youth, wanting to tangle. I loved it, as I do to this day.)

I took advantage of the generous spirit of many of these artists by asking them to listen to my songs. Armed only with my guitar and that aforementioned chutzpah, I would make my way backstage after shows with hopeful determination. They were a sweet and gentle bunch, and not once did they turn me down.

Steve Goodman was unique among great songwriters in that he could write a brilliant song, such as "City of New Orleans," which became a hit for Arlo Guthrie, but would also sing and record classics by other great songwriters. It was Steve who introduced John Prine to the world, as he did Michael Smith. Songs by both Prine and Smith represented to me the greatest a songwriter could achieve, the distant star toward which I aspired.

Steve gave me my first songwriting lesson. And to this day the most important one. It was after one of his greatly spirited shows. In a dressing room with lights and mirrors surrounding, I asked if he'd listen to my new song. He smiled, said sure, and handed me his big black acoustic guitar.

I was fourteen then. My song was "Troubled Winter," which had a plaintive, pretty melody highly influenced, admittedly, by the chords of "Sisters of Mercy" by Leonard Cohen. It had a true tonal center too, starting and ending in D major.

He listened carefully, gentle smile in his eyes. When I was done, he waited a beat and said, "Yeah, you know that was good. That was *good*. But I could have written that entire song in *two lines*."

Brutal criticism! And not what I had expected, having previously received almost unanimous praise for my efforts. But, I recognized, now I was in the major leagues. I wanted to play with the pros, after all, and this was a healthy and warranted dose of reality. It was a little painful initially, but ultimately greatly appreciated. Because I knew he was right: the song did amount to perhaps two lines of actual content, and no more. And rather than be crushed by this criticism, I took it as a challenge. I decided to write songs that made sense. To write something like a Steve Goodman song. Or a John Prine or Michael Smith song. A true story song. With lyrics poetic and musical but that told a story someone could understand. That was the goal anyway. I didn't always reach it. But I aimed high.

My next song was called "Shades of Color" and was inspired by a newspaper story I saw in the *Chicago Sun-Times* about convicts who painted. This was the story of one such artist, who used art to escape.

This songwriting journey is one every songwriter takes and plays out against the soundtrack of the time one is in. Mine was a time of momentous, meaningful songwriting. In only a handful of years The Beatles progressed from "She Loves You" to "Strawberry Fields" and beyond. I was hyperaware of this evolution, which was intoxicating and electric to me. Nothing seemed more vital or meaningful. Dylan, Simon, The Beatles, and the others—they expanded the popular song. Without sacrificing anything that made songs great, they showed, as Robbie Robertson said, that anything goes. That a song could contain any topic, and the only limit was the songwriter's imagination. It was a brave new world. Then came other geniuses like Randy Newman and Tom Waits into my life, who showed me other parts of town I'd never even considered and where I soon wanted to live. Also there was James Taylor, Joni Mitchell, Laura Nyro, Carole King, Stephen Stills—all doing glorious work but in different ways, and each valid and beautiful.

And as modern standards emerged, enlivened and expanded by this evolution, the world was changed.

I never took any of it lightly. Each new miracle song that arrived in my world was momentous to the extent of changing everything. I remember countless examples, but the most stunning was 1970. I was still in my first year of writing songs. After my dad picked me up from weekly Sunday School at Temple Sholom in the city, we went out for lunch in what was then called Old Town, a hip part of town along Wells Street with great cafés and cool poster and record shops. It was the counterculture realized, the world I was experiencing through song though rarely seeing firsthand, living as I did in a mostly wealthy, white suburb.

After lunch we went to one of these shops. The weather was cold, gray, and biting outside in typical Chicago fashion, making these interiors ever more glowing.

It was there I heard it as soon as we walked in: "Bridge Over Troubled Water." The new single by Simon & Garfunkel. Released prior to the album of the same name.

I nearly swooned. I knew who was singing it. I knew it was our friend Artie. That golden voice so friendly and dear to me, even then, like a brother singing to me. But this was something new, something different. It was something so sweeping, so majestic and triumphant—and yet so warmly amiable, a song of true friendship—that it was utterly enthralling. My dad sweetly purchased the 45 for me, probably knowing there was no way he could pry me out of this store if he didn't.

I brought it home, went directly to my room to play it, and essentially lived inside that song for months. On the flip side was "Keep the Customer Satisfied," which I also loved. But "Bridge"—I couldn't get enough of it. How anyone could write something so beautiful? It was something I really couldn't fathom. But I sure thought about it. How exactly did Paul Simon sit down with only a guitar and a pad of paper—same tools that I have—and come away with "Bridge Over Troubled Water"? He looked like a normal human, after all. Like a member of my own family, in fact, which is how I always thought of him, to this day. But no one I ever knew could do *that*.

It's that hunger for understanding, that passion for these musical concoctions, that led me to these questions and these volumes. At that time these heroes of mine were often interviewed in the press but rarely queried about songwriting and hardly ever about music itself. Yet internally I was compiling my own personal lexicon of questions I'd like to ask Paul Simon—or James Taylor, Carole King, Laura Nyro, Randy Newman—or any of those songwriters I revered. How did they do it? Does it seem as miraculous to you as it does to us, your listeners? And how about *this* song, and this one? How did you write *those*? And does the process seem as magical to you as it does to me?

I knew then of the connection between all songwriters and proudly included myself in this club. As the late great Pete Seeger said in the first interview in the first volume, "All songwriters are links in a chain." It's that wisdom that guides this journey and repeats like a refrain through all these pages: the understanding that all songwriters—regardless of genre or generation—are united by this singular pursuit of combining words and music to make songs. No songwriter learns how to write songs—or even acquires the inclination to do so—in a vacuum. Inspired and enervated by the songs of others, songwriters begin by using these templates of songs known and loved and then expanding from there. We imitate and we emulate that which we love until we discover, ideally, our own voice and our own song. Even Dylan started by imitating Woody Guthrie. (And he wasn't even the best Woody imitator, according to Woody's wife, Marjorie, in our opening chapter.)

I also wanted to ask about a phenomenon I experienced from the start and knew wasn't particular only to me. Which was when lines for songs, both musical and lyrical, would simply arrive, like a gift. A line that does everything and more that you need. Where did that come from? They always seemed to come from beyond, as if I was tapping into some timeless and mystic source. And it still feels like that.

Because in that experience exists the essence of songwriting. It is a conscious act to reach beyond the conscious mind, to discover and invent things outside of our usual reach. That is both the challenge and beauty of the thing. Every single songwriter I spoke to had some experience of it, although they perceived it individually. The especially intellectual ones, with no faith in anything spiritual, attribute these experiences to the artist connecting with his own unconscious. Sure, it *feels* as if it comes from beyond, they say. Because it is beyond your conscious mind, from your own subconscious.

The others—the spiritual ones—scoff at the others' inability to grasp the truth—and understand songwriters tap into a source that is beyond them but connects all. Rickie Lee Jones, who embodies the faith and openness of the spiritual ones, laughed and said, "Where *else* would it come from?"

Soon after "Bridge" came another song that, to me, also resounded like a miracle: "Let It Be," the single by The Beatles, written by Paul McCartney. Again, exalted consciousness. It seemed nothing could be more beautiful. Obsession—I listened to it nonstop. It was all I needed.

Other remarkable songs emerged, songs that stretched and redefined what songs can do. "Mr. Tambourine Man," written by Dylan but performed by The Byrds. "Fire and Rain" by James Taylor. "Suite: Judy Blue Eyes" by Stephen Stills. "American Pie" by Don McLean. "Hello in There" by John Prine. "Louisiana" and "Sail Away" by Randy Newman. Everything by Laura Nyro. And so many more.

These songs, if I listen to them today, still send me. They bring me back to when I first heard them—but forward too. Their power is undiminished by passing time. And therein lies the beauty and magic and power of the song: it is a forever renewable source. It is a vessel of grace and spirit, impervious to the wear and tear of the physical world.

This exalted song consciousness doesn't belong only to the distant past. To this day I am forever excited and even surprised by the extent to which great songs can still send me. So many times in recent days I have found myself walking down Hollywood Boulevard and confronting a song so utterly compelling, I need to stop and take it in. Whether it's something fairly new, such as "Chandelier" by Sia, a recent favorite, or something classic, I will be transported. There's one store that only plays Michael Jackson, and whether I go by and hear "Billie Jean" or "Man in the Mirror," I have to stop. Stop and feel the magic. Every time.

So when I got the lucky job in Hollywood, 1987, of becoming editor of *SongTalk*, which was the journal of the National Academy of Songwriters, my mission became to interview legendary songwriters—and ask them only about songwriting. Of course, it's a big subject and encompasses a lot of corollary issues. But the main focus was always on music and the creative process, which invariably led to good places. Music, after all, is the realm in which these people live and in which their genius flourishes. Yet rarely can they discuss the actual technicalities of music itself with the press, as most writers are not musicians.

But if I asked Brian Wilson, for example, about colors associated with musical keys in his mind, he opened up (insisting darkly, however, that every minor key is black). Or if I mentioned to Paul Simon, for example, the cunning of the subtle key change in the last verse of "Still Crazy After All These Years," his eyes lit up, and we connected in a whole new way. Or when I spoke to Dylan about the essential nature of the key of A minor in "One More Cup of Coffee," our conversation instantly deepened. ("Try it in *B minor*," he said. Why? "Because it might be a *hit* for you.")

This was the pattern always. As soon as I would let on that I was a fellow musician, the conversation would shift. Musicians simply speak differently to fellow musicians, and songwriters to fellow songwriters, than to civilians. It is a whole other language. Yet it's an abstract and vaporous thing to discuss, a genuine mystery even to those who have written music for decades. But it's where we live.

Because as songwriters know well—and was exemplified in Volume I—there are no easy answers about songwriting. Not one of these legendary songwriters divulged a secret or a trick that would make songwriting easy. Because it is not easy. When I first realized that Simon, for example, while writing songs for *Graceland* and subsequent albums, had jettisoned his old tried-and-true method of writing a song with voice and guitar and was, instead, writing songs to musical tracks, I thought it was an especially hard way to write songs.

He agreed. "Yes, it is hard," he said. "But *all* of songwriting is hard. There are no easy ways."

And, of course, he's right. There is no formula or no repeatable method for the writing of a great song. Because as Lennon said and all songwriters understand, any one of us could sit down and write a song right now. Given a title—even a key, a tempo—we can sit down and write a song. But a great one? A timeless one? That is the goal. And how you get to those ones—the songs that seem beyond, even beyond the songwriter who wrote them—that remains a mystery.

But part of being a songwriter is the passion to embrace this mystery. As Leonard Cohen said in Volume I, "Songwriting is much like the life of a Catholic nun. You're married to a mystery." That level of devotion resonates with songwriters because it's accurate. It's a daily pursuit of something unseen, even unknown, and you fling yourself directly into this unknown, sustained by nothing but faith and courage. And love. The love of songs, of music, sustains us. The religiosity in Mr. Cohen's words rang true in my heart and mind, as I know it did for songwriters everywhere, because we recognize that songwriting is a high calling and perhaps the purest and holiest thing we do.

"The world doesn't need any new songs," Dylan told me with a sly smile. But to this he added the qualification: "Unless someone comes along with a pure heart."

A pure heart. That is the essence of great songwriting, the well from which Woody Guthrie drew, as did those who came in his wake. They came for the pure love of song. Even when writing on a commercial assignment—as did Leiber and Stoller when writing songs for the movie *Jailhouse Rock* starring Elvis, or Jeff Barry and the Brill Building writers, or Norman Whitfield and the Motown gang—they connected with the pure heart of music, the love of song.

For songs—and songwriting itself—is a source of joy. We don't *work* music; we play it. Being playful and connecting with joy is the essence of the thing, even for those who find the process torturous. It's only tough up to that point when you get something that works. Then it becomes joyful.

As Laura Nyro said, for her songwriting was a "serious playground." When writing songs, she said she felt that "you are really with your essence. . . . There can be delight there. There can be self-discovery. You can dance there." Jimmy Webb said, "I am like a kid with a jigsaw puzzle. A glittering, magical jigsaw puzzle."

It's a journey of joy I've been on for a long time. The year I wrote my first one is also the year The Beatles broke up. It was one of those occurrences so significant, as was the death of John Lennon, that it seemed the world wouldn't go on. But it did, and it always does. As Stephen Stills wrote, "We have no choice but to carry on." And it's the songwriters who make life endurable in these times, who give us hope to carry on even when it seems all hope is lost.

To this day music still matters as much as ever, if not more. Songs still matter. Though I am well known as an author of this and other volumes, my greatest joy is the writing of a new song. I quote Van Dyke Parks's statement that the writing of a song is a triumph of the human spirit all the time because it is so true.

And concurrent with writing these books and other writing about music (and Hollywood history: *Hollywood Remembered* is another compendium of my love and obsessions), I have continued on the golden path of writing songs, and it's been a rich and wonderful journey.

Songwriting is an ancient endeavor, dating back to the dawn of man. The first book about a songwriter was the bible, with the psalms composed by King David. Psalms that spoke to man more directly and fully than mere words ever could. There is no epoch of history or any culture that existed without music. Many historians maintain song preceded spoken language.

Songs, for successive eons, have been integral to every human occasion, from momentous events such as weddings and funerals to mundane ones like elevator trips and supermarket shopping. Songs fan the flames of war, celebrate victories, and envision peace and a world beyond war.

Songs are written and sung in rage and protest, in an effort to change the world. Songs are also there to celebrate the beauty of the world and the greatness of existence. The need for song—for this attempt to make sense of the world with words and music—is deeply rooted in humans and as primal and necessary as the need for love.

Now headlong into this twenty-first century, with miracle technology forever at our fingertips changing our world profoundly, still nothing has surpassed the power of a song. New technologies have forever changed the way we acquire, collect, and listen to songs. But never have songs and the need for songs in our lives been supplanted. Despite what Dylan said, the world absolutely needs new songs.

The truth remains that whether a song is heard by millions or by only one, it matters. It is truly a triumph of the human spirit. Here is a deep and joyful journey into the heart of the mysteries from which these triumphs emerge. It's there, in that timeless place where words and music meet, that Bob Dylan's words resonate forever: "Thank God for songwriters."

Marjorie Guthrie

On Woody Guthrie

New York, New York 1981

It's New York City, 1981, and we're more than twenty floors up above 57th Street and the everyday mayhem of Manhattan. But here there is calm. And joy. And music. It's the office she shares with Harold Leventhal, famed manager of legendary folk stars like Pete Seeger, Arlo Guthrie (her son), Judy Collins, Peter, Paul and Mary, and others.

"You want to see something wonderful?" she asked with an impish glint in her eyes. "Look at this one." In her hands was a timeworn cherry-red spiral notebook. Inside were epic poems, song lyrics, romantic entreaties, expansive erotica, musings, jokes, sketches, drawings—all inscribed there by her late husband, Woody. Woody Guthrie.

For years they lived on Mermaid Avenue in Coney Island, where they raised their three kids, Nora, Arlo, and Joady, and would take the train between there and Manhattan, where they worked. During those commutes Woody would get busy and devote all his exultant energy to filling entire notebooks thusly, dedicated to his beloved.

Now here I was, Woody's notebooks and songs at my fingertips. I had somehow crossed the mystic river, and I was on the side where Woody was. Anything was possible. I could go to the source.

Woody's old pal Pete Seeger said, "All songwriters are links in a chain." And who did Pete learn to write songs from? Woody. Who so inspired and enervated a young Bob Dylan that he had to leave his Midwest home, change his name, and head east to start his life? Woody.

So it seemed an appropriate place to begin this volume, as Pete's interview was the first in the previous volume, with an interview I did with Marjorie Guthrie back in 1981 about her late husband, Woody.

One of my very first jobs out of college was to work for Marjorie at CCHD—the Committee to Combat Huntington's Disease—in New York City, 1981. She'd created this organization to fight this disease that robbed not only Woody's life but also the last decade of his life. They needed someone to do publicity and other chores. I signed on, not so much out of any great desire to battle this disease but, admittedly, to be with Marjorie and her treasure trove of Woody's world—his abundant archives, overflowing not only with the thousands of songs he wrote but also with those beautiful notebooks of poetry and prose and erotica and cartoons. Also the tools of his genius were preserved so lovingly, his pens, pencils, crayons, and notebooks. This proximity to the stuff of legend—to the cornucopia of expansive song wisdom and wonder that all poured out of this one miraculous little man—and the very crayons of this famous kid at heart was all I needed to sustain me.

She was born Marjorie Greenblatt on October 6, 1917, in Atlantic City and lived until March of 1983. She danced with the Martha Graham troupe starting in 1935 under the name Marjorie Mazia. She first met Woody in 1940, as described in the following, and was with him on and off until the end of his life on October 3, 1967. She was a brilliant and beautiful woman who put up with Woody while he was alive, though it was never easy. He wasn't a man who stayed still for long. But long before he was gone they both knew the legacy—the body of work—mattered. And though I was there before legions of great songwriters wrote new melodies to his unfinished songs, the lyrics that lived in the exalted archives, the recognition of his lasting legacy underscored all other endeavors. Like Dylan who came to be with Woody before he was gone forever, I wanted to get near this source too, and Marjorie was used to all sorts of folk-inspired pilgrims being drawn to all things Woody. So she kindly allowed me to interview her about Woody on more than one occasion, a dialogue I am happy to include here.

After all, Pete Seeger was our hero growing up. He was in our world. But he always spoke and sang of Woody. And perhaps he cleaned up the dark aspects of Woody's outlook more than necessary—Woody was no saint, after all—but what was undeniable was Pete's respect for Woody as a songwriter. As *the* songwriter.

"Woody is just Woody," John Steinbeck wrote. "He is a voice with a guitar. He sings the songs of a people and I suspect that he is, in a way, that people . . . there is nothing sweet about Woody, and there is nothing sweet about the songs he sings. But there is something more important for those who will listen. There is the will of a people to endure and fight against oppression. I think we call this the American spirit."

Woody's work was remarkable—some two thousand amazing songs— songs of love, outrage, beauty, faith, humor, death, sex, and pretty much every other human experience under the sun. Some became famous, such as "This Land Is Your Land," "So Long, It's Been Good to Know You," "Roll On Columbia, Roll On" "Deportees," "Union Maid," and "Do Re Mi," but most of his songs have hardly been heard once, if ever. And there was also so much else that he created: volumes of poetry, love letters, journals of erotica, books, drawings, doodles, paintings, and stories.

When he was married to Marjorie, he was so thoroughly in love with her that he'd write her entire inspired daily notebooks of love poetry and cosmic musings while on the subway, hurtling through the subterranean tunnels toward their Coney Island home. Marjorie kept all of these—and every letter he ever wrote and every song he composed along with every crayon, pencil, and pen he used to conjure his magic—in her New York archives, where she'd share it with his admirers, a legion of artists, musicians, and vagabonds that increased every year and continues to expand.

Born in the heart of the Dust Bowl—Okemah, Oklahoma—in 1912, his childhood was spent in the oil boomtown of Pampa, Texas. In the depression-ravaged thirties he hitched and rode the rails along with thousands of others to reach the world of their dreams, the Promised Land—California.

Of all those wanderers, thousands more than there were jobs, Woody was one of the fortunate few able to make money by singing, playing guitar, and painting signs. He managed to get a fifteen-minute daily radio show that paid him a dollar per show. And when he wasn't broadcasting he could be found singing at saloons, parking lots, rallies, and union meetings—anywhere people would listen. Their struggles were the impetus for his talent—he always knew his mission was to translate their hearts and minds into song. Using what his pal Pete Seeger called the "folk process"—writing new words to old songs—he gave these people a voice.

Radio gave many people their first taste of Woody's songs. One listener, Ed Robbin, commentator for the Communist newspaper *People's World*, was surprised to discover that the man he had pegged as a hillbilly was actually quite politically savvy. He invited Woody to perform at rallies, first warning him that they were left wing. "Left wing or chicken wing, it's all the same to me," Woody said. And with that he connected with a new audience, one that was charmed and inspired by his unique fusion of country simplicity, Okie humor, and political sophistication. His popularity spread quickly across the country and even preceded him to New York City, where he eventually fell in with new friends such as Josh White, Leadbelly, and the actor Will Geer.

Opportunity kept knocking. In an attempt to cash in on the popularity of John Steinbeck's novel *The Grapes of Wrath*, Victor Records hired Woody to write a song about it. Though he didn't read the book, Woody saw and loved the film and understood its subject matter better than most. With his guitar and a jug of wine, he got behind a typewriter in Pete Seeger's apartment and proceeded to work into the night. The next morning Pete found him slumped over the typewriter with twenty-six verses of "The Ballad of Tom Joad" still in the typewriter.

"I learned a lot about songwriting from Woody," Pete said. "I learned something that was *awful* important. And that was: don't be so all-fired concerned about being original. You hear an old song you like but you want to change it a little, there's no crime in that."

By today's standards Woody's records sound rough. Mostly guitar and a ragged, often off-tune voice recording on the spot by Moses Asch for his Folkways label. But each of these recordings contains the essence of pure and brilliant songwriting, the dynamic and delicate marriage of music with words.

Woody well understood the inherent power of this combination—words to express the timely and timeless needs of the people and music to underscore that expression while engaging the soul and lifting the spirit. He knew few forces were as effective in uniting people as a good song, and as he constantly traversed America by walking, hitching, or riding the rails, he would constantly connect with new people and translate their lives and dreams into songs.

Woody wrote his most famous song, "This Land Is Your Land," as a response to Irving Berlin's "God Bless America." Woody felt Berlin got it wrong—that America was already blessed by God—and wrote "God Blessed America for Me." He kept fiddling with it for a full decade and eventually realized that if he substituted the line "This land was made for you and me" for his title line, he had a song not just about himself but about all of America. Not only was he a great thinker, he was a crafty songwriter.

He died in 1967 at the age of fifty-five. But his songs have lived on, performed and championed by a big range of singers, including not only Arlo, Dylan, and Seeger but also Ani DiFranco, Bruce Springsteen, Ry Cooder, and even U2, who cut Woody's song "Jesus Christ." Though Woody's been gone now for so many decades, his songs and the spirit of human hope instilled in them have been resounding with more force than they have for years. "The worst thing that can happen is to cut yourself loose from the people," he wrote. "And the best thing is to vaccinate yourself right into the big streams and blood of the people."

I conducted this interview on a sunny autumn day in Manhattan, in the 57th Street office. She sat at her big desk, always calm and joyful many floors above the tumult of a New York City business day, with the archives of Woody's songs and writings always within easy reach.

It's been suggested that, for both Martha Graham and Woody Guthrie, you were the organizer behind the genius.

Marjorie Guthrie: This is true. Some people felt that Martha Graham was difficult to work with, but when you know you are in the company of a great artist, you minimize their negative aspects and are grateful for the opportunity to see how a true artist works. Let me say that she was a very good rehearsal for Woody Guthrie.

When did you first meet Woody?

On one of the Martha Graham tours, in St. Louis. My sister called me from Columbia, Missouri, and wanted me to visit her. So I got Martha Graham to let me leave the company for a day, and I took the bus over to Columbia, and when I got there my sister said, "Oh Marge, I have to play something for you."

And it is so vivid to this day: I sat on the arm of a chair and she played Woody's "Ballad of Tom Joad"—first time I had heard his voice. And I was so moved, when it got to the end I started to cry. I am an emotional person, and I love being emotional, and when he got to the end I was just in tears.

I said to my sister, "How does anyone put into words what I'm thinking about myself?" Funny, I related it to myself: growing up, going through the Depression, seeing what happened to our family, coming to New York. Then Sophie Maslow, who was with Martha Graham, had choreographed two of Woody's songs from that same album, "I Ain't Got No Home" and "Dusty Old Dust," and she said to me, "Guess what? Instead of using the record, I'm going to use Woody Guthrie, if he'll do it, because he is in town. And I'm going to ask him to appear on stage with us and sing those two." And I practically fainted and said, "Woody Guthrie is in town? Sophie, I'm coming with you!"

I went with her and we came to what was then the Almanac Singer's Center on 6ᵗʰ Avenue, a big loft with great big wide posts. First of all, they didn't want to let us in. Finally, they did, and I saw Woody from the back first.

He was looking out the window at 6ᵗʰ Avenue, and he was nothing at all in stature like the way I pictured him. When I had heard his voice I thought of this tall, Lincoln-esque figure with a cowboy hat. But then he turned around and he had this *wonderful* face. I loved his face immediately.

I don't remember anything he said. I just kept looking at that face. And then remembering that voice and the quality of those songs. I fell in love with him right then and there. And he said to me later that when Sophie and I came up he was talking to her but looking at me. And I was looking at him.

In a few days he started to rehearse with us. He was to be both a narrator and a singer in a production called *Folksay*. And here I loved this guy, and everyone was picking on him. Why? Because he sings the song differently each time. Here we have twelve people on the stage, and he puts in an extra verse, he takes out a verse. What do you do? Everyone was angry with him. I was just dying for him.

What I did was to take cardboard sheets and type up all the words of the songs and put them in measures and say, "Woody, why can't you sing it just like the record?" He would say, "The day we made that record, Lee Hays had asthma, someone had just given us $300, and we were on our way to California. I don't have asthma, I don't have $300, and I'm not going to California, so I can't play it the same way." But I worked with him, using these little cards, and before you knew it we were living together.

What was he writing during this period?

That was the year he was writing *Bound for Glory*. He would be writing—by hand—and I would come home in the evening and he would read me what he had written. Then we would take turns, reading and typing. It was then that I first learned about his mother and all of her problems and that she had Huntington's Disease.

Was he a disciplined writer?

Oh yes. Take a look at any of his notebooks. He loved to write. He had great respect for his work. He signed every piece of paper and dated almost everything and wrote a little background about each song, like why he had written it. He did have a highly organized mind.

So he had an understanding of his own historical significance?

Absolutely. We used to tease about it. He would say, "We can be poor now, but maybe someday this stuff will be worth something." But you see, even knowing that didn't stop him from doing things the way he wanted to. And that was something else that I loved about him. You see, in the thirties and the forties dancers were the poorest people on the cultural ladder, and I didn't have much. But that didn't matter to me because the dancing was so important.

Woody had that same feeling. It wasn't important whether everyone loved him or every song made money. It was important that he was doing what he wanted to do and what he was compelled to do. He couldn't have done anything else anyway.

Did he have moments of self-doubt?

Very few, I have to tell you. He had confidence in what he was doing, that there were important songs, not whether they were commercial successes or not. That he didn't know about. But what he knew was that in his songs were the voices of people he had known, and he felt better suited to represent these people than anyone.

Could he take criticism of his work?

He would argue with me. Very rarely would he change something. In the song "Jesus Christ," I felt that one verse was wrong, that it misinterpreted Christ. He argued with me about it and won the argument. But he let me argue.

Did you have a sense of how famous he would become?

I never thought of him being famous commercially. I always had the feeling that when you speak for the downtrodden you might be famous among the downtrodden, but nobody else hears about you. And again, I don't care. I wanted him to do what he was doing, and I felt that what he was saying was important. But the first hint of his real importance didn't come from me or him. It came from Alan Lomax. It was Alan who said to me one day, "Don't throw anything away. Save everything." And I looked at him as if to say, "Why?" And he said, "Woody is going to be very important."

I knew that what Woody wrote was good because it moved me. But it would move other people too, and maybe cause them to want to be "wherever little children are hungry and cry" [from "Tom Joad"]. When Alan said that to me, it was the beginning of my appreciation that other people loved what Woody was saying.

He already had a little recognition when he came to New York. I was not yet involved with him; he was here with [his first wife] Mary. He had a radio show, the *Back Where I Come From* show, and he was commercially successful. But he left this show and he let me know why: "They wouldn't let me say what I wanted to say or sing what I wanted to sing, so who needs them?"

He gradually started receiving recognition, especially after the publication of *Bound for Glory*. Did that change him at all?

It didn't change him, but he was very pleased. He wrote "My first copy" in the first edition of it. He was very proud of himself, especially when people began reading it and enjoying it.

Besides writing songs, he was always writing letters and poems and doing drawings. Which was most important to him?

The songs were most important. They came first. He had a wonderfully organized system, something most people don't realize. Every morning he read the paper first thing. Then he would tear out of the paper things that he wanted to write songs about and then make a list of songs that he was going to write. Then he would write a few songs, read some of the books that he had gotten from the library, usually two or three at a time. He would read standing up because he got tired of sitting. Then he might sit down again and do some writing.

Yes, there were times when he did do some drinking, and when he did it had a very bad effect because of the Huntington's disease. HD puts you off balance, and drinking puts you more off balance, so Woody was sometimes *very* off balance.

His writing has a dizzying, almost drunken power to it. Do you think the HD affected his style?

No. I don't agree at all with the suggestion that Woody wrote the way he did because he had HD. It does sound logical, but even with Martha

Graham I saw the same kind of intensity and determination and creativity that Woody had. And look at Whitman and Jack London. They didn't have HD, and yet they had similar writing styles.

Also, he was encouraged by Joy Home, who edited *Bound for Glory*. She said to him, "Woody, don't worry about what I'm going to cut out. Whatever comes to your mind, just do it." And he enjoyed that freedom to just let it go.

I read that she'd suggest a few changes and he'd return with a hundred new pages.

That's right. And she would say, "Woody, why didn't you bring them in yesterday?" And he would say, "Well, because I hadn't written them yet."

Did he talk the same way that he wrote?

Nothing like that. Nothing like his writing. We were opposites: I am as verbal as anyone can be, and he was just the opposite.

If he were sitting with us right now and you were interviewing him, he would probably answer in a very slow, halting voice, kind of like [*very slowly*], "Yeah . . . welllll . . . way back . . ." Nothing like the flowing quality of his writing. He simply loved to write. He loved pencils, paper, typewriters. You know, I have to show you something. [*Brings a box of pens and colored pencils.*] This is all Woody's. He loved this stuff.

Did he have dry spells ever, times he wasn't inspired to write?

Very few. He was always churning them out, as you can see by the archives, which hold about two thousand of his songs. And he was just as creative a father as he was a musician. He could spend a whole day on the beach, starting with just our three kids around. By the end of the day he would have these *tremendous* sand castles and about thirty kids who helped him build them. And they were beautiful, really beautiful.

Was it because he was so much of a kid at heart himself that made him so great with kids?

Yes, for sure. He had a great sense of playfulness, of fun. And both of us have great respect for young people because you are tomorrow, you are it. Anything we had is going to die and go away before you know it, but you have years ahead of you.

It is true that Woody and your mother wrote a song together?

My mother, who was a Yiddish poetess, wrote the words to a song and he *corrected* her. They didn't write it together. It was called "I Gave

My Sons to the Country," and he was opposed to it. "Why do you want to give your sons to the country?" he asked. "Shouldn't that be the question?" But my mother was really a much better writer in Yiddish, and Woody never really knew this.

I was astounded when you showed me all the letters he wrote you and the full notebooks of love letters and poetry and erotica he would fill up for you.

Every night when I would come home [commuting from Manhattan to Coney Island], I would look forward to two or three letters from Woody, especially when he was in the Army. I was a woman alone, and it was wonderful to have these. But you know, I am a prude, and I used to *die* from embarrassment all by myself. Nobody would be in the room, but I would be reading those sexy letters and I would be *dying.*

And then he would say to me, "Why don't you write back in turn?" And I would say, "I can't write those kind of letters!"

I know Woody was a great fan of Chaplin. He always seemed Chaplinesque himself—

You're right, he was very Chaplinesque. You know, he used to play the harmonica and dance at school when he was a kid. And don't you think Arlo did the same thing when he was a kid? Certain people have that elfin quality. Arlo had it as a child; Woody had it all his life. Kind of half-singing, half-dancing, I'm the little guy on the block, but I'm no dumbbell.

In 1969 Arthur Penn made a movie out of Arlo's great song "Alice's Restaurant," starring Arlo.

Yes. I loved that film, because there was a lot of truth in it.

There's a scene in the film where Pete Seeger and Arlo come to Woody's hospital room and sing "Car Car." I've read that Woody loved hearing the song "Hobo's Lullaby" the most.

They sang all those songs and more. They sang a lot of songs. The only thing that wasn't accurate was showing Woody in a private room. How I wish he had a private room and his own nurse!

I know that in addition to Pete and Arlo, a lot of other musicians came to Woody's bedside during that last decade when he was at Greystone in New Jersey. Most famously, Bob Dylan made the trek to meet his hero. What were your impressions of Dylan from then?

He impressed me with his quality and intensity. I knew that he was determined. I didn't like his diction when he sang, and I couldn't understand the words. But I loved many of his songs, and I felt that he was a creative artist who was going through, even now, the ups and downs that an artist must go through. Everything that you do isn't always top-notch.

At first did he seem like just another Woody imitator?

Well, I had already spent a couple of good years with [Ramblin'] Jack Elliott, who Woody said was more like Woody than he was! But I had no resentment whatsoever of people imitating Woody, because if you are around a great artist, their influence is bound to get to you. It's like osmosis. Later in your life maybe you can find your own style. After all, I learned to love dance from someone who learned to love dance from someone who learned to love dance and so on. You must carry on the tradition of whatever you are doing and do so with integrity. I think Bob did that.

Woody's life ended too early, and during his last years he wasn't able to work. Had he more years, what do you think he would have done with them?

I can't answer that easily. Woody would have changed with the times like everybody else to a certain extent. And Woody loved all kinds of music, something that not everybody knows. Moses Asch, who was a kind of mentor to Woody, gave him many free classical albums, and often I would come home and find him listening to Prokofiev. He knew *Romeo and Juliet* backward and forward.

He liked all different kinds of music, depending on what time of day it was or what he was doing right then. Nothing can better express the essence of the moment. Music is the soul of man. Woody used to borrow music from everywhere and change it around a little for his own songs. But it was the honesty and the quality of the songs that mattered.

◆ ◆ ◆

Jerry Leiber and Mike Stoller
A Bridge Built on the Blues

Los Angeles, California 2006

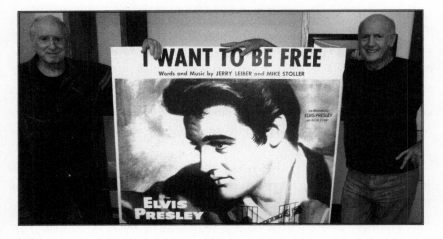

Though they were among the chief architects of rock and roll, having written "Hound Dog" and other songs recorded by Elvis, they never thought rock and roll would last. Like Elvis's manager Colonel Parker and others, they thought rock was a fad that would quickly fade. Though they wrote successive rock classics in addition to "Hound Dog," such as "Stand By Me," "Jailhouse Rock," and "Kansas City," they were prouder of songs such as "Is That All There Is?," which they wrote for Peggy Lee. Though they are forever implicit in the creation of rock and roll, its lasting cultural impact took them as much by surprise as anyone.

It was one of many reasons why talking to Leiber and Stoller was a remarkably revelatory experience. Two Jewish boys from LA united by a love of the blues, they earned world fame and fortune for writing in a black genre, and became purveyors of this genre they didn't truly embrace or respect, rock and roll. Today they are American icons, yet have rarely spoken to the press in the fifty-six years of their celebrated collaboration, and have never really participated in their history as it's been written.

Their feelings about their now-mythic songs are bittersweet, and quite often more bitter than sweet. And almost every one of the published stories that purport to get their history right are wrong, including those surrounding the writing and recording of their most famous songs, such as "Hound Dog" and "Jailhouse Rock," both recorded by Elvis, or "Kansas City," recorded by The Beatles, among many others, or "Stand By Me," recorded by Ben E. King originally and later John Lennon. (The Beatles also recorded two other songs by Leiber and Stoller on their first demo, "Searchin'" and "Three Cool Cats.")

Their career stands as a turning of a page, a transition from the age of Tin Pan Alley, the era of writing the standards that now form the proverbial Great American Songbook, the epoch in which not one but two people toiled to churn out songs—a lyricist and a melodist—into the age of rock and roll. Jerry Leiber and Mike Stoller, who shared a suite of offices in the 9000 building of Sunset Boulevard, a building where some august veterans of the Tin Pan Alley such as Sammy Cahn once had their offices, have met here on this autumn day in Hollywood to give a rare interview about the career that created many of America's most famous songs.

Though they came together just as the legendary writers of old, they were the architects of a new sound, a new craze, a new era of wild rhythm-and-bluesy tunes. It was rock and roll. It was a bridge from the blues—in which both Leiber and Stoller were well versed—to popular music, a bridge they built themselves.

This suite of offices was appointed with large, brightly colored folk-art paintings of the blues heroes who painted their youth with blues tales of urban centers like Chicago, far from their sunny Angeleno homes. Muddy Waters, Robert Johnson, Willie Dixon—these fathers of the blues hang over their heads in chromatic glory, sharing the wall space with only one messenger of rock and roll—a young man who, in black and white, remains as electrically vital as these blues beacons—Elvis Presley. Their lives and his are forever entwined, and though his image is monochromatic here, his presence in their life is full of technicolor radiance and unfaded glory. Their memories of the King—which are frank, forthright, and unqualified—related here for the first time in unexpurgated detail, remain as alive as Elvis himself is said to be.

It is true, though, that, as reported, Stoller didn't like the idea of writing songs with Leiber when they met in 1950. It's not true, though, as has often been quoted, that he said he didn't like songs. What he said he didn't like were *popular* songs. He preferred jazz. But when he realized that the young Jerome Leiber had written not pop songs but blues, a bridge was built between them that still stands to this day. It's a bridge built on the blues.

Because their most famous songs came fast and easy to them, "hot off the griddle" as Leiber put it, they don't tend to value them to the extent they value their songs like "Is That All There Is?," an existential theatrical ballad made famous by Peggy Lee. To this day Leiber, the lyricist, and Stoller, the melodist, yearn to be known as more than writers of simple rock and roll. When I lingered on the writing of "Jailhouse Rock," for example, Leiber looked me squarely in the eyes and said, "Why are you spending so much time on 'Jailhouse Rock'? Is it that important?" Though they've written some of the most lasting popular songs ever, they didn't think any of them would last. As soon as they were off the charts, they felt, the songs would vanish.

Leiber and Stoller have long felt their famous rock and roll songs were kid's stuff, and they wanted to write songs for adults—deeper, more musically and lyrically complex songs, of which there exists an abundance in their mythical "vault." But except for "Is That All There Is?," it's their simple, easy songs that have connected them timelessly to popular culture. Although countless songwriters attempted to approach the same kind of lofty heights Jerry and Mike reached, they were attempting to write songs like Brecht and Weill wrote and to translate into words and music the synthesis of sorrow and humor found in the writing of Thomas Mann and other writers. Out of the universe of albums that have been recorded containing their songs, the one they speak of with the greatest pride is *Peggy Lee Sings Leiber & Stoller*, a collection of their "adult songs" sung by the legendary vocalist.

And although you might assume any songwriter would be forever proud to have had a song recorded by Elvis or The Beatles, they never liked the King's rendition of "Hound Dog" (and have never referred to him as the King or even Elvis; in the following interview he is "Presley"). Nor did they like The Beatles' record of "Kansas City" (for reasons also explained in the following). They only wrote "Jailhouse Rock" because the movie's producer refused to let them out of their hotel room until they came up with some songs. "Hound Dog" was written on the fly and not for Elvis but for Big Mama Thornton (and not on a piano but on a car, as explained here). From the first second Jerry uttered its title, he didn't think it was sufficiently explicit and still doesn't feel it's as biting as he wanted (nor does he see much value in other legendary titles he's created, such as "Jailhouse Rock" or "Spanish Harlem"). Elvis's rendition of "Hound Dog"—perhaps the most famous record ever of one of their songs—doesn't even use the right lyrics; instead, it copies improbable lyrics written for the song by Freddie Bell—who introduced the whole notion of a rabbit to the song, a notion Leiber and Stoller regard as nonsense.

They were the first independent record producers to be officially designated as producers—"producer" being a title they invented themselves (they wanted "director")—but they started producing records only in self-defense, as they explain it, to ensure that their songs wouldn't be wrecked.

Even with their most famous nonrock creation, "Is That All There Is?," they are forever dismayed by Peggy Lee's insistence on changing one word—an alteration, in their opinion, that dilutes the entire point of the song.

To this day, like any couple who have stayed together through many decades, they sometimes irritate each other. Often they finish each other's sentences, though their memories frequently clash. "Our relationship is the longest-running single argument in the entertainment business," Jerry said, only half-joking.

But the connection that led them to write words and music like one person over the decades is still powerful, and as often as they argue, they laugh, and it's clear that there are few people they'd rather spend time with than each other.

We met on a sun-bright day in Hollywood that had a shaft of darkness piercing through it—it was the fifth anniversary of 9/11. But that tragedy didn't darken our time together, which was originally only slotted to be less than an hour and extended, thankfully, to several hours. Mike, who so seemed the embodiment of pure energy that I was prepared for him to leap up and run several miles at full speed, sat in front of a giant blow-up of the sheet music for their song "I Want to Be Free," which was recorded by Elvis. The King's iconic profile shone like the sun over Stoller's shoulder throughout our talk, a presence that was both ghostly and vital, as is the enduring presence of Elvis in their lives. Stoller sipped Snapple out of the bottle as Leiber drank coffee from a white china cup and saucer, and the distinct dynamics that have been at play within this duo for more than a half century were very much alive, as the memories ripened and shape-shifted and the sparks flew as they have since the very dawn of rock and roll.

Now, the legend goes that Jerry wanted to get together with you, Mike, when you were both seventeen, to write songs. And you didn't like the idea of writing songs.

Mike Stoller: Well, that's not really true, but, you know, when you're interviewed, frequently you give a very quick answer. The thing is, I *assumed* that Jerome Leiber was not writing something that I would be interested in. I had very specific tastes. I was a musical snob. I was a big bebop fan. So I thought he would, somehow, be writing songs that I just wouldn't care for. That I'd consider *commercial*, which was a terrible word among jazz musicians. I wasn't a jazz musician. I played a little bit. But I had that kind of an arrogance, if you will. And when he came over, of course, I discovered that he was writing *blues*, and I loved blues. 'Cause it's great stuff. I was a big boogie-woogie and blues fan, as was Jerry.

Before meeting Jerry, were you hoping to make your living as a musician?

Stoller: I was hoping to make it as a composer, yeah.

Of jazz? What kind of music?

Stoller: Just music. Of jazz, or of, quote, serious music.

Were you considering being a songwriter?

Stoller: No.

And so you, Jerry, were writing blues without music?

Jerry Leiber: Yes.

Had you worked with other songwriters before working with Mike?

Leiber: Well, I worked with one other person who I wouldn't really characterize as a songwriter. This was in high school. Going to Fairfax High School. I hooked up with a drummer. Whose name was . . . Jerry Horowitz. Is that his name?

Stoller: I can't remember, and he can't remember. [*Laughs*] I remember what he looked like. Nice fella.

Leiber: We worked for maybe two months, three months. One day he didn't show up for a writing session. And it sort of went out the window. I needed a composer. Tunesmith. He told me he had a musician's name written down who was a piano player that he played a dance with in East LA and he thought was pretty good. And he *might* be interested in writing songs. And he took his number down and gave it to me.

I called—it was Mike—I called him up and I said, "My name is Jerome Leiber, and I was given your number by a drummer. Said he played a dance with you in East LA. And he said you might be interested in writing songs. Can you write notes on paper?"

He said, "Yes."

I said, "Can you read music?"

He said, "Yes."

I said, "Do you think you'd like to write songs?"

He said, "No." I thought what a tough nut to crack here. And I talked to him for a few more minutes. And sort of wrangled an appointment with him.

I took my school notebook, which had all my lyrics in it, and I went to his house. Which was at—

Stoller: 226 South Columbia Avenue. Right where Belmont High School is.

Leiber: I can't remember the address. It's been, what, forty years?

Stoller: Fifty-six. He's a great lyric writer, bad mathematician. [*Laughter*]

Leiber: I don't have a very good memory either.

Stoller: That's true.

Leiber: So he was adamant. He didn't want to write songs. He made it clear that he was doing me a favor by talking to me. He really wasn't interested. He told me he was interested in Charlie Parker, Dizzy Gillespie, Art Blakey.

Stoller: Bela Bartok. [*Laughter*]

He was good too.

Leiber: Miles Davis. And I thought he was a terrible music snob. And I think so did he. But he did take the book out of my hands and wandered toward the piano.

And he set the book down on the piano, and he started playing licks. Sort of blues-jazz. And he looked at the book and he said, "Hey—these aren't songs. They're not the kind of songs I dislike. These are blues, aren't they?"

I said, "I think so."

He said, "I like the blues. I'll write with you."

And that's how it started.

The legend was that you said, "These aren't songs, these are blues." But did you consider them songs?

Stoller: Well, they weren't the kind of songs that I thought that he would be writing. Most of the blues that I knew—almost all the blues—first of all, were written by black people. And most of them by black singers, and as a matter of fact, many, many of them were piano players, and I bought their records for the boogie-woogie instrumentals, which might have been considered, in those days, the B-side. You know, in the old 78 records? But I always played both sides. And the other side, frequently, which might have been the A-side, had the same person playing a blues and singing. So I did become somewhat familiar with the poetry of the blues and certainly the structure of the blues, and Jerry's work was in that mode. It had the blues poetry in it.

Leiber: Almost all of our audiences thought we were black. And when we took some of our music to a performer to show it to him for approval or to teach him how to sing it, they were absolutely amazed. I remember we went to a little hotel down on Central Avenue. We were taking some songs to Wynonie Harris, who at that time was pretty hot. And we knocked on his door, and he opened his door and he looked at us in *shock*. At first he really didn't believe that we were songwriters. That's how it went for years, actually. It wasn't just the first five minutes. That's how it was for *years*. And some people today still think of us as black songwriters. In fact, LeRoi Jones wrote an article about us. He said we were two of the best black songwriters in the business. And he meant it.

Stoller: But when *Smokey Joe's Café* went into rehearsal for the Broadway production, three of the guys met us for the first time and were *shocked*. And this was ten, twelve years ago. They thought that we were *black*.

Those first lyrics you wrote, did you intend them to be blues?

Leiber: Well, they *were* blues. The form, the structure. There were repeat lines—

Stoller: Yeah. I looked at it, I said, "There's a line, a line of ditto marks, a rhyming line." I said, "These are twelve-bar blues." I didn't know that you were writing blues.

Leiber: He turned to me and said, "These are blues. These are the blues . . . I *like* the blues."

I understand one of the first songs you wrote together was "Kansas City."

Stoller: It was the first big hit. Actually "Hound Dog" and "Kansas City" were both written the same year, 1952, when we were nineteen. Yeah, I remember very well both of those songs, the writing of them.

Was "Kansas City" first?

Stoller: I'm not absolutely sure. I do know when "Hound Dog" was recorded—it was recorded in August 1952; it came out in 1953.

"Kansas City" might have been after that, but it came out in December or thereabouts of '52. There might not have been as long a wait. 'Cause I remember—

Leiber: "Hound Dog" waiting—

Stoller: We were waiting and waiting and *waiting* for "Hound Dog" to come. We knew, if one can know, it was a smash—

Leiber: In the blues.

Stoller: In the blues field. We went down to Pico. We went and waited and waited and said, "When will the goddamn thing come out?"

Leiber: I remember it came out when I was in Boston. Visiting my sister. I think it took eight or nine months to come out. Then it came out, and it was out for twenty hours. And it *broke*. Like the atom bomb. In *Boston*. And I found out that it broke every place else within five minutes. It was one of the biggest hits ever.

You wrote that song after you went and heard Big Mama Thornton sing?

Stoller: In between seeing her sing and coming back to a rehearsal at Johnny Otis's house.

You pounded out the rhythm on your old car—

Stoller: Yeah, on my old car. [*Laughs*]

Leiber: A green Plymouth.

Stoller: It was actually gray. It was a gray 1937. . . . It was *greenish* gray, you're right.

And that main line, "You ain't nothin' but a hound dog," just came to you?

Leiber: Yeah, it did. And I felt it was a dummy lyric. I was not happy. I wanted something that was a lot more insinuating. I wanted something that was *sexy* and insinuating. And I told Mike I didn't like it. We were driving, and he said, "I like it, man."

I said, "I like the song idea, but I don't like that word. That word is kind of replacing another kind of a word."

He said, "What are you looking for?"

I said, "Do you remember Furry Lewis's record 'Dirty Mother'?"

He said, "Yeah?"

I said, "Well, I'd like to write something like *that*."

Mike said, "You'll ruin it. If you write something like that, they won't play it."

I said, "I don't care if they don't play it. I want this word in the song."

He said, "Jer, leave it alone. I think you're making a mistake."

Stoller: Well, I liked "Hound Dog." I liked the *sound* of it.

Big Mama Thornton's version is in E flat. Did you write it in that key?

Stoller: Didn't write it in a key. I probably played it in C 'cause it was easier.

When you say you didn't write it in a key, did you write it away from the piano?

Leiber: The two of us walked in his house and walked into this sort of a den, where this upright piano was. And I was singing. I started singing it in the car on the way over. "You ain't nothin' but a hound dog, quit snoopin' round my door." And I didn't have all the lyrics. And we walked into Mike's house, into the den, and he walked over—and I will never forget it, the moment is *indelibly* etched on my memory—he walked over to the piano, and he had a cigarette in his mouth, and the smoke was curling up into his eye, and he kept it there and he was playing, and he was *grooving* with the *rhythm*, and he was grooving, grooving, and we *locked* into one place. Lyrical content, syllabically, *locked in* to the rhythm of the piano. And we knew we had it.

We wrote it in about twelve minutes. And I will *never* forget it. He had the smoke from this cigarette curling up into his left eye, and I was watching him.

And he was singing, "You ain't nothin' but a hound dog," and I said, "*Yeah, yeah, yeah*—that's it."

Stoller: And we drove back to the rehearsal. Because we had been invited. We had worked with Johnny Otis on a couple of sessions with Little Esther and Little Willie doing duets with Little Esther and so on. And [Johnny Otis] called me and said, "Are you familiar with Willie Mae Thornton?"

I said, "No, I'm not."

He said, "Well, I need some songs." The procedure, before that, was that we'd get a call from Ralph Bass, who was the head of Federal Records, a division of King. He would call and say, "We're cutting Little Esther tomorrow. Two to five at Radio Recorders. Bring some songs." And we would write two or three songs. And sometimes during the session, during which we'd try to get some of our ideas done. Even though we were just newcomers in that field, we'd go out in the hall and write *another* one.

So Johnny called and said, "Come over and listen to her and write some songs," and that's the way that happened. We went over and heard her and said, "Whoa!" We ran over to my house in my car, wrote the song, came back.

Leiber: I just remembered—we came back, and I had this sheet of paper. And we walked in. And I think I said, "We got it." And Big Mama walked over and she grabbed the sheet out of my hand and she said, "Let me see this." I looked at her and I looked at the sheet. And I saw that the sheet was upside down. And she was just staring at it, looking at it, as if she could read it, right?

She said, "What does it say?"

I said, "You ain't nothing but a hound dog, quit snoopin' round my door."

She said, "Oh, that's *pretty*."

She took the sheet back and she started singing [*slowly and melodically*], "You ain't nothin' but a hound dog . . ." She's singing a *ballad*. She's *crooning* a ballad.

And I said, "Mama, it don't go like that."

She grabbed the sheet and she said to me, "Don't you tell me how to sing." And she started to sing it again. And Johnny Otis had witnessed this little contretemps, and he came over, and he was getting a little bit *salty*. And he said, "Mama, don't you want a hit?" And she said yes. And he said, "These guys can get you a hit."

Stoller: He said, "These guys write hits." Which was—

Leiber: Not true. [*Laughter*] He said, "These guys can write you a hit." She accepted that, and he said something like, "Now be *good*." Like he was punishing a *child*.

Then he turned to me and he said, "Why don't you perform it for her? Why don't you demonstrate the song?" And I was a little nervous, because there was about a twelve-piece band sitting on a platform—it was a pretty big band—and I was always used to performing a song wherever, whatever, with Mike. He played the piano, I sang the song—no big deal.

I got up to sing the song, and half a dozen of the men—the rhythm section more than anybody else, guitar and drums, bass, whatever—sort of accompanied me. Mike was *not* playing the piano when I turned around. And he was standing by the piano, smoking. And Johnny Otis said, "What about your buddy?"

I said, "He'll play in a moment. He's just getting ready." And I said, "Mike, play piano." He was very self-conscious in those days and didn't like to perform. He was gonna sit it out. And I almost pleaded with him to play the piano.

The groove she was singing was not right. I said, "Mama, it don't go like that."

She said, "I know how it goes. It goes like this . . ." I didn't know how to deal with this. I said, "Mike, play the piano." And the groove fell right in, 'cause he had the groove.

So Jerry, although you are the lyricist, you sort of had the music for that.

Leiber: Just a road map. Mike wrote the melody.

And you wrote the melody apart from the piano—you just sang it?

Stoller: More or less. Based partially on what he was singing and how I felt it should do. But it wasn't written out on a lead sheet and handed to Mama. We didn't have time to sit down and write out *anything*.

Leiber: I think I had the music for the very first line. [*Sings*] "You ain't nothin' but a hound dog . . ." And Mike picked that up and *went with it* and developed the rest of it. And then she got it. She understood.

It's amazing to learn you didn't like the name "Hound Dog," given that it's such a classic now—

Leiber: The line was not what I wanted. Sometimes you make mistakes.

Stoller: Thank goodness. [*Laughs*]

That the two of you met each other at the time you did and that you ended up writing so many great and important songs together, do you attribute that just to good luck, or was it something bigger—was it Providence?

Leiber: Now I look at it different. Forty or fifty years ago I thought it was Providence. Or just dumb luck that happens to people kind of mystically or magically. But then about eight years ago my cousin told me that my father was a songwriter—he used to write religious songs in synagogue. And then I thought that Mike's aunt was a great musician.

Stoller: That's something else. It's a genetic strain. But I think what Paul is asking is something else. Which has to do with—from my point of view—great luck—

Leiber: That's because you're a gambler.

Stoller: Well, that's true. But in those days I think that two white teenagers that loved and knew enough about black music to begin to write it and meeting each other—

Leiber: Fortuitous.

Stoller: Absolutely. Because you could have come over, and I could have been not interested in writing with you. I could have wanted to write "Floatin' down a river on a Sunday afternoon." Or you might have written that kind of a lyric, and I'd say, "What is this? I'm not interested. Bye."

The original "Hound Dog," by Mama Thornton, was in E flat, but Elvis sang it in C.

Leiber: That's because he got the song from Freddie Bell and the Bellboys. He did not learn the song from Mama's record.

Stoller: He knew her record, but it was a woman's song, and he never sang it until he heard Freddie Bell and the Bellboys, who had distorted the song so that they could sing it—

Leiber: Lyrics and music.

Stoller: Yeah, both. And that's how he learned it. Though I'm almost *positive* that Big Mama's record was in D or E. I know they were *playing* it in D or E. It depended on the piano in the studio, which might have been out of tune. I'm sure it was D or E. It was Pete Lewis playing that guitar solo. And he had *retuned* his guitar to what was, ostensibly, a Southern tuning. It was not standard E-A-D-G-B-E. It was tuned differently. So I am also positive—I would *think* E. And "Kansas City" was *probably written* in C. Because at that time I used to write a lot of things in C because it was easy to whip them off that way. And that was done by Little Willie Littlefield. That was the first record. He was a boogie-woogie blues pianist. And it's possible that it was in E flat. It may be. We taught the song to Little Willie at Maxwell Davis's home.

Leiber: He chipped his tooth on the microphone.

Many articles written about you say that Elvis knew Big Mama's version of "Hound Dog"—

Stoller: He did. But that's not where he learned it.

Leiber: He didn't do her version.

Stoller: Her version is a woman's song. It's a woman's lyric and she did it in that way. He heard a white group called Freddie Bell and the Bellboys. We learned this later. They were hired as a lounge act in Vegas, and when he walked through Vegas, he heard them doing it.

Leiber: It was what you heard from him. Ostensibly it was like an English skiffle shuffle band.

So Elvis got his lyrics from Freddie Bell?

Leiber and Stoller: Yeah.

And it was Freddie Bell who rewrote the lyrics?

Stoller: Yeah. Or somebody did.

Leiber: I wrote, "You ain't nothin' but a hound dog, quit snoopin' round my door, you can wag your tail, but I ain't gonna feed you no more.

You told me you was high class, but I can see through that, you told me you was high class, but I can see through that, and Daddy, I know—"

Stoller: "—you ain't no real cool cat, you ain't nothin' but a hound dog." Freddie Bell's is, "You ain't nothin' but a hound dog, cryin' all the time—"

Leiber and Stoller: "—you ain't never caught a rabbit and you ain't no friend of mine."

Leiber: Nonsense! He liked the lick. He liked the sound.

Stoller: She was singing to a *man*. And he was singing to a dog. [*Laughter*]

Leiber: She was singing to a *gigolo*, to be very precise. Somebody that was *sponging* off of her. *That's* what it was about.

So were you unhappy with the lyric as Elvis did it?

Leiber and Stoller: Yeah.

Leiber: I didn't like the record either. Mama's record was *it*. Pete Lewis playing that guitar solo, with her screaming her heart out. That was *it*. And Presley, he did records that we really loved. One of the best records we've ever had of a ballad of ours was "Love Me" [recorded by Elvis]. One of the very best. And he did a great job on a lot of songs.

Stoller: "Jailhouse Rock." I mean, that's *great*.

Leiber: But his biggest song of ours, I think, I feel—Mike does, I think so too, I can speak for you—was just not up to snuff. It wasn't up to his standards either, I don't think.

Stoller: Well, I think "Jailhouse Rock"—

Leiber: Is *it*.

Stoller: —is, at this point, one of the biggest songs. Bigger than "Hound Dog." Though "Hound Dog" is his signature.

Bigger in what sense?

Leiber and Stoller: Sold more.

Leiber: It's more famous too.

Stoller: It's hard to say whether "Jailhouse Rock" is more famous than "Hound Dog."

Leiber: Not than "Hound Dog," no. "Hound Dog" is one of the greatest performed songs of all time.

Some people consider it your greatest song. People have said if you wrote nothing other than "Hound Dog," that would have been enough.

Leiber: That is, in a sense, true. The point is, though, the record that is celebrated is not the record that should be celebrated. It should be Big

Mama Thornton's record. That's the way it was conceived, and that's the way it was written, and that's more or less—and very much *more*—Mike's bag, because the rhythm pattern that Mike played that day on Columbia Avenue is the rhythm pattern that was used for Big Mama Thornton.

Did you produce Big Mama's record of it?

Leiber: Just about.

Stoller: I'll tell you what happened. Johnny was running the session, but Johnny had played the run-through at his house. He was the drummer. It was his garage. When we went to Radio Recorders to record it, he went to the booth, because he had to make the record, and he was ostensibly *making the records*. There was no named producer. That word hadn't come into the lexicon in recorded music yet. So he was making the record, and Jerry said to him, "It ain't happening." His drummer was "Kansas City" Bell. Layard Bell.

Leiber: Bell. You're right. Again! [*Laughs*]

Stoller: And Jerry said, "It's not happening. And you've got to get out there on the drums."

Johnny said, "Well, who will run the session?"

And Jerry said, "We will."

Leiber: It was the beginning of it. Of producing.

Stoller: And he went, "Okay," and he went out there and played the drums. We did two takes. The first one was fabulous and the second one was *magnificent*. [*Laughs*] And that was it.

And needless to say, everything was cut live. No overdubs—

Stoller: No. Mono.

So the first time both of you heard Elvis's "Hound Dog," neither of you liked it? You didn't like the words or the sound?

Leiber: No. Mike was more tolerant than I was. We really didn't like it.

Stoller: It was nervous sounding. It didn't have that insinuation that Big Mama's record had.

Leiber: You know what's strange about it? It's something that really is sort of an imitation that never really turned out well. It became one of the biggest smashes of all time. And lots of songs and records that we made that were really great never made it at all.

Stoller: It's a matter of aesthetics. It's where you live. And what really gets to you. That's really the most important thing. And once in a while you do something that you feel is just right, and everybody else thinks so too. Then you've really accomplished something.

Aside from the groove and the lyrics, did you think Elvis, on "Hound Dog," had a good voice?

Leiber and Stoller: Yeah.

And you knew nothing about him when you first heard it?

Leiber: No. But when we heard him, I think we thought he was an *animal*. He had a voice, a *range*, that was unreal.

Stoller: Animal in the most positive light.

Leiber: He would go out there. He was like one big champion in the recording studio. We'd tell him we need one more. It was take fifty-eight. And he'd do it. And he'd do it with the same kind of zest and energy as take one.

Stoller: He loved to perform.

Leiber: That's when he was really himself. He was *very* self-conscious. Very, almost always, openly, *embarrassed* about being anywhere socially or being anywhere where it had to do with his *mixing* with anybody. He carried his entourage, the Memphis Mafia with him, and they were his family, and they *knew* him. If he wanted a peanut butter sandwich with tomatoes on a *bagel*, they all understood.

Stoller: [*Laughs*]

No bagels?

Stoller: No, I don't think he ever ordered a bagel in his life—

Leiber: No, I know.

Stoller: I know. Orange pop and peanut butter and banana sandwiches.

Leiber: But when he was behind the microphone, that's where he *lived*.

I know that when you worked with him, he would do lots and lots of takes. Did you feel at the time he needed to do that many takes?

Leiber: He was so good, we kept going—

Stoller: He loved to *perform*!

Leiber: —he'd *improve*. Yeah, you don't know when he was gonna stop improving. And when you felt he did, and you got take twenty-five or thirty, and it was good, we'd often go for take thirty-one. Because we felt it might be greater. And often it would be. So we'd always go for one or two more after he did a great take.

When he was singing in the studio, would he be moving in the way we now know Elvis to famously move?

Leiber: No. No way. You mean shake his hips? No.

Stoller: No. But he was constantly singing. Between songs he would sing a *hymn*. He would go to the piano and play a few chords and sing a hymn.

Leiber: "Nearer My God to Thee." Stuff like that. White Baptist hymns.

Stoller: He had The Jordanaires with him. And they'd come in behind him. That's what he wanted to do all the time.

Would he ever play guitar while doing vocals?

Leiber: No.

Stoller: Once in a while he'd pick up an electric bass guitar—it was in those days, it wasn't real electric bass—and fool around with it. But usually he just sang.

Would you give him ideas of how you wanted a song to sound?

Stoller: We'd demonstrate it as best we could. The feeling. And that's what we did.

After he did "Hound Dog," did you like the idea of doing more with him?

Stoller: Well, we submitted songs. His music publisher asked if we had any other songs that would be good for Elvis. And Jerry thought of this song "Love Me" that we had recorded with this black duet, Willie and Ruth, and then had been picked up and recorded by a dozen other people, including Billy Eckstine. None of them were hits. And Jerry remembered the song, and it was submitted, and he did a *fantastic* job on it.

So you were happy with that one.

Leiber: Oh yeah.

Stoller: Very. And then they asked us to write songs for the movie. We did "Loving You" and then "Jailhouse Rock." Then we were informed that he wanted us to be in the studio. Because he knew the records that we were making.

Leiber: He was a fan of ours. In fact, he was a fan of ours before he started making records for Sun Records and Sam Phillips. He knew what we did.

Do you remember how "Kansas City" came about?

Leiber: Yes. There was a blues with a big band that I loved. And it was one of the only blues with a big band that I really cottoned to. There was one song that I really loved, and it was "Sorry, But I Can't Take You." "We're goin' to Chicago, sorry, but I can't take you." I was influenced by that song, and I wanted to have something like that.

So I sang "Kansas City" to Mike like I sang "You ain't nothin' but a hound dog." And Mike said, "Yeah, I like that, but I don't want just a blues shout. I want to write a melody to that. I want to write kind of a jazz-blues-oriented melody for Basie, or someone like that."

Stoller: What I said was that I wanted to play a blues—

Leiber: With a melody—

Stoller: With a tune, so that if it's played instrumentally, people will recognize it as that song.

Leiber: I said, "I *want* it to be a blues shout. I don't want it to have a predictable melody, some jazz melody. I want it to be a blues. I want it to be really raw. I don't want it to be phony."

He said, "Well, who's writing the music—you or me?"

I said, "Well, I guess you are." So he wrote the music, and it became the big standard that it became.

That's fascinating. With both "Hound Dog" and "Kansas City" you had disagreements about the way they should be—

Stoller: We've had a disagreement about everything since 1950. [*Laughs*]

Leiber: Our relationship is the longest-running single argument in the entertainment business.

You are both the same age—so it's kind of a sibling rivalry—

Stoller: Absolutely.

So many of the famous entertainment duos, from Martin and Lewis to Simon & Garfunkel, are famous for their fights.

Leiber: I think out of those confrontations come very good work.

You came up with the idea of "Kansas City" 'cause you liked the use of Chicago in the other song, so you came up with another Midwest city? Was Kansas City the first city you considered?

Leiber: Yeah. I loved the sound of it syllabically. Kan-sas Ci-ty. Chicago was good, but I liked Kansas City better. Because Chicago is halting consonantly wise. And Kansas City just rolls out.

Stoller: And Kansas City was the center—

Leiber: Of jazz, yeah.

Stoller: Blues and jazz-blues.

Leiber: Jay McShann. Charlie Parker. It was kind of an homage from us to Kansas City.

Stoller: Count Basie put together one of his first bands *in* Kansas City and had the Kansas City Seven, which had Lester Young. So it was that amalgam of blues and jazz. And Joe Turner—

Leiber: It was a breeding ground for great musicians.

Stoller: It was a lot of history of that kind of music.

With a song like "Kansas City," would you finish the whole lyric before giving it to Mike?

Leiber: Rarely. It was later on in our career that I got accustomed to writing the lyrics on my own. But even then there would be a line or two that he would help with.

Stoller: To my memory, it was always like that. Same thing with the music. I would write the music, and Jerry would make suggestions. He'd say, "It doesn't fit what I'm trying to say"—

Leiber: "Would you change that note?" He'd say, "No"—

Stoller: No! [*Much laughter*] But eventually things smoothed out. I'd say, "If I have to change it there, I'd have to change it there . . . well, that could work . . ."

You once said that "Kansas City" came together like spontaneous combustion—

Stoller: Even including the argument, I would venture to guess that the whole thing, within forty-five minutes to an hour, was complete. *Including* the argument.

Leiber: The songs that were tooled and worked on for weeks did not happen that way. "Is That All There Is?" did not happen that way, was *not* spontaneous combustion. "Hound Dog" was. "Kansas City" was. "Stand By Me" was. "Down Home Girl" was. A lot of things were. A lot of the early blues things would be finished in ten minutes, twelve minutes. At the most a half hour. But other things—the Peggy Lee songs—took a lot more craft and a lot more working. And I would spend a lot of time on my own trying to get it right. Because I didn't want to waste his time with me struggling with a line that could take me a day or two or longer. Jokey songs for The Coasters, like "Charlie Brown" and "Yakety Yak," also came quickly, but not as quickly as the blues. They were technically more refined in terms of *form*. There's a lot more rhyming. There's a lot more acknowledgment of structure.

Did you write the melody of "Kansas City" at the piano?

Stoller: Yes, I did.

It has been recorded so many times—by Joe Williams, Little Richard, James Brown, Peggy Lee, Little Milton. Even The Beatles recorded it.

Stoller: I didn't like The Beatles' record of it because they neglected to sing my melody, the way it was written.

Leiber: We don't like the greatest records, the greatest names.

Stoller: But Joe Williams and Count Basie, you know—

Leiber: —were killer.

The original version by Little Willie Littlefield, released in 1952, is in D flat—

Stoller: Do you have perfect pitch?

No.

Leiber: I do, but I'm a baseball player. [*Laughs*]

Stoller: Well, you never can tell because sometimes we would record things in one key and then you'd pitch them up or down.

Leiber: Presley never did that at all. Presley would sing the song in the key that the demo was in. Even if he had to strain his larynx and everything else.

Stoller: Because he learned them—

Leiber: In that key.

To write the songs for the film *Jailhouse Rock*, I understand you went to New York—

Stoller: Well, we didn't go to New York for that *purpose*. We went to New York because we had started making records for Atlantic Records. And we also had some notions about writing for theater.

Leiber: Actually we went to New York because Nesuhi Ertegün had discovered us in LA, and he liked the stuff we were doing, and he realized that we were making records at that point for our own label with Lester Sill. And were making records like "Riot in Cell Block No. 9" and other songs. And they used to get very good reviews in the trade papers, but they never really sold very much.

Stoller: Not outside of LA. 'Cause we didn't have any promotion.

Leiber: Nesuhi approached us and said, "You know, you're making great records. But you're not gonna sell them 'cause you don't know how to merchandise records." He asked questions about who we had doing promotion, who we had taking records to the radio stations. We didn't have anybody doing anything. We thought all you needed was to make a record and send it to twenty-five or thirty disc jockeys and that was it. Well, of course, that wasn't it. And he talked to us about going to Atlantic. And I thought of an idea that might work for us. And something I wanted to do very much. And I talked to him about it, and he wasn't sure we could do that, but he thought if we made records for Atlantic, they would put them out and distribute them.

Mike and I finally talked it over and decided to ask the guys at Atlantic to consider us producers since we were in the studio making the records. And in many cases Mike was making the arrangement. In many cases I was directing the rhythm section. They fought like tigers to keep us from getting credit on the label. It had never been given to anybody else.

Stoller: Actually they came up with the title "producer." We didn't invent that title.

Leiber: How did we get it? I was fighting with Jerry Wexler.

Stoller: Yes, we *were*.

Leiber: Or was it just about money?

Stoller: No! It was about some kind of *credit*. For making the *record*.

Leiber: Oh, I know, I know.

Stoller: Finally, when they agreed, they came up with the name "Produced by." Because I would have thought "Directed by" would have been more appropriate.

Leiber: That's what I was gonna say right now. That we came up with "Directed by," and they didn't buy it for whatever reason. I think it sounded too consummate—

Stoller: That may have been so. All I remember is saying we wanted credit, and they finally gave in, 'cause they said, "Man, how many times do you want your name on the record? You *wrote* the song. We tell Waxie Maxie in Washington, the distributor, we told him you made the record." [*Laughs*]

So you were the first official designated record producers.

Stoller: As far as I know.

Leiber: With credit.

Stoller: Independent record producers.

Leiber: There was Buck Ram, who was making records for The Platters. He was making records at the same time. I *just* remembered that. I haven't remembered that in forty years.

Stoller: But he didn't have a producer credit.

Leiber: There was no credit. There was no credit at all.

Was there any name for the person doing that job?

Stoller: The A&R man.

Leiber: But he never got label credit.

Stoller: That's true.

Leiber: The A&R man—

Stoller: —was a hired—

Leiber: —producer, actually.

Stoller: In effect, a producer. But in some cases they selected the song. Then they called the take numbers. They hired an arranger, and frequently that was it. They hired an arranger, and they selected a song for the artist. What *we* were doing, because we were writing and we wanted to protect the intention that we had when we wrote the song, was outline—not only teaching *how* to sing, which Jerry frequently did by demonstrating over and over certain phrases, and I would write an arrangement, and frequently I would play the piano on those early sessions. I played on all of those Coasters records—

Leiber: Nobody could ever play like Mike could. And there were *wizard* piano players. But they never got the feel.

Stoller: I was not a wizard piano player. I'm still not. Apparently I had the feel for the songs that we were writing. Especially at that time.

I never understood why the name "producer" for records was chosen, as a record producer, of course, is much different than a movie producer.

Stoller: It should have been "director."

Leiber: That's why I came up with "director." I was looking for a word they might accept. And then they refused to use the word "director." I put a lot of pressure on Jerry Wexler. And to some degree we both intimidated him. We got to a point where we more or less stood our ground, and we indicated that if we couldn't get a credit and a royalty— we wanted a two-cent royalty—they didn't want to give us either, but then they gave in, and we got the royalty—

Stoller: They gave us a royalty?

Leiber: It wasn't two cents?

Stoller: It was two cents, but then after that we wanted three. And we went up to three.

Leiber: Mike is right. And they gave us producers credit. And we went from there.

Stoller: And we made their first million-selling single, which was "Searchin'" and "Young Blood" [performed by The Coasters].

Leiber: "Searchin'" was designed to be the B-side, and it became a big hit. "Young Blood" was a big hit too, but nothing compared to "Searchin'."

And you would completely produce the sessions—

Stoller: Between the two of us—

Leiber: Between the two of us we did everything.

Stoller: Including the mastering. In fact, even before there was multitrack, we were doing overdubs. When we had to. And cutting an S off a word because it wasn't supposed to be there. Because in those days you couldn't reach into one track and adjust it. There was only *everything*.

Leiber: We used to do it with [engineer and producer] Tommy Dowd, who was a *wizard*, at Atlantic.

Stoller: Well, first we did it here, with [engineer] Bunny Robine. At Master Recorders.

Leiber: On Fairfax. Right across the street from my high school.

Stoller: But with Tommy, we had a *major* advantage, because Tommy had—

Leiber: —a four-track machine.

Stoller: Eight.

You had eight-track?

Leiber: Not the first one.

Stoller: Yeah. Guarantee it. Three people had an eight-track machine. Tommy Dowd, Les Paul, and the US Navy.

Leiber: I remember that Tommy had, by himself, a four-track machine for six or eight months, and then he graduated to an eight-track machine.

Stoller: Well, when I worked with him, that I recall, he had a small studio—234 West 56th Street, top of an old brownstone building. My memory of it was that working there with The Coasters was with an eight-track machine. But we didn't do any of that stuff where you start with the bass and drums and then add a guitar. We did *everybody* at the same time, but we had the ability to make little adjustments. And we had the ability to have the group, or the lead singer, sing four or five bars or do a whole performance again. We'd pick the best stuff.

But you wouldn't overdub the lead vocal. You would do it live.

Stoller: Oh absolutely, it would have to be.

It's surprising to me you had eight-track so early on. The Beatles, at Abbey Road, didn't get eight-track till 1968.

Stoller: We didn't except if we worked with Tommy Dowd in New York. He had an eight-track machine *early*. I'm talking about, I think, 1958. And there was an eight-track. Like I said, there were only three at the time. Tommy was a *genius*.

You said that you overdubbed prior to having a multitrack?

Stoller: Yes. Going from a mono to another mono. The original tape, with whatever was on it, and adding a new element.

And it sounded okay?

Stoller: Well, it wasn't fabulous. But we got what we wanted!

So many of the stories written about you are inaccurate, according to what you've told me. Another is that when you were asked to write the songs for *Jailhouse Rock* you were in a fancy hotel in New York, and you spent the nights partying and clubbing rather than write the songs—

Leiber: It wasn't a fancy hotel. We were in a small hotel, and Mike was a real jazzophile, jazznik, and he *schlepped* me all over New York to small clubs to watch jazz players, the greatest jazz players, and Mike was excited about the whole scene, and couldn't care less—

Stoller: But we were given a script by Gene Auerbach, who said, "We need songs for the new movie." I forget what the movie was called then. Somebody told me this, that the original title was *Ghost of a Chance.* We kind of tossed it in the corner with some other magazines, and we were having a great time in New York.

Leiber: And then they came looking for us.

Stoller: Yeah, Gene came. [*Laughs*] And he locked us in, more or less. [*Laughs*]

Leiber: He came over to lecture us on fidelity in delivering work, and we hadn't done *anything.* And he came over, and he stalked around the room, and he talked about the necessity of being on time, etcetera. And finally he shoved the sofa against the door. And he stretched out on the sofa and said, "Boys, I'm gonna stay here until you give me the score."

We wrote four songs, and one was "Jailhouse Rock."

Stoller: The others were "Treat Me Nice" and "(You're So Square) Baby I Don't Care" and "I Want to Be Free."

Leiber: We wrote those songs in about three hours, all four of them.

Stoller: And then we wanted to get *out.*

Leiber: He finally took the songs and said, "*Great!*" and left. And we split.

Stoller: [*To Leiber*] Let me ask you a question: Did we make demos of those songs?

Leiber: I think you played them live and taught Presley directly, 'cause I don't remember a demo.

Stoller: That's what I *thought!* I played them and you sang. 'Cause I don't remember—

Leiber: Yeah, I remember. And I'll tell you where the piano was. It was in the right-hand corner.

Stoller: I remember you and I teaching Presley the songs.

Leiber: Some session was over. I think it was the *Jailhouse Rock* sessions, and one of the guys in the entourage of mechanics and doers and coproducers and associates came over to me and said, "Jerry, we'd like you to show up tomorrow at seven in the morning. We'd like you to play the piano player in the film." And I said, "But I'm not a piano player. Mike is the piano player." "That doesn't matter. You look like a piano player."

Stoller: You look like one. [*Laughs*]

Leiber: What nonsense. So I go home that night, and at ten o'clock that night, my face was swollen out to here—I have an impacted wisdom tooth. So I call Mike up, and I said, "Mike, you're gonna have to go at seven in the morning. They wanted me to be the piano player." He said, "Jerry, I can't do it. I have a beard." I said, "So shave it!" He said, "No." He's always like that.

Stoller: I've got to protect myself.

Leiber: He was, "How do you want your 'No'—fast or slow?" But then he said, "All right, I'll do it."

Stoller: I didn't say that to you about the beard. You said, "They won't know the difference."

Leiber: I said, "Yes they will! Shave your beard off!"

Stoller: No, no. My memory is this. Your memory could be right, but mine could be righter. I went over, and they put me in a Hawaiian shirt, and they said, "You start Monday morning, seven in the morning every day." And they said, "Shave the beard off—it's a scene stealer."

And you did?

Stoller: I did.

Leiber: The dialogue is a little different from how *I* wrote it.

Stoller: Yes, but the result was the same. And that was my debut!

Leiber: He became a star, and I became a no-name *schlepper*.

I had assumed *Jailhouse Rock* was the original title of the film, and you wrote your song to the title. But you invented that title.

Stoller: There was a scene. We didn't read the script that carefully, but we thumbed through, and Jerry saw that there was an amateur show in a prison. So he wrote "Jailhouse Rock." The only title song we wrote to their title was "King Creole."

Good to set the record straight. It's been written that you wrote the songs for the movie *Jailhouse Rock*—

Stoller: We wrote songs for the movie that *became Jailhouse Rock*.

It was also written you were staying in a "ritzy hotel."
Leiber: Ritzy?
Stoller: No, it wasn't.
Leiber: The Gorham Hotel.
Stoller: The Gorham Hotel.
Leiber: Did they mean fancy, expensive?

Yes. Fancy like the Ritz.
Stoller: No.
Leiber: The Plaza was ritzy. The Waldorf was ritzy. They don't pay expenses when you do movies.

When you wrote "Jailhouse Rock," did you have a sense that it was a great song?
Leiber: No, we never felt that. See, you can write a great song and you can end up with a lousy record. Because record production is sometimes not up to speed. As Mike once said, "We don't write songs. We write records."
Stoller: [*Laughs*] He's giving me the credit for saying that.

Yet you produced many of the records yourself, so you ensured the songs would become good records.
Leiber: We started producing in self-defense because a lot of our songs got wrecked. And we started moving closer and closer to having hands-on producing situations. We were the first independent producers.

In what ways were your songs wrecked? Was it the wrong feel?
Leiber: Yeah. You give an A&R man a song, and he'll misinterpret it. It'll be like a Texas shuffle, and he'll do a Benny Goodman swing arrangement of it, instead of Tiny Bradshaw or James Brown, or the right stuff.

So with "Jailhouse Rock" you both wrote words and music simultaneously?
Leiber: Yeah. Most of the blues were written that way. Once I had a couple of lines, it created a groove. And once the groove was in, he could groove with it and extend it, if he wanted to, and that's the way a lot of the blues were written. The cabaret songs were not written that way.
Stoller: On some ballads sometimes it would start with a melody. A beginning of a melody. Then the words would come in. In the early days we worked a lot—
Leiber: Simultaneously.

When you wrote all four of those songs in a handful of hours, did you feel there was something phenomenal about that?

Leiber: No. "Hound Dog" was twelve minutes.

Stoller: We wrote songs for Little Esther when a phone call came. As Sammy Cahn would say, "What came first, the music or the lyrics? The phone call." We would write three songs in a few hours and finish one in the car on the way to the studio.

Leiber: Tell the story about the Christmas song.

Stoller: Oh yeah. [*Laughs*] They were doing a Christmas album with Elvis, and he wanted us in the studio all the time.

Leiber: Like lucky charms. He believed that. We were lucky charms.

Stoller: We were in the studio, and they said, "We need another song." And we went out into the utility closet at Radio Recorders, and within eight minutes we had written "Santa Claus Is Back in Town"—

In the closet.

Stoller: Yeah. And pardon the expression, we came out of the closet— [*Laughs*]

Leiber: Well, he did, not me. As you can see, I stayed in the closet.

Stoller: And we came in with the song. Colonel said, "What took you so long, boys?"

So again, no instrument. You just wrote the melody in your head.

Stoller: Well, yeah. It's kind of a vagueish melody.

Leiber: It's also blues oriented. And Michael would often, in a song like that, add sort of a touch of polish of a melody.

Stoller: Well, we sang it to them.

Many songwriters have written great songs fast, but to write four great songs fast—

Leiber: They're not all great.

Stoller: We'll let you decide which ones are and which ones aren't.

Do you think it was the pressure of having to write that enabled you to come up with four songs so quickly?

Stoller: No.

Leiber: No.

Because the Motown writers and the Brill Building writers had that kind of pressure, and they came up with great stuff.

Stoller: Well, the Brill Building writers—and they didn't write in the Brill Building, as you know [1619 Broadway], but across the street at 1650 Broadway—they had to compete with each other for cuts.

As did the Motown writers.

Stoller: I guess so. We didn't compete with anybody. We chose our own productions. The only time we wrote for assignment was when we wrote for movies.

When you would teach a song, such as "Jailhouse Rock," to Elvis, would he do the song pretty much as you did?

Stoller: No.

Leiber: I don't remember him copying me behind a microphone. I remember him going behind a microphone, and what he did for the first two or three minutes was crack bad jokes.

Stoller: He had one of his entourage, also—

Leiber: —on the microphone.

Stoller: —comedian. Talking like a phony airport—

Leiber: "Boarding on a 707, gate twelve . . ." And they all laughed. [*Laughter*]

Stoller: And they ate lunch in the studio too.

Leiber: He was right about that. Peanut butter and banana sandwiches. The idea made me *ill*.

Stoller: That was amazing to us. We were producing *records*. And we would go into the studio with the Robins or with the Coasters, and we had to get four tunes done in *three hours*.

Leiber: It was the union's rules.

Stoller: Because, what was it in those days? Four dollars and twenty-five cents per musician, and if you went overtime, you know, that was *heavy*. These guys took over the studio. RCA booked the studio from ten in the morning till whenever—they just blocked out the whole week! So they stayed in the studio, and nobody was worried about them.

Leiber: That was the only pressure, actually, that we put on ourselves. Because we were just *trained*, we were *brainwashed*, not to go over three hours. And to get four sides. And we *always* did. And we learned how to move *very* quickly and very effectively. But that's the only pressure. The other pressure didn't exist for us.

Stoller: No. First of all, we were very young, and we could work eighteen hours a day without being concerned about anything, about being tired—

Leiber: And smoke four packs of cigarettes.

Stoller: And drink endless cups of tea.

Leiber: Can I ask you a question? Why are you so interested in "Jailhouse Rock"? Is it that important?

Yes, it is. It's part of our culture. It's one of the most iconic and classic songs performed by Elvis, who is considered the king of rock and roll. When you hear that record he is alive—his spirit is alive in that performance.

Leiber: Yeah, that's him.

Stoller: Absolutely. That's true.

Leiber: But there's a whole other dimension to our collaboration. We wrote "Is That All There Is?" in three shots, as I remember it. Before it was even recorded, it was part of another song called "Black Is Black No Longer."

Stoller: Well, it wasn't part of it. What happened—this is my memory, again, which is pretty good—Jerry presented me with spoken vignettes. And I set them to music. They were all set to the same music. And Georgia Brown, the British singer-actress who had been on Broadway in the show *Oliver*, she came over with her—

Leiber: Manager.

Stoller: Her manager, and an arranger, Peter Matz. And we played this for her, and she said, "It's great, it's great. But it's all talking. I need something to sing." And we had this other refrain, "We all wore coats with the very same lining," and we stuck it in and she said, "That's it. I'm gonna do that on my television special in London on the BBC." She left, and we looked at each other and said, "This doesn't make any sense." [*Laughs*] We both vowed to write a refrain—he the lyrics and me the music.

The next day I called him and said, "I've got a tune that I think is really right for this."

And he said, "Okay, but listen, I've written a lyric already. And I know that the lyric is right. And you might have to jettison what you wrote." I came over and I insisted on playing and he insisted on reciting, and finally I won, and I played it. The tune.

And he said, "Play it again." And I played it, and he sang the lyric. And it fit perfectly. We didn't have to change anything.

Amazing.

Leiber: That is pretty amazing, yeah. That only happened once in fifty-six years, but it happened.

Stoller: And there's only one rhyme in the entire piece. "Let's break out the booze and have a *ball*, if that's *all* . . . there is." That's the only rhyme in the piece.

Does that phenomenon—of having written words and music separately that matched perfectly—give you any sense that there is Providence at work guiding your collaboration?
    Leiber: No.
    Stoller: No, no, not at all. [*Laughs*]

As you know, many songwriters have said they don't feel they write songs but that songs come through them. John Lennon said that—
    Leiber: He got that from me. That you're a vessel.

You feel that?
    Leiber: Sometimes.

Had you ever written a song like "Is That All There Is?" before—a song with spoken vignettes?
    Stoller: We wrote "Riot in Cell Block No. 9" that has spoken parts. It's very different. That's talking blues.
    Leiber: That's talking blues.
    Stoller: And this was not exactly talking blues. And yet—
    Leiber: It was *Sprechstimme*. It wasn't blues at all.
    Stoller: I know it's not blues—
    Leiber: The closest thing you can get to a model for it is Bertolt Brecht, and that kind of articulation. It's in "The Black Freighter"—
    Stoller: But *Sprechstimme* is almost—
    Leiber: Tonal—
    Stoller: Tonal. This is just a recitation. It's not even *implied* to be sung.
    Leiber: Yeah. I tried it. I tried kind of a dummy tune, and I realized that the tune created a synthetic kind of unreality that is so far from the tough attitudes about living I was trying to express. So I decided to try and just *say* it. But I was afraid to do that because I didn't think it would be acceptable.
    Stoller: When I set it to music, not having really discussed it at length with you at that point, I said, "You know, I think these should really be spoken," and you said, "Of course, that's what I meant."

A lot of people have likened it to Brecht and Weill.
    Stoller: We were influenced by Brecht and Weill because we liked their work.

Leiber: I was influenced by a long short story by Thomas Mann. Called—

Stoller: "Disillusionment."

Leiber: "Disillusionment." And I decided—all of these decisions came at about the same time—both Mike and myself were getting tired of writing for the market. And also the market was changing to a point where a lot of stuff that we liked to write was not going down, was not happening. A lot of the groups from England were happening, a lot of that other stuff was happening, Kennedy got killed. And the stuff we were doing was kind of fading from the scene. And we both wanted to write some material that was more adult and more theatrical.

So I was reading this story by Mann, and the thread in it was this kind of terrible, negative thing. But it had, at the same time, a parallel line that was very Germanic and very funny. So I felt I'd like to try to translate this material. At least the *feel* of it, the *sense* of it. And I wondered if it would work. And I did a lot of work on the lyric, and I gave Mike the material. And we usually always, as you know, worked together, on whatever we were doing, simultaneously, and on this piece I just handed him a lyric—

Stoller: The original, the vignettes, you handed me on a piece of paper.

Leiber: I gave him the song, and he took it home. And he had written, on his own, without lyrics, a refrain. And I came in the next day, and we hassled over who would play it first.

I said, "Let me play it first, because then lyrics come first before the music."

He said something like, "Not in this case," and it was another argument.

Then he played the melody. And I was in *shock*. [*Sings refrain*]

Stoller: I wanted to play it first because I thought he would love it. And I wanted to play it so he would be inclined to adjust his lyric to it rather than me having to tear my beautiful new tune apart to his lyrics. I wanted to get there first for that reason. But fortunately neither of us had to adjust.

The lyric is so beautifully constructed, with the repeating refrain tying together disparate subjects: first a fire, then the circus, then love, and then life—

Leiber: That last one is suicide. "If that's the way she feels about it, why doesn't she just end it all? Oh no, not me." Oh, you want another secret about that? In Peggy Lee's version she sings, "If that's the way she feels about it, why doesn't she just end it all? Oh no, not me, I'm not *ready* for that final disappointment." Which is wrong. And which changes to some degree the meaning of the song which was intended. By one word. And that's a great lesson in writing anything. *One* word can change it quite a bit. And that is, "If that's the way she feels about it. Oh no, not me, I'm in no *hurry* for that final disappointment." Which is the joke. I'm not *ready* for that final disappointment—is not a joke.

But she *insisted* on singing "ready" because I think she felt that it sounded more natural. And she missed the point.

Interesting you started the song with a description of a fire, which can be both beautiful and disastrous—

Leiber: It can be very dangerous and uncontrollable.

What brought you to start there?

Leiber: I never know what brings me to think of anything. I'm not one of those writers who gets an idea from looking at something. The words, the ideas—I don't know where they come from.

Stoller: We made a demo of it, and Jerry brought it to Peggy. She said, "This is my life story." She said, "I was in a fire like that."

Leiber: She said, "You wrote this for me. I know it. And if you give it to anyone else, I don't know what I'm gonna do." And she was convinced, on some mystical level—she wasn't joking—she thought that was true.

It is a perfect song for her.

Leiber: But we really wrote it for Lotte Lenya.

Stoller: Oh, that's a lotta Lenya. [*Laughter*]

Leiber: I like that.

Stoller: You got it. [*Laughs*]

Leiber: Leslie Uggams recorded it first. Mike wanted to test the arrangement out—really, that's the truth. We both knew that she wasn't really appropriate. But we couldn't get anybody—

Stoller: But we didn't have anybody ready to record it.

Leiber: Yeah, some record. I would have done it with Mae West. In fact, she made a record for us. She did the Elvis Presley Christmas song that we told you about.

Stoller: "Santa Claus Is Back in Town."

Leiber: And it's pretty good.

Stoller: It's funny. [*Imitates her*] "Christmas, oh . . . Christmas, oh . . ." That's the way it starts. [*Laughs*]

Leiber: I love the record. That's one of my favorites. And of all the "Kansas City" records, out of all those great stars—Little Richard, Joe Williams, you name it—I think the best take is Little Milton. You've got to hear it.

Stoller: For me it's Joe Williams.

Leiber: Well, I mean, it's Joe Williams for me too.

What was it about the Joe Williams record that made it the best?

Leiber: It's really what it oughtta be.

Stoller: The intention. It was, finally, the intention of a real kind of Kansas City blues-jazz feel.

Leiber: It was stylistically perfect. A lot of people who did it before did it as kind of a country, semicountry version, semi–big city blues. Tiny Bradshaw.

Stoller: Or dropped most of the tune and just shouted.

And that was what The Beatles did, in your opinion?

Stoller: Well, The Beatles copied Little Richard's record. The Beatles' version is good, but it isn't what I wrote. It doesn't have the melody that I liked. The first record was Little Willie Littlefield in 1952. And the other weird thing about it, if you want to talk about something mystical, was that this one has a certain mysticism in my mind: Jerry and I were meeting at his townhouse in New York. We both lived on the east side then. I lived on 17th Street; he lived on 72nd in brownstones. I went up to work with him, and I said, "Remember that old song 'Kansas City'? That would really be a great song for Joe Williams and Count Basie."

And he said, "Yeah, yeah, I can see that." He said, "I'll pick up the phone and call Teddy Reig at Roulette Records," because Teddy Reig produced all of the Basie stuff there at Roulette. So he placed a call—it was a Friday, I think—and left a message.

And Monday the trades came out, and they had a pick. And the pick was "Kansas City" by Wilbert Harrison. Plus three other cover records mentioned. And we had not had a cover in *seven* years. We were just thinking of the song, [*laughs*] and on Monday it came out as the big pick hit of the week. And this is after seven years.

Leiber: And that was a big hit. It went to number one. I still can't figure it out.

Stoller: He remembered the song, Little Willie's record. Which was originally called "K. C. Loving," though the lyrics were the same. And I always thought Ralph Bass screwed up the possibility of a hit by calling it "K. C. Loving" instead of "Kansas City" because he thought it was hip.

Of all the great writers of classic rock and roll songs, such as Little Richard and Chuck Berry, there's not one who also has written songs like "Is That All There Is?" Your stylistic range is amazing.

    Leiber: Well, it's obvious that we're just geniuses. [*Laughs*]

I know you're joking, but it's true.

    Stoller: He's not joking.

So you wrote the melody for the refrain of "Is That All There Is?" as just pure melody, with no lyric idea at all?

    Stoller: That's true. But I knew the subject matter from the vignettes. Each one of which ends with "Is that all there is . . ." And although I didn't specifically, consciously write the melody as "Is that all there is"—

    Leiber: He wasn't writing to a lyric. He was just writing notes that obviously sounded—

    Stoller: That felt right to me.

    Leiber: And I came in with the lyric, syllable for syllable.

And it actually matched perfectly—you didn't have to change a single word?

    Leiber: Not at all.

That's amazing.

    Leiber: It is amazing.

On the song "Stand By Me" Ben E. King has writing credit with you. Did he write it with you?

    Stoller: Yeah.

    Leiber: Yes.

There's been countless instances of singers getting their name on a song without really writing it, a tradition that dates back to Jolson and certainly extends to modern times.

    Stoller: There has been, but not in this instance.

    Leiber: We were scheduled to have a rehearsal with Ben E. King, and Mike and I got there early, and a couple of other guys were in this rehearsal—

    Stoller: I have a totally different memory. Go ahead.

    Leiber: —were in this rehearsal hall. We had a small auditorium in a junior high school with a piano. Ben E. came in and "Hi, hello," you know. And he said, "Hey man, guess what? I wrote a song." Ben E. was not a songwriter. A very good performer, but not a songwriter. And he went [*sings softly, to the tune of "Stand By Me"*], "When the night has come and the land is dark, and the moon is the only light we'll see . . . I won't cry, I won't cry . . ." He said, "That's all I wrote."

I said, "That's pretty good. You want me to finish it for you? You want me and Mike to do it?"

He said, "Oh yeah, man, that would be great." So Mike and I finished it. And Mike put that incredible bass line on it. And when I heard that bass pattern, I said, "That's it. That's a hit." And I didn't do much predicting of hits. But I knew that was in there. I also knew "Hound Dog" by Big Mama Thornton was a hit. And "Kansas City" by Wilbert Harrison. Which I wasn't crazy about, but I knew it was a hit.

And we started writing "Stand By Me." And it became what it became.

Did the two of you take it away from Ben E. and work on it on your own?

Leiber: No, we finished it right there. Like we did most of the stuff. We did it there. I mean, these were not assignments that you took home and worried over for a week or two or three or a month. These were hot off the griddle, and we always felt that way, that when they were hot they were more effective and more attractive.

So he had a melody and lyrics.

Leiber: He had the first few lines and the beginning of a melody.

Did he have the chorus?

Leiber: Yeah, I think he did have it. Because it was only one phrase, one line. But he said he couldn't get the rest of the lyrics. He's not a songwriter, but he came up with something pretty good. A couple of sentences and a hunk of the refrain, or maybe all of the refrain.

Stoller: As I remember, it was in our own office. We had an office on 57th Street. And Jerry and Ben E. were fooling around with the lyric on "Stand By Me."

Leiber: And then you came up with the bass pattern.

Stoller: And I came in. Ben E. was singing it in the key of A. And I sat down at the piano, and I just felt this bass pattern, and I started working on a bass pattern, and within five minutes I had the bass pattern, which is the bass pattern of the song and is a big part of it. And in the orchestration, it starts with bass and guitar, and it goes into strings playing it, and it builds up, and this pattern is from beginning to end. But Jerry was working with Ben E. on it, and I think most of the melody of the tune is Ben E.'s. I wrote the bottom part. Which is kind of a signature of the song.

Leiber: The bass pattern.

Stoller: [*Sings bass line*]. "Boom-boom, boom-boom-boom, boom, boom-boom-boom, boom . . ."

It's in A and has that beautiful shift of chords to the VI chord, the F sharp minor—did you invent that or—

Stoller: It's kind of implied. I thought it, to me, it was implied. I think the melody may have shifted a little with the chords I was using. But it's basically his.

And he was just singing it a cappella?

Stoller: Yeah.

John Lennon, years later, made a famous record of it. Also in the key of A. Did you like his version?

Stoller: Yeah. It was a different kind. But it still had the bass pattern. It wasn't like the difference between Big Mama and Elvis. It was the same song; it just had a very different feel. But it was legitimate. It felt right. It felt good, also.

Leiber: It was too fast.

Lennon's was too fast?

Leiber: Yeah. It felt too fast.

Stoller: It was *stiffer*. It was definitely a stiffer feel.

Leiber: Ben E.'s was more syncopated.

Leiber and Stoller: [*Sing rhythmic bass patterns of both in unison, in which Lennon's is straight-time, and Ben E.'s is more fluid and syncopated.*]

Stoller: That's really the difference.

Leiber: Unison! Did you hear that unison?

Stoller: It felt good. I like it.

Leiber: It felt *white*. That's what we're trying to say. And as Mike said, it's somewhat stiffer. It doesn't really have that loop in it.

"Stand By Me" is a phenomenal song. It's got a beautiful melody, but it's also visceral. It's a rock song but it's a ballad. It's got everything.

Stoller: But, you know, it was a hit when it came out. But when it came to be this wedding song and this *everything* song is when Rob Reiner made this movie.

I met Rob at a party, and he insisted on singing all of the Leiber and Stoller songs. And he insisted I go to the piano while he sang. And he called me up months later and said, "I have this movie. It's called *The Body*. And it's been in the can for a while, and I like it. *The Body* is the right title for it. But it's not good, because it's based on a short story by Stephen King, and people will think it's a horror film. It's really a coming-of-age movie. So I want to call it *Stand By Me*."

I said, "Great! Be my guest."

And then I thought about it and I called him back. This was 1986. The record came out in '61. And I said, "Hey, who do you think we can get to record it and put it into your film?"

And he said, "We talked about that. But I view this movie as a period film. So I'd like to go with the original record."

I said, "We produced the original record." So it wasn't that I wasn't *flattered*, but it was that I thought that, well, this'll be an album cut, and if we got Tina Turner [*laughs*] or somebody else to do it, it might become a *hit*. And it did become a hit again. The same record. Nothing was done to it.

Leiber: I couldn't make heads or tails out of that choice. I thought it had nothing to do with that movie *at all*. And I still think so. I think he was in love with the record and the song, and—

Stoller: Hey—listen—

Leiber: And he wanted it in his movie. And the movie was about a dead body in the woods. And what does "Stand By Me" have to do with that, with *children in the movie, what*—?

Stoller: *Whatever* it is, I am so grateful to him. Because it *became*—

Leiber: Yeah. A monster hit.

Stoller: I think people liked the song [when it first was released], but it didn't become that powerful. It became a much *bigger* hit twenty-five years later. Which is really great. I mean, *five* years, maybe. But twenty-five years?

Donald Fagen did a version of your song "Ruby Baby"—

Stoller: Yeah, I love that arrangement.

He took your chords and extended them.

Leiber: Yeah. And he did a terrific job. The original "Ruby Baby" was Dion.

Stoller: No, Dion's wasn't first. The first was The Drifters. Nesuhi Ertegün recorded it in 1954. But I love Dion's record. And I love Donald Fagen's record. [*Claps syncopated drum rhythm from the Dion record.*]

I'd like to ask you about the song "Spanish Harlem." The story goes that Phil Spector wanted to write a song with you for a long time, and he came over and had a chord pattern which he played you—

Leiber: No. He didn't have *anything*.

What happened is that Phil had bothered me for three months, four months, to write a song with him, and I didn't want to do it for a couple of reasons. And the main reason is that Mike and I had sort of a tacit understanding that we were exclusive partners. A number of people wanted to write with Mike and a number of people wanted to write with me, and we just didn't. And [Phil] wanted to write with me, and he was signed to us. Lester Sill [their music publisher] sent Phil Spector to us. For safekeeping. Did a bad job. Lester called me up one day and said, "Jer, I got a kid out here who's really talented. And he's nuts about you guys. He worships the ground you walk on."

I said, "Well, be careful. Watch out. That's usually dangerous. Why do you hate me so much? I never did anything to you."

He said, "He wants to come out and work for you guys."

I said, "Lester, that's like fattening frogs for snakes. Why should we take Phil Spector in and teach him everything we know so that he can go out and compete with us? Who the hell needs that? Let him go find out for himself."

He said, "Jer, you owe me real big. Do me a favor. Take him on for six months or a year. You don't have to sign him to five years or anything like that. And let him hang out with you, in the studio, and let him observe what you do."

So I said, "Okay. Will do."

He said, "By the way, will you send me the fare for a one-way ticket?"

And I went to Mike and told him what had happened, and he said, "Do it." So I did it. And [Spector] was with us for three or four or five or six months. And he wanted to come over and work on a song with us.

I was somewhat annoyed because he was supposed to come over at six thirty, and he came over at five. Mike was supposed to come over at six thirty to work with us. He came over while my kids were having dinner. They were just finishing up. They went, and we were sitting there talking, smoking, having a drink. I got a call from Mike, and he said, "I'm terribly sorry, but I can't make it."

Stoller: The problem was that we had been working on some other things, and some studio stuff, and I hadn't had dinner with *my* kids in weeks. And my wife said to me, "When are you going to see your children?" I canceled out because I wanted to have dinner with my kids. So I called Jerry after dinner—

Leiber: After your dinner?

Stoller: After my dinner.

Leiber: What time was that?

Stoller: Well, it might have been eight thirty.

Leiber: That late? No, it couldn't be, not with children. It couldn't have been eight thirty.

Stoller: Oh, we ate later.

Leiber: Really?

Stoller: Or maybe it was not only after dinner but after bedtime stories and all of that. I called, and they said, "We finished writing the song." And I said, "Fine."

Leiber: Both versions could use some examining. But that's of no consequence. As far as I was concerned, I waited and waited for Mike to come over, and he didn't, and then he finally called. And in that time I wrote "Spanish Harlem" with Phil.

What actually happened was that I had this collection of LPs that were related to Spanish themes. I had Segovia and I had *Rhapsody Espanol*. I had one by Ravel. And I had this idea: "There is a rose in Spanish Harlem, a red rose up in Spanish Harlem . . ." I told them the sentences. And he started to play a melody that was like Jeff Barry rock and roll. [*Sings the lyrics to a rock groove*] Sort of jazzy and wrong.

I said, "Let me play you some stuff that is in the right bag." And I played him two or three of those pieces. And he has a good ear, and he picked up *something* in there. I think he even picked up a three- or four-bar lick in one of the pieces that were in the strings. And we wrote it together.

That's completely different than stories I've read, which stated specifically that he came to you with some music, and you picked up on the Spanish flavor in his music and were inspired to write this lyric.

All the stories about Phil Spector—almost *all of them*—are distorted and wrong. Almost all of them.

Did you have that idea—about the rose in Spanish Harlem—before working with Spector?

Leiber: Yeah. Absolutely. It was a quatrain in search of a melody.

But you never brought it to Mike—

Leiber: It wasn't in enough shape to bring it to anybody. I mean, I don't come in with two lines.

Those are great opening lines. It's visual, it sets the scene, like "Kansas City," there's a sense of place—

It's nice. It's not *special*. "There is a rose in Spanish Harlem, a red rose up in Spanish Harlem . . ." Big deal.

I'd say it is special.

Leiber: "It's growing in the street right up through the concrete" is a special line. But not those opening lines. They're rather ordinary.

Stoller: I agree with Paul.

When you were writing your rock and roll songs did you ever consider that they could become standards?

Stoller: No, we thought all the standards had already been written. Irving Berlin, Jerome Kern, the Gershwins. And those are still great standards, but now they refer to them as the Great American Songbook. And they're putting them in a package as if they are old. Well, they are old. But it's separate from any new works. Just about.

Leiber: We thought our songs would just disappear after they were on the charts. We didn't think that they had any staying power like the old standards. We didn't think they were as good and specific. A lot of them were comic and not serious love songs. For a number of years we had trouble writing love songs. Then we fell out of love, and it was easy to write love songs. [*Laughter*]

Stoller: I think we were—and probably to some degree still are—in awe of the writers I mentioned before.

As songwriters today are in awe of you.

Leiber: If they are, I wish they would remember to tell us that more often. [*Laughter*]

Stoller: I'd say most writers today don't know who we are.

If they don't, they certainly know your songs.

Stoller: Yes, that they do.

Leiber: I'd say that's true.

◆◆◆

Richard Sherman
Writing Songs for Disney

Beverly Hills, California 2010

"People usually love or hate me for it," he said with a smile about writing "It's a Small World," a song that is literally in constant rotation, accompanying the ride of the same name at Disneyland and the other Disney parks throughout the world. It has the distinction of being the only song in existence to receive constant, nonstop airplay all day, every day, as it's performed in all the parks around the world, overlapping time zones. This phenomenon makes it the most performed—and most translated—song in history.

A humble and humorous man, Richard Sherman is quick to point out that a goodly portion of people are seriously annoyed by the song, as it spins on endlessly. But others love it. (As I told him, my mom loved it. It was always her favorite part of Disneyland—that ride—and "that charming song.")

It was also the source of a songwriting myth, which is clarified here, that Richard—and his cowriter brother Robert—got paid every single time the song was played. Untrue. They are paid performance royalties for anytime the song is used outside of the park, in a movie, or on radio. But for usage on the ride, they got paid one time only. "The Mouse," as many refer to Disney here in Hollywood, is notoriously tight.

But the Sherman Brothers made a fortune at Disney—absolutely cherished and coddled by Walt himself, who always admired genuine talent and hard work—and they wrote some of the most magical movie songs ever written. They wrote the entire song score to several Disney movies, including *Mary Poppins* and *The Jungle Book*.

Richard Sherman was born on June 12, 1928; Robert came first, on December 19, 1925. (He died in 2012.) Music was in their blood. Not only was their father, Al Sherman, a Tin Pan Alley songwriter well known for his funny wordplay; their grandpa Samuel was a composer and violinist in the royal Austrian-Hungarian court of the Emperor Franz Joseph.

He had his first taste of the opposite coast at the age of seven when a producer heard some of his dad's songs and put him under contract. "So with only that promise," he remembered, "and some enthusiasm, Dad packed the family up. He uprooted the family. The day we got to California he found out this fellow, this producer, had dropped dead from a heart attack."

Not a propitious beginning for his dad's California songwriting career. But because Bob was always a sickly kid who suffered through the harsh winters of New York, Al Sherman decided to keep his family in Los Angeles and lived forever in locomotives between the two coasts. He found the music business in Hollywood somewhat of a closed club to which he was uninvited and kept returning instead to old New York to sell his songs. Ironically, his sons were not only invited to join that elite songwriters' club that banned Al; they were also soon to become among its most celebrated and successful members.

"We loved it here," Richard said. "If you live in Southern California, this is God's country." Raised in Beverly Hills, he went back east to study music at Bard College (where Becker and Fagen of Steely Dan also went, decades later). During World War II he was in the Reserve for seven years and active duty for two years. "I wasn't in combat. Mostly I counted the days till I could be out. I had just started writing songs." His brother Bob did see combat, was injured in the knee, and was awarded a Purple Heart.

For reasons unbeknownst to this writer, the brothers in later years had a falling out and put an ocean between them, with Bob in England and Richard remaining stateside. But during our interview no indication of any dissonance between them surfaced, and Richard had only kind things to say about his brother. "[Bob] was a natural writer," Richard said. "He wrote stories and poetry. I was in music. I could pick up any instrument and play it. Together we did what we did. We couldn't have done it separately. I needed him as much—if not more—as he needed me.

They belonged to an old songwriting world, the one in which songwriters were hired by movie companies to be on staff and to come in every day and write songs for various projects. But before getting that dream job the Sherman Brothers began by writing pop songs and early rock and roll such as "You're Sixteen," first recorded in 1960 by Johnny Burnette and later by Ringo Starr, who had a hit with it in 1973.

From their dad they learned the value of writing unique and humorous songs, such as "Tall Paul," which was cut by Annette Funicello when she was still a kid and Mouseketeer, a cast member on the Disney TV show *The Mickey Mouse Club*, which started in 1955. That song connected them with Disney, and they wrote more for Annette before being invited to join the Disney writing staff, a dream come true, all related in the following conversation.

We met at the Hamburger Hamlet on Sunset Boulevard in Beverly Hills on a radiantly clear and crisp autumn day in 2010. Many well-wishers came to our table during our discussion as if he were mayor, and he greeted each with warmth and gentle humor. He's a beloved man, with good reason—soft-spoken, whimsical, and genuinely grateful for a life writing songs.

Except for the Gershwin brothers, I can't think of many other songwriting teams of brothers.

Richard Sherman: Well, that's the miracle of it. Bob and I both recognized it. We were both very different people. I'm an extrovert; Bob's an introvert. I'm very talky; Bob's monosyllabic. He's a deep thinker. Very solid brain. It was mutual respect.

We didn't go together through life. We always left each other alone socially. But in the room, when we were working, especially when we started working on projects like films and stage shows, there was no sibling rivalry—it was strictly work. And we both respected each other enough to listen to each other. We would discuss everything. It was kind of a ceasefire when it came to writing music and lyrics. We just sat in the room and *sweated* out the thing. And there were no happier guys than we were when we got an idea that *socked*, and we'd say, "Oh yeah, yeah, this is good."

Whether it's gonna be a hit or not, who knows? But you got that hook, that little something, that special thing that makes it listenable. There's always something, always one little thing that makes something happen.

I remember when I went into the service we didn't write together for five years. He was writing with another writer, and I was writing by myself and with another fellow. We had had dozens of songs recorded, but nothing big where you can say, "Hey, look at that big hit."

One day, through a series of circumstances, we started working together again. The respect sort of happened at that point. At the beginning there a bit of a rivalry going. But then after the five-year period, then it was really business. We respected each other and got along as songwriters and partners. And with a brother, you trust. So there was no problem with trust; it's just a matter of respect. And that's it. We spent the next fifty years writing songs.

There is so much musical talent in your family. Not only was your father Al a songwriter, but your grandfather also was a songwriter, yes?

Yeah, he was a musician and composed a little bit. But mainly his thing was he was a great violinist. When the family migrated to this country Grandpa Samuel was versed in the Strauss waltzes and this marvelous, *marvelous* music of yesterday—of course, it wasn't yesterday then—but he wasn't into ragtime or rhythm music of any kind. He was square. He didn't really manage too well in this country. He did have little ensembles and things, and he played riverboats and other kinds of things. And he made a living at it, but he was never the great success that he should have been. 'Cause in Europe he was the concertmeister of Emperor Franz Joseph's orchestra in Austria-Hungary.

He was a member of the royal court.

Yes. My father used to reminisce. He'd tell about how as a little boy he used to love to listen to his daddy play, and one day Grandpa brought him in—he was five years old—to the court and smuggled him behind the curtain so he could listen to the music. And the empress noticed this—there was jiggling behind the curtain—and the emperor had a guard go over there, and they found a little boy listening, and he said, "That's my papa playing."

So the emperor said, "Oh, come listen to it better" and put him on his knee. And he sat on Emperor Franz Joseph's knee to listen to his father play marvelous music and polkas. He had a little ensemble, called a salon orchestra. Back in the grand days when great music was being played in courts.

So then Grandpa came over here thinking that the world was waiting for them but found the miserable fact that he was not hip. It was kind of a shattering blow. Nobody here cared that he was in the royal court. You didn't bring your résumé. So basically Grandpa, kind of shattered by it, didn't want Dad—my father—to go into it. Because Dad was a natural pianist. Self-taught. A *fabulous* pianist. He was terrific. And he had a great sense of melody. He could invent gorgeous melodies. And he was very successful. He wrote many, many big hits in the twenties and the thirties.

But despite his daddy's warnings and everything, he started his own band and played music. Then he had some hits and some giant hits and became a full-time songwriter. And Dad, God bless him, told us, "Do not go into this crazy business. There is no security in it whatsoever. There's no paycheck at the end of the week. You can slave away at what you're doing and get all sorts of turn-downs and wind up with absolutely nothing at the end of the week." He didn't want us to have the heartbreaks.

He wrote songs with many people. Was he writing the music and not the words?

Dad was an idea man. He was a great natural composer. So 90 percent of all those melodies are his. But he came up with wonderful word sound songs like "What Do We Do on a Dew-Dew-Dewey Day?" and "Aha Me Too," and "(Tomatoes Are Cheaper) Now's the Time to Fall in Love." He'd come in with a catch phrase. And then he'd go to a really sharp cookie like Al Lewis, and they'd sit down and work on words.

But he was always looking for great word sounds and titles. And he taught us. He was the one who sat us down and said, "You've got to get a hook. To get somebody to listen. You don't use the same old words every time. Come up with something special and new. It doesn't matter how good your tune is. If you don't have a good lyric and a good solid idea and follow it through with some surprises, you got nothing." And he was right. He said, "Keep them simple, singable, and sincere." The three S's. And also original. That was the big O surrounding the S, S, and S.

Bob and I, throughout our career, try to write very sincerely, very singable, and very simple. So at least you can understand it. We are not writing for ourselves or somebody else.

When you saw your dad being a songwriter, did that look like an exciting life?

I never thought of it as exciting. I thought about it that he was aggravated a lot and worked very hard at it. He sweated on songs. I wondered why, and he said, "To make 'em better, sonny." He was a hardworking natural composer. A great idea man. And in later years wrote a lot of lyrics too. But in those early years, being an immigrant, he didn't have the versatility with language that a lot of people did. So if he'd get a Buddy DeSylva to write a lyric for him, or Howard Johnson, he'd be in great shape. Later Al Lewis and other people. He had a lot of wonderful friends in the business who worked with him. But Dad was always relied upon to come up with an idea. Like "if you saw what I saw swimming in a see-saw in Nassau by sea . . ." And the guy would write a hell of a song based on Dad's opening line. And he told us, "If you can't do that, don't be a songwriter."

That's why we have so many unique words. We were always digging for something nobody else had done. Like "Fortuosity" or "Bratifaction" or "Supercalifragilistic," I mean nobody did them. That's why we did them. It was Dad's teaching. He said, "You've got to grab hold of somebody. You've got to make them turn around and say, 'What's that?'"

You said he initially didn't want you to become songwriters. Did he ever change his mind?

Yes. Bob and I were both going off in different directions. We were both out of college and living in this little tiny apartment. Out of necessity. There was no question [*laughs*] that we couldn't afford two apartments. We had a little apartment over a cleaning store. Right on Pico Boulevard. Bob is typing away at his novel every day. And I am at the piano, writing my great musicals and my great thematic statements that I was gonna put into a symphony one day. We were just kids, and I was in my early twenties. Bob was about twenty-four or twenty-five. One day Dad came in and sat down and said, "I bet the two of you don't got enough brains between the two of you to write a pop song that some kid wouldn't give up his lunch money to buy." [*Laughs*] "And, you know, I don't think you have the brains for it."

Then he got up and left. It was the gauntlet.

He was challenging you?

Oh sure! I remember he said, "Listen to the radio. Listen to what's being done. And then do one *better*."

And it wasn't easy. It was hard. But we said, just for the hell of it, let's try one. So we started toying with ideas. And once a week Dad would come over and listen to our stuff and say, "This has been done a thousand times. There's nothing new here. I *expect* this tune to go from here to here because that's your statement. But you've got to surprise me."

He kept making us jump hurdles. To make it better, better, better. And one day we got a real hook, a genuine hook. Because we were talking about money. And wanted to write a song about money. We thought, "Gold, that's a good word." So we started playing with that. And we thought, "You know you can buy everything but you can't buy love with it. You can't buy love. Gold can buy anything—but love." And there was our title. "But Love." The "But Love" was the trick. So we had a hook. And that was the first time we actually had a hook in a song. We had a statement: "Love, love, love, you can't buy love. Gold can buy most anything. Anything but love." It was just a gimmick, and we felt, yeah, now we have something strong.

Dad came over and said, "Yeah. Vine Street's over there. There's a lot of publishers there. I'll tell ya a couple of publishers who might want a song like this." He gave us some names, and he *steered* us. He told us where to go and who to speak to and how to demonstrate it. He said, "Dickie, you're gonna go demonstrate it. And *sing it with all your heart.* Don't be shy." 'Cause I used to hold back. He said, "Sell it!" And we got our first song recorded. And by none other than Gene Autry, the number-one country-western singer in the country in 1951. On Columbia Records. And we were absolutely over the moon.

Our song was called "Gold Can Buy Anything (But Love)." And basically what happened was that it started breaking as one of the biggest hits in the country. And at the time General Douglas MacArthur made a speech in front of Congress. He'd been called back by Truman because he'd over-stepped the 38th Parallel. He had overridden the orders of the president. And like MacArthur thought he was God. So he was recalled and he had to retire from the Army. And he made a very famous speech and ended by saying, "I want to conclude with an old ballad we used to sing when I was a cadet," and it was "Old soldiers never die, they just fade away." And that same day Autry recorded "Old Soldiers Never Die," and our song was pulled off the presses and never saw the light of day. And we wanted to kill ourselves. We were up on top of the world, and all of a sudden we were crashing.

Our dad said, "That's called a curve. If you can't stand a curve, you get out of the game."

We learned that real fast. And many a curve occurred over the next several years. We had songs recorded; we had activity. But no hits for a long time.

Would you both work on words and music?

We sat in a room together—I'd sit at the piano, he'd sit at his desk—we'd scream at each other and write ideas. And I'd say, "No, no, no, let's do it this way." It was a mutual thing. We both collaborated on everything.

That's unusual, as you know. Often one does music, one does lyrics.

Yeah, it's not that way in our team. I write music, I write words; Bob heavily edits what I do. And he also writes lyrics very well. And we both come up with ideas—it's a mutual thing.

Will he have musical ideas?

Well, he can say, "Maybe you should do a lilting ballad." He would start me on something. We'd always start with an idea. With every single song we have done there are three parts: the reason for a song, what it's going to be about, why write it. And therefore we didn't just say, "I love you, I need you, I miss you, I want you, I lost you, you've come back to me, please." Everybody has written those things. You've got to come up with something *special*. It's different. Our songs usually had a hook or a twist. Even if they were lousy, they were original. They were different.

So at first you didn't have one publisher—

No, no, no. [*Laughs*] Whoever would take our things. Eventually what happened is our luck broke when Bob decided he had enough disappointments with various publishers who would take the songs and forget them or lie or cheat or do something else. So he decided to be his own publisher, and he started a company called Music World Corporation; that was his company. One day I saw him he said, "If you have any song ideas and nobody else wants them, bring them to me." I was writing by myself and with people. One day I came over to his office with a song idea, and he and his partner were working on a song. To support myself and to keep my head above water, I was an artificial flower installer. Doing that in dentists' offices and mortuaries and private homes and wherever I could do it. And writing at night and selling my songs in the afternoon. But in the morning I'd get up in the bright, early part of the day and build a manzanita bush [*laughs*] or build a rubber tree somewhere. That's the way I made a living. I made enough money to pay my rent and pay for my demo records.

One day I had this idea. I was driving along going to a job, early in the morning. On Melrose Avenue at the time there was a store, and it was called the Tall Girl Shop. And the word "tall" was not written horizontally, it was written vertically. TALL girls. And I looked at it and all of a sudden a new world happened. And I thought, "Tall. That's a wonderful word. What rhymes with 'tall'? Paul rhymes with tall. Tall Paul, that's a good title! Nobody's written 'Tall Paul.' Now there's a *grabber*. You can go over every book in the business. See, nobody's written Tall Paul." I thought, "Hey, there's an idea about the tallest kid in the class, and there's his girlfriend." I had this whole concept going, and I came into Bob's office, not with that idea but with a ballad I had written. And he was working on this song with this fellow, and they were writing a song with "Chalk on a sidewalk / Initials on a tree, everybody knows it, he loves me . . ." They were playing like a teenage pop song.

The phone rang and a guy named Frank Babcock called and said he had a little girl named Judy Harriet and "She has a terrific voice. I need a little teenage girl song. Do you got anything?" And Bob said, "Do we got anything for a teenage girl?" And I said, "I got a title," and he said, "Okay, we got a song. Come over." So in about thirty-five or forty minutes we wrote "Tall Paul." We changed the words they had to "Chalk on the sidewalk / Writing on the wall / Everybody knows it / I love Paul / Tall Paul, Tall Paul, he's my all." It sort of rolled out, and it was a teenage rocker, which was exactly what he was looking for.

It was really the turning point in our career. We had never written anything like it before, and so my brother, Bob—and Bob Roberts, his collaborator at the time—we wrote this song. [Babcock] came over, and he loved it. Judy made a record, and it didn't break. Nothing big happened with it. Except a guy named Moe Briscell in New York City, who had gotten a memo from the Disney people, which said that Annette Funicello still has about five months to go on her contract, she's the last of the Mouseketeers, and we were looking for some teenage rock songs for her because she's still very popular. So he was listening to the radio going to work from New Jersey, on his way to the bridge to get over to New York, and he heard this song by Judy Harriet. He turned his car around, went to the radio station in New Jersey, and found out who wrote this song. Then he made a deal with Bob to get the rights. So they split the copyright between Disney [*laughs*]—the major Disney company!—and my brother's little company. And they published "Tall Paul."

It was then recorded by Camarata with Annette Funicello. We doubled her voice 'cause she had a little voice. We added echo to her voice, and it became the Annette sound. A fantastic thing. And it became her sound. And it was a huge hit.

So you produced it yourself?

Yes. We worked with Judy, and we had recorded so many bad singers who couldn't sing, so we used to use a trick, having them sing one version and dropping it into a deep echo and then duplicate it on top of it so it sounded like a bigger voice. And with Annette it worked perfectly, because she was perfect with her synchronization. So it was a great sound. It penetrated.

She was not a great singer, but she was a good singer. She sang right on pitch. And so we doubled her voice. And then she had one successful record after the other. Many were ours, because they asked us to keep writing for her. "Pineapple Princess" was another record she had, and "Jo-Jo the Dog-Faced Boy," "Wild Willie." Fifteen songs.

"Tall Paul" was rock and roll. As were those others. Was becoming rock and roll writers something you wanted?

We said, "We've got to write a song. What's selling?" Rock was selling. We started studying rock. Listening to how Leiber and Stoller wrote a song. I mean, they were the *masters* at it.

And like you, they produced their own records—

We were more interested in the writing. Although we did have to produce records. Because not everybody was running after us. We were on the periphery.

But then we had a giant hit with Johnny Burnette, "You're Sixteen." That was another gimmick. We wanted to give the listeners something they hadn't heard. They heard so many hard rock beats. But nobody had heard shuffle rhythms. So basically we said, "Let's do a shuffle rhythm for the verse, and then when you get to the chorus, you hit them with a hard rock beat." So basically it was all thought out before we wrote anything. But we had the idea: "You're sixteen, you're beautiful, and you're mine." And we did it, and it's exactly the way Johnny Burnette recorded it, because we did a demo. And we just happened to do the demo with Dorsey Burnette, who was Johnny's brother. It was just *pure coincidence*. The powers that be, out of Chicago, heard it and said they had Johnny Burnette. And Johnny was such a talented kid, and he heard the demo his brother did—not knowing it was his brother—and said, "Hey, I can do that. It sounds just like me!" And he had a *huge* hit with it.

So we were not rock and roll writers. But we wrote some songs in that style.

Funny that "Tall Paul" is about a football hero, which was the subject of your dad's famous song.

Dad's first song that he ever wrote that was published was called "Good as Gold." And our first powerful song was "Gold Can Buy

Anything." Though it wasn't more than a flash in the pan, it was our first major published song. So a lot of coincidences happen in this life.

So through Annette you met Walt Disney?

Yes. He decided to put her into one of his films and wanted her to sing one of her songs. So he told the people at the studio, "Why don't you get those young guys who are writing songs for Annette?" 'Cause we had done a lot of songs for her. Four albums. We'd write three or four songs and then get standards, all classics, and put them together. And her albums were all selling lots of stuff.

So Walt recognized our stuff and liked our songs. He said, "Get those brothers, I want to meet them," and that's how it all began, really.

What was your first meeting with Walt Disney like?

We met in his office suite at his studio in Burbank, California. We drove out there with a little song we had written. We played it for Jimmy Johnson, who was head of the music department. He liked it very much and said, "Now you've got to play it for Walt." We said, "Walt who?" He said, "Walt Disney, of course."

I said, "Walt Disney? We've got to make a demo for him. We can't just sing it." Jimmy said no, that's how he likes it—he didn't like demos. Because he could hear through to the end result. He knew what he wanted to hear and could hear it through the performance. He was an unusual man. He was a great, great producer, the greatest I have ever worked with. An imagination beyond anybody's belief. He could grasp an abstract concept and refine it right there on the spot. He was an amazing man.

Was he intimidating?

Anything but. He was very sweet and friendly and nice. I mean, knowing who he was, you were intimidated. But he was very friendly. His opening line to us was, "Are you two really brothers? Or is it just an act like in vaudeville?"

We said, "We're really brothers, Mr. Disney."

He said, "Walt. I don't like Mister." He put you at your ease. Then he'd say, "When I was young I was in a vaudeville act with my friend Walt Feiffer. We called ourselves The Johnson Brothers. And why? Because we found some cards that said The Johnson Brothers. And it was just a business." So I told him, no, we had the same mother and father. And he got a kick out of that.

When he'd listen to a song, he'd never, ever say, "Great, wonderful, perfect." He only said, "That'll work." With a straight, bland face.

Basically he gave us one assignment after another. Always different. He gave us something to write for *Zorro*, the TV show. He had us do songs for a Western series. An assignment for German lieder. He was testing us and accepted everything. For *The Parent Trap*—which was called at first *We Belong Together*—he wanted to have a song about divorced parents. He wanted to find out what was their song. So we didn't just write a song; we figured out that if this picture comes out in 1961, and the girl is fourteen, we had to think 1946. Get a love song from 1946. So we wrote a song called "For Now for Always," which sounds *exactly* like something Dick Haymes or Perry Como would sing from back then. Very smooth lines. A very warm, lovely, loving concept. Totally different than anything that was being played in the popular market. And we played it for Walt, and when we finished he said, "How come you wrote it like that?" We gave him our concept. So he said, "You think story, don't you?" We told him we always thought story. 'Cause every time we wrote a song we'd think who's singing it, where is he singing it, what year is it happening. If we wrote a Western, it sounded like a Western. Everything we ever did, we always would box in where we were going. Those were the buttons we'd push. I hate anachronism in music. When you're doing modern music in a period piece.

The first day we met him he reached around and pulled out a book and said, "You know what a nanny is?" We said, "Sure, it's a goat." We thought maybe this was a story about an enchanted goat or something. He laughed and said, "No, no, no, I am talking about an English nursemaid." So he handed us this book and said, "Read this and tell me what you think." Now, he never said that to us before. He always said, "I need a title song for this," or "Here's a lonely girl missing her boyfriend—write a song for her." But this time he said, "Here's a book. Tell me what you think." The book was called *Mary Poppins* by Pamela Travers. The rest is history.

Mary Poppins is something we worked on for three and a half years. It didn't come out till 1964. We were at the studio for four years. We came back with our ideas about *Mary Poppins*, and he must have flipped 'cause he put us under contract. He put us to work for him. We worked on everything that came out of the studio. We wrote *song after song*. He loved everything we did. Rarely did he ever tell us to do something again. He was very succinct in what he wanted, and we could read him.

And you always would bring a song directly to him.

Yes. Every time. God, we had something like 160 songs published by Disney. We wrote every day. Sometimes seven days a week.

Anyway the success of *Mary Poppins* established us as writers who could write musicals. Full-fledged musicals. So we never really did pop music again. We never wrote straight for the pop market. And thank God, because that's the hardest thing of all. To sit there in a room and think, "What are we gonna write about?" I mean, that is so hard. But when you're given a story, a situation, a character—it's a pleasure. It's great.

Is it true that you and Bob had a lot to do with shaping the story of the film?

Yes. In the books there is no story line whatsoever. It's only a series of brilliant, wonderful, imaginative adventures. But there is no reason for Mary Poppins to come in in the first place. She doesn't actually change anything. It's magical. Mrs. Travers had invented this wonderful, magical nanny who brings kids on wonderful adventures. But never explained anything. So when we read these stories, we realized it needed a story. What we did was create a story line and used six chapters that we really liked out of that first book as our basis. It had the jumping into sidewalk picture and things like that. Which we felt was a marvelous idea. And Uncle Albert floating around in the air. And the old lady who sells bread crumbs. We thought that could be not just the lady but the meaning of the story. The father is not paying enough attention to the family, and the mother is busy doing her thing. So Mary Poppins teaches them a life lesson—that it's important for them to stick together and care for each other. This was our concept.

And you changed the time it took place?

Yes, we did. It was in the Depression, London, 1934 era. Yucch. There was no character in the music; everything was imitation American pop songs in England. But at the turn of the century they had a *wonderful* music flavor. They had music hall. And I *loved* that music hall. They had a wonderful ragtag sound they used to do, funny novelty songs like "Boiled Leaf and Carrots." Things like that. "Any old iron, any old iron . . ." Crazy songs. I *loved* those songs. And that's what gave us the trigger to do things.

I remember sitting in our little office with this little red book and thinking, "What are we gonna knock Walt's socks off with? Let's do something with one of those crazy words like we used to do in summer camp. An obnoxious word. Yeah, let's start with 'obnoxious.' And it has to be super-colossal." So that's how we started. Because Mary Poppins will teach the kids to say it, and it will feel good. And we felt "obnoxious" is really ugly. So why don't we say "atrocious"? It's an English story. That sounds a lot better, and you can sound like you're really smart and you're precocious. So you have atrocious, precocious, and that could rhyme with "docious"—yes. But super-colossal—everybody and their Uncle Harry would write that. So we dropped out the "colossal" and said, "Supercalifragilistic." It just sounded like something big. 'Cause we would yell out of the car when we were kids, "Your galvinator rod is dragging." And everyone would say, "My galvinator rod?" And there is no galvinator rod. So we went with "supercalifragilistic"—from galvinator. That was Dad's trick. He came up with these great word sounds and put them together.

We thought it wouldn't be sung by anybody but these Pearlies. These guys who would dress up with pearly buttons. At the racetracks in England, they have pearly bands, families who would dress up with pearly buttons. And it was the kind of song they would do.

Walt said, "Why do you call this the 'Pearly Song'?"

We said because there was nobody else who could possibly pronounce "Supercalifragilistic." He said, "That's your title!" We said, "Okay, Walt."

Was that the first song you finished for *Mary Poppins*?

No, the first song was "Feed the Birds." We wrote that before we met with him. That first meeting was a turning point in our *life*. We played him "Feed the Birds." Said this is the story of the lady who sells breadcrumbs. We think it means a lot. We spent a lot of time with him. He sent out for sandwiches, and we had lunch with him. He was as enthusiastic as we were. He said, "Play me that bird lady again." We only had sixteen bars, the feel, and the main chorus of it. He said, "That's what the whole story is about, right?" We told him how Mary is needed to help this dysfunctional family. And then when she sets things up, she leaves. He liked the period thing.

We said, "Yes, Walt, that is what it's all about."

He said, "How would you like to come and work for me here?" And that was the day he put us under contract, and it changed our lives.

Bob had an office on Sunset Boulevard in Hollywood. But when Walt put us under contract we gave up the office. And we went to work for Disney and moved to the studio. For eight years we were full-time contract players out there. And we have had a fifty-year relationship with the studio. We've done things for [Disneyland]. We did things for Epcot.

As a kid we so loved the *Mary Poppins* album. We cherished it, and in a good part because of the great range of music on it.

That was a big turning point in our lives. We wrote thirty-five songs for it. We were exploring chapters and exploring situations and ways to do things. When we weren't working on other things we would always work on *Poppins*. It was the back-burner project. Eventually the best writer in the whole studio, Bill Walsh, wrote the script. Using our story frame. The story frame was Walt Disney, Don DaGradi, Bob, and myself. We made a story out of it. And that's when Mrs. Travers came and gave us the okay. Because she was a tough cookie. Walt didn't have the complete rights until she said yes. She finally signed off on it. That's a whole story in itself. She finally acquiesced. And Bill Walsh wrote a witty script, and we added some new songs.

Did you write the arrangements?

No. That was a musician named Irwin Kostal. He did *West Side Story* and *Sound of Music*. He read the way we felt, and I could sing it for him, and he could hear the end product. So many guys can't. They put their own personal stamp on it. We said, "We want it to be vanilla. We want it to be 1910." So you would have none of these diminished chords or things you heard in later contemporary music. And he said, "I am going to make this song the way you want it." And that's what he did. We did five movies with him. We did *Poppins* and *Chitty Chitty Bang Bang*, *Charlotte's Web*, *Bedknobs and Broomsticks*, and *The Magic of Lassie*. All with Irving Kostal. He was *great*. And a sweetheart. A wonderful guy.

Your song "Chim Chim Cher-ee" from *Mary Poppins* won the Oscar for Best Song of the Year. And became the most famous song from that show.

We were playing around. Don DaGradi found a chapter in a later *Poppins* book. Mary Poppins shakes hands with this sooty little man, this chimney sweep. And she says, "Don't you know it's lucky when you shake with a sweep." Don found that story and drew a picture of a chimney sweep whistling, walking down a foggy London street, with his brushes slung over his shoulder. And Bob and I saw that picture. Don told us about that chapter, and right away we knew this was a song. We're gonna write a song about a chimney sweep. It was born right there. We went back to our room and started playing with the word "chimney." We started playing with how we would get into the word "chimney" pronounced "chim-a-ney"—then "Chim, chim-a-ney." And nobody had ever written "Chim Chim Cher-ee." That is a completely created word. So we said that is what it's gonna be. Now we have to find out what it is.

So we said, "Now that the ladder of life / Has been strung / You might think of sweeps on the bottommost rung / . . . Spending time with the ashes and smoke / . . . There is no more happier bloke . . ."

Basically we're telling the story of this little chimney sweep. Later we learned that if he blows you a kiss, that is lucky. So we added that: "So blow me a kiss and that's lucky too . . ." We put that all together. It was this magical thing. That the moment we got inspired by the chimney sweep, it was magic.

That one has a lovely minor-key melody. In C minor, I believe?

Yes, it's C minor, but it changes. Because there's that chromatic line that keeps going down. So it isn't too Russian or Middle Eastern. It adds a kind of English flavor too. Because originally it was written with strictly all minor chords. And I loved it but I hated it. I felt, why is it so heavy? And then I thought I would reinvent the thing. And I put that descending line in. And already it changes the color: you get a pastel color, and it's not so heavy.

Which many people have imitated since, in so many songs—

Yeah. A lot of times. But imitation is the highest form of flattery. This is stuff musicians know. I reharmonized the basic feel. And it sounds like a folk song. Which is cool too.

We thought maybe we should put a bridge on it and going into another key. And my brother said [*in gruff voice*], "This is *it*. This is right. Don't change it. *Christ*, you're gonna screw it up."

Did you two generally agree on most stuff?

We came from different angles. Which was nice. We were totally different. Built differently. Many times he's right, and many times I'm right. And we had to find a middle ground. We never showed a song to anyone if we didn't both agree that this was as good as we can do it. That is what kept us going. These little simple agreements that kept us going over the years. Because all brothers have differences and disagreements. So we sort of kept apart so that nothing would get in the way of the work. We always agreed.

"Chim Chim Cher-ee" was a major song in our life. It won the Academy Award. Perhaps if I had prevailed and we put a bridge into it, it wouldn't have been quite as charismatic. And perhaps if I hadn't have been sick of that Russian sound in there—it was a good lyric, the lyric stayed the same, I was happy with the feeling in it, and it was driving me nuts.

Or the song "Jolly Holiday." That's the only time you play the melody in the key of C. It starts on D, on the second chord in the key. But in order to get that, you need five chord changes to get there. And I never had those chords to make it work. For two years I was working on it! And one night I got it! And that is what everybody takes for granted. [*Sings*] "You feel so grand, your heart starts beating like a *big brass band* . . . *boom*." Six different chords to that phrase. If I had a piano, I could show you better. These are things, I remember them, because it's such a key element in my career having that credibility. Because once we succeeded with *Mary Poppins*, other producers would give us a whole picture. Not just one song but a whole picture.

You wrote many songs for *Mary Poppins* that weren't used?

Yes, many.

Weren't used because Walt didn't want them or you didn't want them?

No, no, because the story didn't need them. We wrote four songs for a sequence called the "Magic Compass" sequence. Which we didn't use. We worked on it for months, and one day Walt said, "You know, that compass sequence, you really don't need it, because we can go from here to here and you'll have a much smoother line . . ." And when you're working for a master like that and you have so much love and respect, you say, "Okay, Walt."

Walt Disney—

And he could hear through my singing to what a gorgeous, beautiful little girl's voice or what a beautiful little character voice would sound like, through my performance.

Were you the one who would always sing?

I'm the demonstrator, yeah. I did the singing and playing. Bob sort of suffered along with me. [*Laughs*]

Would you work nine to five at Disney?

No. We'd come in when we'd feel like it. Nine thirty or ten in the morning. That is when Walt was there. When Walt left it became a machine. A different kind of studio. You had to have your time cards and garbage like that. With Walt, just turn in the work. And we'd sometimes stay till seven or eight working. We just loved it. We'd come in on the weekends and worked. We could always do it when we wanted to. As long as we met our deadlines and things he needed, we were free. He was that way with all his artists. Nobody punched a clock.

The songs you and Bob wrote for *Poppins* and others all seemed so inspired. Could you always come up with something, every day, or were there days you ran dry?

[*Sighs*] See, that's the good thing about having a collaborator. If I was dry, Bob would come up with something. If he was dry, I would come up with something. We both were workhorses. We loved to work. I don't think there was ever a time when we both looked at each other and said, "I can't come up with anything." One of us would come up with something. And we'd come in the next day with a fresh idea. We'd scribble down some idea or title. And come in and say, "*Hey, yeah!* We can do something with that!"

And Bob and I were professionals. A professional doesn't wait for the muse to come and loft in—you sit down and you *work*. If you have the ability to do it and you're inspired by an idea, Bob and I have always said, "The idea, the idea, the idea." Anyone can write notes and words. It's the idea that motors the whole thing.

We were very lucky. To be in the right room at the right time with the right producer. Here's your work with the right recording artist. You know you can have the most marvelous song in the world and the wrong ears hear it or somebody doesn't hear through your rendition of it to a final performance. But I was lucky. Bob and I were signed by the finest storyteller of the last century.

◆◆◆

Jeff Barry
River Deep Mountain High
Burbank, California 2015

"You know what Kitty Hawk was?" he asks with laughing eyes. "That's where the Wright Brothers rolled their first plane off the hill to get it to fly. And that's what we were doing. We were inventing modern pop. At least the New York sound of it, and it was great."

There was a "vacuum," as he put it, into which he and his partner in song and life, Ellie Greenwich, introduced a remarkable profusion of exultant hit songs and records that painted the sonic landscape of the early sixties and beyond. In 1964, the same year the music of The Beatles was first played on American radio, they had *seventeen* songs on the pop charts. Seventeen songs! And each a deliciously infectious pop treasure concocted by a husband-wife team in love with the unchained promise of the new American pop song.

The previous year, 1963, they wrote "Be My Baby," which is not only one of the most famous songs of our time but also equally famous as a record, produced by Phil Spector. Brian Wilson (see page 271) called it "the greatest pop record ever." Others have declared it "the Rosetta Stone for studio pioneers." It was tailor-made for the siren sound of Ronnie Spector and the Ronettes. She possessed the perfect voice for the task: soulful, deeply in the pocket, expressive, and full of yearning. It was also right in that sonic zone where it cut through all the production like butter, delivering that beautiful tune and lyric with remarkable power and grace. John Lennon so loved the record that not only did he listen to it repeatedly for weeks, he cut the song himself years later for a solo album.

Brian Wilson famously said that he first heard it on the radio while driving on the Pacific Coast Highway and had to pull over and park so as not to crash while taking in this miraculous song. "It blew my mind," Brian said. According to legend confirmed, he'd go into the studio and listen to it over and over. The engineer said, "I'd like to have a nickel for every joint Brian Wilson smoked trying to figure out how I got the 'Be My Baby' sound." He's said to have listened to that song in excess of a hundred times a day. "Don't Worry Baby" is the song he wrote for The Beach Boys' response.

"To this day, all these years later, it still does it for me. There is *so* much love in that record, in that song, in that vocal. It's a miracle."

Had Jeff written only this one song, he'd matter. But he and Ellie, in love with each other and with music, wrote successive classic songs together, including "Chapel of Love," "Leader of the Pack," "Hanky Panky," "River Deep—Mountain High." He wrote "Sugar, Sugar" with Andy Kim, and with Peter Allen he wrote, "I Honestly Love You," a giant hit in 1974 for Olivia Newton-John.

Jeff is also one of the rare ones who has given back to this industry in so many ways. He was the chairman of the board for several years of the National Academy of Songwriters, the nonprofit organization that also employed this author, for twelve great years, to be the editor of their journal, *SongTalk*. Jeff worked there in an unpaid position to educate, inform, and support songwriters at all stages of their career.

He was born Joel Adelberg on April 3, 1938, in beautiful Brooklyn, New York. Before meeting and working with Ellie he recorded several singles for RCA, including "It's Called Rock and Roll," which he also wrote. Then the great Sam Cooke recorded his song "Teenage Sonata," which became a hit. And "Tell Laura I Love Her," which he wrote with Ben Raleigh, was a number-one hit in the United States by Ray Peterson and a number one in the UK for British singer Ricky Valance.

Jeff and Ellie officially met in late 1959 but quite possibly had met earlier, as they were actually distant cousins. But it was at a Thanksgiving dinner when they formally met, bonding over turkey and talk of music. Before even teaming up as a songwriting duo, they put out a record. The song was written by Jeff and called "Red Corvette," and the band was credited as Ellie Gee and the Jets. At the same time Leiber and Stoller [see page 26] had offered each a job as staff writers for their publishing company, Trio Music.

In October of 1962 they got married and decided to write together exclusively. It was through Ellie that Phil Spector came into their picture, and the Barry-Greenwich-Spector triumvirate created successive classic records, all the essence of the girl-group sound: The Crystals' "Da Doo Ron Ron" and "Then He Kissed Me," The Ronettes' "Be My Baby" and "Baby, I Love You," and more.

In that magic year 1964 Leiber and Stoller invited Jeff and Ellie to become staff songwriter-producers for their label, Red Bird Records. Some fifteen Barry-Greenwich songs hit the charts, and all became hits: "Chapel of Love," "People Say," and "Iko Iko" by The Dixie Cups, and "Remember (Walkin' in the Sand)," and "Leader of the Pack" by the Shangri-Las. "Do Wah Diddy Diddy," originally recorded by the girl group The Exciters, became a reworked number-one hit by British Invasion darlings Manfred Mann.

Although they got divorced in 1965, they continued working together. Always on the lookout for genuine talent, they found Neil Diamond and brought him to the attention of Bert Berns, a famous songwriter who also ran Bang Records. Berns signed him, and Barry and Greenwich produced Neil's famous first records, including "Solitary Man," "Cherry, Cherry," "Kentucky Woman," and "Girl, You'll Be a Woman Soon." It was the same time they teamed up with Phil Spector to work on "River Deep—Mountain High" by Ike and Tina Turner, and "I Can Hear Music" by The Ronettes and The Beach Boys. All of which is discussed in the following.

One of his most poignant songs, however, was never a big hit but remains one of his most beautiful songs and most moving song-origin story. "Walking in the Sun" was recorded by soul legend Percy Sledge and revolves around a single line of truth. It's a line, like many we find in pop songs, that we might find perhaps insubstantial but is, in fact, the core of the thing. It is also, to me, an ideal organic metaphor for recognition of the divine and does resonate that way. But Jeff, whose father was blind, insists this is literal and not a metaphor: "And even a blind man can tell when he's walking in the sun."

Either way it's a deeply personal image for Jeff Barry, and it's there that our discussion begins.

This interview was conducted in front of a live audience at the Songwriting School of Los Angeles as part of a web series I am doing with the school called *Songwriters on Songwriting Live*. Jeff agreed to do this because he's a steadfast believer in the value of songwriting education and even offered to take home songs by any students wanting his feedback. Throughout the show we had many great vocalists sing his famous songs, a delightful musical journey—that ranged from complex ("River Deep—Mountain High") to very simple ("Hanky Panky") to exultant soulful pop ("Be My Baby") and beyond—that said more than words ever could about the great span of this one man's body of work.

I took advantage of the opportunity to perform myself his song "Walking in the Sun," and it's with that song that our conversation began.

Jeff Barry: I'm probably the only songwriter in the world who could have written that song—or would have—because my father was blind, and I grew up with a blind father. And also a mentally retarded sister. So that's probably one of the reasons I don't use metaphor. I like to say I don't even use meta-*three*.

Because if you think about it, when you try to communicate with someone who can't see, your references have to be other than the visual. And when you're trying to communicate with someone who is mentally handicapped, you have to be simple, succinct, and very clear to *both* of them. And I realized way into my life and career that first I'm a lyricist, melody second, and chords a distant third.

I was fourteen years old. I was with my father, and he was an insurance salesman, and we lived in Brooklyn, but he'd have to go to Manhattan once in a while. On this one afternoon I would go with him, and we were coming back, and it was late in the afternoon in New York City. The sun is on an angle, we're walking, and it's chilly. Probably in the fall sometime.

And my father, who's the blind one, [*laughs*] says, "Is the sun out across the street?"

And I didn't think of that, and I look and go, "Yeah, it is."

So we crossed over and walked on that side, probably going to the subway to go back to Brooklyn.

Many years later I had my offices at A&M Records, and Jerry Moss said, "Why don't you write for yourself and make an album?" What the hell—why not? So I had no idea what to write, and this song came out, and it wasn't until years later I realized it was because of that incident that I wrote "Even a blind man can tell when he's walkin' in the sun."

And it's a cool truth that probably I am the only one who might have had an experience like that and gone on to be a songwriter. So that's that.

You wrote the song, and that line just came out?

Yeah. It just came out, because I sat down to write for *me*. I didn't know what that was about, writing for *me*. So whatever came out, came out.

Percy Sledge cut that song—a great, soulful record.

Glen Campbell had it on the country chart too. A whole different record.

That one you wrote alone. But most of your songs you've cowritten.

Yes. I like to write with people who know all the chords. [*Laughter*]

You famously wrote with Ellie Greenwich, who was your wife. But before you and Ellie wrote together, you each were writing with other people. So what brought you and Ellie together?

Ellie and I met, as the story goes, when she was three and I was four. [*Crowd laughs*] Her cousin married *my* cousin, and we were at some family thing. Fade out, fade in. Twenty-some-odd years later, she was graduating from Hofstra College, studying music. And I had had some hits already, and they said, "You guys should meet," which we did. And we kept on meeting. And we were married for about three years and had a whole bunch of hits. And unfortunately Ellie passed on a couple of years ago. She was great, obviously—a great singer, great person.

It's unusual that there were several husband-wife teams writing together: Goffin and King, Mann and Weil.

That's what it was. It was Barry and Greenwich, Goffin and King, Mann and Weil. We were the three married couples. We were all friends; we all kind of started out together. The sixties is when this is all happening. We were actually *in* the Brill Building. And it was what I call Kitty Hawk. You know what Kitty Hawk was? That's where the Wright Brothers roll their first plane off the hill, and hey, it *flies*. [*Laughter*]

And that's what we were doing. We were inventing modern pop, at least the New York sound of it, and it was great. I mean, the word "retro" didn't exist. We were creating what's today's retro. [*Laughter*] And there was really nothing to look back at. It was all just making up the rules.

Now, my understanding of the Brill Building is you go in, and you'd be in cubicles.

They called it cubicles. They were *rooms*.

Okay, you're in your own room.

Yeah, we had a room. It was kind of nice.

So you'd go in and work every day, every day, on songs, writing songs?

Yeah, but no, it was *fun*. We didn't work. I feel like I've never worked a day in my life.

With Goffin and King and Mann and Weil, one did the words and one the music. But you and Ellie did both, is that right?

Yeah. I mean, I kind of did the lyrics.

But you also brought musical ideas.

Yeah, I don't write lyrics; I sing 'em. And the melody—it would either stick or not.

And she would bring the chords?

Yeah. When Ellie passed away, somebody sent me an obituary from someone in the Midwest somewhere saying how remarkable it was that she had the ability to tap into the teenage girl's psyche.

And Ellie was a really great singer and performer.

Absolutely.

You guys had a group called The Raindrops. Were some of the songs you were writing for yourself?

Yeah. We formed The Raindrops. I'm not sure really why. I guess because we *could*. Know what I mean? We could do anything we wanted. We had twelve things in the Top Ten. No one's going to say no.

Did you write "Hanky Panky" for yourself?

When you book a band, you have them for three hours, period. Three hours, you're done. Anyway, whatever song it was we were going in to record, we made the tracks first for the Raindrops. We got done in, I'd say, *two* hours.

A lot of the time in a session is at the beginning, when the engineer has to get the sounds on the drums. The kick, the snare, the hi-hats, and all that. And then get the sound on the guitar and the piano and the bass. That can take at least a half hour. And then you have *two and a half* hours left. But whatever it was we went in to do, we were done.

So I said, "Wait a minute. When we put an album out, if you put a single out from the album, if somebody buys the single, they already have two of the songs on the album. Doesn't seem fair." I said, "Look. Let's go out in the hall and write a simple, simple song that we will *only* put on the B-side of the single for the next Raindrops single. And if somebody buys the album, they'll have *nine* new songs," which I thought was pretty nice. The lesson is, be nice. [*Laughter*] I'm very serious about that, by the way. So we did that, put out the next single.

Tommy James was a fan, he bought the single. He turned it over and listened to the other side and cut "Hanky Panky." So because of being nice, we had a big hit. It's true.

And how long did it take to write "Hanky Panky"?

Twenty minutes. [*Laughs*] If that.

It's interesting that you guys had your own group, because that was right before the time when the singer-songwriter emerged, and Carole King obviously became a singer-songwriter. Songwriting shifted when people started writing for themselves.

True. We were still looking for artists, and sometimes they were great songwriters too. We discovered and produced Neil Diamond, who was one of the biggest stars ever.

He wrote "I'm a Believer," which you produced.

I produced that with The Monkees. That was the Record of the Year.

I produced Record of the Year twice. That and "Sugar, Sugar" by the Archies. That one I get a real kick out of because the Archies didn't *exist* as a real group. It was a comic book that they were bringing to TV, and they called and said, "Do you want to do this?"

I said, "Well, yeah, but I don't want to just, like, rewrite 'Happy Birthday' and all those PD [public domain] melodies."

They said, "*Duh*, that's why we're calling you." [*Laughter*]

So it was a group that didn't exist—Record of the Year, 11 million singles, by a group that did not exist, a song that was written for pre-schoolers. [*Laughs*] Really, that was the assignment. It was going to be on Saturday morning TV for preschoolers. Which I had at the time. I had a three- and a four-year-old.

It came out in 1969, when I was ten and just starting to write songs. We were a little past preschool, but we all loved it. That was the essence of what they termed "bubblegum" pop—but it was great.

You know where the term "bubblegum" comes from? A song called "Yummy Yummy Yummy (I Got Love in My Tummy)" [written in 1968 by Arthur Resnick and Joey Levine; recorded by 1910 Fruitgum Company]. Some writer dubbed that "bubblegum," so anything that was cute became "bubblegum."

But someone was talking to me about it and why I don't write other things. She said, "Because I'm not stupid. Write something for an adult, will you?"

And I said, "You know, you're right." I said, "The other day I was reading a poem by Rod McKuen, and it said something about 'the loveliness of loving you.'"

She said, "*That's* what you should write."

I said, "Really? That's from 'Sugar, Sugar.'" [*Laughter*]

It is remarkable that you and Ellie wrote and produced so many great songs in this one time, and at the same time, your peers were writing some of their greatest songs. Do you have any idea what enabled so many powerful songs to emerge at the same time?

There was a vacuum. A disc jockey by the name of Alan Freed said the words "rock and roll" on the radio for the first time in 1955. That's the cornerstone of when rock and roll, modern pop, whatever you call it, began. And that's when the rhythms of the South were coming up, and lo and behold, the guitar and drums were the center of everything.

Some of the northern writers were starting to write young songs by young people for teenagers. Teenagers, kids, were not a market in the monetary sense until the fifties, when Eisenhower was in and things were good. There was no war at that time. It was a decade of peace. It was very strange. And things were good, and kids literally had a buck as allowance. The word "allowance" was there then.

So the adult writers who were writing for all the artists and bands, the big bands in the thirties and forties, they tried to adopt and adapt to this burgeoning market, and I think that's where songs like "(How Much Is) That Doggie in the Window?" came from. You know, the writers felt, "That's good—the kids will like that."

But then young people, like myself and Carole and Gerry and Ellie—literally teenagers—started to write for teenagers about what we were interested in, which was not puppies. [*Laughs*] And from when no one was writing for kids, by the end of the sixties no one was writing for *adults* anymore. The market was all kids, all young people. And it was absolutely wonderful to be there. I mean, I was at ground zero.

I joined BMI in 1958, had my first hit in 1960—first big hit in 1960—and was pretty much on the charts all through the sixties, and these were crazy times. There was a vacuum that needed songs to fill it.

Would you guys be always writing, or only when you'd go into work?
Always. I'm writing right now.

Would you come in with ideas—
Probably. [*Laughs*] I was probably in charge of ideas.

"Be My Baby" famously starts with Hal Blaine on drums. Was that drum figure your conception?
Yeah, you know, I used to bang on this file cabinet in the office when we were writing. And that beat is basically called a *baion*. It's on every record today. It's either that or four on the floor, right?

Yeah.
It's a Latin *baion*. Leiber and Stoller (see page 26), they used that on a *lot* of stuff. In my fledgling production days that rhythm was always in my head. It's constant today. You cannot listen to the radio and not hear [*plays beat*]. It's just there.

Ronnie Spector's vocal on "Be My Baby" is so powerful. Was that written with her voice in mind?
No. We would just write songs. [*Laughs*]

Some of your songs came very fast. Would you distrust them if they came fast without much work?
No. It all comes easy. We used to feel that working on a song forever, something's wrong. It's a problem. Seriously. It's maybe an unnatural idea or title or something's wrong. If you can't figure it out, it's not happening. It could very well be that there's something wrong.

Ordinarily would you and Ellie finish things pretty quickly?
In a normal flow. I would say usually it would take two sittings and the song was done. Not that it wouldn't necessarily change, even in the studio, last minute. Somebody'd get an idea about something. It's never done until it's out. Then it's too late. [*Laughter*]

Were there ever times when your well ran dry and you had nothing?
No. I have never had writer's block. Well, there were times when I'd write something like "Hanky Panky." Pretty close to writer's block. [*Laughs*]

The challenge of songwriting is how to try to find some angle on this stuff that hasn't been covered, because that's what songs are about. Ninety-nine and a half percent of things on the charts are about the human condition, and *love* is the word that is literally undefined. "Love" is the most important word, unless you're not healthy, and then "health" is. We all want to be, to use the pedestrian word, *happy*. That's the word. You need love to be happy. And for something that's so important to human happiness, there's absolutely no education to it, let alone definition of what the word means. There's no education on how to find it, recognize it, keep it. None. We all get pushed out into the river of life, and it's like, "Good luck." [*Laughs*] You know?

Some part of me says that if someone would ever figure it out, besides divorce attorneys being out of business, I think songwriters are out of business. Because part of the psyche leads us to believe that one of these songs is going to have the answer.

[*Laughs*] I have nineteen-year-old twins, a boy and a girl, and at this point I'd love to be able to pass along *some* advice, something to save one dark night, one heartbreak. There really, really isn't much you can say and pass along, really. So what we're doing is trying to write about something that we have no idea what it is. It's kind of interesting.

You wrote songs with your wife, so that love was not something outside of you but always there when you were together. Did that affect you?

Did it? I have *no* idea. I have no idea. We didn't have kids yet. We had *songs*.

So what is the definition of love? Is it not love if it doesn't last? Is it only love if it lasts for frigging ever? I don't know. I don't profess to know. Were we in love? Is the answer, "Well, evidently not, because we were only married for three years"? Or maybe love is for however long it is? It could be for a "Hi, how are you?" and a chat and be absolutely, totally in love and never see each other again. I have no idea. Or it could go on and on and on until death do us part. [*Laughter*] But that's another hour and a half we could do.

You and Ellie continued to write songs after the marriage was over. How hard was that to do?

That was momentum, honestly. We were never enemies, so it wasn't like some ugly thing happened; it just *wasn't* anymore. That part of our relationship which was about the writing, that was still there. So we kept writing.

After all these years of writing songs, have you any advice to offer about how best to do it?

I can't teach songwriting. But I can inspire. You get an idea, something you want to say. You sit down and you write that verse, and it's just great. And then you have a chorus, where also the title is. You write your chorus.

Now, second verse, right? *Nothin'*. Nothin' comes! Have you had that happen to you? Consider this: you already wrote the second verse. It's your *first* verse. You said the meat of it. Take your first verse, make it your second verse. You'll see how easy it is to write the pre-, the setup.

I have done it so many times. You say it, and it seems there's nothing more to say. But there's a lot to say.

The other advice is to learn the rules. Here comes the joke, so you'll know what not to do. Know the rules, but then see what happens if you make up your own, because there *are no rules*. I mean, yeah, if there's a C chord, there's going to probably be a G chord somewhere, you know. [*Laughs*] But the important thing is, all art, all creativity, is about one thing. All art, all showbiz, is about one thing: creating emotion.

The oldest adage in showbiz is, "If you leave 'em like you found 'em, you blew it." You've got to make them *feel* something. People pay to have their emotions move. Make 'em cry, make 'em laugh, make 'em sad, make 'em happy. Make 'em *something*.

The shape of the audience for your song is like a football. Your audience is that fat middle of the football. On one end are people who you're not going to try to reach, and on the other end are people you're not going to try to reach. But these people in the middle are like you. We're all issued the identical set of emotions when we're born. So if you're afraid of it, everybody's afraid of it. If you love it, everybody loves it, except the people at the ends. [*Laughs*] I mean, at the ends are the psychopaths and my sister. [*Laughs*]

It's not a joke. People who aren't normal, mentally normal. But we're not writing for those people. I joke around a lot, but I'm serious. We are writing for *us*. If it moves you, it'll move them. So you never have to worry, "Is it good or bad?" Do *you* like it? It's good. It's *so simple*. Twelve notes. We all have the same book of words—it's called a dictionary. And the same set of emotions. So what's the friggin' problem here?

I'm writing now, perhaps, more than ever. I am a better songwriter today. I just have more life behind me, and I'm much more particular. Think about this: in your songs which note, which word, is not important? They're *all* important. And you write the song and then make sure every word and every note is as good as you can make it.

But here's another little hint. I hear myself say this all the time to my people I'm working with: "We *got* that line. We *got* that line. It's not going to go away. Let's see if we can find another way to say it, a more interesting way to say it. Let's not do 'feels so right in the middle of the night.' Let's take that same thought—maybe there's a cooler, edgier, better, newer way to say it."

Don't be lazy. Don't be lazy. It's not genius because it rhymed. Trust me. And it may not be ever genius. "Genius" is the wrong word. But a lot of people are very satisfied because it fit in the right amount of bars and it rhymed. First of all, rhyming is not that important anymore. It's more the thought. Nor do the melodies in the first verse have to match exactly. The chords will be the same and the melody will be close. It doesn't have to match exactly. It's more important to impart the emotion.

In 1966 you and Ellie wrote "River Deep—Mountain High" with Phil Spector, recorded by Ike and Tina Turner. I understand that Phil agreed to do this only if Ike wouldn't be in the studio.

True. I never saw him. I never met him.

Yeah? So he wasn't there.

No.

And Phil Spector famously spent $20,000 on this one record, which at the time was like a million dollars.

It wasn't twenty thousand. I think it was nineteen actually.

Tina said she had to sing it over and over, that she was drenched with sweat. She said, "I had to take my shirt off and stand there in my bra to sing that song."

Right. Phil liked to torture people.

Where did the title "River Deep—Mountain High" come from?

That's about as close to metaphor as I do. People always ask where the ideas come from, and I tell a quick little story about this centipede and this spider. We all know what a centipede looks like: a hundred legs. A centipede's in a limo, and a spider comes over and he says, "Can I talk to you a second?"

The centipede stops, and the spider says, "Look, I have *eight* legs, and I'm always thinking, like, 'Oh, second one from the back, and oh my

God, oh gee, got one over here.' And you have a *hundred legs*. How do you do it?"

And the centipede thinks, and he never moves again. [*Laughs*] That's my little story in answer to where the ideas come from. I don't know. And I kind of don't want to know, because if there is a place, I might go there and see what's in the box.

It seems like there's an endless, astronomical, incalculable number of combinations of those twelve notes, and then when you start to add octaves, forget it. There are less words and even less emotions, so it's amazing that we can write about the same thing using those notes and those emotions and those words and keep coming up with things that are legally nonsueable and are different *enough*. That's our challenge, and it's such fun. And when you do come up with an angle on it and beat it, it's really gratifying.

Well, I asked about that one because it seems different. "River Deep—Mountain High," that title, it's kind of elemental.

So how did that come together? Do you remember writing "Sugar, Sugar"?

I wrote that with Andy Kim. We used to write in my office, and he would sit opposite. I would sit at the desk, and my desk was the drum, and the side of the desk was the kick drum, and the top was the snare. He would play the guitar.

We wrote, "I just can't believe the loveliness of loving you" for four-year-olds. You know? But I was always very conscious back then of what I was writing. I really wanted the parents to like the songs. "Edgy" was not a term then. I actually believe that a baby girl born in the fifties, who was a teenager in the sixties, and a baby girl born early this century that's a teenager today, when they're born they're identical in who they are. So where does the fifteen-year-old girl today supposedly become antilove and doesn't believe in it anymore? Where does that happen? I think it's dictated and they go along with it, but I think every human being on the face of the earth—I don't care how cynical you are—somewhere you've *got* to believe it can be done, and you're going to find it. Love, that is. You believe in love.

"Sugar, Sugar," like "Hanky Panky," is talking about love but using other words for it. It's an adult song, "Sugar, Sugar," though it's written for kids.

Well, I don't know about the "You are my candy girl" part. [*Laughs*] I mean, we do have to realize, as a professional, "Okay, yeah, right.

'Loveliness of loving you' aside, we're writing for four-year-olds. What do they like? Candy." [*Laughter*]

"Pour some sugar on me"—that's an old blues kind of idea.
    It is?

No?
    You got me.

I think it could be.
    Sounds like it.

You wrote "I Honestly Love You" with Peter Allen, which became a huge hit for Olivia Newton-John in 1974. How did that one come together?
    I was going to produce Peter Allen. He had no success at that point at all as a writer, as nothing. And he was an interesting guy, and A&M wanted me to produce him. So I listened to his songs; I didn't hear a radio song at that point. And I started on a song, and he was at the piano—it's one of those snapshots in my head—he was at the piano in my office, and I said, "You know, I have an idea for a song, something that hasn't been said." I thought it would be a really sexy song for a guy to sing. "I'm not trying to sleep with you"—I cleaned that one up—or even stay up with you. In fact, *I honestly love you*. No one had ever said that before. And I thought any girl who would hear that would have to say, "Well, can we just do it once?" [*Laughter*]
    So I sang the opening—I had the opening line. [*Sings*] "Maybe I hang around here / A little more than I should / We both know I got somewhere else to go." I had that. And to me it was like a three-chord country song.
    He's at the piano, and I sing him that. Peter had, like, eleven fingers. And he starts playing these chords. *Holy shit.* And we wrote that in six hours. Three hours that afternoon and three more. That's the only song I know, besides "Hanky Panky," exactly how long it took.
    It was so complicated chordally that I had to make a demo: vocal, piano. Sat at the piano, microphone. Because when I'd get with the arranger for those weird chords, right? For strings and horns. And somebody in the publishing department who was going to play songs for Olivia Newton-John heard the demo, didn't ask, went off, came back the next day, and said, "Olivia loves the song and she wants to—"
    "What song?"
    "That 'I Honestly Love You' song."
    And I said, "Oh no, no, no. I'm cutting that with Peter Allen."

So Peter and I, we sat and I said, "Look, Peter. She's the hottest female artist in the world, and if she has a hit with it, that's really good for you. Not bad for me either," [*laughs*] "but it would certainly kickstart your career. And if she *doesn't* have a hit with it or doesn't even put it out as a single, you can still record it."

So he thought that made sense, and it actually was forced out of the album by radio. She was having hits with mid- to up-tempo kind of nice little radio songs, and the record company, they hated it. I heard from them, and they just hated it. But radio really liked it. It was just solo piano; there's no drums or bass on that record. They made the perfect record. It's her singing a song she loved, with the piano part from what he played on the demo.

And they footballed—you know what "football" is? Whole notes?—they footballed the strings and the voices, so it was just sheer in the background. Nothing's in the way, which is a good lesson when producing. Get out of the way. Your job is to present a singer singing a song. That's your job. No showing off allowed. *Don't bury the vocals.*

That's the story of "I Honestly Love You."

With the Phil Spector productions, there was so much going on. He filled in all the space. Yet it still always focused on the vocal.

Yeah, well, that's just a good mix. You make a pocket. Look at your record from the side view, like you're standing in the wings looking out at the stage from the wings, and leave a little shelf—leave a pocket for that vocal to sit in.

That kick drum is under the vocal. The other stuff's on top of the vocal. The stuff there in the range of a vocal—guitar, certain keyboards, that are in the range of a vocal? They're *behind* it. Don't show off.

These days do you find songwriting is any easier or has shifted?

No. I come from a place of where I hate *everything*. But it's a good place. I mean, I'm like that about myself. I don't please myself that easily. At this point I don't go too far into a song unless I can't wait to finish it and show off with it. You know, I can't wait for somebody to hear it because that's really fun to do.

I don't fool myself. You've got to be honest with yourself. The hardest thing—I almost wish I never heard it, but I'm going to do it to you too—is, "Who *cares*?" Ask yourself, "Who *cares* about this song?" It's, ugh, terrible. But it's of value if you can answer it. If it's like, "Uh, I don't care myself," move on. Junk it. Go on.

Preparing for this, it's been a joy to hear so many of your classic songs. And none of them seem old or dated—they are as great as ever. "Be My

Baby" is undiminished by time. If anything, it sounds better. Do songs still matter as much as ever?

Yes. There's never been a civilization we've discovered that doesn't have a form of song, music, and I think even dance. And for some reason we need it, and it's part of the human condition. I don't know if we have time, but I can tell you my theory of *why*.

Please.

When we were coming out of the caves and the brain was developing, it was all about one thing, and that was *survival*. Fashion didn't exist. Nothing existed except survival: stay alive. Which is the first law of nature: self-preservation. Second law of nature? Anybody know what that is? Propagation of the race. Third law of nature. Anybody? It's a joke—there is none. [*Laughs*]

But seriously, nature says, "Stay alive and do it." It's true, right? Think about it. So the brain is developing. It's all about survival, right? There's no language even. Language comes along. I'm trying to shorten the history. [*Laughs*] There's forty to sixty people in a club, whatever they call them. Tribe. And they would literally move all day and pick and find things to eat.

Until *fire*. And they knew how to keep fire burning when they found it: keep putting stuff on it. And fire was good. So they would stay there. Why do we stare at fire today? If somebody has a fireplace? They advertise the house. Who cares about a fireplace? We rarely use them. You have a fireplace—do you turn it on? No, but it's good. They advertise it. Because the fireplace was so important. The fire would give us safety and light and warmth and scare the saber-toothed tigers away.

So all we knew was that when the fire got low that we'd have to put more fuel on it, and it was so important that they would stare at it. They had to stare at it, and when it got low they would get excited and get wood and put it on it. Before we learned how to start fire. But that was a long time. Anyway, we still stare at fires.

So people are dying. Why? What happened? They ate those red berries. *Ahh, that's why.* Everyone who died ate those red berries. Don't eat the red berries—you'll die. Very important. Not funny. You don't know whether I'm joking or not. When it's death, I'm serious. [*Laughs*] Don't eat the red berries—you'll die. Pass it on. Tell everybody. Don't eat the red berries—you'll die. It goes on for a hundred thousand years, whatever.

Now, rhythm and tonality are realized, and they've discovered they were always there, obviously. And somewhere along the line, they realized that [*sings*] "Don't eat the red berries / You'll die" *sticks* better.

[*Laughs*] And you can all sit around the fire and sing it and pass it on to generations.

So the brain said, "This is *good*." And I think that's why, to this day, the singer of songs is revered. Probably, come to think of it, as this tonality thing caught on to survival, there was probably a singer of the "red berries" songs. You know, he would sing these songs and was a very revered person who passed along this life-saving survival information. And to this day we will buy someone's CD and then get in the car and drive in traffic and pay to park the car and pay a lot of money to go into this huge place and see in the distance that same person who's singing on your CD.

Why? Because we like to sing songs with the singer of songs. We still go and do that. Justin Timberlake working in a McDonald's. Girls, would you look at him twice? With the goofy white hat? You put anybody on stage, they're *better looking*. Why? Because now they are the singer of songs. And we still revere that. We've not giving any life-saving information anymore, but we're out of the caves, they say, for a split second, right? It's been a split second since the caves in the full context of time. And it is still ingrained in us, and we still stare at fires, and we still want to hear the singer of songs sing whatever it is. And that's my story and I'm sticking to it. And our job is to supply the singers of the songs with songs.

That's an important job. The industry has changed, technology has changed, the world has changed. But people still want songs. They don't want something instead of—

The twelve notes, the book of words, and the emotions have not changed.

The words and melody together? You can't beat that.

It's called a song. The song, to me, is the part the singer sings: words, melody. And the chords, totally important obviously, those are the makeup and the lighting and the costume and the scenery in the film. And the words and the melody are the script. And you can sing a cappella, and theoretically, if it's a good enough song, they'll still get the message. How many records start with vocal and one instrument?

And then, because of radio, somewhere along the line here comes the bass. You have to make a record out of it. I may try changing that, actually: if the song is that great and the singer's that great, before they realize it, the record's over and nothing else ever came in. You get away with it.

◆◆◆

Paul Anka

From "Diana" to "My Way"

Los Angeles, California 2013

The man wrote "My Way." For that and that alone he deserves a chapter in this volume. Not only is it one of the most recorded and sung songs of all time, it was also the signature song for the man many consider the greatest singer ever, Frank Sinatra. It was a song that reflected the paradigm shift the world was traveling through, reflected in our music—as the songs of Sinatra were supplanted by rock and roll. When Frank confided to Paul that he was considering retirement, as rock and roll had made him irrelevant, Anka embraced the moment and created an iconic song.

Its full origins—written to a modest French pop hit—are related in the following conversation with Anka. When he wrote songs for people, he didn't write insignificant ones. He wrote their essential songs. Their theme songs. "She's a Lady," for example, was handcrafted for Tom Jones like a fine suit. And there's none more famous than "My Way." What he reveals in our following conversation is that Frank had been asking for a song for years. But Anka felt unworthy of putting words and melody into the mouth of the man he considered the greatest of all singing stars—until the poignant and unlikely birth of "My Way," which is related herein.

But he also wrote one of the most famous theme songs of all time, the theme for *The Tonight Show Starring Johnny Carson*, the origins of which he divulges (it went through three incarnations), setting that record straight once and forever.

Born in Ottawa in 1941, he started playing piano and writing songs when still a tot. By fourteen he already wrote and recorded his first single, "I Confess," and by sixteen was taking on "Diana." The subject of that famous unrequited love ballad was real, as he recalls here. Throughout the decades he surmised that reality underscores the themes of songs better than anything. "Yes, there was a real Diana," he said, "a beautiful girl. I never spoke to her. I was too shy. So I put it all into the song." It also taught him a lesson he has always embraced: the beauty of lyrical simplicity, of saying the most with the fewest words. Though it earned him a hit as a singer, he knew it paved the way for the career he most wanted: to write songs. Though he continued to record his own material through the decades, it was always about the writing for him.

He also learned early on never to trust anyone's opinion of a song. In 1974, when he wrote and recorded "(You're) Having My Baby," everyone he knew told him that it was unsuitable for pop radio. They were wrong. It went to number one.

He also wrote several songs with Michael Jackson, including "I Never Heard" (later reworked and retitled as "This Is It"). Although rights to these songs were disputed following the death of Jackson, Anka's memories of working with MJ remain pure.

His hero was not only Sinatra but also those who wrote songs for Frank, especially the composer Jimmy Van Heusen and lyricist-genius Sammy Cahn (interviewed in *SOS I*). "Sammy was my guy," Anka said when I mentioned our shared love of Mr. Cahn. "Sammy," he said, "I stayed at his house. I learned a lot of my craft from him."

But unlike Sammy, who always wrote the words for others to sing and record, Anka began by singing his own, one of the first to do so in a business not yet used to this phenomenon of one artist doing so many jobs—singer, lyricist, composer—all in one. Today it's normal. But he was one of the first in pop music, and it's there our conversation commences.

Although he was one of pop music's very first singer-songwriters, scoring number-one hits with his songs "Diana" and "Lonely Boy" in 1958 when he was all of seventeen, he says he was just doing what needed to be done. "I needed some good songs," he said during a recent talk at his sun-kissed California studio. But what he created was more than a good song; he stretched the boundaries of what pop songs are about from the very start with classics like "Diana" and "Lonely Boy" long before he wrote his most famous songs. He went on to become not only a beloved artist and singer of his own songs but also one of the most recorded songwriters of all time. "My Way" shares the same realm as "Yesterday" (by Lennon and McCartney, his pals) as being one of this world's most covered songs. ("But when you add up all the karaoke versions," he said, "my song is number one.")

He's written countless other classics, including "Puppy Love," "Put Your Head on My Shoulder," "She's a Lady" (which became Tom Jones's signature song), "You're Having My Baby," and the theme for *The Tonight Show Starring Johnny Carson*, often called "Toot Sweet." The origins—many quite unlikely—of all of these songs is related in the following conversation.

Carole King often gets credit for being the first singer-songwriter, but you were writing and singing your own songs before she did.

Paul Anka: Yes, she came after me. I started about six years prior to her. When I first met The Beatles in Europe before anyone knew them here, they said, "Yeah, we are patterning ourselves after you. Doing your own songs, your own lyrics." It was kind of unheard of back then.

Many songwriters back then who wanted to be performers had a tough time making that transition. Was it a challenge for you to be the singer of your own songs?

It wasn't a challenge as much as a necessity. When I started, pop music was in its infancy stage. I was a kid in Canada. Fourteen, fifteen—writing. There was no *American Idol*. Television had barely started. Everything was radio.

So I was listening to all that music, and I just wanted to sing. My parents didn't know what to make of it. My mother supported me, but my dad wanted me to do something more tangible. I was working at a local newspaper to become a cub reporter, and he wanted me to be a journalist. I studied shorthand. But I also studied music. But I realized there was nobody who was going to write [songs] for me.

I was singing, and I just sung what I saw. And I *wrote* what I saw. I was a teenager, so I saw this girl Diana, and I wrote about her.

"Puppy Love" was for Annette [Funicello]. Just observation stuff. "Lonely Boy" came because a lot of my friends and guys you talk to, and they're lonely. Back in the day when sexuality was repressed. We didn't have such broad parameters.

You wrote "Diana" and "Lonely Boy" when you were very young. Did you write some bad songs first, or were those your very first songs?

They were pretty much near my first songs. "Tell Me That You Love Me" was on the back of one of the records. That was one of the first ones. I was just playing make-believe stuff. Stuff that I didn't even put to paper. It happened so young. I wrote "Diana" when I was only sixteen years old.

Yeah! And such a wonderful song.

I didn't have fifty-eight songs that were bad. Tinkling on the piano led me to *land* on those songs. "You Are My Destiny" also came then.

Is it true that you wrote "Diana" for a girl in church you didn't really know?

I saw her at church and saw her around socially. I saw her in the community, which was a small community. You know, teenage girls always have been a lot more sophisticated than guys. Certainly back then. So I'd see her in the distance, and there'd be a smile and a wave. And the girls would go off, and she'd date older guys. I'm just a little guy, you know? I was no teenage heartthrob. So I just looked at her and got inspired, and that is how I expressed myself. Kind of like Cyrano.

I sat there and just wrote it for her. And I would play it at parties, and kids would like it and look at me and see me doing it. But I didn't get near her until after it was a hit. By then I'd already been to France and Italy and everywhere and I was back.

So, yeah, we knew each other.

As you said, pop music was in its infancy. Soon great writers like The Beatles would learn how to write songs by imitating your songs and those of some of your peers. How did you learn how to do it?

I didn't. I played piano. I was listening to R&B music and country music. All the R&B groups. Had my own group called The Bobbysoxers. Emulating Bill Haley and "Moonglow" and all that stuff that was around.

When I started piano I just started writing for myself. I would read whatever books were out there. I had *Hit Parade*—remember that magazine? I'd read a bunch of books. But there wasn't much about the *craft* of songwriting. It was pretty simplistic back then.

So I just sat down to write for myself and write from my feelings. Because nobody would write for me, and I wanted to be a singer. Once I broke into Chuck Berry's dressing room when he was onstage. Because I wanted someone to hear me. He listened and said, "That's the worst song I ever heard. Go back to school."

So I just wrote for the sake of writing. But nobody was teaching me. I would just study the way songs were built.

Remember, pop music was in its infancy stage. Television was just starting, and everything was limited. It hadn't really evolved yet. I remember when I saw The Beatles, and all the kids and the fans and how remarkable the sound was. I came home to my agent and tried to explain it. There was no media then, there was no CNN, no way of knowing. All he had was a telephone. Nothing else whatsoever.

Not surprised The Beatles would appreciate your songs, because like them, you have rock and roll songs with some really interesting chord changes. "Diana" is like that—it starts off simple but then goes to unexpected places harmonically.

Well, when [the arranger] Don Costa and I would create those records, we'd throw in those off-chords for intros. You know, he was a genius, not me. He was a great engineer, great arranger. I'd be singing lines and licks and playing chords. You had to realize you only had a vision and a sound in your *head*. You didn't have the technology then like today to be sitting there with drum machines and all that stuff and work it out. You had to take what was in your head and put it on paper, but you still don't hear it.

And when you get to the studio and you've got it on paper, you've got musicians there and a quarter-inch tape, mono, right? And you didn't know what you had until you were hearing it. And you were changing it as you went. And then you stood in that room, and you *sung* it. There was no sitting around for three years and spending two million dollars. You'd get a record done in a *day*!

So what I'm saying is that you worked at it. You really worked at that, licks. [*Sings lick from "Lonely Boy"*] You'd sing *licks*.

But would Don suggest chords or—

No, he would take it off of my chords, and he would do the blocking of the chord. I would go out and do licks to it, and he would translate it to the music. He was brilliant with strings and all that.

About The Beatles' emulation, they admired what I did, they got what I was doing. But they liked Chuck Berry more. And Buddy Holly, my friend, who I wrote "It Doesn't Matter Anymore" for, which was his last tune. They liked *those* guys. Because they were guitar driven. I wasn't. Even though I used [guitars] in experimental ways in the studio.

I think they admired what I was doing; they got what I was doing. But they were a group. I wasn't a group. The only group they liked in the United States then was Sophie Tucker. They called her America's favorite group. [*Laughs*] Poor Sophie!

But like you, they were serious craftsmen of songs—

Well, that guy [George] Martin. He was very instrumental there. Like Don was with me. Those guys are the unsung heroes. The George Martins and the Don Costas. One and one makes three.

That's generous, but in terms of songwriting, you wrote the song and chose the chords. What they did was arrangement and production— but songwriting is different than that.

Well, let me tell you something: success has many fathers. And I know that process. Yeah, I brought the chords and the licks, but I still like to give credit to those guys. I really do. George could really pull it together till your hair stood up. I couldn't do that. I can't do arrangements. And make those notes happen. I can *sing* licks, but they fucking *do* it. A lot of guys don't get enough credit. I'm not for that. I can craft a song. I know how to do something like "She's a Lady." I know where to put it. But there's still guys there who get the other half of that tape rolling. I've always been an arranger guy and respect guys who can do that.

The other link with you and The Beatles is that they wrote their songs for themselves, but those songs began to get covered a lot. And that is certainly the same with you. "Yesterday" and "My Way" are the two most covered songs of all time.

Yes. "My Way" is the bigger karaoke sing-along. A lot of that. "Yesterday," yes, a lot of play. "My Way" is a whole other song.

As a singer yourself, were you as happy when other people cut your songs, or did you prefer to be the singer?

I realized early, as much faith as I had in myself, the business began to change, and we looked up at the Rat Pack, and there was nothing quite like that till The Beatles. And I realized that I wasn't going to have the hits all the time, and I was a writer first. I was always a songwriter first.

Sometimes I had to do the songs because there was nobody else who was going to do those songs. You can't walk up to any modern-day singer and say, "I have a song called 'Diana'—'I'm so young, you're so old . . .'" Who's that? That's the first line.

I knew it was all about songwriting, and I knew if I was going to last and if I was going to have any gravitas, that's what really worked for me—Shakespeare: "The play's the thing." What a creator was. They're always going to have the clout.

I remember seeing the evolution into when if an artist *didn't* write their own songs, they couldn't get signed. And that was never a problem for me. I instilled that in myself, that I was always going to put myself in the place of someone and write for them, whether it was Buddy [Holly] or Connie Francis or the *Tonight Show* theme or "Longest Day" [the theme song for the movie of the same name]. An eclectic array of stuff that I was writing for, honing my craft. Knowing if I wasn't making it on record that I would be writing and would still have the gravitas 'cause I was an entertainer. I was schooled with Sinatra and those guys. I was sort of a strange sort of enigma. I was the one who lasted from the fifties. You know, when new shit comes, they don't want to know about yesterday. And here I was still surviving. And then I'm running over to Italy and selling millions of records writing with Italians. Nobody was doing it. And I was still the odd guy out with what was contemporarily happening. [*Laughs*] It was very weird because that's from the fifties.

So that became my life. Be the writer first. Because then it gets you to "My Way." Then it gets you to "Let Me Try Again." Then it gets you to "Havin' My Baby." The writing came first. The fun became the performing. That gave me the lasting credit, the longevity.

You sound like you've got some vintage, you've got some brains there. I think you understand what I'm saying to you. I was never the star of the sixties. I was a guy from the fifties that was lasting. And everyone was wrestling with why and how? Here's this guy with the Rat Pack in Vegas. Everyone laughed at Vegas! Now they became hypocrites because they're all working it now that they can make a lot of money. It's always about the money. So the songwriting was really important to me because I didn't think I would last without it. You wouldn't be talking to me without "My Way" and all that.

Yeah, I'd say you did pretty well with that decision. As a songwriter, your success is phenomenal. If only for "My Way," which is a truly iconic song. And one with unusual origins. I know you adapted a French melody—but how did that happen?

Really simple. I vacationed a lot in France and spent a lot of time over there. Took my family over, married my wife there. I was really into that scene, and I know everybody. I like the diversity and the balance of it. And I heard this song on the radio. A mediocre hit by a French singer called

"Comme d'habitude," which means "as usual." It's about a couple in a very boring marriage, a relationship, which is as usual—they get up every day, and "the smell of your breath, I love it . . ." Very graphic French shit.

So I heard it, but I knew there was more in it. 'Cause it wasn't a huge hit. I knew the publishers up in Paris. You got to remember this is '66—and I called them up to see if I could get this song. I mean, we weren't buying the pyramids here. It was done in thirty minutes: [*in French accent*] "Yeah, here take it." It was a two-page contract. I had a vision. They were so-so about it in France, which wasn't a big market.

So I brought it back. And I was just keeping it in the drawer. I'd play it on the piano. I didn't refer to the French record at all lyrically.

So all through this period, knowing Sinatra and working with him—you know, he *hated* pop music—he hated Presley and The Beatles. Never got it. He didn't understand it. He was from the real pure world, old standard American classic. He wanted to be with it, but he couldn't. He tried. And then he married Mia [Farrow]. But he never got it. He would sit there and say, "What is this shit?"

So Sinatra's teasing the shit out of me all the time, saying, "When are you gonna write me a song?" Which I knew wasn't going to fucking happen. But it *bugged* me. Because I loved him and adored him like all of us did. And I decided that one day I was going to do it.

The long and the short of it is that I was down in Miami, he's doing a movie. I go to dinner with him. He said, "I'm quitting." Kennedy was all over, Bobby Kennedy. The Rat Pack was waning. He said, "I'm quitting. I'm getting out of here."

That really motivated me. When I went back to New York, sitting there at one in the morning, thinking, "This is for real." I called Costa and said, "The guy's done. He's quitting."

And I started at one in the morning at the typewriter-piano. I wrote it as if Sinatra were writing it. I used a lot of his language. I started metaphorically: "And now, the end is near, and so I face the final curtain." I wrote it just for him. And put the demo together. Brought it to him.

Two months later he calls. He's in LA, I'm in New York. I put the phone on the speaker. He said this was the one. And that was it for me. I started to cry. It was a turning point in my life. Even though I'd been nominated for an Academy Award when I was a kid, for *The Longest Day*, even though the *Tonight Show* theme was cooking every night, for me to get a Sinatra record on a song like that, which I knew was the most different I'd ever written, was a monumental day in my life.

I can imagine. And that explains where that song came from, because you were only twenty-eight when you wrote it, yet it's about being an older man.

Well, it shows you about writing, when you know your craft, when you're a writer, there is no age barrier. But when you're the singer performing the song, there is. RCA was pissed at the time that I gave it away. I said, "Hey, I'm young enough to write it, but I'm not old enough to sing it. It belongs to Sinatra. He's the guy who's gonna get it out there. That's his song." You check your ego at the door. And I would never, *ever*, ever try again.

And to have any song recorded by him would be great, but that became his signature song.

Yes. And he came back and said, "I'm gonna try again."

Why is it, when he first wanted a song, you didn't write one for him?

I didn't have the capability. All through those early years I did not feel ready. You have to remember, as you're growing and maturing and working at your craft, that's not overnight. There's a certain kind of song that you write for your age and your intellect. It comes from learning your craft and maturing as a person. I never would have written that song when I was younger. I wasn't capable.

Were you worried that writing that the end is almost near would upset him?

No, because he always talked about age. He hated getting old. He hated old age.

And the song admits to being old.

Yes. You're old, you're vintage. But curiously enough, people are living into their nineties. Look at the life expectancy.

You mentioned the *Tonight Show* theme, which was the theme song during Johnny Carson's long reign. Is it true that started as a different song?

It started as a song for Annette [Funicello]. It was called "It's Really Love" [also known as "How Will I Know Love?"]. But it was going nowhere. And it meant nothing. Written for her. "Puppy Love" was the biggest one I wrote for her. So I just copped that song, because no one was ever gonna hear it, and that's it.

It always seemed like the ultimate dream for a songwriter, to have your song performed every night on the *Tonight Show*. And the real one. With Johnny Carson.

Exactly.

Do you remember how that felt when they accepted it?

I remember going to the studio. It was nowhere near the vibe of what I had originally written. I took a big band in, because that's what was on the show, with Skitch Henderson. I did the demo and sent it to him. Skitch didn't want it 'cause this kid was coming in, cutting in on his turf. And then it wasn't going to happen. So I gave Johnny half the song.

So it was that melody with a full set of lyrics?

Yeah. I wasn't sure if they were gonna take it, accept it. I was covering myself. But knowing it didn't really matter because they were only going to use ten seconds. There wasn't a full song needed, though I presented it as a full song. So I didn't know if they were gonna use it, if Skitch would throw it out, or if I should keep it with Annette. I was just juggling basically.

When I was growing up I knew you mostly for "Havin' My Baby," which was a big hit in 1974.

After "My Way" all that stuff started over. I was maturing, and I got a record deal. And experiencing what I was going through. Having kids. Five girls. That was the next real decade in my contribution.

And like "My Way," it had new lyrical content for a popular song. Nobody else was writing that song.

I tested it with disc jockeys, and they said they wouldn't play it. Can you believe that? With all the shit that's on the radio now, with the rap and all they talk about, that back then you couldn't talk about having a baby! [*Laughs*] Now anything goes, the language. What were they getting on me about having a baby in a song, but the *Washington Post* and *Time* magazine came to my rescue. They got on it, which drove it to number one. But those DJs, they weren't going to play it.

It's a great lesson for songwriters, that some of the greatest songs get resistance like that.

Exactly. Don't compromise because you're going to get nowhere. Don't ever compromise to please everyone and be liked. You've got to take those chances. Good is the enemy of great. You've got to push it.

Some of your songs are enormous hits, and others are great but aren't as well known. Are the hits the best ones, do you think?

No. There are greater ones. Today it's scary because there's so much stuff out there, and it's all about marketing or other dynamics. But there are other songs that I have that I think are better. There are tunes of mine, they weren't as big as the hits, but that doesn't make them any less.

"She's a Lady," I like it. Would I have done it myself? No, it was for Tom [Jones]. It was what he's about, and I just wrote it in a commercial sense. It's a huge song. Known all over the world.

I didn't realize you wrote that for him. You are great at writing the perfect song for an artist. As Sammy Cahn did with Sinatra.

Well, he was a great guy to write for. And Sammy and Jimmy knew him inside and out. Sammy knew how to do it.

And you do as well. "She's a Lady" became Tom Jones's theme song.

Yeah. It was his only number-one song.

One of your most beautiful songs is "Hold Me 'Til the Morning Comes," which you recorded with Peter Cetera.

Yeah, I love that song a lot. See, to me that should have been bigger than it was. Even though it was a top AC record. I love that.

You've written so many great songs. Any advice you can offer about how you get to that place where a great one can come?

Well, I got to where I did with the young stuff without really knowing how. It was just honest and pure stuff. But later, in the early sixties, you just know when you study the rudiments of rhyming and structure and melody. When I got there with "Longest Day" and the records I did for RCA, I knew there was a certain level that you needed to get to if you were wise enough to know what was good and what was mediocre. You were still writing to write a hit song. Not that any of us know. We don't have that crystal ball. But you know, as a craftsman, that you're at the level that you want to be at. And you think it's got a shot.

I was never a craftsman, writing all the time. I did write all the time. But I always had the avenue of performance. I only wrote songs because I had to write. I was writing to cover the French, German, Italian market. So I was writing and writing and writing. At least I had the outlet. I didn't have the rejection. A lot of guys would write songs every week and get rejected and not get any records. And that's tough.

Would you start songs with music or with words?

Sometimes a key line that would start me off. Then I would get the structure of the melody. Because it's only as good as the word on it. But I needed that infrastructure of that note, and I need the infrastructure of what the vibe of the song is, what's going to carry me through. And then the words would come later, even though I'd get my key line. A lot of the lyrics would be dummy lines. So what I'm saying is that I need to get a structure. And then the word starts falling in—where the vowel belongs or what the emotion is.

Do you generate melodic ideas from chords or separate from chords, just pure melody?

It's mixed. It's eclectic. I play chords to generate melodies. Sometimes I think of only melody, because I want to keep it simple, and put the chords around it. It just depends on the song. I would hear it and then work on the chords, to get the chords where I want it to go. But it has to have a bass line, and sometimes the bass with the melody will define the chord. [*Sings melody to "Longest Day"*] It depends. It's not always the same.

You wrote a song with Michael Jackson in 1980 called "I Never Heard," which was later reworked and retitled "This Is It."

Yes. Michael took all the tapes and, unbeknownst to me, rerecorded them. He had obviously kept them in a drawer after rerecording what he took into the studio. After his death his people thought it was a new song. The original title was "I Never Heard," as you said. "This Is It" was actually the first lyric I had.

What was it like working with him? Did he bring as much to the words and the music?

Yes. We worked at my studio in Carmel, and he was my houseguest. We just sat in a room. I was banging away at the piano, and we came up with ideas.

So he brought as much to it as you did?

Oh yeah. Absolutely. He was very talented. We just played off of each other, like all duets. He was talented, shy, but confident. He had a great knack for melody, and he loved music.

He was such an astounding singer and performer that his talent as a songwriter is often overlooked.

They don't know because some of his hits were written by other people. But he contributed. You sit in a room and hear things. He wasn't a craftsman, really. But he did all of the background vocals.

One of the main tests of a song is how many different versions there are by different bands and singers. And your songs have been recorded by a remarkably diverse array of people. The Sex Pistols recorded "My Way." And The Misfits recorded "Diana." What did you think of those versions?

You know, you're always pleased. Some of them didn't thrill me, obviously. But an interpretation of a song by someone who has honestly put their soul into it, you can't be judgmental about it. But I have my choice to say what my favorites are. Were the Sex Pistols my favorite? No, but I think the guy did an honest attempt. I think he honestly felt it. I think he did it to the best of his capabilities in interpreting it. So I can't judge them for that. I liked Presley's version, I liked Sinatra's version, I like Brook Benton's version.

Did you know Elvis?

Yes. I knew him all through the years. But when he came to Vegas and I was working there, we'd sit and talk. And you get to know a guy like that. We saw the whole physical change he went through. Just by sitting with him. And I loved him. He was a great artist and a great guy. Not a malicious guy in any way. He was a great singer. He had a black man's voice, frankly.

He would sit with me in the seventies, and he'd go [imitating Elvis], "Hey Paulie, I love that 'My Way.'"

I'd say, "Elvis, it's not your kind of song."

And he'd say, "I love it, man. It says so much to me."

And I said, "I wouldn't recommend that you do it." You know, he would do that other stuff, the three-chord stuff. But it meant so much to him be- cause of what you're going through. And you can't shut a man down.

He tired of three-chord rock and roll songs early on. He wanted to do the kind of ballads that you were writing—

Yeah. So he went in and did it because I think internally he really was going through something.

During his Vegas time, according to so many of the books about him, he was miserable. Is that right?

Part of the time, yeah. He was getting old. And he was no dummy. He could see what he was doing to himself. It was not easy for him. I'd say to him, "Hey, you're Elvis! You're gonna get old—we're all getting old. You just got to be graceful. You're Elvis!"

Many songwriters have said it seems songs come through them. Does it feel that way to you?

Yes. Absolutely. Through the experience that you're going through. And then some from when you've got a definite project in mind or some- one in mind, and you're putting your brain to it. Thinking as the artist. But the others are coming from something that's affecting you, and it is coming through you, that's absolutely true. And it's a beautiful feeling, to be the one who brings one in.

◆◆◆

Kenny Gamble

Inventing the Philly Sound

Philadelphia, Pennsylvania 2008

The idea was to have a catchy melody so closely linked to a title that you could never think of that title without the tune. Think of any of their famous titles and listen to the music they conjure: "If You Don't Know Me by Now," "You'll Never Find," "Me and Mrs. Jones," "Love Train," "I'm Gonna Make You Love Me," and many more.

All of those songs were written by Kenny Gamble with his partner in song and business, Leon Huff. Together Gamble and Huff were the architects of the Philly sound. Like Motown in Detroit, Gamble and Huff built an empire on song. They wrote the songs and produced the records, teaming up with a phenomenal group of musicians, arrangers, and engineers to create a remarkably unbroken chain of soul masterpieces.

Besides being tremendously savvy songwriters, Leon and Kenny had a great ear for talent—always on the lookout for not only strong voices but unique ones. Voices you never forget once you hear them, like Lou Rawls or Aretha Franklin.

Kenny Gamble was Philly born on August 11, 1943. His first records were cut when he was a kid at penny arcade recording booths. He started his own group, Kenny Gamble and the Romeos, all about great harmony soul vocals and smooth songwriting. Teaming up with Thom Bell, he met Leon Huff and split up the work: Gamble and Huff would write the songs while Thom Bell arranged them.

As related in the following, the very first time Gamble and Huff sat down to write a song, they wrote ten.

Rather than attempt to truly compete with Motown, as was the conventional wisdom around them, in fact the Philly sound, as Kenny explains herein, was created entirely in the image of Motown and with great reverence. Gamble and Huff didn't only create a catalog of songs, they started their own label, Philadelphia International Records, for which Clive Davis of CBS did the distribution. Their records crested the R&B and pop charts, romantic and soulfully infectious classics such as those by The O'Jays ("Back Stabbers" and "Love Train"), Harold Melvin and the Blue Notes ("If You Don't Know Me by Now"), and Billy Paul ("Me and Mrs. Jones").

In his native Philly on a sunny but snowing day, he spoke. It was soon after the election of Obama, leading us to a talk of the African American impact on music, of which he was a fundamental and lasting force.

You and Leon Huff together created a phenomenal chain of classic songs. Is there a feeling you were meant to meet? Was it providence that brought you together?

Kenny Gamble: Yeah, I think so. Because we just fit together like a hand in a glove. The day I met Huff I met him in an elevator. And we were working in the same building. We was on the sixth floor and I was on the second floor, and I had never seen him before. I had never seen any African American people in there, period. And when I saw him, we struck up a conversation. I told him I write lyrics and play guitar a little bit. He said, "I play piano and I write songs," so I said, "Let's get together." We got together [*laughs*] that weekend, and we sat down to write. And we hardly even knew each other then. But we sat down, and we must have written seven songs together in a couple of hours. *Unbelievable!* That is forty-eight years ago now. It really was destiny that we got together. And the beautiful thing about Huff and my relationship that, I always say, is that not only did we have the ability to write together and to come up with some great concepts and ideas, but we opened the door for so many other great writers, like Thom Bell and Linda Creed, Sherman Marshall. The list goes on and on and on of some of the great writers we were able to bring into our company.

Had you written songs before working with Huff?

Yeah, quite a few. And he likewise had written quite a few songs before. But the magic of Gamble and Huff was that Huff was a piano player—and an extraordinary piano player—and basically I'm a lyricist. My strength was writing lyrics. His strength was playing the piano. So when we got together it was magic, it was unbelievable.

We inspired each other. I inspired him and he inspired me.

That inspiration comes across in the songs. Would you both do both words and music? Would you sometimes have musical ideas and would he sometimes have lyrical ones?

Oh yeah, yeah. Sometimes I'd play some chords for him and he'd take the chords and embellish on them. And sometimes he'd have ideas for songs, and then I'd take them and finish writing them out. The way we really worked was we would have a legal pad, and we'd write down hundreds—hundreds—of titles. And when we'd go to work, we'd say, "Who are we going to write for today?" And we might say, "Okay, this is for Lou Rawls today" or something like that. We'd be in a Lou Rawls state of mind.

In fact, when we first started out, we started to name our publishing company Tailor-Made Music. We settled on Mighty Three Music. That was the name we settled on. Because we figured that we tailor-made the songs especially for the artist we were writing for. Like the O'Jays. When we would come in and write for the O'Jays, we'd be thinking like Eddie and Walt and William and all these guys.

You'd notice that the amount of artists we did was substantial. And none of them sound alike. The music was different, and the songs were all catering to their abilities. Like Lou Rawls, he had such a wonderful baritone voice that we would write songs that would be in his register. We knew the keys that he sang in best. And when he would come in to record, we would rehearse with him, and the songs would fit him just like a tailor-made suit for you.

I was wondering if that was the case, because I think of your song "You'll Never Find." And I can't think of that song without thinking of his voice with it. It is so perfect for his style, his voice, and delivery.

Yeah. We were lucky on that one. We really were lucky. We got a gigantic record on him, the first song out. "You'll Never Find"—it sounded just like him. When we were writing the song I thought, "This sounds just like Lou Rawls." And man, when he came in he gravitated to it just like a duck to water. [*Laughs*]

And then you would tailor-make these songs also in the studio by producing the song around the artist.

Yeah, but that's the hard part. Well, *all* of them are hard. But writing the song was probably the easiest part. Then going into the studio and having to relate that to a group of musicians, the kind of atmosphere and the mood that you wanted to create with the music. So we had *tremendous* musicians that worked with us.

You sure did. The MFSB [Mother Father Sister Brother, a pool of more than thirty great Philly musicians].

Yeah, the MFSB was a *tremendous* orchestra. And we had great arrangers, Bobby Eli and Thom Bell. We were all like a great team working together. In addition to that, we had great arrangers. Because the fidelity on our records is just unbelievable. When you listen to those records today you say, "Wow, these are great-sounding records."

You said the writing of the songs was the easy part. Did it always come easy? Or were there times when you would work and not get anything?

Oh yeah. Quite a few times we'd come in there and be empty. [*Laughs*] So we'd have to take a few days off. Or sometimes we'd fly to Jamaica or someplace like that. Jamaica was a wonderful place to write because, boy, we might write ten or fifteen songs down in Jamaica when we were there. Jamaica is beautiful. The environment is beautiful, and you'd have somebody to cook for you. And the phones weren't ringing all day long. So you didn't have anything to do but write songs all day long.

Is it true you and Huff would work together on songs and then you would take them home and finish them?

Well, sometimes we would write and then I would take the songs home and work on the lyrics to make sure the lyrics were just right. Sometimes maybe I wouldn't even have a lyric, and I'd sing "la-dee-da-dee-doo" or something like that. [*Laughs*] Then I'd have to go home and think about how to make the story and the song work its best.

Would you and Leon discuss what the song would be about before you would take it home?

Oh yeah, no question. No question about it. When we had all those titles we'd sit down and discuss. Let's say, for example, a song like "Love Train."

We were talking that day about how people all over the world were so disunited and there was so much trouble in the world! So we said, "Hey, let's write a song about people all over the world, and let's make it a love train." When you hear the lyrics to "Love Train," you see we tried to mention every country that we could. [*Laughs*] Every country from all over the world.

At Motown all those writers would compete every day to get a cut. Same thing with the Brill Building writers. They competed and wrote amazing songs that way. But for you and Leon, since you owned your own record company, there wasn't competition like that, was there?

Yeah, but we competed. We followed the blueprint of Motown. Yeah, Motown was the blueprint. That was my favorite record company. I'd say Motown is the greatest record company that has ever been in the music business. We followed that same blueprint, where we had an office full of great writers. And the O'Jays would come in, or Harold Melvin and the Blue Notes would come in on a certain date. And we'd say, "Listen—bring your songs in." And then we'd review the songs and we'd pick the best ones out of the batch, and then those songs would go into the studio to be recorded.

For example, if the O'Jays came in to record, during those days you might have eight or ten songs on an album. But we would record maybe twenty. Twenty songs to get the ten best. It wasn't easy. Taking a song and going into the studio, you don't know what's going to come out. It doesn't always come out the same way you heard it.

And you and Huff would make those decisions—which song would get on the album?

Yeah, we would make the decision on what songs would go on an album. And that would be pretty much it because we were pretty much responsible for that. Somebody has to make the last decision, you know? When you look at the albums, you'll see Huff and I used to write maybe 50, 60 percent of each album. And the rest of it would be other writers and producers.

And when the other writers would bring you a song, would you tell them how to change it, or would you accept them as they were?

Oh no, no. I'd tell them how to change it. Yeah. As a matter of fact, today I look back and think I should have gotten the piece of royalties on that song. [*Laughs*] Sometimes I'd have to write a whole verse.

But it was a good camaraderie. We had excellent relationships with everyone who worked there. We had a great team. It was *teamwork*—that is what made it work.

Motown, of course, had the Motown sound. And you and Leon created the Philly Sound. Was that a conscious choice, to create your own sound, or did that just happen organically?

Like I told you, we followed the Motown blueprint. And at that time they had the Memphis sound, they had the Motown sound, so we said, "Let's call ourselves the Philly sound." And then that's how it all happened. We basically did what Motown did. Motown was the blueprint that we followed.

Yet the Philly Sound itself was different. You "put the bow tie on funk," as the saying goes—

[*Laughs*] Yeah, that was Fred Wesley from James Brown's band who said that.

Our sound was different for a couple of different reasons. One is that Motown was basically doing it in the early sixties, and pretty much most of the music and technology was mono. When we came along, which was the late sixties and the seventies and the eighties, everything had changed to stereo. So of course, stereo is much, much more appealing to the ear than mono, and it's a whole other recording technique. And in addition to that, the technology had changed tremendously.

Also, we had a tremendous orchestra, the MFSB. That orchestra was unbelievable, and I think stereo really showed that sound off. And then, again, during the time of Motown most rhythm and blues stations were AM stations. When we came along that was during the time rhythm and blues stations had changed to stereo stations. So we were able to reach a wider audience. And it was all because of technology. Just like technology is changing today.

Among the great songwriters of our time, not many were also great producers. Leiber and Stoller obviously were, and you and Huff. When you would write the song would you think in terms of the arrangement and production, or did that come after?

That came along as we were writing it. Because the whole arrangement of those songs were designed in the song. And that's what we were trying to achieve. 'Cause you can hear it in your head. You can hear how you want it to sound. And pretty much you just have to go in the studio and relay that to the musicians. 'Cause they don't know. They come in cold. And you have to relay it to them. And many times what we would do is play the tape with Huff and myself singing it so they'd get a feel for it. And fortunately it worked out very well.

So you and Leon would record the song like a demo first?

Oh yeah. Well, when we were writing we would write with a cassette player on the piano. So we have *thousands* of tapes of us writing. All the mistakes and everything. [*Laughs*]

And you both would sing?

Yeah, sometimes we'd both sing. And sometimes it sounded pretty good! I look back on it, and probably some of them songs Huff and I could have done. [*Laughs*]

When I listen to your records I'm always impressed by the great vocals you always got. Of course, these were wonderful singers. But what was your technique for how you enabled singers to get such a great vocal performance in the studio?

Well, I think we were very fortunate to be able to have some exceptional singers, number one. I mentioned Lou Rawls. We went for the *uniqueness* in a person's voice. That they would have a sound of their own. Like Patti LaBelle. When you hear a record on the radio and you listen to it and you know. You say, "That's Patti LaBelle, right there." Or you'd say, "That's Lou Rawls," or "That's the O'Jays," or "That's Aretha Franklin." Because they had their own individual sounds. And that's what we were looking for when we signed an artist. How unique was this particular person and the sound of his voice?

Would you and Huff equally guide a recording session?

Yeah, no question about it. We collaborated. We collaborated like one person. We're like one person in the studio.

You would always agree?

Yeah, no question about it. Because we'd talk it over so much. It was almost unanimous, everything that we did together.

You've written so many great melodies. Any way of explaining what makes a melody good?

Well, I think what makes a song and a melody good is you putting your heart into it. And as far as the melody is concerned, it just has to be something very simple that people can actually sing along with. You have to have a great sing-along. And that's what we always tried to do, was have great hooks so that they would stay in a person's mind for a long, long time. For example, if you think of a song like "If You Don't Know Me by Now," you can hear that song in your head.

Yes. And that's true of all of them. You name a title like "Me and Mrs. Jones," and you hear the music when you say those words.

Yeah, you can hear it. You know, you can hear it. And look at Billy Paul—look at how unique his voice is. And he was a friend of ours. And he was a longtime favorite in Philadelphia as a singer. In the local nightclubs. But he was so *unique*. That he was able to come off. And he performed "Me and Mrs. Jones" tremendously.

The other thing too, with most of the artists we had, is that they were great performers onstage. And that, in my view, was maybe the biggest compliment that we had. That the artists were not only able to not only perform the records, but they would be able to go on tour. And dazzle the audiences. And that made it easier for us to write for them. It made it easier for them to build up fans all over the world.

"Me and Mrs. Jones" is about a guy having an affair—

Yeah, well, that song alludes to it. It doesn't say that it is, it just *appeared* that they were having an affair. Because Huff and I used to go down to a little café that was downstairs from our office at the time. And as a songwriter you're always watching and looking at everything. Everything you do, everything people say, what they *do* can potentially be a song for you.

So on a couple of days we used to watch this guy come into the café, and he would go sit in a certain booth. And then maybe fifteen or twenty minutes later, a young lady would come in. And they would play certain songs and sit there, maybe have a drink or whatever the case might be. And then they would leave, and the next day they would come in again.

And Huff and I would say, "Hey, this guy was here yesterday! And the girl, the same girl!" And we thought, "Yeah, it's 'me and Mrs. Jones, we got a thing going on.'" And we went upstairs and started writing the song.

That's called inspiration. Inspiration. The whole world around you is a great inspiration.

Yes. And some songwriters, we can connect with inspiration at certain times. But not always! Yet you guys seemed to be on a roll. You wrote so many great songs for so long.

Yeah, we used to write every day. *Every day* we used to write.

Is that part of the key to doing it so well for so long—to do it all the time, constantly?

Yeah, and also, too, we had an outlet with CBS Records. Which was a *wonderful* thing. Because the greatest thing that a songwriter can have is an outlet for his songs. To get the temperature and find out if the audience and people really like their songs. So once we were able to get a couple of hits, it was like hitting a vein. And then you just keep draining from that vein. You think, "If we did it before, we can do it again." And thank God, we were able to have a long, long successful run, being very prolific. And the only thing I can credit that to is that we were really blessed, and we were inspired to write all those songs and have a great relationship, Huff and I, as friends first and also, too, as business partners.

That is good advice for songwriters—that you shouldn't sit around and wait for inspiration. You guys were working. It was a mixture of hard work and inspiration.

Yes. You can't just sit around. We were always working. And were always looking for new artists. And people that would inspire us. Certain artists, you look at them and they become a challenge. It was a *challenge* to write for the O'Jays. Or a *challenge* to write for Teddy Pendergrass. Because their vocal ability was just *unbelievable*. When they came in to record we had to be *ready*. We couldn't hand them no halfway songs. Those songs had to be almost perfect, you know?

I think the artists help inspire us. And the world around us. That we were able to talk about through our songs.

Was there a feeling sometimes that songs came from somewhere that was beyond the two of you?

We always used to say, "Wow, where did that song come from?" Because once we finished a song it was just so amazing that we could even come up with the song. And then, on top of that, once we recorded it and released it, and then within a couple of months it would be a number-one record, we'd say, "Wow. What's going on?"

It's unbelievable.

Where do you think the songs do come from?

I think we were really blessed. Really blessed to even have the gift for writing songs. I think that we wrote songs from our heart. And from our soul. You kind of spill your guts out in the songs. You make things a reality. You're writing for people, and you're putting words into their ears and words into their mouths that they will say themselves. Like our song for The Three Degrees, "When Will I See You Again." Now this is something that people say every day. When will I see you again? So that song came from a conversation I had with a young lady. I saw her outside of my office, and I said, "I haven't seen you in a long time." We would talk for a few minutes. Then at the end of the conversation I said, "So when am I gonna see you again?" And right then it popped into my head. I said that's a great title.

Every day you hear people say certain things. Another example. The O'Jays' "Family Reunion." That was from a time, especially throughout America, people were having family reunions everywhere. So a guy came into our office, and we were talking, and he said, "I just got back from North Carolina, and I went down to a family reunion." And, wow, that was it. That sparked off that song, you know?

One of my favorites is "If You Don't Know Me by Now."

Yeah. That comes from *another* conversation. Like with one of your girlfriends or your wife. And they always ask you, "Where you been at?" and "Whatcha been doing?" So that song was, "If you don't know me by now, you'll never know me." This guy was telling her, "You know, I love you, and we've been together for ten years. Come on now—this is who I am."

When you would work on a song, would you sometimes have to work to find the perfect melody that worked—or did it always come easy?

To be honest with you, most of the songs that we wrote, we used to write those songs fast. When it comes, it comes *quick*. That's why we had it on tape. Because it's hard to remember it when it's—what is it the rappers say, freestyling? We were freestyling writing songs. [*Laughs*] It was something that you had to catch it when you could.

You talked about how much heart these songs have. And that's been proven over the years that a song like "If You Don't Know Me by Now" became a hit again—when Simply Red did it. The songs weren't just about the time you wrote them; they were just great songs.

Yeah, they're timeless. These songs are timeless. In fact, when we started Mighty Three Music, Thom Bell, who was our partner in Mighty Three, he came up with a logo first, which was three elephants. And I said, "Why did you pick three elephants, Thom?" And he said, "Because they say that elephants have the longest *memory* of everyone." And he said that our slogan would be "You'll never forget our tunes." And that's come true. And it's really happened. Because the songs are being recorded still. Rod Stewart just did "Love Train." He also did "Only the Strong Survive." And so the songs, people still record them, and so many of the young new artists, the rappers, have sampled our songs, it's hard to even count. [*Laughs*] So, I mean, it's timeless. The music we are a part of, it's timeless.

So you always felt that the songs would transcend the time and always be loved?

Well, you know, we always said, when we were writing, let's write standards. We used to drill that into our heads. To write standards. A lot of the songs, we just discarded because they're not good enough. And that's why when we came up with something special, we'd say, "Wow, where the hell did *that* come from?" Sometimes you've got to dig deep to get the best out of yourself. So Huff and I, we literally put our heart and soul into writing those songs.

I always thought you wrote "I'm Gonna Make You Love Me" with Huff, but you wrote it with Jerry Williams and Jerry Ross, is that right?

Huff was writing under an anonymous name at that time, Jerry Williams. That was him. He was writing so much he decided to use an anonymous name. That was me and Huff and Jerry Ross. That's Leon Huff right there. And the thing is, we wrote that song for Dee Dee Warwick, Dionne Warwick's sister. She was the first one who recorded it. It didn't do that well with her, but a few years later Nick Ashford, from Ashford and Simpson, he took that song and he produced it on The Temptations, and The Supremes, and it became a number-one record. Beautiful.

Did you write "Back Stabbers" with him or was that one he wrote alone?

No, Huff wrote that with [Gene] McFadden and [John] Whitehead. Yeah, I didn't get in on that one. I tried to get in on it, but they finished it by the time I got there! [*Laughs*]

You produced a great album with Laura Nyro—one of my favorite artists of all time—*Gonna Take a Miracle*—with LaBelle on it. It's a classic. She is not your usual artist—how was it working with her?

Yeah. She was *great*. I enjoyed working with her. Because she was different for us. She wanted to come to Philly to record with us.

A lot of people don't understand the difference between a record and a song, that you can write a great song and not make a record out of it. What was the key to making a great record out of a good song?

Well, I think the key to making a record out of a good song was Huff and I, we wanted to make sure it sounded just like we heard it. Being able to relate your feelings to the musicians and the musicians responding to you. We worked with this band every day. We were like one. And a lot of that had to do with the musicians and the engineers and the technical people so that they would record the efforts of what we were trying to do. And then the song took care of itself. Once you got the music right, the song took care of itself. And if you had a *great* artist, like Teddy Pendergrass or Patti LaBelle or The Jones Girls or whoever we were working with, then it becomes a lot easier.

Would you have the vocalists perform live with the musicians? Or overdub the vocals?

Not that often. Every now and then we would do a live session with the artists singing with the musicians. But generally we would do the tracks first. Then we would bring the artists in to overdub their voices. And then we'd do the arrangement after that. We'd put in the horns or strings or whatever else we were going to put on that record. And then we'd mix it.

When writing songs to be standards, were you thinking of what would get on the radio or just trying to write a great song?

Well, we were trying to write a great record and a great song. Because if you have a good song and a good artist, the rest takes care of itself. You only can do the best you can do. So we really wanted it to sound the way we wanted it to sound. And we were very fortunate so many people gravitated to our music.

Now with this election of Mr. Obama, we see America shifting. And perhaps one of the aspects of that shift is a real recognition of the black impact on our culture. What would songwriting in our lifetimes have been without you and Motown? The world would have been a much different place. And less soulful.

[*Laughs*] It's true. The contributions that have been made are unbelievable. As a matter of fact, I was talking to some people the other day about slavery and about how our people were brought over here. I said, you know, the way it's going, with Barack Obama being president and the African American influence in America, it's almost as if we were sent here. For this time. Instead of being brought here, we were *sent* here, and we were put through a cleansing period. Our ancestors were put through the fire so we could bring some kind of balance to how great America really is. As a people. So African American people have a tremendous role to play in the future of America.

Are you hopeful about America?

No question about it. I just think that the spirit of America is so powerful that we as American citizens, we have to educate the citizens of America so they can comprehend the environment, comprehend the value of America, this life here. Once the country is focused on educating everyone, especially African American people who have been denied so many of the rights that this country offers. And I think when you're educated, you pick better leaders.

You look at Barack Obama and his presidency, and that wasn't just African American people voting for him; that was the whole country voting for him. So creed and color doesn't matter anymore because we are all human.

I think once you can come to that consciousness where we're all humans and we all come into the world the same way and go out the same way, it's not when you're born or when you pass away; it's what you do in between that time. It's the dash that matters on your tombstone, when they have the date of your birth and the date of your death—it's that dash that counts. This creation is incredible, and everything you know has been created for a reason. America can lead the way in showing the world why we're here. And that is to be the managers of earth and to keep it. So far we haven't been doing such a good job. [*Laughs*] But I think we can learn from our past.

Speaking of that dash, most humans spend that just getting by. Taking care of business, of their families. But some humans—like you and Leon Huff—have created something lasting that impacts all of us and gives us something to hold on to. You've created something which will transcend your lifetime. How does that feel?

It feels great. Because it's something that I always wanted to do, and I feel very blessed to have met Huff and have written those songs. Those songs were from inspiration. We were inspired to write those songs. And I'm very thankful that I had an opportunity to participate in the music we wrote. Music that uplifted people's spirits.

◆◆◆

Norman Whitfield

Through the Grapevine

Hollywood, California 1991

He lived in Detroit because his dad's car died there. The family was driving cross-country, from New York to California, for his grandma's funeral. But heading back home, the car broke down in Detroit, and so the family stayed there. For years. And it's there, in the Motor City, that he established his career.

"Words and melodies are forever," he said, and in his own work there lives the truth. With his partner, Barrett Strong, he's written some of this planet's most soulful and enduring songs, classics such as "I Heard It Through the Grapevine," "Just My Imagination," "War," "Papa Was a Rolling Stone," "Smiling Faces," and more.

More than anything, these masterpieces emerged from the fierce, fighting environment of Motown, where Whitfield and Strong had to compete on a weekly basis to have their songs cut. "If you're in a basketball game and everyone is a six-footer, you can't come in at five foot eight and expect to win," he said, referring to the Motown giants against whom he competed, prolific geniuses such as Smokey Robinson and Holland-Dozier-Holland.

Whitfield, who embraced the challenge of being creative under this kind of pressure, also had the job of evaluating new songs from Motown and sometimes had to admit that his own was simply out of the running, such as the week when Smokey Robinson brought in "My Girl." But rather than get defeated, Whitfield and Strong would write an even better song and cut a hotter track. Such was the world of Motown.

Though Smokey beat them out a couple of times with The Temptations, Whitfield had his greatest successes with the group, writing songs for them with Strong and producing them by himself. When their song for the Temps, "Unite the World," actually failed to go Top Forty, Strong and Whitfield changed direction again and wrote a romantic ballad for the band called "Just My Imagination." It went to number one within eight weeks.

The first song Strong and Whitfield wrote together was "I Heard It Through the Grapevine," now one of the most recorded songs of all time. Artists who have recorded it include the Temptations, Ike and Tina Turner, Creedence Clearwater Revival, Gladys Knight and the Pips, Elton John, and many more.

In 1971 Strong and Whitfield parted ways. Strong moved to California to launch a solo career and to release two albums. Whitfield kept working, writing, and producing the entire *Masterpiece* album for the Temps as well as other records. He scored a hit in the late seventies with his title song and track for the movie *Car Wash.*

This interview was conducted in my Hollywood office. He came dressed as if ready for a basketball game, in jersey, shorts, and sneakers. In fact, he was heading to a nearby game after our talk. The man, as he discusses in the following, loves to compete.

It's true you ended up in Detroit because your dad's car died there?

Norman Whitfield: Yes. I was born and raised in Harlem, in New York City. When I was fourteen we came out to California to attend my grandmother's funeral. And on the way back my father's car broke down and we wound up staying in Detroit.

We stayed there for most of my early career. That was where the actual interest developed to become a songwriter or to have something to do with the business that would be lucrative enough to keep me interested. [*Laughs*]

When did you decide to make music your career?

When I saw Smokey Robinson driving in a Cadillac. To be absolutely point-blank honest. That's what inspired me. And I actually ran up to him one day. I scared him a little bit. I ran up behind him and asked him, after he was halfway frightened by then, "How do you get started?" And he gave me the most ridiculous answer I've ever heard in my entire life. He said, "Make your own bed, brother, because you've got to sleep in it." [*Laughter*] I later dethroned him, dealing with the Temptations. [*Laughs*]

You know, the Motown experience was really quite an experience. It was an absolute philosophy of music over there. This was the Berry Gordy period: the Hollands, Dozier, so on.

Is this when you met Barrett Strong?

I knew him before I ever got in the business. Barrett is the guy who wrote and played "Money" a long time ago, and it was a number-one record. It was on a very small label called Anna records. Berry Gordy produced and cowrote the song.

I was like anybody else. I was very young, and I had seen him perform. And we got to know each other because I was hanging around Motown long before they let me participate, writing and producing. And we had some run-ins with some girls . . . [*Laughs*]

Did you and he begin collaborating on your own, or did Berry Gordy team you up?

We kind of got together on our own. I was down in one of the Motown rehearsal rooms, and he was much more familiar with the Motown thing than I was, to be honest with you, but what happened was that I had a hit record on Thelma Records called "I've Gotten Over You," and Berry Gordy was dominating the town then, Detroit, and Berry Gordy sent his A&R director to find out who I was. The song got picked up by a larger label, and Berry made me a little offer. He said, "Look, man, why don't you come over here? We've got this big machine over here. You'll probably love it, and it'll give you a chance to make a lot of money . . ."

Of course, I was only making $15 a week then when I did go with Berry Gordy. And another $15 a week he paid me for any or all royalties. Which I didn't mind, because I knew in order to make money, you needed to be around a situation where there was some real money being made. And it was an opportunity. The absolute opportunity of a lifetime.

I was down in the rehearsal hall one day, and Barrett came in and we started talking. We talked about some old times. About girls, you know.

We were never really very fond of each other. There was a subtle rivalry there because of the girls; the only difference was that I had the girls, and he was always trying to get them.

We sat down. I said, "Look, I got quite a few hit records." I played him a few things. I said, "If you are interested, I can at least guarantee you $100,000 a year. To write together."

He said, "Well, yeah. Sounds pretty good."

I said, "I can only guarantee it to you verbally. I can't put it on paper because it would have a lot to do with how much we would put into it." So it worked out pretty well. From that point on, we were writing.

What was your first song that you wrote together?

"I Heard It Through the Grapevine." That was a lot of years ago. There's a tremendous story behind that song, and nobody knows the story. Barrett doesn't even know the story.

Can you share that story with me?

I *wish* I could, I really do. It's a story in itself because of the political obstacles and things that happened. And I personally wouldn't want to incriminate Berry Gordy. He's like a father to me. It would be something very special for you to have, but I've got to be honest with you, there's a deal pending, and I wouldn't want to dilute the value of it. Other than the fact that it has been a song that, since day one, Barrett and myself, we've always had a very strong feeling for this song. And I guess it didn't transcend to other people till later on. Because the first version was done on Marvin Gaye, but it never got released. Then I did it on Gladys Knight and the Pips, and it went to number one. I had just come off their first hit record for Motown called "Everybody Needs Love," and it was a perfect chance for me to take a song that Barrett and I had felt so strongly about and put it on an artist who just came off a hit record.

I personally went and looked up where the saying "heard it through the grapevine" came from. It went all the way back to Confederate black soldiers. They had a grapevine in order to pass on their words and experiences to each other.

You wrote the songs with Strong but produced them alone?

Yes, I shared in the writing, but I always produced alone. Kind of like a solo. I'm such a loner when it comes to music. I think it would be a strain for somebody to produce with me because there are so many things that I envision. What my mind can conceive, I can achieve. I've lived by that code for a long time.

Does that make it hard to write with somebody else?

No, because I've come to a certain level of writing. I've mastered every style of writing there is.

Where did you and Barrett write?

At my home or in the office or at his house. And Barrett is a very good piano player, and a lot of time, from being a percussionist, I can figure the rhythm out, and he'd be struggling with a little piano lick and trying to keep the intensity up. When you go over it so many times it gets hard, especially when you're writing up-tempo songs.

When we wrote "Cloud Nine" on the Temptations, I started studying African rhythms on my own, and I wanted to know how to make a song have as much impact without using a regular 3/4 or 4/4 backbeat. And it turned out very successfully. It went to number two or three.

So you can have a hit without a backbeat?

Yes. It has a lot to do with the feeling. Of course, nowadays the kids are pretty dance oriented and the records don't have as much substance. But it's something you have to learn to live with.

Melodies and good lyrics are forever. That's the philosophy we were raised on. Also that competition breeds champions. We had a *very competitive* atmosphere at Motown. *Very.* But in some cases it made people stronger. In my case it made me stronger. I went through a tremendous amount of adversity. I don't even want to *go into it!* [*Laughs*] I was really the new kid on the block. Everybody else was pretty much established there. But I managed to hang in there and make my way. I was probably the fastest-growing producer in the history of Motown. At least, that's what Berry Gordy told me. [*Laughs*]

I also worked in quality control. Because Berry discovered, when I first got there, that I have an absolutely perfect ear in terms of picking hits. So he gave me the job in quality control, which would justify the $15. [*Laughs*]

Did you pick a lot of hits?

Oh, I picked many. I picked "Where Did Our Love Go?" I mean, a lot of hit records. I enjoyed it because I *felt* something, and when I felt something, I was always right. An alarm would go off inside me emotionally when I would hear something special.

Did you do that with your own songs as well?

Later on it got like that because I realized I had to be the recipient of the bad news, and the good news for Smokey Robinson when he sent up "My Girl." You know? It came up; I had to evaluate it. [*Laughs*] I had to take it into Berry Gordy. I said, "Berry Gordy, I do not have a record to submit at this time. This record is *absolutely* a smash."

And it stirred something inside of me to make me say, you know, "Norman, you're really going to have to step into this." And eventually I changed the sound. And Smokey was doing records that I thought were not as *intense* or as lyrically strong, and I got a chance to beat him out. And then once I beat him out, nobody ever got a chance to have the Temptations again while I was there.

Your songs all are timeless. They sound great today if not better as ever. Can you explain how you write a song that will last?

Yes. It has everything to do with the standard that was instilled by Berry Gordy. There was no sense in turning in things that were basically mediocre. And the standard was so *high*; the competition put the edge on it and would carry you over. And I enjoyed it, I enjoyed it. I actually found out that when the going got tough, the tough got going. And I wasn't like that in school. When I played basketball I would react just the opposite. But with music there was a certain tenaciousness inside of me and something that would always drive me to make something very special out of a common situation.

Do you remember writing "Just My Imagination"?

Yeah. I wrote that in Barrett's basement. We kind of felt that it was a step back because we had just come off of "Can't Get Next to You." And we've always enjoyed driving the other groups crazy because we were the leaders. We would take the Temptations and make a left turn, even with everyone saying, "Well, you know, they're going to turn right again," so we just go left. That's part of being a front-runner and being the best in the field: you are allowed to be innovative and do anything you want as long as you keep in mind the standard.

Did you like doing your song "War" with Edwin Starr?

Yes. I also had offered this song to The Rare Earth. I did it on the Temptations first. It was a much different version then. I cut a track that was strong enough to be a single, and I tried to give it to The Rare Earth. And they refused it. They said, "We want to play on our own records."

And Edwin was walking down the hall, and I said, "Edwin, I got a song for you." When we got ready to dub it in, I got a couple of classes of school kids to share the experience with him, of them coming to Motown. They were between nine and eleven. I did that from time to time because I realized there was no vision there because of the poverty.

Did you like Springsteen's version of "War"?

Yes. I was very thrilled when I heard it because I thought it was really quite a compliment to have it on his first live album. I was very excited and very grateful.

How about the Rolling Stones version of "Just My Imagination"?

[*Laughs*] Well, it was different. And I can't say that I absolutely liked it. I can't say that I accepted the fact that they did it because they were who they were. And it was such a beautiful song—it was very close to me and Barrett, you know. When I heard it, Mick Jagger had such a different rendition. It totally caught us by surprise.

After a while you start accepting that somebody else has a different rendition of it. But it was anything but romantic. But it did pretty good in the dollars-and-cents category.

Can you talk about writing "Papa Was a Rolling Stone?"

First I better say this: The Temptations didn't do the first version of it; The Undisputed Truth did. And it did about three hundred thousand. And I thought there was more to the song. So I went and cut it a whole different way because I wanted to stay away from the original version. And the Temptations were a little reluctant because they felt it was a used tune. Eventually we saw eye to eye and we worked on it very hard and got excellent results on it.

Do you have a favorite song you've written?

It's not "I Heard It Through the Grapevine." Because that one was written and produced with the same intensity as all the songs we did. It's one of my favorites. The phenomenal success it has had is undeniable. I like a song very much, like "Too Busy Thinking About My Baby," which Marvin Gaye did, it did a quiet 2 million. I love "I'm Losing You." I thought the song had pie-in-the-face, so to speak. It said what it said, and it said it so cleverly.

How does it feel to have written standards?

I am still experiencing the thrill of it. It's phenomenal, and I thank God that whatever He gave me, that the songs have longevity. And the people are really the people that make the songs what they are. We as writers, we only do what we do, and then we have to give it to the public. They're the ones who determine if you're a genius or a failure. So it's an exhilarating feeling.

I've had it for so long, but I don't take it for granted. I try to remember what it took to get it to that level. Lyrics and melodies are forever, but music can change. It changes with the times. I'm always going to be a chancy person and a nonconformist. I conform only to my feelings.

◆ ◆ ◆

Loretta Lynn

Songs from Butcher Holler

Nashville, Tennessee 2014

So overflowing with inspiration was she when writing "Coal Miner's Daughter," combined with rich remembrance, that she wrote ten verses. Owen Bradley, her producer, said it was too long, so she threw away six verses. Completely. Not saved for some future boxed set. We're talking gone.

But the song, as the world knows well, was so beautifully crafted, so rich in the textures and times she was in, that it became an instant classic. A standard from day one. And after that, she didn't throw away anything.

Miss Loretta. She's royalty, of course. The first lady of country music. She's been mythic for decades, both for her beautiful voice and for those vivid songs from Butcher Holler she wrote herself, painting an American picture so poignant and real, you never forget them. Yet as mythic as she is—having been portrayed, after all, by Sissy Spacek in the movie of her life—she is a real person, and an especially warm, funny, charming, and gracious one. The time spent with her is time I will cherish always. And I have a feeling everybody who has met her feels the same way.

Some people are just born with it. With the gift for writing songs. Songs come to them, and they simply need to write them down. It doesn't take any agony or even much thought; it just takes time with a guitar alone to capture them as they fly by. It's how she started. Right out of the gate, Loretta Lynn wrote songs richer and deeper than the finest songs emerging out of Nashville. And she sang them with robust bravado, this little girl "dressed up like Annie Oakley," and ascended swiftly to Nashville royalty as one of country music's greatest singers and songwriters.

Born in 1932 in Kentucky, she married her beloved Doolittle when she was only thirteen and had the first four of her six kids before she was an adult. He gave her a guitar for her twenty-fourth birthday, and she started playing and singing as if she'd done it her whole life. Her first two songs, "Whispering Sea" and "Honky Tonk Girl," were also the twin sides of her first single. And when people heard that voice with those songs, songs that reflected country life as it was really lived, they fell in love.

After those two, the songs kept coming. When the Nashville crowd first heard her songs they were stunned. Roy Acuff said he couldn't fathom how she could write such astounding songs—"every one a little movie"— after never writing before. Gradually she created a bounty of work, a deep well of country music splendor from which singers have drawn for years— and continue to. She attributes it all to telling the truth. Her most famous song, "Coal Miner's Daughter," is entirely autobiographical—every detail, every fact. Plugged into her rich memory of the past, she overflowed with verses—writing ten for that song alone (and cutting out six, throwing them away forever). But sometimes the truth wasn't what the good ol' boys in Nashville wanted to hear because it reflected too closely the reality of the changes America went through in the sixties, such as "The Pill" and "Rated X," both of which were promptly banned from radio and both of which went to number one, sparked by controversy.

Today she's home in her sun-dappled writing room, tending, as she often must, to the business of being Loretta Lynn. But as anyone who knows her will attest, she is no diva—quite the opposite. When told that it's an honor for this writer to interview her, she just laughs and says, "Honey, don't say that. You can interview me *anytime*."

You once said you would rather be remembered as a songwriter than a singer—

Loretta Lynn: I would. Way before I started singing I was trying to write. I lived out in the state of Washington, and I had my four babies out there. I was trying to write every day, and I didn't know how. So I looked at the songbooks and thought that anyone could do that, so I just started writing. "Whispering Sea" was my first song, and then "Honky Tonk Girl" was my second song.

Did songwriting come easy to you?

Yes. When I started writing, my husband was out on the ocean, fishing, and I wrote "Whispering Sea": "Whispering sea, roll on by, don't you listen to me cry."

"Honky Tonk Girl" came from a lady who kept coming into the little club. Doo got me a job working for five dollars on Saturday nights, a little club. She came every time I worked. She told me that her husband had left her for another woman. She'd set there and cry. And I wrote "Honky Tonk Girl" from that.

Some songwriters never write story songs.

Yes, that's true. I always do. I start with an idea. I thought, "Well, 'Honky Tonk Girl.'" I turned it into a song because she picked strawberries with me during the time when strawberries were ripe. And then when strawberry pickin' was over with, she kept coming to the club and cryin'. And I've always had to have something to write about.

So you have an idea first before you start writing?

Yes. The idea first. I had to have a real reason to write a song. I wrote them about true things. And I just kind of kept that up. I'd write the words by thinking and watching.

Do you write a whole lyric before music?

No. I start the music on guitar with the first two or three lines.

Many of your songs are in odd keys, not normal guitar keys. "Honky Tonk Girl" is in C sharp.

Yeah, I know it. [*Laughs*] I don't know why. They told me in Nashville they couldn't believe it, what you're writing! All your keys are funny. 'Cause they wrote D, G, and A, you know. I was going out on a limb a little bit, but I didn't realize that. I started playing rhythm guitar with my brother and a steel player when I first started singing. And I played barre chord rhythm. I had all sorts of notes on the guitar at that time. Now I probably wouldn't remember all of them.

Since I learned all the keys, I just thought everybody did it that way. And evidently I was different. I was so far away from country music. I was a long way from Nashville, Tennessee.

I never knew another songwriter until I came to Nashville and met Harlan Howard. And he said, "Who in the heck taught you to play rhythm guitar like that?" I said, "I taught myself." He said, "I can't believe you're the writer you are and taught yourself to play rhythm guitar like that." But I did.

How old were you when you started playing?

Twenty-four. Well, I had four kids, one right after the other. And when all four kids were in school, I started writing. My husband got me a job making $5 on a Saturday night and I thought I was gonna get rich. [*Laughs*] I saved my money up and bought me a black skirt with fringe and these cowboy boots—they were $14—and, well, I looked like Annie Oakley. I didn't know that people didn't look like that. I come to Nashville, and I'm the only one who walked in looking like a country singer, with my boots and my guitar 'round my neck—I've come to sing. [*Laughs*]

When I first started singing, although I was writing songs, I did other people's songs, like "I Walked Away from the Wreck." Owen Bradley told me, "You start doing your own stuff." But I was afraid they wouldn't go over. I put out records, but they didn't do nothing until I started doing my own songs. And they went to number one. I was hitting home with them, I guess, with the honky-tonk music.

Your songs are so rich in detail. Did that come naturally to you?

Yeah, it just come naturally. I think anyone could do it. I think a lot of people try to write songs that are a little out of reach. And they should just sit down and write what they know. And what they see.

"Coal Miner's Daughter" is such a vivid picture of your childhood.

I had more verses. Owen Bradley said, "Loretta, there's already been one 'El Paso' and we'll never have another one. [*Laughs*] Get in that room and start taking some of those verses off." Yeah, I took six verses off.

Six? It has four we know, so it had ten verses altogether?

Yeah, I had a whole story going. I wished I'd never thrown them away. If I'd kept them, I could record them now and put them back in the song.

You don't remember them at all?

No, but I should sit down and start rewriting on that song and come up with some more verses. I threw them away, and I should never have done that.

Do you remember writing it?

Yes. I wrote it on a little $17 guitar. It didn't stay in tune. And $17 was a lot of money, 'cause at the time we didn't have any money. But then Gibson gave me a guitar, and I wrote all the others on that one.

Every word is true. My daddy would work all night in the coal mine. During the day he would work in the cornfields. There were ten of us. He had to make a living for us. Eight kids. I was second, so I would take care of the kids while Mommy did the sewing and the cleaning and everything else. I think that's why I sing. I'd rock the babies to sleep and sing to them.

The song says your mother's fingers were bleeding.

Yes. I'd seen them bleed many times. In the wintertime we had these old clotheslines made out of wire. It would be so cold that her fingers would stick to that wire. She'd pull them loose, and I'd see the hide come off of those fingers. I would hide and cry. Monday was wash day. She'd scrub on those washboards all day, and her fingers would bleed. But she didn't complain.

My mommy, to me, was beautiful. I'd see everything she'd do, whether it was crying or laughing. She would rock the babies by the coal oil light, like in the song. That was our light. We didn't have much light. Butcher Holler, Kentucky, was dark at night. You go up a long holler, and there's trees everywhere, and it's very dark.

There is the line about having no shoes—

We would wear our shoes out before it would be warm enough to be without shoes. We'd have holes in our shoes and put paste-board in our shoes. But halfway to school the paste-board would come out.

One time my daddy found me by the creek with my shoes off, just crying, 'cause it was so cold from those shoes with holes. And Daddy picked me up and carried me home. And Daddy only weighed 117 pounds. I don't know how he did it, but he did.

You know, you hear about poor people in other countries. There are a lot of poor people in our country if you go to the right places. There are a lot of hollers, not just Butcher Holler—I've seen them. I guarantee you there's kids right to this day in the Kentucky hills that don't have shoes.

So touching is the line, "Daddy always managed to get the money somewhere."

Parents do what they have to do. Daddy would usually try to get two hogs, one to raise and one to sell. So the other hog would pay for itself. We had a rough life. It was a hard life. Mommy would raise a garden in the summer, and we'd help her. She would can, and I would pick wild blackberries. I would go and pick from morning till night. And Mommy would pack up a hundred quarts of blackberries.

The song doesn't tell half of it. If I told the whole story, nobody would believe it now anyway.

Owen knew it was about my life, and he didn't care about my life and figured nobody else would. So I cut out, I think, four verses. And I cried the whole time. And I have lost those verses, I do not remember them. I wish I did.

We cut it in Owen's studio in his barn.

Did he arrange it, or did you?

It was my arrangement. I told him exactly how I wanted it, whether I wanted the steel to start it or the fiddle. Then I sang the song to the band and said, "This is what we're gonna do now." And I sang it live with the band. Just sang. I didn't play guitar. Just a couple takes at the most. I never did many takes of anything. The more I sing, the worse I get. I like to make it fresh.

It was my husband Doo's idea to put a banjo on it after. He was right. It added so much to the song. None of us could believe it.

It was a fun session. I stopped at the store before going to the barn. I'd get a half a roll of bologna cut up and cheese, bread, onion, potato chips. We made everything fun. I didn't have a drink, but whoever had a drink had a drink. A hillbilly party. I didn't want my sessions not to be fun. Because if you go into a recording studio and you think you're a better singer than the boys that's gonna play behind you, then you better not go. It's a thing you are feeling and you can sense, and I know the musicians can sense it.

It's amazing to think of you writing a song like that so easily. Not only is it richly detailed, but you have great craft in there, like rhyming Butcher Holler with "poor man's dollar."

Well, that was the truth. Everything that I put in that song was true. I lived all of it. I've lived a lot of stuff that I wrote. Of course Doo, my husband, wouldn't have wanted to heard that. [*Laughs*] But I did. I never had to lie about anything I was writing about. That was my problem. I didn't lie. And sometimes Owen would say, "I don't know whether you should put that out there now. Doo might divorce you." [*Laughter*] And I'd say, "Let him divorce me—it's the truth."

And he never did.

No, he never did. He knew they were true.

Would you always play new songs for him?

Oh yeah. I let him hear it first.

Was he honest in his response?

Yeah, he never denied any of it. He was always honest. If he liked it, he liked it. If he didn't, he'd say, "I don't think that's so good." And I'd throw it away and start again.

What inspired "You Ain't Woman Enough"?

"You Ain't Woman Enough" come to me when a little girl come backstage and said her husband didn't bring her to the show—he brought his girlfriend. This was before the show started, and she wanted me to look out the curtain and see what this girl looked like. I peeked out, and there she was, painted up like you wouldn't believe. I looked 'round at the little girl that was talking to me. And she didn't have no makeup at all. And I said, "Honey, she ain't woman enough to take your man."

I went right straight to my dressing room and wrote it in ten minutes. Ten minutes and a lot of money I made on that song. [*Laughter*] A lot of people have recorded it.

Is writing a song in ten minutes unusual for you?

Sometimes they work, and sometimes they just won't. Sometimes you get hung up on them. When that happens, you just throw it back, and maybe come back to it two or three weeks later.

Some of your songs were quite controversial and even banned—such as "The Pill," about birth control.

Oh yeah. "The Pill." Also "One's on the Way." They started hollering about some of the songs and banned them from the radio. But immediately, when people would hear they'd been banned from the radio, they'd hit number one in a hurry. [*Laughter*] And then [radio] would have to play them. If they had listeners, they'd have to play the one that was banned.

Did you enjoy making the album *Van Lear Rose* with Jack White?

That's the country-est album I've ever done. I told [Jack] that, and he said, "Well, thank you." [*Laughs*] And he's not a country guy—he's rock and roll. But when my movie came out he said he was nine years old, and he said, "I sat in the theater and watched it all day long." It just kept coming back on and he kept watching it. He's a good guy, Jack White is.

I didn't know he was gonna sing with me on "Portland, Oregon." I walked in the studio, and I said, "Who is that man singing it with me,

Jack?" and he said, "That's me." [*Laughter*] I like Jack. Anything he did I thought was cool.

Do you write the music for a song before you finish the words?

Yes. I write the melody as soon as I finish the first verse. It's got to fit the song. If it don't fit the song, I don't think it'll come easy. But I think if it comes easy, then the melody is gonna be okay.

How do you create melodies yourself?

When I write a song, the melody just comes in my mind to fit that song. And if it's a slow tempo, I think of a slow melody to get in that mood. I let the song come to me. I just gotta get by myself and get that song. And if it don't come easy, I lay it down. And sometimes I'll pick it up, and sometimes I won't ever go back to it.

Can you write at any time of day?

Night is best.

When you come up with an idea, do you always write it down right away?

If I don't, I'll never remember it. [*Laughs*] I've got to write it down right then, or I'll lose it.

Do you remember "Miss Being Mrs."?

Oh yeah. You know, that just come—to be truthful with you—from one of those things where I just thought, "I miss being Mrs. tonight." When you're not married anymore—which I'm not, my husband passed away fourteen years ago—naturally you're gonna feel that way. And you just miss being Mrs.

You're good with wordplay like that. Like in "Coal Miner's Daughter," when you say "I remember well the well where I drew water." A beautiful use of language.

Well, when I thought of that I felt it was a good line to use. And then I got to thinking maybe nobody will really understand that line, so maybe I shouldn't use it. But I let it go anyway and thought, "Yeah, I'm gonna use it."

And we understand.

[*Laughs*] You knew it was good, didn't you? Well, bless your heart. Boy, I've drawn a lot of water out of that old well back in Kentucky. That was my job. To go and get the water.

Do you remember writing "Rated X"?

Yeah, that was about a married woman. Things didn't work out and she was divorced. I probably sat down and talked to her. She told me the story, and I just wrote it.

I love your song "Van Lear Rose."

I had to talk about Mommy in there. She had the biggest bluest eyes I ever seen. She was a beautiful woman. I remember back when she was thirty-two, thirty-three years old. Mommy was *so* beautiful. I always wanted to be as beautiful as Mommy. [*Laughs*] Never made it. She had long black hair, beautiful blue eyes, and a dark complexion. She was Indian and Irish. My father was Indian and Irish. And the Irish have great personalities, you know. And most of them sing. People from Ireland, you know, they come into this country singing. There's a couple of them in Branson right now singing. And Indians are in touch with nature. That's me. I wrote about things that have happened. I probably took after the Indian part on that.

Do you remember writing "You're Lookin' at Country"?

Yeah. I remember we came home. We've got about twelve or thirteen hundred acres. I was out riding around, and I looked over toward the field. Doo and Hattie all planted some corn, and I thought, "Now you're looking at country." And immediately I come into the house and went to the writing room and wrote it.

Are there songs you start that you can't finish?

Oh yeah. I've had a lot of them. I don't know why I don't go back and finish them. I just kind of quit writing. I haven't written a song in a long time.

Why?

Lazy. But I'm gonna get back to it.

You've written so many classics that you have nothing left to prove.

True, I don't have a thing to prove, but if I write, I'm gonna prove something. Don't do anything that you can't do best. I don't believe in doing something that I don't know is good. If I go back to writing, I bet there will be a good song out of it. If I write ten songs, there will be three good ones out of it. I won't dedicate my life to something that's not good.

What advice would you give songwriters about how to write good songs?

Write about the truth. If you write about the truth, somebody's living that. Not just somebody—there's a lot of people.

◆ ◆ ◆

Sheldon Harnick

Of Fiddlers on the Roof

New York, New York 2015

Considering the old American songwriting tradition of Jewish songwriters submerging their Jewish identities to write, instead, gentle songs like "White Christmas," the writing of an entire Broadway show about Jews in the old country—*Fiddler on the Roof*—seemed brave. Courageous, if you will.

He'll have none of it. He being Sheldon Harnick, the lyricist who wrote the famous songs with his partner in song, Jerry Bock. Of course, like my father as well, he was a member of the greatest generation who went to Europe to fight in World War II. "We were fighting *Hitler*," he said. "*That* took bravery. But to write a Jewish show and hope it gets on Broadway? That's not brave."

Okay, granted, compared to fighting Hitler and ultimately saving the world, creating this celebration of Jewish culture for Broadway was relatively risk-free. Still, it was unprecedented and even considered forbidden territory. To bring Jewish culture, humor, myth, and even language to Broadway was bravely brilliant. "To Life (L'Chaim)" not only introduces Yiddish exultantly into song, it also provides the translation.

But it's not the bravery for which his songs from *Fiddler* are most remembered; it's for their poignancy. A tremendously savvy comic songwriter, a genius with rhyme and meter, he's also deeply gifted with serious ballads. He's the man, after all, who wrote the words for "Sunrise, Sunset." It's a song that has reverberated through our lives, one of the best ever in capturing the sorrow woven into our lives, the swift passage of time as our children grow up and change so quickly. He wove it all into one line, a beautiful natural image that matches perfectly the organic simplicity, the enduring ascension and descent of the title sun. Here in the garden we see infinite unfolding as "seedlings turn overnight to sunflowers." With those few words he gives us the full span of life, with people blossoming as naturally as flowers under the perpetual sun.

Born in Chicago in 1924, he attended Northwestern University (a sentence I like, as it applies to my dad as well in every respect), but he started writing songs as a kid. Words came first, and before he wrote songs, he wrote poems. Meeting up with a pal in high school led him on a path to musical theater songwriting. "I was writing poetry, and it was getting published in our school paper," he remembered on a crisp autumn day in Manhattan. "One of my classmates who was interested in the theater looked me up, and we began to write sketches. Then we also wrote parodies of songs."

This early songwriting training served him well when he enlisted in the Army, and it was determined early on he was better with words and music than rifles and ammunition. Fellow soldiers, recognizing his gifts, would invite him to write songs for their girlfriends, which he did, thus honing his craft while serving his country.

At Northwestern he wrote songs for their famous Waa-Mu Show, the original student musical comedy they produced each year. Though he was adept at piano, his main instrument was violin, and he intended to play it in Chicago dance bands upon graduation. "My ultimate dream," he confessed, "was to be in the second violin section of a second-rate symphony orchestra somewhere because I knew I wasn't good enough to be in the first violin section of a first-rate symphony."

It was hearing the musical *Finian's Rainbow*, with beautiful tunes by Burton Lane and brilliant lyrics by Yip Harburg, that led him to understand writing songs was to be his life. An early meeting with the great Yip, who wrote the lyrics for *The Wizard of Oz* (with music by Harold

Arlen), gave him a glimpse of the world in which he could live, and he devoted himself to musical theater.

His most famous show is *Fiddler on the Roof*, based on the writings of Sholom Aleichem, which he wrote with his longtime partner, Jerry Bock. But he wrote many other musicals, including *Fiorello!* about the legendary mayor of New York, as well as a musical—*Rex*—with the legendary Richard Rodgers (who normally wrote only with Hart and Hammerstein).

On a cold and gray but snowless Manhattan day he took time to amply delve into the annals of his remarkable career. Although he was past ninety years old when we spoke, he was sharp, funny, and in happy awe of the remarkable life he's lived in song.

When you were growing up what was the music that you were listening to, and what was the music in your home?

Sheldon Harnick: Ahh, it was on the radio. It was whatever popular music there was. I loved hearing songs, all kinds of songs. There was not much classical music except for what my sister was playing on piano.

I read that Yip Harburg was one of your idols. So at some point you became aware of who was writing the songs and who he was, yes?

That happened when I was in college at Northwestern. I was contributing songs to the Waa-Mu Show, and the first song that I had done in this show was sung by a performer named Charlotte Lebowski, who later became Charlotte Rae and had a lovely career in television. Charlotte was terrific. We became good friends, and when I was a junior, around 1948, she went to New York on the Christmas holiday. When she came back she sought me out and she had an LP in her hand. She said, "Sheldon, you of all people have got to hear this." And she loaned me a copy of *Finian's Rainbow*, and when I listened to that, I suddenly thought that is what I want to do with my life. I hadn't paid too much attention up to that time about who was writing the songs, but I wanted to know who wrote the lyrics to *Finian's Rainbow*, and it turned out to be a man named Yip Harburg, and he became my idol.

Finian's Rainbow has such beautiful songs but also a social consciousness. Was that part of what attracted you to it?

Yes. It was the fact that he had the social consciousness but that his lyrics were so playful. I thought you have to listen to what he's saying even if you should happen to disagree with him. Also, when I got married Burton Lane was a neighbor, and so we became very good friends with Burton.

I understand that when you met Yip Harburg he gave you some advice to work with many composers and also to write comic songs, not ballads. Is that correct?

More or less. Charlotte called me, I came to New York, I had written this song for her, and she was working at the Village Vanguard. She called me and said through a friend that they had invited Yip Harburg down to the Village Vanguard to see her act, and if I wanted to meet him, I should come down. And so I did. And he was very gracious. I asked whether I could play for him, and he said sure. So I went to his apartment. I'm not a pianist, so I got a pianist and I went and auditioned. Mostly what I was auditioning was the stuff I had written for the Waa-Mu Show. I hadn't written that much new material in New York, but he was very encouraging and he did say, "Oh, I had an uncle in Chicago who had done a lot of theater," and when I came to New York he gave me introduction to a composer named Jay Gorney, who by coincidence had written with Yip Harburg. "Brother, Can You Spare a Dime" was their big song.

So I went to see Gorney, and Gorney's advice was to write ballads because producers want to make sure that you were able to write a successful ballad. That was his advice. When I met Yip, his advice was to write comedy songs and character songs because they're the most important part of doing a show. His advice was that if you can do a good ballad, that's terrific, but he said more important are the other kind of songs, the comedy songs or the character songs. Yip knew that I was writing my own music, and he suggested that if a good composer invited me to work with him, I should accept that. He said that it would facilitate my career to work with other people, other composers as well as myself.

And he did something else that was just so incredibly gracious. About three days after I had auditioned for him I got a card from him in the mail. It was a greeting card. And on the cover was a picture of a bare-footed harp player, a woman playing the harp, and the message was:

"Dear Sheldon:

Keep doing what you're doing. I am sure you will be successful if you keep wanging that lyre."

And it was signed "Yip." That's the part I treasure most.

That's great. And it's interesting that you got that advice to write ballads and that advice to write comic songs. You ultimately did both very beautifully.

Well, you have to for a musical, or any imaginable kind of song for any imaginable kind of character.

When you were writing your own songs, did you do it at the piano?

Yeah. I had to. I was not a pianist, and it was a very arduous proposition, just so. And as a matter of fact the first songs I wrote, the piano accompaniments I wrote just did not serve the songs well. And when I got pianists to play what I had written I thought, "Oh my God, that's terrible," because what I had written kept getting in the way of what the singer was singing. Little by little I learned how to write a proper accompaniment that supported the singer without competing with them.

That took a while. If I had been a pianist I think I would've, like so many pianists I know, accompany singers so they get used to what proper accompaniment is supposed to sound like.

Before Yip suggested you write with other composers, were you thinking along those lines or were you thinking you would do it both yourself?

I was thinking I was most interested in doing it myself.

When you first started writing songs did it come easy to you?

The lyrics came fairly easily. The music did not. But lyrics, from the time I was in grammar school, [*pause*] it was fairly easy to write poetry. Right now I can look back and realize I had a gift for it. I didn't think of it in those terms in those days. My mother used to celebrate every bar mitzvah, every wedding, and so forth by writing a piece of poetry, and so my sister and I began to do that too because we were influenced by my mother.

My sister was actually a very fine poet and a serious poet. So when I started to write poetry I thought I will write light verse so that I don't find myself competing with my sister.

Although my sister wrote a two-line poem that I think was very funny. Which was "In the summer, it is warmer." [*Laughter*]

That's like Ogden Nash. That's great.

Yeah. Well, we were both great fans of Ogden Nash. And as a matter of fact, I was Ogden's assistant on one television show he did. Burt Shevelove arranged it. He was a friend of Burt's, and Burt knew that Ogden was not musical and would need help. He had been hired to set lyrics to Prokofiev's melodies. It was a television program, *Art Carney Meets Peter and the Wolf*. The centerpiece of the program was going to be Art Carney narrating *Peter and the Wolf*. But on the rest of the program they intended to have songs with music by Prokofiev and lyrics by Ogden Nash.

Ogden needed somebody to give him dummy lyrics so he could tell what the rhythms were because he didn't read music. I got the job, and I wrote a lot of dummy lyrics. I wish I had saved them because I was trying to write dummy lyrics that might amuse Ogden, and the only pattern I can remember was one where there was a Prokofiev melody that went "da da da dum, da da da dum, da da da dum, da da dum." So I wrote a dummy lyric that was "Canada Dry, Canada Dry, Canada Dry, Alaska." [*Laughter*] And Ogden laughed.

Ogden, by the way, was an absolutely charming, warm human being. He was just wonderful to work with.

Wow. That's really interesting to hear that you worked with him, because like him, you are a great rhymer of words but also so playful with words—there's always humor in there.

I asked him whether he had ever discovered that somebody had anticipated a rhyme of his. And he laughed. He said when he read Robert Browning he was always constantly finding rhymes that he thought he had originated but Browning got there first. [*Laughter*]

You've always been an amazing rhymer. Spanning your whole career there is great rhyming throughout.

Thank you. Thank you. Well, I must say, rhyming is great fun.

Yeah. That fun is reflected in the songs.

That's nice to hear. I hope so.

Speaking of funny songs, I was listening last night to "The Merry Minuet," which you wrote alone, correct?

Yeah. I remember when that got written, it was early in the 1950s, and I had been reading the newspaper and I kept the news, it was like today, the news was constantly bad. I would turn the page, and I would start to read an article, and I would start to shake my head, and I would go, "*Oy!* Oh my God, oy!" Then I started to laugh at my reactions, and I thought that it might be fun to do a song like that. Where the singer keeps saying "Oy, Oy." Then I thought, "No, rather than that, I'll have him whistle."

I was playing a lot of chamber music at the time, so it was natural that the song took the form of a Mozart minuet.

It's a brilliant song, and I'm sure you know that often people assume that Tom Lehrer wrote it because of the dark humor. And Tom [featured in *SOS I*] confused the matter more by performing the song himself.

Yes. I've met Tom, and he did a darling thing. He was performing in Australia, and he sent me a copy of the program just to show that he was singing "The Merry Minuet," but on the program he gave credit to me, and he wanted me to know that.

It seems tailor-made for him and his delivery.

Well, I was very flattered that he chose to use it because I love his work. As a matter of fact, I'm embarrassed to tell you this, but he is my son's favorite lyricist.

I love him too. I had the pleasure of interviewing him, and like you, he's a great craftsman. He's obviously very funny but such a great rhymer and good craftsman.

Yeah. He's terrific.

Sadly, "The Merry Minuet," like most of his songs, is still so relevant. Maybe more now than ever.

I know. I loved writing the song. Harry Belafonte once asked me if he could use the song and if he could change the lyrics to be about Southern bigotry, and I allowed him to. And a number of people have done that because it can be done in a very bitter way. I don't think I did it in a particularly bitter way but it expressed what I was feeling which was sad, very melancholy.

It's so beautifully crafted. Talking about a great couplet, you have, "We can be tranquil, grateful, and proud / Because man's been endowed with a mushroom-shaped cloud." All those interior rhymes—that's such great writing.

Thank you.

Also it rings true now with global warming and the idea that what nature doesn't do to us will be done by our fellow man.

Oh right. I did a song about global warming after reading the book about that forty or fifty years ago. I wrote a lyric, "When the Sea Is All Around Us," and music by David Baker. It's remarkable how that song has held up. It's unfortunate how that song has held up.

The Kingston Trio recorded "The Merry Minuet," and afterward they say, of the song, "That was written in 1949, and due to our consistent foreign policy we didn't have to change any of the lyrics."

Hah! [*Laughter*] It was written in 1950 actually. I hadn't come to New York until 1950.

So with them doing that song, did that encourage you to do more songs along those lines or were you ready to go to musical theater?

I was looking for somebody to write a musical with. I wasn't particularly interested in writing more songs like "The Merry Little Minuet." I was interested in writing songs that expressed how I felt, so it's possible there could've been more songs like that, but basically I was looking for somebody to team up with to write a musical.

My understanding was "Boston Beguine" was your first song that was produced.

Yeah. That was the result of a trip to Boston. My first wife was in a show they were trying out in Boston, so I went to visit her. While I was there, in the newspapers there was a kind of miniscandal, a new book, a standard sex manual. It wasn't an erotic book—it was an educational book—but several of the churches had written big articles trying to get the book suppressed, and it infuriated me, so I wrote this song about a young woman, an inexperienced woman in Boston who has an affair but is unable to consummate the affair because she's never read the proper manual on how to go about it. That was the story of the "Boston Beguine." Leonard Sillman had done a series of [Broadway] shows called *New Faces*, and he wanted to do another. Alice Ghostley was the star, and so I played "Boston Beguine" for Leonard, and he said this would be perfect for Alice, so for heaven's sake, finish it! I did. And Alice did it superbly. That was my introduction to the world of musical theater, my debut as a Broadway songwriter in *New Faces of 1952*.

So how did it happen that you met Jerry Bock?

That was through the actor Jack Cassidy. Jack and Jerry Bock had worked in the Catskills together at a summer resort. Jack had been an actor on the staff, and Jerry had been a composer on the staff. They met and they became friends, and there was a musical version of *Shangri-La* with a score by [Jerome] Lawrence and [Robert Edwin] Lee. When the show went on the road they found they were in trouble and needed to stay on the road longer than they thought they would. But Lawrence and Lee already had commitments to go work on *Mame*, so they had to leave the show, and they needed somebody in case any new lyrics needed to be written. I got the job, so I went out to join the show on the road.

One of the actors was Jack Cassidy, and we became friends, and Jack said, "You have to meet Jerry Bock." He said Jerry had been working with a lyricist he met at the University of Wisconsin and they'd been fairly successful—as a matter of fact, they did the score for the first act of the Sammy Davis show *Mr. Wonderful*. But something had come up, something had happened in their relationship. They broke up, and Jerry Bock was looking for another lyricist, and Jack Cassidy introduced me to him and the meeting took. We hit it off immediately.

When you said you hit it off immediately, did you talk about music and songs that you like? Is that how you bonded?

Well, I knew his work. I had seen his songs in the off-Broadway revues that I went to, and he knew my work and liked it, so that was a good beginning. We respected each other's work right from the start.

I was fascinated to discover, reading an interview with you, that when the two of you would write songs, generally he would give you a whole bunch of melodies, and then you would go through those melodies and choose ones, and then later you might write words first.

He was very generous. He would go into his studio while we were working on a show and write songs and record them. Then he would send me a tape with anywhere from eight to twelve or more songs on it, and I would listen to the songs. On any one tape there might only be one or two songs that coincided with ideas I had, so he was very generous because all the rest of those songs went back into his trunk.

That's the way we always started. Sometimes when we were in the midst of a show I would write lyrics first. So when our relationship broke up I was curious to see which came more often—the music or the lyrics. I went through every song we had written, trying to remember whether the music had been written first or the lyrics. To my surprise, it turned out to be almost exactly fifty-fifty. We always started with music first, but then a moment would come where I had an idea for a song and nothing Jerry had written fit that lyric, so I had to write the lyric first. Ultimately I wrote about half of the lyrics first and I wrote to music about half the time.

It's just hard to fathom there's all those Jerry Bock melodies that you didn't use. So were those never used, those ones that you didn't choose?

I don't know because Jerry did a lot of work that I didn't know about. And as a matter of fact, after we split up he worked in Texas, and he might very well have used a lot of those melodies. I don't know.

And would those be just him playing piano, or would he be singing as well on the tape?

Yeah. He would be singing nonsense syllables, yeah.

Were they totally complete songs—verse, chorus, the whole thing—or just sketches or ideas?

Usually they were complete—verse and chorus. Sometimes they were just chorus.

And what kind of process was that for you to listen to those? Did you listen carefully to each one with ideas of what the content needed to be, or did you go through them quickly?

No, I couldn't go through them quickly because it was on a tape, and I had to wait until the song was over. But I was always excited when I got a tape because, you know, in a way it was a world premiere. I was the first person besides Jerry to hear these songs unless it was Jerry's wife.

I would listen, and on every tape there were always a couple of songs that really excited me, and I thought, "I can't wait to put words to that." I, almost invariably, didn't have any words kicking around in my head that fit what I heard, but when I got excited by the melodies I couldn't wait to put lyrics to them.

It's especially surprising because the words and music of your songs work so beautifully together, it almost sounds like someone sitting at the piano with him and crafting them both at the same time.

Well, I am a good musician and I'm very comfortable with music, so it's fun. It's fun to be that kind of craftsman and to make the lyrics fit the music as comfortably as possible.

When you would write lyrics to one of these melodies would you then learn it and play it on the piano to work on it, or would you work with the tape?

I would work with the tape. I would memorize the music, and then I would just walk around singing the tune in my head and trying to fit lyrics to it.

I remember I almost got killed walking doing that once. I had this melody of Jerry's going through my head, and that's all I could think of, and suddenly I heard this loud horn blow, and I looked up and there was a huge truck that was about four inches away from me. I had walked right in front of the truck, and he had honked the horn and saved my life. I've made a joke out of it by telling people that I told the driver, "It's okay, driver, I got the lyric." [*Laughter*] But that wasn't true. I was scared to death when I saw how nearly I had been killed.

I'm glad you weren't hurt. But it's such a chapter from a songwriter's life that even while walking around you were working on the songs.

I find, especially when there's a problem with a lyric that's not coming, if I walk, it facilitates the process for some reason, so I love to walk when I am working on a song.

Paul Simon told me he would drive his car with the tape going, and something about the movement helps sometimes to get to the words.

Oh, I wouldn't dare do that! I was doing that once. I was driving down to East Hampton, and luckily there wasn't another car around, but suddenly I hear this siren behind me. I was working on a lyric, and I pulled over and the cop came over and said, "Mister, did you know that you were doing eighty-five miles per hour?" I said no, I was working on a lyric. He laughed, but he gave me the ticket anyway. [*Laughter*]

Besides walking, when you are having a hard time and the words aren't coming, any other advice besides walking? How you finish a song and get to the right lines?

The other thing I do is work on the song shortly before I go to sleep because I have found quite often I will wake up with the solution to a lyric problem.

What do you think allows that to happen? Is your brain working on it while you're sleeping?

Yeah. My brain unconsciously is working on it. And does the work for you at night. It's a curious phenomenon, but it seems to be true. It's true of me, and I've talked to some other lyricists who have had the same experience.

It's the amazing thing of the lyricist's job, especially writing to a melody, that when you're finding words, you can't dictate what the words can be—you have to really discover the words that fit. Yet if they're being written for a play, you have strict content and dialogue and plot things you're trying to advance.

I know. It can be very tricky. As you probably know, we had *Rothschild & Sons* just open at the York Theatre. There's one song in particular there, it's called "Rothschild & Sons," and I remember Jerry had sent me the music that I loved, and I remember how hard I worked on that song because I loved that melody and I couldn't wait until I had the right lyrics for it. But you're right—it had to fit the situation. It had to fit the characters, and it was hard.

Do you generally write more drafts for songs until you hone in on the perfect lyric?

I don't know if that would be the way to express it. I have yellow pads and just keep writing. Of course, I try different things until I begin to see the shape of the lyric that I want. But along the way I will have done different line lengths, different stanza forms, just searching for something that makes sense to me.

Sometimes your rhyme schemes are quite intricate. I was surprised at all the different lines that rhyme. Does that come from the music suggesting where the rhyme should be?

Quite often that's the case. The music rhymes, and so you feel the lyric has to rhyme. When I first came to New York I remember I was very aware what other people were writing, and I thought there are so many clever writers who are doing these wonderfully intricate things. I decided to go the other way and keep my lyrics more simple, which I tried to do. Then there was a period where I got interested more in rhyme, and then when I began to write with Jerry, sometimes I had to write rhymes because, as I say, the music called for it. The music rhymed, and so it would have sounded odd if a repeated musical phrase was not rhymed.

Yes. Did you create any writing routine? Any time of day best for writing?

No, I'm very undisciplined that way. Whenever the muse strikes. Of course, one of the things that make the muse strike is a deadline, [*laughs*] and when I get worried that I'm not going to make that deadline, then I begin to really work around the clock.

Were there times when it was just impossible and stuff was not coming, and if so, what would you do?

Oh yeah. I was working with Mary Rodgers on something, and I was stuck. And thank God, Mary was also a capable lyricist, and because Mary was able to come up with two or three lines, we were able to finish the song. I just couldn't come up with it, but she did. That can happen.

So the first show you did with Bock was *The Body Beautiful*?

Yeah. We didn't choose it. Tommy Valando was Jerry's publisher. Tommy performed an absolute miracle. Somehow he persuaded the producers of *The Body Beautiful* to hire Jerry Bock and me to write the show even though we had not written a song yet. This was a real leap of faith on their part and of course for me. Ooh, I had been longing to write a Broadway show, and here was the opportunity. So it didn't matter at that time that the show was about boxing. And boxing was something I was *totally* unfamiliar with and actually didn't particularly like. But I did the show anyway, and I think the show may have suffered because I really was not a boxing fan.

But it was a Broadway show, so we started to work on it. There were problems with the show, big problems with the book. We did a lot of work on the road, and a lot of good work. But there was just too much wrong with it, and we didn't have time. A director needs at least four to six months to just study the show before it goes into rehearsal, and that did not happen.

You didn't have to go through many of those kinds of experiences. Your next show was a huge success, *Fiorello!*

Yeah. That was [producer] Hal Prince, and he knew that and [director] George Abbott knew that, so we did work on it a long time before it opened.

The show is about the New York City mayor Fiorello La Guardia. An unusual topic for a show.

The director Arthur Penn had been asked to do a documentary about Fiorello, so he started to work on it, and the more he learned about Fiorello, the more he began to feel that he was such a colorful character that instead of a documentary, it should be a musical.

So he went to Hal Prince with his idea, and Hal loved it. They went to George Abbott and presented the idea, and at first Abbott was against it. He had done a musical about a mayor of New York, Jimmy Walker, and he said, "I don't want to do a political musical." But Hal and Arthur Penn said, "George, it's not just politics. Fiorello had two very important love stories in his life," and that was what interested George Abbott. He said, "Really?"

So and then they hired Jerome Weidman to do the book, but Weidman was a novelist, not a theater person, but Weidman knew that his cowriter would be George Abbott. And the two of them worked together and created a wonderful book. Then they had a competition for songwriters. My reputation was from the revue songs I'd written. Steve Sondheim had seen a preview of *The Body Beautiful*, and although he had great problems with the show, he thought that Jerry Bock and I were very talented, so he called Hal Prince and said, "You should acquaint yourself with the work of this new team, Bock and Harnick."

And so, sure enough, on the opening night of *The Body Beautiful* Hal Prince was there. At the party afterward the first reviews had been read—they were bad. Most people had left the party. Hal came over and introduced himself. He said, "I had problems with the show, but I *love* your work, and I hope to be working with you guys soon."

And sure enough, when he did *Fiorello!* he hired Jerry immediately, but they thought that when they went to the book writers, the book writers would express their wish to write their own lyrics. So that turned out to be true, and that included Jerome Weidman. He wanted to write his own lyrics, and I asked Jerry Bock, how are his lyrics? He said they are like small novels—they just went on and on and on, and at some point Hal Prince said, "Mr. Weidman, we want you to do the book but not the lyrics."

At that point they began to look at various teams, and they gave Jerry and me the opportunity to write four songs on speculation. They told us the spots in the script where they wanted the songs, and then Jerry and I wrote them. We went to Hal's apartment and auditioned them, and we got the job.

Did the topic of Fiorello seem in any way unwieldy to you, or were you up to the challenge?

All I knew about Fiorello at that point was that he was a particularly colorful character, and when I read what they had written so far, I was *so* taken with it. I thought that it's really not about politics as much as it is about this man and his love stories. I read the script and thought it was *wonderful*, and I couldn't wait to get involved.

Had you and Jerry already adopted that process of him doing melodies first and sending you a tape?

Yeah, we had. On *The Body Beautiful*, yeah. So I knew that that's the way we would start.

When he would send you these melodies, they would be specifically written for this show?

Yeah. He would designate that this was written in such and such a scene by such and such a character. He was very careful about that. Once in a while he'd say—and it me made me laugh—"I don't know what in the hell this song is but I like it!" [*Laughter*] Then he would play me a melody, and quite often those were among the most appealing melodies of all.

That show went on to not only win the Tony but the Pulitzer Prize.

Yeah. It's a good show. Unfortunately around the rest of the United States people tend to think, "Well, it's such a local New York show that our audiences wouldn't understand it." And of course, every time it's done somewhere, the audiences absolutely understand it. There was just a very successful production just opened up in California.

Yeah. It's a wonderful show. You've written great songs for shows that were hits, but also great songs for shows that flopped. But the songs were always great. How is that, as a songwriter, to have your work attached to a sinking and, ultimately, sunken ship?

It's depressing. It is depressing. I have to confess it, yeah.

Like in 1960 you did *Tenderloin*.

Yeah.

That show didn't succeed, but you wrote the great song "Artificial Flowers." Which became a hit for Bobby Darin.

Well, at least that one we had some action on because Bobby recorded it. When Kevin Spacey did the movie about Bobby Darin, he not only did the song but he did the complete version of it. I was surprised when he started to sing. I thought he's just going to do a little bit, but Kevin Spacey sang well enough to do the entire song. So we did get action on that song.

It's a great song. And a hit. Went to number twenty on the charts.

Well, it came because of Burt Shevelove, who suggested that as a theater lyricist that I should go out and find a set of six books by a newspaper man, called *Our Times*. It went from about 1900 to the early 1930s. It was written as a popular history of the times. Instead of political events, it was about the fashions and the songs and the movies. I bought the set, and I remember when I was looking in the Fiorello era there was a picture of a young girl who was working on a hat, but she was supporting herself because her parents had died, and I thought that's a very melancholy thing, but I think it could lead to a song. And that led to "Artificial Flowers."

Yeah. A great song. So 1964 is when *Fiddler on the Roof* emerged. I'm Jewish, and at the time it came out I was a kid and didn't understand that shows about Jews weren't that common. To me that seemed, "Great, these songs are about Jews." [*Laughter*] Now I see how brave it was in a lot of ways and also beautiful.

I know. So many people have told me how brave we were. We never thought of that because, look, I was a soldier in World War II, and we were fighting Hitler. *That* took bravery. Right now to write a Jewish show and hope it gets on Broadway. That's not brave. And we thought these stories [*Tevye and His Daughters* by Sholom Aleichem] were wonderful. Why not work on them? Why not do a musical on them?

My dad, born in the same city and year as you, also fought in World War II. And I agree, compared to fighting in World War II, it's not the same level of bravery at all! Not even comparable.
    Yeah.

But in terms of songwriters, all the great Jewish songwriters, like Irving Berlin, didn't write Jewish songs. Berlin was writing "Easter Parade" and "White Christmas."
    [*Laughs*] That's true.

Generally Jewish songwriters haven't written about the Jewish experience.
    Not very much, no. Though when Irving Berlin was starting, some of his special material songs were about Jewish subjects, but very few people know those songs.

You and Bock then not only wrote these songs but songs so authentic and beautiful. Did they start like usual—with Jerry giving you a tape of tunes?
    Yeah, he gave me a tape, and I remember one of the songs on the tape turned out to be "Sunrise, Sunset." I put a lyric to it and went over to Jerry's place and we worked on the song. I had to do a little polishing, but then when we were finished we invited his wife to come down, and we auditioned it for her.
    And I've learned not to look at people when I audition—I look over their heads. But we sang the song, and then when we finished it, I looked at his wife. And to my astonishment she was crying. I thought, "My *goodness*, we must have something special here."
    And then, because this song is very simple, I learned the accompaniment, and I played it for my sister, and the same thing happened. I finished playing, I looked at her, and she was crying. And I thought, "My *God*, this is a very special song."

Yeah. So many people have cried to that song since. That's just remarkable to me that the music came first, because that lyric, "sunrise, sunset," so fits that tune—it ascends on "sunrise" and descends on "sunset." Did that title come when you heard that song, or did that come after?
    When I heard the music, for some reason almost immediately those two words came to me. It was a "dee dum, dee dum," and almost

immediately I began to sing, "sunrise, sunset." There must have been something in my life that suggested that.

Harry Chapin wrote "Cat's in the Cradle," which touches on the same topic—how quickly our kids grow up. My son is sixteen now and seems like it was yesterday he was a tot. And I sing that song to myself all the time. There is no better song for the subject.

Thank you.

An ordained minister was performing a wedding ceremony for two guys, two gay guys, and they wanted to know if I would consider rewriting "Sunrise, Sunset" so it could fit—they wanted it performed at their wedding. I thought that was such a charming idea. It was such a simple change that I did it, and they had it performed at their wedding.

What was the change?

The line was "When did she get to be a beauty?" And I changed it to "When did he get so handsome?" Yeah. An easy change.

[*Laughs*] That's wonderful.

You were talking about using such simple language. I think part of the beauty of it is the simple language, but then there's the poetic line that has always touched me so much: "Seedlings turn overnight to sunflowers." Such a lovely and natural way of saying that.

Yeah. Reading so much about that part of the world, where Sholom Aleichem was writing about, the word sunflowers kept popping up. There were a lot of sunflowers there. So that was in my mind.

You said how this now-iconic title, "Sunrise, Sunset," just came to you. Other songwriters have described that feeling, that they arrive like gifts sometimes. Do you have any understanding of where that comes from?

Usually I find there is something going on in my life. It may be unconscious, but there is usually something important going on, and so when I hear a new melody, words spring to mind unconsciously because of what's going on in my life.

John Lennon said he felt sometimes like a channel, channeling things from somewhere else.

Yeah. It's the same thing.

You feel that? That there is a spiritual source?

I don't think of it that way, but now that you mentioned it, sure, yeah, I would agree with that.

The song "If I Were a Rich Man"—did that come melody first?

That was a melody first, but as I heard it, there was an interesting genesis to that song. Jerry and I went to a Hebrew actor's benefit because we thought we might find some performers there who were right for the show. A mother and daughter came up and performed a Hasidic song. There were no words to it; there were just Hasidic syllables, sounds. I didn't know it at the time, but Jerry was simply *enthralled*, and he went home and he worked all night.

He called me the next day and asked me to meet at our publisher's office. So I went to Valando's office, and Jerry played me the melody for "If I Were a Rich Man" and he sang his version of those Hasidic syllables. And I *loved* the song, and he said, "Look, when you write the lyrics, I think it might be fun to have a couple of bars where instead of words, we use some Hasidic syllables."

I thought that's a terrific idea. My problem was I had no idea how to spell those Hasidic syllables. So I had to come up with something that sounded a little like them, and I came up with "digga digga didle digga dum." [*Laughs*] Whatever I put in there. Which is meant to sound a little bit like those Hasidic syllables.

It does, and it's so joyful too. And spoke to all of us who grew up with that sound, which is a joyous sound. That lyric seems like it would be a special challenge to write because they are very long lines: "I'd build a very tall house with rooms by the dozen."

Oh, but that, if you go back and read the story about Motl and Shpil, you will practically find all of those lyrics in there—or the ideas for them. When I read that story there was just the whole image of Tevye kept saying, "Ah, if I was a Rothschild." And it was easy enough to change "if I were a Rothschild" to "if I were a rich man."

And he talked about what being rich meant, so many of the lyrics in the song are just based on sentences that Sholom Aleichem gave Tevye.

And that one has an interesting rhyme scheme. It's two pairs of three lines, and the second and the third line of each section rhymes.

I'll take your word for it.

It's a perfect rhyme scheme. It rhymes perfectly every time.

Thank you.

"Miracle of Miracles" is a beautiful song. Decades before Paul Simon wrote, "These are the days of miracles and wonder," you wrote these

words: "Wonder of wonders, miracle of miracles . . ." Which is from the Bible, yes?

Yes. That was written on the road. That one, the lyric came first. Motl was singing a love song, a ballad. I think we were still in Detroit, and after one of the matinees we had a meeting with Jerry Robbins, and he said, "You know, instead of him doing a ballad there, I think he should have an up-tempo number to express his excitement and his elation." And we agreed.

So I went back to my hotel room, and there was a Gideon Bible. I began to look for the idea. We already had the dialogue, and there were the lines "It's a miracle, it's a miracle." I thought that would be a good idea for a song, so I looked in the Bible and checked for some miracles, wrote a lyric, and gave it to Jerry Bock, and he set it.

As a matter of fact, this song was originally longer than it is now. And when Jerry Robbins heard it, he said, "It's wonderful, but there's a section in the middle that we don't need." So part of the song was cut.

That song rhythmically is simpler and more normal than some of the ones you wrote to melody. When you would write a lyric first, would you have a dummy tune in mind? How would you go about structuring the lyric?

Yeah, I had a dummy tune in mind. I have to be careful not to get too wedded to those dummy tunes because when I hear the tune the composer likes, I might not like it as much as my dummy tune, and that causes a problem.

Yeah.

So now I have a kind of nondescript dummy tune running through my head, but it helps me establish the rhythmic patterns.

There's such beautiful language in that song. "When Moses softened Pharaoh's heart, that was a miracle / When God made the waters of the Red Sea part, that was a miracle too!"

That's from the Gideon Bible. [*Laughter*]

But the Old Testament, right? Not the sequel. [*Laughter*]

Yeah.

The song "Tradition" is also wonderful. Was that one a melody first?

Yes. Amazingly. Even all the counterpoint parts—Jerry did all that first.

How about "To Life."

That one, the lyric was there first. That was written once we knew what the scene was with the butcher and Tevye. That was fun to write too. I am pretty sure the lyric came first on that.

Talking about great couplets, that has "One day it's honey and raisin cake / Next day a stomach ache." A perfect couplet. "Anatevka" is such a beautiful song. A very beautiful melody.

That music, it came first.

How did "Matchmaker" come about?

That came about because we had a different song for those three daughters. And it had a wider range. And when we went in to rehearsal we discovered that one of our daughters was primarily an actress, not a singer. One was primarily a dancer, not a singer, and only the third one was a real singer. The song had ranges in it, and they couldn't handle it. We learned very quickly that they were not able to sing the song. And we realized, oh my God, we are going to have to write a new song. And so we wrote "Matchmaker" instead.

Jerry took the theme; I gave him a lyric. He took the theme. At the time we had had a different opening number called "I've Never Missed a Sabbath Yet," which was Golda and the daughters trying to get the house ready for the Sabbath. Jerry took one of the melodic themes from that and turned it into "Matchmaker."

So there were several other songs that you wrote for *Fiddler* that weren't in the original production?

Oh, a *lot* of them. Yeah, we wrote a lot. One of the ones that was hardest to give up was a very funny song we wrote for the butcher called "The Butcher's Soul," where he felt he had been insulted by Tevye, so he defended himself. When we played it Jerry Robbins roared with laughter and then said, "But we're not going to use it."

We said, "Why not?" He said because the scene is about Tevye, not the butcher. And if we give it to the butcher, it just spoils the focus of the scene. So the song was cut.

But there were a lot of songs and a lot of outtakes from *Fiddler.*

I understand there was one called "If I Were a Woman" that Jerome Robbins loved but felt there wasn't time for?

Yeah. We had used it; it was a very successful song. But after one of the matinees he said, "We are going to cut that." We asked why— because it worked. He said, "I know it works, but the show is too long and I can accomplish the same thing in thirty seconds of dance that this song accomplishes in four minutes." He said, "Look, if my dance doesn't work, we'll go back to the song."

So he did his dance, and of course the dance was charming and we lost a song.

As a songwriter, does it feel that song is lost, or is there a feeling like it could come back at some point? That it can work elsewhere or outside of a show?

No. It's lost. Jerry and I wrote songs that just were specifically designed to certain shows, times, and places and certain characters, and they just don't seem to fit in other shows.

After that you did "Apple Tree," which is a wonderful song and musical— and revolutionary.

Yeah. Instead of one book, it was three one-act musicals. That was fun.

You wrote the musical *Rex* with Richard Rodgers.

Yes. And as a matter of fact, it was a failure. But the book writer was Sherman Yellen, and we had revised it since then. We had a production in Toronto, and it worked wonderfully. We did turn it into what I think is a really lovely show.

What was that like writing with him? One of the great melodists of all time. Would he give you a melody to write to?

Only once. Only once did he do that. He used to do that. But when we worked together he had had so many illnesses and strokes, all kinds of illnesses, that a doctor once explained to me stroke patients lose the ability to think abstractly. Music is a very abstract art, so it's not surprising that Rodgers now needed to see a lyric before he can write music. And that's what happened. All the lyrics, except in one case, had to come first, which was a challenge, but he met it. He did a lovely job.

But he was not healthy during that period?

He had cancer of the larynx. He had his larynx removed, and as soon as he could, he went back to work. And he was able to do the score, but he could no longer sing.

I've read that he was not generally a happy guy and didn't seem to find a lot of enjoyment in music. Is that accurate?

No. Not accurate at all. The first day of rehearsal I saw this man who had been looking so ill after his operation, and when he was involved in music he just came right back to life. He was rejuvenated. I think music was his life.

Were you happy with the music for *Rex*?

I was, yeah. Yeah. [*Laughs*] I think that it was Noel Coward who said Richard Rodgers *pisses* melody. [*Laughter*] It's just endless.

***Rex* has the beautiful song "Away from You," which Sarah Brightman recorded.**

That was one of [Andrew] Lloyd Webber's favorites of all of Dick Rodgers's songs.

It's a classic Rodgers melody too. A funny, interesting melody for which, once again, you found an ideal lyric.

Well, I was trying to channel Oscar Hammerstein. I was thinking, what would Hammerstein write here? And then I tried to do that, and I would show it to Rodgers, and he would say always, "It is a Hammerstein lyric. This is lovely. Beautiful song."

You did the English translation of the opera *Carmen* [by Bizet]. Was that experience similar to writing songs?

It was similar, because *Carmen* is like a musical. It's not an opera that is sung from beginning to end. The original *Carmen* was a collection of songs. There would be a complex song, a long aria, but then there would be a dialogue scene, just like a musical. And then there would be another musical moment and then another scene. So it was structured like a musical.

Then at some point a student of Bizet's took all of those dialogue scenes and condensed them and then set them to music. They were much shorter so the whole thing could be done musically. The job I was given was to do the original version, which was songs and scenes, very much like a musical.

I love the show *She Loves Me*. I understand it's coming back next year. Is that correct?

Yes. It closed at first after only eight months, and we were *so* disappointed. Because it's maybe the most gratifying experience I've had theatrically. When it closed we were all very depressed. Then about a year later we had a production and then another production and more and more productions. And since then it's become a musical that's produced a lot. It is extremely gratifying.

You wrote the title song of the movie *The Heartbreak Kid* with Cy Coleman?

I miss Cy a lot. You couldn't be with Cy two minutes without finding yourself laughing. He was a joyous person and a wonderful composer and pianist.

Did you two work together at the same time?

No. He wrote the music first and he gave me the music.

Even with all the new technology and all the changes in our lives, songs seem to matter as much as ever. They have not come up with anything that's important as a great song. Do you think songs will always matter, and is there a need for new songs, do you think?

I do. I don't know what it is that makes people want to express themselves in song, but it's very gratifying to sing, to whistle, to hear melodies. I'd love to read a study on that. I never have. But there is something innate in the human being that just seems to respond to music.

Do you still enjoy songwriting?

Oh yeah. Very much so. Jerry Bock left me a lot of music, but when I wrote the lyrics I looked at all the music he had left and nothing fit. So I had to write the music myself.

Had you written only "Sunrise, Sunset," that would have been enough. It is one of those miracle songs.

Thank you. You ask very good questions. It's been fun answering them.

Speaking of that song, many years after we wrote it, Jerry called me in great excitement. The country of Iceland used to honor a composer every year, and they were honoring Jerry. So Jerry went to Iceland to be honored, and when he got back I said, "How was it?" He said, "It was thrilling. A symphony orchestra played some of my songs, some of yours and mine." He said, "The choirs all sang our songs, but they changed one of your lyrics."

I said, "What was the change?"

He said, "They sang 'Sunrise, Sunrise.'" [*Laughter*]

◆ ◆ ◆

Peter, Paul and Mary
The Power of Song
Los Angeles, California 1996

An angel and two cellos playing guitars. That's how Peter, Paul and Mary were described in the liner notes of their self-titled debut album of 1962. It was an apt description even then, encompassing both the earthy and angelic qualities of the trio. You see it in that first famous photo of them on the first album, against a wall of dark bricks. Both Peter and Paul are bearded and warmly smiling—collegiate in suit and tie—but with guitars. And in between them is the angel, and she's radiant—Mary Travers—luminous and joyful. And from these three figures came harmony remarkable, like three voices from a shared soul, each voice distinct yet blending into a remarkable whole, a sound both modern and also ancient and timeless.

This interview was conducted around a giant table in a record company conference room in 1996. There were four of us there: Peter, Paul, Mary, and me. It's a funny sentence, admittedly, and a funny place to find myself. Because I grew up not just loving Peter, Paul and Mary—I revered them. They were heroes to us. They had number-one hits and were up there on the pop charts and on our radios along with The Beatles.

But they belonged to us. They were connected directly to the heritage of American folk music, the legacy of Woody Guthrie and Pete Seeger and, ultimately, Dylan and beyond. It was Peter, Paul and Mary who brought many of Dylan's most famous songs such as "Blowing in the Wind" to the world in the biggest ways.

And their harmonies were phenomenal, as inventive and yet perfect as the songs themselves. How I used to delight in their recording of Dylan's "Don't Think Twice, It's All Right," at the intricate way their three vocals would intertwine on the melody and harmonies of the song. Each line, each verse was always different and always viscerally linked to the meaning and intention of each lyric. It was a kind of singing based on traditional folk music but wedded with rock and expansive songwriting, unlike anything before or since.

Even then, back in 1962, prior to the British invasion, prior to the advent of the electronic, often mechanical music as we have come to know it, Peter, Paul and Mary were significant for being real, for employing "no gimmicks." As the liner notes went on to say, "maybe mediocrity has had it. One thing is for sure in any case, honesty is back. Tell your neighbor."

Recognizing the inspirational power inherent in their vital mixture of acoustic guitars and three-part harmony, they turned to the most vital music they could find—folk music, both traditional and contemporary—and breathed new life and passion into it. Whether starting with an old folk song, such as "The Cruel War," or a new folk song, such as Dylan's "Blowin' in the Wind," they merged their musical souls to solidify the bridge between the old and the new. They carried on the traditions of Pete and Woody, making many of Pete's songs world famous, such as "If I Had a Hammer" and "Where Have All the Flowers Gone?" Like The Weavers before them, Peter, Paul and Mary showed the world that folk music not only sounded good but could also sell records. As The Weavers took Woody Guthrie songs and turned them into radio-friendly records without sacrificing their substance, Peter, Paul and Mary did the same with the songs of Pete and Woody as well as those of Dylan and other new writers.

It started in the clubs of Greenwich Village, Chicago, and San Francisco and spread to all corners of the land. The new sound of folk generated a lot of satellites, and Mary Travers was one of the brightest. A member of the group The Song Swappers, who had recorded with Pete

Seeger, she was well known in the Village both for her great beauty and her beautiful voice.

Peter Yarrow came to the Village from Cornell University, where he graduated with a degree in psychology. Noel Paul Stookey was always referred to as Noel by all friends and family but took on Paul because it sounded better with Peter and Mary. He started off as a stand-up comic, coming to New York from Michigan State University mostly to pursue comedy, a humorous proclivity that came to the surface not only on "Paultalk," a delightful comedy routine on the trio's first concert album, but also in the comic verses of songs such as "I Dig Rock and Roll Music" and others.

Encouraged by Dylan's manager, Albert Grossman, to team up, the fledgling trio holed up in Mary's three-flight walk-up apartment and rehearsed for three solid months before making their public debut. When they did—at the Bitter End in 1961—the audience was entranced and thrilled. Soon the group was launched on a tour of folk clubs around America. Within a year they released their first album, and, as *Billboard* recognized at the time, it was an "instant classic," remaining in the Top Ten for some two years.

Singing the songs of Seeger, Dylan, and others inspired Peter, Paul and Mary to write their own, and all three developed into fine songwriters. With his friend Leonard Lipton, Peter wrote "Puff the Magic Dragon," the first of many famous songs written within the trio. Paul Stookey became experimental in his writing and recording, influenced by the expansiveness of The Beatles to record and write great songs like "Apologize" as well as comic commentary in the aforementioned "I Dig Rock and Roll Music."

Mary collaborated with friends to write lyrical songs with beautiful melodies such as "Moments of Soft Persuasion," ideal for her angelic voice.

At the same time, they continued to embrace the songs of new songwriters and, in doing so, launched many careers. They had a number-one hit with "Leaving on a Jet Plane," written by John Denver, and also a hit with "Early Morning Rain" by Gordon Lightfoot.

Peter, Paul and Mary disbanded a few times to pursue solo projects and to walk their own paths. But they reunited often. In 1978 they came together with a great reunion album called *Reunion* and tour and continued together on and off. It was in 1996, soon after the release of their album *LifeLines*, that I had this occasion to interview all three at the same time.

I'll admit: I was both proud and somewhat amazed when, with much laughter, they told me I knew more about them than anyone who had ever interviewed them. Of course I came in knowing their famous songs on their famous albums. But I also came in knowing—and truly loving—some of the very obscure but remarkable songs on their solo albums. One was on Paul's first solo album, *Paul And*, called "Edgar," a song both funny and mysterious that had long perplexed me. "Nobody has *ever* asked about that song," he said with wonder. (It's about the mystic Edgar Cayce, he said.)

Sadly, Mary Travers died in September of 2009. Peter and Paul have done shows together since, but of course, she's impossible to replace. But go back to the records. There is her spirit as alive as ever, wonderfully intertwined with the musical spirits of her two best friends into one of the best things humans can achieve together: perfect harmony.

Peter Yarrow: When you inherit the tradition of the Pete Seeger point of view, the songs are not pieces of entertainment. They are the communication of a long tradition that has a particular meaning historically. And if you're singing something that you know, historically, has really affected people, you're not going to treat this as if it's just entertainment and doesn't matter. It really matters.

For instance, Pete Seeger recently said something very wonderful about us. We were doing a festival he was in too, and he called on us to sing "If I Had a Hammer" with him. And as you know, we do a different chord structure from his.

Your version has all those pretty minor passing chords between the chords he plays.

Peter: That's right. He talked about "Where Have All the Flowers Gone?" as well, and there was a sense of his blessing in the changes that we made. And for us that's very, very important. Because that was more than a song; that was a piece of shared feeling and ethos at the march in Washington with Martin Luther King, where he gave his "I Have a Dream" speech. So it really matters to us, and we really go head to head on the stuff.

Mary Travers: We fight about songs all the time. Not angry fighting, but philosophical fights. Because we've always believed that we'd never ask anybody to sing something they don't like. I mean, what greater punishment could you give somebody than to make them sing something they don't believe in?

Peter: And the premise is so one person can say no.

Mary: There's a great copyright story that we must tell. It's the best copyright story in the world.

Paul Stookey: The Reverend Gary Davis story.

Mary: Absolutely.

Paul: It was about the song "If I Had My Way," which we recorded.

Peter: They weren't sure if he wrote it or not, so they called him up at the house—this is very important. Artie Mogull, our link at Warner Brothers, called him up at the house and said, "Are you Reverend Gary Davis?" And he said yes.

They said, "Did you write this song 'If I Had My Way'? Because Peter, Paul and Mary recorded it, and it's gone gold."

He said, "No, I didn't write it."

Artie said, "So who did?"

He said, "Nobody. It was revealed to me."

That's when Artie explained to him what royalties were, and even though it was revealed to him, he got the royalties. He called his wife to the phone and told them to start over and tell her. It was hard for him to believe.

Mary: When you're dealing with some of those traditional songs— when you're dealing with the body of music from the 1920s and early 1900s—those songs really traveled from one black church to another. And the essence of folk music has always been that each person that sings the song, traditional or not, imprints it with their own feelings and sometimes their own lyrics.

You famously recorded the song "If I Had a Hammer," and you changed the lyric from "all of my brothers" to "brothers and sisters."

Peter: Well, Pete [Seeger] said Peter, Paul and Mary did not do that. Indeed, he talked about a fight that he had—well, not a fight, a discussion—with a cowriter who wanted to say "all of my brothers," and Pete said he insisted on it.

His cowriter being Lee Hays, of course.

Peter: That's right. So although I know you think that we made that change, according to Pete, that was his change.

I've noticed how well your voices blend together, and I realized that all three of your voices make up the sound and that if you changed any one of the voices it would alternate radically.

Mary: I've often thought that, like the decorating, it's the weaknesses that make the strength. If you have a house that is absolutely square, it's very difficult to make something creative happen. None of us have perfect placement. Peter is sort of a tenor with baritone thrown in there, and Noel is a baritone with a little bass thrown in there, although he's got a pretty good falsetto. And I'm an alto.

Paul: Contralto.

Mary: And contrary too. And getting lower all the time. But it's because they are not perfect that they make us have to deal with each piece anew, taking into consideration those elements so you get a unique sound.

Do you have any recollection of the very first song you sang together?

Mary: [*Laughs*] Peter and I probably knew more folk songs than Noel did. But we knew different versions of everything. Every song we tried, we would sing differently, so we went through this for about twenty minutes, trying to find a song that we could agree on. Finally we threw up our hands and we said, "Oh, let's just do 'Mary Had a Little Lamb,' just to see what it sounds like." And that is what we did—that was the first song.

Paul: We each took turns singing the melody, and the other two people took turns singing a third above, and it was nice, and it was so obvious that we had sung in groups before. Because there's a kind of giving, a kind of bending. It's not pitch, exactly. If you had sung in a group, you know the same thing. You can either sing out or you sing out with an invisible touching. That's what we did, and simple as the song was, the three of us obviously had a relational capability, and I guess that's really what it is. And now we even rejoice in it. We have this thing, this confluence, where we decide we all go to bend the jet stream.

Mary: That's the most exciting thing in the group, is that kind of ESP you get. You're listening so carefully that you hear the subtlety of somebody who's decided tonight to sing the song with a completely different attitude.

You made the song "Blowin' in the Wind" by Bob Dylan world famous. Do you recall how you first heard it?

Peter: We heard it backstage at the Gate of Horn [in New York]. Albert Grossman was managing him at the time, as well as Richie Havens, Gordon Lightfoot, Joan Baez, The Band, Janis Joplin, and the list goes on and on. And he played us the record, and on that record there were a couple of songs that we hadn't heard before. One of them was "Don't Think Twice, It's All Right." And the other one was "Blowin' in the Wind." And we felt so strongly about it that it was the only song that I remember we ever recorded as a single. We went in and recorded the song, and it was so, so powerful. It was riveting.

Mary: Sometimes you need a translator. You don't need a translator for "Blowin' in the Wind." You just say, "Yes."

When Dylan first arrived on the scene he had a unique voice. Not one that was easily accessible, and one can, I think, say safely that the world fell in love with Bob Dylan's words before they fell in love with his voice. After they'd fallen in love with his words, they began to find his uniqueness in terms of vocal quality.

I remember with Dylan, I played him for everybody, including the delivery boy that came to my house. Anybody. Stop and listen to those words. I mean, this was a poet.

With "The Wedding Song," Paul, you put that song immediately into the public domain. Is that correct?

Paul: Well, yes, not into public domain actually but a public domain fund, which I get to manipulate and administer. If you don't specify, somebody else will administer the funds, and those funds for "The Wedding Song" would've gone to pay BMW car payments for some record executive somewhere. So this way I can't touch it, but I can spend it.

Mary: Why did you do that with "The Wedding Song"?

Paul: Because it was revealed to me. [*Laughter*] It's another one of those, isn't it?

Was it written for Peter's wedding?

Mary: Yes, written for Peter's wedding.

Paul: The song was revealed to me as an answer to an open prayer. Because when Peter asked me to write a song that will bless his wedding, I said, "Okay, I'm Christian. I know the source. I'll go and I'll pray. I'll say, 'Okay, well, how would you manifest yourself at Peter's wedding?'"

And honest to goodness the words came: "I am now to be among you at the calling of your hearts." It was all in the first person. "Rest assured this troubadour is acting on my part, the calling of your spirits here has caused me to remain, for whenever two or more of you are gathered in my name, there am I, there is love."

Peter: This is interesting news! I didn't know this.

Paul: This is the original lyric. We're at the motel room at Wilbur, Minnesota, and nobody's ever heard the song before, not even my wife, Betty. So I get out the twelve-string, and I start playing it, and she says, "They're not going to understand." See, the sensitivity of the times was that Noel was a Jesus freak. Which is true, to a certain extent—

Peter: I wouldn't have used the term. You were more of a born-again Christian who had the book burning a hole in his pocket.

Paul: Well, so Betty said that anybody who hears me sing that song is going to say I had gone over the edge: He is now declaring himself as God—who is now to be among you. They're not going to be able to make the transition.

And so I changed it from first person into third person: "He is now to be among you" rather than "*I* am now . . ."

Well, the curious thing to it is that now in the struggle among the church for gender righteousness, there's a problem. By introducing "*He* is now to be among you," I deposited God, or the Spirit, into a place where it was never meant to be. Isn't that curious? Because it has no gender when it says "I," which is the way it came to me.

It's such a beautiful song and story and interesting because it's ostensibly about the marriage but it's really a song about the presence of God.

Paul: Yes! About a larger marriage.

Did you find that most of your songs came that way?

Paul: Personally, just as I divide concept, lyrics, and music up, I also walk this walk, what I understand what's inspired and what's just experiential. If I write a song that's based on the experience of me, then I thank God for the insight. But it is, after all, me describing my life. But if I move into areas like "The Wedding Song," I do still put songs in public domain because I think they belong there.

Paul, the song "Sebastian" was written about a twelve-string guitar?

Paul: Yeah. It started off that way, and then it became a kitten, and then it became a little boy.

How about your song "Edgar"?

Paul: Goodness gracious, you do know our songs. No one has ever asked me about that song. Edgar was Edgar Cayce, who predicted that the West Coast would fall into the Pacific sometime before the year 2000.

Peter, "Puff the Magic Dragon" seems like a traditional folk song now. Do you remember writing that song?

Peter: I have to say that ultimately we had the strange reinterpretation of the song by *Newsweek*, where they were writing about "Lucy in the Sky with Diamonds" and "Mr. Tambourine Man," and at the time, since poetry was the nature of lyrics, it was much more involved in thinking and analysis of what the lyrics really meant. But they never just have anything to do about drugs.

Leonard Lipton wrote the original lyrics on a piece of paper at Cornell University. I then added to the lyrics, so that I actually wrote at least as many lines as he did even though the original concept was his. The music was written at a later time. The fact of the matter is that the inspiration for it was really an Ogden Nash–like point of view on Leonard Lipton's part, and that was the positive view. And on the flip side of that piece of paper he wrote a very dark fragment, which was not grist for the songwriters mill.

Did all the drug interpretations of that song bother you?

Peter: No, but it did seem stupid and some people took it seriously. It's still forbidden in Hong Kong and Singapore.

Mary: Is there a last question that you must know the answer to?

Do you foresee the three of you staying together in the future and continuing to record?

Mary: On canes and walkers. [*Laughter*]

Peter: As a matter fact, I suggest that ten years from now that might be the perfect title of the album. *Canes and Walkers.* [*Laughter*]

◆ ◆ ◆

Herbie Hancock
On a Journey of Jazz
Beverly Hills, California 2010

Rare is the chance to talk to a genius, and even rarer when that genius is not the troubled kind but one with great focus and inner peace. That is Herbie Hancock, a genius of music, a living link to the revolutionary jazz of Miles Davis. Miles was both Herbie's mentor and boss, teaching him, mostly by example, the meaning of space and silence in music and the unlimited potential always inherent within the limitations of music. Miles also taught him the power of metaphor to set musicians on the right track, as discussed in these pages.

But Herbie also learned lessons Miles didn't teach, lessons informed by the wisdom of Buddhism, which has freed him from turmoil, chaos, and self-obsession to focus on what matters the most and what lasts. Before our interview he went to a nearby Buddhist center to chant for a full hour. "It keeps me grounded and grateful," he said softly with a smile. A multitude of birds were singing in the trees, which he regarded with joy: "Dig it: it's several jam sessions at once!"

Two years prior we were both at the 2008 Grammy Awards, where Herbie beat out Kanye West and other stars to take home the biggest prize of the night, Album of the Year, for his beautiful tribute to Joni Mitchell, *River: The Joni Letters.* For a jazz guy to beat out the immense mainstream success of the other nominees was too difficult for many in the press to bear, especially with a collection of songs by another artist they found unworthy of their attention, Joni Mitchell. And so they literally screamed: *"Kanye got robbed! He got robbed!"* It was only the second time in history that a jazz artist won Best Album. (The first was *Getz/Gilberto* in 1964, by Stan Getz and João Gilberto with Antônio Carlos Jobim.)

But although the press was enraged by this perceived travesty, music lovers the world over—fans of jazz, Herbie, Miles, Joni, and all combinations thereof—united in celebrating this rare mainstream acknowledgment of classic songwriting mixed with jazz. All due to the heart, mind, and prodigious musicality of this humble and gracious man.

In our ensuing discussion we touched on the creative courage necessary to artists like himself, Joni, Miles, and more. Artists who necessarily embraced artistic evolution and followed a singular vision even when prominent voices urged them to play it safe. When Joni decided in 1979 to write lyrics to the expansively exultant, complex jazz of Charles Mingus, her audience mostly turned their backs. They didn't want her to move forward artistically or even to stagnate; they wanted her to go *backwards* and make music like *Blue* again. She was the one, after all, who said famously in concert, "Would people ask Van Gogh, 'Hey, paint "Starry Night" again'?" But Joni was on her own journey of jazz and bravely brought together the world's greatest jazz players. First she turned to her friend, the beloved bassist Jaco Pastorius, who assembled the band and brought in Wayne Shorter on sax. And Herbie. Joni's vision of purity and faithful allegiance to Mingus and his spirit delighted and impressed him, as discussed here, especially when he learned she didn't want him to play it safe—she wanted him to "fly." Those miracle flights are preserved forever on the masterpiece of *Mingus.*

Born in Chicago on April 12, 1940, Herbie started playing music when his folks bought him an upright piano for his seventh birthday. He studied classical at first, which forever informed his music, and gradually turned to blues and then jazz. The R&B trumpeter Donald Byrd gently ushered him into the jazz world and taught him the fundaments of business and craft both, as discussed in the following conversation.

His life changed profoundly when Miles Davis invited him to join his quintet, teaming up with Wayne Shorter on sax, Ron Carter on bass, and Tony Williams on drums to create one of the greatest groups in the history of jazz. Herbie, like Miles, always welcomed musical evolution, and although he became one of the true masters of the acoustic piano, he lovingly embraced funk and electronica and the new sounds that synthesizers afforded him. And with those tools he made magic.

Although his first song, as related herein, was a pop ditty written with his brother and sister, he evolved into a gifted composer. His compositions were always distinguished by the fusion of a hip groove with clear, shining melodics. Asked what the single-most important ingredient of a melody is, he said, without hesitation, "simplicity." That love of singable tunes, even against the most complex harmonies known to man, has always been at the heart of his work. Great tunes abounded in all eras of his career, including "Cantaloupe Island," "Watermelon Man," "Maiden Voyage," "Chameleon," and "Rockit."

Today wind chimes are ringing in the trees, ongoing birdsong jams are mingling in the air, and an orange-blossom sweetness is singing on the breeze from nearby trees in his hillside yard, ripe with fruit. Herbie's sitting on the patio of his Angeleno home, where he's lived now for decades, looking as if he hasn't aged through any of them. His newest project at the time of this interview was *The Imagine Project*, for which he assembled a mighty international array of musicians and vocalists to record inspirational songs such as Lennon's "Imagine" and "Don't Give Up" by Peter Gabriel.

When told of my desire to discuss composition, he laughed and said, "Too bad I didn't write any songs on this record." Of course, he does have a lifetime of compositions to discuss and a world of wisdom acquired both from fellow geniuses and from the inner river from which all songs flow. Munching a sandwich that he graciously offered to share, he took time to seriously ponder each query and then generously shed ample light into the joys and challenges of musical creation.

Among jazz artists, you are one of the few to always show such respect for songwriters and their songs. Certainly songwriters of previous generations but also current ones such as Peter Gabriel, Bob Dylan—and a whole album of Joni Mitchell songs. You've done the standards but now have established these as new standards. A lot of people feel songwriting itself has diminished since the Gershwin days. Do you feel there are still great songs being written?

Herbie Hancock: Yes. That was the idea for that record. There's still great songs being written. How can you deny songs by The Beatles being great songs? On the same level as a Gershwin. I went to a Paul

McCartney concert at the [Hollywood] Bowl just a few weeks ago, and he started doing all these songs, and *wow*. What a legacy these guys left.

Yes. Such a body of work and such a rapid evolution. Which is not unlike your work, which encompasses so much music and such a profound evolution. I have been immersed in your whole body of work, and it is wonderful because a whole universe of music is there.

Thank you. I've been very fortunate to have great parents that encouraged me to pursue whatever I wanted to pursue. They said, "Whatever you decide to be, son, we'll back you up all the way."

They said that before you chose music?

Yes. I started playing music when I was seven. On my seventh birthday my parents bought me an upright piano. We didn't have one before. I took lessons. I didn't take lessons from day one—a few months later I started taking lessons. My older brother, younger sister, and I—we all started taking lessons.

Classical?

Yeah. But we were already exposed to classical music. My mother in particular wanted us to listen to classical music. She said, "The other stuff you're gonna hear in the neighborhood. But you're not gonna hear this."

What was the music you were listening to then, apart from the classical music you were playing?

I was listening to R&B. In the forties groups like The Midnighters, The Five Thrills. A bunch of groups that were named for birds. [*Laughs*]

Right. The Penguins—

Yeah, The Penguins, Nightingales.

So you were drawn to popular songs before you were drawn to jazz—

Yeah. I listened to R&B. And they had a thing called the Hit Parade at the time. It was kind of corny. Not as hip as pop music is today. Not as hip as what had been popular music in the thirties. Which really was what's called jazz. At that time Frank Sinatra was a jazz singer.

Big bands were jazz bands.

Right.

Were you considering being a classical musician?

Yeah. As a matter of fact, when I was graduating from elementary school we didn't have a yearbook; we had this newsletter thing. It had a picture of all the students. And he asked us what do we want to be when we grew up. And I said, "Concert pianist."

Did you share that with your family? Did they know that was your goal?
Oh yeah, that was fine with them. They began to get more worried when I got into jazz. [*Laughs*]

And that happened when you were still in the home?
Yeah, I was in high school when I first really started paying attention to jazz. My folks both were jazz fans. They played Count Basie's band and Duke Ellington. People like that. They were big fans of Fats Waller. Though I don't remember them playing much Fats Waller.

When you got into jazz did you leave classical behind, or did you do both?
I was doing both.

And classical, I would presume, helped to shape your style in jazz?
Yeah. I mean, I had to make that transition from being a classical musician to being a jazz musician. And it helped in a lot of different ways because I already had a choice of musical balance and flow. And on a completely different level the correct body position, the correct way to hold my hands so I wouldn't do anything to injure myself. Or to get the most out of controlling the instrument. I run into a lot of musicians who have problems with their backs and shoulders. And I never had any of those problems because of my classical training.

At what point did you begin writing your own music?
Right at the beginning. I remember my brother and sister and I wrote a song called "Summer in the Country." I must have been about ten years old. And we wrote this song together. [*Laughs*] Sort of a corny song. It had words. It was more like a pop song. [*Sings to a sweetly melodic tune*] "Summer in the country / We'll have a lot of fun . . ." [*Laughs*]

So your first song was a pop tune—
Right!

Even with that song I could hear a sax play that tune, and it would be a great jazz tune. And it's well known that your famous jazz songs are all beautifully melodic. You can sing them.
Yeah. I guess that was something I was conscious of right away. A melody, you know, is not just an extension of improvised lines—it is something that can stand on its own, being something singable to one

degree or another. So constructing a melody with that in mind, there's a better chance of it being palatable to nonmusicians, to the average person.

Yeah. A lot of your famous songs, whether "Chameleon" or "Rockit," they're singable. And people love melodies. And you've been a champion of other great melodies in your work for decades. Do you have any thoughts about what makes a melody strong?

Usually simplicity. Yeah. Usually it's a simple idea. Something really fundamental. Like something that you could reduce to either two or three elements. And that's what I try to employ on some of the songs that I wrote, even instrumental ones. Like "Chameleon" is in patterns of two. [*Sings melody with two note passages*] Then the answer to that phrase.

And it's based around two chords as well—B flat minor and E flat.

Right, right! That too.

I was surprised, while analyzing your songs, by that simplicity. Your harmonies and chords are often quite extended and complex, but your melodies are often, like you said, single enough that somebody could sing them.

In order to explore harmonic variety, which I like to do, there's got to be some balance. So if that's going to be complex and involved, the balance would be a melody that is based off something more towards the simple side.

When you compose melodies do you do it by generating them from chords you play, or do you think in terms of a pure melody line, apart from chords?

Well, in the beginning I used to do it in a tried-and-true way that a lot of jazz musicians utilize, and that is to start with a bass line. Sometimes it's a bass pattern. Sometimes it's a harmonic movement. That used to be kind of the formula that I used.

I can hear that. Often the bass part is the foundation of the whole thing. Like "Watermelon"—

Yeah. That particular piece, when I wrote it, I was actually thinking about the real watermelon man in Chicago. You know they have alleys in Chicago. Cobblestone. They used to be cobblestone when I was a kid. And the watermelon man had a horse-drawn wagon. Now they have trucks, but they still had horses then! And what I tried to capture with that bass line and the harmonic pattern and that rhythmic element,

I tried to simulate—I tried to capture—the spirit of the wagon wheels going over the cobblestone, and the horses' movement, and their hooves hitting the cobblestones. And that's what [*sings rhythm*] came from.

I remember that the watermelon man, he used to have a little song that he sang. And it was [*sings*], "Wat-y melon, red ripe watermelon." He had a little song that he sang. But that wasn't so melodic in a traditional sense. It was melodic germane to his job. That was their thing. And that's not something that other people can easily sing. So I thought, "What else is happening?" I remember. We had back porches then leading to the back alley. When we lived in an apartment building we still had back porches. And women would yell for the watermelon man. They would yell, "*Heyyyyyyyy, Watermelon Man!*" So I made the melody that. That's what I tried to capture with that melody.

It's interesting that even when you write an instrumental like that, you had such a clear subject and image. Is that something you normally would have, a story attached to the tune?

Well, in this case it was for the first record that I did under my own name—1962. I had already been told by the person who discovered me, Donald Byrd, great trumpet player that brought me to New York. I became his roommate for a couple of years. We shared an apartment in the Bronx in New York. And he kind of *raised* me. And he's the one who really encouraged me to make my own record and help make that happen with the record label.

He said, "Look, let me tell you how the music business works. As far as jazz is concerned, half the record is for you, and half the record is for the record company."

I said, "What does that mean?"

He said, "Well, half the record can be your songs. But the other half will be to help sell the record." [*Laughs*] Of course, the obvious implication is that my songs are not going to help sell the record because nobody knows any of my songs and I have no track record or anything. What helps sell the record is something that's a blues or a cover of a standard or a Gershwin tune or "If I Were a Bell" or "My Funny Valentine." Or whatever. A Cole Porter tune.

So I said, "Okay." But then I started thinking about it, and I thought, "Well, why don't I try to write something that would help sell the record? What would that entail?" So my first thought was Horace Silver because he had records that were selling to the jazz public. And he became very popular, and it went beyond the standard jazz sales. And what was it that he had? His tunes were funky. I had already had a background listening to rhythm and blues and funky stuff anyway, so why don't I try to write something funky like that? So I started to think, "I'm a jazz musician. I wanted to be true to jazz, and I don't want to write something commercial just for the sake of it being commercial. If I write something, I want it to be connected with something true, connected to me and my life."

When you think of the word *funky*, that really comes from an African American tradition. So what can I write that is ethnic? That I can relate to with a song? I had heard songs about chain gangs and the South and discrimination and things I hadn't been consciously experiencing. But what I could relate to was a watermelon man. That was definitely ethnic. Also, the idea of watermelons had a big stigma attached to it. That was a negative one among blacks. The pickaninny eating a watermelon, you know, with big eyes. That kind of thing.

So black people—of course, we love watermelons! But in the hood, no problem. But outside the hood it was something. We kept some kind of distance from it because of that association, because of that connotation. So I kept trying to avoid it. But it kept coming back so strongly. Inside. That *that's what it has to be.* And what really convinced me was that I started thinking, "Is there anything really wrong with watermelons? No. Is there anything wrong with the watermelon man? No. You either got to be a man or a mouse. You either stand up for what you believe in or you're a coward." I had to stand up for what I believe in. And it was funny because when I told some other black musicians that I wrote a song called "Watermelon Man" they said [*in a hushed whisper*], "You're gonna call it *that*?"

See, it sounds now like it wouldn't be an issue. But back then it was. 'Cause this is before Martin Luther King; it's before James Brown and "I'm Black and I'm Proud" and all of that. And so a lot of things that were associated with *blackness*, we kind of hid. We had a tendency to hide in a lot of cases.

And Chicago was—and still is—a pretty segregated city.
Right. Exactly.

And I also remember, growing up in Chicago, the arrival of fresh fruit— and watermelon—in spring. It was always momentous. We sure didn't get it all year. And the song has that happy springtime feeling to it.
Yeah, right. I wanted to capture that. But *who knew* that it was going to be such a big hit? I had no idea. So the funny thing was, when I went to present the songs to the label—I was going to present three songs one

day and three songs on another day, to get their approval. So I brought my three songs the first day, and "Watermelon Man" was one of them. I played those songs for them, and I said, "Tomorrow I'll bring you my blues piece and a standard." They said, "No, why don't you write three more pieces?" [*Laughter*] And that was *highly* unusual, to take a new artist and have all the songs be originals—that was not something they normally did.

Yeah. They recognized what they had.

Yeah, I think they did.

Did you have enough of your own compositions to use, or did you write new songs then?

No, I think I had started on a couple of things. I went back home, back to the Bronx, and worked on them that night and brought them the next day. And they said, "Great."

Then they said, "Of course, you're going to have to put them in our publishing company." All the record companies had their own publishing companies. And I had already been warned about that from Donald Byrd. He said, "They're gonna tell you you're gonna have to put your tunes in their publishing company. Do *not* let them do that. No matter what they say, tell them no."

I said, "But supposing they say they won't put out my record—"

He said, "Trust me. They'll still record you."

And it went exactly the way he said. They said, "Yeah, you need to put your songs in our publishing company." Meanwhile I was crossing my fingers.

And I said, "Uh, no."

They said, "Why not?"

I said, "I've already published them in my company." It was a *lie*. I hadn't even set it up yet. [*Laughs*]

They said, "You did? Well, I guess we can't record them."

So I turned around and started to walk towards the door. And just before I grabbed the doorknob they said, "Wait a minute. Okay, you can publish them."

I said, "Great." And because of that, I'm the proprietor and publisher of "Watermelon Man." Solely. And all the songs on that record.

Byrd gave you great advice. Not only what was right but how to deal with the guys.

Oh, it went *exactly* the way that he said. [*Laughs*] I am eternally grateful for his advice.

Almost all songwriters I've spoken to talk of those times when songs are coming through and those other times when nothing comes. Are you able to control when things come through? Is it there for you, or something that only comes once in a while?

At this point in my life, as opposed to when I was in my twenties, [*laughs*] it's very difficult for me to write something. Stuff used to just flow out of me all the time. Over time, as I got older, it became more and more difficult for me to write. And it became more of a struggle. And it's still a struggle. But I do know one thing: it's struggle that is a necessary ingredient to overcome and win over. It's winning over yourself. And that victory is an element that stimulates creativity and growth.

I learned that I need a deadline [*laughs*] to actually do something. Sometimes I don't get anything done until the *last* minute. I don't care what it is. The first thing that comes out of my pencil is going on the paper. And I'll do that. And I'll go, "This is a piece of *crap*." But it leads to something. And I keep working, and it leads to something else. And eventually I'll have a piece.

So even though your initial voice says it's no good, you know to go beyond that. Not let that guy stop you from going on.

Oh yeah. Right. I mean, I've had this ongoing struggle for half of my career. For twenty-five years. Movie scores, same thing. Albums, same thing. Most of the recent albums, the songs are not my compositions. But the focus of the records is the concept and the direction. So my energy has been placed in that and the development of the overview, which was never really apparent to me in the beginning of my career—I used to just write tunes.

And you'd record them all at one session, everything at once—

Yes, exactly. My more recent things, over the past few years, have been concepts. As a matter of fact, starting back with probably the record called *Dis Is Da Drum*, there were major concepts putting that record together. It came out in 1995, but I started that record in 1991. And it took all of that time to put it together. I originally wanted to have that record be a surround-sound record—long before it was really possible. [*Laughs*] And I had a lot of musicians that signed off on an album that believed in the project. Then when I did *The New Standard*, that was also an answer to the question, "Will the standards always be those songs written in the twenties and the thirties? Or will there be some new standards?" So this was my reply to that. Not that the songs I chose were standards. But what I did with that record was the same thing we used to do with the old standards—which is to turn them into jazz songs. [*Laughter*]

And by doing that with these new songs you establish them as standards. It helped elevate them to that place.

I don't know how much I had to do with that. [*Laughs*]

There does seem to be an elitism among some jazz artists that these newer songs aren't worthy and aren't as harmonically interesting as the standards of the previous generation.

At least maybe I helped dispel that myth. That is what I like doing. What I can to expand the boundaries that we set up for ourselves. And to promote the idea that our creativity is stifled by boundaries. That the human being has *infinite* potential, infinite potential for creativity. I firmly believe that. I believe that you have to be what you believe and be an example of what you believe. At least strive towards that.

It's why your work has always been so vital and exciting. Whereas other musicians are content to be segregated always into separate genres, it's in the fusion of genres that the future of music lives. You've been a pioneer in this.

Yeah, I like that goulash.

And that's uncharted territory in a lot of ways.

Yeah, it is. Because it hasn't really been encouraged by the business. Certainly not by the pop business, which is *very* money oriented and the stakes are really high. So there's a tendency for pop artists to do the thing that they're known for. And in most cases what they're capable of creating—including their interests—go beyond that. But it's kind of stifled. They stay on that safe path.

But my training is from Miles Davis. He would *fire* you if you tried to be safe! [*Laughs*] So I have to answer to *that*. As if Miles judges everything I do. [*Laughter*]

To this day you think of his judgment?

Yeah! The whole spirit of that is really in me.

And there are certain artists, like you—or Miles, or Dylan, or Joni— who bravely moved on even though your audiences might not have wanted that change.

Yeah. Well, I never think of my audience as being a stagnant audience. I always hoped for, for one thing, for the sake of the life of jazz, to continue to grow a new audience. Because people die. [*Laughs*] If you don't grow a new audience, there won't be an audience for the music. And then who will you make music for? Yourself? Then you won't be able to make a living. And you won't be able to be a contributor to the culture of the world. It's the culture of the individuals who make up the world.

Speaking of Miles, I have been watching films of you in his quartet with Ron Carter and Tony Williams. There was so much freedom and yet also precision. Would Miles talk to you about the music? Would he give you verbal guidance about what he wanted, or was it beyond words?

He *never* talked about music. [*Laughs*]

He didn't seem like a very talkative person—

No, he was talkative. He would tell us stories about him and Bird, or him and his relationship with Dizzy [Gillespie]. Or the scene back in those days. Funny stories. Miles was always funny. Or something that he saw on the street. Even if we were working on a record, if there was something that he wanted to transfer to us, he wouldn't tell us *what* to play; he would find some metaphor. Which really is the heart of what he wanted. 'Cause with a metaphor you have to translate them into your own terms and figure out how to describe in musical terms that metaphor. Because even if he had a single idea—and this is something that I came to believe long after those first experiences with Miles—and that is that the musical idea is one example of the metaphor. [*Laughs*] And so the metaphor carries the heart of what that is really about. So it can express itself in many different ways.

But if you tell a person what to play, first of all, it's you, and you're not playing that instrument. [Miles] is a trumpet player. He's not going to play piano. He's not playing drums or the bass. So he wanted each of us to create our own parts and create our own avenue or our own character within the performance. So the metaphor would give us a chance to ponder the spirit of the idea he had and come up with an expression of it that *we* create. See, that's what a master teacher does: he doesn't give you the answers; he tells you a way to find the answers for yourself.

That was reflected in the music, that it was a journey of discovery for each musician. Also he chose such astounding players, so that the level of musicianship was extremely elevated.

Yeah, Miles was like that, he was a *master* at being able to do that. And I had the great fortune of working with the best musicians around.

[*Laughs*] It doesn't get better than that. To have Ron Carter on bass, Tony Williams on drums, Wayne Shorter on saxophone—you know? And Wayne not only on saxophone but the great composer that he was and continues to be. I mean you should hear what he's writing now! He's writing for a full symphonic orchestra. The stuff is *fantastic*.

Really? Can't wait to hear it.

Oh yeah. It's new, fresh stuff. You can't compare it to Wayne's tunes. It's a much larger vision than that.

Would Miles ever tell you after a gig if he didn't like something you did?

[*Pause*] No. [*Laughs*] He never told us if he liked something either. [*Laughs*] But the fact that we still had a gig—I had that gig for about five and a half years—that meant he must have liked it. [*Laughs*] I could just tell that Miles loved for us to create with a lot of question marks. That he would have to *maneuver* through. To create music. He lived in that. If he knew what we were going to play, he would be bored to tears. If we threw a curve at him, he loved that. That's what he could do. He could turn lemons into lemonade every time.

When you said that composing is now a struggle, why do you think that is? Is it that it requires energy that is easier to summon when younger? Because your playing sounds as amazing as ever.

Thank you. [*Pause*] I don't know exactly. I suspect that perhaps it's a combination of things. I can't really pinpoint it. It's easy to say age. Yet Wayne Shorter hasn't slowed down one bit of constantly writing and composing songs. Chick Corea, too, hasn't slowed down one bit. And Wayne is a few years older than I am. Chick is a year younger than I am and hasn't slowed down. So age isn't really the right answer.

For me, striking the balance between what was, for me, a new vision of myself, which was a product of my Buddhist practice, and how to achieve a balance is something I am continually trying to grow in that area of balance. And that is, back in the day I didn't pay attention to politics. I didn't pay attention to the news. I never read the newspapers to see what was going on. I didn't watch news shows if I watched TV. It's a whole different ball game now. I listen to talk radio. Not the music stations. I watch the news on television. Sometimes I watch movies. I love playing with my computer. That's part of a special interest that I have that stems from my interest in science. But the process—the change of being a musician to being a human being—is a process of growth for me.

We usually define ourselves by what we do: I'm a writer. Or I'm a doctor. Or I'm a dancer. Whatever it is. Or I do construction. That's usually how we define ourselves. There's a big trip with all of that. If we take a look at Christopher Reeve. He was an actor. Something happened in his life to curtail his acting career. It could happen to anyone. So what did he do? He stopped being limited by a concept of being an actor. He didn't go into deep depression. Well, I never knew him, so I don't know. But the end result is that he came out finding a position where he could use his being for the advancement of humanity. So the end result is that he wound up contributing more towards humanity and his legacy from being denied the possibility of continuing his acting career. His life became greater with that "handicap."

Yes. Limitations can create possibilities. As Krishnamurti taught.

Right. Exactly. *Exactly*. So Buddhism really promotes the truth and the fact that the human being really has limitless possibilities. And that the core of what we are is not that thing that we normally define ourselves as. The core of what we are is a human being. And when we define ourselves as a human being, it changes everything. So music now, I look at it from the standpoint of being a human being and use *that* as the foundation. And then I use what I do to translate what initiates from my humanity into musical terms. That's why I'm able to make every record be different from every other record.

And that comes across. And I find with many of the greatest musicians and songwriters there is a humble acceptance and a gratitude for musical gifts received. Whereas some great musicians—maybe Miles even—let their egos get too large and thought of themselves as more than human beings.

Well, I never perceived of Miles as having a big ego. I know that his reputation was that. If his ego were that big, why is it his ego was not big enough to overcome his demons? So Miles was wrestling with a lot of things. He was tormented by his demons. But what I saw in Miles, fundamentally, was this person who sought the truth and tried to express the truth in everything that he did. He was arguably successful at that. The reason I say that is because I know some people—one, in particular— who had a horrible physical experience with Miles. But in my opinion [Miles] wasn't himself. His demons came out in various ways. We all have our demons. It's a part of life. [*Laughs*]

Yet you seem to have transcended demons—

No, I haven't! [*Laughs*] A bunch of them attacked me for this record.

But you're seventy and you are young, healthy, vibrant—productive, prolific—

Oh, thank you—

So many great people, including many you worked with, aren't with us anymore. Many died very young.

[*Softly*] I know. A lot of them are gone.

Like Jaco [Pastorius], for example. Sometimes it seems people with that much talent burn out quickly. Too much current for the conductor. Hendrix too. And you've sustained it for a long time.

I'm really fortunate I was able to discover Buddhism. It helped me develop a clearer idea of my relationship with the environment. My personal relationship with everything that's outside of my personal self. Which includes the people and circumstances that manifest themselves externally. Buddhism really helps you to understand what that is. And in doing so, you have a much better chance. If you recognize something, you stand a fighting chance of dealing with it in a more positive way. It's when something blindsides you and you don't see it coming, then you can be knocked over and defeated. So I continue to chant. That is where I went this morning. I went and chanted for an hour at a center that's near here. In Buddhism we practice and we chant every day.

The other thing I was going to say is that seventy is the new forty. [*Laughs*]

Do you feel musicians hear music differently than nonmusicians do?

Yes. [*Pause*] Well, let me qualify that because I can't speak for every musician. Because my training and my expertise, if you will, is in jazz, there's a tendency for jazz musicians to hear the harmonies and the textures and those things and are basically interested in examining those and finding out what they are if something is interesting to them. Whereas the average listener might like a certain texture, but there's no avenue for them to even question examining it. It becomes part of the vessel. And people evidently [*laughs*], judging from what the public supports, there is a tendency for people today to be more cognizant of vocals than they are of instrumentals.

As a matter of fact, some people—and I've heard this expressed, it's pretty weird—that when they hear an instrumental it sounds like a partial piece of music because the vocal isn't there. [*Laughs*] Which is weird to me.

Do you think of musical keys as having their own colors or character?

Yeah. They do. There are some musicians who might think more in terms of color. I don't think more in terms of that, but I recognize it if someone uses that as a description.

But do you see specific colors attached to keys yourself?

Sometimes for me the keys that have sharps in them seem to have a brightness to them. A lift, maybe. And the keys that have more flats in them, I love them. [*Laughs*] G sharp can be A flat. There's usually a darker, not necessarily somber, but mellower character to it.

I've been just astonished listening to your accompaniments on piano and keyboards—whether with Miles, or on Joni's beautiful *Mingus* album or on Peter Gabriel's "Don't Give Up," which is so beautiful. Your choices are always revelatory—often sparse but magical and unexpected. I was wondering: Are you equally fluid and conversant in every key on the piano, or are there certain places where you are more comfortable?

[*Laughter*] Unfortunately there are places where I'm more comfortable.

Really? Where would that be?

F. [*Laughs*] From the standpoint of piano I have more of a tendency to be more comfortable in F than anything.

It's a good piano key.

Yeah. [*Laughs*] F sharp is more of a challenge.

Irving Berlin played exclusively in F sharp.

That's what I've heard.

It seems when I listen to your accompaniment that you know every chord. Is there still music on the piano or the keyboard that you haven't reached or are still trying to discover? Or have you encompassed it?

No. I'm always [*laughs*] discovering, certainly for myself, new sounds and approaches. But what I'm trying to do now is get away from being motivated from the standard chord structure and think more in terms of a landscape. Objects in a landscape. Textures. Colors. Shapes. Degrees of emotions. Degrees of tension and release. And other characteristics that are nonmusical terms.

Your version of Peter Gabriel's "Don't Give Up" is a great example of that. The melody, sung by John Legend, is quite close to the original. But your accompaniment is a whole other landscape, adding a different depth and texture to the thing but without pulling it into another place. The song still comes through. It is amazing and hard to conceive how you would achieve that.

Well, fortunately [producer] Larry Klein continues to push me that way. He and I really see eye to eye. And he knows I'm capable of utilizing space and textures and other devices than just placement of chords. So he encourages that.

When you approach a song like this, do you think of what you are going to do in advance, or are you following the emotion of where the song leads you?

I try not to think. I try to react. And find a space that is cognizant of the meaning of the lyrics and the emotion that I am experiencing moment to moment. And let myself respond to that.

You chose inspirational songs for this album, such as "Imagine," "Don't Give Up," and "The Times They Are A-Changin'." What draws you to a specific song?

For this project, because the purpose of this record is about peace through local participation, because of that I was looking for songs that would fit into that general concept. But by peace I didn't confine it to world peace. There is inner peace. The peace inside an individual. "Don't Give Up" is about that. And it translates itself to all the various levels of what peace can be. That is what I wanted to do. And all the pieces relate to the struggle against adversity and the hope for a peaceful solution.

A song like "Imagine" and also "The Times They Are A-Changin'" are both pretty simple harmonically. Diatonic. How do you come to something like that? Does it seem restrictive to play within that kind of harmonic framework?

I learned many years ago that if something, at the onset, seems to be confining, it's only confining because of my lack of perception. To perceive how to remove the barriers. Of incarceration. [Laughs] Because if something is confining, it's like you're in jail. But I am developing the experience now of trusting that there is a way of looking at a piece of music where what might normally be perceived as confining walls, the walls are removed. So if my first reaction is from hearing a way a song

was done before or when it was written by the composer it was written a
certain way. If my first reaction is that it can be confining, then I know
there must be a different way of looking at it.

So there are two ways of trying to approach that. One of them is
to reharmonize things. And in many ways that's the coward's way out.
That's easy. It's much more valuable to still keep the essence of the simplicity of the original song. And within that, create an external framework that's more open. But it's not just external—it's internal too.

What I find is that if a piece, on the onset, seems to be confining, I
look to myself, to free myself internally from that feeling of being confined. I mean, look how many things I have to work with! Space. [*Laughs*]
It's easy to forget about space.

Yes. Your music shows that. The use of silence.

Yes. But you have to use it wisely. That's something I was learning
from Miles. He's a master at that. And also you have to trust what's in
your heart and develop the ability to trust what's in your heart and not be
swayed by external forces. 'Cause it's easy to be swayed by external forces.

**It seems some musicians, certainly certain pioneers you have worked
with, are impervious to that.**

Yeah, exactly. A lot of pioneers, the reason they appear to be impervious to it is that they have the courage to fight for what they believe in.
And to stand up for what they believe in. And they demonstrate their
vision in what they do, and they don't back down from it.

**Yes. Like Joni doing the *Mingus* album was very brave. And a lot of her
fans, to this day, don't like it. Yet it's one of the most amazing albums
of all time.**

Oh yes. Let me tell you, I never expected Joni to be like that.

**What a band on it too. You and Jaco and Wayne Shorter. *Wow.* Beyond
words.**

Yeah. [*Laughs*] I was sitting at home in my living room, and I got this
call from Jaco Pastorius. Jaco says, "Herbie, come over here."

I said, "What?"

He said, "We're making an album with Joni."

"Joni?"

"Joni Mitchell. You know, you got to come over. We're trying to put
this thing together. And the piece that's missing is you."

I said, "With Joni Mitchell? Who else is on it?"

He said, "Wayne."

I said, "I'll be right there." [*Laughs*]

But when I got there I thought I would have to hold back things. Simplify things. In the traditional musical words. Simplify. And Joni didn't want that at all. She wanted us to *fly*. Of course, the roads that we had to construct had to include her in it. [*Laughs*] We couldn't just traipse off with our instrumental stuff and play all over the place.

Were you guys leading the sessions?

Uh, no. [*Pause*] It was her and Jaco.

His horn charts on that album are remarkable.

Yeah. Jaco was doing a lot of the talking because he had been working with Joni and he understood what she was looking for. I didn't ask her what to play; I asked him. I said, "How do you think she wants this?" He said, "Man, just go ahead. She wants you to just go ahead and fly."

Were there charts of the songs?

Yeah, there were charts. She didn't want us to just play what was written. I remember Jaco saying, "She wants you to *paint*. That's something you can do, Herbie. *Paint*."

I said, "Okay, here we go." And she just ate it up.

Because Joni has such a big heart, she is always saying yes to charity things. She called me up and asked me to do things. And I always say, "Sure, Joni." I did that for a couple of years on and off. Once she gave me a watch. A Corum watch. A very expensive watch. On the back of it, it said, "He played real good for free." [*Laughs*]

Did the jazz community respect that project, the *Mingus* album?

Yeah, I think so. I don't remember hearing anything negative about it.

◆ ◆ ◆

John Stewart
Daydream Believing

Malibu, California 1991

When John Stewart was a junior in high school he had his first real run-in with rock and roll, an experience so profound, he never forgot it. "I saw Elvis on TV, and a light went off in my head," he said. "It was like the monkeys touching the obelisk in *2001*. I saw my destiny."

He purchased his first guitar, a Sears Stella, learned a handful of chords to get started, and began playing Elvis songs such as "Hound Dog" and "Jailhouse Rock," both written by Leiber and Stoller (see page 26), and writing songs at the same time. His father was a horse trainer, so the family moved all around Southern California, from Pasadena to San Diego to Riverside and on. He started a band called The Furies while still in high school, composed of himself, two more guitarists, and a drummer. But this band was different from all others at the time because they wrote their own songs.

Songwriting from the beginning was a means of expression close to John Stewart's soul. Though it's not the only one for which he had a natural gift: he was also a fine artist who showed me many of his recent paintings and works in progress. I went with our mutual pal Henry Diltz, legendary musician-photographer, to John's Malibu home, which was in the hills overlooking the big blue Pacific. We spoke over coffee and cake in his sunny kitchen, his own paintings all around. We flew through a history that stretches from his time with the Kingston Trio, performing for and befriending the Kennedys, through his work as a solo artist, writing hits such as "Daydream Believer" for the Monkees and Anne Murray and songs like "Gold," which was a hit for himself.

The first song he wrote was called "Before the Night Is Over," which was intended for high school dances. "At these dances all the girls sat on one side of the room, and all the boys sat on the other. It was the trauma of the acne age," said Stewart. At first it was Elvis and Buddy Holly who provided his primary inspiration, but when rock was infiltrated by Frankie Avalon and Pat Boone, it lost all of its appeal for him. "It didn't have any soul, so I gravitated toward folk music and started writing folk songs."

He organized a folk group called The Wanderers and eventually landed a record deal, at which time he became wise about the industry. "I discovered how much money was in publishing, so I realized I should be working on my songwriting."

He wrote to Dave Guard of the Kingston Trio and invited him to a gig his band was giving at Shrine Auditorium. Guard came to the gig and told John afterward that he didn't think the band was ready for the big time. He did like some of the songs, though, and suggested John send him some. Stewart took him at his word. "Every time he was in town, I was backstage playing songs for him," John remembered. Finally Dave liked two of them, "Molly Dee" and "Green Grasses," which they recorded. That album was a hit, and John Stewart, who was in college at the time and living at home, suddenly became a successful songwriter.

His story, below, tells about how the official version of "Daydream Believer" altered one word, substituting "happy" for "funky." Of course, the distance between happy and funky is a vast one, and it shows you, in a song, just how important one word is.

Do you remember the day you wrote "Daydream Believer"?

John Stewart: Very clearly. For some reason I was writing songs all day, every day. It was part of a trilogy, a suburban trilogy. I remember going to bed that night thinking, "What a wasted day—all I've done is daydream." And from there I wrote the whole song.

I never thought it was one of my best songs. Not at all. And then when I heard The Monkees do it, I said, "My God. The line was supposed to be 'You once thought of me as a white knight on his steed / Now you know how *funky* life can be." You know, after the wedding how things can get funky?

And then Davy [Jones] sings, "Now you know how *happy* I could be." The record company wouldn't let them say "funky." Within three months it was number one around the world. Then Anne Murray did it, ten years later—another version.

Henry Diltz: And she's singing "happy" because she learned it from The Monkees.

John Stewart: It *is* "happy." It'll always be "happy."

I lived off that song totally for more than a year. And then Anne Murray recorded it, and it came up again. It was just a song I wrote in a few minutes, and I have written many other songs like "Runaway Train" and others just as fast.

How do you do that?

Clear your mind.

How do you do that?

Write early in the morning when you first wake up—take your guitar to bed. That's before the critical voice kicks in. That doesn't kick in until about a half hour later. At five in the morning you can be pretty clear. And do some sort of breathing and meditation to learn how to turn off that monkey-conscious mind. It just gets in the way. Monkey-conscious mind—like a little wild monkey that goes to all these things. That's what a critic is, and that's the one that tells you that you can't and then tries to get cute and clever.

I like to write while I'm watching TV. 'Cause it's just interesting enough to keep my mind occupied and just boring enough to let it wander. Ideas sort of frees the bird. And driving in the car is great.

Sometimes I'll put two radios on at the same time—and the audio chaos short-circuits your brain, and you can focus on what you have to write. It actually works.

Is it true you wrote "Gold" while you were driving?

Yeah. I was on RSO Records, and Al Coury said I had to have a Top Ten record or I was off the label. I was hanging out with Lindsey Buckingham at the time, who would just sit there and write songs that were making millions of dollars. And so I wrote this song about people who get hits and the guy at the gas station trying to get a hit, and I wrote that whole song driving over to see Lindsey.

It's an okay song. It's catchy, but it didn't dig deep in the thing. Artists that I love, they really dig deep. Francis Bacon goes too far. No, you can't go too far, but Russian artists, they go for this essence beyond the essence and really dig deep for their subject matter. And then there's painters who just paint nice pictures—they're nice; they never dig deep. And I felt that song was just a nice song and just because a lot of people like it, it doesn't mean it's a good song.

That's why Paul Simon and people who are about art rather than about their income, not about being a star, people who really dig deep to give us great songs—that's why they matter so much.

Others besides Simon who matter that much?

I like John Hiatt and Springsteen and Chris Whitley. Also Jesse Winchester and Peter Gabriel. Sting manages to dig deep. Very philosophical.

And look at The Beatles: they wrote these great songs that everybody got. I just don't have the knack for a hook like they did. I mean you don't get any better than "Imagine" and "Walrus" and "Let It Be."

Do you have any idea where ideas come from?

They come from the consciousness that is not the real day-to-day, walking-around consciousness. It's the collective consciousness. Several people can get the same idea at the same time. It's the consciousness that elected presidents and makes hit records. That consciousness that is the link of all of us. All of us are that consciousness. It makes things work. And a writer's above that. But I think it's from that consciousness that is, not to be too philosophical, but if this was a big Halloween party with all kinds of costumes, if we took off all the costumes, we'd all be the same person. It's that consciousness, where it all comes from.

When you try to get your ego in there, try to get your own licks into it, you smell it, and it's kind of repelling. And something that's really honest, someone making an honest statement, people gravitate to that. Those who surrender to that consciousness write the best songs.

There are some who are just given it. They don't even work at it. But that's where I feel the songs come from. They can come from the ego mind, but I just feel those are ego songs. Very Vegas. I won't mention any names. But we all know who writes those songs.

Any advice you can give us on how to tap into that consciousness?

I think just realizing it's there and surrendering to it. And all I have to do is be invited and get out of my way. Constant practice—there's nothing better than you out there doing it. I think surrender is the ultimate trick. You have to hear it without trying to.

◆ ◆ ◆

John Sebastian

A Loving Spoonful

New York, New York 1998

He grew up in the very belly of the blues, with living legends like Lightning Hopkins, Leadbelly, and Mississippi John Hurt coming by the family apartment in Greenwich Village, showing him around both the guitar and harmonica. His world was a world of music, art, and showbiz.

Born John Benson Sebastian in New York City on March 17, 1944, he grew up both in Greenwich Village and in Italy. His father, also named John Sebastian, was a classical harmonica player, and his mother wrote for radio shows. Vivian Vance, famous for being Ethel on TV's *I Love Lucy*, was his godmother.

A gifted singer who also played autoharp, he got his start playing on others' albums, including those by Billy Faier, Fred Neil, and Tom Rush. A trusted pal of Bob Dylan, he played bass on several tracks of what became Dylan's *Bringing It All Back Home*, although those parts were unused. Invited by the gone-electric Dylan to join his touring band, he elected instead to stay in New York and start his own band. He became one of the members of The Mugwumps, which included guitarist Zal Yanovsky as well as both Cass Elliot and Denny Doherty, who became one half of The Mamas and the Papas with John and Michelle Phillips.

He wrote his first music in high school, an extended suite. "In and around those last years of high school," he recalled, "I started to write a piece that would work within a Shakespeare play. It was called something like 'The Rain It Raineth Every Day.'" The reason given for starting to write normal songs: "desperation." The Spoonful had run out of covers and needed some material. Up to then they were playing what he called a "rock and roll smorgasbord," which included revamped jug band music, songs by Chuck Berry and Fats Domino, and some "unlikely blues and country things."

The band took its name from the song "Coffee Blues" by Mississippi John Hurt, which carries the line, "I left my baby by the loving spoonful." Sebastian, who was on vocals, guitar, harmonica, and autoharp, was the heart of the Spoonful, joined by fellow Mugwump Zal Yanovsky on guitar, Steve Butler on drums, and Steve Boone on bass.

He evolved into a serious songwriter and wrote many of the band's hits, including exultant anthems such as "Do You Believe in Magic" and "Summer in the City."

We met at his studio in Greenwich Village to discuss these and other songs. Surrounded by a beautiful collection of guitars, both electric and acoustic, he fell into the story of how he learned to play guitar and how that changed his life and the world he knew.

John Sebastian: I think there was a unique thing happening with guitar playing at the time that I was learning, which was that there were so many of my contemporaries learning, to different degrees of proficiency, that you could get on and off the train. You could learn all the chords and then say that's all I need, I'm just strumming and learning "Tom Dooley." And then maybe someone like Lightning would come along, and you say, "I want to dig a little bit. Be able to play in that polyrhythmic way." And that would take you to the next step. That was the process. It was social. Summer camp was a way. There were always six or eight people learning.

By the time I was eighteen I had actually been able to learn from people like Lightning. By then he knew me so long that I carried his guitar for a year and a half while he was doing gigs. Whenever he came to New York to do gigs he stayed at my house. I'd carry his guitar. So I learned that way. He was not an instructive person. John Hurt, who I later accompanied on harmonica, really was. A real teacher. So John Hurt was somebody who really did show me the rudiments of thumb-picking and that style.

I would think both of them played in open tunings. Am I wrong?

Yes—you are wrong. Lightning was playing often in a standard tuning, sometime down a half step or so. John played a lot in both standard—and standard with a drop D. He had a sliding Delta he used to do in a G tuning.

That was mostly for my curiosity. I just wanted to know.

[*Laughs*] That's fine. Hell, we'll stuff them with a little bit of unexpected knowledge.

You wrote your first songs, you said, out of desperation?

Yes. We had found all the cover songs that we could do, and there were a couple of tempos that we were missing. We needed a big shuffle to create more of an exciting dance floor. It didn't amount to much more than that. We just wanted to get the people up and moving. You have to remember we were playing for the most dour of audiences in Greenwich Village. As much as I love my hometown, the audiences were all the beatnik audiences, so nonverbal and noncommunicative—the folk music audience, which was very complicated and sort of snobbish to their own particular likes and dislikes, so if you were a little vocal trio that was imitating the Kingston Trio, you were out with them. Or you would be out with the commercial crowd if you played blues. It was segregated. I hated it.

So it was out of the need for different songs that caused you to write your own?

That's really what it came from.

Do you remember the first one?

I wrote two songs pretty much in the same two days. The first was called "Don't Bank on It, Baby," and the other was called "Good Time Music." They both ended up on an Elektra compilation album that included four cuts from The Bluesbreakers with Eric Clapton, four from The Butterfield Blues Band. It was called *What's Shakin'*.

Were those blues songs your first ones?

They were bluesy, not too ambitious chordally. But they fit the bill.

When you started writing songs, did it come easy to you?

It was fairly easy. I had had enough failure to make it work fairly easily. You do it a couple of times, and then it starts to roll.

Then did you start to write a lot?

The demand has so much to do with songwriting. And part of my continuing life is to create situations where I have a demand. I really don't believe in writing a song just for the sake of writing a song. If I could leave with two and a half minutes of silence, that suits me really fine. I need the pull of whatever demand there is.

As a matter of fact, Sammy Cahn was the guy who said, when asked what comes first, the music or the lyrics, he said, "First comes the phone call." That applies to me too.

Sammy was proud of his ability to write songs fast, soon as he got an assignment. Could you do that?

I was in a few of those kind of dramatic ensemble works—animated film projects, movie projects. It does have to have a certain momentum, and I function well in those circumstances. I did find I could do it when it was called for.

When you started writing songs for the Spoonful, would you go to it in a disciplined way or wait for inspiration?

Yes, it was more of an undisciplined way. But it was writing all the time. Because there was just too much material needed. As fast as I could write it, it was coming out. Everything we did we put out.

Do you write songs on guitar?

More so than other things. But I sometimes like the strangeness of writing on a keyboard, because it's not my instrument. I am pretty primitive on a keyboard. I'll make mistakes, and that is where you will sometimes find fertile areas.

To preserve those mistakes, do you tape yourself while doing it?

Yeah. I usually get a Dictaphone running or something.

And so you work just on music, without lyrical ideas?

Yes, very often. I was listening to a stub of me coming up with "Welcome Back" the other day. Kind of in preparation of this. And the thing that made me laugh the hardest is that I started at the beginning of the A-side of this tape. Which really takes the whole tape to get anywhere close to "Welcome Back."

On side one I'm playing a kind of country and western thing—no-where *near it*. Then I'm playing this kind of shuffle thing on the piano. And I'm going "Welcome back . . ." But nothing. Then somewhere about halfway through the tape I abandon the whole idea and then start again. And then by the second side of the tape it's starting to make sense [*laughs*] and starting to actually fall into place. And that's the way song-writing can be sometimes. In that particular instance I did have some-what of an agenda. I knew what had to be spoken about. I knew there had to be a certain mood that was the mood of these underachieving students, shall we say? And you had to be in that vernacular; you had to have the right attitude. By the second side of the tape I'm starting to get into the right attitude. And that's what wrote that song.

On keyboard you wrote that?

I worked on keyboard right up till I began to play it with other people.

That song was an exception among TV theme songs in that it was a theme song people loved but it also became a hit and a song people love. It transcended the TV show. Did you feel that, when writing, that it was a great song as well as a good theme?

Yeah, I won't do any false modesty. I was about three-quarters of the way through the aforementioned tape, and I felt I've got a hit song here. And I know that doesn't fit the normal course of events with television shows. They have a little visibility because of the show. Even though I didn't have the power to put it out right then. It was actually a two-and-a-half-minute thing for a TV show first. And then it got write-ins. And phone-ins. People were calling their record shops and saying, "How do I get this?"

Nothing makes a record company react like this. I had no idea. I found myself in a studio all of a sudden trying desperately to make an album that they all of a sudden had green-lighted after not really paying attention to me for a number of years. It was a pleasant accident. And I was enjoying it, certainly.

When you went into the studio did you expand the song?

Once these requests came in, I realized if this thing was gonna go out as a single, it had to be longer. So I said, "Look, I'll take one of the verses and copy it, and then stick it in the middle and play a harmonica solo over it." So what you hear is the heart of that original demo with an additional verse. Then you go back to the beginning and play some extra parts. A few electric guitar parts that I put on that gave it more of a sequential nature. So it wasn't just a repeat when you came to what would be the third verse.

Seemed wise, from a songwriting perspective, that you kept it a universal song. You used the phrase "Welcome back" but kept it general enough and not so specific that it could apply only to the TV show.

I did ask them not to make me write something called "Kotter." There's "otter" and not much else.

"Potter."

[*Laughs*] It was a tough rhyme, and I didn't feel like it. I got this ten-page synopsis, and here are these guys just trying to schlog their way through school, and here's this guy—Kotter—who found his way all of a sudden. Somewhere along the way he must have gotten inspired because he became a teacher. So now he's coming back, and these guys have to tease him. That's what has to happen. So it was sarcasm that was sort of the key to it.

That song, like many of your songs, is upbeat. It makes you feel good when you hear it. Not a lot of songwriters can write good, happy songs without being trite. You've done it in so many of your songs. Does that come naturally to you?

[*Laughs*] It does feel a little strange to have so many people relate to me as this songwriter of happy songs. I'm really glad that they came out that way. But there are songs like "Summer in the City" that, when I wrote them, I was not having a good time. I did not think I was creating a song just to have fun with. This is one of those benefits you kind of have to sit back and say, "Well, great." I would much rather be a writer of happier songs than sadder songs. But I wouldn't want to have just one flavor.

A lot of songwriters don't enjoy the process of songwriting. Do you?

No, I hate it. [*Laughs*] Yeah, it's very hard to do it because there's so many other things that are more fun than staring at a page. And they're all in my house. It comes down to a reason. You need a reason. An idea can be a reason; a project can be a reason. Or it can be a group.

You mentioned "Summer in the City." Do you remember writing that one?

Oh yeah. [*Laughs*] In point of fact, the original core of the song, the chorus, is written by my brother Mark Sebastian. He came to me with this song that was most of the way written, and it had this "But at night it's a different world." This chorus that really struck me as so resonant. I felt if the verse was different, then it would really hit you like a ton of bricks. So I tried to write this angular thing in a minor key that then opens up like a Jewish folk song by going to the subdominant chord in a major way. Like "Exodus." [*Sings*] And "Evening of Roses"—from which it was stolen. So the idea was to start with something that has that minor mode and then move into the major for the chorus.

And it worked. Then we had the verse and the chorus. And in the process of recording it Steven Boone, the bassist for the Spoonful, had a fragment that he played constantly in rehearsals. And I thought this could be the bridge. And it was also in a different time signature, so it did a thing that was almost classical in really taking you from one mood to another. And between that and just a nice accident, then it started to sound like Gershwin, like "American in Paris" to me. [*Sings section of "American in Paris"*] And in that he was imitating traffic. So let's imitate traffic. Let's get some traffic! So we hired this old radio sound man who came in and helped us find traffic and particular car horns. And then we ended it up with that pneumatic hammer.

I also love your song "She's a Lady." Such a pretty song.

As a matter of fact, it was at a very difficult time. I was splitting up with somebody. It was sort of trying to take the sadness of the situation but not the difficulties of the situation. A little idealization works good in songs.

Do you remember writing "Did You Ever Have to Make Up Your Mind"?

Yes. I had spent five summers as a camp counselor. And in this community of counselors, there were two different pairs of sisters that were my age. We were all falling in love with each other. Basically fifteen-year-old stuff. Nothing was ever consummated or anything. It was kid's stuff. But though nothing worked out in actuality, it gave me the basis for the song.

You wrote it then?

No, I wrote it later. I wrote it in a cab on the way to a session, when I needed a song.

Was that unusual for you, to be able to write something in a cab?

No. I'd say it does happen. It's happened more than once. But it ain't the way I like to work all the time.

I think of your song "Do You Believe in Magic" as a great example of one of our happy songs.

That was really the first visible song that I ever wrote. It has a special memory for me. At that time the Spoonful was playing in a little club that really hadn't had a teenage audience yet. We really hadn't found our audience. On this particular night we looked out into the audience, and there was a young girl dancing. This was in a setting where most of the other people were beatnik types sitting around playing chess. And so this really made a difference. It was like seeing the beginning. We knew that if she was there, she would tell her friends next week. Suddenly *we* were gonna have an audience. We were cocky enough to think that. It's a good thing we turned out to be right. But that is what the song was all about.

How about "You Didn't Have to Be So Nice"?

The core of that also came from Steve Boone. He wrote the music for that, and he said, "How about if it's called 'You Didn't Have to Be So Nice'?" And it was so easy to come up with lyrics after that. That song was written very fast. That's a collaboration between he and I.

Did a lot of your songs come fast?

Oh yeah. I've written songs—no hits, but a few that I am proud of—that took all summer. A song called "Face of Appalachia," I kept tinkering with it for most of three or four months.

Sometimes they just slide through faster than others. That's all you can say.

How about "Daydream"?

"Daydream," I think, came out so different than it was intended. The Spoonful was traveling with the Supremes. On a bus, about 1965. Down south for a summer tour. And they had "Baby Love" out there. Also known as "Where Did Our Love Go?" There was something about the groove in that song. We called it, in those days, a straight eight. Because it didn't have any inflection on the two or four or the one and three. Like a lot of music stresses one or the other. The way they got it was by getting people to stomp on a big choir stand. And part of the sound on that record, when the band cuts out and there's just this *whock whock whock*, it's people on a choir stand.

So I tried to write something that was in that groove. And I thought, "Wait till we play this. It's gonna be our baddest thing." [*Laughs*] And instead it comes off as a croony jug band thing. I don't know what it was! But it wasn't what we thought we were copying so well.

◆◆◆

Gene Clark

Still The Byrds

Hollywood, California 1991

"You look like *you* got some sleep," Gene Clark sleepily said as he sat at a table in Hollywood's oldest restaurant, Musso & Frank Grill. From his weary tone and half-opened eyes I concluded that he hadn't gotten much sleep, if any, the night before.

He didn't look too good. Painfully gaunt, his weathered face had been badly battered in a recent car crash, a few front teeth were missing, and his left ear was bandaged à la Van Gogh. Even so, his spirits were high; he seemed happy about embarking on a concert tour that was to begin with a five-night stint at Hollywood's Cinegrill, just down the street from here. He had been gone for a while, but Gene Clark was ready to come back.

"I'm going to record a new solo album," he said. "And I've got about four dozen beautiful unrecorded songs." He smiled happily. "It's going to be a good year for me."

We talked about his past before, after, and during his time as a founding member of The Byrds along with bandmates Roger McGuinn,

David Crosby, Michael Clarke, and Chris Hillman. We spoke about the famous songs he wrote for the band, such as "I'll Feel a Whole Lot Better" (also recorded by Tom Petty) and "Eight Miles High," and the famous people he's known, including his fellow Byrds as well as Jim Morrison, John Lennon, and Bob Dylan.

But he never got to go on tour or to record all those unrecorded songs. Sadly, just weeks after our talk he was found dead in his Sherman Oaks home. The day he died, May 24, 1991, was Bob Dylan's fiftieth birthday. Gene was forty-six.

Because the sound of Roger McGuinn's voice and electric twelve-string guitar is so closely associated with the greatness of The Byrds, McGuinn is often thought of as the sole guiding force behind the band. In truth both Gene and Roger led the band, with both usually singing dual lead vocals, as Paul and John did in The Beatles. It was Gene who insisted, over Roger's objections, to make an arrogant but angelic-voiced singer named David Crosby a member of the band. And it was Gene who wrote the majority of the band's first songs—until the other Byrds caught on to the fact that his royalty checks were bigger than theirs and started writing more.

During our lunch he drank a lot of coffee and ate some pounded steak with gravy, saying he wanted to gain back some of the weight he lost in a recent stomach operation. His countenance was not unlike that of a prize fighter the day after a big fight. He seemed battered physically and emotionally but not defeated. Despite sickness, despite problems with drugs, a generous spirit and a soul of sweetness shone through.

About halfway through our talk he got a serious coughing attack that he wasn't able to suppress, so we decided to continue our talk over breakfast days later.

On the morning of our meeting the stomach flu arrived in my home and refused to leave, so I had to cancel our breakfast, leaving a message on his answering machine, explaining my absence. We spoke the next day on the phone, but before I had a chance to apologize for missing our meeting, he apologized to me, saying it was he who got the stomach flu and marveling at how sudden and severe it was. This was confusing, to say the least, but I took it as part of the conundrum that was Gene Clark. We concluded the interview a few days later, after both of us had recovered completely.

He was born on November 17, 1944, and raised the second oldest of thirteen kids in Tipton, Missouri, near the Ozark Mountains. All his brothers were natural musicians, as was his father. "My dad was one of those guys who could pick up any instrument and make it sound good," he remembered. "We always had instruments around the house—cellos and violins and guitars. My favorite was the guitar, and one of my earliest memories was sitting in front of my dad and watching him play guitar and asking him, 'How do you do that?' And he taught me."

His father was a farmer, and besides the bluegrass music he provided, all of the food the family ate came from the earth. But Gene turned to other places for his music as well, and the radio linked him up to early idols such as Elvis Presley and The Everly Brothers, inspiring him to want to be a musician. "I wanted to be a singing star from the time I could think," he said.

His first band was called The Sharks, with whom he recorded a single. He then returned to folk music and abruptly was discovered and enlisted by the Christie Minstrels, an extremely popular folk group at the time. The instant notoriety he gained was a shock to his eighteen-year-old system almost as strong as the one he felt when his next group, The Byrds, became world famous in a matter of months.

I was among those at his final show at the Cinegrill, which was the nightclub in the Hollywood Roosevelt Hotel. It was more than a concert; it was a party. Gene bought drinks for the entire audience. "It's on me, tonight," he said. The place wasn't full, but those who were there were the devotees, the ones who had been there since the start, when The Byrds played the Whisky just up Sunset from here.

Wearing a white tuxedo with tails and strumming a dark Washburn acoustic, he played some great old Byrds classics as well as some Beatles songs—"Don't Let Me Down" was a highpoint of his set—and songs by Bob Dylan. His final song was Dylan's masterpiece "I Shall Be Released": "I see my light come shining / From the west unto the east / Any day now, any day now / I shall be released."

Do you remember how old you were when you wrote your first song?

Gene Clark: I was about five years old when I wrote my first song. I wrote tons of songs. From there I started getting around folk music, singing lots of harmony with banjos and guitars, like Peter, Paul and Mary.

When did you meet Roger McGuinn?

Met him at the Troubadour [in Los Angeles]. He wasn't performing there; he was just hanging out and sitting in a corner, playing a Beatles song. I said, "Wow, man, you got the right idea."

And then David Crosby joined in, so there were the three of us. And then we saw Michael Clarke walking down the street, and he just *looked* the part, and we said, "Hey, can you play drums, man?" He said, "Yeah, I play drums." So I said, "Why don't you join us?"

Did he really play drums?

No, but he could fake it. And he faked it good, man, until he learned. When we started out, we couldn't even afford drums, so we got some cardboard boxes with a tambourine on one side and a cymbal on the other one, and that's what he played. But you'd be surprised how good the recording sounded.

Were you playing electric guitars?

We were playing our acoustics through an amp with pick-ups on. We all had acoustic twelve-strings—me, Crosby, and McGuinn. We were all twelve-string players.

When did you switch to electric instruments?

Well, we got somebody to back us a little bit and give us enough money to go and buy them. We had to buy a set of drums and electric guitars.

When you started the band, were you thinking of it as a rock group or a folk group?

We didn't have any particular concept. We just wanted to have a group. The Beatles were rather folk-rock themselves because they used a lot of really melodic melodies and a lot of harmonies and minor chords.

And so when I first started to hear The Beatles I said, "These guys are hot! I mean, they're wonderful, you know?" And immediately with McGuinn and Crosby, when people heard us sing, man, we were an instant success. *Instant.*

Everybody had us play at their parties. I remember Ian and Sylvia and us were all staying at the Tropicana Motel, and the two of them were flipping out. Hoyt Axton too. They all thought we really had something happening. Everybody else was putting us down, but Hoyt Axton and Ian and Sylvia, they loved us. They said, "Man, if you guys catch on, this could be really *big*."

Were you doing your own songs at first?

We started right out with our favorite Beatles songs, and then originals because we already had original stuff in that vein.

Did you and Roger switch off singing lead vocals?

On most of the records it's really him and I singing together in one voice.

In unison?

Yeah, in unison, exactly. And a lot of people don't know that. And David would sing harmony. Roger and I sang lead together; that's why the voice was so big on the early records.

On "Eight Miles High" and "Turn! Turn! Turn!" that's all McGuinn and myself singing dual leads. Because by himself, he has kind of a thin voice. And by myself, I have a very broad voice, right? You put the two together, right? If you check out some of those early Beatles records, Paul and John are singing in unison. Both harmony and unison.

I heard you say that Crosby was arrogant for someone with such an angelic voice.

Well, Roger and I went to watch him at the Monday night hootenanny at the Troubador, and this guy came onstage who I thought was a total jerk. Because he had such an arrogant, uppity attitude. But then when I heard him singing, it *blew* my mind.

I said to Roger, "There is our high voice. That's like our McCartney, right there," and Roger said, "I don't know, man. I've tried to work with him before." [*Laughter*] But David actually literally begged us to let him sing with us—that's no shit.

He literally begged us, and I said, "Yeah, let's do this," and Roger said, "I don't know, I don't know," and I said, "Come on, man, come on. You got to try. This is too good . . ."

And we'd go in the stairwell of the Troubadour, where there was an echo, and we would sing in there. People would hear us and just go *nuts*. They'd come in and say, "Wow, where are you guys at?"

Who came up with the name of the band?

McGuinn and I. At the Troubadour. And he added the Y. I came up with Birds, B-I-R-D-S, because of flying, you know, very high, evolved creatures. And then he said, "No, let's call it The Byrds, B-Y-R-D-S, like the A in Beatles."

Speaking of flying, do you recall writing "Eight Miles High"?

It really started when Roger and I were sitting on an airplane together. And I asked him, I said, "How high do you think we're going?"

He said, "Well, about forty thousand feet or so."

I said, "Well, how high is that?"

He said, "Maybe six miles high?"

And I said, "What a neat name for a song—'Six Miles High.'"

And he said, "No, six doesn't sound right. It's got to be eight miles high." [*Laughs*] That's how it started.

And then me and Brian Jones worked on it. Brian, he never wanted credit for it. But then he and I picked it up later down the line, the idea, and we groomed it for months. We presented it *back* to Crosby and Mc-Guinn, and they liked it so much that they really went really *deep* into it. So it ended up all three of us writing it, with Brian Jones uncredited.

Did you and Brian work here in Los Angeles?

No, in St. Louis, Missouri. To Pennsylvania. [*Laughs*]

You wrote the words?

I wrote all the words except for one line that David wrote, and then Roger arranged it, basically. So I had to part with something with those guys. I decided that I wasn't going to get a single out of this deal because I'd already written so many songs with this group that they were going to grab up the singles for their own stuff, and so I split it with them so I could get a single.

The Byrds, famously, had a big hit with "Mr. Tambourine Man" by Dylan. And that sound pretty much defined folk-rock.

Roger and I knew it was a hit. We were the only two who did. We were the only two people who did. Roger and I knew it was a hit; we knew we had a big record. Nobody else would believe it.

I loved the Dylan version. But, you know, we put it out before Dylan did. We sent him a letter asking him for permission to record a song that he hadn't recorded yet. So Albert Grossman, Dylan's manager, and Bob sent us back "Mr. Tambourine Man." It was so long that we had to cut it down to one verse and two choruses in order to keep the record under three minutes.

That was one of the most important records of my childhood—both the song itself and the sound: your harmonies and the guitars.

It was for a lot of people. You'd be surprised by how many people come up to me and say, "Hey, the first time I heard 'Feels a Whole Lot Better' I was laying in the mud in Vietnam getting shot at. Some guy had a little pocket radio. That song gave us faith, man." Guys would really say that.

Did you write that one yourself?

Yes, and Tom Petty gave me a great favor by recording it last year [on *Full Moon Fever*]. It sold 4 million copies. Their version is almost exactly the same as mine.

Do you remember writing that song?

It wasn't really *about* anything. It just kind of came along. It was just a feeling that came along. I wrote it in about twenty minutes, which is unusual. "Eight Miles High," as I said, took months.

"Turn! Turn! Turn!" was a huge hit for The Byrds, a song Pete Seeger adapted from the Bible. Whose idea was it to record that song?

McGuinn's wife at the time suggested doing that. He adapted it to an arrangement, which I worked on with him. I remember coming up with the intro lick and all that kind of stuff. Most of the really great things we did were mostly collaborations.

Pete Seeger said that he loved your version of the song, with all those jangly guitars and all.

That's cool. I would imagine he would like it. [*Laughs*] At first I didn't know if we should do it. But when I heard what McGuinn had in mind, how to execute the actual arrangement of it, then I realized we had something great there.

Did you want The Byrds to break up?

[*Loud sustained whisper*] No, no, certainly not. I think it was just that everybody was not ready for that kind of success. All at once we are thrown into being international and gigantic, international gurus. Nobody was really prepared for it. The management wasn't; the guys ourselves weren't. It was a mob scene on the street in daily life. What could you do? How could you handle it? Everybody sort of had a nervous breakdown. I know I did. And that's what really caused the breakup.

It had nothing to do with fear of flying or any of that stuff that the rumors said. It was just that none of us were really prepared to handle that kind of impact.

Would you like to have a reunion?

Sure, but I don't know if it will happen. It's hard to say.

Well, unlike The Beatles or The Stones or The Doors, everybody in The Byrds are still alive, so it could happen.

Yeah. I just don't see it happening for some reason.

Do you still spend a lot of time writing songs?

Yeah, that's why I am so tired today. Once I get going, I get this great streak going, and I can't stop. I write all the time. I write constantly. I have so much material that I have never recorded.

Writing is total sacrifice. People ask me what it takes to have the kind of reputation I have. I tell them total sacrifice. It's like being a ballet dancer. If you want to do it, you do it 100 percent. If you don't do it that way, you'll never get there. You have to give up a lot.

Being a good songwriter has to do with being a visionary, but what can you envision? I have maybe four dozen unpublished beautiful songs. I can't wait to get some of the new stuff I've written out. Some of it is very bouncy and up, and I'm very excited about it.

So I started a solo album next month. This is going to be a good year all the way around for me.

◆ ◆ ◆

Stephen Stills

The One You're With

Beverly Hills, California 2007

When he was a kid, just a few years after learning to walk, he learned to tap dance. One of his clearest memories is being three and sitting on a chair with tap shoes on and tapping rhythms onto a metal board. Rhythm is in his blood. The first instrument he mastered was not guitar but drums. "Rhythm is my thing," he said.

Today this same man is in his sixties and looks relaxed and happy as he sits in his location of choice, the legendary Polo Lounge at the Beverly Hills Hotel. It's a place one might more likely meet Liza Minelli than Stephen Stills, but I soon discover, upon his arrival, that he's quite at home here. He's got his own table under the sun-streamed windows, and the waiters all know him. He's got on sunglasses and a blue floral shirt and looks rested and healthy.

Not only is he forever famous for writing a profusion of classic songs, including "Suite: Judy Blue Eyes," "Love the One You're With," and "For What It's Worth," he was also the architect of the Crosby, Stills & Nash sound. His voice was one-third of their miraculous vocal blend, and his soul was thoroughly injected into all their records—in his passionate acoustic and electric guitar playing and also in his arrangements of their famous songs.

In fact, when bandmates Crosby and Nash were out at parties socializing and spreading this miracle news of a superband—Crosby from The Byrds, Nash from The Hollies, and Stills from Buffalo Springfield, united in song—Stills preferred to stay in the studio and work on the music.

"Stills played almost everything on the first album," said the late Dallas Taylor, who was their drummer. "Except for the drums, which I played, he played almost all the guitars—acoustic and electric—organ, piano, bass. He put it all together. He doesn't get that credit much, but Stills is a genius at production."

A great example is Graham Nash's "Teach Your Children," which started as a gentle and wispy ballad before Stills gave it a groove and transformed it into the country-tinged masterpiece we know. He scrutinized David Crosby's abstractly ingenious chords, figured them out (usually), and created a solid foundation for Crosby's asymmetrical musings. And when Neil Young joined the band, not only did Stills have a new sparring partner on guitar, he also had more songs in which he could infuse fire.

With a Groucho-esque glint in his eyes, he expresses admiration for the many long-legged women who pass by and peppers the conversations with a variety of funny non sequiturs, such as "I don't know about you, but I am *so* over tattoos." Asked if he's been writing any new songs lately, he says no and explains, "It's busy stuff with little kids." He has two kids at home right now, one three and one eleven, which he refers to as "the last litter." Asked how many he has altogether, he pauses and says, soberly, "Seven. So I'd better write some more songs," and then he laughs.

"This is all too complicated," he says to the waiter about the elaborate lunch menu we are offered, featuring dishes like osso buco that seem especially heavy and convoluted at eleven in the morning. "Can I get a breakfast menu, please?" he asks, and the waiter says, "Sure, you can have anything you want, Mr. Stills. You know that."

"Yeah, I know that," he says knowingly to me. He smiles 'cause it's true. He can have anything he wants—not just in terms of this morning meal, but in life. And he's earned it. The man has been in the trenches and emerged triumphant, a real guitar hero whose chops only get better as time goes on and a man who has succeeded in fusing expansive lyricism with visceral music better than just about anyone this side of Bob Dylan. "I'd like a bacon sandwich, or something like that." Soon he orders eggs Benedict, apologetically explaining, "It's bad for me, but I'm gonna do it anyways. I love it." It's the same apologetic tone he adopts when, later, waiting for cars at the valet, his giant Mercedes is brought to him. "I'll get a Prius one of these days, I promise."

Not only is he a great songwriter and singer, but as his fans know well, he is also a real guitar hero. He was pals with Jimi Hendrix back in the day, and there are recordings of them together, each matching the other's intensity and soul. Though the man, like Neil Young, can play the part of a folkie quite convincingly, at his heart he is a rocker—and a great one.

Last time I saw him perform with CSN was in Orange Beach, Alabama, also known as the Riviera of the South, in 2010, while working with Henry Diltz on a documentary about CSN and their pals and peers called *Legends of the Canyon*. [To make the tour work best, each member of CSN had their own bus.] The singing of CSN was as beautiful as ever. But Stills's electric guitar playing was simply transcendent. He was on fire. He's always a fine lead player, but on this night he seemed to reach a whole other realm.

After the show, I told him how amazing the guitar playing was. "It should be," he said with a laugh. "I have been doing it for more than forty years. You would think I would get better!" I mentioned that he's also been writing songs for that long—so did that get better too? "No," he said flatly. "No, that just gets harder."

Born on January 3, 1945, in Dallas, Texas, he was raised in a military family that was always on the move. His childhood included time in Florida, Louisiana, Costa Rica, Panama, and El Salvador—a mixture of cultures that shaped his musical soul. His music was all over the map, literally and figuratively, from joining the rock band The Continentals early on to joining the folkies onstage solo at Gerde's in Greenwich Village, where Dylan started. With Richie Furay he became part of the Au Go-Go Singers before the two of them ultimately teamed up with a Canadian named Neil Young to form Buffalo Springfield. Their biggest hit, "For What It's Worth," was written by Stills, discussed in the following interview.

His genius for writing songs then—and a lot of powerful ones—is reflected now in a remarkable recording just released prior to this conversation, *Just Roll Tape*, an album he made in a couple of hours in April of 1968 after his girlfriend Judy Collins wrapped up recording for the day and he wanted to preserve some of his new songs. Successive master-pieces came rolling out: the expansive, amazing "Suite: Judy Blue Eyes," in which he expanded the song form into a suite in a way nobody—save those Liverpool lads on their *Abbey Road* medley—had done quite the same way. Also "Helplessly Hoping," "Change Partners," "Wooden Ships," and more. Even delightful and mysterious fragments that could have been expanded into full songs or more but were never developed are there, such as "Dreaming of Snakes," which has all the makings of a Stills classic.

Hearing him play and sing these famous songs is a revelation—the confidence and power he exudes even solo in the studio is stunning, and for the first time we discover which part was the actual melody. "We were very clever boys," he says coyly about the intricate harmony arrangements he cooked up with CSN.

No sign of the notorious Stills temperament surfaces except for the occasional slightly irritated "obviously" offered as an answer to questions he doesn't feel need to be posed. But mostly he seems quite happy in his life, in his world, and he kindly subjugates himself to a gentle interrogation.

You seem happy. Can you write when you are happy?

Stephen Stills: Sometimes. I have these little starts of songs, and then I have to think hard if I have already written that. [*Laughs*]

Do you need turmoil or melancholy in your life to write good songs?

Yeah. Or they come out sounding like Lawrence Welk. [*Laughs*] Go to work for Disney when you feel like that. [*Laughter*] Some songs are hard to write when you're happy.

I Love the *Just Roll Tape* album—

Yeah, my briefcase was such a mess, I had to get those down on tape before I forgot them. [*Laughs*]

Many of those songs, such as "Suite: Judy Blue Eyes" and "Wooden Ships," became famous with CSN. But did you write those before you guys got together?

Yeah. I think I'd just come from Miami and David's boat. "Wooden Ships" was brand new. Of course, timelines back then. You know the old saying, "If you remember the sixties, you probably weren't there."

Right. Though Graham Nash seems to remember a lot.

Not everything, though. [*Laughs*]

"Wooden Ships" is credited to you, Crosby, and Paul Kantner.

Yes. They were on the boat when I arrived. Crosby had a little bit of the first part and Kantner had a little bit of the second part. And then it kept drifting around. So I went down below deck and finished it off. Everyone else was up watching the stars or whatever, and I polished it off. And then I came back and said, "How do you like your song?" [*Laughter*] And you could sort of hear that in that rendition.

Did you three discuss what it was about, or did you write it instinctually?

Dude, there's no telling what we discussed that evening. [*Laughter*] It was one of those overwrought hippie things. I don't know—it's hard to say now what we were talking about. The boat was humming, if you will.

It's interesting that back at this time all your peers were writing songs of the conventional length, and then you wrote "Suite: Judy Blue Eyes," this expansive and amazing suite, which expanded the song form in a way nobody had considered. How did that happen?

It started out as little bits, and all of a sudden I realized that they fit together, and one thing led to another, but nothing was finished. I actually liked the way that I did it on *Just Roll Tape*, but I realized that with other people involved it would be hard for them to pick up. Because only half of it is half-time. Three-quarters of it is in the same tempo as the first part, and then it changes. It's a little more legato.

On this version you stop and change the tuning.

Maybe. Maybe. I'll tell you the truth about that. I figured that if I stayed hands-off I would have a better chance of getting it in pure form. So when I listened to everything [on that tape] I only listened once and made notes and just said that we're keeping everything in the same order. Just put it out that way. So I know there were noises in it, and I said, "No, leave that in," and there was talking.

I had a little chart that said, "The good, the bad, and the ugly, and conclusions." There were only three things that I knew would never see the light of day. There was some babbling. Some people liked that, but it wasn't even musical babbling.

It's cool to hear you tuning, in that everyone nowadays uses tuners to tune, but you tuned very fast between tunings, and there's a confidence there.

[*Laughs*] That's cool. If you notice, at Woodstock, in the film, at the beginning when we first start. A warm, wet wind had just hit the guitars. So there were a few seconds of tuning the guitar and then we walked out. But if you notice on the film, we start "Suite: Judy Blue Eyes," it was horrifyingly out of tune. And luckily I was the *only* one at Woodstock who was straight. There were too many people, and I didn't want to relinquish any control whatsoever. At least until after I played. [*Laughs*]

When you were putting "Suite: Judy Blue Eyes" together, did you think that a song shouldn't be that long?

No, no, no. I'd been to school and had played lots of overtures and things like that. I grew up on "Rhapsody in Blue" and things like that. So this was just doing the same thing with words. I certainly never worried about it. And it wasn't that long anyway; it was only seven minutes. But they still wouldn't put it out as a single. And I said, "You guys are nuts," and then, sure enough, it wasn't eighteen months until somebody put out something just as long. And how long is "Stairway to Heaven"?

Part of the reason we had gone to Atlantic was because they were adventurous. I mean, Ahmet [Ertegün] loved it. But he wouldn't put it out. So I said, "Do what you did with Ray Charles. Put out half of it." I didn't care.

On *Just Roll Tape* you don't have the ending of "Suite: Judy Blue Eyes," the "doo doo doo doo doo" part. Did that come later?

That was an afterthought that seemed fun. Basically what happened is that we sang that whole album in people's living rooms ad nauseum. So things had time to develop. It was almost like road testing it. Which is what I like to do before I make records now. Teach it to the band and play them in the show and see how people react.

The vocal blend of CSN was miraculous—

That's your word, miraculous.

Yes, it is. But when the three of you would sit down and sing, were people blown away? What kind of reaction would you get?

I guess they were blown away. Crosby thought so. [*Laughs*]

You were at such a creative peak at the time of *Just Roll Tape*. What happened to allow so many great songs to come then?

I don't know. The *Manassas* album ended up being a double album because I had so many songs. I don't know if they were all so good. There was a period there when I was writing lots and couldn't keep up. But I could never be like Neil [Young] and basically write an album and record it in a week. You know, *fuck* him. There are people who can do that—

Not many.

No, not many. Who can do that? I take them as they come. And right now I'm waiting. Or gestating. I don't know which.

Some songwriters feel they are receivers, and songs come through them from beyond. Others feel it's a conscious process and comes from them. How do you feel about it?

Both. [*Laughs*] When you're compelled to write, as I am sometimes, when you are writing social commentary, it comes through you. It's conscious and unconscious. Sometimes you feel I have to say something about this. But there are a lot of them that are the result of a lot of good craftsmanship.

A lot of them come from just keeping yourself open. I mean, where could "Eleanor Rigby" have come from other than taking a walk and seeing this little church. I mean, what a great story. A couple of my friends, actually, when they have got to write some songs, they can write on assignment a lot better than I can. They go for a walk. New York City is better for that than LA.

But these songs, I didn't write them all at one time. This was just the first crack at a tape recorder I had. There were some other demos. Judy [Collins] wanted me to play guitar, and then I took the studio after she was finished. The last thing she said was, "Don't stay all night, 'cause I need you fresh tomorrow." And I didn't. I stayed just as long as it took to record all those songs one time. *Just Roll Tape* was my way of keeping my word to Judy.

She left?

Yeah, I couldn't have done it with her there.

"Suite: Judy Blue Eyes" was written for her?

Yeah, of course. She called me up and said, "Gosh, it was like getting a love letter after all these years."

Yet it has mixed emotion in it. You say, "You make it hard."

Yeah. But she does. She did. It was so long ago. And that's another charm of it. It was so long ago.

As you said, your songs are both consciously and unconsciously created. There's that expansive poetic feeling but also a conscious focus on craft elements, such as the alliteration in "Helplessly Hoping."

A lot of alliteration for a cautious cowboy. [*Laughs*] When I did the first few lines like that, I thought, "How long can I keep this going?"

[*Laughs*] It's basically a country song, and it sings like that. It really wants the brushes on the drums. That's what we intended it to be, and we still do it in the same key. It was meant to be sung like that. It's in G, though it starts on an A minor.

It's fascinating to hear, on *Just Roll Tape*, songs like "Helplessly Hoping" and "Suite," because it was never obvious, from hearing the CSN versions, which part was the melody, and now we hear it.

Yeah. In some cases, being the one with the highest falsetto, I was the one who ended up with the castrato part. And basically when I do it myself, I'm happy to be back on the melody.

I always thought Graham had the highest parts—

Graham doesn't have a falsetto. He just sings really high. When we sing "Suite," for example, I'm way on top.

Is that how you would always do the vocals for CSN—with you on top?

Well, we were very clever boys. And we changed it all the time. For no reason at all. It's kind of like "stump the band."

Graham told me CSN was born when you and David were singing your song "You Don't Have to Cry," and he heard it, listened a couple of times, and then added the third part.

Right. It was at Cass Elliot's house in the dining room. Some people said it was at Joni's house, but they're wrong and I'm right.

You are so self-contained. You could have easily done a solo thing then instead of getting into another band—

Yeah, but I'm a band guy. Back in the day, when I was in New York City doing the solo coffeehouse circuit, I was miserable. Yeah, 'cause I played drums in school. I'm a band guy, I really am. I love the camaraderie and stuff. I must say, my more recent tours, we do "Helplessly Hoping" with the band, and then I do an hour solo set, telling stories and singing, and I love that. But I love when the band then comes back and I get to play rock and roll. I'm in a really good spot now—I can do both.

You're one of the few who is a great acoustic guitarist, but you've always been a burning electric player too.

I want to keep flaming while I can.

And you're playing better than ever lately—

The longer you do it, the better you get.

Is that true with songwriting as well?

No. Those first passionate ones are really special. And later in life you might get deeper and more resonant and more crafted, but they're not as free as those first ones. That's kind of logical, isn't it? Sometimes you end up out-crafting yourself. Which is why I admire Bob Dylan so much. He's managed not to do that.

What do you mean by out-crafting?

You get too cute. Losing the point. Getting contrived.

James Taylor told us he was able to write his first songs like "Fire and Rain" because he felt no one was listening. Yet with these songs you were already famous, having been in Buffalo Springfield.

True. But it took a while for my craft to develop. And you have to remember, James is a really shy guy. I know that because I am too. Though there's this ham in me.

Your song "For What It's Worth" is a classic and reflective of a chapter in American history. How was that born?

I had a house in Topanga. Me and a friend of mine drove the 101 and went over Laurel Canyon, figuring to go clubbing. We were young and bored. We come down to the corner of Crescent Heights and Sunset. On one side of the street was that silly little bar, and on the other side was this whole troop of cops, this battalion. Full Macedonian battle array. I thought, "What the . . .?"

I had been working on this song about guys in Vietnam. And of course, we did consider turning around. But we got out of the car to see what was happening, and they said there was this funeral going on for [the club] Pandora's Box, and the cops all showed up, 'cause it was spilling out onto the street. But the cops were really testy. They just went *nuts*.

So I said to my friend, "Get me back to my guitar." I wrote it in about fifteen minutes. Everyone heard the song and loved it, and Ahmet [Ertegün] said, "You have to record it." We had a record in the pipeline, and he said, "Stop the presses," and we had it out in seven days. Which is a trick that people have been trying to replicate ever since.

Such inspired, powerful writing. "Paranoia strikes deep, into your life it will creep"—

That's an example of it just flowing.

You said you needed to get back to your guitar to write. Do you always write at the guitar?

No. Sometimes I write them in my head. And I'm very shocked when it comes out like I thought it would. Sometimes I write at the piano. Sometimes at the typewriter, and then work on the music. Get a little hook line. But those can turn into real torture. I recorded one of Dylan's songs. For phrasing sake, I changed a lot of words, mostly adjectives and pronouns. Graham *freaks out*! He said [*in British accent*], "You changed seventeen Bob Dylan words!" [*Laughter*] I got Bobby on the phone, and he said, "Does it still mean the same?" I said, "Sure it does." He said, "Well, send it to me. I'm sure it will be fine. I never know how they go until I sing them." [*Laughs*] He said, "I wrote too many words, and getting them out is tough."

In CSN not only did you write amazing songs, but you also powerfully guided the shape of others. Graham played me the original demo of "Teach Your Children," and it was kind of a lilting English folk ballad. You created that great track—with Dallas Taylor on drums—and made it groove.

That's part of the fun of being in a band. Graham saved me from a couple of disasters too. Mainly I have the whole line, but I was missing a payoff. And we really wanted to cut it. And Graham is really great at coming up with a missing line. And it was like, "Of course!" 'Cause I'd been all around the park, trying to come up with something. And that's part of being in a band.

But when it would come to the groove of a song—

You don't argue with me. I'm the groove guy.

Yeah, it seems like that. 'Cause your songs are so rhythmic—

I played drums first. And basically the first thing I did artistically, when I was about three, I took tap dancing lessons. So rhythm is my thing.

You have the rep for being the guiding spirit in the studio of CSN, like the Brian Wilson of the band. Accurate?

Considering how many hits Graham Nash had, it was pretty cheeky of me. But Graham was my biggest fan. He would egg me on.

To get the CSN vocal blend in the studio, would you all sing at the same time?

Yes. And we'd all sing on one mic. Then we got lazy and were impatient. I'm a little slower in learning parts that are odd. And in some of those intricate ones I would be slower and Crosby would get frustrated, so we ended up singing them one at a time. Which I thought was a big mistake. But that was later on.

At first we always sang them gathered around a big mic. If you have a beautiful Neumann 87 in front of you, it sounded so good. Back when I started singing with ensemble singing groups, the mic would be at least three feet away. And you'd stand back from it, and the mic would capture the blend. And then when we started playing electric, everybody had to get really close, so the sound engineer said we had to be real close to the mic. Well, no, you need to put a wall of foam in front of the band. I still think at least six inches away from the mic. My voice sounds too heavy if it's miked too close. Where you stand from the mic is everything. Miking is all. You can learn what everything does, but what separates the men from the boys is where you place the mic. With relationship from the band or the voice or the strings. Often it would sound almost right and the engineer would say, "Okay, Crosby, take one step backward," or "Graham, take one giant step backward."

With a song like "Suite" did you do the entire song from start to end?
Yes.

Would it take many takes?
Yes.

On *Just Roll Tape* you have the song "Dreaming of Snakes," which is great.
I hardly remember it. It was probably after some nightmare. And I woke up and made myself write that right away.

It's great, but it seems unfinished.
Someone ought to finish it. And it would be great for strings. And it moves at the tempo that a snake does.

I also like the song "Bumblebee."
Yeah, it's great, had a great groove. But it's fast. It sounded like the Chipmunks playing B. B. King. [*Laughter*]

Did you ever want to do more with that song?
A lot of those lines ended up in different songs.

Yeah, it's the first mention of a "love gangster," which became an entire song.
Yeah. Poaching. Like cannibalizing a car for parts. I would do that song a lot slower. A *lot* slower. I would do it like a Tex-Mex shuffle, like Stevie Ray Vaughan.

Dylan said one of the saddest things about songwriting is trying to re-connect with an idea you had before and didn't finish.

He's absolutely right about that. That happens to me when writing prose. You start digressing and think, "Shit, I got to get back to that."

"49 Bye-Byes" was another one which was a suite, with many sections and tempo shifts. Did you also write that one in separate parts?

No, that one I planned that way, because it worked so well the first time. [*Laughter*] There's a version out there in which I play everything. It's when I realized I totally lost all my drum chops. [*Laughs*]

When we, as your fans, first heard the sound of CSN singing together, it sounded so amazing. How did it sound to you?

Obviously it was the same for us. But it ceased to be so miraculous after the first temper tantrum. [*Laughter*]

Were all three of you having those?

I could be temperamental back then. But I got over it. It was a deal I made with my wife. I don't like yelling. I heard enough of it from my father.

Your songs have a folk-rock feel, but there's so much soul in your singing. "Carry On" is a good example of that—

Well, when I was a kid I would listen to the Wolfman Jack show, and I got that. And also there was a black station that played all the soul groups. All of what would have been called race records had it not been for Ahmet Ertegün. I *loved* that stuff. Old blues. Me and my best friend, Mike, who is still one of my best friends, we would think nothing of driving two hundred miles to go to an old record store and sift through old 78s looking for blues records on Arhoolie and Brunswick or whatever.

This album has a great blues, "Treetop Flyer," in which you really jam on the blues, but solo, like a great old bluesman. You play lead and rhythm at the same time.

Yeah, that's why they call me Captain. [*Laughs*] That's one of the first times that it was performed. And I'd just taken delivery of a dobro made of brass, and that's why it sounds like two guitars, 'cause I was just fingerpicking it and it had so much resonance. I was fingerpicking and using a bottle neck. And that is pure, that track. There's no overdubbing on it, no electrics. It's an acoustic album.

I understood you brought Neil Young into CSN because you wanted another guitarist with whom to spar.

I definitely wanted another musician. And first we wanted John Sebastian. But he had his own plan. I was thinking a keyboard player. But Ahmet brought it up, getting Neil. But it was odd, because he [Neil] had already walked out on me once, in Buffalo Springfield. At a pretty critical time. It turned out to be a pretty good match. There was always a bond between us from the very beginning.

You are an accomplished and prolific songwriter. Was it tough to have to share songwriting with the others and only have a few songs on an album?

Sometimes. But that turned into solo careers. Neil quickly discovered that's where you get *all* the money. [*Laughs*] It got crowded. But that's okay. Life gives you the curves it does.

When you would write a song for the group, would you think of the harmonies, or would they come up with them?

Both. Sometimes I would have it all planned, and they would pretty much expect that. And David was really good at finding the really cool, weird part.

Is he usually the middle part?

We really wanted you guys to be just as confused as you obviously are. So I'm not telling. [*Laughs*]

Those parts cross and overlap, so it's impossible to figure it out.

Exactly. One of the secrets of singing ensemble is imitating each other.

Would it take intense rehearsal to get the phrasing so perfect?

No, we were very lazy. But it was so much fun to hear ourselves that they were easy.

What was it like in CSN or CSNY when someone would have a new song?

The torturous time was when you would go, "Huh? Okay." [*Laughs*] And then you wouldn't know exactly how to put it. "I don't know what to do on this one, so I'll just be quiet for a while, and maybe something will occur to me." [*Laughs*] When Crosby got more and more into unusual tunings, so that I couldn't play along, I had to go through hell. A lot of those chords wouldn't have a root. The bottom note on the guitar was not necessarily the root, so I had to go find them for him. And then he would say, "That's the wrong chord." I'd think about it and play it again and say, "No, it isn't." [*Laughs*] I had enough training so that I was *usually* right. And then there were chords that escaped me for years. Then I'd finally figure out one little thing. And I'd say, "Oh, I've been playing this wrong. Like for ten years. [*Laughs*] I'm so sorry!"

Were the arrangements for all the songs usually something you did?

As time has gone by, everybody says no, but actually, yes. [*Laughter*]

Did you cut things live with drums and bass?

Because of the way we wanted to do vocals, we had to do them separately, which we got used to. But now I have learned how to sing the lead vocal live while playing with the band, usually by having a long guitar chord and getting in an iso booth.

Would you sing a scratch vocal back then when laying down the rhythm track?

Yes.

"Love the One You're With" is another classic you wrote, and it's one people respond to—

Actually I was sitting with Mac Davis. He wrote a whole bunch of songs for Elvis. And there was a civil war back then between Elvis people and Beatle people. And Elvis lost me at "Blue Moon of Kentucky." He lost me when he took on Colonel Tom. Who wrapped him in a Confederate flag.

There's a song Mac wrote for Elvis about "a little less conversation, a little more action." He and I have written the two most sexist songs alive, between those two, if you take "Love the One You're With" on the surface level. But it has a lot of other meanings. It's multilayered. But it can be called a paean to promiscuity, if you will. A lot of people said, "Yeah, I got laid to that song." [*Laughs*] Which I used to consider my job. It was the seventies, you know?

Was there somebody you were with when you wrote it?

Not really. It was basically what was going on with everybody at that time. I was in London at the time, and everybody was changing partners. There was a lot of that going around. Being on the road. It evolved.

Did you write "Change Partners" then too?

No. I wrote that earlier. That was about being in high school and the tea cotillion parties then. Being a teenager in the late fifties, early sixties, that was what life was like.

The song "4 + 20" is a mythical song. Did it come from the old nursery rhyme about "four and twenty blackbirds"?

A miracle of free association.

The line that always got me was "I embrace the many-colored beast / I grow weary of the torment, can there be no peace?"

Hey, when you get that deep into depression you feel that.

Did that come out of deep depression?

Obviously. I mean, listen to the song. It's pretty self-explanatory.

But many songwriters only write about deep depression after they've come out of it, not when they're in it.

That ended it. I wrote that song, and the minute I sang that last line I knew the depression was over.

Do you have favorite keys to play in?

There are easy keys to play in as a guitar player. That's why people use capos. But capos are a trap. I hate them. If you want to play in B flat, I'll figure it out. But for songwriters who play with a band, it can get you into trouble.

So you never use a capo to write a song?

No.

Do you feel each key has its own color or feeling?

Of course. It's a sonic thing.

I know you use E minor a lot. You like that one?

Yeah. And I like B minor. I like B flat too. It's a horn key.

"Carry On" is a joyful song.

We needed an opener for an album. A lot of songs would come that way. We would need a song. And I would figure out a song to fill the hole. And it would be a race between me and Graham to figure out a song to fit. I'd say, "I know what we need. I'll be back tomorrow." And I'd go home and get the majority of the song. "Carry On" was one of those. And putting it with the song "Questions" was a studio afterthought.

Was there always a competition among you, like as to whose song would be the opener?

A friendly competition. At least in the first years. It was like puppies. Like little kittens.

And then by *Four-Way Street* **there was a sense that you were each going your own way—**

Yeah. That turned into a difficult time. As he will readily admit, some of that was Neil's doing, because the man has control issues. [*Laughs*] As he will freely admit.

Did you want to leave the group at that time?

Yeah. I was overburdened with songs. And rather than jamming the songs, I wanted to get back to more organized stuff. That whole San Francisco Grateful Dead, just play whatever you want, it will all be great—sorry, it was lost on me.

When you were with the group did you envision that it would go on for a long time, or did you always intend there just to be a few albums?

We have said this at least a million times in interviews: the whole reason for using our names was so we could do that. Like Merrill Lynch. We found a way to sound mellifluous. Rather than some animal name or the Electric Prunes. Or some ridiculous thing that would come out of Crosby's imagination.

Who devised the order of the names?

It just sounded best that way. And I said to David, considering your personality, how could you not be first? [*Laughs*] But Neil and I, unfortunately it was taken, during the 2000 rehearsal we came up with the name SYNC. [*Laughs*] Stills, Young, Nash, and Crosby. [*Laughs*]

You said you and Graham would go home and compete as to who got the opening song. Was David outside of that equation?

No, he just wasn't that fast, and he'd be the first one to admit it. He said, "I can't do that."

Were there songs that got rejected?

Yeah. We'd say, "That's not ready yet." It was friendly.

Do you recall writing "Dark Star"?

Yeah. Actually, the version that got recorded—and I think it was a drug-induced mistake—we didn't remember how to stay in the same key, and we ended up with a key change. The way I do it now has no key change. I remember people saying, "What are the changes?" and I came up with them, and they were wrong. The way it is on the live album is how it should be.

Did drugs ever help you write songs, or did they get in the way?

Getting in the way was not an option. People would come in and finish off lines. That's part of being in a band. But there were manners involved. People might have thought that I got in the way, but that was only later. Way later. In the eighties. I hated the eighties. Bad drugs, bad music, bad everything.

With you guys, Dylan, and The Beatles, music changed so much. And it never really got better than that. Did you feel that, that it would change more?

I thought more new than this. There's a throwback every now and then to something great. But the rap has had a terrible influence. They squash too many syllables into every sentence. But it's not like Dylan. It's like running off at the mouth. Like recording your coke rap. [*Laughs*] I can't stand it. There are some profound things in hip-hop, but for the most part I don't get it. Are you a poet or a musician? I just don't want to be yelled at.

Are you surprised that the music you made and that was made by your peers has as much meaning today as it does?

Well, when I was a kid, the music of World War II was still just as meaningful. I think our music will last about the same amount of time. There's always a resurgence of the old stuff. Look at Tony Bennett. He hasn't changed his style. It's *adorable*. It's wonderful. It's everything it's supposed to be. It's good to refer back to that kind of stuff, even before us and The Beatles and the Stones.

I love the Rolling Stones just as much as The Beatles. Keith still inspires the fuck out of me. And watching Mick Jagger do forty-yard wind-sprints at the age of sixty-five is devastatingly annoying.

With you guys, it wasn't only the music; it was the image. I know Henry Diltz well, and his photos of you just showed what seemed to me like the coolest guys alive, like on the first CSN album.

Well, that whole concept was born in England, because of the light in England. The Beatles looked like really interesting cats in all those photos, but when you actually got next to them, they were pretty homely looking. Except for Paul. But the light was really gray—for that whole decade—from the mid-fifties on. Somebody pointed out to me, I think it was Billy J. Kramer—that it rained in England from 1957 to 1959. Virtually 365 days a year. So everybody was inside all the time. And that's when everybody got good because they were always inside listening to music and playing music. Because they weren't adept at playing football or any sport, and even cricket was very hard in the mud. But they also created that wonderful covered light, which was great for black and white photos. So you guys did need a visual aid? [*Laughs*]

Well, those photos were great. Henry said that first CSN cover was taken at an old house on Palm in West Hollywood.

Yeah. It was torn down the next day.

"I Give, You Give Blind." Where did that one come from?

I don't remember. It came quickly. It needed strings. And it needed slowing down. It was recorded too fast. Too quickly for what it was. It needed to be just a little bit slower. It was a little rushed. And if it had real strings doing that line, it would have been better.

Were you a kid when you wrote your first song?

I was nineteen, I think. I was already out of the house. Already been in and out of college.

A lot of your friends felt that they would stop playing music at thirty-five or so.

Not me. I always knew I'd keep doing it. Everything else seemed like a crushing bore. Sportswriter, maybe.

Are you optimistic about your future, where you're going musically?

No one in their sixties is optimistic about their future. [*Laughs*] Except politicians. You remember back in the day when nothing hurt and you had a thirty-inch waist.

◆ ◆ ◆

Paul Simon
Love and Hard Times
Beverly Hills, California 2011

"It's all I do," he said more than once in regard to writing songs and making records. Which, to students of songwriting, is tantamount to Picasso saying, "All I do is paint." Yeah, true, but those paintings, Pablo, you know, they're pretty good.

Of course, Picasso did more than paint—he also sculpted and wrote poetry and danced and loved. And Paul Simon, who, weeks away from his seventieth birthday and seeming more than ever like the Picasso of popular song, does do more than write songs, of course. He also turns those songs into records, an art and science perhaps more tricky and elusive even than songwriting itself—and one that, he says in the following, he prefers to writing songs.

He's also, of course, one of the planet's most beloved and familiar vocalists; the sound of his singing, like that of his friends James Taylor and Paul McCartney, is one of the most consistently compelling ingredients of popular music through the past several decades. Also, like both

McCartney and Taylor, he's a seriously gifted musician, a guitarist who has consistently found new ways to express himself on this instrument he's been playing since he was a kid.

"Nothing I do on guitar is very difficult," he said. Which might be technically true, but what he does is ingenious, using the range and tuning of the guitar to find chords and harmonic passages that, though simple for him to execute, sound anything but simple. He's done it since the start— the cascading introduction to "Scarborough Fair" is a good example.

To show an example, he took out his acoustic Martin and played me the haunting chord that starts "Questions for the Angels" (B minor-add 2/D). It sang like an extended jazz chord but with the guitaristic sweetness of open strings resounding. He also showed off a nifty transition from an Eb/Bb to an Em7/B that he said he'd used several times and that sounds very Simon: both simple and complex at once—and elegant.

It's not the first time over the years that, in place of words, he's shown me passages on guitar that he discovered and that served as the foundations of certain songs. (And being a Simon devotee, admittedly, I always have practiced and learned them. To me, it's like being given baseball tips from DiMaggio.) It's always been revelatory to recognize that something both musical and momentous—a Paul Simon song—is built on humble origins, these inspired guitar progressions he shows off with a gentle, parental pride.

After his work on *Graceland* he did the same thing, happily showing the partial chords in different registers he learned from African musicians and that—although simple to play—aren't in the usual American bag of tricks. He's a guy who collects this stuff and keeps it all close at hand, like a painter with many brushes.

"Songwriting is like you're wandering down a path," he said, sitting in the soft morning sunlight that sings of Southern California, "and you don't know what the destination is. Somewhere toward the end you can sort of see what the destination is and you can understand what the journey is about." It's that mystery that distinguishes songwriting from more conventional human pursuits, the fact that, unlike most professions, in songwriting there's no repeatable method of accomplishment. Even someone as dedicated, brilliant, and studied as Simon still essentially reaches into the darkness, uncertain of what will be received. It's about a conscious reach into the unconscious, a knowing venture into the unknown, the destination forever unknown until you find yourself there. It takes a certain kind of creative bravado—chutzpah, if you will—to even want to go there.

Even Herbie Hancock, who surely knows the piano keyboard better than almost all other humans, told me that there's always new musical ground to be discovered right there on the same keys he's been playing forever. "It's endless," he said.

When I told Paul this, he laughed and said it's endless for him as well. "If it's endless for Herbie," he said, "you can be *sure* it's endless for me too."

Unless, of course, you're content repeating yourself. But Paul Simon, more dramatically than most of his peers, has gone to great lengths, literally, not to repeat himself. He's gone around the globe—to Jamaica for the track that became the first reggae-tinged hit ever in America, "Mother and Child Reunion," to New Orleans for "Loves Me Like a Rock," to Africa for the tracks that became the landmark *Graceland*, to Brazil for *The Rhythm of the Saints*.

This interview was set up to coincide with the release of his album *So Beautiful or So What*, for which, instead of traveling to distant lands, he journeyed into the past. Lovingly looped on several tracks are great recordings from the dawn of recorded music. "Love Is Eternal Sacred Light" boasts a great locomotive-charged harmonica exhortation by none other than Sonny Terry, sampled from his 1938 "Train Whistle Blues," while "Getting Ready for Christmas Day" is woven tenderly around samples of a 1941 sermon delivered with much fire and brimstone by the Reverend J. M. Gates and his congregation. Rather than ignore the potential of digital innovations such as loops and samples, Simon embraces them: not only is the potential for discovering new music endless, so is the sonic potential of any record, now more than ever.

Graceland was the start of a radical new approach to writing songs for Simon, which was creating the record first—the musical track—and then writing the song to fit the track. It led to some of the most exultant and dimensional music of his career. And so he continued using this method for the next many albums, concocting compelling music tracks, editing them into a song form, and then writing words and melodies to fit.

But for his latest album, evidently ripe to walk a fresh musical avenue, he returned after more than a decade away to the simple dynamic of acoustic guitar and voice. Asked how he felt doing it, he said, "Awkward at first."

The first song he created this way was "Amulet," which he then felt was too complex for lyrics, and so he kept it as an instrumental on the record. But the next one that came was also a composition of much complexity but with a melody that led him to one of his most poignant lyrics, "Love and Hard Times." In a narrative that crosscuts remarkably from a funny earthly visitation from God and Jesus to a remarkably intimate glimpse of a marriage, in language both literary and domestic, with the home so quiet that you hear it breathing in "clicks and clacks," comes the ultimate conclusion, the one we reach in that still middle of the night, gratitude for real love.

Today he's staying at the grand pink lady of Beverly Hills, the Beverly Hills Hotel, where movie stars have stayed and played for many decades. It's the day after three sold-out concerts in Hollywood. Rather than play large arenas, as he has often done in Los Angeles, he's playing some old, intimate theaters, like the Henry Fonda Theatre. His concerts, weaving together as they do so many decades of beloved songs, are inspirational and euphoric.

A friend worried aloud that Donald Trump is making waves, and Paul dismissed it like a bad joke. "Nobody's listening," he said. He's more interested in what Ben Witherington, a seminary professor at Asbury Theological Seminary, wrote about him in *Christian Today*: although the previous album was entitled *Surprise*, this one is the surprise, as its message throughout is spiritual. "I think Paul is being made God's music even now," wrote Witherington. "He just isn't fully aware of it."

Asked if he felt this was accurate, true to his nature, Simon wasn't sure. "Generally I feel it's just a lot of good luck. Or the harder you work, the luckier you get. But I look on it as luck."

He's seems happy, relaxed, and very much in love with his wife of many years, Edie Brickell, and their kids. It's a sense of spiritual harmony that permeates all of *So Beautiful or So What*, the only album he created in his own home. This native New Yorker, long one of Manhattan's most famous faces, has actually left New York—but not too far—and moved with his family to rural Connecticut, and it's there, in a little house next to his big one, he created a studio to record this album.

It's also a warmly familial lifestyle change and speaks to the depth of his love for his wife and kids. As opposed to the isolated soul "stranded in a limousine" whose life slip-slides away as depicted in earlier songs, he's happily working on lyrics in his head while picking up the kids from school or coaching Little League. "You know that motion you make with your arms to call the runner on third to run home?" he said. "I do that a lot now, even when I'm not coaching."

Last time we spoke you told me you were more interested in what you discover than what you invent. Is that still the case?

Paul Simon: Yeah. It's like you're wandering down a path or a road, and you don't know what the destination is. Somewhere toward the end you can sort of see what the destination is and you can understand what the journey is about. At which point, if I want, I can go alter some of the things that occurred to set it up. But usually I don't. It usually just goes along as a story that I'm telling, and I'm a listener, and at a certain point I say, "Oh! That's what it's about."

You said you can intuit meaning when lines start emerging. Do you give a lot of thought to the meaning while writing?

No, I'm not giving a *lot* of thought to it. The only thought that I give to it is "Is that something that I really believe?" It doesn't have to be *insightful* or anything. It just has to be not a lie. I can't say, "I'm setting out to write a really deep, philosophical song." I would never say that. I have no idea.

And most of the time, most of the songs have jokes in them or almost little sarcastic things or purposely kitsch or something. So that's going along with a story, like I do in life, just talking to myself and making fun of stuff and laughing at stuff that's serious. And sometimes it's a good idea to put the laughing into the songs. Sometimes it's not. Sometimes it's all right just to be serious. But most of the songs have some kind of joke in them.

"Love and Hard Times" is so rich melodically, and the tune is, as you said, quite complex. But I find that complexity gives it more strength and richness.

Well, thank you. You know, it's more literary as an idea than I usually write. Meaning that it started a theme, it wandered away from the theme, and then came back at the end to refer to the theme again, but from a different angle and in a different way, which made for a complete cycle lyrically—that was interesting. Because it started with God and God leaving and then it ended with "Thank God I found you." That was really the payoff to the whole thing. Because He left.

We generally think of songs as confessional, about the songwriter, or a story song. Yet this is both: it starts with the story of God and his only son visiting Earth, and then makes the transition to "I loved her the first time I saw her," which is very much—

Edie.

Yeah. That's different. We don't get that in songs much. It's like a cinematic shift from one scene to another.

Yeah, that's right. You could say that. That it shifts. Because once the first two verses were over and I'd finished that part of the story, I realized that the rest of the song was going to be a straight-ahead love song. There was enough cynicism in the first two verses, and now I didn't really need to go any further, and now the rest had to be pure love song. So in a sense it is cinematic in that it now changes to another story. As if you did a flash ahead in time or something. Or a flashback. But it's two different places.

But the thing about it that's interesting is that they do connect up. At the end. So that's why I mean it's more of a literary device than a song device.

In the past we've spoken about how you can combine enriched, poetic language in lyrics with colloquial language. In this song you do that musically as well. Lines like "Well, we'd better get going" sound melodically conversational, whereas "there are galaxies yet to be born" is enriched and poetic.

That's right. And also it sort of changes key and shifts into a Jimmy Reed shuffle for a couple of bars—when I sing "can't describe it any other way," it slips into a blues, a shuffle.

Well, that's one of the advantages of writing a song with no drums, just guitar. You can change on a *dime*.

That's the only song on the album we heard prior to the album release because you performed it at a bookstore in New York when you were writing it. And it's on YouTube.

Right. I started to do it live. After I finished it. To see what the reaction would be to it and whether people would understand what I'm talking about.

It was amazing to me, having gotten to know that live version well, that on the album version you changed the melody and harmony at the end of one of the bridges. That melody is so complex, and yet you were still working on it. And your change was better.

Did I? I don't know what that might have been—maybe the first quarter bridge where it went from a major chord with a seventh to a minor chord with a seventh. I changed that. I don't know what it was really.

But yeah, as long as the process is going along, the opportunity for change is there. At a certain point you close it down, and you're finished. And you try to finish the record. *Unless* there's something that's really irritating about it. In which case I'll go back.

When I originally recorded "Love and Hard Times" it was just with the guitar and the voice. And then I did the string session with Gil Goldstein. And when it was finished I said, "Gee, I had hoped this was going to be more." And that's when I decided I was going to take Philip Glass's advice and put a piano on it. He also said it was a piano song. And I said, "Oh, well, I just worked out this guitar part, and I hate to give it up." And he said, "Well, you can do both, you know. You can have both on it." And that's when Mick Rossi came in and did the overdub. And that's when we met, and now he's in the band, which I'm thrilled about.

He's a wonderful player. That song seems very much like a guitar-first song—

It is. It's the second song I wrote for the album; "Amulet" was the first.

"Amulet" is a beautiful guitar instrumental. Had you considered writing words for it?

No. I was thinking of it as a song, and then it was too complicated for me to figure out how to write a song over it. So I just left it. I sort of abandoned it, actually. Then Luciana Souza, who is a really wonderful jazz singer from Brazil, she heard it a couple years ago at BAM when they did a month of my music and she was singing some of the songs. I played that for her, and she said, "I'd like to record that." And I said, "It's not even a song. It doesn't have words." She said, "I *like* songs without words."

Did that song emerge from just experimenting on the guitar?

Yeah. All of the ballads were the first things I wrote. They were all just sitting with the guitar and play.

Which hasn't been your process for a long time.

No. That's why I decided to do it.

How did it feel to go back to that?

A little bit awkward at first. And then, you know, I was a little bit apprehensive about whether I could do it. "Amulet," which was my first attempt, was much too complicated. So I said I'll have to think more like a song. Not so much like whatever my fingers do. I have to try to put it into a structure that can be made into a song. Although "Love and Hard Times" is a pretty complex structure for a song. It has different parts and changes key several times. But nevertheless, it is a symmetrical structure. And then I realized, well, of course I can do this. And it's just a question of patience.

So those were the first three songs I wrote, and the fourth one that I wrote was "Rewrite."

You wrote that one on guitar?

I just tapped the guitar and made a loop. Which is still in there. It sounds kind of like a drum, but it's just me tapping at the wood of the guitar. And then I made up that guitar thing. [*Sings fast line*]

I played with a kora player at this show at BAM. And I liked the idea of the kora and the guitar. So I just added a kora. And that's really all there was essentially, other than the percussion sounds. And there are a lot of nice colors in there.

For the percussion I would send the tracks off to Paris to Steve She-han, who worked with me on *You're the One*. But I would never send the vocal. I just would say, "Here, put anything and everything that you want on this." I didn't want him to hear the vocal. I didn't want him to *accompany* me. I wanted to hear things that you didn't expect. And then I'd take out all the things I didn't like and keep what I wanted.

Why did you call it "Amulet"?

[*Laughs*] I don't know. Didn't have any title. I don't know. I might have been reading something and saw the word and said, "Oh, there's a good title."

With "Amulet" you said you wrote all the music before you even considered words. And then decided it wouldn't have any. In the past you've come up with words and music at the same time. How was "Love and Hard Times" born?

I think I had the opening line, "God and His only son," which I thought, "That's got to be a good opening line for me. What am I gonna do with that?" It's pretty far away from home for me. But otherwise, I didn't have the story or anything.

That part of the process, I really can't explain it. I don't really know why an idea comes to me. But all of a sudden an idea comes to me, and then I understand now, because it's all I've ever done, really. So from experience I can now intuit what something's going to mean when an interesting line pops up. Or at least I can intuit what an interesting choice might be. And I can try a couple of different choices and see which one feels right and then continue the song to see where it goes.

You once said that the mind, while writing songs, will always pick up on what's true, even if it's not the truth you want to face at that time. Besides the humor, one of the constants in these songs is God and spirituality. Why do you think that's coming out now?

Well, I don't know. But there was just some big piece in [the *Christian Times*], and the writer [Ben Witherington] said, "Paul is writing God's music. I don't think he knows what he's doing now. I don't think he's aware that he's a vessel for this."

So I found that very intriguing because I would never say, "Yeah, I'm doing this—"

Is it accurate?

You know, I really don't know. I really don't know what *exactly* all the songs mean. Sometimes other people have meanings, and when I hear them I think, "That's really a better meaning than I thought, and perfectly valid, given the words that exist."

So part of what makes a song really good is that people take in different meanings, and they apply them, and they might be more powerful than the ones I'm thinking.

You've always done that.

I think it's just a natural thing. I'm not being purposely *vague*, but that seems to be true. Not just of me, but of a lot of songs, where they turn out to mean something really powerful that wasn't meant to be. Like "Born in the U.S.A." It's a powerful song, but it's not what Bruce [Springsteen] was writing about.

"Mother and Child Reunion" is that.

Yeah, "Mother and Child Reunion" is ambiguous enough that you could think a lot of different things with that.

And you intentionally leave mysteries in your songs, such as "what the mama saw" [in "Me and Julio Down by the Schoolyard"], so that enables us to bring our own thoughts to it. When I mention that line to friends, everyone has their own idea what the mama saw. Some think it was definitely that she saw them smoking pot.

Right. Yeah.

And you've always had a lot of questions in songs, but these songs seem to have more questions than ever.

You think?

Yeah. "Questions for the Angels," for example, is about questions. Questions for God, or for angels.

Well, really, it *seems* to be that. But the last question is almost a rhetorical question, really. The last question is *the* question: If there were no human beings on the planet, would any other living creature really care? Would the planet be suffering in any way? I mean, that's really like a rhetorical question, because, I mean, obviously the answer is no, not at all.

But you don't say that in the song. To me that's not obvious.

Well, do you think a zebra would really have any suffering if there were no human beings left?

Probably not—

Definitely not. What did we ever do for zebras?

[*Laughs*] You're right, except wipe out their habitat—

Exactly.

But when I hear that, I think more about the character asking the question, and the choice of words, the zebra and zebra's tears.

Well, the zebras, I think, were in my mind because the whole family took a trip to East Africa a couple of years ago and saw the great migration of animals that takes place every August. And there's thousands and thousands of wildebeest and zebras crossing the river from Kenya into Tanzania. So it was a really powerful memory. I think that's where the zebras come from. There's a lot of zebras there. There's more wildebeests than zebras, but a lot of zebras.

Do you recall where the opening lines came from?

Well, that's one of those first lines that just popped into my head— "A pilgrim on a pilgrimage / Walked across the Brooklyn Bridge." I have no idea why that came to me or what I was thinking about or anything. Nothing, as far as I remember.

But if a song begins with somebody setting out on a journey, that's a perfect metaphor for what the song is trying to do anyway. So that's fine. I've written quite a few traveling songs. People are going from one place to another.

So that's what that one was, and the questions that he asks, they sort of get deeper as he goes along: Who am I? Where will I sleep? Things like that. And then they get a little bit more deeper in the next one: If you make a bad choice in love, do you have to pay for it, or can you not pay for it? And if you get called to a certain destiny, do you have to choose it, or can you avoid it? Those are bigger questions, but they're all adding up to the last question, which is, what defense does the human race have for its behavior?

Musically, it's really nice. I love the shift in the chorus to that chord on "questions." And the shift into the three-quarter time bridge is nice.

Yeah, that's the guitar. Where your hands go on the guitar. It's, let's see what I have. B minor. I'm in B minor and then I go to a G and a C. Yeah, B minor, so it's like D, and then I go to C minor, so it's sort of like the key of E flat. But that's basically what's happening. And then that bridge in three-quarter time goes to B major.

When you say "your hands on the guitar," does that mean you are actively trying to find music on the guitar you don't know?

I'll show you. [*Gets guitar out*]

I asked Herbie Hancock if, when he's playing, if there are still places on the piano he's never gone, and he said, "Yes, it's endless." You feel that as well?

Of course, it's endless, yeah. If it's endless for Herbie, you can be *sure* it's endless for me. [*Laughter*]

It is endless, of course. [*Begins to play*]

So I'm playing this. [*Plays*] It's a Bm with a D in the bass. This is making it a Bm9. [*Plays more chords*] See what I mean? With me on these guitar things, they're always really pretty simple. Because I'm really a pretty simple player.

Yet it doesn't sound simple.

No, it doesn't sound simple. It's nice voice-leading.

Does that come just from experimenting?

Yeah, just sitting there. [*Plays more*] So there I am, that's in D. Then I go over here to B minor, C minor, G, E flat, B flat, B—I use this in a couple songs. This is in "Love and Hard Times." And I'm back here, but when I go to the bridge I have the minor third in the bass and move it—

Now it's B major.

Right. It's not that hard to play, really. But the mind has to say you should go somewhere now. You should go to B major. But sometimes I go into a place and it's no good, and I say, "No, that's not it."

I use this chord a lot. [*Sings with it*] I use that as a way of navigating between C and A flat and B flat. It's very guitaristic. And useful. If you're in that key.

I compensate for what I can't do on guitar by finding interesting things that I can do. But they're not hard to play. I usually don't play it when

I'm onstage. I usually give the guitar parts to Mark [Stewart] or Vincent [Nguini]. Because there's too much for me to sing about to play some counter-line and singing. I can do it, but I won't play it *accurately* all the time.

Yet you did "Wartime Prayers" solo, which is quite complex on the guitar.

Yeah, that was complex. And I did "Love and Hard Times," which is complex. And I still do that. But for the most part I give the parts over to Mark or Vincent, and then I play something really simple, or nothing. But when I'm making them up, they're fun, and I can just keep playing them until I get a good take, and then that's the take that sits there.

With "Questions for the Angels," the bridge about seeing Jay Z is nice, not only that it's an unusually modern reference for you but that it sings so beautifully: Jay Z is a lovely name, and singability matters.

Yeah, that's very important. But as it happens, that's a true image. I was doing this month at the Brooklyn Academy a couple of years ago, and every time I would come over the Brooklyn Bridge, I would see this big billboard of Jay Z. So it's real. It was a real image.

So Beautiful or So What **is such an inspired album. It's clear that you are aiming as high as ever—and getting there—whereas it seems many songwriters peaked long ago—**

Well, I don't know. Can't really address *that*. Although I must say Leonard Cohen's doing pretty well at seventy. And Randy Newman's last album—*Harps and Angels*? Fabulous. Really great work. So he's definitely, *definitely* at the peak of his powers.

I don't know on the others. The creative impulse is varied. Paul McCartney's writing a ballet. Neil Young is very involved in film. Bob [Dylan] paints. He makes these incredible gates, iron gates. Really beautiful, where he welds things together. So they're very creative.

You know, there's not too many songwriters that I've actually had a really sort of forthright conversation about songwriting with. Not too much. Yeah, I have spoken with other songwriters, but I haven't spoken to my generation of guys. I never had a conversation with Bob [Dylan], *barely* had a conversation with Paul [McCartney] about it. We had some conversations about composition.

I know Bob is very interested in you. A friend of mine who dated him said he knew "Boy in the Bubble" perfectly. He could sing and play it.

Well, I don't get to talk to him much. But when we did tour together, we chatted and chatted about lots of things, but we never talked about that.

I saw your tour with him when you played the Hollywood Bowl. It was really cool to see you two together, but so different from what you normally do, to sing with him. How was that for you—to sing with him?

Fun. [*Laughs*] And funny.

Funny?

Yeah. He doesn't sing the same thing twice, you know? So if my job is to sing harmony, I don't know where he's going to be.

A challenge others have had. Like Joan Baez.

Yeah. But I think it's just sort of fun that the both of us were standing up there singing together.

Do you think that the changes in the industry have discouraged some great artists from doing new work?

Maybe. This is just pure speculation, so I don't know. But because the record business changed so much and kind of imploded and *evaporated*, it might be that there's not so much of incentive to go and make a record. Even the record companies don't seem incentivized. They all seem afraid. Well, not this company [Concord] that I'm with. I'm very happy to be with them.

They're doing a good job.

They are, yeah, and they were very enthusiastic.

But in an environment that doesn't seem to value the album form as much as it does the single download, that might have some effect. But it's pure speculation. Because none of those people that we're talking about, they've never said anything to me, so I don't know how they feel.

But as far as I'm concerned, I feel like it doesn't really matter what happens with the record business because I'm just following the path that I set out on in the sixties. And I'm just curious to see where it leads. And I don't expect it, really, to lead into big commercial success. But I am very curious to see where it will take me.

And I'm not particularly creative in any other field. [*Laughs*] You know, I can't paint or make gates or make ballets or films or any of that.

But you are very talented not only in the writing but in the record making. More so than most songwriters.

I like the record making more than I like any other part of the process.

You recorded this new album in your own home studio in Connecticut?

Yes. I did one track, "Christmas Day," in a studio. Because my place is a little small. It's a tiny little house that I use for a studio, and I didn't think I could fit drums in. But I can. I can just about fit drums in. So then I started to record drums in there too.

That's a very different process, being in your own place—

It's *very* comfortable. Very comfortable. And [producer] Phil Ramone lives fifteen minutes away. So it's easy for him too. We don't have to drive into the city for an hour and then park and then at the end of the day be exhausted and then drive back home on the Merritt Parkway when you're tired. It's very comfortable to do that.

Also, I have so many choices of instruments there. I have all my guitars there. So if I decide that I want to choose a particular guitar that I wouldn't normally carry to a studio with me, for example, if I say, "Oh, let's try a Dobro on this sound, or let's try a requinto, or maybe I should try that Country Gentleman." I have, whatever it is, twenty, thirty guitars that are there. So I have a pretty big palette to choose from in terms of guitar.

Also, I've started to collect a lot of percussion sounds. Especially bells. There are a lot of bells on this album. Overtones of bells used in different ways to create echo sounds.

That kind of thing, using bell overtones for echo, reflects the level of comfort you feel there—

Well, I am comfortable. With all this time available to me and no particular pressure—like I don't have just two days in a studio or something—I have a lot more time for trial and error. And the trial-and-error aspects of this record were significant. Because a lot of things didn't work, so they're not in there.

Really?

Yeah, I mean I'm playing different bell sounds or overdub sounds. Or, the example before, let's try a Dobro. You take it out and spend an hour figuring out the part and playing it, and then you say, "You know? It's not that great, actually. So let's go back to the Strat or something like that." There's a lot of trial and error.

I was impressed with how much electric guitar—lead lines—you played, that I don't normally associate with you.

I can play leads. But I have to do it a bunch of times. [*Laughs*]

That's how George Harrison did it. He'd work out his parts.

Yeah. They sound like that, kind of composed lines. But, you know, that's fun for me. To make up all the different parts.

Would you work in the studio all around the clock—

No, no. No. We'd work from eleven to six. Something like that. Eleven thirty to six. Or five. Or maybe six thirty. Depending upon whether I had to go pick up the kids at school or if Edie was going to. It was kind of loose, but those are roughly the hours. That's about it for intense concentration for me.

Given your full vision and love of recording, I wonder what Phil's job is. Does he come up with ideas, or is he there to get your ideas down?

He does have some ideas, but he's more a facilitator for what I want. And more than that, he's somebody whose opinion I trust. So I don't have to be an editor of my work constantly. I can throw out ideas, and if he says, "That one's the best," I don't have to say, "Well, can you play them all back so I can check and listen?" Same with vocals. I do my vocal tracks. And I'll do a lot of passes on a vocal.

Then do we hear the whole vocal, or are you punching in lines? Because your vocals always sound very natural.

Yeah, they are natural. This is my typical thing: I'll do four takes, combine them into one, do *another* four takes, combine *that* into one, and take the two combined takes and make that into a master, and whatever I don't like after that I'll usually just go specifically for what I didn't get. *And* I could come back two weeks later and say I don't really like this vocal; I'm gonna do it again. And end up keeping one line from an earlier one.

It's the same thing. I'll just stay with it till I like it. Or I could get it in a take or two. It's the same principle, really. The ear goes to the irritant. And if you don't like it, eventually it has to go away. And if you like it and you capture something, then you keep it.

That's interesting. "The ear goes to the irritant." That applies also to your lyrics in that the language is also so beautifully smooth and polished. There are no irritants. And I've found that since your first songs.

Well, thank you. I don't have a clear picture in my mind of how that works. I have a very clear picture about how I do the music. The words come. [*Pause*] Usually it's a long time before they come. And then when they start to come, it doesn't take so long for it to be finished. It takes a long time to begin. And then it sort of gets finished.

Sometimes I'll be stuck on a verse or some aspect of a song. Could be for a *long* time.

Really?

Yeah. "Love and Hard Times" took a long time.

On the album liner notes you thank Philip Glass for helping you get out of "harmonic tangles" you would somehow "miscreate." Was that about "Love and Hard Times"?

It could have been about "Love and Hard Times." Sometimes I'll just ask him about a modulation and how to think about that, what notes I might want to have to solve the problem of it. Eventually I'd figure it out. But with Philip, he's like Google. [*Laughter*] You ask Philip, you pretty much get a quick answer. Unless he decides it would be better for me to just work it out. In which case he says, "Hmmm, I don't know." He knows. [*Laughs*]

And you use his answers when he has them?

Yeah. Yeah, I mean, often his suggestions are absolutely appropriate.

Is "Getting Ready for Christmas Day" a track-first song—

Track first, yeah. Well, the guitars and all that first. Then I said, "Let's put that sermon on and see if that sermon works." I didn't have the idea of using that sermon in anything. Till I made that track.

I assumed it was the other way around, that you made the track to fit that sermon.

I did hear the sermon before making the track, but I didn't have anything but a liking for that sermon.

Seems you even chose the key, A major, to match his voice. It seems perfect there—

Yeah, it does. Yeah. There was a lot of good luck on this album.

Do you think it's just luck?

Yeah, that was luck. That his voice fits perfectly and seems to be right in the right key and the right tempo.

I think many, including the Christian writer who wrote that you're doing God's work, would ascribe it to more than luck, to God or Providence—

You *could*, you know. Or the harder you work, the luckier you get. But I look at it as luck.

You took the sermon and chopped it up to fit it in rhythmically?

Yep. It sort of laid right in. The tricky part there was to write a song that went around the sermon.

It's something you haven't done in your records—using a sample of a spoken voice—since "7 O'Clock News / Silent Night" in 1964.

Oh, that's right, yeah. "7 O'Clock News / Silent Night" wasn't even a sample. That was something that was written, and then we gave it to an announcer. And he read it. We hired a radio announcer.

But that combination of spoken word with your track, when you thought of that with "Christmas Day," were you confident it would work?

Oh no, no. That's why I said there's a lot of luck in it. I just said, "Put that up there. Let's see."

As soon as it was there, it was really compelling. If I were just a producer, I would have said, "Just leave that—with that track and that sermon. That's fine. No need to do anything else." But as a songwriter who's making a record, I have to figure out how to get me into the track. [*Laughs*]

It's a cool groove—

Yeah, it's a good groove.

The guitar has a great sound. What is that?

It's got a really good tremolo on it with a dotted eighth note attached to the click and a foot stomp.

Acoustic guitar?

It's both. It's an acoustic-electric guitar that is miked acoustically and at the amp. And the acoustic is treated differently than the amp.

Did you do that in "Amulet" as well, where there are two different guitar images?

Yeah, but there I just overdubbed myself. There I'm playing acoustic guitar. I did that on "Questions of the Angels" and "Amulet."

Sometimes I'll just double a thing, and I'll keep whatever little thread seems to enhance the guitar. I'll throw away 95 percent of the double and just keep 5 percent, and it seems to work. Again, the ear goes to the irritant and you throw out all the irritant, and what is left is nice.

So many of your peers have no interest in any of the new digital recording technology, whereas you have embraced sampling and loops on this album in a big and amazing way. Was that an easy understanding for you?

Andy. Andy Smith. He's very good. He's been my engineer now for about twenty years. He's really good with the technology.

I love how you use a sample of Sonny Terry's harmonica [in "Love Is Eternal Sacred Light"]. Sounds like he's in the studio with you.

Yeah, it does. It's fabulous.

Now you played that harmonica part yourself live, right?

Yeah. Part of it. I'm playing along with him, and then they take that sample out and then I play the end of it.

The title song, "So Beautiful or So What," is built on a great guitar riff. Is that a loop?

No. Well, it might be a really long loop. It might be sixteen, twenty bars or something like that.

It's similar to the "Mrs. Robinson" riff.

Yeah, it has the same kind of right-hand move to "Mrs. Robinson." I do that a lot too. I use things that I made up before. Change them around a little bit. Licks that I made up.

That song has a verse about the shooting of Martin Luther King. Such a provocative verse—"Dr. King has just been shot," and this very vivid picture of the three men on the balcony. And yet the song isn't just about MLK.

No, but he's the embodiment of that choice—so beautiful or so what? He was a person who clearly said we have the potential to be living in a paradise, or we have a potential to live in hell.

When that verse emerged, did you feel it should be removed or that it distracted?

No, just the opposite. I thought that the song was a little bit unfocused until that came about.

Again, that's very cinematic to cut to Dr. King, and the way you show us that famous image.

Right. That's an iconic photo.

The sequencing of the album is interesting—you put the title song last.

That was the last one I wrote.

A songwriter friend of mine said, "He put his hit last." She considered it the hit.

Oh yeah? I'm not sure that there's any hits in there. Or what the hit is. You know what seems to be the hit in concert? "Rewrite." "Rewrite" gets a lot of response. Which is sort of interesting. And a lot of people who have had the album for a long time have said that "Rewrite" has emerged as their favorite song.

Maybe people like them when they're simple. When they're really simple. Eventually. They don't get on your nerves.

The lyric of "Rewrite" was published in the *New Yorker* as a poem.

Yes. Paul Muldoon, who is the poetry editor, asked if he could use one of the songs from this album in the *New Yorker*, and he chose "Rewrite." That felt good. Though I didn't think of it as a poem; I think of it as a lyric. But yeah, it did. It was nice.

Patti Smith, who writes poems and songs, told me she writes poems for herself, but songs are for the whole world, and for that reason songwriting is harder than poetry. Do you feel that, that when you write a song, the whole world could hear it for years?

I don't think that way, but I don't write poems. No, I don't think this is something that the whole world will hear for years. And I don't think I ever did. Most of the time when I had hits, as a soloist—maybe not so much with Simon & Garfunkel—but most of the time when I had hits as a soloist, I was surprised they were hits. I didn't know what the hits were.

I never thought that "Loves Me Like a Rock" was going to be a hit, or "Mother and Child Reunion" was going to be a hit.

"Kodachrome"?

"Kodachrome" I thought was a hit. It sounds like a pop song. All the other ones sound odd. "50 Ways to Leave Your Lover." They didn't sound like what the hits sounded like at the time. Radio was more open to things that weren't exactly what every other hit was.

Definitely. And hearing those songs in that context was always wonderful. We loved it.

Yeah, that's right. People liked it then. That's sort of gone away. It's too bad.

It is too bad.

Your previous album, *Surprise*, was a collaboration with Brian Eno, and quite an amazing album.

Some people didn't like *Surprise*. They didn't like the combination of me and Brian. Not personally. They didn't like the combination of our sounds. But I did.

I know a lot of people who loved and have imitated that sound. Acoustic instruments with techno. It influenced a lot of people.

Oh well, that's nice. That's nice.

This album is more simple than *Surprise* was. Every time I finish a record I say, "Now what was it about that record that I really liked? And what about it could I just leave and not repeat?"

I think what I took out of *Surprise* was that I don't need to have complicated, polyrhythmic drumming, which I happen to like. But I also like that really straight 4/4 rock and roll, like fifties rock and roll and African. Really just 4/4. Not even a backbeat.

"Christmas Day," no backbeat. So is "So Beautiful or So What." And so is "The Afterlife." And I've said this many times, that my two favorite records, my two favorite records are "Mystery Train" and "Bo Diddley," and neither of those had backbeats either. If you think of a bunch of my songs—"Me and Julio" doesn't have a backbeat.

I guess that's right. But such a cool rhythm.

Yes, it has a good rhythm. It's not that I don't like backbeats, I do. But I really like it when it's not. And I guess there were a bunch of fifties things that had that. Especially the foot-stomping records.

"How Can You Live in the Northeast?" from *Surprise* is an astounding song.

"How Can You Live in the Northeast?" was a good song. And a good question . . .

The ending quatrain about three generations off the boat, wearing your father's old coat, reflects an American experience so few songs have ever touched, that so many of us are so recently off the boat.

Yes, that's true. It was not my father but his father who came off the boat. My parents were born in New York. But yes, three generations. It's true, it's a big leap in three generations. In a hundred years, it's a long way. That's the American story.

"The Boy in the Bubble" is just amazing in concert, and it's such a special song.

Yeah, "Boy in the Bubble" is Sutu rhythm. That might have been my favorite of the South African grooves, the Sutu.

That lyric is just phenomenal, so interesting with all those modern and mysterious images, like the lasers in the jungle and the bomb in the baby carriage.

Thanks. That's a song that I wrote—I *completely* wrote it—and didn't like it at all and threw the *whole thing out* and said, "That's *awful*." And then I rewrote it as "Boy in the Bubble."

A whole other lyric?

Yeah.

Do you remember what it was?

No, I don't. It would be interesting to see. I just said, "You know, this is a great track and this lyric, but I don't *believe* it. I don't really believe it. I don't believe that. Sounds like I'm *trying* to say something." Instead of it naturally coming out of me, it sounded like I was already saying something that I knew.

I can't remember what it was. And either I threw it all out or I threw 90 percent of it out and kept a line or two. I don't even remember. That's happened a couple of times to me. Not too often, but a couple of times. Very aggravating when it does happen.

"Love Is Eternal Sacred Light" is like that. That song was called "Brand New Pre-Owned Automobile." Like the last verse. And when I sang it, I said, "Nah, I don't believe it." And as I said to Phil, "You know, I don't like it. I'm not gonna do this," some voice in me said, "This should be called 'Love Is Eternal Sacred Light,'" which, actually, I didn't even like as a title. But you tend to give credence to these voices that come from within. Not always a good idea, but we tend to do that.

That's interesting, because it didn't strike me as your kind of phrase. I can see why that writer felt you were preaching God's songs here.

Yeah. I was surprised. I was surprised that all of these God references had come up. Five out of the first six songs. I noticed it, but it was unintentional.

And you listened to that voice and trusted that was the right title, even though you didn't like it at first—

Well, you know, it has that title, and then you can see me take another angle at the title by the time you get to the middle of the song.

Very much so—

So I wasn't *totally* committed to that title. Or to that thought. I let the thought play out, and then I came at it from another direction.

"Love Is Eternal" has that remarkable section of short lines starting "Earth becomes a farm / Farmer takes a wife." You're describing the origins of mankind on Earth.

Right. "Farmer takes a wife" is from a children's song, "Farmer in the Dell."

It has that kind of nursery-rhyme rhythm—

Right.

But with the fast passage to man becoming machine, "oil runs down his face," it's very quick—

Yeah, very quick description of evolution.

It goes into a section about the Big Bang being just a joke. Is that the voice of God?

I think so, yeah. Or somebody.

It's got that poignant line, "I love all my children, it tears me up when I leave."

It's the second song where He left.

Also, being a native Chicagoan, I like that the song is placed in the Midwest and you mention Lake Michigan. Which is rare in your songs. Why did you place it there?

Well, when it came it just felt like it was really fresh. And the song felt like it was a Midwest song, that end part about driving along, all that stuff. It's sort of vaguely Chuck Berry–ish. Rock and roll-y.

And you kept in the line about the "brand-new, pre-owned '96 Ford"— you knew it was a good line but not a title.

Yeah. I liked "brand-new, pre-owned." It's just a bullshit line that salespeople use. Brand-new, pre-owned.

Years ago you told me you found the structure of "Slip Slidin' Away" boring because it doesn't have a bridge, a third section, and you said the normal song structure seemed a bit restrictive. In this album and others in the past years you've exploded the song structure—you have C sections which aren't just bridges you hear once, they are whole other places you go to.

Yeah. That's been going on for quite a while now. "Darling Lorraine" has five different sections. But both ways are good. Other songs really never change their structure, like "Christmas Day." It's the same chord pattern through the whole song, and then there are different structures laid over it, but it's the exact same chord pattern. Same with "The Afterlife" and same with "So Beautiful or So What." Same with "Rewrite." Same chords. Never changes chords, never changes key.

And that's a great sound—when a melody moves over a repeating riff like that. The words to "So Beautiful" start with the image of making chicken gumbo—and then you step back and say, "Life is what you make of it / So beautiful or so what"—

I had that title very early. Way before, years before, I had that song. I had written down a sentence: "Everything is either so beautiful or so what." So again, that is what I mean: there was a lot of luck in this album. I come up to the last song, and this phrase which I like, it fits, I can call it that, and then I thought that's a good title for the album. It does sum up the album, and the cover, with the DNA on it, same question. Same things as "Questions for the Angels."

Have you done that before, taken lines from the past and used them in new songs?

No, I don't use the lines from the past. Actually I probably should, but once I finish, I put the stuff away, put the box somewhere, and I don't go back to it. But I keep a notebook, and I use lines or thoughts from the notebook when they're appropriate for the song. There's still a bunch of stuff that's not used, that just didn't fit in anywhere, or I lost interest in it, or you know, I did like it, but I just couldn't find a place for it.

What was your writing process like for this album? Did you work on songs every day?

Well, in a way I was. But it's not like I go and sit down at my desk and do that. In fact, I don't really like to write at a desk. I like to write when driving in a car.

With the track going?

Yeah. Which is why I am one of the guys you want to avoid when you're on the road. [*Laughter*] I'm more listening to the track than I am paying attention to driving.

So do you mean you finish a track for every song before you write the words?

Quite often. Not always. On the guitar songs, that's why I did have to sit in the room and play. And it makes me restless to sit in the room and play.

Does it?

Yeah. I like the car. Because you're passive; stuff is passing. You know you can look, and things are going on. You get bored and you turn it off and you turn on a baseball game or something.

I've had good ideas come to me when I'm away from work, like in the car or something.

Yeah. Once you're working on it, you're working on it all the time, and sometimes stuff'll come in the middle of the night, in a dream or something. Your mind is working on it all the time.

"The Afterlife" is a funny song about death. How did that come to be?

I think it's another one of those songs that had a first line.

"After I died and the makeup had dried—"

Yeah, "I went back to my place." I didn't know what that song would be about. I thought it was a *pretty* good first line, not really good. It was a little too complicated for a really good first line. The first time you hear that, it's not like you really grasp, what? "After I died . . ." Because it's a concept and it has a little bit of a joke in it, all that stuff, all coming in that line. But anyway, I didn't find anything else, so I stuck with that. I like that track a lot.

People pick up on your lines in a way they don't with most songs, it seems. I hear people already saying, "Well, we'd better get going . . . these people are slobs here . . ."

I really put the lyrics up front. I don't really get it why people bury their lyrics. Especially if they have something to say. A lot of indie bands. Or Radiohead, I can't hear the lyrics when I first put the record on. I think if these guys have something to say, why stick it there in the track where I'm kind of straining to hear? But everybody has a different aesthetic. I put mine way out front. And that's sort of part of my sound.

And your lyrics are meant to be heard. Interesting you say they are songs and not poems. They are meant to be sung, not spoken.

Yeah. Sometimes they have elements that could be shared with poetry. But they're not poems. They're lyrics. They're meant to be sung. They come out of the rhythm of the music, as opposed to creating your own rhythm of the words.

Also, there's much more use of cliché in songwriting than there is in poetry, because a song is going at a certain tempo and it's going fast, and if you miss a line, you missed it. But when you're reading poetry, you read it at a much slower pace. So the lines can be much more dense. And have words which are not usually in a speaking vocabulary and which carry multiple meanings. Because you can slow it down so you can get it.

But in a song, it's clocking along, and if you missed it, it's gone. And if you miss enough of it, well, the song is gone, and you sort of lose interest.

You've told me you've read poetry a lot, and the influence of poetry on your work is especially evident in some songs—I think of "Cool, Cool River": "moves like a fist through traffic"—the language is quite charged and poetic—

Thanks. Yeah, there are poets who have definitely influenced what I write. There are poets who write in a way that is good for songs. For simple kind of songs, straight ahead, Robert Frost is very touching and simple. Who I like, especially if it's an American kind of song, maybe if it's set in the woods or the country or something like that.

There are other poets who influenced me. I learned a lot from Derek Walcott when we wrote *The Capeman.*

Speaking of him, I remember back when you were working on songs for *The Rhythm of the Saints* you had a line about your head "resting on a rented pillow" for the song that became "Thelma." You said Derek Walcott told you not to use the alliteration because alliteration is easy.

Yes. I enjoyed the collaboration. I thought when we really did mix the two of our styles it created an interesting song. Lyrically. But even if the song was mostly Derek's, which a couple of them are, they still had my melodies, and I would still say, "No, you can't do that. I need this," and he would change it around. And a bunch of those songs are all me too.

But the ones that are combined, they have a quality to them that's sort of a mix of pop and poetry that I think is very interesting, like "Can I Forgive Him."

Well, all your work has that quality—since the start, they're all poetic songs.

But with the Derek work, it sounds like his poetry a lot.

I loved those songs you wrote for *The Capeman.* And I loved the show, which I was lucky to see on Broadway.

The Capeman is, I think, coming back. It played last summer in Central Park. It was very well received. I think *The Capeman* was, perhaps, ahead of its time. Well, it was also a flawed piece of work. But it was an interesting piece of work. And it got *unusually* beat up. More beat up, actually, than it deserved.

So I think now there is a willingness—it took ten years—I think there was a willingness to take a listen to it again. And it was treated much more kindly. It came back twice, once at BAM and once last summer in Central Park. It was fabulous in Central Park, outdoors. Right in the middle of the world I was talking about.

It's not unlike Gershwin's *Porgy and Bess*, which was attacked brutally at first and then became accepted like a classic.

Yeah, *Porgy and Bess* was ripped apart too.

I love the song "The Vampires," and your version of it is great—the timing of the dialogue is great.

Yeah, I like that rhythm too. I think it's a *guajira*.

And then it explodes into a great horn section and solo.

That's Oscar Hernández. He's great, Oscar. His album just won a Grammy this year. His band is called the Spanish Harlem Orchestra. *Really* good. I just saw him the other night; he came the other night, lives out here [in Los Angeles].

In "Love and Blessings" you have a wonderful verse: "If the summer kept a secret / It was heaven's lack of rain . . ." Which to me seems to be about global warming—

Yes.

Interesting how you touch on that but obliquely, as in "Can't Run, But," when you discuss the cooling system that burned out in the Ukraine—

Chernobyl.

Yeah. But you don't do it too overtly.

Yeah. You know, I don't want to be preachy. I don't think anybody really needs to be preached to. And people resent it if they think that you are preaching to them, and I think I would resent it. I don't need to be told things that I know, or lectured, or any of that stuff.

So it's just a comment on what's going on. It's not saying anything. It doesn't tell you a moral judgment. It assumes that you have already taken the issue into account and you have an opinion. That's all. And just move on.

With "So Beautiful or So What," the song, and like many of the songs on this album, the rhyming is playful and fun. And in that song you rhyme to the title—rhyming the "what" word with different words each time. How do you make something like that, which needs to be contrived to work, sounds so natural and noncontrived?

[*Pause*] I don't know the answer to that. As I say, there's a significant part of writing songs that I have no logical explanation for. Just seems to be something that comes from me. And I sort of recognize it, as opposed to *shaping* it. Oh, that's a good idea, that's a good line. I wonder where I can use that.

But with rhymes, you have to be conscious to make rhymes work, don't you?

Yeah. But you know, when you get into a rhyme group like "not," you got a lot of rhymes; you got a lot of choices. Whereas if you get into "climb," for example—

"Time," "crime," "lime"—

And "I'm." And you're pretty much gonna go for "time."

"Love" doesn't have many rhymes.

Yeah, you got "of," "above," "dove," and "glove."

Yet one of the great things you've always done is use rhymes in a way that doesn't call attention to them, that one is there as a setup. It just seems inevitable, and that, to me, seems like the greatness of great songs.

Well, the more you do it, as I say, the better you get. I really never had any other job since I was fifteen. I made my first record at fifteen. It's really all I ever did. I went to school, but all I've ever done is write songs and make records. Now it's a long time, and I've had a lot of experience at it.

You've gotten pretty good at it.

[*Laughs*] Thanks. But a lot of it is just, you know, good luck.

◆◆◆

Ringo Starr
The Beatles and Beyond
West Hollywood, California 2014

Once on the BBC soon after the release of their film *A Hard Day's Night*, John Lennon was talking about how great Ringo was in the film. The host says to him, "A lot of people are saying Ringo is like a young Chaplin," to which Lennon replies, "No, he's like an *old* one."

Today Ringo is no longer a youngster but is still as spry and Chaplinesque as ever, in great shape, and exultant about his life making music. Rather than rest on his prodigious laurels, he continues to write songs, make records, and tour, almost every year, with his remarkable All-Starr Band, a superband of great proportions in which countless legends have appeared, including Edgar Winter, Todd Rundgren, Steve Lukather, Richard Page, Joe Walsh, Nils Lofgren, Dr. John, Billy Preston, Rick Danko, Levon Helm, Clarence Clemons, Felix Cavaliere, Eric Burdon, Ginger Baker, and many more.

As anyone who has seen these shows knows, the spirit of Ringo reigns. Rather than be the star in the spotlight the whole show, as he's happily done his whole career, he shares the stage with famous friends. He gladly celebrates the greatness of others with a quiet generosity he's always possessed. But when he comes out front to perform, he doesn't hold back. Unlike the other three Beatles, he's the only one who always dances when he sings. And it's a dance of joy.

"Inspired?" he said with a laugh when I used that word to describe the joy that infuses all the songs he wrote for his newest album, *Postcards from Paradise*. "We need to have you around more often!"

Seemed like a great idea. His band The Beatles, as the universe knows, was the greatest ever, and the love they brought the world through their short but miraculous reign continues to permeate every day. With John, Paul, and George, he came together to churn out miracle songs from 1963 to 1969 almost nonstop, forever evolving and changing the art of songwriting as we know it.

He was born Richard Starkey (of course) in Liverpool (of course) in 1940, the same year as John Lennon's birth. Before joining The Beatles and supplanting Pete Best in 1962, he was the drummer for Rory Storm and the Hurricanes, about whom he wrote a song on his newest album, discussed herein.

It was Ringo, of course, who often came up with The Beatles' titles and phrases ("A Hard Day's Night," he confirmed, was his, though "Eight Days a Week," often attributed to him, he said, was not) and also discovered distinctive drum parts as extraordinary and right as the songs themselves. A songwriter's dream drummer, he always crafted soulful parts that served the very essence of each song. Even his fills are legend: all soulful grace and visceral power without ever overwhelming the song.

But in addition to all that—the man is a great songwriter. Besides "Octopus's Garden," written for The Beatles, he wrote "Photograph" and "It Don't Come Easy" soon after the big break. He's since written many albums of great songs. Sure, he had some seriously great teachers. In the movie *Let It Be* we see him writing "Octopus's Garden" on the piano, in C major, trying to discern where its verse would end. Fortunately for him, George Harrison was there and suggested the famous return to tonic, back to the I, C major.

With direct education as well as osmosis by proximity to authentic geniuses of songwriting, he swiftly became a great songwriter. "Octopus's Garden" was as magically surreal, whimsical, and beautiful as any Beatles song. Like George, who established himself in leaps and bounds as an equal of Lennon and McCartney, here came Ringo—the comic

Beatle—with some serious songwriting. In 1970, after The Beatles, he immediately wrote and sang two great songs, "Photograph" and "It Don't Come Easy." He also had a hit with "You're Sixteen," written by the Sherman Brothers of Disney song fame (see page 65).

Now, well versed in the knowledge that collaboration with gifted friends leads to greatness, he's made a brand-new masterpiece of inspired songwriting. *Postcards from Paradise*, all new cowritten originals, includes the magical, Beatles-detailed title song written with Todd Rundgren; the New Orleans gumbo of "Bamboula," written with Van Dyke Parks; and the opening song, "Rory and the Hurricanes," about his famous pre-Beatles band and life, written with fellow northerner Dave Stewart.

Lest one assume that this artist took unwarranted songwriting credit, both Stewart and Parks confirmed that Ringo led the collaboration, coming in with substantial musical and lyrical ideas. For "Bamboula" Ringo had a whole drum track, inspired by the Afro rhythms of 1820 New Orleans. Van Dyke, a scholar of musical history, delved into that time and spirit to inform the lyrics. "The collaboration was swift and projectile," said Van Dyke, "as was the recording. And it seemed like another great way to confirm Ringo's adaptability to his adopted home. He is, after all, as all-American as he is royal loyal."

Decades past, when Paul and John wrote about their early years in "Strawberry Fields" and "Penny Lane," Ringo now shared this early chapter in "Rory and the Hurricanes," written with Dave Stewart.

"Ringo and I are both from the same part of England," said Stewart. "And we have the same passions and the same sense of humor. So when it was time to write about our mutual past, that was fun, and it was easy. And Ringo always comes in with ideas, both musical and lyrical. He's quite the brilliant songwriter and, as you might know, a very good drummer as well."

That he's still making music at this stage of his life is testament to his lifelong passion for music. "Ringo's vitality," said Van Dyke, "his interest in others and athletic approach to making this a better world—with peace and love his signature—is totally uncommon. He needn't prove anything. He already has. This makes him a role model. When most guys as seasoned as he is are resting on their laurels, he's creating new works, with emphasis on mutual empowerment."

That Ringo, like his late great friend Harry Nilsson, is famous not only as a musician but as a friend is understandable the moment you're in his sphere. He's always been kind of adorable, in a way both funny and sweet. His delivery of lines, any lines, always was delightfully funny, often more for the way he said the words than the words themselves. That each of his bandmates was a genius was pretty clear early on, and Ringo always provided them a foundation—both rhythmic and human—they could fall back on. In an early radio appearance in 1963 Paul and John do all the talking while George laughed and Ringo was in the other studio, adjusting his drums. But although he was separate, the others constantly referred to him lovingly, like a musician repeating a pedal tone, holding down a song. "We brought you the flowers, Ring!" said Lennon affectionately. "And the *grapes*."

Short pause, and then in the distance the drummer intones laconically: "Oh, I like grapes!" And everyone folds inward with laughter. Despite the madness and chaos that swirled around the ceaseless phenomenon that being The Beatles was, Ringo was the comic constant, the endearing spirit that gently but soulfully kept everything in place.

I always think of you in the movie *Let It Be*, working on "Octopus's Garden" on the piano, and you ask George where you should go. He shows you to go back to the I, the C major. You had some kind of good teachers around for songwriting.

Ringo Starr: There's also a bit before that where I'm playing. [*Sings*] "I'd like to be . . ." And he's lying on a settee? Is that in the movie? I don't think so. And he's going, "G!" [*Laughter*] You might as well shout "asparagus" to me. I can't play G. I play everything in C on piano. "F flat!" Yeah. [*Laughs*]

Yes, they were all helpful. George was more helpful in the end because he produced "It Don't Come Easy" and "Photograph." He really produced it, and then Richard Perry redid it. But it was sort of George's arrangement.

I'd have a couple of verses. I'd always have a chorus. And I wasn't good at ending in those days. I actually have a song that is like twenty-seven verses. And I gave it to Harry Nilsson and it was still too long.

I loved Harry.

Yeah, I loved Harry too. He was my friend. So George came out and produced the record, and he really helped me.

Did you write "Photograph" together?

We never wrote anything together. I came to him with "It Don't Come Easy," and I came to him with "Photograph." Because I'd written "Photograph" in Spain, and I had it. "Every time I see your face it reminds me of the places we used to go. And all I've got is a photograph, and I realize you're not coming back anymore . . ." I had all of that. Now I see some publishers are saying it's a Harrison song.

Yes.

No, I promise you, I'm not trying to build myself up. It was Starkey-Harrison when it started. And George was trying to put Krishna into it. And I said, "No, no!" Then he put God. And I said, "No, no!" In those days I wouldn't sing about God or Krishna. Now I'll sing about God or Krishna, but not then. That was a battle we had. But we have peace and love.

It's Starkey-Harrison, no matter what anybody wants to say.

It's an unusual song, in that it's so sad, especially now that George is gone. But musically it sounds happy. I never really thought of it as sad until now.

Sure. Well, I do it every night onstage, and people think it's for George.

And you've said that.

Well, no. Well, you can check me and call me a liar whenever you're ready. [*Laughter*] I might have said it one night. It's not something I would say every night, it's just . . . understood.

How was "Octopus's Garden" born?

I had left The Beatles. It was mad, it was just one of those mad periods, and went to Sardinia with Maureen and my two kids at the time. And Peter Sellers had a boat down there. And they gave us octopus and chips. [*Laughs*] And I said, "What the hell is this?" [*Laughs*]

These were the days of marijuana days. I was sort of hanging out, and the captain was there. I said, "Man, octopus—you got no *fish*?" And somehow we got into a conversation that octopuses build gardens. They go around the sea bed and pick up shiny objects and put them in front of the cave they're hiding in. I thought, "How great is that?" And I had the guitar and picked it up and played in E. Because I only play E on guitar, C on piano. Though I have threatened for so many years to take lessons.

And I had the line, "I'd like to be under the sea." It started there.

We were all a bit mental in that period. If you need the lead-up, I went knocking on John's door. He was in an apartment with Yoko. And I said, "I'm not playing good, and you three are so close."

He said, "I thought it was *you*! *You* three!"

So, okay, I went to Paul's door, knock knock. I said, "I'm not playing good, and I think you three are really close."

He said, "I thought it was *you three*!"

So I thought, "Fuck it, I'm off. I'm off! It's too mad now."

Anyway I went away. They sent me faxes. Telegrams! And then I got "Come on back. Come on, we love you." And George had the whole place filled with flowers.

They missed you.

They did! We were really good pals. We were all good pals.

"Octopus's Garden" was only your second song after "Don't Pass Me By." Yet it's as magical as any Beatles song.

I was shocked with that. Yeah. I've just done [a tour of] South America again. And I do "Don't Pass Me By." And they *all* sing the words. To "Don't Pass Me By"! Not "Yellow Submarine"—they do sing that. I mean, you expect it. But [*sings*] "I listen for your footsteps . . ."

This new album is phenomenal. The songwriting is great—"Postcards from Paradise," written with Todd Rundgren, and "Rory" and "Bamboula," which you wrote with our friend the great Van Dyke Parks.

Well, you know the story with "Bamboula." I always do the basic track on a synth, just to get rhythm patterns. It's in E. In fact, I do it all in C. And I just then drummed to this. There's no song or nothing. I just drummed. And I sort of got this idea in my head that I was in New Orleans drumming. And so it's a Liverpool–New Orleans sound. [*Laughs*] And I thought, "Wow, Van Dyke, he *really* knows about New Orleans, and he's a great songwriter." And he's a friend.

So I called him over, and I said, "I got this track. Don't have a song yet." And we were sitting around, and he mentioned bamboula. And I said, "Never heard of it—what is bamboula?"

And then he was telling me about in New Orleans—'cause the track is New Orleans-y—the guys that were brought to New Orleans [*laughs*] would play these drums. Then he went on the Internet, and then there's a sheet of paper giving us the whole rundown on bamboula.

So we wrote this song. But it's still like a love song. But once we had the word "bamboula," that's all we need as writers, and we're *off*—yeah, and the idea that the drum *led* this song.

Anyway, we finished it. And we tried it in a New Orleans-y way. He did all the brass arrangements and that, and we think in a New Orleans way. But then I thought, "You know, I want it to sound more like a street band." And it's like a song they all sing.

So I played every drum I had. I have these three huge African drums that Joe Walsh sent me from Africa. And so I just hit them. And I hit everything else. And I didn't hit everything perfect, because I wanted it to seem like the whole town was playing drums. And I thought, "Well, we'll fade it up, like it's coming from, you know . . . the Sunset Marquis." [*Laughs*]

You can hear the band. Okay! It's excitement. Then you get the song, and then they go past. And so that's why I did that to it. And I did bring him over, and he was smiling all the way through, so I thought, "Okay, he likes it." Because I didn't want to do anything that would upset any of the other writers.

Van Dyke's synth playing is amazing. I thought it was Stevie Wonder.

Oh yeah. And he's playing accordion. Well, he's always been great.

Your drumming on that is wonderful.

Well, that's great. Does it sound New Orleans to you?

It does. But it sounds like Ringo too—

Well, that's what I'm saying. Liverpool–New Orleans.

Did you think of writing "Rory and the Hurricanes" before working with Dave Stewart on it?

Yes. Because I'd written down, suddenly, a stream of consciousness of a time. And this was an absolute fact, that when I was with Rory and the Hurricanes we rented a van and went to London. Had never been to London—the big city—like going to LA. And we had no money. We bought the gas to get us there. And we all stayed in one room. Slept on the floor, whatever, we didn't care—we were lads. And we lived on bread, butter, and jam. And the butter ran out. And we just had bread and jam. And it's in the song.

And we did go to a dance. And no London girl would dance with us because of our accents. Because we were from the north.

Is that right?

Oh yeah, they wouldn't. We'd say, "Excuse me, love, do you want to dance?" But no. Then I asked this French girl, and she said, "Oui." And it's in the song.

So cool you chose to write a song about being in Rory and the Hurricanes, this famous but distant chapter of rock and roll history, which hadn't yet to be written in song.

Well, it was big in my life. Rory and the Hurricanes. You know, Johnny Guitar was incredible. And Rory was the ultimate showman. And in Rory and the Hurricanes, I left the factory. That was big news. I said, "No, I am a musician." We sort of turned professional overnight. We didn't know if it would *last* or not. And look where it led me.

Yeah, you did pretty well.

[*Laughs*] Yeah, but you didn't know that then.

You even did a drum solo on this album, on "Rory and the Hurricanes." Which you famously don't like to do—

I don't like to do.

What led you to do the drumming on this?

Because the next time I had gone to London, it was different. If you listen to the song. But still playing the drums, like I always do. [*Sings drum groove*] I love the end of that fill, that *dat-dat-dat*—all very simple. But I thought it was emotional. Because I wanted it to *feel* like those days. I didn't want it to sound like John Bonham or something. And I think we captured that, you know?

And also when I called Dave—now we just pass back and forth, e-mails, which in the song, you can send them to each other—I wanted him to put voices on it. Girl's voices. But I wanted them young, like we're trying to get to those days, when the girls' voices were really pitchy and up there. And he got these two fourteen-year-olds. One of them he owns. [*Laughter*]

His daughter Kaya. She is quite a singer.

She is quite a singer. I went to see her when she played the Troubadour. That wasn't easy, at fourteen.

What led you to writing all these songs with your friends? Of course we think of you singing "With a Little Help from My Friends."

Well, it is a little help from my friends. And the last three records were all cowritten. Because it's a *perfect* excuse to hang out with writers and musicians. And I haven't sort of written a solo song in a long time. I have the idea, and I want to know where it's going. If we start writing together, and it's going somewhere, I'll turn it into where I want it to be because it's my record—that's what I do. But I'm hanging out with musicians, which is just great.

These songs seem so inspired. Seems like you guys were having fun.

We were having fun. But I should have you around more often— *inspiring!*

The title song, "Postcards from Paradise," is quite remarkable—using all those iconic titles from Beatles songs.

That was a lot of Todd Rundgren in there. Because I had the track. And Todd took it and brought all that to it.

You famously came up with some titles that Paul and John used, such as "A Hard Day's Night" and "Eight Days a Week."

No, not "Eight Days a Week." Paul straightened me out. He was in a taxi with a guy who said, "Oh, I've been working so hard, eight days a week." [*Laughs*]

And he and John wrote the song. But I've always claimed it was me.

Did you ever think you should have your name on the song when you came up with the title?

Well, no. That's *these* days. When Gary Brooker, who was being sued by the organist [for "Whiter Shade of Pale"] 'cause the organist was saying, "My line." And I thought, "Oh shit, my drum fill!" [*Laughs*]

Yes, if not for coming up with titles, every drum part was so distinctive, it was just remarkable.

I think you should talk to the camera and tell them they should give me half. [*Laughs*]

I think of your part on "Come Together," for example. It is amazing. No drummer has ever played it right, like you did, since. Even [Jim] Keltner.

I had dinner with Jim the other night. He's still talking about my drumming. But he was great. I was really with John, Paul, George, and Ringo when we came here. As musicians. Like the new boy. And he was telling me—and other drummers—man, they're making us all play like you! In the studio we have to play like you.

So no matter what they said, it didn't bother me. I knew the reality of it was real out there.

Songwriters know it because you so served the song—

I do.

Every fill was part of the song in a wonderful way.

That's what I do. I've *always* had that concept that the song—if a guy is singing, they don't need no damn drum fill over it.

So many of those songs and those records blew our mind when we heard them, whether it was "A Day in the Life" or "Strawberry Fields." Was there any one, when you first heard it, you thought was really mind-blowing?

Well, I was laughing the other night with Jim because I mentioned "Rain." He said, "You always mention 'Rain'!" Well, I say it was like an out-of-body experience. I have never played that way since.

Or "Tomorrow Never Knows"—the one with the drone, and I hit the tom twice. And so just a fun story, my boy Zak said, "And that loop you had!"

[*Laughs*] I said, "Loop? We didn't have any loops!"

He said, "It's a loop! It's perfect!"

I said, "Phone this number."

And he phoned the number. And George Martin said, "Yes?"

He said, "Is that a loop?"

And George Martin had to tell my boy, "Look, Zak, we didn't have loops in those days. [*Laughs*] Your dad had great time."

It seemed you worked out amazing parts almost immediately. You'd hear a great song and find the perfect part for it.

Well, I was always pleased when I found a part, you see.

When you heard something like "Strawberry Fields" for the first time, do you remember how you felt about it?

Yeah, but it didn't sound like that the first time. It sounded like [*sings quietly*] "Let me take you down . . ." And then I would try different things. And we could *always* tell when it was coming together. We *always* knew when, yeah, that's a good move. And we always knew when we were fed up with a song. Not that song, *a* song. Just give us a cassette. We all knew that when we were coming in the next morning—

Like "Ob-La-Di, Ob-La-Da"?

Yeah, we had to do it again, you know. [*Laughs*] A lot of that went on. It was just a love of each other and playing and supporting. Even when, in the late sixties, it was a little tense. It was never tense after the count-in. Everybody gave their all.

You can hear that.

Always. And that's a great credit to any band.

Your drum part on "Get Back" is amazing.

I know. I thought I was a *genius*.

You are.

And Billy Preston, how lucky that he came to see us that day. That's all that it was about. It wasn't like a big plan: and then we'll have Billy Preston do this. It was, "Hey Billy, you can play. Play whatever you want."

And in my estimation—Billy was a good friend of mine—and Billy never put his hands in the wrong place. *Never.*

Your music has so impacted the world. Clearly as profound as what Beethoven or Mozart did.

Well, that's what we all say. And we'll see in five hundred years.

I don't think there's any doubt anymore.

I don't doubt it. I don't doubt the music. We were the best band in the land. Inventive. And anyone who is honest in a band today will say they recognize that. A lot of bands have used what we created.

You know, The Beatles were a cover band too. It's a bit different now because the writer is there already. But when we started, George Martin brought songs. And we had to make a decision. We said, "No, no, we only want to do Lennon and McCartney songs." And that was a *huge* move on behalf of The Beatles. To stand up for that. But every song he brought us was a hit for somebody else. It wasn't like he was bringing us trash.

But early on, the quality of the original songs was so high.

Yes. All love songs. "I Want to Hold Your Hand." I mean, how hard is that? The drumming on it was good.

And it was musically ingenious, going to the minor V chord on the bridge—

I wouldn't know a minor V chord if it trod on me. [*Laughter*]

But there's so little music we know that is so universally loved by almost everyone. Almost everyone loves The Beatles. What do you think led to that?

Well, I think those emotions still play today. And a lot of kids are buying our records. Few artists still sell records. And we actually are still one of them. How is that?

Because there's no better music.

Well, I think the atmosphere we came with, we gave out. And musically it's still cool. It's emotional. It's laughter. It's tears. It's love.

◆ ◆ ◆

Brian Wilson

Beyond The Beach Boys

Beverly Hills, California 1995

"Okay, I believe you," he says unconvincingly. We're having breakfast at his daily deli, moments from his home up here in the Hollywood hills, and I'm trying in vain to communicate to Brian Wilson the level of joy people receive from his music—and have received for years. He's not hearing it, looking up at me with his face downturned and a decided "if you say so" expressed in his weary eyes.

As anyone who knows anything about him already knows, he's not the type to revel in joy at his own greatness. Quite the opposite. His endless summer is a season of perpetual discontent. In an immaculately blue Angeleno sky, the sun a distant jewel of radiance, he sees only crows. "See those two?" he whispers, pointing out two distant birds outside the window, perched on a tall palm. How and why he noticed such faraway birds is beyond me. "They have been watching us this whole time."

I mention, in a musical tangent that seemed related at the time, that the composer John Cage composed melodies based on telephone wire birds he saw.

"I *know*," Brian smiles.

"So what would that melody of those crows be?" I ask.

He pauses for a moment and giggles softly to himself. Then he intones an ascending pair of notes (the interval of a major sixth, from E to C above) and sings it again, looking inward.

"You know what that is?" He sings it again and then sings, "Be-*cause* . . . be-*cause* the world is round . . ." It's "Because." By The Beatles!"

"Aha. So John Lennon is singing to you through the crows?"

"Yes," Brian says, still smiling. "Wouldn't be the first time."

Many times he sings his answers. Rather than using words to describe a certain groove or melody, he sings. Asked to describe how he composes harmonies, he sings each part. Which is impossible to transcribe into written language, of course, but still a joy to behold. And which is why interviewing him is a perpetual challenge—the fullness of his thoughts, as the world knows well, is devoutly musical. His genius is for that which is expressly beyond words. Which is why he enlisted others such as Mike Love, Tony Asher, and Van Dyke Parks to write the lyrics that fit his melodies. It's that singular focus that has enabled him to write so much gloriously tuneful and timeless music as well as harmonies to make heaven smile. Today, over a big breakfast and two bowls of strawberries, he patiently listens carefully to each question. "Let's eat first and then talk," he says, and I agree.

But first it's time to sweeten his strawberries. "They just aren't quite ripe yet," he says and opens up several tiny white packets of artificial sweetener to sprinkle on his strawberries. "It's fake sugar. Real sugar can kill ya, you know," he says with a sly smile. "But as long as it's fake, it can't hurt you."

I've had the privilege—and the challenge—of interviewing Brian several times. He's not an easy man with whom to have a conversation, as his soul is so troubled that personal darkness sometimes sadly obscures everything and it's impossible to get in. The very first time we spoke, back in 1988 (which is in *SOS I*), he was under the care of the doctor Eugene Landy and laid on a couch as if I were his analyst. One of Landy's assistants also taped the interview, and Brian spoke carefully, almost painfully, not unlike a prisoner of war knowing he's going back to his cell after this talk. He gave full and complete credit to Landy, testifying that "he rejuvenated my soul." Months later Landy, who cowrote songs with Brian and put his own name and that of his girlfriend, Alexandra Morgan, on many songs, had his license revoked for entering into a business arrangement with a patient.

The next time we met was at his home up off of Mulholland Drive, where he sat under a red tartan blanket pulled up to his chin on a couch far from the windows overlooking the San Fernando Valley. He sat motionless as an iguana, his face ashen, never facing me, and saying very little. He was so distant that day and so deeply sorrowful, I could barely reach him.

The next time I was to meet him, almost exactly two years later, he disappeared. Set to meet me at the deli where he daily dines, he didn't show up. With other people this might have been a minor concern, but with Brian it was major. I contacted his wife, Melinda, who was panicked. Brian's life was well arranged so that his whereabouts remained known. Perhaps he drove off of Mulholland this time. Or into that big Pacific Ocean that inspired so many of his songs and into which his beloved brother Dennis was lost.

Fortunately he soon surfaced. No attempt was ever made to explain to me what happened, only that our interview would take place the very next day, same time and place. And on that day, unshaven and in a billowy Hawaiian shirt, Brian appeared. Asked where he went yesterday, he paused for a long time and then said, "I went to see a friend. And she took me to see another friend, and before I knew it, it was sundown and we were in Venice. Having Thai food."

This time around the talking came easy. Sometimes the clouds that obscure that lucky old sun are clear, and he shines. And having known him now for all these years, I have learned those things that wake him up and inspire him to come alive and participate. There are others, certainly, but the best I know are women and song. One time at a party for our mutual friend Henry Diltz, the legendary photographer-musician, Brian was sitting alone, unsmiling, withdrawn. I mentioned to him that my son, who was eleven then, had discovered The Beach Boys and loved especially Brian's beautiful ballad "God Only Knows." A change came over him as I said this, like he was returning to his body. With a slight smile he said, "I love that one too. Maybe the most of all."

I asked if I could take a photo of him, and he consented, but without smiling—*without* is actually an understatement: he looked terrified. Fortunately the lovely Michelle Phillips was at the party, and I invited her to pose with Brian for a photo. Rather than stand next to him, she immediately got on his lap. His eyes opened with surprise and joy like

Stan Laurel. She snuggled up to him and purred in his ear. This worked. Suddenly the big ice melted, and Brian Wilson was smiling. A big smile.

Afterward I said, "So is that what it takes to get you to smile? To have Michelle Phillips in your lap?" He nodded and said only "Yes."

But the other dynamic that brings Brian back is music itself. Over our lunch, during which I conducted the following interview, when I brought up nonmusical topics he was nonresponsive. But as soon as I got into music he was there with me. The man is a musician's musician. He lives inside of music. It might be why it's hard for him to communicate to the nonmusical world; it's a whole other language. Brian didn't write lyrics, after all. But he made those lyrics come to life with music of great complexity and beauty. That he was a major inspiration for The Beatles—and Paul McCartney especially—is well known and not lost on Brian, who during lunch sang for me all of "Back in the U.S.S.R.," McCartney and The Beatles' most overt Brian-inspired composition.

He even was game to play along with my musical key/corresponding color query, based on the fact that many songwriters and musicians have colors in mind that correspond with each or most of the musical keys. Brian had specific ones for the major keys, but unlike every other songwriter I've ever spoken to, he had only one color in mind for the minor keys. Black. Every single one. Black.

In fact, almost all of his songs are in major keys. He's famous for being a dark soul forever tied to the task of writing sunny songs. He was the Beach Boy who didn't surf and preferred to fill his entire living room with sand than actually go to a beach. Yet the entire weight of The Beach Boys was on his shoulders. In the following he compares his situation to that of The Beatles, noting they were a unified group who worked together. Paul, John, George—even Ringo—wrote the songs and then made the albums together. "They were a *unit*," he said. "And they couldn't be torn apart."

Not so Brian and The Beach Boys. He would write and produce the albums himself, often staying home in LA when the group went on tour, and bring in the legendary members of the Wrecking Crew to cut the tracks, rather than his own band. Of course, Brian being a keen musician, got the best players in the world. Though his brother Dennis was the ostensible drummer for the band, on the record we get the soulful precision of Hal Blaine, one of the world's greatest drummers.

But all of it was Brian's vision—the songs, the sound, the spirit. And the pressure to be a genius—and to do it all—overwhelmed the fragile human at the center of it all, and Brian Wilson cracked like a cymbal hit too hard. But the man survived. He's still here with us. Long after so many of his contemporaries are gone.

And it seems impossible for him, sadly, to fathom, even after all these years, his actual impact on the world. I have said to him on more than one occasion that his music has brought joy to so many people and brought sunshine into the darkness of so many souls. But saying that to him is like talking to a man down in a well. It doesn't seem like the words ever really reach him.

As Dylan said, people have a hard time with anything that overwhelms them. And the music of Brian Wilson is overwhelming. His use of multitracked vocals over many concurrent harmony parts changed the sound of popular music. Suddenly there was the richness of a choir with the precision of a quartet. It was the arrangement of the vocals that provided the timeless infrastructure, a brilliant blending of barbershop quartet chords, doo-wop, and rock and roll.

Then came the magic of the studio. Six or more separate harmony parts would be sung often against a counterpoint of other vocals, and each part doubled or even quadrupled to tape, creating a deeply dimensional and lush landscape of sound. He took everything he could absorb from the Phil Spector Wall of Sound school of recording and then added his own harmonic genius to the mix, and his singular sweetness.

He was born on June 20, 1942, in Inglewood, California, not far from where the planes of LAX take off and land. Absolutely terrorized by a tyrant of a father, Murry, Brian retreated always to the piano and into the music. Boxed so hard in the head once by Murry, he became deaf in one ear, making this musical innovator unable to hear stereo. Into the heady days of Beach Boys success, like his idol Phil Spector, he became obsessed with perfecting records and would work endlessly on them. He spent half a year and a small fortune on "Good Vibrations" alone. But he made masterpieces. Working with another genius, Van Dyke Parks, who contributed not only lyrics but also musical ideas to the songs and recordings, Brian created the astounding and expansive "Heroes and Villains" and other great songs. It's with that song that our discussion begins.

How did you get the drum sound in "Heroes and Villains"?

Brian Wilson: I played the bass drum. I played it with a mallet. That is the *only* record I ever cut having the bass drum be the backbeat. [*Sings first verse, emphasizing the backbeat*] Great boom boom. People across the street were saying, "Hey—whatever you're doing sounds great!" Thank you very much!

Van Dyke Parks wrote great words to that—

He wrote some of the music too. He wrote some of the arrangement, not the melody. [*Sings horn line*] Like that Gershwin stuff, he wrote that. Gershwin got his way into rock and roll. Gershwin's music *was* rock and roll.

How so?

How? [*Sings melodies from "Rhapsody in Blue"*] What's more rocking than that?

Gershwin was like you—wrote amazing music, but others wrote the words—

Yes. I think Ira [Gershwin] resented having to live in George's shadow, but he wrote some wonderful lyrics, he really did.

Having famous brothers is something you obviously understand. Your brothers were famous, but in your shadow.

They were. They probably felt some envy for me.

Did they ever express it?

No. The only guy I ever really had problems with was Mike [Love]. Because he was sarcastic.

The Beach Boys still go out on tour each year without you, yet they're doing your music. How is that for you?

Well, they're keeping the music alive. But you know what they're doing? Driving the name into the ground. In the overall scheme of things it really doesn't matter. But some things do matter. The things that matter is if someone is happy with a melody. If someone says, "I want to do the lead!" And you say, "No, Mike, I want Carl to do the lead." "But I want to do that lead!" And I say, "Okay, Mike, you can do that lead."

Michael and Carl both achieved a good place with their singing. Carl Wilson was one of the greatest singers in the whole damn business. Michael too. Michael was a good rock and roll singer. And I'm a good soft-rock singer—ballads, soft-rock kind of songs. So we all did our best.

Is it true that you don't like the sound of your own voice?

You know what? I did like it some of the times, but most of the time I didn't. On my solo albums I didn't like my voice. I don't think I sing as sweet as I used to. On some songs, like "Let Him Run Wild," I hated my vocal on that. On "California Girls" I liked my vocal. "Don't Worry Baby" I liked it. "I Get Around" I liked it.

When you would write a song would you know who it was for?

No. As soon as I had the song done, then I figured it out. As soon as I was done writing the song I'd say, "Who is this song for—me, Carl, Mike, Al, or Dennis? This is for Dennis."

Your songs are so much about being in California. Had you been born elsewhere, would your music have been totally different?

Probably. They wouldn't have been as much about surf and cars.

Do you believe that Providence, or God, has guided your career?

Yes. I live my life under God's help. God helped me through my life.

Many of your songs are happy and make people happy—

Like "Wouldn't It Be Nice"?

Yeah. Or "Good Vibrations." And yet we know you've not always been happy in your life.

Yeah. Though the songs I'm writing now are not ballads anymore. I'm trying to write hard-rock songs that will sound like [*sings strong rock rhythm*]. Because I think Phil Spector paved the way for me to learn how to write rock songs.

Was "Don't Worry Baby" influenced by him?

Yeah, it was.

When you're writing a song like that, what are you aiming for?

I'm trying to think about pleasing people with harmony. I like to make people happy with harmony. That's what I'm trying to do.

Your songs all have amazing harmony parts. How did you create those?

I work them out in the studio. Phil Spector taught me how to do that. I have to hear them over the speakers to know what is there. First I put down the melody, the lead part. Then double it. Sometimes quadruple, four voices on one part.

Some songs would only have two parts and two voices doubling them, so that's only four parts. But on other songs we had up to twenty-five vocals.

Do you think a normal listener can hear all those parts, or is it something they feel?

Can you hear them?

No. I can't tell how many voices are there. But I feel it.

I don't think anybody can. But they feel it.

The Beatles imitated that sound on "Back in the U.S.S.R."

Yeah, I remember that. [*Sings entire song*] I remember the first time I heard it. It *blew* my mind!

Blew your mind in a good way?

Yeah, of course.

Unlike The Beatles, you not only wrote all the songs, you produced the records.

Well, I was producing, writing, arranging, and singing. I learned that from Phil Spector. I don't know if I did more than The Beatles did. I think Paul did some producing too.

But they were a unit. And they couldn't be torn apart. They were one unit. And Harrison came into his own later on. He wrote some really good music. It really surprised me to see what Harrison was up to musically.

Yeah, he reached their level. And they realized to do great albums, they had to stop touring and work. Whereas you did that while The Beach Boys toured without you—

Right. I sacrificed the tours in order to make great music. It gave me the freedom and the liberty and the space to make good music. I told them I needed to record, and they got Glen Campbell and then Bruce Johnston.

What you accomplished on your own is miraculous, really—

Well, I had to do it. It was my life work.

True, but you did more than work. You created masterpieces—

There is a big ratio of those.

Absolutely. "Heroes and Villains," "God Only Knows"—

"California Girls."

How do you get through writer's block?

The key is not to try to write when you're not inspired.

Last time we spoke you were having trouble writing new songs. How did you get through that?

Slowly. Very slowly. I wait until I get inspired. The key is to not try writing if you do not feel inspired. If you feel up—if your energy is up and your strength is up, then I think it's a good idea to try to write. If not, don't try to write. I won't touch the piano unless I'm very inspired.

The songs on *Lucky Old Sun* sound inspired—

Two summers ago I wrote all the songs.

But you never force it if it's not coming?

Yeah, well, sometimes I'll give it a little goose.

Do you write at an acoustic piano these days?

No. I write a lot at my synthesizer. That's where I wrote all of *Lucky Old Sun* stuff. Lately I have been at the piano again, but I might go back to my synthesizer.

Why?

Because the synthesizer sounds so *good*. It inspires melody.

Do you use different sounds?

No. I always use one called Full Grand. It's a mellow sound. Very mellow.

Your songs have always been very sunny, from The Beach Boys up to now. Do you write during the day when it's sunny?

Yes.

My current favorite song of yours is "Midnight's Another Day."

It's very dynamic. The dynamics of that are very different. I wrote the melody and then Scott Bennett wrote the lyric. He had full rein on the lyrical content. He was interpreting me. But we don't talk much except when we work. We blow all our karma on work.

I had that lyric, "lucky old sun," so I bought the Louie Armstrong version, learned the melody, and then reconstructed the chorus to make it updated and modern.

I started with that and then I wrote sixteen songs. We only used ten of the sixteen.

"Lucky Old Sun" is a suite of songs—and it's something you've done as far back as "Good Vibrations," write songs that are suites really, with many parts.

Yeah. "Good Vibrations" has six, seven sections, right.

It showed us pop songs can do more—

I think pop songs can do much if not more than people think, depending on who writes it, what the content is, how far the range of the melody is, the intimacy of the lyric, and the delivery of the vocal—they all matter. [*Laughs*]

And back then "Good Vibrations" was one of the records that changed the idea of what a record could be.

Oh my *God*, yes. Music was changing in psychedelic terms. I think *Sgt. Pepper* was a psychedelic album. I think it was a drug-inspired album. Just like *Pet Sounds*. Marijuana inspired *Pet Sounds*.

You spent a long time just making one record, "Good Vibrations"—

Six weeks.

Was the band okay with you taking that time?

No. They'd say, "Brian, what's goin' on here? Why do you want to go to another studio and another studio?"

"Because I want to get *different sounds* for *different parts* of this record."

"But Brian, we want to get this done! We want to get this done."

"Guys, take it easy. I got to do it my way or we're not gonna do it. Look—I'm gonna do this in as many studios as I want."

What led you to using theremin on it?

My brother Carl, believe it or not, said, "Why don't we use a cello and a theremin?" And I had never thought of that. So we called the Musician's Union, local 47, and we got a cello player and a theremin player. I sang the part to the guy and he played it. [*Sings part "whoo . . . oo"*] I came up with the arrangement. But he had the idea for the instruments. Without him we wouldn't have had "Good Vibrations." It wouldn't have been as good a record.

You rerecorded the entire *SMiLE* album—but all alone. You used the same arrangements, yet it sounds way better.

It was a kick. It was fun. I had to figure out all the parts—I didn't remember them. That was very difficult.

I love the album *Orange Crate Art*, which you did with Van Dyke Parks.

Oh, that's a *great*, *great* album. It's a masterpiece. Only he could have done that. Nobody in the world could have done that but him.

Do you have favorite songs of your own?

Well, yeah, I have favorites. "God Only Knows" and "California Girls."

"Good Vibrations"?

No. I like "Good Vibrations," but it's too arty for me. It's not rock and roll. [*Sings strong rock beat*] I just didn't like it.

The chorus is rock—

Yeah, it isn't rock and roll. It's pop. Rock and roll has drums in it, and guitars and bass and piano, keyboards.

So many great songwriters I know had dads who were tough on them.

Oh yeah?

Yeah. Many said how much it would have meant to get their dad's approval. Your dad was tough on you, wasn't he?

Yeah, he was rough on me. He lit a fire under my ass. He set me on fire is what he did. He got me going. He got me producing. He was a coach. Like a football coach.

Was he harder on you than on Dennis or Carl?

No, he was harder on Dennis than on me. Carl he let go. He went easy on Carl.

It's true that you are deaf in one ear?

Yes. I can't hear stereo. When I would mix I just had to do my best. It's sad. My right ear is shot, doesn't work. I just can't hear out of that damn right ear. My right ear is gone.

Your music impacted The Beatles, and their music impacted you. Music was changing fast then, whereas it kind of slowed down—

It reached its peak in the sixties and the seventies. And after that it started to descend a little bit.

Any idea why?

You want to know the truth? I think songwriters went out of business. It's hard to write a song. An original song. I think that's the reason that the business went down the tubes.

Was it the songwriters or the industry who caused that?

Both.

In doing my homework, I noticed that almost all your songs are in major keys—

Yeah.

Any reason why?

No, only to say I like major chords.

Guitar players use keys like E, A, and G a lot. Whereas you use keys they never use, like F sharp. Like "Forever She'll Be My Surfer Girl."

Do you like that key?

I *love* it. Because it resonates in my ear very well. The sound of that key, F sharp, appeals to my ears.

Irving Berlin only played in F sharp. It's the only key he knew.

I can't believe that. That's hard to believe.

I know. Though he had a transposing piano, so he could stay in that fingering of F sharp. Do you feel each key has its own color or feeling?

Yeah. I'll tell you my favorite keys, okay? D, B, F, and F sharp. A's a good key too, sometimes. A has a strong vibe, very powerful vibe.

A happy vibe?

A happy vibe to me would be E and B. A is not a happy key, just a powerful key.

"Mexican Girl" is in B.

Yeah. [*Sings chorus*] Yeah, B is not a common key, is it? I think "Whiter Shade of Pale" was in B, wasn't it?

I think it's in C.

I thought it was in B. [It is in C major.]

I'd like to name keys to see if you have colors associated with them.

All right.

A.

Red.

E.

Red.

F.

White.

F sharp.

Green.

G.

Black.

A flat.

Turquoise.

A.

Red.

B flat.

Brown.

B.

Yellow.

E minor.

Black.

A minor.

Black.

C minor.

Black.

B minor.

Black.

Are all the minor keys black?

Yes.

"God Only Knows"—that's in F sharp minor, right?

You know what? It's not really in any one key. It's a strange song. That's just the way it was written. It's not written in any one key. It's the only song I've ever written that's not in a definite key, and I've written *hundreds* of songs.

Yes, it doesn't start on the I chord.

Right.

Which is part of its beauty. It is an utterly stunning melody. And the words to that are perfect.

Tony Asher. He expressed it beautifully. With that one I wrote some of the melody and then he'd write some of the lyric, and then I'd write more. We kind of wrote it together.

Your drum parts are unique—quite intricate and unlike normal drum grooves. Rarely would you have a backbeat on the snare in a normal place, often turning that around and other cool anomalies. How did you do those?

I would write out the manuscript. Like with Hal Blaine, I would write out the chart. With other drummers who couldn't read charts, I'd have to teach it to them without the charts.

Was Dennis a great drummer?

No. He was a good drummer but not a great drummer. Hal Blaine was great. He was my favorite. A great drummer is important. But you can't forget the bass lines. Drummers are like [*sings simple drum beat*]. The bass player sometimes plays that bass, but sometimes he'll play a third instead of the tonic, like in Motown. You're in C, but you play an E in the bass. Or you're in the key of F and you'll play a C, which is the fifth. You can't forget Motown.

Besides being a pianist, you play bass and played bass with the band. How did being a bassist influence your music?

I learned how to write bass lines. I'm self-taught. I taught myself how to write bass lines. Knowing how to play bass affects how you write. You write the melody then and the changes, against the bass line, and build a strong structure. If you start with the bass line, you can be sure of having a firm structure.

That structure is what causes your songs to resound. They are timeless—

Depending on who you talk to.

Do you feel your songs are timeless?

Well, yeah, I think my music is all-time music. I think if you listen to any of The Beach Boys records ten years from now, you'll like them just as much.

What makes a song great? What's the most important thing? Is it the melody?

I think the most important thing about a song is the melody and the lyrics.

More important than harmony?

Harmony, like with "Don't Worry Baby," the harmonies are very sweet. The harmonies on "California Girls" were very sweet, but they were nice. The harmonies on "Good Vibrations" are not real sweet and pleasant, but they were right for the song.

Do you think of harmonies while writing?

No, that's a later thing in the studio.

With The Beach Boys would you record each part separately?

Well, it depends on what year you're talking about. In the sixties we would do it all at once. In the seventies and the eighties we would do it, sometimes, one part at a time.

You've gone through lots of hardship in your life. Without that pain do you think you would have written the masterpieces that you did?

Probably not. No. Because I went through a lot of bullshit in my life, and that's probably why I had to squeeze out some good songs.

First time I interviewed you, back in 1988, you were working with Dr. Landy. In retrospect was that a good thing?

Yes. Well, he yelled a little bit, you know. He yelled at people. He didn't have much control on his temper.

Do you have any sense of how much joy your music has brought to the world?

I don't know if it brings joy or not. I don't know.

It does. There are so many people just in my life who turn to your music to make them feel better.

Oh. That's amazing. When people say, "Brian, you brought a lot of joy to me with your music," I don't know if they're telling the truth or not.

They are.

Okay. I believe you.

◆ ◆ ◆

Kris Kristofferson
Another Word for Freedom

Nashville, Tennessee 1999

Only two times in my life have I seen women actually swoon. I mean total, fall-down *swoon*. The first was at an event that Gregory Peck attended. And though Peck was in his eighties then, he was still tall and debonair, and upon seeing him in the flesh, a young woman swooned. Her knees seemed to buckle backward, and she folded softly to the ground. Peck smiled and offered her a hand, as if this happened all the time.

The second time was with Kris Kristofferson. We were walking together in the lobby of the old Wiltern Theatre in Los Angeles, where he was taking part in a show I helped write and produce called *The Salute to the American Songwriter*. There he swiftly charmed everyone with his acoustic renditions of classics he wrote such as "Me and Bobby McGee," "For the Good Times," and "Help Me Make It Through the Night."

The afternoon of the show we were strolling through the lobby, and being with this legend of songwriting, who also happened to be a movie star who had done not a little but a lot of acting, I asked what meant more to him, the music or the movies. "Oh, the music," he said immediately. "By *far*. The music means everything. Movie acting is fun, and I can do it. And people pay me for it. Sometimes a lot. But it's not like writing a song."

He said this while we turned the corner, at which time a young woman in a floor-length white gown saw me and then saw the man I was talking to. She seemed to faint with her eyes open, but vertically. With an odd smile she softly tumbled in on herself like a rag doll, collapsing softly to the floor. There were people all around who came to her immediate aid, and she was fine, her head still spinning slightly as she still focused on him and said meekly, "Hi, I'm Karen!"

When I interviewed him for this discussion I related the swoon story, and he said, "Really? Who was she?" I told him I wasn't sure and asked if that happened a lot. "Not as much as it used to," he said.

He was born Kristoffer Kristofferson on June, 22, 1936, in Brownsville, Texas. His father, Lars Kristofferson, was a US Air Force major general who encouraged Kris to become a soldier, which he ultimately did.

His first song, written when he was eleven, was called "I Hate Your Ugly Face" (which, he said, his kids love). After the first, he kept honing his songwriting chops through high school and wrote more seriously when he got into college. A Rhodes scholarship came with a ticket to England, with study at Oxford University and exposure to the Soho folk music scene. Paul Lincoln, the manager of UK pop star Tommy Steele, placed an ad in the paper, which Kris answered, looking for singers to make records. They changed his name to Kris Carson. He cut a few songs, but legal entanglements kept them from being released, and Kris Carson became Kris Kristofferson again.

But he hadn't paid any dues, he said, and he felt he had some life to live. His father's pressure to join the Army worked, and after receiving flight training in Alabama, he became a helicopter pilot and worked his way up to captain. Stationed in West Germany in the early sixties, he formed a band and wrote some songs. "Once I started writing again," he said, "I decided when I got back into the music that I wanted to start at the bottom. Fortunately that's where they put me." Soon he was sweeping the floors at Nashville's famed Columbia Studios.

Proximity to country legends allowed him to peddle his songs. When June Carter Cash was in the studio he gave her a tape for her husband, Johnny Cash. Which she accepted, but it seemed to get lost in the piles of tapes people sent to him. So to get his attention, and using skills he learned in the Army, he borrowed a helicopter and landed it right in Cash's front yard, where he delivered his tape. It got his attention. Johnny cut "Sunday Morning Coming Down," and his career was officially launched.

But he didn't stop flying. To support himself while writing songs and trying to get them cut, he worked as a commercial helicopter pilot for Petroleum Helicopters International. Many of his songs were born—or worked on—while in flight or between flights while sitting on an oil platform, as related in the following conversation.

In 1966 he started recording his own songs and, in 1970, recorded his first full album, *Kristofferson*. Though it didn't sell much at first, many of his songs were recorded by many singers, including Ray Price ("For the Good Times"), Waylon Jennings ("The Taker"), Sammi Smith ("Help Me Make It Through the Night"), Bobbi Bare ("Come Sundown"), and others. In a very short time he went from student to sweeper to songwriter-singer to legend. Somewhere along the way he also became a movie star in *A Star Is Born*, with Barbra Streisand, as well as one of the most famous flops of all time, *Heaven's Gate*, directed by Michael Cimino. When I told him I actually loved *Heaven's Gate*, which I did, he said, "You're the one!"

His most famous song is "Me and Bobby McGee," recorded by Janis Joplin. As he explains in these pages, he never heard her record of it until after she was gone.

Do you always write your songs on guitar?

Kris Kristofferson: Usually. Often I write them in my head. Then when I can get next to a guitar, I see if it works.

When I was real young the tunes used to come first. But then once I went to Nashville and started being serious about it, then it went just the opposite. And finally, after watching some songwriters like Mickey Newbury, I realized you had to have a combination of the two. But still the words and the ideas come first to me now.

And then you'll think of the music in your head before going to guitar?

Yeah.

Bacharach said he did it that way. But most songwriters write with an instrument.

I'm not that good a musician, I don't think. I probably have more freedom in my head.

Do you remember writing "Casey's Last Ride"?

I do. I remember starting it years and years ago. The imagery goes all the way back to London, when I was hanging around there. But I didn't finish it until I was driving around one night. I used to work out of Morgan City, Louisiana, for a helicopter company. Flying out to the offshore oil rigs. And I used to drive back and forth from Nashville, every other week, right up to 1969. Anyway I can remember driving through a rainstorm. One of those jungle storms [*laughs*] they have down there in Louisiana. At night. Those verses in the middle of "Casey," that pretty part starting with "Oh," she said, "Casey it's been so long . . ." Those just came to me. It seemed I didn't know whether they would fit together or not. That's always been one of my favorites.

Is that unusual, that lines to a song like that will just come to you?

No. No. Some of my best songs have come like that. But, I mean, I'm always thinking about them at some level of my consciousness. [*Laughs*] Running through my computer up there.

The mind never really stops working on them, does it?

Yeah. I think that's the way mine organizes my experience. Lines just keep going through it. Especially here where I live now. I go out and work, clearing weeds and trees and stuff. And I'll be working for eight hours out there, and you've got a lot of time for stuff to run through your head.

You come up with songs out there?

Yeah. And some of them never go anywhere. But lines are always going through my head.

Do you need to write down the good ones to remember them, or do they stay with you?

I count on them to stay with me. If they're good enough, I stick with it. Unfortunately I've lost some stuff that way. [*Laughs*] My wife just pointed out some things she found that I put down on tape and just totally forgot. But they have good stuff in them.

Are you always working on songs, or do you take time off from writing?

I think both. But I think on some level my brain is always writing. Probably always will be. I noticed one of my youngest kids—he's five years old—he does it all the time. He just walks around singing his experience. Whatever's happening.

You've written several songs that are standards now, such as "Help Me Make It Through the Night." Was that one where the title came first?

No. No, I had the title last. Which is kind of odd, because that's probably the best-known part of it. I was sitting on an oil platform fifty miles south of New Orleans [*laughs*], out in the water. I had my helicopter tied down on top of the deck, and I would sit up there with my guitar by myself. I had an old twelve-string at the time. And I remember the images were first. The images of the verses. "Take the ribbons from your hair / Shake it loose and let it fall . . ." Probably just what a guy thinks about [*laughs*] when he's out there on Alcatraz! No wine, women, or song out there on those oil platforms. I think I got the title from something I read that Frank Sinatra said one time. He said he would take a bottle or a broad or whatever it took to get through the night. [*Laughs*]

When you get to that place, where you reach a title that is perfect, is there a sense you are finding something that is there or inventing something new?

Well, I never thought it was that unusual—help me make it through the night. I thought the whole song was good. I thought it was a sensual kind of sexy song. Feedback that I got from my friends—Sammi Smith was one of them—was so positive that I figured this one worked. And actually Sammi got her record out. I think Waylon and Ray Price were arguing over who would record it. While that was going on, Jim Malloy recorded Sammi, and she had a hit with it. And then Gladys Knight had a hit with it.

And Jerry Lee [Lewis]. When Jerry Lee sang it, it was a command: "Help me make it through the night!" [*Laughs*]

Jerry Lee has a way of transforming everything he sings and makes it his own song, whether it's an Al Jolson song or Hank Williams or whatever. I remember the first time he recorded a song that Shel Silverstein and I wrote called "Once More with Feeling." And we were just blown away because it was an okay song, but he made it *wonderful*. [*Laughs*] It's one of the special joys of being a songwriter that a novel writer or painter doesn't get. That you can see someone else take your work and transform it.

And transform it positively?

Not always. But more often than not. Because most people who are making music are doing it for a reason—they're good at it.

Shel Silverstein was such a brilliant songwriter. And one of the very few people with whom you've collaborated on songs.

I've never really got my name on a collaboration with a lot of people. Because I just wanted to see the credit, like sitting in the same bus or something. But Shel's one of the few people that I actually cowrote with. A couple of songs. One of them, he just gave me the idea and I went and wrote it myself. "The Taker," that Waylon [Jennings] cut, and "Once More with Feeling."

Why did you end up writing with him?

Shel, he showed up in Nashville at a time when I was a couple of years away from making it as a songwriter. He hung out with us song-writers. He was a respected writer already as well as being a guy who sold books. He was kind of famous when he came to town. He hung out with all these broke songwriters. Loved songwriting. And he was such a good one. To me, some of his songs are just perfect. Like "Boy Named Sue." It's a perfect example of a Silverstein song to me. Because it grabs you with its great imagery all the way through, and then he hits you with the surprise ending. And then, just when you are saying wow about that, he hits you with another one—the last line. [*Laughs*] I mean, you never saw it coming. I really appreciated working with Shel.

I understand you and Willie Nelson tried to write a song together, but you only got one line.

[*Much laughter*] Actually Roger Miller was in the room too. And the three of us should have been able to come up with something wonderful. We didn't, though. We were having too good of a time, I think. We had one which started, "'Hello,' he lied . . ." That was as far as we got. [*Laughs*]

"Me and Bobby McGee" is your most famous song. Do you remember writing it?

Yes. I wrote that, again, while I was working down in the Gulf of Mexico. At the time I was flying around Baton Rouge. That is probably why Baton Rouge and New Orleans were in it. But it was an idea that Fred Foster had given me. He told me he called up one time when I was about to go back down to the gulf for another week of flying, and he said, "I got a song title for you: 'Me and Bobby McGee.'" Boudleaux Bryant, the songwriter, had an office in Fred's building. Fred was the guy who owned Monument Records and Columbine, which I was writing for at the time. And Boudleaux's secretary was named Bobbie McKee. I thought he said "McGee." And he told me to go write this song. And God, I can't write on assignment. It gives me the worst case of writer's block that I'd ever seen. [*Laughs*] So I had to hide from him for a couple of months.

But then the idea just started growing in my head. And I can remember when the last line came to me. I was driving to the airport in New

Orleans, and the windshield wipers were going into the line about "the windshield wipers slapping time and Bobby clapping hands . . ." And it finished the song for me.

And I went back. Found Billy Swan back at Columbine Music, he was the only guy who was still there when I got back to Nashville. So we stayed up all night making the demo of it. It just blew Fred away.

So the only idea he gave you was the title?

No, he said Bobby McGee is a *she*! And I thought, "Oh God, I've got to start over." [*Laughs*] But I don't know, we sort of talked it over, what could happen. I was thinking of it as two people traveling around. I thought of the movie *La Strada* with Anthony Quinn. He's traveling around with Giulietta Masina in this little funky circus thing they had. He leaves her by the road. She's kind of half-witted. And he's getting tired of taking care of her. Anyway, he leaves her there.

And at the end of the film he hears this song she used to play. And this woman, who's hanging up laundry, is singing it or whistling it. And he goes up and asks her where she learned that song. And she said, "There was this little girl who came into the village, and nobody knew where she came from, and she died." And later you see Anthony Quinn out there in this tavern getting in fights. He goes out on the beach and ends up howling at the stars. It was like the double-edge sword of freedom. He was free from her. He left her sleeping by the road. He wheeled his motorcycle off so he wouldn't wake her up. But he lost her. And that was the feeling that I wanted to get out of "Bobby McGee." And freedom's just another word for nothing. Nothing left to lose. Then when I wrote that, [*laughs*] one of my songwriter friends, at least one of them, tried to get me to take that line out. [*Laughs*] They said, "You've got so much good concrete imagery all through the song, and then you get all philosophical in the chorus." I'm glad I didn't listen to them.

That's why it so works so well. That line works so well because you set it up with all that imagery, so it's a departure point. That's a song, of course, which has been so transformed by different versions of it. None more famous than the Janis Joplin version.

You can't think of it without thinking of Janis. Because she made it her own. But I love the way Jerry Lee [Lewis] sang it too. And Willie [Nelson]. And Roger [Miller]. And *shit*, Gordon Lightfoot, Ramblin' Jack Elliott. It's one of those great songs that a lot of different people can own.

And like a lot of your songs, it can be done in many styles. It can be a fast rock song or a country song.

Yeah. I've done it every different way.

Did you have anything to do with Janis's recording of it?

No. Janis and I hung out for a couple of months right before I started performing at the Troubadour. She was going off on this rock and roll train. That was a tour that was in the east. I was starting to perform at the Troubadour and the Bitter End. And then I went over to the Isle of Wight. And I was starting to do my own performance. I wasn't around her much then. When I came back from the Isle of Wight, I came back to do the Monterey folk festival, that Joan Baez was putting on. And the day after it was over we got the word that Janis had died. And so I flew down there and we were hanging out in the motel where she died. The Landmark. And Paul Rothschild, the producer of the album, told me to come by the studio the next day, and he wanted to play me that. And I did. It just blew me away. Just blew me away. I heard later—many years later—a tape of her singing it at Threadgill's in Washington. She had a big old teary introduction and everything.

Of course, the Grateful Dead used to do the song too. And they changed that line to "Freedom is just another word for nothing left to do—"

Nothing left to do! [*Laughs*] That's the most hippie thing I've ever seen. Freedom's just another word for nothing left to do. God almighty, how can you do that? [*Laughs*]

Do you remember writing "For the Good Times"?

Yeah. I was at the end of a relationship. Pretty way to say good-bye.

That is a great thing about being a songwriter, that even when the relationship is over, you still have the song.

Yeah. Don't cross a songwriter. He'll get you back. [*Laughs*]

How about "Sunday Morning Coming Down"?

That was just autobiography. It's funny—that was Sam Peckinpah's favorite song. And Robert Mitchum liked it. And Kurt Vonnegut told me it was the best song [*laughs*] that he'd ever heard. I tried to figure out what we all had in common. And I think it was drinking. Waking up with no way to hold your head that didn't hurt. And that was just walking around on a Sunday in Nashville. In those days I didn't have any family there in Nashville. I was living in a slum tenement. [*Laughs*] A condemned building. And the *bars* weren't even open on Sundays. So it seemed like a perfect day for that song.

How old were you when you wrote your first song?

I was eleven.

Is there one song of yours that is a favorite?

Oh no. It's the last one I've written. But they're like your kids. Somebody was trying to put together a collection from my different albums, and they wanted to do about thirty songs. And I started going through the different albums, most of which nobody ever heard. And taking songs out that I liked. And I had it down to like seventy-five. And that was too many.

◆◆◆

Bernie Taupin

Writing with Elton

Hollywood, California 2009

He loves cowboys. And all things of the American West. As Elton John's lyricist for three decades, Bernie Taupin is one of the most famous British songwriters of all time. Yet his passion is planted firmly in all things American—he lives the life of a working cowboy on his ranch near Santa Barbara, and even when he comes to his Hollywood office to tend to business, he is forever surrounded by immense posters of *The Wild Bunch* and other vestiges of the Old West. Though this fervor has been reflected in his songs dating back to 1970's *Tumbleweed Connection* and most pronounced, of course, in the words and spirit of their *Captain Fantastic and the Brown Dirt Cowboy*, it's a subject matter to which Elton John no longer related at the time of our talk. So Taupin created a new outlet for such songs, his own band Farm Dogs, with whom he recorded the gloriously acoustic *Last Stand in Open Country* and was at work on the follow-up.

And when the time came to write new songs with Elton, Taupin restricted himself to neutral content that met his partner's approval, a process entailed in the following discussion. "I write songs about desert nights and horses and guns because I'm around them," he said, laughing. "That's what I do. I spend most of my life on a horse. Elton doesn't. He spends most of his life in Versace."

Born in 1950 in Sleaford, Lincolnshire, England, he met his lifelong partner in song in 1967, the year of *Sgt. Pepper*, by answering an ad in the UK music paper *New Musical Express* placed by Liberty Records. They were in search of new songwriters. Elton answered the same ad, and whether it was providence or happenstance that brought them together, they were the perfect team. Bernie was known to famously labor for months, if necessary, crafting a lyric. He'd deliver a bunch of these, typed, to Elton, who would quickly page through, land on one that spoke to him at that moment, and compose the perfect melody.

It was a wedding of great craft and instinct, of determined diligence and unconstrained genius, and it produced miracles. From early classics such as "Your Song," through multidimensional suites such as "Levon" and "Tiny Dancer," to the explosion of chromatic narratives and adventures in *Goodbye Yellow Brick Road* and beyond, Elton and Bernie wrote songs for the ages.

Taupin spoke softly and with much humor and British self-deprecation about this challenge and others that exist in the life of a world-famous cowboy-lyricist.

Is it true that Elton will take one of your lyrics that you've worked on for a long time and write the music in ten minutes?

Bernie Taupin: Yeah, yeah. It's *ridiculous*. He has written four songs in a day sometimes. Sometimes he doesn't even write songs before he goes into the studio. He goes in the studio on the morning that they are going to start recording and writes a couple of songs, and when they come in he starts recording. Go figure.

How do you explain it?

I think he's a borderline genius. I think because of Elton's persona— because he is larger than life—sometimes people forget that. He is an unbelievable singer, an amazing musician, and an incredible writer. He's just got a natural flair for melody.

What he does is very interesting, because sometimes he'll play me something, and I'll think, "That's not so great. It's quite good, but it's not so great." And suddenly you realize that there are little nuances in that song that come back to haunt you. And you'll hear it again and you'll go,

"Shit, this is good. I didn't realize it, and now I know better." That's his ace in the hole. He just has these little elements where he'll twist the melody to make it interesting. He's still doing it. The songs that we are writing for this new album, they're for the most part human condition songs. They don't venture out of that. They're just really, really good songs. Real classic material. And he executes that stuff just brilliantly.

You said you just wrote thirty new songs for Elton. Does he take them all and decide which one to work on?

When there's that many, I put them all in a folder. And he just goes to the piano, puts the folder up, and sees what catches his eye. He'll skim through it. I'm sure he looks at titles too. Sometimes he won't even read through a lyric. He'll just start. [*Laughs*] He won't even understand what the song's about till probably it's recorded, and six months later he'll come up to me and say, "You know, I just figured out what that song's about!"

Do you think the lyric and the music are of equal importance in a song?

I think it should be. I don't necessarily think it's the truth. I think the melody sells the song. I don't think the lyric sells the song. But if you've got them both, it's even better. But melody is what sells a song.

Can a song be great even without a great title and lyric?

Well, I think the perfect example is that Eric Clapton song that won Best Song of the Year.

"Change the World." [Written by Tommy Sims, Gordon Kenny, and W. Kirkpatrick]

What sold that song, I believe, is production. And it had a good melody. But don't listen to the lyric. Because the lyric is appalling. [*Laughs*] It's a bad lyric. There are some rhymes in there that are really awful. But that's not what sold the song.

Presently you've been writing songs both for Elton and for the Farm Dogs. Might a Farm Dogs song ever work for Elton or vice versa?

Oh no. I had to put myself in a whole different frame of mind because when I work with Elton—and I credit him for his honesty—he likes the material to be ambiguous. No "he" or "she." The references are important to him. He wants people to believe that what he is singing about is true. That it's honest. So the subject matter is different. When I come back and write for Farm Dogs I get gritty and write about things that I want to write about.

So many of your previous songs for Elton were story songs—

Yeah, but the thing is that times change. Elton could never make a *Tumbleweed Connection* now because he wouldn't want to. He wouldn't feel himself honest doing it. Because his personality has developed into something larger than life. And that's not what he's interested in. In a way Elton's a lot more advanced than I am. I'm a bit more retro than he is. He's very into what's going on in England. And it doesn't interest me. It's all too parochial for me. I can't relate to bands singing about bus shelters in Newcastle.

In the past was Elton open to all kinds of subject matter?

Well, in the past we were finding our way. I think that's why people love all that old stuff. Because it was very evocative and it covered every musical source. He's developed his style, he's developed his personality, he's developed his character. And now his music reflects the character he is now.

Do you always write down your ideas to preserve them?

Oh yeah, I have to. If I get too drunk, I'll forget them. I've been in horrible situations sometimes where I've not been in the vicinity of paper and pen, where I've come up with several lines strung together and driving along and repeating them till I can get somewhere where I can write it down.

I came up with the first verse of "Rocket Man" like that. It was in my head as I was driving to my parents' house in England many years ago. I drove like crazy down these backroads trying to get there in time so I'd remember it and rushed in the door to write it down. I had the whole opening bit: "She packed my bags last night, pre-flight / Zero hour, nine a.m. / And I'm gonna be high as a kite by then." That all came to me at once.

When writing a lyric, do you work from titles?

Yes, very often. I have my word processor, a writing pad, my guitar, and hopefully I have a title. I always work off titles. I have a tape recorder in my car, and whenever I get ideas I just talk them into my tape recorder. I love titles. Titles have always fascinated me. I usually got the title on the top of the piece of paper, and I will start basically at the beginning and work my way down. Sometimes I'll just write all the verses first and then come back and write the chorus. I never usually write the chorus first. It's almost like I create a song like writing a story. The story comes alive.

Do you generally grasp the full meaning of a song while writing it?

In the old days I didn't really think at all about what I was writing. It used to just fall into place. That's why some of that early stuff is very, very esoteric. Some of it I haven't got a clue what it means anyway. Things like "Take Me to the Pilot"—I haven't the *foggiest* idea what the song is about.

Do you always designate specific song sections for Elton?

Yeah. Always. Even if you look at my early files. My assistant just dragged out a big trunk, and the first lyric on top was the very, very, very first song that Elton and I ever wrote. "Scarecrow." It was never recorded. It's on a little piece of schoolboy note paper, and it's very meticulously written, and it has verse one, verse two, chorus, and so on.

"Your Song" is also one of your first, and it's such a timeless, beautiful song.

It was one of the first songs we wrote when we really got locked into writing and when we had really honed our craft after writing all this sort of early bits and pieces that never surfaced.

I wrote that song one morning when Elton and I shared an apartment in Northwood Hills just outside of London. And I remember writing it as I was having breakfast—the original lyric had tea stains on it. He wrote it the same day. We went into the room where the piano was and just hammered it out.

The great thing about that song is that the naiveté of it is truly honest. It's real. It's not somebody pretending to write a song that is simple and naive. It *is* a simple, naive song. And it still stands up.

It's one of many standards you've written with Elton. Is it satisfying for you to have written standards?

Oh, sure. I'm very proud of my songs. I'm fiercely proud of our catalog and what we've done. I think it's pretty remarkable. I think it's remarkable that two people had been writing consistently well for thirty years. That's over half of my life. And still writing, still being prolific, still writing great songs.

◆ ◆ ◆

Paul Williams
Only Just Begun

West Hollywood, California 1992

His first job was as a sport parachutist in air circuses. "It was a very brief period of my life," he said, "but it has that nice carney ring to it. There I was, high over Albuquerque on the wing of a biplane, barnstorming."

He first came to Hollywood not to write songs but to act in movies. "But I looked like a little kid with a hangover," he recalled, "so it wasn't easy to cast me."

Unable to land any acting roles and finding an abundance of time on his hands, Paul Williams turned to songwriting. "I didn't have any money," he remembered over breakfast at Hugo's in West Hollywood, "and I couldn't get any work. So I started writing songs mostly for my own amusement. And once I started writing, that's all I did. I was constantly writing. When I got an office at A&M, which was a few years later, I was there around the clock. I loved it."

Recognizing Paul's intense drive and inherent talents as a lyricist, the publisher Chuck Kaye teamed him up with the composer Roger

Nichols, a collaboration that started slowly but lasted for many years and produced countless hits, including "We've Only Just Begun," "An Old Fashioned Love Song," and "Rainy Days and Mondays."

It was Nichols from whom Paul learned the basics of song craft: "For about four years he was my music school. He was a trained musician, and I learned a lot of the basics about how to put a song together from Roger Nichols and from Chuck Kaye."

For four years the team of Williams and Nichols turned out songs and had no hits. And although they would work solidly for hours, when the day was done and Nichols would go home, Paul would stay in the office and continue writing. To eliminate the need for sleep, he turned to artificial means, as he remembered. "I think I discovered amphetamines by then. So many of the songs were written by Paul Williams and those little yellow pills."

He's sober these days, and this change is foremost in his thoughts. "I can talk to you about songwriting," he said, "or I can talk to you about my life. And my life right now is about being in recovery."

He was a "construction brat" born Paul Williams Jr. in Omaha, Nebraska, in 1940. On the road with his family since he was an infant, he lived all around the Midwest as well as South Dakota, Wyoming, and Ohio. His father, an architectural engineer, was killed in a car wreck when Paul was only thirteen, after which Paul was sent off to live with an aunt in California. After high school in 1958 he moved first to Denver, where he learned to parachute, before moving to Hollywood to pursue acting.

He was raised on the music of Crosby and Sinatra, making him the perfect choice to write the hilariously inept songs for the movie *Ishtar*. But it was the beginnings of rock and roll that truly fueled his fire in the fifties. And when he heard The Beatles his life was altered forever: "The Beatles made me crazy. *Sgt. Pepper* was a turning point in my life."

His collaboration with Nichols resulted in worldwide fame, thousands of recordings, and many awards. It also led him back to the world of movies. He wrote the entire song score for Alan Parker's delightful debut film, *Bugsy Malone*, starring a teenage Jodie Foster. For the 1976 film *A Star Is Born*, costarring Kris Kristofferson (see page 286), he collaborated with Barbra Streisand on "Evergreen," which won the Oscar for Best Song that year.

Although he has written so many standards known the world over, when asked what his favorite song is, he answers with one most people don't know, "A Perfect Love," which was recorded by Gladys Knight and

Ray Charles. "The lyrics say a lot about my own life: 'Old enough to know when I've been wrong, and fool enough to think I might still change.'"

This interview was conducted in 1992. He's since not only remained sober but also became the president of ASCAP in 2009, and he has worked diligently ever since as a champion for songwriters' rights and education.

Instead of looking back and mourning the business as it was, as do many of his peers, Williams looks forward with both realism and optimism. "Yes, the business has changed," he said at an ASCAP event in 2014, "and a lot of us don't even recognize this business that it has become. But we must recognize that songs matter as much as ever. How people are buying and listening to them now has changed profoundly, but as the creators of songs, we must adjust to the new world and recognize that songs are still in the very center of people's lives. And we will fight to ensure that songwriters receive fair compensation as they always have up to now."

How did you learn to write songs?

Paul Williams: I learned by doing it. I would write all day with Roger Nichols, and then at the end of the day Roger would want to go home. And I had a tendency to not want to do that. So I'd stay up all night and write with anybody who wanted to write with me. And out of that came other collaborations.

Did you and Roger develop a routine for writing together?

Nichols would write a melody that I'd like, and then he locked me into the office and wouldn't let me out until I finished it. Roger's like six foot five, and he'd make me stay. So all of my lyrics were written to existing melodies.

When writing words to a melody, I always thought the words were already in the music. The music is the key that opens certain emotional rooms in me. I hear the music and it touches certain places in me, and then I speak about how I feel about those places.

One of my favorite songs that you and Nichols wrote is "Traveling Boy," which Art Garfunkel recorded.

"Traveling Boy" was written in the embryo. We wrote it and it laid around a long time before anyone did it. Garfunkel recorded it beautifully on the *Angel Clare* album. I usually closed my show with it when I performed. I loved it. I ripped off [Garfunkel's] arrangement and used it for myself.

You and Nichols wrote many hits for The Carpenters. Were those songs written specifically for them?

The Carpenters were good for me. The songs that they did were not written with them in mind.

"We've Only Just Begun" had all the romantic beginnings of a bank commercial. Roger Nichols and I were asked to write a song for a Crocker Bank commercial. It was something that really hadn't been done yet, to use a song instead of copy for a commercial. Roger wrote the music, and since it was a commercial about a young couple starting out, I wrote "We've only just begun / White lace and promises / A kiss for luck and we're on our way." That takes us through the wedding. Then driving off into the sunset—"Before the rising sun we fly . . ."

We wrote the bridge after the fact and just strung together what we had as a song, just in case anyone wanted to record it. It never occurred to us that anyone would. I mean "In-A-Gadda-Da-Vida" was the big song at the time, so to come along with something as schmaltzy as this and to have it take off like it did . . .

Mark Lindsay recorded it first, and his record was on its way up the charts when The Carpenters, who had also heard me sing it on the commercial and had asked if there was a whole song, recorded it. They released their single, and it just raced up to number one.

Some songs take months and some take minutes. "Old Fashioned Love Song" was about a twenty-minute song. That's how long it took to write.

"Rainy Days and Mondays" took months to write. I knew that part with "rainy days and Mondays always get me down," but I didn't know why or what I was going to do with it.

I think the interesting thing about the song is that it sold more than 3 million copies of sheet music. Which means people were buying it and learning it. To me that was a sign of something going back into the family structure—learning the song and playing it at home.

It's an interesting dichotomy that you were writing these beautiful old-fashioned ballads, although your life and lifestyle were anything but old-fashioned.

Yes. It was very Norman Rockwell for someone who was as *Mad* magazine in their personal life as I was. Because just as my success was ascending, my lifestyle was getting more and more like Dante's *Inferno*. I never looked like the kind of guy who wrote the songs. I wore round black glasses and had shoulder-length hair, a top hat with a feather in it, tie-dyed pants, and took a lot of psychedelics.

I remember Bing Crosby driving off the lot at A&M, pointing at me, and talking to his driver with great disgust. And I thought it was interesting because I was probably the only guy on the lot who wrote the kinds of songs he would sing. So I felt very rejected. I think I went out and drank.

I am a very romantic person, but I had a dark side. I think I had a spiritual awakening, and it's the reason I can sit down at this table and talk about this stuff.

Do songs come from spirit?

It feels that way. So much of songwriting is on a subconscious level, where what you're writing just comes out of you. And it's totally different from what you've been concentrating on consciously. It comes from a totally different place, and I think that if I can trust that work is being done on a subconscious level, then it kind of flows out.

I used to use drugs to get to that place; now I have patience. Have a little patience, give it a little time—it will come. You don't have to write down every single line. If you just sit quietly or go about your business, the right line will come. I write just what I need.

I'm a big fan of your songs for the film *Bugsy Malone*. How did that originate?

It was Alan Parker's first film. He came from London with these amazing drawings of what he wanted to do. I thought he was crazy. But I loved the idea. Because these were kids dressed as adults driving cars with pedals. It seemed to me I could take that twist and use it in the songs. It was creating a nonspecific period music. It wasn't really thirties or forties. Jodie Foster played Tallulah in that, and she was wonderful.

You wrote the beautiful song "Evergreen" with Barbra Streisand. Was that a melody that she wrote prior to you writing the lyrics?

Yes. She had the melody down and played it for me on guitar. She was really shy when she played it, really charming. That melody was full blown and complete when I got it. I didn't change a note. I think I would have been picked up by the hair if I had.

As I started working on the lyrics she got really excited, as if she had never heard the song before. It was really charming. Her performance in that movie [*A Star Is Born*] was brilliant.

When I heard her melody for "Evergreen" I knew we had a love ballad that's a classic ballad. Now all I had to do was write words for it. No wonder I did drugs—when you set yourself up like that. It was a classic melody. I'd like to see her write some more. She writes with two instruments, the guitar or keyboard. And this amazing voice and this head that thinks melody options against chords that I don't know where they come from, but they're beautiful.

What was it like to write those intentionally bad songs for *Ishtar*?

I became possessed with my absolute belief that Chuck and Lyle were real guys, the characters that Dustin Hoffman and Warren Beatty played. I worked months on that project. Oddly enough, a lot of the underground bands in LA started to do those songs.

I enjoyed that; it was like therapy finding out who those guys were. I crawled into their heads. It was a safe place to go because I was busy losing myself, and I wasn't comfortable in my own head, so I climbed into their heads. I had to write good bad songs.

I was surprised the critics panned it to the extent that they did. They didn't review the movie, they reviewed the budget. I thought it was a great film.

I did too. One of the great songwriting films. When they're crawling through the desert, about to die, and start coming up with lyrics— that is the essence of the songwriter's life. This is a bad situation, but maybe there's a song here.

[*Laughs*] Yes. I'm glad I did it.

Everything I've done has brought me to where I am right now, and I'm the happiest and most serene I have been in my life. There was a time in my life when I first got sober, I didn't know if I would ever write again. Not just my songwriting but my entire life was caught up in drugs and alcohol use. But I now know that my ability to communicate came from God. So I'm running a little slower now, but at least I'm still writing.

◆◆◆

Maurice White

Inside Earth, Wind & Fire

Hollywood, California 2008

He was the shining star, the drummer turned songwriter turned singer and producer extraordinaire, the heart in the heart of the soul, the founder of Earth, Wind & Fire.

Earth, Wind & Fire. The elemental poem, connecting the natural elements at play forever on his astrological map to form his universe of song. *Earth* is the rhythmic bedrock, the groove, the foundation for the tower of soul. *Wind* is pure melody, notes in succession, the expression of the human soul, the voice, the tune forever flowing, and with harmony entwined, perpetually in motion, flowing forever forward. *Fire* is elemental passion, the heat in the blood that pumps the heart, the sparks that catch when words of love and spirit fuse with groove and melody and everything ignites. All these disparate elements he wired together and connected like miracle clockwork. Everything to accentuate everything. Pure precision yet infused with authentic soul. Always crested with that element that always sent the thing home and connected directly with the heart: human voices in harmony. In a world of chaos, as he knew well, few things go deeper than that sound of humans combining their voices in perfect harmony.

He was the guy who did it. The unifier.

First came gospel. It's there he got that fire, that deep knowledge of passion injected directly into the bloodstream by way of singing. Many voices, many timbres, many different ranges and frequencies and textures, all united into one rich, joyful sound, linked by one melody and one message. It's the reason song is forever linked with religion, with all religions—that holy connection that comes when humans stop clashing to sing together and to harmonize about God and man and heaven and earth.

He sang in church and he sang at home. Then came the drums and the passion for pure rhythm that propelled him on a forever path toward one of the most essentially soulful, exultant musical experiences ever preserved on record: Earth, Wind & Fire. As the guiding light of this expansive group, the unifier of all elements, the heart in the heart of the soul, Maurice White wrote or cowrote all of their signature songs, including "That's the Way of the World," "September," "Fantasy," and "Shining Star." He won seven Grammy awards and a total of twenty-one nominations.

He was also an artist highly respected by his fellow musicians and industry folks and universally beloved by all those whose lives he touched. But like other shining stars that burn so brightly, his light is already gone. Just weeks past turning in the draft for this book, February 4, 2016, Maurice White died at the age of seventy-four in Los Angeles from Parkinson's disease.

But that shining-star spirit shines forever bright in his chain of inspirational songs and in those deeply dimensional musical tracks he concocted, always anchored with solid grooves and colored beautifully with horns, strings, synths, and rich vocals. The sound Maurice made.

He was born into a musical family in the musical mecca of Memphis, 1941. His father was a doctor who also played saxophone, and his grandmother was a gospel singer. Gospel was the only music he knew for years, and it was enough. Raised by his grandmother at first in the Foote Homes projects in South Memphis, music infused his soul.

He started singing at six. At twelve he started playing drums. He took to them like he'd played them his whole life. His great rhythmic prowess on the snare itself inspired him to join the school marching band, becoming its shining star. Not only was he a naturally gifted musician, he also had a flair for performance and dug the shiny uniform he got to wear while dancing down the field with his drum. It was a taste of things to come.

In time he moved to Chicago with his grandmother to be closer to his mother and stepfather. It's there he fell in with Chess Records, or "Chess University," as he called it, as it's where he gained experience and wisdom about how great records are made and how the business works.

At Chess he became an in-demand house drummer, playing on records by their legion of legendary artists, including Etta James, Ramsey Lewis, Muddy Waters, Betty Everett, Buddy Guy, and Sugar Pie DeSanto. In 1966 he went off to become the drummer in Ramsey Lewis's trio.

His own band began to coalesce when he first teamed up as a songwriting trio in Chicago with Wade Flemons and Don Whitehead to write jingles for commercials. This led to a record deal with Capitol as The Salty Peppers. Their first single, cowritten and performed by all three, was "La La Time." When the second single failed to fly they realized it was truly "La La Time," and they moved to Los Angeles to regroup.

Maurice renamed the band after the elements that united like harmony parts in his astrological chart, Earth, Wind & Fire. He was the guiding light of the group always, the chief songwriter, lead and harmony vocalist, and producer. Always yearning for new equations of sounds to distinguish his tracks, he began to weave in the acoustic kalimba, a thumb piano, with early Moog synths, rich horn sections, and lush strings. It all came together like magic, and it was a magic that emanated from his singular soul. He redefined his own group, gave funk and soul a new depth and grace, and impacted all in his wake, even fellow geniuses like Stevie Wonder.

Stevie was known to be reverential in his love of Maurice, a love that was mutual. At the 2016 Grammy Awards, only eleven days after Maurice's death, Stevie expressed that love as he does best, transcending words to pour his soul into a song. With the glorious five-part groove vocals of Pentatonix joining him in exultant vocal richness, Stevie lit Maurice's "That's the Way of the World" on a fire that burned so brightly the entire audience was on their feet, dancing with joy, only moments in. Such is the power of song.

Having momentously stepped out front from behind the drums, Maurice was always impeccably and chromatically attired—this shining star shone in shiny suits ever since the marching band showed him the way—and he danced his exultant way up the soul and pop charts, shaping the sound of the late seventies. In time his band would sell more than 90 million records.

Eventually the Parkinson's caused him to cease touring with the band, but like Brian Wilson with his Beach Boys, Maurice stayed at home and wrote songs and produced records—the music never stopped flowing. He also wrote songs for and produced a host of great artists, including Minnie Riperton, Weather Report (he did the vocals on "Mr. Gone"), Barbra Streisand, Neil Diamond, and Barry Manilow. All turned to Maurice as the magic man, wanting an infusion of his chromatic soul in their music.

Personal aside: I always remember, personally, being in my freshman dorm room at Boston University, 1977. These were the days long before computers. We didn't even have a TV in our room—we didn't want one. We had a stereo. And my roommate, who was a terrific dancer, had Earth, Wind & Fire records. It's when I discovered what true soul— the heart of R&B, with harmonies and synth textures transcendent— sounded like. It sounded like Maurice White and his band.

We spoke on a resplendently sunny day in Los Angeles, where he graciously and generously expounded on his remarkable life in music.

Maurice White: When I moved to Chicago I was seventeen. In order to go to college. I went to a junior college first, and then to Chicago Musical Conservatory. I wanted to be a schoolteacher. I wanted to be a music teacher.

What happened?

What happened is that after about a year or so I started to work at Chess Records. Chess Records was like Chess University. [*Laughs*] It gave me an opportunity to really spread my wings. I got an opportunity to play with all of the artists I had dreamed about when I was a kid. I would pick up their records and follow their careers. I had an opportunity to play with just about everybody.

Were you already writing songs before this time?

Well, what happened, as a result of being in the business, going to Chess every day, I kind of got the knack of understanding the simple songwriting, you know. That was what it was really all about.

I kind of experimented a bit with some of my friends as far as songwriting, but we just did, like, local stuff. We did commercial jingles and things like that. So it wasn't anything on a large level at that time.

And at Chess you got to work with Willie Dixon—

Yes, I played with Willie. I got to play drums on a lot of his records, and he played stand-up bass. I learned a lot from him.

Etta James?

Yes, Etta James. She was extraordinary. I worked with everybody on the roster.

And when you were playing drums were you also beginning to produce and arrange?

Not at first. Mostly drumming at that time. I was just getting my feet wet learning the structure of song and learning how to apply it in the proper way. It was like a university, man, it really was. All the production was done in one room, and I just got a chance to pick it up.

How long were you at Chess?

For five years.

Longer than a college term—

Yes. And it was like college and graduate school all in one.

How did you hook up with Ramsey Lewis?

Ramsey Lewis was an artist on the label. And he used to come down to Chess all the time and just watch the band. Because we had a band that worked for Chess primarily. And so he would come down and just watch us. And we all knew each other.

When his own band broke up he needed a drummer and a bass player. So he called on me and a friend of mine, Cleveland Eaton, who played bass. And we'd go out on the road. It started as just an experimental trip to see how I would work out. And we all gelled, so we decided to stay together, and I joined his band. I worked with Ramsey for about four years.

Before Earth, Wind & Fire you started your own band?

Yes. What happened, during the time I was with Ramsey, I had a group on the side called The Salty Peppers. And we made a little record deal with Capitol Records. We had a regional hit in the Midwestern area with a song I wrote called "La La Time." I wrote it with Don Whitehead and Wade Flemons.

What happened was when we wrapped up doing what was the formation of that band, and I didn't know it at the time, but the members of that band, The Salty Peppers, became the original members of Earth, Wind & Fire.

How did that transition from Salty Peppers to Earth, Wind & Fire happen?

We all came out to Los Angeles after I quit Ramsey's band as The Salty Peppers. So we changed our name to Earth, Wind & Fire.

Your name?

Yes. That's my name. I was looking for a name for the band because I wanted to change it from The Salty Peppers. This all happened in Chicago before I had my astrological chart done. It was laid out on the table, and I saw the elements that were in my chart, which were earth, air, and fire. I turned air to wind. The rest is history.

We all came out to Los Angeles to try to make it. There were six of us. In fact, we had a female in the band too. Her name was Sherry Scott.

Then I augmented the band with some members I picked up out here. But it was six of us from Chicago. We stayed together for about eighteen months. Then my brother Verdine eventually joined that particular band as bass player. We began to augment and expand the band, and Verdine was a part of that.

In the band you started by playing drums?

Yes, I was playing drums at first. And I was singing a little bit, but I had to have some main singers because they were away from it.

By that time were you writing a lot of songs yourself?

By that time, because of circumstances and because I didn't have any writers to depend on, there were two other writers in the band, Don Whitehead and Wade Flemons—they had a lot more experience in commercial writing than I had. But I picked up on it because of my experience of my playing, you know.

So we wrote all the songs together. And then Sherry Scott, she was a pretty good writer too. She contributed heavily to the writing.

So the writing would be done in a collaboration of all of you working together?

Mostly the three of us, Whitehead, Flemons, and myself.

Is it true your songs always start with music?

Yes. The way I've always written is that we write the music first, and then the music suggests the lyrics. I've always written like that.

Do you write on keyboard now? What do you usually use to write?

I usually write on keyboard now. I usually collaborate with other people. I like writing with other people.

There are only two songs that I wrote primarily from the piano by myself: "Head to the Sky" and "Devotion."

But the band changed, and after eighteen months we decided to go separate ways. So I had to re-form the band and got Ralph Johnson as drummer, and I got Philip [Bailey] as a conga player and singer, and Larry Dunn and Andrew Woolfolk, and that was expanded from that point on.

How did you hear of Philip Bailey?

A real good friend, Perry Jones, was a friend of Philip's, and he turned me on to Philip.

What a perfect player for your music. And his voice and your voice are perfect together.

My intention in the beginning, when I got Philip in the band, was to put him out front. I was not going to sing. I was only just going to play drums in the back. But that didn't work out because Philip's range was a high range. So I needed to balance that range.

Did you enjoy stepping out front from behind the drums?

It was always hard to get out front. I didn't like it too much. But after the girls started screaming and that stuff—

Then you got used to it.

I got used to it. [*Laughter*] It was pretty easy to get used to.

Also you got a fine drummer in Ralph Johnson. Early on you started using kalimba in your music.

I started playing kalimba while being with Ramsey. Because Ramsey gave me a great forum for exploring my talent. Ramsey, every night during the concert, he would feature me as a drummer. I had a twenty-minute feature. During that period, of course, I played the drums. But then I started to introduce the kalimba as well. That's how the kalimba was discovered.

That's such a great sound. You also began to write songs with Charles Stepney.

Charles Stepney was a great friend of mine. He contributed heavily to my development. During my years in Chicago playing jazz music Charles and I used to have a trio. We played jazz music. Also, Charles was great as an orchestrator. While working at Chess, Charles was an orchestrator there, and he knew about arranging and stuff. Once I got my band together, Charles contributed quite a bit to the sound of ours, as far as strings and horns.

So that's why he has writing credit on "That's the Way of the World"?

No. He has credit on that because he helped to write the melody. But he had started to work with me much earlier. I think the first album was *Open Our Eyes*. And he contributed very heavily to the orchestration because he was really good with that. He was my first real coproducer.

On your records not only is the songwriting great but the horn parts, harmonies, and vocal arrangements are so beautifully conceived, as perfect as the songs themselves.

Yeah. Well, everything enhances, everything enhances the other. That's our objective of it, to make sure everything fits hand to glove.

When you write a song, are you thinking in terms of the parts of the production, or does that come afterward when you go to the studio?

First of all, I think in terms of the melody. Melody and rhythm, that's my first thing, the first thing that approaches me. And then from that point on, I'll start to think in terms of story. But first, melody comes first for me. Melody is always to me influenced by lyrics.

So you generally finish an entire melody before you even consider lyrics?

Yes, I do. And it's worked for me all these years.

Yeah, it sure has.

Yeah, pretty much. The melody complements the words, and the words complement the music. And you also have a string melody that complements the horn melody. It all fits together.

Some songwriters keep the tape rolling while they're writing.

Yeah, I like to do that too. I do.

Do you generate melodies from chords, or do you work on the melody itself?

No. From chords. What I try to do is I try to push chords. I'm concerned sometimes when certain melodies will not fit up with certain chords. And I'll push real hard and try to make something fit.

There's no real formula that I use, other than to start off first with melody or rhythm. I always start from that point, you know.

Speaking of melody, "That's the Way of the World" has such a sweet and enduring melody. It's inspirational.

That melody was written by Charles Stepney, and from that melody and those chords I wrote the words. The music influenced the lyrics. It sounded in a way that suggested those words.

He wrote the melody and the chords sometime before we really approached the song. And I knew it was great. It reaches a climax and just stays there. It was a great song from the beginning. Some songs are just more inspirational than others. And that's one of the few.

It sure is.

Yeah. When it comes on, I think what happened too is that all the pieces fit together perfectly. The melody, the strings, the horn melodies—everything works hand in hand.

It's a song—and track—that never loses its greatness.

It just gets better and better and better. It really reaches the climax, and it just stays there. And one point that made that record good was the contribution of Charles Stepney. Especially with the string lines and the horn lines. By that time he had really developed as a great string writer.

He also wrote "Reasons" with you?

Right. He wrote "Reasons" with Philip [Bailey] and I. That came out of the same batch of songs. There was "Reasons" and "That's the Way of the World." Those two melodies were two melodies that he played for me.

It was very interesting because during our time, that was a rather early time for the synthesizer. And all melodies he had put on tape with the Moog synthesizer, which was brand new and unknown still at that time.

So he didn't sing them at all?

No. They were all done with synthesizer. And that was from the midseventies, '75 or something like that. That sound, the sound of the synthesizer, was very new.

On "That's the Way of the World," did that lyric come quickly or did you have to work on it for a while?

We had to work on it for a while. The overall lyric came easy, but the verses were something we had to labor for a while. It wasn't hard, but it took time.

"Shining Star" was written with Philip Bailey and Larry Dunn?

Yes. "Shining Star" was very easy to write because we came out, and we had just recorded a melody in the studio, like a funk melody, and I was just walking. We actually did it in Nederland, Colorado, at Caribou Ranch, where Chicago used to record.

I love Nederland.

So you know. It's a beautiful place. We were just walking outside, and the stars were so plentiful, it was almost like you could reach in the sky and pluck one out. And actually it was having that experience of the stars in the sky, being able to see them so clearly influenced me to the title "Shining Star."

I had no idea! It's a Colorado song!
Yeah. The environment helped. Had we not been there, I don't think that song would have happened. The stars don't shine as brightly in LA.

Not the ones in the sky anyway. [*Laughter*] Do you recall how "September" was born?
Yep. That was written by Al McKay and myself and Allee Willis.

You came up with that melody?
Al McKay and myself. That was written actually in Washington, DC, in the middle of a riot. We were checking into this hotel in Washington, DC, and I remember there was a riot going on outside. We were just trying to find something to do, so in the middle of it, we just started to write a tune. [*Laughter*] We wrote it while looking outside the window at the riot. And "September" was the song.

Yet that lyric wasn't about the riot at all?
Oh no.

Why did you choose that title?
September had always been a favorite month for some reason. I don't know why.

That's another great melody.
That was another great one, yes. A ballad with big groove.

I understand that the last time the band went on tour that you stayed at home to work on the record?
Yeah, while they were on the road. I am basically retired from the road. And after twenty-five years on the road, that's long enough for me. I'm getting more into production. I am basically a producer now. It was the first time, and we wanted to see if they could do a performance without me.

You think it works okay without you in the band when they are out there?
It works pretty well. I make an appearance every once in a while. [*Laugher*] I stay at home and work on a live album. We have a live album that's coming out pretty soon. We recorded in Japan. So at first I stayed home to work on that.

Many great artists, such as The Beatles or Brian Wilson, did some of their greatest work when they stopped touring.

Yeah. You can really concentrate on the work. Touring takes a lot out of you. It takes *all* your concentration.

Also, at the same time I'm dealing with a company now. I'm actually building a studio right now.

Is there a favorite Earth, Wind & Fire song of yours?

Probably "That's the Way of the World."

Yeah.

Probably is my favorite. There's another tune that I like pretty much. It's called "Love's Holiday." I like that too.

It's a great song.

Yeah. We've recorded quite a number of tunes [*laughter*] throughout our career, you know.

◆ ◆ ◆

Bryan Ferry
Of Roxy Music

Los Angeles, California 1993

Bryan Ferry is poolside. It's a posh Los Angeles hotel bustling with midday activities: limos and taxis arriving and departing with doormen handling luggage and palming tips, banquets of businessmen and women congregating around big circular tables in formal dining rooms, a ballet of waiters and bellboys and clerks circling, tending to wishes and conflicts. It's one of those glorious Southern California days during which the sun is sumptuous, a cool breeze is blowing, and some people are very, very busy while others are anything but.

Ferry is calm and comfortably shaded beneath an umbrella, reflecting elegance and luster in country-club white at a table by the pool. He's wearing dark shades, hair slicked back, drinking a frosty glass of bottled water. Occasionally he casts a glance toward the turquoise pool, where people are wetly frolicking, while others lie around the periphery in pastel suits, reading papers and paperbacks and sipping cold tropical drinks. After dispatching a friend for a particular hair tonic, he happily agrees with my estimation that *Avalon*—one of the many wondrous albums he conceived with his group, Roxy Music—remains one of the best albums ever.

At the time of our talk he had been toiling away on a still-unfinished album of originals called *Horoscope*. But he put that on hold to record *Taxi* instead, an entire album of covers.

He was born on September 26, 1945, in Washington, in the north of England, near Newcastle. It's the town, he tells me, where George Washington was born, a coal mining area surrounded by farmland. There were never any other musicians in his family before him. His father, Fred Ferry, was born on a farm and farmed himself until the Depression, at which time he went down in the coal mines to work with the horses—the "pit ponies" that pulled the trucks. "He was an old-fashioned man," remembered Ferry, "so we never had a telephone or a car, but we had a radio."

Before becoming a professional musician, Bryan was a pottery teacher at Holland Park School in London. From there he formed his first band, The Banshees, and later The Gas Board. In 1968 he moved to London and formed Roxy Music in 1971. It was composed of many friends, including Graham Simpson, Andy Mackay (on oboe and sax), and none other than Brian Eno, who played Andy's synth and also recorded the band. Other musicians who ultimately joined included Dexter Lloyd, David O'List, Paul Thompson, and Phil Manzanera. Their first hit was "Virginia Plain" in 1972. Eno left the band before the second album, and Bryan took over. In 1976 he disbanded them for the first time to do solo work. They got back together in 1979 and did several more albums.

Their first and only UK number-one single was the song "Jealous Guy" by John Lennon. It's classic Lennon, an aching melody of great beauty with words of dark candor, so ideally suited to Ferry's smooth delivery.

He was a visual artist and painter before he started songwriting, and he continued in that vein by designing all of his album covers, videos, and stage shows. Today he has about forty minutes to talk before being limoed to Burbank for a rehearsal of *The Tonight Show*, then still hosted by Jay Leno. On the show that night he talked about including the late Anna Nicole Smith in his new music video for "Will You Love Me Tomorrow," the famous ballad by Goffin and King. Today at poolside he's talking mostly about music, origins and goals, and the technological burden of the modern recording studio, with its limitless possibilities. With swimmers and sleepers reflected in his sunglasses, he joins in a recitation of lyrics from one of his own songs, the hauntingly beautiful "More than This" from *Avalon*. Speaking of how the lyrics delighted me,

I mentioned the first lines, which slowly turned into the two of us, pool-side, celebrating these lyrics in unison: "More than this, there is nothing." That said it all.

I know you had no TV or telephone growing up. But you did have a radio. What did radio mean to you?

Bryan Ferry: It meant everything. Radio—and music itself—was very important to me growing up. One of my aunts who babysat me would play me all the American crooners: Nat King Cole, Billy Eckstine, The Ink Spots.

So I was brainwashed into that kind of music at a very young age. Later came 78s that my sister played: the early Elvis records, Little Richard, Fats Domino.

I got into blues and jazz from about the age of eleven and got obsessed with it. I got an EP of the Charlie Parker Quintet with Miles Davis and learned every note of that. When I went to university I studied painting for four years, from '64 to '68. After graduation, since music meant so much, I thought that maybe I should try to write some songs. I knew that if I didn't try to do it, I would always regret it.

So I started learning piano. Actually a harmonium was my first keyboard. I remember pumping away furiously at it, playing these rather modal, droning things.

After writing a few songs I thought, "This is what I want to do. This is what I want to do all day."

Do you remember your first song?

Yes. It was called "Psalm." Maybe not the very first, but the first one that mattered. I held back until the third Roxy album. It was hard at first to write songs. It's even harder now. The music always comes to me much easier than the words. That's always been the case. Especially in the last ten years. Ever since *Avalon*. I started to work in a larger format, which, looking back now, I realize was a big mistake. With this album, *Taxi*, I've gone back to twenty-four-track analog, but for all those years after *Avalon* I had doubled up to forty-eight-track and, lately, fifty-six-track. Which was a nightmare.

Why?

I have a habit of writing in the studio and using the studio as an instrument. When you're working twenty-four-track, that method is just about workable because, at some point, you have to stop filling up tracks and do the vocals. When you use forty-eight-track, you double all your options, and it becomes a torturous process—a very interesting one, because you can experiment with textures. But it creates problems too. And that whole time I was producing myself.

When I did my own work, my own songs, I'd build this abstract soundscape and then try to find lyrics to fit that. And the more sophisticated the abstract instrumental composition became, the harder it was to find lyrics that would work.

So finding the words is harder than finding the music?
Yes. Melodies come to me easily, I think because I have eclectic tastes.

I work on melodies at the piano, playing chords. Sometimes I just get a mood, a chord structure, and not even know the top line. Or sometimes I get a top line, but it changes radically. I work on it for weeks and months. Sometimes I get tired, and I find a melody that is a negative to the positive. I start singing in the spaces. It's like painting. You work on something and rub it out and do it again. It's not finished until you sign it. Or till you go to the mastering room.

Sometimes I have an idea for a song and write it down in the notepad, and months or years later, when looking for an idea, I find something that will fit a chord sequence with a melody I have. Sometimes something completely spontaneous will come up musically that will match an idea. There was a song called "Kiss and Tell" that was inspired by some English *National Enquirer*–type paper about some girl's revelations. I first did a real slow, haunting version of it. Which sounded quite better than what the original record turned out to be, which was a faster version.

When it comes to writing the lyrics, any advice about how best to do it?
No. It's a nightmare writing lyrics. I'm still looking for the answers about writing lyrics. I loved reading about novelists who get up early and write solidly from seven until noon and then take the rest of the day off. That sounded wonderful to me because I always worked late at night. But things are beginning to change for me. For this new album I got into singing during the daytime, and it was much better. I used to think that I can only sing at night, at concert time, or much later. Similarly, with writing lyrics, the next time I do it I will try to write lyrics during the day.

You said you used the studio as an instrument for songwriting. What kind of track would you start with?
When I would write songs in the studio I would often start just with some percussion. I like electric percussion. So it's not heavy drums, but

something lighter. Then usually piano, electric piano, is the first thing that goes on, and then maybe some strings or a sound that fits the music.

"More than This" is one of those magic songs that sounds as great as when it first emerged. How did that one come to be?

I composed "More than This" on a keyboard with a string sound. But maybe it was piano.

I think it's one of my best songs. I wrote the lyrics in different places—some of it was England, some of it was Ireland, some was in Nassau, some in New York.

Did you write "Avalon," the song, at the same time?

Yes. When I wrote the song "Avalon" I made a little, private keyboard demo of it, and it was quite fast, a much faster groove. Seven months later I came to cut the song and did it in a slow way, and it suited it much better.

To those of us in Southern California, when we think of Avalon, we think of the little town on the island of Catalina. But that had nothing to do with your song, did it?

No, it didn't. The title came from some reverie, and it seemed to suit the music very nicely. I was in a hotel in New York when I wrote the finished lyric. I finished it up on a Saturday night, desperate because I had to go in the next day and sing it.

When I went into the Power Station [recording studio] the next day to sing it, I discovered the girl who sang on it at the coffee machine. It was Sunday, and this girl from Haiti [Yannick Etienne] was getting downtime and was strumming an acoustic in the corridor, practicing a song.

I heard this voice, this beautiful voice, and I thought that I must get this girl to sing on the record because her voice was just amazing. And now you can't imagine the song without her. I just got her to do some scat singing on it.

Do you have favorite songs you've written?

I think, of my own songs, I have a few favorites: "Do the Strand," "Dream Home," "Mother of Pearl," "Windswept," and "Avalon."

Each one of those, though they're very different songs, shares one element: a strong melody. Do you have any idea what makes a melody great?

Good melodies are often infuriatingly simple. You realize that when you sing some songs by other people. I sing "Rescue Me"[written by Raynard Miner, Carl Smith, and Fontella Bass] on this album, and if you analyze the original Fontella Bass version, you see that. It has a great female, diva-like performance, a wonderful bass line, and that was it. If you take the bass line away, there's not much there. We changed the bass line to change the entire feel of the song, which is quite nice.

In your lifetime—and mine—we have seen the popular song go through some serious changes. Do you think there are new places to go with the song form?

Yes, absolutely. Some people think the song form has exhausted itself. I don't think so. It would be depressing to think so. I think people need songs in their lives. They always have and always will.

◆ ◆ ◆

Elvis Costello
A Man Out of Time
New York, New York 2015

"There's no *one* way that I know songs to be written," he said in the midst of discussing the miraculous multitude of songs he's written. And so he wrote every kind of song that can be written. His vast lyrical span is matched only by his tremendous musical range, quite unlike most songwriters. It's not only that there are a lot of songs—and a lot of great ones—but such a vast array of songs in every style. From the pumped-up and frenetically brilliant first work through the expansive, cubist stylings of *Imperial Bedroom*, to the Americana of *Blood and Chocolate*, to the sophisticated and complex songs written with Bacharach on *Painted from Memory*, and beyond, his work has spanned more kinds of music than most people ever listen to.

But it's all him. All united by a charmed gift for melody, a penchant for sophisticated chords and harmonies, and endless lyrical ingenuity. He's one of the few songwriters who is as equally inventive and inspired with lyrics as with music.

That vast musical range was instilled into him since he was a kid. Early on, he heard a lot of songs. All kinds of songs. His father was a professional singer who would do dance band versions of standards as well as songs from the Hit Parade—all kinds of songs. He'd come home with a weekly armful of records, and father and son together would absorb them. His dad even appeared on the same 1963 Royal Albert Hall bill as The Beatles, the show most famous for Lennon's cheeky remark that the people in the cheaper seats applaud while the wealthy should just "rattle their jewelry." In that very show Ross MacManus, who used the pseudonym sometimes of Day Costello, performed "If I Had a Hammer," written by Pete Seeger and Lee Hays. (See *SOS I*, page 1.)

Elvis delighted in the range of music his dad would deliver, always in search of the right song to sing in the dancehall. "Every weekend he'd come home with a stack of records," he said. "And they were anomalous records, really, for someone who was singing with a dance orchestra. He'd bring home the hit tunes of the day and learn them. When he struck out on his own he started to make his own choices of songs because he no longer was told what to sing, and by then he had opened his mind up to all sorts of music that you wouldn't expect a man his age to be interested in. But he *was*. He would be listening to the new Marvin Gaye record and then the new Jefferson Airplane record, and then he'd say, 'Okay, I got that now,' and he'd give it to me. He was always my conduit of new music. I always had much more music than my allowance would have allowed me to buy."

Not only did his dad come home with records, he also came home with sheet music. And it's there that his young musical son discovered a musical and magical realm that forever enriched and expanded his own musical vocabulary—all the rich and often complex chords, wrapped around sumptuous melodies, used in standards. He already knew the basic chords, the I, IV, V, and VI found in rock and roll. But suddenly he learned all the chords between the chords—the minor sixths, major sevenths, and even those beautiful adult chords—the diminished and augmented ones that many rock- and folk-based writers never learn. Although he didn't theoretically analyze these chords, he used them early on in his own songs—bringing sophisticated harmonies to rock and roll—as if Buddy Holly and Cole Porter collaborated. And like both Buddy and Cole, who were gifted wordsmiths as well as great composers, Elvis had a love for wordplay and the delicate dynamics of fusing language and tune.

Elvis always had a reverence for great songwriting of every generation and genre. After his first albums, while many of us were listening to
him, he was listening to Sinatra and others sing the songs of the past—
the standards of Cole Porter, Gershwin, Jerome Kern, and the rest. He
even went so far as to invite Sammy Cahn, lyricist for so many Sinatra
classics, to write with him, a story shared in the following conversation.

Like his dad, he's joyfully journeyed through periods of immersion
in different flavors of music, times that forever shaped his own songs.
Father and son bonded in their happy inclination to slip on different
styles of music others never would consider and making it their own.
"[My dad] had a similar thing that I seem to have experienced," Elvis
said, "when he would be all about one kind of music for a little while.
When I was a kid, he was all about Irish music. Then Spanish music.
Then there was this period when he was only playing the *St. Matthew
Passion* [by Bach]. He was that kind of creature."

It's the same kind of creature Elvis is, as he admitted, though he's
always been a fan and practitioner at the same time: "Often I only listen
to one kind of music exclusively for a period of time. Partly enjoying it,
partly learning from it."

In his dad's later years, after Elvis had become a famous songwriter,
father and son continued their listening parties: "We always enjoyed
listening to music together. I would go over to his house and play him
something I was working on, and he'd be playing some records for me."

Unfaithful Music & Disappearing Ink is his memoir, published in
2015, just in time for this conversation to take place. Though we were
only officially allotted one hour, he kindly spoke for more than two. I
thanked him for giving so much time and thought to this, and he said,
"Actually I hadn't noticed how much time had gone by. I guess we must
be doing something right."

In fact, it was one of those conversations that only scratched the surface of his genius and could have gone on for many more hours and still
be incomplete. His mind, as is evident in his often gymnastic lyrics, is
agile and leaps from subject to subject—each with its own validity.

He's a humble guy and, like others in these pages, deflects any pomposity or, as he calls it, "piousness" in regard to his own prodigious gift. Instead
he insists he is lazy and that the word "prolific" does not apply to him.

Regardless, he's written a vast amount of remarkable songs in every
style and form and approach, starting with his remarkable 1977 debut,
My Aim Is True. Masterful collaborations with Bacharach, McCartney, and

others proved that which we already knew, that he's a deeply gifted crafts-man; his descriptions of writing those songs sheds substantial light into the joyful mystery of songwriting. Although he allows that much about making music is often "beyond language," his explanations of the delicate dynamic required in discovering—as opposed to inventing—a song is revelatory and is as beautifully expressed as thoughts within his lyrics.

At the time of our talk he was discussing returning to his work with Burt Bacharach on a stage musical that would incorporate new songs they have written together but remain unrevealed. "I am writing things you can't hear right now," he said, "but there are very extraordinary songs that we have in our folio, which we have expanded to create a stage musical. *Beautiful* ballads. I am just now starting to go back to work with Burt again. Since the very beginning, with 'God Give Me Strength,' we have this powerful collaboration which leads to a lot of things. And I am thinking of how I take all the songs in this folio and connect them for the stage. That would be a contrivance. When you are facing the puzzle of how to get a story to credibly run through songs, sometimes you have the songs you need already, and sometimes you simply have to write new songs. So we have the opportunity to write another ten songs. Hopefully that will happen and you will see them produced."

Because Elvis took on the tough task known so well to this writer, the challenge of using words to write about music, we started our con-versation there.

You wrote in your book how certain aspects of music are "beyond lan-guage," which is a good understanding with which to start this discus-sion, as much of this is about that which transcends words.

Elvis Costello: Yes. Writing about music is tricky. There have been erudite books about classical music using all sorts of big words which are often misleading and probably not that expressive to the casual lis-tener. So those things suffer. Steel guitars are always lachrymose [*laughs*] if not *weepy*.

I think you can probably put yourself into the mood of a song and as-sume that listening to it will burn away that gap between elusive things in music and what is literally beyond words. It's part of the reason people are inspired to go to their own train of mind while listening to music.

It's much easier to describe where words from a lyric come from be-cause they are a direct recitation of experience or they're an imagina-tion of someone else's experience or an observation or commentary on something in the world. Or in praise of something or in lament. There's not that many different things that we do with songs. Not to say that they can't have a great number of variations.

You meet the challenge in the book of using language to get inside of music and also inside the job of the songwriter. The way you described the dynamic necessary when working with Bacharach was perfect in showing the songwriter's goal. You wrote, "Those songs required me to listen to what the music was really saying to me. Sometimes it was speaking quietly and I had to listen very intently." That songwriting isn't a process of imposing yourself onto a song as much as it is discovering what the song is.

Particularly when it's music that someone else has written. Or for that matter, even if it's music that you've written yourself. [Bacharach] wouldn't disagree with the fact that there are many of those songs for which we both shared responsibility for the music. There's an assumption that says because I am better as a lyricist and he is better as a melodist, it must have all been divided along those lines. In fact, that's not true at all. There are some of those songs where the initial statement of music is mine. But then his intervention—sometimes quite small— would change and expand that music.

And sometimes I'd have a story and I couldn't quite grasp all of it and put it into workable language because the melody was so big and unwieldly. So it would require me to recognize what the story was and then puzzle out how to say that thing in the right amount of words.

Then I started to think more that way so that when I wrote the next one it worked even better. And that is why I was able to write so much with him even though we came at it with wildly contrasting styles. It is something that could seem like an awkward joint. I tried to think in his language a little bit.

And you did so beautifully. These songs you have written with him are stunning. I admit, like everyone else, I thought you did the words and he did all the music. Not because you are not a great composer yourself but because Burt writes only music and not lyrics. So I assumed you became his Hal David. But I was fascinated to discover that for "God Give Me Strength" you actually wrote the initial melody that started the song, and then he altered it.

It was very subtle. He took one of the phrases of mine and stretched it over twice as many bars. He kind of elongated one of the phrases, and he added the introductory figure. Some of the others, like "In the Darkest Place," also started like that with my music. Then the things he did in response to my music were so dramatic.

It was always a conversation. Some conversations are even longer. When I was working with Paul McCartney the volley back and forth was much swifter. After a while it got hard to say who came up with what line because it was all happening so fast. I can't break those ones down in the same way. But I have sheet music for the Bacharach cowrites, so I know exactly where the starting place was on certain songs and where they ended up.

You wrote that he composed the bridge music for "God Give Me Strength," and then you wrote the words "instantly." Yes? That is an astounding bridge—the music so dramatic, and the words matching that intensity.

Yes. The bridge came very quickly, the lyric there. It took the writing of a dummy bridge that I wrote. Burt looked at it and said, "No, that music doesn't quite work." And then he realized it did need a bridge structurally, even though it's quite a long song. It needed to get away from the original statement of music. And then he wrote this beautiful passage. It's one of my favorite parts of all of the songs we wrote.

It was all a very good experience. The one song that took a really long time to puzzle out was "This House Is Empty Now." Though I had the sense of what kind of song it was, it took a while to get the words.

It's interesting you use the word "puzzle," as it applies to how you construct a song. It's a word you use in the book as well. Does the puzzle of a song have only one ultimate solution? Or can you solve that puzzle in different ways?

Not every song is actually like a puzzle. Some are more like an electric shock. They appear too quickly. And they are too complete. I wrote "The Angels Want to Wear My Red Shoes" while standing in the rain. Ten minutes or fifteen minutes, and the song just presented itself. I wrote six songs for *The New Basement Tapes* end on end in something like ninety minutes. Of course, I then had to go back and work with the raw material.

There are these strange things, when it all comes beaming in. Is that inspiration? I don't know. And then there are other times when you have disconnected bits of language and fragments of music, and you might think there is something to that, and then one day something emotional will trigger something, and that fragment will return and fit perfectly. There have been times when I discover a lyrical passage or a couplet and I see how to make sense of it now because I have lived three more years and am in a whole new place. So sometimes you have to be patient and wait for the thing to happen in life before you can put it down in a line in a song.

All songwriters know that great experience, when a song arrives just like a gift. Any explanation of how you get to the place where that can happen?

No, I can't explain it. Some people want to be mystical about it, and that's completely legitimate. I think a song can have a precious little secret or sentimental dimension, but I don't go around with a pious face on feeling that I'm above everything because that can happen once in a while. I think it's *shocking* when it happens.

There's the famous story of the composer getting up every morning in his pajamas and going to the piano and saying, "I've got it, I've got it!" And writing a little ditty. You could have written a nursery rhyme and think you've written the most original tune in the world. Because it gets in your mind and it's seductive. And it's deciding whether that tune is really an original tune or a cliché.

That's what makes Hal David so great. To write so economically and with such unshowy language and yet write such indelible words. It's so confounding to someone who doesn't do that.

I agree. In your book you mention how songwriters are often complimented by being called poets, as in "He isn't just a songwriter—he's a *poet*." But as you wrote, songwriting is not an inferior art. In many ways songwriting has become the poetry of the masses. Would you agree?

No. *Poetry* is the poetry of the masses. They're different.

It can seem patronizing to say, "Well, you're quite good. For a *songwriter*." The way in which words work in songs is unique. It is not the same as poetry. I personally resisted having my lyrics printed on the sleeve because I was quite earnest, I suppose, early on that I wanted the words to be heard as part of the whole picture. And then people really asked for the words to be written down, so I accepted it. I tried to make them interesting to look at, when we laid it out. And then that becomes a different thing. It makes the whole package into something that seems worth your time.

I didn't mean to denigrate poetry in any way, but I find in these modern times, if you long for rhymed verse, it is in songs and not poetry where you find it.

I can't agree with that. It depends on what kind of song you're talking about. There are some pretty dreadful songs out there that make a poor case for the art of songwriting. And there are perhaps a greater number of rhymed verses being declaimed on hip-hop records for a much larger audience. So does the ubiquity of it make it inherently superior? Well, in the case of some records, yes. Some of those have a level of dexterity and daring that some songwriters don't even approach.

Regarding your resistance to printing your lyrics on an album's sleeve, on *Imperial Bedroom* you printed the lyrics but without punctuation. Yet it showed me how much of a difference punctuation can make, as in the great chorus to "Man Out of Time," which begins, "To murder my love is a crime." Leading me to believe it was a contemplation of the murder of your beloved. But in your book you provide the punctuation: "To murder, my love, is a crime." Which has, of course, a whole other meaning, that you are discussing murder with her but not contemplating murdering her!

Well, I think, to be honest, the way it's sung it can have both meanings. That was also because you can't convey a dual meaning—you either leave the comma out or not. It gets into hair-splitting and a very good case for not having written it down originally and not having the punctuation. Because it does mean either, in the song, as I sing it. But when I wrote it down on this occasion in the book I felt it was more accurate to punctuate it that way.

In the book you discuss this issue, the way words can be used on more than one level at a time in a song. You wrote, "If you can do this in a painting you can do it in a song, using words in a manner that don't necessarily accumulate to literal sense." Which was fascinating to read because often your songs are like Cubist paintings that are multidimensional and can be seen from several perspectives at the same time.

[*Laughs*] That's a very nice comparison. I think Barney Bubbles [the cover-painting artist, credited to Sal Forlenza] might have been alluding to that on the cover of *Imperial Bedroom*. He painted the cover of the album after hearing the record, and he, of course, made this reference to Picasso in it. And I [*laughs*] never had this grandiose idea that I was writing Cubist songs. But I did definitely have a feeling that you can have more than one reality on the same plane. So I suppose without giving it that actual title, that was what I was doing.

But I didn't stand back from the page enough to say, "Okay, I'm now doing this." I was just doing it. Quite often you have to think about it later, what you were doing.

Yet without thinking about it too much, you were stretching the limits of what you can do in a song—

I wasn't doing it so other people would notice it, because then it would seem self-conscious. I was following my instincts and emotions, which is really all that ever drives it. And I was also writing at the same time songs which, as you say, have these multiple planes. Like "Beyond Belief" and so forth.

There were just different ways to present a song. A feeling for a song comes to you, and you use the tools that are at hand, whether it's a complex tune or a simple tune. Is it an elaborate melody with unexpected harmonies? A big, bright open tune in a major key? A dark ballad? You can actually select any one of these things.

I relay in the book the story of my calling Sammy Cahn and asking him to write the words to "The Long Honeymoon" on *Imperial Bedroom*. But I wasn't really able to convey coherently what I was after. Because that was the way I was in those days.

I sent him a rather rambling piano demo—music without words—but he wasn't able to get a handle on it. He said he couldn't hear the structure of the song. So I ended up, two days later, writing the lyric myself. In the end I ended up with a good song. But I wished I'd have had a cocredit with Sammy Cahn—it would have been lovely to have a connection. Because some of the songs I wrote then were inspired by my exploration of the shape of his songs from his period. He was really one of the *last* songwriters of the time, in the fifties and sixties, when he was writing songs with people like [Jimmy] Van Heusen and other composers as well. [See Sammy Cahn, *SOS I*, page 27.]

Having interviewed Sammy, I know he always stressed the architecture of a melody, its sturdy structure. You gave him a complex melody, but had you given him something more traditional, like "Almost Blue," I think he would have jumped on it—

Yes. I think if it had been something perhaps more obvious, it would have worked. [Jazz trumpeter] Chet Baker had a hard time with the structure of "Shipbuilding" because it isn't a normal by-the-bar form. I could have narrowed the shape of the song, and obviously there was great invention within that, and there was *con*-ventions I didn't obey. And that came because I was playing the piano instead of Steve [Nieve], so it was my own piano playing, not unlike a gorilla wearing boxing gloves.

Chet Baker had some trouble memorizing the form of the song. Not the harmony—he had no problem with the harmony. On some of the takes, when he was really flying and playing beautifully, he anticipated the change in the harmony, and it didn't go where he thought it did. Because the form of the song was quite unconventional in his experience. It is not a standard thirty-two-bar form.

"Shipbuilding" is a magical song. So haunting and yet so specific and cinematic. How was it born?

I came up with the melody first, which I put on cassette. I was singing it wordlessly, maybe just humming, while playing the melody on an organ. I sang just the vocal melody over these beautiful changes. It was for Robert Wyatt [of Soft Machine]. He had the hope that I would write something bright and optimistic that would be the way Robert intended it, sort of like Neil Diamond's "I'm a Believer." Maybe something more poignant, but it should be like a conventional pop lyric. Instead of which I wrote a very specific song about something else entirely, and that reflects what was happening at that moment, that particular conflict of all these dilemmas that blew up and came out of the lyric of "Shipbuilding."

That song, as you said, stretches the song form. And many times you've stretched and reinvented the forms of songs, more so than most songwriters who stay within the usual verse-chorus structures.

Yes. When I was working with The Roots, with Steve and Questlove predominantly, we wrote a whole song based on a loop of us playing "High Fidelity." I wrote a song called "Waltz," which was somewhat of an answer song to "Shipbuilding," looking at that same conflict from the other side of the ocean.

You can travel as a songwriter. Like a novelist can. Crime writers kill people all the time, willy-nilly, but they never go to jail. So I could imagine this girl watching the victory speech from London, after the fact.

So I think I learned something valuable from that. You can tell a three-dimensional story, and it didn't obey any of the structural rules of any of the songs I'd written over the last forty years. There's something very refreshing to have yourself confined by a loop like that. I've written a number of songs that are based on something like this, by the tension created by something coming round and where you've got instincts to go, "Okay, we're going to the IV now; well, we're not! We're going back!"

Yes, and music is always about playing with expectations.

Yeah. And if you're also dealing with a textural sonic realm, where you're dropping things in and out, like a dub record does, you create these holes, this negative space, also into which the words drop. And then if you add other voices, and singers singing in Spanish, it is like making a little film almost. The continuity was completely different than any song I had ever written before.

It's good not to be so self-satisfied that you know all the ways that you can tell a story. That was just one occasion where it was markedly different—structurally, texturally, even in terms of the language, going in and out of English and Spanish.

One of the greatest examples of song expansion is "I Want You," which throws away verse and chorus and ties the song together with emotion and a haunting repeat of the title. It broke the form in a remarkable and powerful way.

At the time it had written itself before I had the chance to think, "Oh, this is different." That is similar in a way in that the monotony of the form reflects an emotional claustrophobia that is going on in the lyric. And it's also prefaced by this strange, lullaby-like melody. I think I wrote that intro part, that acoustic lullaby section at the top, in a Japanese restaurant with Japanese music going at the same time.

"I Want You" is also a great example of your greatness as a songwriter in that both the words and the music of that are equally intense.

I think it's very specific. But lots of songs are. But that one carries it on for six minutes. A song like that certainly would not work if it lost the intensity halfway through. If it suddenly drifted off and started talking about the pattern of the curtains, it wouldn't be right.

It arrived before you had time to think about it?

Yes, the bulk of it I wrote on a train. The preface was written afterward as another form and then was used as the introduction in the recording. But the main body of the song was one long appearance.

So you wrote the lyric on the train only, or did you write the music as well?

Well, the music was sort of very obvious. The music was sort of there. Often with words, you can just hear the music. There was a little bit of panic having to get from the train to my mother's house to make sure I didn't forget.

Same as when I wrote "Red Shoes." There were no portable tape recorders at that time. Well, I didn't have one, anyway. So I didn't have any way to capture it. The only way I could ever remember a song, I would just have to sing songs over and over until I was sure I wouldn't forget them. And that's some test of how indelible a melody would be, would be that you could retain it and play it for an evening, and wake up the next day—and could you still recall it?

["Red Shoes"] appeared whole in a ten-minute burst, and I had everything in my head playing like a record. But there was a panic that something else would enter it and alter it somehow. Like something ambient, like a radio playing in a car or a station announcement that had a note in it.

With "I Want You" I was going in the opposite direction on the train. And obviously it took a longer portion of that journey to write that song because it is a longer song. And there were probably images that got edited out. It was perhaps even longer originally. But when I got to an instrument the music was already there. And then the preface came at a separate occasion.

It's rare that another artist can do one of your songs with anything approaching your intensity, but Fiona Apple's rendition of that song is simply chilling.

Oh, Fiona turned it into Shakespeare. It was like Lady Macbeth's version of "I Want You." [*Laughter*] You know, I was standing next to her while she was doing that. We just couldn't believe it. It was very thrilling to do that. You know, she has that intensity in her songs. She's a wonderful, wonderful musician.

I agree. Does that often happen, when you get a song completely like that?

Oh no, no. Songs came in all sorts of different ways. And that's the beauty of it. If you knew how to do it, you'd just keep doing that. If you knew how to get the jackpot out of the fruit machine, you'd keep pulling the handle.

Of course, sometimes it's a big sheet of paper with lots of words thrown on it. Sometimes it's a tiny little notebook with scrawled handwriting. Sometimes a couplet that you stored away might suddenly connect up with a new set of thoughts, something with a brand-new exterior for something in the world you want to remark upon. And it'll all just fall into place.

I suppose the often manner by which it all falls into place is fairly swift. But there have been songs, like I described, that I pondered for a long time before I found the right words for the melody.

There's no *one* way that I know songs to be written. I have written a number of songs in collaboration, and then you have to think about the other person's rhythm of creation, the rhythm of their creative process. You can't hurry it up if somebody else takes a different path to it. It would be inelegant and presumptuous.

It's instructive to learn that a great songwriter such as yourself doesn't have an easy answer, because there are no easy answers.

Yes. You know, there are a lot of examples of writers in every form who get up very, very methodically and go to the desk and do something every day. I'm talking now about writing books. But there are some writers of songs who do that, and it doesn't mean they always come away with complete songs, but they may do something. It might seem an odd thing to say, as I remarked in the book, but I'm quite lazy. I feel as though indolence is my main vice. Yet somehow I've managed to write a lot of songs. Heaven knows what it would have been like had I been hardworking. [*Laughter*]

You've not only written a lot of songs, you've written a lot of great songs. If someone writes one song that impacts the world, that is a great thing. But you have done that in so many songs and sustained your songwriting over a long time. So however you've done it is clearly the right way.

It's nice of you to say. I don't know that they matter anymore than anybody else's songs. But they mattered to somebody. If only to me, or I wouldn't have written them in the first place.

And it's a curious thing to think after a number of years that anyone wants to hear a number of these songs that I wrote a while ago. At different times I've resisted that. But I've come around to ways of approaching them. That is why I keep trying to change the way I'm approaching the material so that it's not a ritual that can be anticipated.

When you say you're lazy as a songwriter—

No, I'm just lazy *generally*. [*Laughs*] I'm making a joke, but it feels that way to me. I don't get that prolific thing because there are long periods when I don't write. So I suppose what it must be is that I must write intensely when I do write. I don't keep a diary, so I don't notice that.

When you approach a song do you think about the story you want to tell before writing it, or does that happen while writing?

That really depends. I think there are times when you're letting yourself be guided. Perhaps by an enigmatic phrase that had been intriguing to the imagination—or just to the mind, not necessarily the imagination—and what the implications of that phrase is. Sometimes it's the opening line of the song; sometimes it's the title. I have notebooks in which there are lists of titles. Sometimes titles predate the song. The title was there. And there's a whole story you can paint in that title.

I often wondered if you started with titles, as so often you have evocative titles. In the book you mentioned one of your first songs was "Poison Moon," which is a strong title—two words that conflict, a good dynamic.

Well, because people wish upon the moon, that immediately suggests that it's not a good-luck song; it's a hard-luck song. At that time I didn't know how to write in realistic language about my life, so I borrowed these idioms and tried to write more like a Tin Pan Alley songwriter in a way. I wrote in a romantic idiom. But it was a slightly sour one in this case. I took something which people often wrote joyful songs about and twisted it, and it's got this little sadness that things are not going to work out.

The song is about looking in the mirror and not being what you want, the dream not being fulfilled. That was a real feeling. That part wasn't romantic. But the rest of the language that I used was sort of a borrowed idiom. I found songs that I wrote right before then that sounded just like Robert Hunter songs. 'Cause that's who I listened to. They were filled with these paradoxes, and his songs have a lot of that in them. I was so enamored of that, I tried to copy it. But I never recorded any of those songs; I just put them away. They didn't sound real.

Yet so early on it seemed you completely found your voice and your own world with "Watching the Detectives," which, to this day, is a revelation, a rock and roll love letter to crime fiction, even with camera directions. It was unlike anything we had heard and remains so to this day.

It's a device. It has to be one that has a reason to exist. I have returned to that idiom a few times because you can tell different stories. There's the Mingus song ["My Flame Burns Blue"], and there's "Church Underground," which is a complicated idea.

"Watching the Detectives" also has this arch A minor melody and slinky electric guitar, linked to a "Secret Agent Man"–like riff. It's another example of how in your songs the music speaks as eloquently as the words.

It does for you. And whether it communicates to anyone else in the long run, it actually doesn't matter. Unless you are a gun-for-hire writer, where you have to hit a certain mark and you know a song is a failure unless it says something specific. I have dozens of songs which the meaning is specific to me. They express something I wanted to say very much.

But are there songs that are unclear even to you?

Yes. Songs are like mysteries that you can go back to. And they can change on you. They can turn around and bite you, even, while you're holding them. And that's a great thing to have that, as well as songs that are very clear. To have songs which are mysterious even to the person who wrote them is exciting.

There are songs that transform themselves as you are performing them. I have as many of those as I have songs that are clear. I like the fact that I have those songs. Maybe some of them don't get aired very often, but that's for the very reason that I have to be in exactly the right mood to sing them. Otherwise they just sound confusing. I've stood on the stage and sung "All These Strangers" and it's been exactly clear to me what it's about, and other times I've sung it and it just sounded like I don't know what is going on in this song. [*Laughs*] I'm not entirely certain where that came from.

I have a few songs which are like mysteries to ponder for all time. And they're companions. And that's a comforting thing. It's good to have songs which are very, very clear and obvious, like "Indoor Fireworks," where you've got a very strong central image and you run up to it with something that is full of emotion. Or "Stranger in the House." These are songs I wrote a long time ago. And then it's good to have mystery songs too. It's good to have them.

Leonard Cohen said being a songwriter is like being a Catholic nun, that you're married to a mystery. Embracing the mystery is part of being a songwriter.

Well, you can hear it in his songs. The precision of his words in the greatest of his songs, that everyone agrees about, doesn't mean that the songs that are not as universally embraced are not great songs as well. There are many of his songs which are mysteries. And in a beautiful way, in a beautiful way.

But so many songs contain mystery. Whether they're old Tin Pan Alley songs, you go, "How did they come to that image?" Such as in "I left my heart in an old cathedral town," in "Boulevard of Broken Dreams." Well, "old cathedral town"? Why that? That seems so strange to me. Every time I hear that line.

"God Give Me Strength" has a melody with a big range. Is part of the secret of a great melody a big range like that?

I don't think so. The idea that a melody has to have a big range, I think, is a mistake. There are songs that are written in the thirties, and in some ways the harmony's more complex on those songs. Those songs have the appearance of greater development because of the genius way they're harmonized. It is true when snobs who like jazz go on about "It was all better then," the only part of what's true about that is that the harmony in those songs written in the thirties and even some in the twenties gave the appearance of the melody traveling farther than it actually was in register.

Also, those songs were written to be sung by anybody. The song didn't really have one definitive version. Something like "Side by Side" [by Gus Kahn and Harry Woods], there must have been five hit versions of that song in the year it was written. And yet some of those songs have the appearance of great drama. In different times the way people created that drama was different. Power chords, power ballads. There are other solutions to creating the drama. Another way is making people lean forward. Jobim songs. The Bacharach songs, even. Some of them are very dramatic and have a big range, but some of them are very intimate. But they're very ingenious in the way they use the harmony to create the development and tension.

You had very ingenious harmonies and even modulations—but often at a very fast tempo—such as "Oliver's Army," which is complex and even has a key change.

Yes, it's one of the rare songs of mine that modulates, and I don't know why, but that is how I heard it. I heard it doing that when I wrote it—it's not something that the arranger added, that modulation to the bridge. That song also shows my indiscipline as a songwriter, particularly early on, in writing three verses that were superficially the same but actually had crucial differences in the harmony or in the length of the lines. It makes it a nightmare for musicians to remember them. And you have to pay attention. I'm not saying they're wrong to be written like that.

In the book you describe poring over sheet music your dad would bring home and discovering all the chords you didn't know—the major sixths, the augmented fourth, even diminished, as you wrote. From an early age you were bringing what we sometimes call the adult chords to rock and roll.

I learned to play the guitar from following chord symbols. To learn to play this quite complicated song, "Man of the World." And then I realized I had enough chords, and then I learned more chords to play these Beatles songs and things that I knew. I knew them all the way through, but I didn't know how to play them. I thought they were completely beyond me but then found some of them were very simple.

Then I bought chord books with my buddies, they were these simplified chord books. I don't know why, but they'd write them out in these beginner chords. So they would write something which, if you weren't paying attention, sounded okay. But there's a big difference between a minor chord and a diminished chord. Quickly it would become dissatisfying. I'd listen to the record again and I'd go, "That *can't* be the chord." And then I went and just saw what it was. And once I saw it, then, of course, I could *hear* very clearly that that was the *correct* harmony that I'd heard on the recording. Because my ear was good. I could always hear all the parts of the vocal, all the vocal harmonies.

Your songs have always been distinguished by these chords. I think of "Almost Blue," for example, which is such a passionately sad melody in A minor. It goes from the A minor to A major, which then leads into D minor, which is like something Cole Porter would do. It lifts us up and is also beautiful.

I didn't think of it, truthfully, in that analytical way. But of course, I was spending a lot of time listening to—guess what—Cole Porter. And Jerome Kern and Gershwin. I wasn't listening to rock and roll in 1980. I was writing some rock and roll records, but all my listening, all my records that I carried around with me, were Billie Holiday records, Miles Davis, Debussy. I was just curious to hear other harmonies. I suppose some of it got into some of the songs in a very limited way. If I could write a song as good as "Ghost of Yesterday" [by Irene Wilson and Arthur Herzog Jr.], I'd be very happy. But I can't. Or at least I haven't yet.

Another one of my favorite songs you have written is "The Comedians," which you wrote for Roy Orbison. But I really love your version of it and the way you sing that melody.

I never really cared for our recording of it. I felt I let the melody get away from me by breaking it that way. And it had different lyrics. That was one of those times when changing that lyric didn't come back to me later as being that satisfying. Generally, when I sing it now, I return it to the original bolero rhythm and play it something like Roy's arrangement.

I love to sing it. I have to be in very good voice to sing it because it's quite the challenge. I do sing it now and again, and it has a big impact when I play it right. It's a very emotional song, and one of the most amazing experiences in my career as a sideman, which is a very short career, was to be behind him when he sung it live [*Roy Orbison and Friends, A Black and White Night*, 1988] at the Coconut Grove. [*Laughs*] That's the sort of experience you're not going to easily forget.

And he was singing like that all night long doing his own songs. I'm just sitting there, behind my little music stand, trying to get the changes right. He's doing one after another of those huge crescendos.

In our remaining time might I name some of your songs and invite you to share any thoughts about them?

Sure, we can try, yeah.

"Pidgin English."

As I recall, it's one of those songs that I really took apart and reassembled in the process of rerecording. I'm sure there was a much more straightforward version on the *Trust* model. And then, of course, there's all these overlapping vocals. I recomposed some of the songs in the studio. That was the hallmark of that—"Kid About It" and "Beyond Belief." "Beyond Belief" being the most extreme example, because I completely retitled that song. That's what I most remember about it. Superimposing incoming ideas over the blueprint of this idea about communication.

You wrote in your book that "Beyond Belief" was originally titled "The Land of Give and Take." Did you then rewrite that lyric to the track?

Yes. Some of the same melody stayed there; it was just the spacing. Rather like what Burt Bacharach did with "God Give Me Strength"—it was like stretched, the music over more bars, the melody over twice as many bars in some cases. Or I compressed some sections and made some things stretch out and change the register.

"Pills and Soap."

This was a song that was written as a bulletin. I recorded it as The Impostor, with just a drum loop. And I'd written it sort of like a Ramsey Lewis–style figure. And then Steve [Nieve] played on it, and he didn't know any of that kind of music, so it came out much more dramatic. When he played it, it took on an orchestral scale. I'd have this kind of vamp thing that was there. It was more proclaimed than it was sung. So it was definitely influenced or affected by hearing the first hip-hop records out of New York.

The war was going on in the country at that moment, and I tried to sum it up in that lyric. And Steve kind of played over it. I didn't want it to be played by a band; I wanted a very mechanistic aspect of the literally switch-it-on-and-let-it-run kind of thing, finger clicks and backbeat. It was very simplistic, very spare. And the only other orchestral elements were the background voices that were tracked.

We got it out on record a week later and had it in the charts by the following week. That was really the instant part of it.

"Clowntime Is Over."

That's one that went through a couple of transformations. I can't remember which came first, but it was both a ballad and an up-tempo song. And there were a lot of sessions of *Get Happy!* when we would try many versions of that. There was a lot of drinking going on. Some of their reactions were very exaggerated by that or our ability to realize things we were trying to do. So at some point it was done one way and then the other. And I like both versions now. I'm glad we cut it twice. Both versions emphasize different parts of the tune.

Again, it's the sign of a strong song, that it can stand up fast or slow— as Dylan did "Forever Young" both fast and slow on *Planet Waves*. The song isn't dependent on one record or tempo—it stands on its own.

Yeah. The slow version has one of these anthemic organ melodies. If I could have sung like Mavis Staples, then the ballad version would have been a killer. But I can't. That was as close as I could get.

"Suit of Lights."

That's a very emotional song in a couple of different ways. I wrote it about my father. It's the only song The Attractions played on *King of America*. The original idea for that record being one side electric and one side acoustic. But then I went to Hollywood and cut so many acoustic songs the first week that it completely unbalanced the record, and I had to go with what was best.

You dedicated your book to "My Three Sons," and you also have a song with that title.

Yeah, that's a very truthful song about the discomfort of people who want you to remain angry and be the angry guy forever. I thought I'd explained that pretty well, the emptiness of that. "My Three Sons" is one rendition of that feeling. I could write a number of different things about that perspective—I'm a father and a son.

I love the record of it that we made. Particularly having David Hidalgo, who is one of my very favorite musicians, playing on it was great. It's just a very simple bedding, you know? I also really like to play it in the chamber arrangement that I made. Where the lines of the second verse are interrupted by the melody of the Welsh hymn "All Through the Night." And that's used as a motif that then answers each line in the song from the second verse onward. That's a completely different version of the song, which I don't have a recording of.

"Pump It Up."

Well, I mean, it wasn't a song I felt needed a huge amount of explanation. It was some verses that I wrote late at night, the first time I really ran up against rock and roll mayhem rather than just being in a band playing at a local bar. I suppose I was sort of intrigued, thrilled, and revolted at the same time. So the song is disdainful, [*laughs*] but it's also a rock and roll song. Is it a contradicted song or is it having your cake and eating it? Probably a bit of both.

In the book you said "Alison" is a work of fiction. Is that different from how you feel about most of your songs?

Well, I thought of it as a work of fiction. I think the point being that I don't suppose it was in the long run. Obviously it's based on somewhat of an experience. I mean, I think of all of the songs, anyway, none of my songs are literal, real-time experiences. I mean, a few of them might seem that way, like when you get the longer, more concentrated songs like "I Want You." Even then, that was edited after the fact.

When you write out of a direct experience and don't transpose it, it's more readily understood that this is from life. But the songs on *Painted from Memory* are called that because they are displaced only by time; they're not distanced from the *feeling*. And the songs on *North* don't employ any tricky lyrical conceits. They are pretty straight recitations of feeling. There are some people who *mistrust* that when they come from somebody who is better known for wordplay. But of course, that was just how I felt at that moment, to actually speak clearly and say something like, "You turned to me, and all at once I knew I was betrayed." And what kind of clever, arch way would have made that more sincere?

At other times you want to put a little distance between yourself and the feeling, and obviously that is what I'm talking about with "Alison." There's something very real, some real dread in that song. The fact that it's endured this length of time is probably down to people being able to imagine themselves or somebody they know having that kind of conflict.

That and a tremendous melody. The words are so evocative and visceral, with music that is pure yearning. And the visuals were immediate, as when she took off her party dress—

It was something that you don't analyze when you're writing it—you just go with the instinct. But then when you sing it you realize it has an impact on people.

Randy Newman suggested all songs a songwriter writes, even story or character songs, are ultimately about the songwriter. Do you feel that?

Well, don't you think "Simon Smith and the Amazing Dancing Bear" is a personal song?

Yes. About one's aspiration to be part of showbiz and about exploitation.

Yes. About a dancing bear. And about exploiting *yourself*. I think I found those songs very moving when I heard "Davy the Fat Boy" and these things. The insecurity of the person standing outside of the party.

"This House Is Empty Now."

That's the song that I really had to ponder a long time with Burt's music until I got the right balance of words. And it was, funnily enough, from recalling these lines from an ABBA song that made me realize it was that mood that I wanted to capture. It was very affecting about the way they didn't over-emote. That made it very feeling, that recitation of "Walk into this empty house, tears in my eyes . . ." And once I thought about that, well, what if it were an inventory? That was the solution. In the end the song became an inventory.

"Do you recognize the face / Fixed in that fine silver frame? / Were you so unhappy then?" The picture in a frame idea is in a lot of songs. The thing that Burt's melody allows me to say, because there was space to say it, was "Were you really so unhappy then? You never said . . ." It's "you never said" that says so much and shows how intolerable it was. It's because of the length of the melody, I was able to do that. It's beyond recognizing that someone is unhappy but the fact that they couldn't say it out loud.

You wrote in the book that with the Bacharach songs you'd find the title first. And that title so perfectly is wed to that melody—did you find that first?

Yes. I knew it was called that. But I didn't know what all the fill-in was.

That's an example of a title that tells the story. Of course, how deep that story becomes is another thing.

Yes. The weight of the words. The first couple of drafts I wrote were much more strong, and I had to chill it out. That's where the ABBA song became the key, because it was much more dispassionate in the recitation of the inventory.

You spoke of writing drafts. Are there many songs for which you also wrote many drafts?

Oh yeah, I have whole notebooks. There's drafts of "Oliver's Army," but it has different rhyme schemes. I put a reference to Solsbury in there at one point. And then that didn't survive into the final version. Some of it is just technical.

What allows those words to come through when you are in that first stage of writing? Is it necessary to get out of your own way?

I don't think the way of getting out of your way is to just keep writing. I wrote it out like twenty times in some cases. Some songs came quite quickly, while others I wrote them out, wrote them out, many times.

Some songwriters say they start judging it too soon and get in their own way in terms of letting it come out.

I have friends who have done that. But they're sometimes listening to other voices. They're listening to their sisters or to people they should more cheerfully want to strangle. [*Laughter*] And they get whispering in their ear about stuff. But you've just got to do it. You've got to do what you feel.

Some songwriters I've spoken to, like Randy Newman, complain about songwriting and don't enjoy it, while others love the process and find joy in songwriting—

I've heard Randy say that. I sat with him not very long ago, and he described the most beautiful song that he was working on. It was overwhelming to me that he was telling me about it. He *described* a song to me, which was just a magical thing, seeing someone struggling with how to write this song, and I saw what he was going through. And of course, if you got me on a certain day I might say the same sort of distracted stuff. There are things I've been wrestling with. I have had experiences with writing without so much effort. And because this prolific thing has become attached to me, it makes it seem like I have it all figured out. But of course, there are some songs that are obviously frustrating while you're working on them.

It's just like injuring yourself in some way, or heartbreak, or toothache. In some ways you forget about it. Like why do people get drunk and get a hangover and say, "I'll never drink again," and then three days later they go out and do it again? You forget quickly. Toothache, heartache, and drunkenness, these three things we forget very quickly, otherwise we'd never live. And songwriting is the same.

When I interviewed Dylan he said, "The world doesn't need any new songs. If no one wrote another new song we'd be okay."

Well, you know, that is what he said one day. And then he wrote *Tempest.*

Exactly—

[*Laughs*] He said that to me before. And I've said it too. I was on a plane a couple of years ago, and I happened to be on the plane with James Taylor, and I told James that, and James gave me a real talking to about it and said "You can't say that."

I was on tour in Bloomington, Indiana, and Bob was there, and [John] Mellencamp came to see me. And John obviously knows [Bob] well, and we were just standing together in the loading bay, waiting for the trucks to get out of the way so we could get to the coaches.

And John said, "You writing any songs?" And Bob said exactly what he said to you. That the world doesn't need any new ones. And I thought, "Well, yeah, I believe *that.*" And I don't believe it. You don't want to believe it when somebody good like that says that. And heaven knows, if he never got round to writing another song, we've got a lot from him, wouldn't you say? So, you know, you have to sort of take him at face value until the next time he's moved to write one. Then he writes "Long and Wasted Years."

I felt maybe it's a joke—

Of course, it's a joke. I mean, what he actually said that night to me is "What is it I need that I don't already have?"

And I thought when he said that, is that a song title? Is he quoting a *song title*?

Well, I thought, if it wasn't, it fucking is *now*. And I wrote it down.

◆◆◆

Joe Jackson
Night and Day
Berlin, Germany 2015

Before he ever wrote songs, he wrote chamber music. Expressing himself instrumentally—and with a beautiful range of music, whether orchestra or big band—has been a part of his musical soul since the start. The ostensible purpose of our talk on this day was to discuss his most recent project, *The Duke*, and the big band music it inspired. But as he is Joe Jackson, one of the great songwriters of our time, I indulged his generous spirit by inquiring about some of his own famous songs and his ideas about songwriting.

We spoke over the phone from his home in Berlin, where he'd recently moved. Asked why, he answered, "The cities that I have spent the most time and I know the best are London and New York. And I am kind of disillusioned with both in a way. And I find that Berlin is much more relaxed and more livable, at least right now."

He was born David Ian Jackson on August 11, 1954, in Burton upon Trent, Staffordshire, England, and spent his early years in the Paulsgrove area of Portsmouth before moving to Gosport, England, in his teens.

His first instrument was violin, but he switched early on to piano. He started composing instrumental music at fourteen before he ever wrote a song. "I came to songwriting fairly late," he said. "I didn't really start trying to write songs until I was a bit older, nineteen or so, and playing in bands. Before that I was trying to write chamber music first for various combinations [of instruments] that were around me at school. I wanted to be a composer."

Asked to describe this early music, he said, "It was sort of a strange mishmash of jazzy elements with elements of composers I'd admired, like Bartok and Stravinsky. . . . It was not very good."

At sixteen he started playing piano in bars and won a scholarship to study music at the Royal Academy of Music in London. He joined two bands, first Edward Bear and then Arms and Legs. In 1978 a demo found its way to A&M records, which signed him as the Joe Jackson Band. The debut album was the wonderful *Look Sharp*, with melody, jazzy songs, and smart lyrics. It was a little new wave, a little jazz-rock Steely Dan, and it was fresh and new. The single was a beautifully melodic ballad sung with great urgency, "Is She Really Going Out with Him?" From this song on, we knew he was the real deal.

Subsequent albums sustained this great fusion of smart British pop-rock with jazz and soul. He also was adept at stretching the content of pop songs, as he did with "It's Different for Girls" from his second album, *I'm the Man*, in 1979.

In 1982 came the landmark *Night and Day*, the quintessential Joe Jackson album. Like some beautiful hybrid of Cole Porter, Cab Calloway, and Frank Sinatra, it was unlike anything that came before—well, except his previous albums. But it was the album of the time. As a personal aside, I will always remember working that year, 1982, in a Hollywood recording studio, where I was a second engineer. Often a third engineer, in fact. After long recording sessions we'd have to clean up the studio— all the mics, cords, mic stands, coffee cups, and other detritus of the recent session. Nothing fueled those clean-up sessions like *Night and Day*. We'd put the LP on and blast it over the giant studio speakers, and it was exultant Joe with beautiful, bright, big-band beauty—in great fidelity. It was brand new yet alive with electric spirits of the past, of those big, bright horn sections of the big bands, of those sophisticated harmonies as cool and complex as Duke Ellington yet wed with the persistent, incendiary urgency of rock and roll. It was a new sound, a unique energy, both elegant and raw. It was all Joe.

Since then other great albums have come, such as *Body and Soul* (1984), with the haunting "Be My Number Two," and the live wonder of *Big World* (1986). The following year, 1987, he returned to his instrumental roots with *Will Power*. Then there came *Blaze of Glory* (1989) and *Laughter & Lust*. He then announced he was leaving pop music behind.

Indeed, his next music was a symphony, *Symphony No. 1*. And in 2012 he recorded a beautifully inspired and devoted tribute to Duke Ellington called *The Duke*. It was the release of this album that give me a chance to talk to him over the phone from his new home in Berlin.

This same year, 2015, he released his back-to-form full album of originals, *Fast Forward*. But it was about Duke that our conversation began.

Your own music is so rich and jazzy. I am not surprised you would do a whole album of the music of Duke Ellington. What led you to this?

Joe Jackson: He's one of my musical heroes and role models and has been for a long time. It's a hard question in a way. It's 'cause I like Duke Ellington. But why it is that so many Ellington tunes keep coming into my head, I really don't know, or why I was moved to experiment with different arrangements, I don't really know. And why it got to the point where I saw the possibility of doing a whole album.

For me it's just been like any other creative process of making an album. Although I didn't write any original tunes. But it's a very intuitive process, and it's hard to say why.

It makes sense, as like Ellington, you have had pop hits and written famous songs, yet your music is quite complex, orchestral, and full of big-band sounds—like his.

Yeah, I mean, I certainly don't want to come across as comparing myself to Ellington. But he has been a role model to me, and I think I am a similar musician to him. For one thing, Ellington didn't respect categories or boundaries in music at all and was very eclectic. So there's certainly *that*. And also, he was someone with a big musical vision, who saw the whole thing, the big picture, but still found ways to let his musicians share the spotlight. And that's another thing that I always found very interesting about him that I think I learned from, and I have done the same things.

Interesting you identify the way he'd cross over boundaries of music, and you've done the same thing. In your career you've moved across many genres, whereas most people in your field don't cover as much stylistic ground.

Yeah, I guess I just don't see those. I don't think it's a good thing or a bad thing to be eclectic or to be very much within one genre. I think you just have to be yourself. As Oscar Wilde said, "One should do as one's nature dictates." These sort of controversies about what is authentic and what elements you're allowed to mix together go way back. I was thinking about Gershwin recently, how he got all sorts of shit from the classic people and the jazz people because they said he was neither one nor the other, therefore what he did was not authentic. Yet we still listen to his music. I just went to a performance of *Porgy and Bess*, which is a big hit in New York on Broadway.

Of course, now we recognize that it's not the point whether he was authentically jazz or authentically classical. He was authentically Gershwin.

Exactly. And as I'm sure you know, *Porgy and Bess* was panned when it came out; people didn't like it at all at first.

Yeah, and interestingly enough, Duke Ellington didn't like it much either, although he respected Gershwin.

Why did Duke not like it?

He felt that it was, in some ways, a missed opportunity. Of creating an opera in African American style, which he felt it wasn't. A rare example of Ellington possibly missing the point a little bit. But I don't know. He felt he could do it better.

Did people in the business try to get you to stay in one area and discourage your eclecticism?

Not really. No one comes into the studio and puts a gun to your head and says, "Make this type of record."

No? We felt record companies would do that. Not with a gun, though—

Well, no. I think what happens is that they just won't promote it.

I ask because the thing about you that excited us the most was the new sound you were delivering. It was as exciting as hearing Steely Dan the first time, this heady mixture of jazz, soul, and rock and this recognition that there is a whole new world here musically.

Steely Dan was one of my big influences, I think, as a teenager.

Like you, they have expanded the harmonic vocabulary of rock with extended, complex chords and chromatic changes, yet still with a visceral groove, like the best of rock. And your music is a lot more chromatic than the typical diatonic pop music we hear.

Yeah, I guess so. [*Laughs*] I just try to avoid clichés. And try to avoid things that sound like something I have already heard somewhere. That's as close as I get to a kind of a method.

And you knew how to notate and arrange music—
I learned that when I was eleven. It's not that hard. [*Laughs*]

No, it's not. But as you know, very few songwriters—except Van Dyke Parks, Randy Newman, and Warren Zevon—know how to do that. And you.
Yes, strange.

Strange they don't learn to do it?
Yes. Strange to me that in the pop and rock world generally that people tend to see it like rocket science or something. It's easy. It's really not a big deal. It seems people who can't do it make a big deal out of it. They build strange myths around the whole subject. I've actually talked to people who say they never wanted to learn to read or write music because they think it will take away their *feel* or their soul or something like that. Which I think is just stupid.

Yes, there is that school of thought that too much knowledge of that gets in the way—
I don't agree at all.

I know so many songwriters who say they can't read music as if they couldn't learn. It isn't hard to learn!
It really isn't. [*Laughs*] It's like learning a very simple language that has no exceptions to the rule, very logical grammar, and a small vocabulary.

Did having that knowledge inform your own songwriting?
I think everything informs everything you do. Everything you've learned. But when it comes to actually doing it, speaking for myself, I'm not conscious of it. But everything I've learned over the years I think I'm using in some way. But when I'm actually writing, I'm not conscious; I'm just following my own intuition.

What caused you to shift to songwriting—being in bands?
Yeah, I guess so. And just my openness to pop and rock music, which, for a while, I wasn't that interested in. I went through a bit of a strange trajectory, I think, because when I was ten or eleven I liked all the same pop music that everyone liked on the radio. Then I started with the violin

and got started with classical music. But within a few years I got into jazz, and then into rock and roll. And really everything, really. So I just had to go through that process of learning all kinds of music were valid.

Would you analyze songs musically to learn how they were made?

Sometimes. If they were interesting. [*Laughs*] If they were Steely Dan songs, maybe.

Did you like simple rock or were you more drawn to jazzy Steely Dan–type music?

I liked all kinds of stuff. By the time I was eighteen or nineteen I pretty much liked everything. I liked even the trashiest stuff that was on the radio and TV. I quite liked the glam rock stuff. Apart from David Bowie, who was much more than that, I liked Marc Bolan and the Sweet. I didn't mind how trashy it was. Music either moves me in some way or doesn't. It doesn't have to be complex or clever. Very often I'd rather it wasn't.

When you started writing songs, did it come easy?

Not at all. I didn't know how to write lyrics. It took me years, really. Even a lot of my early recorded stuff, early albums, some of the lyrics make me cringe.

When you would write a song would you usually start with some music or chord changes before words?

No, the starting point seems to vary all the time. But once I have a starting point, I work on words and music together. To write one first and then the other doesn't make sense to me.

Do you work at the piano?

Quite a lot. Not all the time. I mean, I work in my head a lot.

In your head can you hear the whole picture—the chords and melody?

Pretty much. Sometimes I have to go to the keyboard and figure out what it is.

Interesting you say that, as when I interviewed Burt Bacharach he said he needed to get away from the keyboard and think of melodies in his head. Whereas, as you know, a lot of songwriters work from chord progressions on piano or guitar and sing against them.

I think it's a good idea to get away from the keyboard. Because you can find yourself doing keyboardy things. [*Laughs*] For want of a better term. And sometimes being too obvious.

To get back to Ellington for a minute, one of my favorite songs of his is "In a Sentimental Mood." Which I think is one of the most beautiful things he ever wrote. I couldn't come up with an arrangement for it for this album. But today I was playing it on piano and really thinking how so much of the time—really through the whole song—the melody is not what you'd think of putting with those chords. It works. It sounds great. There's a freshness about it. In a way it doesn't sound like someone sitting down at the piano and, as you said, sang against the chord sequence. He always makes unusual and not necessarily logical choices where the melody goes against the chords. And yet it sounds completely right; it sounds logical.

Yes, I know what you mean. He is playing with expectations, so there's a freshness in his music, even though it's obviously not new music.

Yes. That was the idea, where you take the directions which haven't been taken before and have fun with it.

I love the casting of various musicians and singers on it. Especially the Sharon Jones track, which sounds amazing.

Yeah, she's great. She came in at the last minute, the last vocal we did. I'm really glad we got her.

Had you thought of vocalists in advance of making the tracks?

In some cases I did. In some cases I had a few different people in mind. And we whittled it down. I didn't think I would sing "I Got It Bad (And That Ain't Good)" myself. I didn't think I could sing that.

I was wondering about that. You are a great—and famous—vocalist. Why did you choose to sing what you did and not other songs?

I think it was a realistic view of my own limitations. But I also wanted it to have different voices and different colors. Different voices that can do what I can't do.

Does the fact you did this mean you are not writing new songs yourself?

I don't really have the time right now, [*laughs*] to be honest. I have been working on a few ideas. But in the last few years I have been doing a lot of touring. And then working on this Ellington project. It's been pretty absorbing.

Would you generally write songs all the time or just when it was time for a new album?

I sort of would go through bursts. Sometimes I'd write a lot, and then nothing for a while.

Is there any way to explain what affects and allows those bursts?

It's a mystery. A complete mystery.

Many have suggested it comes when doing it a lot, and if you stop, you have to start over. Do you find that?

I think it's more like the cliché about riding a bicycle.

I always remember here in Los Angeles, 1982, "Stepping Out" was our theme song. Everyone used it to get us going. It starts in F sharp minor and then switches to F sharp major.

I thought it was *all* in F sharp major.

Well, that is one of its charms, that the key center isn't obvious.

Yes. It's intuitive.

Many songwriters have expressed that what's instinctual only takes them so far and then they need to be more conscious of musical choices.

I think it's more instinctual than anything. But sometimes I have to think about it more. Somewhere I'll have a problem. For instance, I think one of my best songs is from my last album, it's called "Wasted Time." I was trying to find a way to have a key change in the bridge but have the bridge come back to another section that was in another key. So I really had to use all my knowledge of harmony to structure that bridge. But I think when you listen to it, it just sounds logical.

It sounds natural. It doesn't sound contrived.

I hope so. It actually took a lot of figuring out.

That would be an exception?

Right.

Your song "Breaking Us in Two" also has a deceptive key center, also going to F sharp major.

Yes, that was conscious at the time. To use a couple of the same ideas harmonically but to do something different with it. It was almost like a theme running through the album.

Yes, that theme of ascending major chords. Which is a very triumphant sound. And for "Breaking Us in Two" it's an interesting dynamic between that sound with that lyric.

You've been writing songs for a long time. Does the process get any easier, and do you gain new thoughts about how to write songs?

I don't know. It's changed in one way. I take a lot more time than I used to. It used to be that if I got an idea for a song, then I knocked it out best I could, and that was that. I think that more and more these days I'm more inclined to scrap ideas or to edit myself more or really try something again instead of thinking that however it came out the first time was the way it had to be. I've even scrapped a whole lyric and started all over again. I never used to do that.

Do you judge it while working on it?

Yes. When it's feeling just not quite good enough to me. I don't know. I've got more fussy or something.

Even using F sharp in rock and pop is unusual, as most guitarists don't play that chord except with a capo.

Well, it just seems to be quite often a good key for my voice. I guess I'm unusual in that I've had two songs in the key of F sharp. [*Laughs*] Yeah, "It's Different for Girls" is also in F sharp.

Irving Berlin could only play in F sharp.

Yes. He had a special piano with a lever that changed the keys.

Yes. It is a better piano key than guitar key. Do you find different keys have different tones and moods?

I think the idea is common enough that there must be something to it, but I can't really hear it. I think there might be something to it.

Some songwriters associate different colors with every key. Do you do that?

Not really. I think the colors come from the harmonic movement and the contrast between keys.

So many of your melodies are simply glorious. Do you have any idea what makes a melody great?

Do you?

I don't.

I think it's cool, though, to think about it.

Yes. Because all different melodies can work. There is no one way.

Yeah. But I do like a melody, as opposed to a few repeated notes or a riff. Some songs work okay for what they are, but there's not much going on melodically. It's one of the reasons I always loved standards, and songwriters like Gershwin and Harold Arlen—because the melodies really have an arc and a shape to them.

As do your songs, such as the beautiful "Is She Really Going Out with Him?" It has such a great opening line: "Pretty women out walking with gorillas down my street." Which is a great opening, visually and metrically.

I remember that was one song that started with the title, which has sometimes happened. I hear a phrase or something and think that would be a good song. What would that song be about? And in the case of that song, that song was supposed to be a funny song. It was really amazing to me when some people were interpreting it as being angry.

It is funny. And I love the call and response you have: "Look over there—where?—"

[*Laughs*] It was just having fun.

Have you ever found any repeatable methods for writing songs?

No. There's never been much of a pattern to it.

If something wasn't happening, would you get up and leave or stay there and work?

I am more likely to get up and do something else. It is good to do that. To get away from a problem for a while and then come back to it and really see it. I think that applies to any kind of process, any kind of problem.

Did you find anything made the process easier?

[*Long pause, then laughter*] I really don't know. Mostly it's a mystery. I put one foot in front of the other and try to find something that is exciting to me, and it gets fun, and I am almost jumping up and down.

Is it a sense of following the song more than leading it?

Yes. I feel like that sometimes. I've had this feeling quite often. It's a very spooky feeling; it feels like you're just uncovering it.

And what's the best way to uncover it?

[*Laughs*] Keep working on it.

◆ ◆ ◆

Rickie Lee Jones
Flying with the Cowboys

Malibu, California 2011; New Orleans, Louisiana 2015

Okay, truth be told, even if I had no outlet for this conversation, I would still want to talk to Rickie Lee. I just love being the person who gets to ask her questions and then bask in the sunshine and sometimes rain of her wisdom and whimsy. She's a compelling person, to put it lightly, and any time spent with her is time I cherish and remember always.

Okay, it's easy to remember, as I record our every talk. And then transcribe it faithfully, sure to get the phrasing right. Because she's serious about songwriting. As are the greatest purveyors of this art among us. Although it can be received as mere entertainment, to the serious songwriter this stuff is never to be taken lightly.

And so she speaks in hushed and reverent tones. "The best thing you can do as a songwriter," she says, "is trust the higher part that is writing and don't judge yourself or worry too much about it." That trust has connected all her songs since the start. She wrote her first one at the age of eight and never stopped writing them, a passion, interlaced with her love of singing, that brought her eventually to the western slopes of Los Angeles. Playing solo gigs around town, her music reached the ears of Lowell George, who recorded her "Easy Money" and helped her land a record deal. And unlike almost all songwriters who need a few albums at least to find their own voice, her eponymous debut revealed an astounding maturity and range of expression, from absolute exultation to darkest sorrow.

But despite its meteoric success, fueled by the euphoric "Chuck E.'s in Love," she was wise enough to know "you can't debut twice" and never attempted to repeat herself. She followed it with *Pirates*, a masterpiece of songwriting and singing so sophisticated and soulful that fans were awed and critics fell over themselves trying to capture with words what she did with music. Here was proof that the first album was no fluke and that not only was Rickie Lee Jones playing in the major leagues as a songwriter, she was also one of the most soulful and versatile vocalists ever to grace rock and roll. *Pirates* was likened to the music of everyone from Gershwin to Steely Dan, but none of these comparisons sufficed, as she was then and is now a songwriter and singer unlike any other, playing entirely by her own rules.

Subsequent masterpieces followed, including the mythic soul mysteries of *The Magazine*, the rich desert soundscapes of *Flying Cowboys*, the propulsive electric-acoustic spook-hop funk of *Ghostyhead*, the political rancor and redemption of the Bush-era *The Evening of My Best Day*, and the miraculously spontaneous spiritual exhortations of *The Sermon on Exposition Boulevard*. The gentle and wistful calm of *Balm in Gilead* is as ideal for the cold madness of modern times as she's been. And in 2015, closest to the completion of this tome, came her move to New Orleans and the album written in that wake, *The Other Side of Desire*, a beautifully inspired collection of songs haunted yet joyful, like the soul of New Orleans itself. Interviews that span several of these albums are combined herein.

Like Judy Garland, Billie Holliday, and other singers who invested the fullness of their soul and its sorrows into every song, Rickie encompasses a miraculous range of emotion in her work—"that's my gift," she allows—but unlike the others, she is also the songwriter of these songs, so the closeness to the bone we feel is ever more intense knowing it's genuine. These are not interpretations—although she's great at singing other people's songs—these are songs straight from the songwriter's soul. And in her work—unlike that of her famous paramour of the past, Tom Waits, and those who followed in his insalubrious footsteps—she did not wear masks or hide behind characters. Every song she wrote, to quote Waits, was "one from the heart." And that reality, that lack of distance between the singer and the song, is what gives her work so much poignancy and so much power.

For years she lived in the heart of Los Angeles, in and around the streets of Hollywood, taking it all in. These days she lives high—way, way up high—up above this vast city, up steep winding canyon hills over Malibu in a cottage with lots of land around where she can keep her horse. It seems a good place for those mythic flying cowboys she wrote about years ago to embark on a voyage. And it's from here where she embarks on her journeys—and does so with surprising speed, as one who tried and failed to follow her down winding hills to the Malibu flats knows well. She lost me! I tried to keep up with Rickie Lee Jones and lost. Symbolic? Of course. Everything to songwriters is symbolic.

We met the next day outside of a Malibu café where the sound of people laptopping and cell-phoning and munching on sandwiches around us was punctuated by the high-frequency cries of the gulls. It was an unusually overcast day, one of those spectral afternoons when the lack of glaring light causes the colors to radiate like mystic pastels on a canvas, and she seemed both somber and joyous as she reflected on the myriad paths that led her here. While we were talking, it seemed at first that nobody recognized her, until out of nowhere a lady appeared with a bag of treats for her and said, "Here's some little goodies for you." Rickie smiled for a brief moment. "Does that make you happy?" I asked. I wasn't sure. "Sure, of course it does," she said softly. "But only for a moment. And then it passes."

"Wild Girl" is an amazing song about your past and present and about your daughter. Like most of your songs, it works on many levels at once.

Rickie Lee Jones: Yeah. "Wild Girl," most of it was written in the eighties. It was the first song written after *The Magazine*. But I didn't have the finish, and I kept playing it for people every few months. And it never went away. It was a whole intact song. I couldn't forget it, it just was. Deciding who it was about helped me decide what I wanted to say. As long as it floated around bodyless, you could say anything. I thought of my daughter, Charlotte, and, okay, here's what I want to say. And it finished itself. Without being too revealing.

Were you writing about yourself in it at first?

I was thinking of that girl in high school that everybody sleeps with but nobody likes. Who is she? What happened to her? And how could I save her?

But songs are also amalgams. I was talking to me and to all the girls, when we get all dressed up and we're gonna go out and have fun. What is the line between fun and not fun, and who set it? Did society set it? Did you decide to defy society's line, and how happy are you now? Come back.

That's my guess. It's many years later. I was always expressing myself through other characters. And they're real too. There's a bunch of stuff taking place. I'm talking to me, I'm talking to the future, I'm talking to somebody I don't know. And I believe somewhere in the world somebody hears that and goes, "That was written for me." And they're right. That was written for them.

And it was written for my daughter. Who I hadn't met yet. And who will later find out what the spirit of that song was. My mother loved that song so much. She was the main reason I kept returning to it. Because there was a point where it seemed really quaint and dated. And in the last couple years, whatever the date is, this song has so much innocent heart that we're gonna bring it in. So I don't know how, but I did bring it in. I just transcended all the obstacles in my mind. It was right from my heart.

That sense of innocent heart is a prominent aspect of your work—

It is. I just started to get that picture—I don't know how I got it—but I just started to see if there's one thing that is my gift in music, that's what it is. I have an absolute connection to my emotions when I sing. And that seems to make people feel so healed.

You're able to capture the genuine sense of extreme emotion in your songs, from deeply blue to genuinely joyful.

I think I have to work to write a happy song. I write them carefully—they're simple; they're about when it's fun to walk down the street, you know? Because that's the best thing about when you're happy. It's just one little thing that makes you happy, and you're making friends. The kind of thing I can do is capture this moment. But isn't that what everybody's happy song would be? Like the Rolling Stones are really good at writing happy songs. Even when their content is not happy, there's something about their energies that makes it sound happy.

The mystical thing is that the energy, the *intention*, is what gets translated. Your intention is to express this moment when things go wrong. But what you write about is a trailer court and a blue car in a trailer court. Yet *somehow* when people come back to talk to you, they will say, "You know I listened to that song, and it reminds me of when things go wrong." They *always* understand what you intended.

That's the mystical thing about songwriting to me. We're talking on these other levels that we don't know. And the best thing you can do as a songwriter is trust the higher part that is writing and don't judge yourself or worry too much about it.

Yes, the wrong word or wrong phrase can impede that process, but let it be. Trust yourself; trust your journey and your life. Write the song.

So when writing, you don't judge it—

If I do, it'll die. The *moment* it comes through, the *moment* this little critic speaks up, it dies. You got to really protect it from what you think someone who didn't like you would say—the playground, you know. Because it's *so tenuous.* I am so afraid of losing them when I'm writing. They seem so delicate. They are formed by my intention to them as well as, it seems, their intention for something to say.

It's like the beginning of a love affair. It seems so tenuous. You say the wrong thing on that date and then they don't call for two days and then you get mad and then it's *over,* you know? Just in the beginning you've got to be very courteous with your song. You need to play it every day, every other hour so it doesn't die or you don't forget exactly how you did that part.

When you start a song do you start with an intention of what the song is about?

I don't think I *ever* do that. I think it's always just coming out of me. I never know where it's gonna go or what it's gonna be. I don't watch my process, but I probably write a line or two and then know where I'm gonna go right away. Do I want to do a rhyme scheme or a rhythm thing, or do I want to write free verse? It will usually tell you a direction to go. And what the subject is will be revealed. But it doesn't have the conscious in it. I just get out of my way. Following, not leading it. Not thinking about it at all. I can take the pen and write you eight lines right now. When it's done, it'll probably make sense, rhyme. Because the part just behind my consciousness knows just what it is doing. If my *consciousness* gets in the way, then that unconscious part goes, "Okay, you take care of it." [*Laughs*] And then my ego enters, and the flow stops. So I have to not guide it but just trust that I know what I'm doing. And again, not bothering with it.

Like "Bonfires" was about twelve verses. There were a lot of beautiful verses, but I felt that I was going to lose the impact. What I was thinking about when I wrote that was Bob Dylan's first record. I was thinking of how he played his guitar. This is where I am right now—it's simple. And that's how I wanted to deliver it. I didn't want it to be like Fleetwood Mac; I wanted to be like Dylan. Knowing there's no other way to survive heartbreak than to give love.

"Old Enough" is a great duet with Ben Harper. How did that evolve?

I wrote the verses, and he was brought in to sing one of them, the first verse, which caused me to think about the second one and rewrite the second one. It was like a Van Morrison thing. I ended up with kind of a Marvin Gaye thing. I wanted to say something about why are you rejecting me when I love you? And that was a case of wandering away from a song and finding it difficult to have something to say in four lines five years later. I had four lines I needed to write to connect what was there with what came after. And that was a *lot of work*. [*Laughs*] A *lot of work!*

And the other verse which was there was [*sings strongly*], "I wake up in the morning light / The world is bathed and blue / I take a walk when the sun comes up / I run back home to you / And late at night as the cars go by . . ." That's where he comes in. So it was all one verse. Lately I've been thinking, "God, that was a pretty good verse." [*Laughs*]

When you write a song, do you ever choose a key prior to starting?

No, I've done that in the old days. They do seem to come a lot in G.

Do you think each key has its own color or characters?

Yes.

If I named several keys, could you tell me how it makes you feel?

I could *try.*

Okay. How about C major?

C seems like it would be dressed in a nice cowboy outfit. Friendly, not bothering anybody. It could lead to the sad, it could lead to the happy. It's a kind of middle of the road. It's a little low in my register; I think of it as a boy's key. It's very friendly.

D.

D's much more of a challenge. It's got more tension in it than C. I think of my mother a little bit. Seems like a feminine key.

E.

E is like the dirt. It's where things fall to. E is something to lay down on. It's a really easy key to sing and play. It's a good resolution. Masculine.

F.

I don't know F very much.

G.

Celestial. Very *expansive*.

A.

A. I like A. Strength. It's expansive but it's consoled. It can be masculine or feminine. It can go either way.

A minor?

I like it. It's sad, but it's not without hope.

E minor.

Seems *much* darker to me. Sorrowful. It will accommodate rock. Powerful rock. It can be a pretty dire thing.

I understand that at times when you haven't been writing new songs, you studied certain songwriters to bring you back to songwriting.

That's right.

Paul McCartney?

That was one. And I mentioned him mostly because of the *Ram* album. Which I think is an amazing and still ahead-of-its-time piece of work. When I listen to it, it's kind of the precursor to everything cut-and-paste. But the difference is that he's still got great songs. He's playing everything by hand and it's all homemade. And some of them are just fragments of songs, but they're *all* beautiful.

'Cause normally you'd think you go to John Lennon, right? *Powerful* entity, great, amazing songs, and I do listen to them, but they were never— maybe like the difference between the way one teacher reaches you and another doesn't. When I listened to John Lennon I didn't turn around and go, "I think I'll write something," I'd go, "Oh wow, that's a real great song. I'll never write that song." When I listened to Paul McCartney, I'd go, "Oh yeah, yeah, I can go with that. I could do that." And when I listen to Curtis Mayfield, I go, "Yeah, yeah, I can do that. I know that language."

With McCartney there's a sweetness of melody that your songs share.

I guess so. Yeah. He's very romantic, and he's not afraid to be. Romantic is the perfect word, but there's always something very innocent about being that romantic. You know, I've noticed men are mostly the only people who can get away with that. Women, even though a kind of romantic thing is attached to them, that's not true. It's usually *men* who write the romantic love songs. And women are writing, generally, more aggressive, personal complaint. I'm thinking of *all* the women who are contemporary to me. While the men write an unmitigated [*laughs*] innocent "I love you so much that butterflies are flying around" songs. And I find it just *endears* them to me so much. Although I know men are more inclined to be warriors and all the things we say about them, they're also *this*. They're also fragile and terribly in love and terribly romantic. And I liked learning that.

And you studied their work?

I did. Studied them just by listening to them. But instead of listening just for the pleasure of it, once your door is open, then everything is knowledge. Everything you're taking in, you're taking in to build your house that you're building. You can get it from movies and songs, and everything you look at gets processed.

You went a long time without writing songs. Did you ever feel the need to write during this interim?

Sure. I wanted to write. But, you know, you sit down to write and it *hurts*. The whole thing is a process, right? It's kind of like creating the universe. When you first write, you only have the little grain of sand. You have no idea what it will be. So the first thing you write might be a terrible, uninteresting song, but there's one part of it that reminds you, say, of a kind of emotional freedom you'd like to have. I don't know why. Just a couple bars. And then you go, "I don't know what that is, but I sure wish I could do it." And then a year later maybe that feeling is more sophisticated, and now you've written a *line*.

And so, if I really thought about it, probably in my way I've been working the whole time. Waiting to write a greater song. And be totally engrossed and energized and unafraid of writing. Because writing is *so hard* when you stop. So hard to relearn again. It's really hard.

There are a couple of things: I know how to do it. It's what I *do*. But to do it to the extent that I'd like to do it, to change my life or bring a good thing to the world or shake it up or bring some new style or whatever it is I'm trying to do, like any athlete, you have to just keep *practicing* and *practicing* and *practicing*.

And then the question is, "What is your destiny?" So if you know that's not your destiny to do this, then my prayer is "Can you just show me where I might be content?" This is what I'd like to do. I'd like to write a great piece of work. But just guide me where I'm supposed to go. Because I just don't know where I'm supposed to go.

And I think that maybe if that's your prayer and your point of focus, then you can hopefully find contentment with whatever it is you manifest. If you pray for a specific thing—which also is helpful—that may not actually be what you're setting yourself up to do. I think a lot of times people will pray for a new car, say, but they're not doing anything [*laughs*] to manifest that thing coming through. So you've got to work with your intentions and your muscles and keeping an eye about what your destiny is.

It's all very complicated, and it's kind of easy and silly to say from here. Because from here I could look back, and this is what it looks like. I think contrary things are always happening at the same time. While I was breaking, I was also being restored.

There was a year or two, I remember, in Tacoma, thinking, "You know, I never sing." And now I sing all the time. I wake up singing. It's almost like being manic-depressive. You know, because it's so *consuming* that when you open the door, that's all you're going to do and be. And now that it's open, I'm *very happy*. But it's very difficult to do or be anything else but a musician once that door opens. And [*softly*] I think I've been trying to just be a mother.

You mentioned the tree you drive by, which became the song "A Tree on Allenford." It's a stunning song. It has the powerful and beautiful line, "Every drop of rain that fell or falls is always falling on and on."

I wrote it in my car. There were a couple of songs I started writing as I drove to work. And that was one of those songs.

I would pass this tree every day on my way to work. A child had been killed there, and people left flowers and made it kind of a shrine. And I was thinking how the tree had taken on that burden or that love of those people. And I thought that somewhere in the ether the tree and the children are sitting together.

It's too metaphysical now. It's about trying to offer complete relief to the grieving parent. Not through the lyric but just through my prayer, as I drive by, to say, "All is well, and we're all part of each other. None of us is gone. If we're not in the rain, we're in the tree, or we're in the thoughts. We're all here."

I've had that happen a few times, where I got the melody in my head. And I just keep singing, just keep singing it, till I get to work, don't let anything take me away. Walk right in [to the recording studio] and said,

"Not going to do what we planned—I have a new song," sat down right away, and played it and recorded it. So what you hear is me *writing* it. That's it. That was like that day that I wrote it.

And you played it on guitar?

Actually on a keyboard first. I got that little melody [*sings repeated motif*], and we got a little oboe sound and put that on. And then later we brought in players and put that keyboard way in the back with a little echo on it. So it almost sounds a little accordionish. What's thrilling about it technically is that it's really the day I wrote it, that version.

Did you write other songs in your head like that?

The other one I wrote in my head like that was "The Mink Coat at the Bus Stop." I mean, I remember seeing her very well, so the way that I'm remembering it is that I heard the melody. I'm not sure if I heard the melody then or if I went in and wrote it.

But I saw this girl at the bus stop, a little younger than me, fortyish, early in the morning, when I'm taking my daughter to school. And she was sitting at the bus stop in a mink coat. Every day when I drive her to school I see a lot of people out in the street with nowhere to go. And I knew that people don't look; they didn't see her.

I wondered, "What are you doing there in the morning in your mink coat at the bus stop?" She was looking up, her eyes were cast upward and never changed. The whole time she sat there looking up. And I thought, "Whoa, that's a low-down scene, man." [*Laughs*] And all these people driving by in their brand-new cars. And *all* the people waiting for the bus. What a *hard* way to go in this town. You've got to sit and wait for the bus. And people drive *by them*. They don't even see them; they don't look at them.

And you do really start to feel an incredible class division—the people with the cars and not with the cars. Because that's what *this* town is. And it just made me go, "Hey, I'm that girl at that bus stop. She's not different than me." And in the end how can you look and not extend compassion? And expect compassion to be extended to you from everyone you meet? I mean, what's going on? [*Laughs*] Why is that so hard to give? You know, *give it up, give it up.*

You wrote in that song that everybody is the same and people need dignity, love, and understanding.

Yeah. Dignity.

Did you write the music for that one in your car too?

Yeah. That was fun because I had this nice tough blues thing, but I wanted something else. I think what I started remembering is that I have a great capacity in writing, an unexpected chorus or unexpected bridge. And I *remembered* it, remembered how to do it. I did it a couple of times on this record, and that was one of them.

I said, "I want to go somewhere new," and it said, "Okay," [*sings*] 'I look at the people . . .'" And initially they were so pleased and surprised that it was such a wild turn. But by the time we finished producing the record, I can't tell—does the listener go, "Whoa! What is that?" Or is it just as natural as can be to go there? It is the commentary on the world. So the blues number is we're down at the bus stop, and then the other part is me turning to the camera and speaking to you. Also, it's all kind of urban. Like Curtis Mayfield would have written that melody. So they're all cousins, all these kinds of musics. You just have to find a way to patch them together.

When you write a melody in your head, is it easy for you to go to a guitar and play it?

I think it is, yeah. Now it is. I'm a good enough player now that I can replicate what I hear. I'm better on guitar. I've come pretty close most of the time if I hear something, knowing right where the note is on an instrument. Sometimes I might be a half step or a whole step off. But by now I know the neckboard enough to know where the notes are.

And that's very comfortable, because I can sit with all these men, and I definitely hold my own playing with them. And, in fact, they're really dependent on what I play. That's a *great* feeling, because I think up to now I felt more like a singer who could play. But now I feel like a good player. The thing I know how to do, I know how to do really well. [*Laughs*] I do it really well. Confident.

And I can tell the players feel great. I know how to talk to them now with an instrument instead of just with my voice. And that's *so* fun. It's something I always wanted to be able to do, and I can do it now. So I'm in this kind of great celebration of my life. And I think for many years I would not have been able to say I can do that well. I would have been really afraid. I was afraid of this nameless enemy that would *hit* me. Like a journalist. Or my karma, which would say, "Oh yeah, you think you can do that well? Hey, watch this!" And kick me down the stairs, you know? So I don't have this fear anymore. I know *exactly* what I do. And I've come to do it. If you like it, come and see. If you don't like it, go away. [*Laughs*] I have my feet on the ground.

What affected this change?

Well, I think that was a process. It's a whole bunch of things, really. And they're probably mostly private. But generally, three years ago I had a manager who was a friend who screwed me really bad. And then I had a series of terrible things happen professionally. And they were so *debilitating.*

Actually now as I tell you why I didn't write, I think that's why. There was this series of things that happened—with the band and the bus company [*laughs*]—I went, "*What* is going on? What did I do to deserve this?" Because that's the silly way I process stuff. But somewhere in the back of my mind I thought, "I haven't done *anything.* This must be payment for something really great that's coming. [*Laughs*] Because I don't deserve this. So this hard time must be preparing some ground for me rising."

I guess it's my nature to think, "How can I rise?" It's not my nature to roll over, even though I might complain and cry and be sorrowful. It's just my nature to go, "How can I use this to get back up where I want to go?"

So then that happened. Last year my mom had a stroke. And I think taking care of my mother, being so close that she almost died, looking at the people in my family, thinking of my *whole* life, my dad's life, my grandfather's life, ten thousand years of people who procreated to bring me *here*. Watching my mother. And you know, when she tries to talk, she can't say it, and she *laughs*. Seeing my mom laugh made me go, "What a wonderful world. What a wonderful human being I grew up with." I always loved her, but I didn't realize how *wonderful* she is. Look at her *laugh* at herself.

And I guess it made me turn and go, "Okay, *no more* fooling around. No more feeling sorry for yourself." There's a whole world of people who need my help. They need my help to help them find a hospital for their parents. They need my help with the poem I write. My daughter needs my help; my mother needs my help. And I have *unlimited* energy to give till I *die*. 'Cause once you start giving, you have more. That's just how it is. You don't give, you don't have anything to give. You give, you've a lot to give.

And seeing my mother so close to death made me realize I'm going to die. And some day all these things I won't have done. And I'm still here. I'm still young. I could still do them. So maybe it was like *It's a Wonderful Life*. And I got to come back. With great joy and happiness.

And I'm not sure what happened, but I do feel kind of like him running through [*laughs*] with Zuzu's petals in my pocket.

And I don't know if that's how it will be from now on or if it will subside a little. But I feel the capacity to be part of a larger thing going on as well as helping my career. Redeeming my career. Because I think I'm a great writer and an important character in American art. And I've had my career described as a "downward spiral." And I know I'm a great writer, and I don't want to be tossed away. And have my history rewritten by VH1 as a footnote. That's not *true*. And those kind of things, maybe people think they don't matter to people, but they *do*.

And I think that kind of stuff that hurt so badly might have made it hard for me to get up. It did make me finally decide that it *doesn't* matter. In the end you know what you do. *You* know what you gave; you know what you did. You do need love from the outside, let's face it. If I made the record and nobody wanted to work with me, I wouldn't have this power that I have. But getting love from people and people saying, "It's *so* good to see you working. You sound great. Great song." Then you feel part of the world. People *need* that.

Even when you are talking about some dark subjects, you do it with a lot of joy. The song "Little Mysteries" does that, and it's great.

I started that before my daughter was born. You know, I read a lot of spy novels. I was in France, and four little gypsy children ran up to us, a little boy jumped in front of us and opened up a newspaper and said, "You want to buy the paper, lady? You want to buy the paper?" While he was in front of me kids went through my pockets, and it was *so* fast, *so* professional. I was *so* impressed. Unfortunately they did not get my wallet, which was in my pocket. And I always worried for them that they got beat very badly [*laughs*] when they went back to their gypsy home. But that experience was so *profound*—to see criminal children, I think. I had never experienced organized *small* criminal children before. And it made for a good text.

So I wrote, fifteen years ago [*sings*], "Gypsy boy came up to you and he tried to hide his fingers in your pocket." That's what I had. [*Sings*] "Oh, little mysteries. Little mysteries." That's what I had for fifteen years. Last summer I went, "I have to finish this." I was waiting because I didn't know if I wanted to write one specific mystery or have a series of mysterious scenarios. I wanted to tie those together or just leave them untied. So I decided to write about things that had bothered me.

Your songs have such strong melodies. Do you think people will always hunger for a good melody?

I think they hunger for a great song they can take home and sing. That's what they like. They want to hear a good song. I think one of the problems, as machines get better, is that they divert us from doing the first things. So we get really involved with the machines and all the cool things we can do, but they're not starting with a great song.

One of the things I liked about the idea of *Ghostyhead*, which succeeded sometimes, is I liked the idea of using the wonderful chaotic things you can do with machines but having a great song in the first place. I think that would be fun. That was kind of what was fun about *Ram*. That he did these little funny cut-and-paste things, in his way, but he had a cool melody.

The song "Lamp of the Body" is beautiful. Musically it's like ancient cantorial singing.

Yeah. Yeah it is. It's one of the more challenging ones to do live because it's this droning thing. And it's a real simple text. It's him. There's this moment when he's saying about his journey to meet John the Baptist. This is right out of the book. "He journeyed into the wilderness to listen to John the prophet, the one they call the Baptizer. He spoke to you with truth: he was a burning, shining light, and you were willing for a while to follow him." That's me reading from the book.

I think "the lamp of the body is the eye" is also something that he said. And I just said that over and over. I didn't even notice. I was just opening pages and reading them. So it's very Eastern. It's kind of like the Islamic poets. They write their beautiful poems of love to God. These words of Jesus are so similar to those poems. I never really noticed how they are before. Before I started reading the poets. And I realized these are just all poems of love. To *God*. What a beautiful song, what a beautiful idea.

Did you choose "Chuck E" to be the single from your first album?

They chose it. But I think I probably wanted it. That wasn't my job, so I really can't remember. But I probably thought it was cool as a single because it was so offbeat. And they were very cool. They chose the most offbeat, unusual track on the record as the single.

It's the only hit single ever to rhyme "Pantages" with "contagious."

Absolutely. [*Laughter*]

A good Hollywood rhyme. After that was such a big hit, did you personally have any thought about wanting to do that kind of song again?

No.

A lot of artists wouldn't know not to do that.

No, I knew that would be the kiss of death. With such a huge hit, the only possibility of me having a lifelong career was to absolutely follow my muse. What I thought I did well on the first record was to tell stories. I can say this after the fact; I wasn't thinking this before I did it. What I did well was tell stories, so the only thing I could do that would resuscitate the career from the huge heights it was having to fall from was to be an amazing storyteller. And that's what I did. And I told these stories in a really new and unique way.

I think that gave me credibility with journalists. And [*Pirates*] sold, right away, a half a million records. Which at the time was an incredible disappointment to the record company. I didn't go on tour for about a year and a half before I toured with *Pirates*. And I was always still *defining* myself, so that a year after making that record, who am I gonna be onstage doing this stuff? So I was kind of into doing a New Orleans revue kind of thing. Which is a long way from the impetus of *Pirates*. So you're taking *Pirates* out in a New Orleans revue. If I would have taken *Pirates* out the minute I'd done it, it probably would have been a very different show.

From the first album on, you had a language all your own in those songs. It wasn't imitative at all. I remember hearing that line from "Night Train," "broken like valiums and chumps in the rain," and knowing this was new, this was different—

Yeah. That strange, weird poetry that I remember at the time thinking, this poetry is strange. But I couldn't help myself. That's really the kind of line I would write. And it showed up again in this record too. You pointed out that line about the little dance you do before your mother calls you on the phone. That it was a very Rickie Lee kind of line. Same kind of thing, yeah.

That's why your work matters. You've never contrived anything to be a hit. You have always written what is true to you.

It's so idiosyncratic. You'd think, if anything, that would encumber [*laughs*] your ability to have a hit. And same thing about the way I sing. The strange idiosyncratic faults of my voice are what I find most repeated by singers who sound like me. The things that were kind of questionable are the things they picked up most of all. The pronunciation or the no vibrato or the kind of young-kid tonality. That's what I hear everywhere. The stuff that I wouldn't have done if I could have avoided it.

It's amazing you didn't get blown away by that early success. A lot of your peers, such as Tom Waits, never had a big hit. But you had this huge commercial success and retained your artistic self. Was it tough to balance those two worlds?

Well, you know I was a beginner, so I started out with that. If I had been an artist for a few years and had that happen, it might have been devastating to me. But I think having it from the moment I began, it was just a wonderful, kind of ominous introduction to what my life was gonna be like. It was gonna be unexpected and working with bigger strokes than anyone else. I can't answer that because before that record I didn't have a career. So I wasn't in the water yet to get thrown out of the water.

It's miraculous to me that Warner Brothers was smart enough to leave you alone and let you write your second album in peace. Nowadays they would have you out on the road. They were really taking good care of you.

Yeah. They took really good care of me. I was their girl. They loved me. Lenny [Waronker], Mo [Ostin].

The business sure has changed a lot.

Yeah, I don't think anybody's left there anymore.

Randy Newman told me he wanted to quit during that change-up, but he didn't know anyone left there at Warner's to call.

[*Laughter*] He's *so* funny.

Did you have a lot of time to write *Pirates*?

I wrote it in about a year and a half. I think so. Wrote a couple songs, and then nine months later wrote a couple of more.

An aspect that still astounds me about it to this day is that many of the songs—like "Pirates," "Living It Up," and "We Belong Together"— are more like suites than songs. They have time shifts in them; the tempo kicks in and out. Hardly any songwriter, except maybe Zappa, has time shifts like that. Was it hard to get that sound and dynamic with a band? It's so delicate.

[*Very softly*] Yeah, it was. Really hard.

How did you do it?

We just kept coming back again and again until I got it. "We Belong Together" was recorded about three times, I think. It took a long time. All of them were hard. We were doing "Living It Up," and it was going pretty well. And I liked to talk to [the musicians] about what the story was about or the feeling of the song. And we were playing that song again, and all of a sudden, I'm playing away, and I hear a big *crash*, and [Jeff] Porcaro has stuck his sticks *through* his snare! And he says, "*Fuck this art shit!*" [*Laughter*] And he stormed right out of the recording studio. [*Laughs*] Yeah, 'fraid so.

Elvis is about as iconic as the image of Jesus now.

I think he is, in many ways. Especially since his death. He provides solace and hope. And people just *love* him, idolize him, adore him.

Did you like him when you were a kid?

No. I liked, when I got older, before he died, I saw that comeback film in the seventies. He was pretty good then. But I didn't care for him other than that.

How about now when you hear him?

No. It doesn't speak to me. I think he's an amazing singer. I listen to "You ain't nothin' but a hound dog." That's pretty amazing. I've heard the original version by Big Mama Thornton. [See Leiber and Stoller, page 26.] And both versions are pretty great. Her version is pretty cool, but I think his is better. His takes it to some other places.

That was written by Leiber and Stoller, who were writing rock and roll but were still part of the tradition of two people writing one song—one wrote words and one music. And most songwriters, even today, are better with words or music. But you're one of the rare ones who is great with both elements.

[*Softly*] Thank you. They come at the same time. And as long as they come at the same time, it's usually a really good song. But I spend more time on the lyrics. If I have to hash something out, I hash out the lyric more. To make sure it has continuity and its delivery is somewhere I want to go. And I don't really have to do that *musically*. Musically I'm always a pilgrim. So anywhere I go is okay. But lyrically I have a kind of responsibility.

A lot of songwriters repeat themselves musically, going over the same patterns. You don't seem to do that.

No. Each time I make a record, it's a movie. So some new set of ideas has come upon me. And this one will be flavored like *this*. I think I write movies. If I was just writing songs, maybe they would tend to become the same. But every one is a whole different film, so it's a whole different way of writing. The continuity matters. In "We Belong Together" I was noticing the line "the only angel who sees us watches through each other's eyes." And in *Flying Cowboys*, writing about the "Ghost Train." I'm always talking about the invisible world. *Always*. And that's the continuity that brings me here. That's one reason why I think this record can't be suspicious, because there's something about that which is a total culmination of everything I've ever written. Even though it's different. What's new about it is that I've challenged myself to improvise, and I've walked into somebody else's house. So if I had had to write everything, it wouldn't have been so new. Because I can only write the way I write. And I can't be that raw. It's not in me to write that way. But I can go there and find new places to go.

I would be suspicious of me if I said, "I am just gonna do a guitar-drums-bass record." Even though I would love to do it. I think I would go, "If they hated *Ghostyhead*, I'm not even gonna get this record out." Because people start to say what you can *do*, what they will *allow* you to do. And a lot of my career has been to keep pushing those limits.

I think I could have done probably much more work if I didn't always have to be justifying everything I did and why it wasn't like the last thing I did. If I didn't have to do that, I probably would have done a *lot* more work. And all of it really different. I might have done a cabaret record; I might have done a country-western record. There's so much music to be made, and I love it all. But because of the *career*—if they like that singer-songwriter hat, you can just be one voice. [*Does quick Dylanish singing*] And you only can sing like that. And if you're a real *singer*, they're *suspicious*.

So I just kept defying it. Well, I'm a real singer, and I like a lot of different stuff, and I'm not going anywhere. And I think, finally, at this moment in my life I'm being understood and respected and described in ways I think are accurate. It's a really great moment. When they describe my diversity, they describe it with respect. And that feels *good*. It's hard to always be the itinerant outsider. It's fucked up. And I feel like that has been one of my main identities, the outsider.

It's interesting to me what songs stick in my head, and after days of hearing your songs from your entire career, the song that keeps returning is "Stewart's Coat," from *Traffic from Paradise*. That melody is so haunting.

Yeah, it is. I heard that whole. It was in the back of the cathedral of Notre Dame. And I was walking in back of it over the bridge, and that melody descended upon me whole. With the lyric [*sings*] "Walking in the rain . . ." And it sat like that for many years until Sal [Bernardi] said we should finish it. But I actually started it maybe in the mideighties.

Does that give you the sense that songs come from someplace else, when you receive a song whole like that?

Well, where could they come from but someplace else? Because they don't come from here. [*Points to her heart, laughs*] When they come whole, it makes it feel like it's *somebody* else giving me the work. But I don't know. There are so many answers. It could be made of your confidence, your need to hear it whole. Or it could be being *delivered* to you. In performance is when you most feel like you're a conduit. When I write stuff, I always go, "Thank you *so* much." So if I answer truthfully, I feel like I'm talking to somebody else. Whether or not it's my heart that is setting me free or somebody else's, it feels like there's somebody else to say thank you for what happens.

McCartney said that when he got the melody to "Yesterday," he was sure somebody else had written it. Do you feel that?

[*Laughter*] Yeah, I do. I feel that must already have been written. But I feel, no, no, you're just writing it *now*. But it's almost like we've already been here, and we already know we wrote it. And then when we do, we ask, "Did I write that or did somebody else write that?" I've had that happen, yeah. "Saturday Afternoons" was like that. It seemed to be a melody we all know well, yeah.

***Ghostyhead* is such a powerful album, with songs like "Firewalker" and "Howard." Like some of Dylan's great albums that even his fans rejected, this one didn't seem to get a fair reception.**

Two things happened. It got really mixed reviews. And when we went out on tour we were *really* exploring improvisation onstage. Really *new* stuff. Not so new now. Really new cutting-edge stuff. But my record got sold to Universal, and they didn't put it out, so it was only out six months. So any kind of understanding that could have come to it or sales never had a chance. That's what happened to it.

The fusion of your vocals and the acoustic bass with techno is so beautiful, and one of the first instances of that. A great blend of humans with machines, of warm and cold.

Yeah. And reading poems and making up tunes to that environment. I thought it was a fresh idea.

The newest album, *The Other Side of Desire*, is a masterpiece. I know you did it more quickly than usual. I spoke to Merle Haggard recently, who told me that he recorded his song "Mama Tried" and two other songs in three hours.

So why not? [*Laughter*] Why not?

Why not? Because the way you've always crafted your albums isn't that. Yours have layers of vocals and other studio touches you can't do quickly. Is that incorrect?

It depends. I did do demos for this one, which makes the process of recording quicker. I have an impatience now I didn't have when I'm younger. I've had it for a few years, so it's one reason maybe that I haven't done a record in a while.

In the past I would make myself stay and finish stuff and work stuff out and do it again and do it the best. On this record I haven't. The thing of doing things like *Pirates*, well, *Pirates* didn't really have demos. It was my second record, and I was recording while I wrote. I had a lot of money and I had a lot of authority.

For me, right now, limitations are really helpful, because I am really creative, I have a lot of ideas, and I need somebody just to send me in a direction and tell me that I'm done.

Though you rely on limitations, you break them all the time. "Jimmy Choos," the great opener of this album, is more of a suite than a normal song. You have a verse and then a bridge and another section before you ever get to the chorus. As you have done in other suites of which we've spoken. And that breaks the rules. You're supposed to get to the chorus quick. For which, as you know, you could go to songwriter jail.

[*Laughs*] Uh-oh. Wouldn't be my first time.

[*Laughter*] But by the time you finally do get to this chorus, it's like a Gershwin progression—suddenly we're in this whole other place and it's triumphant and joyful. It's remarkable.

Thank you. Thank you. [*Laughs*]

Maybe that's why I need [limitations] because I find something to do new, to break out of the form, that that helps me go somewhere new. I think that you hit it on the head. I am defiant in nature, and if I have some restriction, I can do that defiance and go somewhere new.

Limitations are like having a tiny room instead of a field. The smaller the room, the more you can do in it. If it's really big, you gotta go buy a bunch of stuff to fill it up, and you're going to need help. The smaller the room, the more I can see where it ends and begins. I can do things to it if I want. I can break the window. That's how I see giving myself restrictions.

When you go to write a song, anything is possible! You can go *anywhere*! And so in order to start, it helps if you give yourself this kind of framework.

Laura Nyro and Carole King both said the same thing to me, that one of the best parts of writing songs it that within a song form you can do anything.

Yeah! Yeah. It's true.

Part of the greatness of the song and the record of it is your performance. It's the essence of being a singer-songwriter in that it's so beautifully designed for your instrument. When you're on that section, "I know about the Motel Six," the first time you do it in a lower octave and then you leap the octave, which is so powerful and visceral. Not every singer could do that.

Yes. Maybe I automatically do that because I know I'm singing it, so I'm not thinking about it. But yeah, I'm writing for myself to sing it, most definitely.

The structure is so powerful, and it's a great lesson for songwriters because it's symphonic. Is that how that song came to be, or did that chorus come earlier in the process?

Let's see. I was laying on my bed, I'd just talked to my daughter a little while earlier, and I started, and I had been working on bluegrass-type of songs, thinking of Louis Michot, the Cajun guy, and wanting to write things in his vein.

I started [*sings*] "Oh cherie, come and take a ride with me, we just need to clear out your mind." That was so heartfelt to me, and so I guess the thing I was thinking of most was the message. Come on, let's stop doing this and, you know, the whole wide world is waiting just at the edge of town—let's go. I still emotionally am always telling the story of the disenfranchised, the lost, defying it and trying, because my mind is like the transvestite on the roof—these people won't give up, they won't get in the car, and now they won't get off the roof. Holy shit!

I mean, [*laughter*] get off the roof! Let's go! No, I'm not going to do it either, and in my mind, I mean, you know, there's a lot of story that doesn't get written down because I'm with these characters, and you know there's whole plays, there's books, there's short stories, so that character is running down the street, and that's where the "Jimmy Choos" came, because he or she is running down the street in the Jimmy Choos shoes [*laughter*] and I thought these Jimmy Choos are going to save us. The Jimmy Choos shoes.

It's such a beautiful use of language. Jimmy Choos, up to now, I just thought of as something rich ladies love, and it had no meaning in my life. Till now.

I know. [*Laughter*] I was thinking that when I wrote "Choos shoes"— of, you know, of this hopeful moment where I might be on stage someday and the big crowd, like at Red Rocks, would be singing "Choos shoes, Choos shoes, Choos shoes." That's what I eventually felt as I wrote that "Choos shoes." I was laughing so hard and didn't know if anybody else would laugh. I sent it to my notoriously cynical manager with a note that said, "Please don't tell me what you think," and he said, "That's a fantastic song—it's so funny." So I knew that if he got it, maybe somebody else would too. I just didn't know if it was going to make people laugh.

It made me happy.

Happy laugh. Yeah.

Songwriters often think you're either writing a song like McCartney, about a character, or you're writing it like Lennon about yourself. But your songs, even about characters like this, are about you as well. You bring the songwriter into it so gently and beautifully when you add a little commentary, "You don't have to tell me about giving up . . ." Suddenly that brings a whole other dimension to it that this is so poignant.

Yeah. That's right. Thank you.

And it says so much that, that even in your position in life, you're still mixing with people like this, characters on the fringe of life. Whereas so many songwriters seem cut off from humanity and aren't writing songs that reflect humanity in the way you still do.

I think wealth does that to people. They get rich and they don't want to be bothered. But if you have money, you don't have to be bothered; you don't have to go do your own errands. But when I do my errands I'm going to meet people. I'm going to interact with people, and when I do that, I'm going to learn about myself.

I had to pick up my suitcase from the shoemaker, and he was so proud of his work, and I was looking at the shop he was in, and when I left his shop I felt good about myself because I could appreciate him and his shop.

So everywhere you go, you know, you're learning about yourself. You're going up or you're going down the elevator. It's all there for your lyrics.

I see that too. People get secluded and afraid of people. Whereas this is a story of a transvestite on the roof, and your embrace of this person's humanity is inspiring and necessary. Whereas most people, I don't think, could necessarily love a person like that so openly.

All the characters are me, ultimately. They're inspired by my life, and when I put them in the song, like a dream, they're me. I thought, "Why must I express my sexuality as a man playing a woman? What are you doing? Why are you always running out of town?" My favorite scenes in movies are when they leave at the end and go to start a new life. I love that!

Even the melody of "Jimmy Choos," which is a bright tune in G major, is happy. Musically there is joy there, even separate from the words. Did you write it in that key on an instrument or a cappella?

That's really perceptive, because I really wanted that song to lift somebody. I think I picked up my guitar, and I think I was playing it from the beginning. Most of what I was writing was in A minor, but I think I went to G for that one. Yeah.

Songwriters often think we need fancy chords to make a beautiful melody. Yet those chords, even for your songs, are pretty simple, yet the melody is just soaring. It's so poignant. Do you have any thoughts of what makes a melody connect so strongly with us?

I think melodies are our true language. You're building something. Like building a little sentence. If you drew it, it would look like an upside down J. Right? I have been thinking about melody, if you draw the shape of it, you can see what it does. I've been thinking that there are certain melodies, certain series of tones, that invoke in us an emotion. And they're picked up in every culture. I noticed, for instance, that certain tunes are everywhere. You can find them in China. You can find them in Western music. It's everywhere. Hank Williams. Japan.

It's interesting you said you started out in A major. That key to me has always seemed maybe the happiest key. And most of The Beatles' songs are in A major, as are Buddy Holly songs.

Are they?

Yes.

Well, as we have discussed before, keys do affect the mood. Paul Simon wrote a little thing on it, and I had never really been aware of it before. But if I do something in F sharp instead of G, like "The Last Chance Texaco," it's a totally different song. It's not just because of what's required for the other players physically or how they have to stretch their fingers; it's the relationship between those tones which is different than it is in another key.

A major is a key I can rock in, whereas G is a key I tend to tell a story in. I wouldn't play a rock and roll song in G. I would play a rocking song in E or A, right? We do it instinctively, even if we don't know how to talk about it.

I know you see keys in color. I don't. I see shapes. But I don't even think of it as keys. I just pick up the guitar and whatever the melody, whatever key it came to me in, I try to play it in that key. At least when I'm writing it. So if I did a melody early in the morning, it's probably going to be really low, because my voice is low in the morning. I might change it from that key later because I can't sing as low later. [*Laughs*]

Some songwriters think it's easier to write a strong melody in a minor key.

Interesting. I don't think that's true at all. For me the minor chord makes a moment of sorrow that we pass through.

Often, as you know, my songs are in several keys. I find the difficult part is to get back to the key you started in. Because you almost end up like you are in a circle that keeps leading to a different key. If you were drawing it, you would have drawn a lotus flower.

I think a major key can take you to a much sadder place, whereas if you start in a minor key, it's pretty hard to write a happy song. But you can go anywhere in a major key.

Talking to you about major and minor is like talking to a Cole Porter in that, like you, he would go in and out of major and minor and change keys brilliantly. Your songs rarely are about one color.

I sure don't think of them that way anyway, yeah. But it's not deep water. I'm not exhausted when I'm done. [*Laughs*]

So many of your songs, such as "Infinity," use music to get us to think about things beyond words, beyond what language can do. Not all songs do that.

Paul, that's really what this record—or this time in my life—is all about.

"Infinity" came from a dream, but I made a decision to make a song out of it which was purposeful. Because the things I think about—space and time and the afterlife—can shape a melody. To me those are the most important things I'd like to say. So I chose to start saying them. I said, "Why don't you go ahead and say what you have to say in your song?" And so I did. I wrote about time and myself.

And the music helps us understand the words much more so than if it was just words on a page. It wouldn't get to us in the same way, where you're talking to our heart and our mind at the same time.

It's true. True.

"Christmas in New Orleans" is wonderful. Bringing in the horns at the end is so haunting and beautiful, whereas other people might have had those right in the intro, those horns. It's so touching.

That song was an evolution. I was living next door to a guy who played a lot of soul music, and it went right through the walls and I really enjoyed it. I liked waking up to his music, and that was good for me because at some other time in my life I would have gone, "That goddamn guy is waking me up with his music!"

But now I went, "That's so cool. I love that music." And I just lay there and listen to it. And I think that the seeds of acceptance got sewn in. So I started hearing this tune, [*sings a cappella*] "She's got her feet on the ground. Life is a merry, a merry-go-round." Just right out of old school, right? And it would not go away. I tried to write some good verses very much in that ilk.

As time went by, I thought, "This is going to be a little too novel. I have to find a way to tell this story." So I had one of those lovely melodies, and I decided to tell the story of the girl with the lovely melody and then go ahead and go to the chorus, which sounds more downtown and shifts tempo.

Thinking of The Beatles, who would have done that, or Neil Young, they used to change tempo. And that's part of my vocabulary, to change tempo. So I allowed myself as much license as I wanted in order to tell you the story of the girl and these families of drug addicts and what is lost and what is never found again and what it's like to wait in line in an office. There's one line about it. I ended up having to edit it just to two verses: say what you have to say. And so that story, clearly to me, is about a drug addict, but I can't tell if anybody else can tell that, and that's okay.

It seems in your music you've always, like, felt things so deeply. I used to think everyone felt things deeply, but sometimes it seems that

songwriters and musicians feel things more deeply, like being a raw nerve in the world.

Lately I've begun to agree with you about that. I've begun to realize that is our part in the collective body. Most people can't express themselves, aren't given the opportunity or numb themselves. I can't tell if we have an apparatus they don't have, but most certainly, for whatever reason, we're *feeling*. We're feeling and expressing—hopefully expressing—but definitely feeling [*pause*] more.

I'd like to see more deeply.

I think that the thing the performer does is to be an empath, to send it back to the people. That's where things get really interesting. It's wonderful to write, but when you can actually stand there and send that music out and see it go back out, it's exciting.

And you've always done that.

I love it.

And all your fans know well, even if you didn't write songs, you do that with other songs. To this day "Rainbow Sleeves," written for you by Tom Waits, just kills me. You touch an intense level of sorrow, and having someone bring us that helps us get through.

But you can only feel it if you have it too. It has to be part of your vocabulary or it wouldn't hit that button for you.

That is a truth I am only now being able to understand. The songs of our friend Laura Nyro do that for me, and I never understood why she isn't as beloved as Dylan to the whole world. And I know that for you, like Laura, being an artist in this industry hasn't been easy. Though you got Grammys for your early masterpieces, later greatness like *Flying Cowboys* wasn't even nominated.

That was all for nothing. [*Laughs*]

How do you maintain a songwriter's soul and connect with great songs when you're in an industry that doesn't necessarily even recognize the depth of what you're doing?

Well, it might be the answer that I came here [to New Orleans] to remove myself from, from the industry. If this record comes out and is ignored again, it's going to hurt me a lot. But I had this profound relationship with people in the world, and for some of us that's just our lot in life. We're not given the flowers at graduation, for whatever reason. I know I'm loved by God, so if this is what it's supposed to be, then it is helping me do better work. It's leading me.

If I turn around and become bitter, then it was wrong. But so far I feel like I'm always finding grace. I'm always finding some new thing to appreciate and love. You know, adoration is really death. If I had too much of it in the past, I think I'm much more balanced now. But I don't like to have too much adoration. Because it's impossible to live up to it.

So all you can do is turn away from it and not read stuff, and you might even become secluded. I'm in a place now where I acknowledge gratefully that I've been around thirty-five years, I've impacted the world with my work, I've impacted people's lives, I understand it now. I accept it, and I really try to check it with humility now. I bow to it, and that's the only way you can do it because otherwise you'll flip your hair and [*laughs*] say, "Yeah, yeah, yeah, yeah." You have to stop and be grateful to those who take the time to tell you that the work has mattered, but then, when you go home, you close the door to all that, you know. You're home with your own world, and it can't come in the house, you know. Or it'll eat you up. [*Laughs*]

Too much adoration. That's a whole subject that I don't know if a lot of songwriters can understand. They feel the opposite. But I understand—

Attention and respect are good—I'm not talking about that. I'm talking about the other thing.

Yes. I also know of some great songwriters who just don't want to do it anymore. They don't even see the point of participating anymore.

Like who? [*Laughs*]

I'd rather not name names.

[*Laughs*] That's when they need to leave their mansions and go live somewhere else. Or not write anymore. I mean it's okay to say, "I'm done."

Is it?

It's okay to be done, you know.

I'm glad you're not done, Rickie. Was part of that the reason these songs seem so inspired, that you took a break from songwriting and you let something build up?

You mean so inspired to you or to me?

[*Laughs*] Both!

It would seem so. It seems to me that until I got to this point, I just didn't have this to say, so it would seem so.

Does the process of getting your ideas recorded get any easier?

No. It really does have to do with the producer. I like having a producer. There are producers who control everything artistically. But for me a producer is someone to share this responsibility with. I want a little bit of interesting guidance. I *really* do. I can do it all myself, but I don't want to. I want somebody to help me.

The only confusion happens when people feel they're not getting their due. They think, "Hey, you know what? I work really hard and I'm really talented, and calling me producer doesn't tell all the things I do here. I want this credit and that credit." And I say, "Hey, you know what? Your job is to do everything you can to make the record great. Wake up every day and be grateful you have the job. Don't be angry. This is just a way of being."

It's so easy, if you feel you should have had something better in your life, then everything you do, you'll try to *extract* from it that thing you didn't get. And you're gonna be a little angry. And it's just a hard way to live your life. Instead, why don't you wake up and go, "I could be at the gas station pumping tires—I am *so* glad to be here every day"?

That gratitude matters so much.

It releases you from your ego. So I really am grateful to be here. The older I get, I think, what a *miracle*. What a miracle on every level. What a crappy life it could've been, or I could've been married. But how *miraculous* to come from where I've come from.

It's a journey. The key is to keep your feet on the ground. Once you've become king or queen, you're screwed. And when you first get famous, it's hard to learn that. People treat you like a rock star. You need to learn how to deal with fame. You know, famous people go to bed lonely, just like other people. Everybody needs to know that. Fame doesn't bring you one thing other than fame.

Does it make you happy knowing that your songs live on?

Yes. It's like creating a universe. When we die, those little universes will be floating around. And people really enter this universe. We are creating places that people go into, and they go into the songs. It's mysterious. I think making songs up might be much more important than we think.

So when I'm gone, those all will be here. And they're places all their own. That's really incredible. I'm excited about that.

◆ ◆ ◆

Daryl Hall

Of Sacred Songs

Los Angeles, California 1994

Daryl Hall is chain-smoking interviews, starting up a new one even before the previous one is over. Journalists are being shuffled in and out as he sits in the darkened end of an LA hotel room, wearing dark shades, drinking Coca-Cola, and smoking cigarettes.

He's not a guy who enjoys giving interviews, as he immediately establishes as we enter and get to work. Yet it's a necessary evil he endures in order to promote his newest work, which at the time of our talk was the joyfully soulful solo *Soul Alone*. Still, he submitted to not one but two interviews, and he patiently and carefully answered every question.

Later he sort of apologized, after what became a spirited musical discussion, for any perceived attitude on his part, which he said stemmed from the fact that "some guys who write about music, you know, they don't dig music. But I get you get it."

Hall is somewhat of an enigma as a songwriter, capable of writing almost any kind of song, from the three-minute melodic pop variety that has catapulted Hall & Oates to the top of the charts, through Philadelphia-rooted R&B that cooks with the best Philly soul there is, into the Peter Gabriel/Sting/David Byrne realm of art songs after years of churning out successive radio-welcome hits in the seventies with John Oates, classic songs like "Sara Smile," and "She's Gone."

In 1977 he released a remarkable solo album called *Sacred Songs*, produced by Robert Fripp, that had been "locked up in the vault" for two years. It established what a lot of people already knew: there's a serious and very poignant songwriter who, when not writing hits, writes oddly beautiful, artistic gems. *Sacred Songs* contains some of Fripp's most moving production work and signature guitar treatments (his "Frippertronics" devised beautifully sustained chordal loops and more before the world went digital and such sounds were simple to attain), while it also captures vocals by Hall that are simply unearthly in the depth of their soul yearning and strength. And the songwriting throughout is funny and beautiful—and unlike anything we'd heard before. Songs like the delightfully strange "Babs and Babs" adjoined stunning ballads such as "The Farther Away I Am" and "Without Tears."

A few years after the release of *Sacred Songs* Hall and Oates released the landmark *Voices* album, which features many hits Hall collaborated on, including "You Make My Dreams," written with Oates and Sara Allen, and "Kiss on My List," written with Janna Allen. It also featured one song that Hall wrote alone, the song closest in mood and color to his solo work on *Sacred Songs*, "Every Time You Go Away." Although, remarkably, it was never released as a single for Hall and Oates, it did become a major hit as recorded in 1981 by Paul Young.

He was born Daryl Hohl on October 11, 1946, in Pottstown, Pennsylvania. Proximity to Philly allowed him the opportunity to play keyboard in sessions for such groups as The Stylistics and The Delfonics. In those days he hung out and learned a lot about the art and business of music from Thom Bell (who, with Gamble and Huff, invented the Philly sound; see Gamble, page 113) and started his own group, The Temptones, whose first hit was written by Gamble and Huff, "Girl I Love You."

Hall and Oates was officially born in Philadelphia at Temple University, where the two men wound up as roommates, realized they were both "soul freaks," and started making music together, a progression detailed in the following interview.

Songwriting, as it did in the life of many great songwriters, emerged organically, without a lot of thought. "I started writing songs when I was twelve," he remembered. "I was really loving music and wanting to try it on my own. I'd be sitting around playing other people's songs on my piano, then my own music started to come out. I started thinking, 'Well, I can use that,' and try coming up with my own words. It was very natural."

Do you remember the name of your first song?

Daryl Hall: It was probably some triad writing, like a Philadelphia dance song or something like that. [*Laughs*] Like, "Do the Mashed Potato."

What was it like to grow up in Philly?

Very rich. Philadelphia is a great place to grow up as far as music goes. It's always been a very strong music scene. Everything from the school systems to the radio stations—music was everywhere. WIBG in Philadelphia was the first radio station in the fifties to have an all rock and roll format. It was a unique place with a unique sound, and I think that's why there is a sound of Philadelphia.

I had the pleasure of interviewing Kenny Gamble [see page 113], who discussed the magic of the Philly sound. How do you describe, musically, what makes the Philly sound distinctive?

It's a certain kind of chord patterns and melodies. It revolves a lot around piano playing as opposed to guitar. The harmonies are very distinct and very church oriented.

That sound goes back to the street-corner people. Like Lee Andrews and the Hearts. Harvey and the Moonglows. All the street-corner groups—that was the rock and roll that was generated. It came off the streets, and it was literally people standing around in the group, snapping their fingers on the corner and singing.

And you were doing that too?

Yes, I was doing that from a really young age.

How long was it before you were writing songs on your own that you felt were good enough to perform and record?

I was seventeen when I made my first record. Gamble and Huff produced it. That was a good start. [*Laughs*] But of course, they were just kids too. It was on Arctic records in 1967, and the song was called "Girl I Love You." Basically it was me copying Smokey Robinson.

What led you to become a duo?

I was going to Temple University, and there's no campus life there, so everyone who goes to Temple generally lives in apartments in Philly. John

Oates and I kept finding ourselves as roommates in all these different places. I would listen to John writing songs over in the corner, and he'd be playing something, and I'd be sitting playing something. It was just constant exposure to what he was doing, and it really came together like that.

We were both soul freaks, and it just kind of came together. We shared apartments when we were students and became friends before we tried making music. There wasn't really any idea of becoming Hall and Oates; it just developed over time in a very natural way.

We really tried writing and doing all that a long time before we really seriously got together and thought about doing it as a team. When we first did say we'll do it, we said, "Well, you write songs, and I write songs—let's share the stage. You play some of your songs, I'll play some of mine. I'll sing harmonies on your songs; you sing harmonies on mine." That was really what it was. We didn't really think of it as pursuing it as a duo, but people started liking it right away. So we said, "Okay, well, let's try doing it together," and it really sort of fell together that way.

You and John wrote a lot of songs together. How did that work?

Well, he added certain things. We did a lot of collaboration on lyrics over the years. But there were a lot of songs where he would come up with part of it and I would come up with the other part. "She's Gone" is an example of that. "Maneater." "Out of Touch." You could go down a list—we did a lot of things where, usually, he would come up with some kind of chorus and I would write the verses.

But at the same time, we wrote a lot separately too. There was always both things going on. Kind of like Lennon and McCartney, the way that I always read about how they collaborated.

Thom Bell said his songs often came like gifts. Do you feel that way?

Yeah. Absolutely. It's there, and it just comes from someplace. I don't know where. I think all the notes are up there. You know, everything has always been there, and these different personalities, different situations, can cause it to come into reality at that moment in time, and who knows why it comes. It's these strange factors. Who knows why?

Have you found, in all your years of writing songs, anything that affects it? Are there times better than other times for writing?

No, no. You never can tell. I mean, I don't beat it to death. I don't try to write if I'm not inspired to write. I don't sit down and say, "I have to write a song today" or anything like that. It usually comes from the excitement of other people. It can either come from that kind of musical excitement or can come from an emotional situation that causes me to feel a certain way. Then I'll sit down myself, and I'll just blurt out whatever is on my mind.

Since I'm a soul writer and a soul singer—without being really heavy-handed about it—it's a spiritual thing. It really does come from the heart. It's just bringing this energy, coalescing this energy into an emotion, channeling through that emotion and making it come out of my mouth.

Does it feel as if some songs exist before you write them?

Yes. I think everything is there, and it's a matter of synthesizing through that moment in time. I don't think anything is created or destroyed. It just is.

Have you ever written a song without really knowing what it means?

[*Laughs*] Yeah, a lot. Right now, in fact.

What makes a great melody?

I think surprises make a great melody. Going someplace unexpected. I hate the obvious. It could be an interval jump, or it could be just going to an unusual note in the chord, a note that you wouldn't expect to go with that chord.

Do you need to be at an instrument to write?

Not necessarily. I usually do it over my own playing, or if there's a track without a melody, I'll sing over it. Usually just takes one run-through.

Do you write all the time, or do you just write for an album?

I go in bursts. I don't write constantly, but in certain periods of time I write constantly.

When it feels like it's time for a new project to come, it just kind of happens. I'll start thinking about things, and as I start thinking and listening to what's going on, environments as much as anything wash over me. I don't listen to the radio hardly ever. I like to have music and clubs down the street and just soak it in that way. Then when I sit down at the keyboard or with the guitar, things just pop out very naturally.

Do you actively look for song ideas, or do you let them come to you?

I let them come to me. I do sit down sometimes and woodshed, but I'm passive about it. Passive-aggressive really. I let it wash over me, then I jump in and do something.

Is it important to have a good title at the outset?

Not necessarily. A lot of times it's just a good chord pattern, and then I come up with some kind of melody. Once I've got that, I'll start thinking about what it sounds like and then start blanking my mind and letting things come in. Letting whatever is subconsciously in my mind come out. I don't know what I'm going to say. I just open my mouth and let things come out.

Do you sometimes start with a dummy lyric?

Yeah, usually just nonsense at first, then I'll start fleshing them out. And what happens is that I'll just kind of riff and scat and sing nonsense syllables, and I'll turn those into words sometimes. I listen back to write the lyrics. Sometimes I'll find I've written about half the lyrics without ever thinking about it.

Do you do much recycling of old ideas that you hadn't finished?

Not really. I may pull an idea out from the past I never used, but most of the time it's new stuff. I tend to let things lay if they're not working and move on. I do have boxes and boxes of tapes, [*laughs*] millions of tapes with ideas on them, which I should probably listen to at some point or give it to someone else, because I'm sure there's a lot of great ideas that were never used.

How do you define soul music?

Soul music is a state of mind. It's bringing things down and being real and singing and playing from the heart, and that can be any kind of music. Bluegrass is soul music; folk music in general is soul music because it's people talking about their lives and writing about experiences.

Do you remember writing "Every Time You Go Away"?

That was a song that came very much from a real experience, and if the person I wrote it about had been in the room, I wouldn't have written the song. So there you go.

That was one of your rare songs that was a major hit for somebody else, Paul Young.

That's really the only one. That was pretty much forgotten as a B-side. [*Laughs*]

You said earlier that you wrote "Sara Smile" with John, correct?

Well, his name is on it, but I have to say honestly he didn't really do anything on that song. I mean, there are certainly a lot of songs that he did do at least as much, if not more than me. On that song I think he was just pretty much in the room, because I think back on that song, and that really came from me, 100 percent. I can't even remember one lyric line that he threw in, so I don't know why his name is on that record! [*Laughs*]

Actually two songs that have his name on them that he really had nothing to do with. One of them was that song, and the other one was "No Can Do." I pretty much wrote that song myself.

How about "She's Gone"? Did he have much to do with that one?

Oh yeah, absolutely. He had everything to do with that song. He really came up with the song. It sounded very different because he had written it on acoustic guitar. But he came up with the melody of both the verse and chorus. I really just kind of added my thing to it and wrote the lyrics with him. But that was really, musically, more generated by John than by me.

How about "You Make My Dreams"?

I wrote that one myself. All I remember about that is just getting a good gospel feel on the piano and just goin' for it and blurting out the first line that came to mind: "You make my dreams come true." [*Laughs*] Then, of course, I thought, "Is that going to work? Is that title too trite?" Then it seemed like it wasn't because it kind of said everything in its simplicity, so I kept the title.

***Sacred Songs* is a wonderful album. We all loved it so much, and it seemed like a secret, which added to its charm.**

It was a different record. That was me really trying to put myself in a context that was very out of what people would expect out of me. I knew Robert Fripp for a few years before that, and we'd become friends. We were trying to figure out how to work together, because whenever I'd mention this to anybody, they would say, "You guys are going to work together? What the hell does that mean?" But I knew it would work. I knew it would work. I knew we'd do something with a unique sound if we did it, and it was a really easy thing to do, to work with Robert, because we didn't think about it too much. The *Sacred Songs* record took three weeks to make.

Did you write the songs for *Sacred Songs* specifically for that album?

Yeah, wrote them right at the moment.

Now I understand all your songs were coming from one songwriter, but at the time it seemed like there were two Daryl Halls.

Yeah, well, there weren't two Daryl Halls. There was the Daryl Hall who is immersed in kind of a rock and soul tradition with John Oates, and then there was the Daryl Hall who does different kinds of things.

I mean, if you listen to the melodies that I choose and the chords, you can tell it's all coming from the same person. I'm not a chameleon in the way David Bowie is, where I completely change styles and sing different. You know, I carry this kind of baggage around with me and put it in different contexts. That's kind of the way I look at what I'm doing.

Why was *Sacred Songs* in the vault for two years?

It was in the vaults for two years because RCA didn't want to release it, to tell you the truth. They were scared of it. What I wound up doing, Robert and I got the tapes and started giving them to people, saying, "Here, listen to this. Review this." Of course, it didn't sell anything—they didn't push it, they didn't do anything. They just put it out. But at least it got out there, which is what's really important.

It's amazing to me you could write all those great songs so quickly.

That happens to me all the time. That's the way most of my songs come.

Do you find that times of turmoil are good for your writing?

Yes, that helps. Complication in your personal life is always good. Anything that stirs up your emotions and brings them to the surface is going to help. It's easier to get it outside of yourself and externalize it. When you're just sitting on the beach in the Caribbean or something, I don't think as much about writing songs as I would if I'm going through a particularly busy or complicated point in my life.

What's the most important advice for songwriters?

Say what you mean, and try to find the right way to say it. Be proficient on an instrument so you can express yourself. And don't compromise.

◆ ◆ ◆

Patti Smith
Still Dancing Barefoot

New York, New York 2010

Since she was a kid she knew she was an artist. And not any artist. A
serious one. One willing to go the extra mile. As early as eleven she approached her own art with a remarkable singularity of purpose that has
persisted ever since. "When I was a kid I wanted to write a poem about
Simón Bolívar," she said. "I went to the library and read everything I
could. I wrote copious notes. I had forty pages of notes just to write a
small poem." Decades later the process persists. She spent months reading every book she could find about Ho Chi Minh before spontaneously
improvising "Gung Ho." She relies on her ability to shamanistically
channel songs and poems—but never blindly: she deepens her well with
information before delving into it.

Of course, she's more than a songwriter; she's an artist who rec-
ognizes that art needn't be restricted to any one means of expression.
Like her great friend, the late photographer Robert Mapplethorpe,
about whom she wrote the beautiful memoir *Just Kids*, she's always been

devoted to making art itself—whether a poem, a memoir, a novel, a record, a series of drawings, a play (with Sam Shepard she wrote *Cowboy
Mouth*), or a song. As a child, art for her was both a refuge and a means
of escape from the monotony of the everyday world. "I did not want to
be trapped," she said. "I grew up in the fifties, when the girls wore really
bright red lipstick and nail polish, and they smelled like Eau de Paris.
Their world just didn't attract me. I hid in the world of the artist: first the
nineteenth-century artists, then the Beats. And Peter Pan."

Unlike Mapplethorpe, however, fame was never a goal. When she made
her debut album, *Horses*, which remains the most visceral fusion of poetry
and rock ever recorded, she never intended to be a rock star and was happy
to return to her job at the bookstore, writing poems and doing drawings.
But she also recognized the unchained potential of rock and roll to speak
not just to an assorted few at a coffeehouse poetry reading but to forty thousand people or more in an arena, all united by song. Although she certainly
never left poetry behind—she's written twelve volumes of published poetry
and several more books of poetry and memoir that are unpublished—she
embraced the electric promise of speaking to the whole world. "Even now
it's an opportunity to have a universal voice," she said, "because everybody,
all over the world, loves rock and roll. It's the new universal language. Jimi
Hendrix knew that. The Rolling Stones knew that. We knew that. People of
the future will know that. What they do with it is up to them." Speaking to
Patti was a fun challenge, as her mind is so agile, she was onto other questions often before they were posed, and it felt like we were having an ancient conversation, one we'd had several times over the centuries. A timeless
talk of art and song and the human condition. Our talk about songwriting
started with a discussion of how hard it can be to talk about songwriting.

Patti Smith: Talking about songwriting is complicated 'cause there's
so many kinds of songs. And so I might seem like I'm contradicting myself, but I'm not. When I wrote "Frederick" I tried to write a song that
everybody loved and everybody danced to. It was consciously written to
be a dance song. When I wrote "Radio Baghdad" that was the last thing
on my mind. For me that has always been such a conflict because I love
natural songs. I love that song "Get in the Groove." [*Sings*] "Hey, get in
the groove." I mean, what's that about? It's such a great little song to
dance to. It doesn't mean to say much of anything.

**Which is a great thing about songs, that they hit us on different levels
at once—our hearts and minds and bodies.**

Yeah. And I think that is the thing why songwriting, to me, has been such a mystery and still something that I haven't completely cracked. How a poet—going back to Jim Morrison—could write such complex lyrics and complex poems and then say, "Hello, I love you. Let me jump in your game."

Yes. People often compliment songwriters by saying they are poets. As if that is a higher calling even in modern times. You are one of the best to explain this to the other humans. How is writing poems different from writing songs?

Poetry is a solitary process. Songs are for the people. When I'm writing a song I imagine performing it. I imagine giving it. It's a different aspect of communication. It's for the people.

We always write a certain amount of poetry for the masses. When Allen Ginsberg wrote "Howl," he didn't write it for himself; he wrote it to speak out. To make a move, to wake people up. I think rock and roll, as our cultural voice, took that energy and made it even more accessible.

When I'm sitting down to write a poem I'm not thinking of anyone. I'm not thinking about how it will be received. I'm not thinking it will make people happy or it will inspire them. I'm in a whole other world. A world of complete solitude. But when I'm writing a song I imagine performing it. I imagine giving it. It's a different aspect of communication. It's for the people.

I write songs when I'm by myself, like walking along the beach, and a song comes in my head. Or I wake up from a dream, like "Blakean Year." I often write songs out of dreams and take them to my musicians to help me. Sometimes I write melodies that are too complex and I can't find them on the guitar because I only know about eight chords. So I take them to Lenny [Kaye] or Tony [Shanahan, her bassist], and they transcribe them into a song.

"Free Money" came to me walking down St. Mark's at three in the morning. It was predawn, but it was so light in New York City, and it came to me, and I sang it to Lenny. He structured it and found the proper chords, and we made a song. It was one of our earliest songs.

Other songs, they just come in my head and I sing them out loud, and the band finds the place, and they adjust it. For myself, the simpler format the better. "Gandhi" is nine minutes on one chord. It's an improvisation. "Radio Baghdad" was completely improvised. I didn't know the lyrics, but I knew I wanted to speak out against the invasion of Iraq. Being a mother, I freely entered into the mother consciousness of the mothers of Baghdad who were trying to comfort their children as they were being bombed. So these lyrics that come to me are self-perpetuated.

It's miraculous that you can spontaneously come up with such amazing work—

It's easier for me than to sit and write verse-chorus. Writing lyrics sometimes is *torturous*. Because I make them too complicated and sometimes burden a song with complicated language. But it's just how I work. So for me it's freedom just to go and focus myself and see where my horse takes me.

Are there times you didn't get there?

I have never been unsuccessful.

How do you explain that?

It's a channeling. Burroughs always called it a shamanistic gift. Sometimes I feel I am channeling someone else. Part of it is experience from performing and understanding that, as a performer, one has a mission, like Coltrane, to take your solo out to talk to God, or whoever you talk to, but you must return. So it has structure.

That's one way that I write. Others take quite a bit of labor. Often the simplest song is the hardest to write. "Frederick" was very hard to write because in its simplicity I also wanted it to be perfect.

Yes. And when people hear them, they think they came out perfectly. But to get to that place is a lot of work?

Yes, a lot of work. But I find, in the past decade, I don't struggle with lyrics as much as I did in the seventies. I think that's partially because, you know, I came out of nowhere. I wasn't a songwriter. A lot of *Horses* was based on poems that I had written. For instance, "Jesus died for somebody's sins but not mine" came from a poem I wrote when I was twenty. I had written it, like, perhaps in '69, and we recorded it in '75. "Redondo Beach" I wrote in 1971 as a poem. But I struggled.

I always thought when we did *Horses* I would do a record—and I was really honored to do the record—but then I'd go back to work, working in a bookstore, writing poems or doing my drawings. It didn't occur to me that I'd be doing more records. Because I felt like I had said what I had to say. *Horses* was based on five years of work and performing and thinking about things, and suddenly when we had another record I found it very, very difficult because I wasn't skilled in writing songs. And *Horses* was such an organic process. So I was learning as I went along.

But now I understand the songwriting process, and it's not so difficult. I mean, it is difficult, but it's not as difficult as it was. I remember writing the lyrics to the songs on *Radio Ethiopia*. At that time I had performed so much, I felt a loss of language and just got very involved with playing electric guitar and making sonicscapes. I was much more happier playing feedback than I was in spewing language. But the language came back.

"Because the Night," which you wrote with Springsteen, is a good example of poetry and song merged. It has beautiful poetic lines and then a very catchy, simple chorus. How did that come together? Did you write the words first?

I got a tape of it, everything completely produced, and the chorus was done. He needed words for the verses, which were mumbled. I listened to it. I sat up with it all night writing a song for Fred, who was supposed to call me from Detroit. And I'm the kind of girl who waits for the call. I listened to it over and over, trying to distract myself from waiting for Fred. And I was so agitated and so antsy that I just took the tape out that I was given to explore the song—Jimmy Iovine gave it to me, and Bruce had given it to him—and I listened to it over and over to try to distract me from waiting for Fred. And that's why the lyric says, "Have I doubt when I'm alone / Love is a ring, a telephone."

I've always wanted to write a song that everyone could love. That's the one thing that I feel I haven't achieved. Writing a song that when you hear it, everybody is happy. When we're in Italy and we break into "Because the Night" and there are twenty thousand people singing, it just brings me to tears. So I know that people must experience a certain amount of joy. When it comes down to it, I might write poetry for myself or poetry for the gods of poetry. But I write a song for the people.

I had always assumed—wrongly, I see—that your poetry and songwriting was intertwined. That you'd write a poem that would spark a song and maybe vice versa—

Well, that can happen. Anything can happen. I have started poems that seemed best served as a song. But that's just one of those things that happened totally organically. It would be false to say everything is black and white; it's either one or the other. It's just that my process is different. My mind-set is different. And I've destroyed many poems, [*laughs*] just lost the thread on a poem and then went back to them and found that it could be the germ of something else. But the initial process is a different process.

Why is songwriting sometimes torturous?

Because I had so much responsibility to others. If I was writing lyrics to someone's music, I had responsibility to that musician. I had to project beyond myself and beyond my world out into the greater world. Allen Ginsberg told me, "If you have trouble writing, just write what you mean." [*Laughs*] And that's a good lesson when you're trying to write a song.

As an artist who has expressed yourself in so many ways, how is it to have written songs which reach so many more people who might never read poetry or books?

I think of my work as relatively obscure. When you look at a poet like Jim Morrison, who is able to write very complex lyrics like "Texas Radio" but also write "Hello, I Love You," this to me is a real gift, to be able to have a span like that.

I think contemporarily Michael Stipe is one of our greatest lyricists, to be able to write such complex lyrics like "E-Bow" and so many other lyrics—the song that ends with "It's the end of the world as we know it, and I feel fine"—and yet write songs that completely tap into the universal consciousness.

With my own work, when I wrote the lyrics for *Horses* I had a particular body of people who I was speaking to, and that was the people like myself, who I felt were disenfranchised. The more maverick person. I wasn't really addressing the masses. I didn't even think I had anything of interest to share with the masses. But I felt that I had something to share with people like myself. So my early work was really written to bridge poetry and rock and roll and to communicate, as I said, with the disenfranchised person. And I think in that way it was successful. But in the eighties, when I stopped performing and I got married and had a family, I became more empathetic to social issues and the humanist point of view. And I think my lyrics had changed. I was speaking to a larger body of people. As a mother, you want to speak to everyone. Because everyone is potentially a son or daughter. So my goal shifted. A lot of that came from my husband, Fred "Sonic" Smith, who was very political and very concerned with the human condition. So a song like "People Have the Power" came from Fred. It was Fred's concept. Even though I wrote the lyrics, he wrote the title, and the concept was his, because he wanted to address all people. So I would say there has definitely been a shift in who I am speaking to, at least in my mind.

That shift seems to have come with the *Wave* album, with a song like "Dancing Barefoot"—

"Dancing Barefoot" begins the shift. That album, *Wave*, came from falling in love and opening up my perspective: "Frederick." *Wave* addressed the fact that I was here, I did my work, I hopefully contributed. And I found somebody who I loved, and now I was embarking on a new life. So, you're right, it's really the album *Wave* which starts that shift.

It took me a while to understand you have license to have abstraction in a lyric. As a kid, I loved dancing. It's very funny I should wind up a songwriter and have to write lyrics. Because as a kid I wasn't so involved with the lyrics; I just loved to dance. Hearing "Gimme Shelter," I didn't really break down what the song was about; I just loved to dance to it.

In the eighties, when I stopped performing and got married and had a family, I became more empathetic to social issues and the humanist point of view. And my lyrics changed. I was speaking to a larger body of people.

I just read *Just Kids*, and it's a beautiful book. I understand there are books you've written that aren't published.

Yes, I have about five of them. I have always considered myself as a writer. I wouldn't categorize myself as a songwriter. I have written lyrics to many songs, and I work really hard on my lyrics, but it's not the thing that comes most easily to me. In any event, it's just one of the things that I do. I do so many things. I just spend my time on whatever way I'm trying to communicate, whatever it calls for.

With the songs on *Wave*, were you working toward writing a more pure song, that is more a song than it is poetry?

All of the songs that I write, I wouldn't consider anything that I record as poetry. You know, poetry is a very solitary process. And when I'm writing poetry, unless it's an oral poem, I'm not really thinking of it in terms of communicating it to anyone; I'm just writing my poetry, and sometimes it's obscure or complicated. But one does not write poetry for the masses or with thoughts of who's reading it. Poetry is a very self-involved, lofty pursuit. I feel embarrassed to call myself a poet. I do write poetry. But it would make me very happy to be able to write songs that are universally appealing. But I think that my language is often— because I am a poet—sometimes my language, perhaps, doesn't speak to everyone. It's not an intentional thing; it's just the way I am. I don't set about to write a song that is obscure. It's just in my genetic code, it's in my blood. But the subject matter is not. A song like "Blakean Year" could almost stand as a poem. But really it's basically a song to remind people that in times of strife, we have our imagination, we have our creative impulse, which are things that are more important than material things. They are the things that we should magnify.

So "People Have the Power," the language is somewhat biblical. But it's simply saying that every individual is important, and as a corrective, we have the power to make tremendous change. So the messages are not complicated; it's just that my language, sometimes, might be a little complex.

When I interviewed Dylan he also said he didn't consider himself a poet. He said, "Poets don't drive cars. Poets drown in lakes"—

[*Laughs*]

But like you, he's combined poetic language with song.

Oh, absolutely. I know Bob Dylan has infused poetry within his work—

As have you—

I believe I have, and Michael Stipe has. And I know that Bob feels, when he was young, he used to sing the praises of Smokey Robinson. And I know exactly why he's done that. Because Smokey Robinson could distill the things that either one of us might talk about in a way that every teenage boy or teenage girl could completely identify with. So it's just kind of our fate that we express ourselves in a certain language. But I think, for instance, [Dylan's album] *John Wesley Harding* has some of the greatest poetic images in our cultural voice.

And in Dylan's work and yours, unlike most modern poetry, we get this language in meter and rhyme, like Romantic poetry—

Well, both of us, I'm sure—I can't speak for Bob Dylan—but I know for myself the oral poets, whether it was Vachel Lindsay or Oscar Brown Jr. or, of course, the beat poets, Allen Ginsberg and Ray Bremser and Gregory Corso, the energy and the language of these poets, the energy that they infused in poetry, really set the stage. We have, chronologically, the beat poets, who were *tremendous* performers, and then you have the emergence of rock and roll. Beginning with Bob's generation, which is just a beat before mine—I mean, we're only a few years apart—the fusing of poetry with social consciousness and, well, with our cultural voice. He opened things up like no other. And so that paved the way for many of us.

And that opening of the song form, as you said, was to infuse it with poetry. So my question to you is, when you would write a song, was it always a conscious choice that you were working on a song and not a poem?

Absolutely. How I write songs usually is when I'm by myself, like walking along the beach, and a song comes in my head. Or I wake up from a dream—like "Blakean Year," I dreamt it, and I quick wrote it down. I often write songs out of a dream. And I take them to my musicians to help me. Because sometimes I write melodies that are too complex and I can't find them on the guitar 'cause I only know about eight chords. So I take them to Lenny [Kaye] or Tony, and they transcribe them into a song.

But do you have the melody first?

Oh, always. Sometimes a melody that Lenny would help me with and find the chords.

When he would do that, would he always come up with what sounded right to you, or would you suggest that he change a part?

Well, we work very organically. We work various ways. Sometimes someone has a song, and I just sit there, and the band plays it over and over and over, and I sit until I feel drawn to it and just go up to the microphone and just start improvising. That's one way we write a song. There's a lot of songs I can point out that were written like that—a song like "Jubilee" or "Cash." A lot of songs are written like that.

Other songs, they just come in my head and I sing them out loud, and the band finds the place, and if we adjust it, sometimes I have to bring them more to where I want to hear it, and sometimes they open it up. They say, "Well, that's very nice, but if you shift it here or add a bridge . . ." Because I tend, for myself, the simpler format the better. I'm really happy to do a two-chord song. And I had it on one chord. And that the band could take it anywhere they wanted, but all based on this one chord. That's another way we write songs. It's completely improvised.

"Radio Baghdad," as I said, was *completely* improvised over Oliver Ray's chord structure. He had the chord structure, the band played it over and over again until it was a long instrumental, and I just said we'll go into the studio and I'll improvise over it, 'cause I knew what I wanted to do.

Your work always seems to be more than channeling something from beyond you—it's channeling it through your intelligence and mind. What do you think is the source of these songs?

I don't know. Sometimes I know they're coming from myself. Other times I feel definitely I am channeling someone else. In fact, when that happens—for instance, when we did "Strange Messenger"—I felt very taken over by another being. And afterward I got a horrible migraine. And that happened also with "Memento Mori." I can't explain it. I don't try to break those things down; they just happen. When I'm performing live I know I'm channeling the people. I remember once we were in New

Orleans I felt like I was channeling the young girls of Storyville. This is something that is a spiritual thing, a mystical thing, and, as you said, some part is coming from one's own intelligence. And I don't feel it's healthy for me as an artist to try to break it down.

I understand. But do you think anyone else could have channeled the songs you channeled? Or are they specific to you?

[*Pause*] All of the songs that I have channeled for myself—you put it better than I did—I think are for me. Because I prepared for them. I read huge amounts of things and writings by Ho Chi Minh to do "Gung Ho." It was just that the moment I get myself focused, I merge with the music, and I do the song. Part of it is experience from performing and understanding that as a performer one has a mission—like Coltrane [*laughs*]— to take your solo out to talk to God, or whoever you talk to, but you must return. So it has structure.

It was Coltrane's birthday yesterday—

I know. We celebrated.

You know, when we did "Radio Baghdad" I thought deeply about how I felt emotionally about what happened, and what I didn't want to do was some political rant. I wanted to speak against what happened but from a humanistic point of view. And so being a mother, I just freely entered into the mother consciousness of the mothers of Baghdad who were trying to comfort their children as they were being bombed through the night. So these lyrics that come to me are self-perpetuated. But I am also inspired by the music. The band is inspiring; the setup is very specific.

But as I said, that's one way that I write lyrics. Others take quite a bit of labor. Often the simplest song is the hardest to write.

Yes. And when people hear them, they think they came out perfectly. But to get to that place is a lot of work?

Yes, a lot of work. A song like "Frederick," which is a simple little song, was very hard to write. Because in its simplicity, I also wanted it to be perfect. But I find in the past decade I don't struggle with lyrics as much as I did in the seventies. I think that's partially because, you know, I came out of nowhere. I wasn't a songwriter. A lot of *Horses* was based on poems that I had written. For instance, "Jesus died for somebody's sins but not mine" came from a poem I wrote when I was twenty. I had written it like perhaps in '69 and we recorded it in '75. "Redondo Beach" I wrote in 1971 as a poem. But I struggled.

Dylan spoke about having to learn to write songs consciously after writing them unconsciously at first. He also made that kind of transition.

Yes. Well, there are songs that I have in me that are always happening, are very simple songs, like Appalachian-style songs. Most of my songs that I write myself around A minor are like Child Ballad songs. But I couldn't call myself a songwriter by vocation. But I certainly would say that Bob is one of our greatest songwriters.

You mentioned A minor. And I noticed many of your songs are in minor keys. Do you choose a key, and does each have a different color or mood for you?

[*Laughs*] I just naturally gravitate toward minor keys. It's a playful argument that I have with my bass player, who is a musician's musician. And he's always trying to encourage me to sing songs in different keys and be a little more diverse. But I don't even know that I'm doing it. I'm not a musician. I can play enough chords on acoustic guitar to write a song. But when I'm singing, I don't know that I'm singing in any particular key. I think my natural voice is sort of in A minor. When I was young it was in A. And now my voice is lower, and I seem to want to start every song in A minor. But I am encouraged, and we sometimes change the key. But it has to be within my range. You can't just choose a key, because my range has its breadth and it has its limits. So I have to sing songs in the key that fits well with my voice.

A major is a very happy key—many of The Beatles' songs are in A major—and now A minor—

I had a higher voice when I was younger—

But A and A minor aren't in different ranges.

Well, I don't know why. Maybe because I gravitated to old rock and roll songs and R&B songs, and that's what I felt comfortable in. Even in the song I wrote myself, "We Three," which is a song about going to see Tom Verlaine play guitar when he was in Television, going to CBGBs, because I was very taken with Tom. It says, "It was just another Sunday, and everything was in the key of A." I was singing about when Television and my band played at CBGBs, and it was in reference to that most of my songs were in the key of A.

You said how you felt some of the language in your songs was too complex, and yet you—and other poetically infused songwriters—stretched the potential of what a song can do by using that kind of language.

Well, I think we've had our contribution. One thing I've really been impressed with in new generations is what interesting lyrics they write. I was a kid brought up on the Animals and the Philly sound and the Ronettes and R&B and figuring out how to write a song like that. It was natural for me to listen to those songs but unnatural for me to write them. It took me a while to figure all of that out. There's such a huge [*laughs*] history now of our cultural voice. I didn't have Jim Morrison to listen to. I was just learning to filter these people. I mean, I did have them, but what I'm saying is I was living within history as it was happening. So now new generations have this huge evolution of rock and roll, and they just keep going. I listen to songs sometimes, and a lot of the ambient music and the lyrics, from My Bloody Valentine to The Decemberists, or whoever I might hear, and their language is so interesting.

It seems, though, that the greatness of your songs is when you have combined poetic language with a great simple chorus, as in "Frederick"—

I just know that sometimes it seemed, from the past, a hindrance. But it isn't anything that I can choose. I just write things the best that I can. I'm not a calculating person. I just do a song. If someone says, "It shouldn't be that way. It could be more appealing," I just have to do things my way.

Have you found ever that a song could not contain something that a poem could, or is the potential of a song limitless?

Well, these days a song doesn't even have to be a song. That's what's so great. At this point I feel like I can do anything. For our new record there is a musical field on one song where I wrote a poem for Tarkovsky, and I'm reciting it. I don't even bother worrying whether it's a poem or not a poem. It's not improvised. It's classic—it's a poem. And I feel the freedom to do whatever I want. Things have opened up, and I would hope our band has contributed to that space. That's one of the things that I wanted to do with our records, was to create space for future generations and to open things up. And now I feel that, really, one can do anything. Now with CDs, everything's changed. It used to be you only had eighteen minutes per side of an album, so if you had a very long song, it was something you had to fight for. Now you can have a forty-two-minute song [*laughs*] if you want. So it's interesting the things that you can do. You can be much more cinematic, and that's acceptable; it's something that's been embraced.

Was there ever content or ideas that you couldn't get into a song?

Well, [*laughs*] I can't think of anything specific. I've always wanted to write a song that everyone could love. That's the one thing that I feel I haven't achieved was writing a song that when you hear it, everybody is happy. At the same time. Like the feeling I got when I was hearing Maureen Gray or some great song when I was young. But of course maybe one cannot hear their own song.

Yes, because at your shows, when you start "Frederick" or "Because the Night"—

I know that people must experience a certain amount of joy. Really, when it comes down to it, I might write poetry for myself or poetry for the gods of poetry. But I write a song for the people. I don't write songs for myself. I don't write songs to be intentionally incommunicative. I write songs with the exact same desires as I write a poem, with the exact same energy and commitment. It's just that the true difference between a poem and a song is I write a song for the people. Whatever the song is, it's for the people. And even if it's a very obscure song, it's for the people; it's not for myself.

That crystallizes the modern difference between songwriting and poetry, in that poems used to be directed at the masses and written in rhythm and rhyme, but they aren't anymore. Yet songs are.

When you said songwriting was torturous, was it that way because you were aiming at the masses?

It was torturous because I had so much responsibility to others. If I was writing lyrics to someone's music, whether it was my husband's or Lenny Kaye's—whoever—Bruce Springsteen [*laughs*], I had a responsibility to that musician. And so I had to somehow meld with their music. And, as I said, I also had to project beyond myself and beyond my world out into the greater world. One of the things I learned is something Allen Ginsberg said: "If you have trouble writing, just write what you mean." [*Laughs*] And that's a good lesson when you're trying to write a song.

Whereas some songwriters, such as Paul Simon, told me the opposite, that he actively steers clear of thinking too much about what he means because then he's too conscious.

Well, I understand that as well. I think if you're overdiligent about that, the song can become didactic. That's not what I meant. I meant that if you're trying to communicate a certain thing, at least understand what you're trying to communicate.

◆ ◆ ◆

Chrissie Hynde
On the Chain Gang
London, England 2009

"Mine is the last act of a desperate man," she says. "I just didn't want to be a waitress." She's in the midst of trying to convince me she's not a great songwriter. But I'm not buying it. This is Chrissie Hynde, after all. But perhaps because it just doesn't jive with her self-image to affect any pretension, any sort of "and then I wrote" songwriterly pride, she repeatedly deflected praise through our conversation, pausing to exclaim, "This sounds *so* lame . . ." She's an antidiva in a sense, the last to adopt any pomposity. When our conversation was interrupted the second time by someone at her door, she came back and said, "You're gonna think I have a life—I don't."

She is, of course, the writer of not one but several songs that have become rock standards, beloved and undisputed rock hits. So let's face it: the market has spoken. Yet her profound reticence to take herself too seriously as a songwriter spoke to a fear that any light shone too directly into that mysterious realm from which songs emerge might destroy it.

And like many songwriters, when songs spill out easily without much work, she's got a hard time taking credit for them. Songs such as classics "Talk of the Town" or "Brass in Pocket" captured her essence of rock swagger and bravado, this American in England. She also deflects praise toward her bandmates, especially James Honeyman-Scott, who died of a heroin overdose in 1982, by saying, "Oh that's all him. That's his riff."

Yet as we all know, songs that come quickly through a songwriter, almost like gifts, are often the most powerful. But could only have come through an instrument that has been finely tuned for years by all the hard work in the songwriting trenches. Of course, she wouldn't hear about any of this. Too pretentiously precious for her. Which is why she's who she is.

And it's undeniable that her songs have stood the test of time. She has written standards. Although she emerged in an era when people were leaning toward booming drum machines and synth pads, she beautifully steered the Pretenders always with a purist's respect for the traditions of rock and roll. She wasn't here to rewrite the rules; she was here to write great songs, songs a great singer can sink her teeth into, songs that have lasted far beyond the era in which they were written. Whether she wants to admit it, she's not only a great songwriter, she's a *hit* songwriter. But every now and then, due to my polite persistence, she gave in and talked about how she's done it. She even indulged my desire to name many of her songs for her immediate response, demurring at first before saying, "Okay, whatever. Go ahead and do your thing."

So I did. And she gave a wonderfully expansive answer to "Brass in Pocket" that was beyond expectations, proving so poignantly how deep these songs do go in her psyche and her history. All songwriters tend to feel that their songs are children—though most don't say it out loud— and it became evident that for Chrissie, taking credit for these songs was like a parent taking credit not only for the child, but for its self-generated success. It's the kid who is great, not the mom.

An Akron native, she was born in 1951. Her dad worked for the Yellow Pages. She wrote her first song at the age of fourteen after learning two guitar chords, recognizing even then that limitations create possibility. "You only need one chord to write a song," she explains. "Look at all those James Brown songs." She hated high school and all it entailed, partly because her eyes were already set firmly on a musical future: "I never went to a dance. I never went out on a date. I never went steady," she remembered. "It became pretty awful for me. Except, of course, I could go see bands, and that was the kick. I used to go to Cleveland just to see any band. So I was in love a lot of the time, but mostly with guys in bands that I had never met. For me, knowing that Brian Jones was out there and, later, Iggy Pop, made it kind of hard for me to get too interested in the guys that were around me. I had . . . bigger things in mind."

She went to Kent State to study art and was there when the Ohio National Guard tragically shot students. Jeffrey Miller, one of the victims, was her friend. She wanted out of Ohio, out of America. Discovering the Brit music mag *NME*, she saved enough money to move to London. She landed a writing gig with *NME*, but it didn't last long—her next job was in Malcolm McLaren's Sex shop. It's there she met Sid Vicious and tried—according to legend—to persuade him into marriage so she could become a British citizen. He passed.

She joined a series of bands, first as singer in The Frenchies, then guitarist in Masters of the Backside, and then the Johnny Moped band. Mick Jones invited her to join a nascent pre–Joe Strummer incarnation of what would be the Clash, and they went on a British tour together, but Chrissie wasn't happy—she wanted her own band. But it would take time.

Her visa ran out and she had to go back to Ohio, but she returned as soon as possible. At last she succeeded in realizing her dream and formed The Pretenders in Hereford in 1978 with three Brits: James Honeyman-Scott on lead guitar and keyboards, Pete Farndon on bass, and Martin Chambers on drums. Everyone in the band sang. Their first single was the Nick Lowe–produced "Stop Your Sobbing," a Kinks song. In 1980 came the eponymous debut album, a critical and commercial success both in the United States and the UK, which led to a great succession of amazing songs penned by Chrissie: "Brass in Pocket," "Kid," "Back on the Chain Gang," "Middle of the Road," and so many more. But tragedy hit the band fast and early: first Honeyman-Scott's death and then Farndon's subsequent bathtub drowning after being fired from the band. Here was one of the greatest new bands on the scene, launching the eighties with the promise of great rock to come, and suddenly half of the group was gone.

But Chrissie was never derailed for long. She also never had any desire to establish a solo career and chose instead to reinvent the Pretenders many times over the years, even replacing Chambers—but later bringing him back, as on the recent tour. "I know that the Pretenders have looked like a tribute band for the last twenty years," she said at their Rock and Roll Hall of Fame induction, "and we're paying tribute to James Honeyman-Scott and Pete Farndon, without whom we wouldn't be here. And on the other hand, without us, they might have been here, but that's the way it works in rock and roll."

The ostensible purpose of this interview was to discuss *The Pretenders: Live in London*, a DVD of a passionately joyful live show with the current lineup: Martin Chambers on drums, James Walbourne on guitar, Nick Wilkinson on bass, and Eric Heywood on pedal steel. Her punk ethic still comes across when talking about it: as opposed to her peers, who involve themselves in all angles of marketing and commercial calculations, she had no inclination to even view the DVD. But when she finally did view it—as required—she was happy.

"You have to keep digging deeper over the years," she says today in regard to parenthood's tendency to soften the edges of a rocker. Nearing sixty, remarkably, she's still one of rock's most fiercely gifted songwriters, and as evidenced by the solid songs she wrote for 2008's *Break Up the Concrete*, she's still very much at the top of her game. Of course she won't cop to it and admits she still feels like a sham—a pretender, if you will—who someday might be found out. "Compared to Dylan and Neil Young," she says, "I'm still in the minor leagues."

Yet few songwriters have talked about the sad suburbanization of America with more poignancy than Chrissie, who often returned to Ohio—even opening a vegan restaurant there—and yet found her homecomings laced always with increasing sorrow at the sight of her hometown's decimation. It's a subject that has recurred many times in her work, most notably in "My City Was Gone" but also in more recent songs like "Break Up the Concrete," a great example of outrage being projected, not unlike Neil Young's "Ohio" about the Kent State massacre, with the assist of a great rock groove.

She did acknowledge at one point that if her fans hear too much negativity from her, they might believe it. But it's her way, and it makes sense. Perhaps it's a clue to her consistency and success. After all these years she's still hungry and still aiming high. Considering the list of classics she's penned, a dimming of her torch by now is understandable. But when you hear "Boots of Chinese Plastic" from *Concrete*, with its distinctive blend of Buddhism, bravado, and a taut Buddy Holly beat, you hear a songwriter engaged, as inspired and inventive as she was back when the Pretenders first emerged.

In conversation she's sharp and funny, suffering fools with a distinctly derisive wit. Asked if her music would have been vastly different had she never left America, she said, "Yeah, because I would have killed myself."

Your most recent songs are as exultant and great as your classics. Do you enjoy writing songs as much as ever?

Chrissie Hynde: Yeah. When it's getting somewhere, it's really enjoyable. It's fucking awesome. It's the best thing in the world. But when it's not getting somewhere, you want to put a gun in your mouth.

When it's not going somewhere, do you force it, or do you walk away?

I don't know. [*Laughs*] I just don't know what to say. It depends on how much pot I've been smoking, how many bottles of wine I've drunk. It's usually just in a puddle on the floor in the morning and is a waste of time. But once in a while it works.

By that do you mean you try to not be too conscious of the process while it's going down?

It's more in my head. So if I don't remember what I had in my head two weeks ago, it's gone forever. So I just keep going over it and over it in my head. And if I do pick up a guitar, I'll go back to that song. It could happen really fast. Or it could take thirty years, like "Boots of Chinese Plastic." When it started out, it was kind of like a Mose Allison song.

I love Mose.

Well, everyone does. The Who and The Kinks—all their songs were Mose Allison songs. That was the way they structured all of them.

Interesting you mentioned Mose, because he told me that, like you, he just remembers ideas and figures if he didn't remember them, they weren't worth remembering. Whereas many songwriters feel you can lose great stuff that way.

Well, he's really sharp. He's one of the greats. I don't think we're all in that class.

Yet the truth is that you've written songs that are beloved to way more people than Mose Allison has.

How do you know that? That could be wrong. Look at how Mose Allison influenced the Kinks and The Who and how many people that reached.

I don't mean to put down Mose. I love him—

Of course. I know you're not. I appreciate you're trying to say something nice.

But you don't find you have lost a good idea ever?

The worst thing is when you're in that twilight moment, when you're kind of falling asleep, because for some reason that seems like a really fertile moment creatively. And I'll be going over a song arrangement or I'll have an idea for a song. It's happened to me quite a few times, where I've thought,

"Well, that's just the best thing that I've ever, ever thought, ever. But I'm just too tired to get up and find a pen and a notebook and turn the lights on and get the guitar." I believe in it so much and I think I'll just remember it in the morning. And I wake up and have no recollection of it. And that's bummed me out a few times. But, you know, fuck it. They're only songs.

Seems like that twilight time is fertile because you're away from the everyday world. Do you find it's necessary to get away from the world, or can you write while on tour or during times of great activity?

No. But all those mundane activities are kind of informing the songs anyway. Like "Break Up the Concrete," that was obviously while I was on tour and I just couldn't *stand* seeing any more concrete. That was an obsession. And then my tour manager told me that something like the size of Hoover Dam of concrete was poured every day. Or some ridiculous statistic that he came up with. That became almost a mantra when I was in my tour bus. So I thought I'd better make a song out of this because otherwise it was a complete waste of energy.

How did that thought come together with that rhythm, that Bo Diddley beat?

Yeah, it was supposed to be Buddy Holly, but it's all the same thing. That whole project happened pretty quick. I had those songs knocking around in my head for a while, and when I got in with the band we had one day of rehearsal without the drummer, and I just said, "Well, here's roughly how the songs are." And then we went in with the drummer the next day, and we recorded everything in about ten days. So we didn't even know the stuff. I just said, "Here's how it goes." And we did two a day.

I love how on that song, in the breaks, you sing the drum pattern before the drums kick in—that funny "dat dat dat-dat-dat . . ."—

Well, that's because I was just trying to run them through the song and tell them how it went. But then when we went back to listen to it—well, I was producing it, though we wrote "Produced by The Pretenders." But I was the only one who knew [*laughs*] how it was supposed to sound.

On the end of one song on the album you hear Jim Keltner, who is obviously one of the gods, and at the end of the song [*laughs*] you can hear him going [*in a low voice*], "Oh, I'm just getting worse and worse now." And I laughed my *ass* off when I heard that, so I insisted that that had to be on the record. Of course, Keltner was *horrified*. But then when we came in and listened to "Chinese Plastic" and you can hear me going "dat dat dat dat . . ." of course I was *mortified* listening back to it. And everyone else was laughing and said we have to keep that in, and I was, like, "Oh, give me a break," and they said, "No, no, no, we have to keep it in." Because I had got my way. So at that point it became sort of a *lurid* free-for-all. Like you can hear me clearing my throat and coughing and stuff, and I said, "Just leave it all fucking in."

And it sounds great. And probably wouldn't have sounded that good if you had intentionally put that in.

Well, I don't think anyone would intentionally put that kind of shit on a track.

Also, Keltner's so solid that you don't need much else on that track. His drumming is so good—

Awesome. And Martin Chambers is like the best live drummer and the most entertaining drummer ever. I mean, to turn around onstage every night and watch him. If I turn around, he'll always do something. He's like a comedian too.

It's one of the most touching things about the new live DVD you put out, to see you onstage with him right behind you, all these years later. The core of the band is there.

Yeah. Weird.

It's exciting to see that you seem as in touch with the source as ever— and the new songs as great as old ones—as opposed to a lot of people, who seem to be repeating themselves—

Well, I hope so. If you're not, then just get out of it, I guess. It's like bring a prizefighter. You got to know when to get out.

But like prizefighters, most songwriters seem to peak young, in their twenties. It's impressive when someone goes beyond that, as have you. A new song like "Boots of Chinese Plastic" is as inspired and inventive as your best work.

I don't know. I kind of don't think of myself as a songwriter. I don't know. It's a moment. I picked up my guitar last night, and I was just *shit*, and I thought, "Ah, I'm just a phony." You know, I go through those down periods of thinking.

Why is it you never wanted a solo career? So many of your peers made a point of leaving their bands and being a solo artist, but even with many different musicians, you've always wanted to stay with The Pretenders.

I like working with a band. I've never joined a club, but I definitely love bands. And as a singer, my place in life is to set up a guitar player and make them look great. And I guess that's how football works. I mean English football. You're always setting up the other player.

Well, you could be Chrissie Hynde with a great backup band—

Yeah, but who wants to see that shit? [*Laughter*]

All your fans.

Yeah. They'll take what they get.

There's something beautiful about that it's The Pretenders.

It is a band. I need those guys. It turns me on to be standing onstage next to a great guitar player. And watching James [Honeyman-Scott] was a fucking *riot*. He was always different; he always pulled something out that you'd never heard. And if one of these guys makes a mistake, it's always fucking *great*. Because they're all musicians. I make mistakes all over the place. But if one of them makes a mistake, they're so mortified. And I enjoy that *so* much. It's so much fun. How can you not have fun in a rock band?

Well, I guess if you didn't have great songs. You have great material each night—

Well, that's a nice thought. But I've got great players around me too.

I do think it would be a lot of fun to play those songs. Your songs, like Dylan's, have so much going on lyrically. Yet they are still great songs—great grooves, melodies.

Well, I think music should make you dance. But, like I said, I'm still working on that. I feel like I haven't done anything that great yet, and that's what still motivates me. I look back on some things and I think, "God, that was *shit*. I'd better do something good to make up for it."

But in truth, among songwriters and civilians both, you're known as someone who has never put out anything that sucks. As opposed to so many people.

I won't name any names of the moments of work of mine which I'd rather you weren't aware of.

I do know some of your fans who only want you to rock out. They don't want ballads from you or any kind of tenderness.

Well, they can go fuck themselves. [*Laughter*] Yes, I have been criticized. Frankly, no one wants a lot of ballads, let's face it. When people go through their householder years and start having kids and stuff, it does ruin the mix for a while. You're in a nice place, and you're preoccupied. And it all goes a little soft—it's not very rock anymore. You have to keep digging deeper over the years. Because when you've got youth and you've got a lot of drugs and a lot of sex and alcohol and stuff, it's a no-brainer. Anyone can do it. But when those things start to fall away, and you try to clean up your act and not be addicted, you just have to dig deeper. And unfortunately that's hard to do with rock and roll.

Sometimes I've gone onstage with the band and we're so horribly hungover that we're all shaking and actually afraid to go onstage. And you think, "I'll never ever do this again. This is horrible." Then you come offstage and one of your more ardent fans who were at the show collar you in the parking lot and say, "That's the best show you've done in the last four years." And then you think, "Well, maybe we do have to go out and get completely wrecked—for the sake of our art."

Mose said a similar thing, that some nights he feels so terrible and then is shocked when he hears a tape of the show how good it was.

Yeah. Well, none of us wanted to go watch that DVD. In fact, we were in New York, and the filmmakers from Canada came down to show us the film so that we could approve it. Because they can't put it out till we approve it, of course. I was so hungover that I called my manager and said I can't face it. Because I can never watch myself back or even listen back— I've learned how, because I have to do that to make records. But I can never watch a performance, television, anything—I just can't. And I was so fucked up in the morning, I called my manager and said, "Look, I just can't watch it. I don't think I can face it. I just can't watch myself. I can't do it. I'll just get too depressed." And she said, "Well, you have to." And I was like, "Oh, can't you guys just watch it? I'm sure it'll be fine. There's nothing I can change anyway now. It's already done. So why do I have to watch it?" She said, "You have to approve it or they can't put it out." Anyway, then I met the guys in the lobby and we walked over to this place. And everyone else is looking pretty green around the edges like I was. And I could see that everyone else was dreading it. And we thought it was fucking great!

It is great.

That was a big surprise. So that's like your Mose Allison story.

That's funny, 'cause I assumed—wrongly—that you watched many films of many shows and chose this one 'cause it's so good.

No. In fact, I only watched it that one time. So maybe it wasn't that great. I think we were all so horrified and not wanting to see it, the only way we saw it was from how we were feeling that morning.

Even the guys in the band?

No, everyone was too fucked up. You know, a day off.

Normally, do you start a song with an idea of what you want it to say?

I don't know. I'm all fucked up at the moment. I think I might lay off the pot and not get too fucked up. It happens all different ways. Sometimes with my limited guitar skills, I just want to hang my head and cry. And then other times I come up with something that is just a couple notes, and it sounds great. It's always changing.

When you write a song, do you finish the music first and then fill in the words?

I don't know. I can't say. It's more like a jigsaw puzzle, and it doesn't make any sense until you find that last piece. I *hate* to make it sound so pretentious or airy-fairy. But it is like that.

[*Pause*] It has to make sense, though. I know that much. It has to make sense or it doesn't work. When people will say, "What's that song about?" the first thing I'll think is, "Oh fuck, they don't know what the song's about, so the song was a *failure* if it didn't make itself clear."

Yet you don't want it to be too obvious—and you want it to be singable—

Totally. That's the beauty of a song. It's only three minutes, and yet you can pack everything into it. The great songs that I like. "You Sexy Thing" by Hot Chocolate. I mean, why is that song so absolutely fucking likeable? You know, his voice is just perfect. It's just great. It's like the perfect pop song.

Much of it is a good groove, and your songs are very rhythmic—

Yeah, I always feel like you couldn't dance to Pretenders records. That's one of my secret shames.

I don't think that's true. A lot of them are very danceable—

Oh, I hope it's not true.

You've mentioned drugs. And so many people were destroyed by drugs, yet you have survived. How did you?

That's the $64,000 question. Who knows? Thank my lucky stars. I don't know. How can anyone answer that? You know, I just didn't quite OD.

I know you loved Brian Jones. Did part of you romanticize that lifestyle—and the thought of dying young?

Dying young? No, we just loved bands. Dying young was really not the thing. I mean, Jimmy Scott, my guitar player, died when he was twenty-five.

I know. Do you enjoy making music as much as ever?

Not really. I get really down on myself, and it actually worries me. I listen to stuff, and I think that I just don't like anything that's out there, and then I start to think that it's just me. And then once in a while something really great will come along, and I'll realize maybe the other stuff just wasn't that good and that's why I didn't like it.

Also, my age. You know I was fourteen when the first Beatles album came out, so if you do the math, I just had all the best music at all the right times in my life. I was there with Hendrix right from the start. Otis Redding. All the *greats*. I went out and got the albums when they came out. It wasn't like I was looking back. I was there right at the right time. You know, we haven't produced another Jimi Hendrix. You know, Prince was not Jimi Hendrix. And we haven't produced another James Brown. And we haven't produced another Bob Marley.

I came up at about the same time, and popular music changed so profoundly from just 1964 or so to 1970. And as a kid I remember thinking that it would continue to evolve as quickly—

It was really an interesting time. Also, because of coming to London and being in Paris right before the punk time happened here, I kind of learned how to really recognize when you're going through a transitional period. When people are going through a transition, you don't know you're going through a transition. It feels like you're on shaky ground and you don't know why. And when the transition is over, then you see that it was a transition. What I'm saying is that I can recognize them now. And we've been going through one for some time. I mean, the whole industry has collapsed. No one knows how to sell records or where it is anymore. And everything's gone on the computer.

But this seems to go in cycles. People keep buying guitars and people keep being in bands.

The last time I saw a really fertile, exciting musical scene was actually on television the other day. It was a documentary on the year that changed jazz, 1958. It was all Lee Morgan and Ornette Coleman, Coltrane—all the greats. And that was really, really exciting music.

Music's also been informed very largely by the drugs everyone's taking at the time. That's always had a lot to do with it. And I'm always trying not to take drugs and not to drink. Like everyone else, I'm trying to get unaddicted. But you know, we worked hard at those addictions to get addicted, and it's really hard to undo it.

Even Dylan's been talking about that, writing without any drugs. He said, "Try writing with a straight mind."

Well, when I've done it in the past and I've gone straight, and I remember thinking, "What is this feeling?" And I felt like I did when I was fourteen, before I started getting loaded. That was the last time I felt like that. Well, it's kind of a youth pill.

So that's what Dylan said, "Try writing with a straight mind"?

Yeah.

Well, it's always been the drugs that have informed the music. But ultimately everyone comes to the same conclusion. If they live through it.

When we were kids all our rock idols did drugs—and attributed much of their greatness to drugs. It was as if they said, "If you want to go on this road, drugs is a part of it."

Well, it was part of it. It was part of that mind-altering place, which has been part of every art and music scene ever. Always. It's fucked up, so there you have it. Where would Lucinda Williams be if it were not for the hangover? We all write songs when we're depressed and crying and all fucked up. So if you don't get depressed and fucked up and you're not crying or maybe you're even in a good relationship, what the hell are you gonna write about?

And it makes sense why a songwriter would turn to drugs—to get away from the everyday world and get to that place where songs are.

Also, I think songwriters and people with that creative way of dealing with the world—I mean, I think that sounds pretentious, so I try to avoid that—but I think artists want to go there. It's only in my recent years I've really taken onboard that some people really just aren't creative. I mean, you meet people who say, "Wow. you can draw. I can't draw. You can sing. That must great to be able to do something." And you look at them and think, "What are you talking about?" And the truth is some people can't sing or draw. And I don't think I ever really understood that. I thought everybody could sing and draw and do stuff like that. I think it was in a karaoke bar one night that I realized, "Wow, some people can't sing." It was pretty shocking. You hear girls at check-out counters at drugstores. They're singing, and they have the most beautiful voices—they're better than anyone on the radio.

Senses are imperfect anyway. Who knows if anyone sees green the same way I do? Obviously they don't. Some people are color-blind. So it's hard for an artist to understand that not everyone has an artistic way of seeing the world.

It might seem to you, when you see me onstage or on this DVD, and there's a collection of songs that I'm largely responsible for, that I'm pro-lific and I know what I'm doing. The truth is that I'm not very prolific. And I feel like a half-assed songwriter and a phony most of the time. Sometimes I paste something down when I'm writing a song, just be shouting. But sometimes I get there in the end. I don't know.

I know other songwriters who feel the same thing, and it seems that need to still prove something is what propels them forward to good work.

No, I just got away with it, man. Come on. There's not anything that's original. I'm just trying to get through it. Mine is the last act of a desperate man. I just didn't want to be a waitress.

Yet you've stretched songs by doing things nobody else has done. And you've written songs that have stood the test of time, which is a major accomplishment. In terms of songwriting, it doesn't get better than that.

Well, I can't wait for you to hear the JP stuff. This is a really interest-ing album we've done, because it's just the two of us.

And isn't this the only non-Pretenders album you've done?

Yeah. I've always said I'd never go solo. And this isn't a solo project. And The Pretenders, I love them. The band is on fire. I love them. And I wouldn't want anyone to think I'm not interested in them. But that's kind of a hard slog to come up with stuff for them. I have some ideas. Of course, I do. The songs I can do with The Pretenders are more get-them-off-my-chest kind of songs. Like I still haven't written songs about barbe-cues and stuff, so there's still plenty of stuff I can moan about.

Are you living in Akron still?

No, I'm in London. I still do spend a little bit of time in Akron, maybe a week or two every couple of months. Which is a *lot* more than I ever used to.

I read a few things about you that said you moved back there to stay, but that's not true at all—

No, that's not true at all. Maybe I kind of implied that. I don't know. I think that was misconceived somewhere along the line. I bought a place there and I have a restaurant there, so it looks like I'm living there more than I am.

It's interesting how much your Ohio roots have colored your music, even though you've lived in England for so many years. Many times you've returned to the theme of seeing how much has changed in America and how much is gone since you were a kid.

Yeah. [*Sighs*] It's kind of weird isn't it? It's kind of been my obsession all my life. And I've tried to go back to the Midwest and rebuild those downtowns. I've thought about it for hours and hours. I've thought about it for years, what happened to America. Then I finally concluded that the way we got that land, that's where we went wrong. We stole that land, and we built our cities on burial grounds. So those cities had to go. Karmically we committed an act of genocide. And what you put out came back. So those cities just couldn't live. Akron and Washington, DC, were two of the largest-growing cities at one time in the States. I mean, Akron was *thriving*. It had all this industry and all these people. But you know, America had all these problems—with the slaves, with emancipation, and all that. I don't think that people like my parents—who were very hardworking, they'd been there for a few generations, like Welsh coal miners, and they were just real ordinary Americans at the beginning—I don't think my parents were racist or anything, but I think that clash of cultures frightens people. You see it all around the world. It's more than racism. Racism, you see it obviously in the South. There was a real problem and there always has been. But people are afraid of other cultures. I live in the most multicultural city in probably the whole world, in London. And you can see people can get along, but there's a real conflict when what is considered blasphemy and what is considered totally unacceptable in one culture is something you're getting your nose rubbed in every single day on the streets where you live.

But then blacks started moving into the urban center, and the whites fled. They went into the suburbs. I'm not entirely hopeful that we can retrieve our Zokolows or our centers. 'Cause it's all gone into that kind of strip-mall mentality. You can't even walk across the street. And what happens is that you lose your youth culture. 'Cause when kids grow up and they get out of school, they want to move out of their parents' house and move downtown and get an apartment with some friends and do something. Well, if there's no downtown, there's nowhere for them to go. So they have to leave the city. What kind of an eighteen-year-old wants to get a job so they can get a mortgage and a car? They usually have other things in mind. Well, that's the story of American cities. For all sorts of reasons, they have collapsed.

When you go back to Akron, is it sad for you to see what it's become, or do you find joy in connecting with what it used to be?

It was sad for me in the seventies when they razed downtown. And I milked it for all I could. No, I just stood there and cried when I went there. I used to walk downtown with my friends. And it would take us *hours*. But there was nothing to do in Akron, so we'd walk downtown. There were only two department stores, but that was the downtown for us, and we loved it. But they just knocked it all down and made great big inner belts. I grew up with it all my life. The house that I was first in, my grandmother's house, you know they picked it up and put it on rollers and moved it up the hill. And that's when the inner belt came through. *All* the streets got cut up. Yeah, I have *obsessively* talked about it. Even on this last album.

You say "when the streets got rearranged."

Yeah.

That theme permeates your work, that so much has changed. But there are some things that don't change. And songs are that way—in that a great song, like "Message of Love" or "Chain Gang," they're unchanged and as powerful and redemptive now as when they first came out. That's why it's hard to understand when you say you're half-assed as a songwriter, 'cause you've written so many timeless and beloved songs.

Well, that's just the way I look at it. I enjoyed being on that last tour, the one you see on the DVD. It was a fucking blast. I love playing with that band. But every year you think maybe you're coming to the end. I've always felt that way, even before The Pretenders. By the time I was twenty-four I thought I was too old to be in a band. Because it used to be a real youth culture.

When you started writing songs, did you write alone?

Yeah, because I had my little guitar. And I wasn't good enough to play along with records, so I had to write my own songs to have something to play. I learned two chords, and I loved singing. So you can get a lot of melodies, and the least amount of chords, the more melodic possibilities you have. If you've got seven chords, you're stuck with those chords. James Brown, some of his best songs were just one chord. It would have sounded *odd* if you played a second chord.

How old were you when you wrote your first song?

Fourteen.

That's an understanding a lot of songwriters don't have, that it doesn't take a lot of chords to write a good melody.

Well, yeah, that's why we have limited skills. It *really* frustrates me that I'm not a better guitar player. I'm good at the one thing I can do. [*Laughs*] But I can't just listen to something and then just play what I want to play. I am a rhythm guitar player, and that's what I always wanted to be. Ever since I heard a James Brown, I wanted to play rhythm guitar.

Your songs are deceptively simple in that when I play them, they seem more complex than they are. Or a song like "Boots of Chinese Plastic," it's only three chords, and yet it's such a great song.

Oh, well, less is more, I guess. That comes from having very little technical skill. Not counting anything or knowing the names of the chords helps. Up to a point.

You said you started with two chords. Do you remember which they were?

Probably A and D.

A lot of your songs are in A. Is that a favorite key?

I don't know. I don't know where I sing the best. I don't know what keys my songs are in. I don't know which side I photograph well on.

[*Laughs*] But your best side to be photographed, that's a lot different than what keys your own songs are in—

But you would think after being photographed for thirty years, somebody would have figured that out. And the rest of it is I just go by the gods.

When you sit down to write a song, how do you avoid going to the same musical patterns you've gone to before?

Well, I don't avoid it. I think I am going to the same patterns. Which is why it's great to write with someone else who is also of that kind of limited skills on guitar. He has great ideas, but he also can't pick up the guitar and express himself the way that James Walbourne can. Or Patrick Murdock, who is in the Fairground Boys, which is the band we're using for this album I'm doing with JP.

You could get three of the best rock musicians in the world, or any musicians, but you've got to have that one focal point to kind of distill it all. Or it's just gonna be lost in space. *They* might enjoy it while they're playing in their basement.

And so many of the greatest songwriters have not been great instrumentalists. Do you think limitations can sometimes create great stuff?

Yeah, I think so. I think you find that even if you're decorating a flat and you have a low budget. Just look at kids. Look at teenagers. If you go on a high street sometimes and you see the kids in a rich part of town, they're wearing designer clothes and stuff and they look like shit. But if you go into the really poor part of town, you'll see kids—ones that are into music, anyway—they have a look. And the more limited is your budget, often you're more creative. That's what I think. If you have unlimited resources, sometimes there's just too many choices. It's all about hunger, isn't it? When you really want something badly, you'll get it. When you're satiated and you've had too much, there's not much creative possibility, is there?

You still sound hungry in your work—a hunger to still do something great or even greater. A song like "Boots of Chinese Plastic" is really inventive and inspirational. People at your level of success often don't write songs like that anymore.

Well, I don't know. It's a song about philosophy, basically. And if you're not thinking about philosophy at my age, you might as well just put a gun in your mouth.

In that song and so many others, you have always been able to balance philosophy and spiritualism with rock and roll. George Harrison did it, but—

Well, I try to keep it hidden. You know, because certain things you just can't express to the light or to the public. My philosophy and where I'm coming from and why I do this has always been exactly the same. And it's all ultimately about child protection and what you might call animal rights. That's something I've had with me since early.

That consistency of message became really clear to me preparing for this and listening to your whole body of work from the start to now. And the message of "Message of Love" and "Boots of Chinese Plastic" is the same. You said how you keep that message hidden, and a friend told me she likes you 'cause you "sneak spirituality" into your songs. But I don't think it's that hidden if someone pays attention. The message is out there.

It couldn't be any more out there. I'd be bearing a cross if it was any more out there. [*Laughs*] The thing is, it's *weird*. It's very, very literal. And I did quite a lot of press for that album, and you know, nobody ever asked me about that song, and I thought that was really kind of far out. Chanting, "Hare Krishna, Hare Krishna, Krishna Krishna, Hare Hare,

Hare Rama, Hare Rama, Rama Rama, Hare Hare, Nam myoho renge kyo." Talking about Jesus Christ. And nobody ever asked anything about it, which is *very* strange. Certain things, you have to keep a veil on. And I thought maybe I didn't on that song. But I seem to have got away with it. Not that it's gonna change anyone's life. But nobody came to me and said, "What are you talking about?"

Well, maybe the sneaky part about it and why people missed the message is that it's a great rock and roll song—has that cool Bo Diddley beat—so maybe people got into that groove but didn't pay attention to the words.

Well, that's good.

Is it?

Sure, if they're still chanting Hare Krishna, if they're still thinking about Jesus Christ and saying, "Nam myoho renge kyo," it can't be a bad thing, can it?

I read that the line you repeat in the song—"every drop that runs through the vein makes its way back to the heart again" is a translation of "nam myoho renge kyo." Is that so?

No. In fact, that line is from a song I wrote when I was trying to get the Johnny Moped band together, called The Unusuals, and that was from before I was in The Pretenders.

Nam myoho renge kyo, I don't even know the literal translation.

It's a beautiful song. I love that line "I see you in the birds and in the trees." I think that's the heart of many of your songs, recognizing God in nature.

Well, that's what I mean. That will be the continuity in my songs— other than heartbreak and fucked-up relationships and that kind of stuff. But I really roll with the punches in my life. I don't get traumatized. But it's the philosophy that can keep you on your path. Otherwise, you've got nothing.

In that song I am not quite sure when you say, "You sure look fantastic in your boots of Chinese plastic" if that's sincere or a statement about the cheapness of much of our lives—

No, I think they're great because they're not wearing leather. [*Laughter*] I guess I snuck that one in.

I thought it was about the disparity of the beauty of nature which surrounds us while people are getting excited by plastic boots, a symbol for disposable culture.

No, it's just part of my endless quest to find the nearest Payless. 'Cause I don't wear leather. Actually, that's a lie, because I actually can afford Stella McCartney boots. Of which I have many.

I thought of you when I heard that the Pope attacked the movie *Avatar* for promoting a "new divinity," that nature is God. An idea which actually precedes the Judeo-Christian idea of a paternal God. Showed me there are always forces working to keep us from the spiritual understanding that's in your songs.

Well, yes. But there's more value in the creator. In the one who created it. So I understand where the Vatican is coming from. I mean, this is only the material world. I mean, if you're not beholden to who created it, then I don't know what you're looking at, really. And of course it's beautiful.

Yet it seems it's that kind of idea, that what is sacred is beyond this world and not of this world, that leads some people to feel fine in destroying the earth and killing animals because they do not consider anything of this earth to be holy.

Well, they're living with a false doctrine then. They're living with an imperfect idea. People will gravitate and be born into and find their own level of their own understanding—they always will. There's not any religions that promotes or condones the killing of animals. What they say in these Halal meat and Kosher laws is all *bullshit*. But nowhere in the Koran or the Torah or the Bible, it never says anywhere to kill or eat animals. In fact, on the first page of the Bible it says, "I give you herbs bearing grain." And "Thou shalt not kill." And yet we're killing billions and billions of animals a year. So we're doomed, 'cause that is murder. That's unlawful killing. Because what we're doing in factory farms, it's Nazi Germany. And anyone who is paying for that and turning a blind eye to it, doesn't matter how much you don't see it, you are responsible for it, and you're gonna get it in the teeth. And that's what we're getting.

All the people who, in the name of their religions, are butchering animals, they are butchers. They're not holy people. Because if you read through the world religions and read those things, they'll make concessions if you have to kill, how not to cause unnecessary suffering to the animals. But believe me, that is not what's going on in these slaughterhouses. So they're liars. They're all fucking liars. My world is a world on a battlefield. As far as I'm concerned, I am a warrior and I'm engaged in a way, which I am very willing and happy to die fighting. And that is my war against meat eaters and that's why I'm in music.

That's why?

Yes. And it always has been. And I don't say that in the songs. But what I can do is at least get this a little attention, have some fun, and hopefully encourage people to stop that.

You have expressed much of what you believe in songs—your philosophy, your horror at the death of our cities—so why haven't you directly put that animal rights message into a song?

I don't know. I guess I just haven't figured out how to do it well yet. Morrissey had that beautiful song. I just haven't managed. I'm also mindful of never wanting to preach to anyone. Because unless someone invites advice, they'll hate you for it. Nobody, nobody, nobody wants advice or to be told what to believe or what they should be doing. Nobody. Especially me. People told me I should be using e-mail for fifteen years and I wouldn't open a computer. I don't like being told what to do. Fifteen years later, after saying, "Oh, you've gotta get e-mail. It's so great," and now they're saying how lucky I am that I'm not using e-mail. I don't know where I got lost in that arc of "you've got to have it" to "you're lucky you don't have it."

But some songwriters who have gotten so involved in nonsongwriting pursuits—working for causes—lose touch with their songwriting—

A lot of animal rights people do that. They lose their human companions. But we're not going to save the world; we're only going to save our own souls. Our job on earth is not to save the world. So if you think that's your job, take your Messiah complex and do what you have to do with it.

In "Message of Love" you say our job is to take care of each other. Is that how you feel?

Yeah, I do. I think we're social creatures. We have to look after each other because if we were supposed to be alone, there would be only one person on the planet. It is obvious, isn't it?

How have you been so passionate about animal rights without letting it get in the way of your work?

Because I know I can lend myself more to it by having a famous name than actually being on the front line. And that's just the way it worked out. You know, I've got stacks and stacks from animal charities and stuff. And it's a creepy society. It's a celebrity society. People are more interested in what someone that they're never gonna meet is wearing or who they're dating than their own lives. It's so voyeuristic.

Why do you think that is?

Because people don't know who they are. They don't know who their real self is. They're confused. They think that they are their body. So they become obsessed with things just related to their body. They stop eating meat because they don't want to put that into their *body*. It's all about their body. They're confused. There are different levels of consciousness. And very few people are fully conscious. I'm sure I'm not. There's a stunted consciousness. Which is more like the consciousness of a tree. And there's a budding consciousness, which is beginning to open. A fully opened consciousness—not very many people have those. And you can't have it when you're clouded over with meat eating and all these other practices which prevent that.

I understand. When I listen to your songs there's a sense of an old soul looking at this world with some sadness.

Well, you know, the soul's eternal, so how old is that?

It seems some are further along than others.

Well, who knows? They say there are 8.4 million species, and we transmigrate through all of them.

Do you think that's so?

Yes.

Among songwriters, if someone writes one song that lasts, that is beloved by the masses, it's huge. And there are some of you who have written many—and that's a great accomplishment.

Well, I haven't written that many. Come on, I'm not like Dylan or Neil Young. I'm still in the minor leagues.

But Dylan is an exception—

Right. No one can compare themselves with him.

But just in terms of hits—and hits are the way many songwriters measure their worth—you've had a lot more hits than most songwriters around.

I could use one now, but you know, I haven't had one in years. You know, I wrote "I'll Stand by You" with Tom [Kelly] and Billy [Steinberg], and that was a cold-blooded mission to get on the radio. I was ashamed of it, to be honest. But then some people who I really like said they liked it, so that made me like it.

I know Steinberg and Kelly, and I remember hearing you were working with them and being really surprised. I didn't expect that you would

**want to work with them. Not because they're not great, but so different
from you.**

The thing is if you've been in the game for a long time, you do all
the things you never wanted to do. You thrive on change. And I do like
change. And I like traveling and moving a lot. And then you actually start
running out of things that you haven't done. And the only things left that
you haven't done are the things that you never really wanted to do.

So you wrote "I'll Stand by You" to be a hit?

Yeah, and I was ashamed because I'd never done that before. I'd never
made an attempt to be commercial and get on the radio. And it started to
hurt, that I wasn't getting on the radio. And I love radio. To me, radio is
everything. Always has been. I grew up on radio. And the radio's always
there for everyone. Although that can be changing now with computer.
Everything's changing now. It's kind of exciting. I'm not saying it's better.
I'm under no delusions whatsoever that things are getting better or we're
progressing. We're definitely not progressing. You know, the dumbing
down of this society—I don't know how much lower it can go. But that's
definitely the direction it's going in. If we didn't have these factory farms
and slaughterhouses, we might have a little chance to have a little bit of
peace.

Interesting you wrote that to be a hit, as that seems so unlike you.

I'd never done that before. It was only when I talked to Noel Galla-
gher and he said, "I wish I'd fucking wrote it." And then Jeff Beck loves
it. And then I thought, "Fucking hell, if he likes it." And melodically it's
got some nice stuff in it. It's a good song. It was just a cold-blooded attempt on my part.

**Did you do something different that you normally would in that one to
make it a hit?**

No. Not particularly. Just writing with Tom and Billy, who are hit
makers, it was a step in that direction. But I have to say it was a blast,
and I loved writing with them. It was really, really fun.

Did you all sit in a room together and write at the same time?

Well, mainly it was like me and Tom ganging up on Billy and trying
to torture him. [*Laughter*] I'd kind of just drink tea and go out and buy
chocolate and hang out and keep thinking of things I had to go out and
buy. You know, I'd stay at the Chateau Marmont and drive to Encino
every day. I hated that drive.

Then Billy would arrive with his little poems. And he'd show them to me, and I'd just pace and eat and drink and get more chocolate and just goof around for hours. And then you could tell that Billy was getting really nervous. And Tom would say, "Billy, can't you see she's trying to surround the moment?" We even hid from him once behind some curtains with knives and were gonna attack him. But my dog gave our hiding place away. So that was some of the most fun times of my life, trying to torture Billy. But I make no secret of my kind of sadistic tendencies. And Tom, I just loved working with Tom. And Billy. They're fantastic. I'd just love to work with them again. It was so much fun.

Would Tom be at the piano?

Yes. And I'd be right in the middle of them, so I would put in musical ideas and change lyrics. And bastardize Billy's sentimental little offerings.

Were you playing guitar?

Sometimes, yeah. We wrote quite a few different songs together in all different ways.

It is true you are working on a duo album with JP Jones?

You know, I just finished an album with him. He's a Welsh singer-songwriter that I met a few years ago. It's a total divergence from what I was doing. I was on tour with the Pretenders, and I came back, and I was sitting here in a bar, and he sent me a song when I was on tour. He just sent me a few songs, and I thought they were good. Really good. And he said we should try writing some songs together, so we did. So we just finished a whole album. So that was a complete out-of-the-blue for me. That's never happened to me. I usually have to wait until I get ideas and then go to my band. We'll have the record finished this weekend. Not sure yet what it's called. We both sing. It's pretty awesome. It's really unusual. And it's a whole other band, different than the people I usually work with. It's just great.

Would it be okay if I named some of your songs randomly for any thoughts you might have?

Yeah, is it okay if I throw up? [*Laughter*] Yeah, whatever. Do your thing.

"Brass in Pocket."

Well, I said that would go out over my dead body. That was my famous quote.

You didn't like it?

I didn't like it because I didn't think it knew was it was. I thought it sounded like it was trying to be a Motown song, but it didn't quite get it. Didn't quite make it.

You wrote it together with James Honeyman-Scott?

No, he had that little riff [*sings opening repeated guitar notes*], he was playing that in the studio, and I thought, "Wow, that's awesome," and I just happened to have a little tape recorder and I taped it. That's the one time I did that. I wish I'd done it more. That's how I did it with him a few times.

But now I like that song because [*pause*] it's one of those songs that served me well. I didn't like my voice on it. I was kind of a new singer, and listening to my voice made me kind of cringe. I shouldn't be saying all this negative stuff, because if people hear me saying all this negative stuff, they'll start to believe it too.

Exactly. We love these songs. As far as this song, one time you said that people think you are that character in the song, and you're not.

Although I loved the anti-establishment nature of rock and roll—that's why I got into it, because I didn't want to be part of the establishment—I still have this thing. See, the thing about rock is there's rules but there's no rules. There's a kind of tradition, like Wayne Fontana and the Mindbenders' "The purpose of a man is to love a woman." So I wrote "Message of Love," and I took the title "Message of Love" from Jimi Hendrix. Like "2000 Miles" came from Otis Redding. I always want to pay tribute to my heroes. And I always think everyone's gonna see that straightaway, and then when no one mentions it, I think, "*Fuck*, someone out there will think I just plagiarized this person and tried to get away with it." I think they're so *obvious* when I do that.

Or maybe they don't have any idea that it didn't start with you.

Maybe. It wouldn't occur to me that somebody wouldn't know that. Anyway, "Brass in Pocket," it's all right. I like it.

It's an interesting title. Why did you call it that instead of "Make You Notice Me" or something like that?

Because I heard a guy from a band up north who had taken his suit to a dry cleaner, and I can't do the accent, but he said, "Was there any brass in pocket?" I hadn't heard that before, and I thought it was a good turn of phrase.

I know you said you worried that sometimes you weren't clear enough in songs, and yet we love that mystery. It's exotic.

It's got "bottle" too in it. Bottle is Cockney rhyming slang. It means bottle and glass. And the way Cockney rhyming slang works is the word you're really saying rhymes with the second word. So bottle and glass rhymes with ass. In England to say somebody has a lot of ass it to say they have a lot of funk. So you say, "That guy has a lot of bottle." There's also reference to Robert Crumb in there where I say, "It's so reet." Another one of my heroes, Robert Crumb. And, well, this is just fucking me rambling. Like I said, I got away from it in that song.

And the other thing about "Brass in Pocket," the tradition of it is that you're supposed to be kind of cocky and sure of yourself. You're not supposed to go onstage and say, "Oh, I'm small and I have no confidence and I think I'm shit." Because you just can't do that onstage. You're not supposed to. And probably you don't have much confidence and you do think you're a little piece of shit, or else you wouldn't have gotten together a rock band in the first place. The nature of the stage—where you're already seven feet higher than everyone and they have to look up to you—you have to use that to your advantage. And so, hence, "Brass in Pocket" is, I guess, a big lie. Name another song.

You mentioned "Message of Love." Musically it's interesting, the way in A you go to C for the chorus—kind of a Beatlesque thing to do. Were you thinking in those terms, that we should go somewhere else here?

I can't remember. [*Pause*] Again, like I said, it was kind of my response as a woman to "The purpose of a man is to love a woman." It was another rock tradition to address.

How about "Kid"?

What about it?

A thing I like about it is that you have a tough veneer, yet that song seems unafraid to be pretty.

I don't know. That's an odd song, because I'm not really a storyteller. God, I feel so fucking *lame* talking about this shit. I'm more sort of autobiographical and more expressing my real experiences, and that was more of a story about a prostitute that her little kid finds out at the end that she's a prostitute. It doesn't say that in the song, but if you listen to it, you'll find out that's what it's about. Maybe that song doesn't work because you don't know that. But then we don't know what Otis Redding was talking about when he said, "I've been loving you too long and I can't stop now, and your love's become a habit to me." Is he talking about heroin, or is he talking about a woman?

Right. But I think "Kid" does work, even not knowing the subtext. The emotion of the subject comes through.

And I use a lot of English expressions that, when I think about it, I know as an American is almost a different language. Like in that song it says, "Your tears are too dear." "Dear" means expensive—they cost too much. But I know from an American point of view, "too dear" might just not make sense or sound really stupid, so fuck it.

Yet from listening to British songwriters all these years, we know a lot of these terms. But would your music have been vastly different had you not gone to England?

Totally. Well, it would have been different because I would have put a bullet in my head. So it would have been very different. It would have been played on harp.

How about "Back on the Chain Gang"?

That was a song I was writing, and I had shown Jimmy Scott some of the chords, and I was working on this song which he liked, and then he died, and it turned into more of a tribute to him.

You made such a great record of it—the guitars, the chain gang vocals. Do you think in terms of the record when you write the song?

No, that comes later.

That one has such a great riff. Do you come up with riffs?

More the guitar player, I suppose. Which is why I don't use my own name on the thing. 'Cause their contribution is so great, that I always keep it as a band thing.

That's unusual to do that, to give writer's credit to the whole band. Why?

Because a lot of people want all the credit for themselves.

A lot of these *cunts*, they take credit for stuff they haven't even written. It's shameful, really. Horrible. There's some who will say, if someone sends them a song, "I'll only perform your song if you give me half of the songwriting."

Right. That's kind of an unfortunate American tradition. Al Jolson, Elvis Presley. They wanted their name as writer.

Well, that's stealing. I don't like cheaters. This year I have a thing about cheaters. People who cut you off when you're driving. People who try to get to the head of the line. I don't want credit for anything else. I don't even want my name as producer or anything, necessarily. Because, hey, I'm a rock star. You can't get any higher than that. Why put yourself down by saying you did the artwork or are the producer?

Yet it's so common. Some people have a really hard time giving any credit, even when it's due.

Well, I have other things to worry about.

"Popstar."

Oh yeah, "Popstar." I like that song. I don't think anyone else really got it. I was trying to write a song like "Get Off My Cloud." It's a very literal song too. People thought it was my take on the new generation of singers. It was very literal. It was me going out with a guy, and when we broke up he found a younger, prettier version of me who wanted to be a pop star. As they always do, of course. So it's really literal. I like that song a lot. David Johansen's on it. He's playing all these ad libs on it. I should have had him play harmonica—he's a much better harmonica player than I am.

I think you sound great. I was kind of surprised how good you are on it.

I never practice or play it. I should play more. I like it a lot. I've been doing that since I was a kid. I've never put "Harmonica by Chrissie Hynde" on it. [*Laughs*]

But we know it's you.

Well, yeah, the inimitable sound.

How about "Middle of the Road"?

That's a real rip-off. That's a total Stones rip-off. I probably shouldn't say that, but *fuck* them. They ripped off so many people in their time. That was kind of my version of "Empty Heart." Same chords. But there's only four chords anyway. And that's another one about exploitation. "The Middle of the Road" is referring to the I-Ching, the middle way. Always stay in the middle. Another one of my philosophical comments.

It's interesting how differently we can understand those thoughts—

Yeah, well, like I said, I like to keep a veil over them.

It's a powerful song because you're saying things in rock nobody has ever said. You're saying, "Hey, I'm thirty-three now, I have a kid. Don't jump on me."

[*Laughs*] Yeah, I like singing that now, "I'm thirty-three," now that I'm fifty-eight. But at my stage I can say what I want. Actually at the time I was only thirty-two, but it didn't rhyme with the word I was looking for. So I said I was a year older. I used to always say I was older than I am anyway.

I've interviewed Randy Newman many times, and he always says how much he loves you as a songwriter—

Wow. *Awesome!*

He said he told you that once, but you thought he was joking.

[*Pause*] Wow.

And he's quite like you. He's very reticent to ever celebrate his own greatness as a songwriter.

Well, come on. It's not the Sermon on the Mount, is it?

Maybe more important to many people. Certainly to me. Songs are one of the few meaningful parts of our lives that aren't just part of our disposable culture. Even now people are constantly walking around listening to songs. It seems that songs do matter.

It is true. No, I agree, I agree. It's just that I feel I'm not worthy. Like, "How did I get here?" Like it was just something that I got away with, like a scam that I pulled off. But I agree with you about songs, because songs inform your whole life. And they really do. And there's no way of telling what's going to turn you on in a song. That's so subjective.

Recently some of my friends who are around thirty were telling me about this one artist. They all just love her. I'm not gonna say who she is, because I've met her and she's a really lovely person. But they were just going on about how great she was. And I was really excited to hear her. And I got the CD and I put it on and I didn't like it at all, and I thought, "God, what's wrong with me?"

◆ ◆ ◆

John Prine
Mailman of Miracles
Nashville, Tennessee 2008

Straight from the streets of Maywood he came, a mailman with a chain of masterpieces. It's Chicago, 1970, and word starts circulating around this close-knit folk music scene that there's a new guy who must be heard to be believed. A songwriter who seems to have emerged fully formed with a voice like Hank Williams and songs that resound like some miracle collaboration between Woody Guthrie and Hemingway. His name's Prine. And almost as soon as the Old Town denizens of the Windy City learned of him, the secret was out, and John Prine belonged to the world.

He was then and remains today a genuine songwriter's songwriter, in that he's written the kind of songs other songwriters aspire daily to write. Evidence of which is the vast array of covers of his songs by his peers, including Jackson Browne, Bonnie Raitt, Johnny Cash, Rickie Lee Jones, Willie Nelson, and so many others. Even Bob Dylan, since the first night Kristofferson brought Prine and Steve Goodman into their Greenwich Village fold, has been awed. "Prine's stuff is pure Proustian existentialism," said Dylan. "Beautiful songs . . . I remember when Kris first brought him on the scene. All that stuff about 'Sam Stone,' the soldier junkie daddy, and 'Donald and Lydia,' where people make love from ten miles away. Nobody but Prine could write like that." Kristofferson, despite unleashing Prine's genius on the world, admitted to being intimidated by him. "He's so good," Kris said. "We're gonna have to break his fingers."

When Prine and Goodman returned to Chicago after landing their deals, a celebration ensued for our local heroes, the entire town welcoming them with warmth and open arms. Unlike other big cities that reject locals who leave to make it big, Chicago has nothing but pride for those who come from our streets and take on the world. "We were like astronauts coming back from the moon," Prine said. "They might as well have thrown a parade for us."

Prine's lines are so evocative, so purely precise and finely etched, that they linger in our hearts and minds like dreams, separate from the songs. There's the rodeo poster from "Angel from Montgomery," the hole in Daddy's arm and the broken radio (from "Sam Stone"), the old trees that just grow stronger (from "Hello in There"). The kinds of lines you carry around in your pocket, knowing they're in there when you need them. His is a prodigious gift for capturing intangibles with language, such as the anomalous texture of Sunday nights he translated into "The Late John Garfield Blues" or the ennui expressed so purely with the flies buzzing around the kitchen in "Angel from Montgomery." Whether writing about old folks so sorrowfully isolated that people call "Hello in there," like talking to a kid in a well, or taking on the phenomenon of celebrity through the unlikely subject of Sabu the Elephant Boy, Prine has melded his staggering penchant for detail and his proclivity to be both hilarious and deeply serious (and often in the same song) with a visceral embrace of roots music. And in doing so he's made the kinds of songs nobody ever dreamed of before—or since.

As a kid his first musical love was country, which kept him endlessly spinning the Roy Acuff and Hank Williams 78s in his dad's collection and tuning into WJJD out of Chicago to hear Webb Pierce, Lefty Frizell, and others "back to back, all night long." Roots music with stories to tell, the kind of songs he'd become famous for writing. And then a new kind of music arrived: "I was coming of age just as rock and roll was invented," he said like a kid on Christmas, and along with his country heroes he added Elvis, Little Richard, Fats Domino, and the one he loved the most, Chuck Berry, "because he told a story in less than three minutes," Prine explained. "And he had a syllable for every beat. . . . Some people stretch the words like a mask to fit the melody. Whereas guys who are *really* good lyricists have a meter so that the melody is almost already there."

He started playing guitar at fourteen, mostly old folk tunes taught to him by his brother Dave, who gave fiddle lessons. He quickly surmised he could take the same three folk chords and, with a little rhythm, play Chuck Berry, but his limitations then, as they have ever since, led him to his own songs. "I learned to write because I'd learn to play a Fats Domino song, say, and it wouldn't sound nearly as good as Fats Domino. So I'd just make up my own melody and write my own words. And anything I made up came out sounding like a folk song because that was the kind of guitar I learned. If my brother would have been into Chuck Berry, then maybe I would have written all those songs as rock and roll shuffles."

When he was old enough he got a job as a postman, which he loved because he could write songs while walking the familiar blocks. "It was like a library with no books," he said. "When you've got your own mail route, day after day, it was an easy place to write."

For a string of consecutive Sundays he started coming to the open-mic nights at the old Fifth Peg, a folk club on Armitage in Old Town. When he summoned up the courage to perform, he played his handful of unheard classics—"Angel from Montgomery," "Hello in There," and "Donald and Lydia"—and the audience was stunned speechless and forgot to clap. He figured he'd failed: "They just sat there. They didn't even applaud, they just *looked* at me. I thought, 'Uh-oh. This is pretty bad.' I started shuffling my feet and looking around. And then they started applauding, and it was a really great feeling. It was like I found out all of a sudden that I could communicate. That I could communicate really deep feelings and emotions. And to find that out all at once was amazing."

And the word spread like wildfire. When Kristofferson heard Prine and Goodman he pulled some New York strings and landed them both record deals. The rest is singer-songwriter history. It was 1971, the dream of the sixties was over, and Goodman and Prine emerged with a new kind of song, eschewing the lyrical abstractions of the past to write instead story songs about real people—"Midwestern mindtrips to the nth degree," as Dylan put it. Songs with the concrete details and imagery of a novelist but compounded, like Prine's hero Chuck Berry, into three-minute masterpieces.

He loves red interiors. He told me this about himself, and it has resounded in my memory ever since, like one of the haunting lines from one of his songs: when he looks in and around Nashville for old cars to buy, as he often does, he starts exclusively looking for cars with red interiors. That, to John Prine, outweighs any concern for how the thing looks from the outside. A red interior, especially one in good shape, speaks volumes. It speaks of America, of our recent past so recently gone, and about his love for the odd, arcane detail. And it points to something beyond words, as he struggled to explain. "Not even sure why," he said, looking skyward. "I just know it makes me happy."

I spoke to him on a sun-bright Tennessee morning, his voice a low, raspy whisper since his recent bout with cancer and subsequent surgery. But his stories were punctuated with frequent laughter—laughter at himself and at the sad folly of a world he's written about so well for decades. Perhaps recognizing that things he's put off forever, like doing this kind of interview, were worth doing now or never, he took a long time to generously delve into his personal history from the streets of Maywood to Germany to the Chicago folk scene to the nightclubs of New York and beyond. Though talking wasn't as easy as it once was, he enjoyed rummaging through the rooms of his own memory, which he found easier to do than recalling what happened last week. "I just gave a long interview yesterday to PBS," he said, "so I might get confused. Sometimes it's hard to separate yesterday from today."

I'm so happy to finally speak to you. When I was growing up in Chicago, you and Steve Goodman were my heroes.

John Prine: [*Laughs*] Man, it was a great place then. I love going back to Chicago. Man, it was a good amount of fortune. That Steve and I came along when we did and got into the Chicago folk scene. It was kind of all ready for us.

It was a great scene for songwriters back then.

It really was. It was just great to see all that blossom. All the people coming from all over and playing at the open stages at the Earl [of Old Town]. Then Goodman took me to New York and showed me all this stuff that I read about—the clubs, the coffeehouses, that whole scene. And that all sprang both me and Steve's record contracts. It was really exciting times.

I remember well hearing about you—this mailman from Maywood— and then the first album came out, and every song was a masterpiece. It was a stunning debut. Did you have those songs for a while before recording?

I really started writing when I got out of the Army in 1968 and went back to the post office; I had done a couple of years in there before I got drafted. So I went back there to work. Especially when you've got your own mail route, day after day, it was an easy place to write. It was like going to a library with no books. You're afforded to just go do your job, and you don't really even have to think about it. You know you're on the right street and you're at the right house, and you're putting the mail in the right box. That's where I wrote a lot of the early songs, walking on the mail route.

When you were growing up, what kind of music did you listen to—and who were your musical heroes? Did you write your first song after you were in the Army?

No, I wrote a couple early on. I learned to play the guitar when I was fourteen. I learned three chords and didn't bother to [*laughs*] learn much else. It got to where, if I wanted to learn a song and it had a minor chord in it, and I really wanted to learn that song, then I'd learn it and the first thing I'd do is take the odd chord, as I called it, the one I had never played before, and put it in a new song of mine. Just to see where it would fit. See where you'd have to go emotionally for that to work. People would always tell me about minor chords: when you're writing a song, to put a minor chord in. For me, it's like doom, you know. You know somebody's gonna be extremely sick or die if there's a character in the song. If it's a first-person narrative, that you're gonna go off to war or something. [*Laughs*] Something bad is gonna happen when the minor chord hits.

That's funny, 'cause throughout all your songs there's hardly one written in a minor key. They almost always start with a major chord.

I wrote in a minor key a couple of times over the years. Mainly just to experiment. Because I always felt that if you start something in a minor key, then you're already down in the mine. [*Laughs*] You don't have to go to the mines; you're already there. [*Laughter*] Because you're in the minor chords.

Do you remember what your first three chords you learned were?

Probably G, C, D. It may have been A, D, E because they're easier. I shied away from B7 for a long time because it took too many fingers. [*Laughs*]

"Hello in There" has that C major 7 chord in it and has more chords than you ever use.

I remember specifically when I wrote it, I think I had learned recently "Nobody Knows You When You're Down and Out." It had about nine chords to it. I learned the song more or less as a lesson so that I could sing and change chords quickly at the same time. And once I did that, I thought, "Gee, I'm gonna write a song with every chord in it I know." And that's "Hello in There." And I'm still surprised to this day that the chords came out that well and sound as pretty as they do.

"Hello in There" is about old folks, yet you wrote it as a young man with a lot of insight into what it's like to be old. Do you remember where it came from?

I just always felt, even when I was a young child, I felt really close to my grandparents. And later when I was a teenager I just felt like a kinship with older people. And I remember for a short time I had a best friend when I was about eleven, he had a paper route, and he'd give me a couple bucks to help him with the route. And one of the streets I had had the Baptist old people's home on it. And you'd have to park your bike and go inside with about twenty papers to the room where the people subscribed to the paper. And some of the people, I guess, they didn't have many visitors. And to their other friends in the home you were like a nephew or a grandson. I picked up on that and it always stuck in my mind. I guess that's what it's like inside of any kind of institution.

Just the title, "Hello in There," is so evocative, as it implies that the person is deep inside himself, hard to reach.

I do vaguely remember that I tied it somehow to the first time I heard John Lennon sing "Across the Universe." He was already putting a lot of echo on his voice on different songs, you know, experimenting with his voice. I played that song over and over again, and it sounded to me like somebody talking to a hollow log or a lead pipe. With that echo. And I was thinking of reaching somebody, communicating with somebody, like "hello . . . hello in there . . ." You know? When I was writing the song I thought that these people have entire lives in there. They're not writers, but they all have stories to tell. Some are very, very down deeper than others. See, you gotta *dig*, you know? And that was all going through my mind when I wrote "Hello in There."

I didn't know what the song was gonna be about, actually, when I came up with "Hello in There." I knew it was gonna be about loneliness and isolation. I was still very much into using names [in songs]. I was a big fan of Bob Dylan early on, and his song "The Lonesome Death of Hattie Carroll" was a big model for me. I modeled "Donald and Lydia" after that song. As far as telling a story and having the chorus be the moral to the story, a wider moral than what the story's saying, like where the chorus is all-consuming and a much bigger subject than what you're detailing. Yeah, that was much in the same way that any upbeat song I modeled after Chuck Berry, I modeled a ballad after specific songs, and that song of Bob Dylan's, "The Lonesome Death of Hattie Carroll," to me was to be held up as a real model for songs, as was a lot of Hank Williams Sr. songs.

It's surprising to me to hear the influence of Lennon and also Dylan to some extent, in that many of their songs were quite poetically abstract and surreal, whereas your songs tell clear stories with precise imagery.

Yeah. I don't know how I made that decision. It's what I was good at, but I might have thought it was a fault at first. I might have thought I used too many words to discuss a minor detail. But I soon found out that the reason that was on my mind is because that's what I wanted to hear. I wanted to hear what was in somebody's purse. I wanted to hear that at the time of this emotional thing. I wanted to hear what paintings were hanging on the wall. I wanted to know whether it was a cheap refrigerator. [*Laughs*] I just did. It was kind of detective work.

You've always been one of the best at using pictures as symbols, like the old trees that just grow stronger in "Hello in There," or the rodeo poster in "Angel from Montgomery."

[*Pause*] Yeah. I'm not sure where that came from. But I'm glad it did.

Was "Angel from Montgomery" also one you wrote during your postman years?

Yeah. That was almost a cowrite. With a guy named Eddie Holstein.

I knew Eddie. And his brother Fred.

God, sure. I knew Fred since I was fourteen and was first going to the Old Town School, Fred used to work part time in the store. Every time I wrote a song Fred would turn on his really good high-class tape recorder, reel-to-reel, and record it. So he's got recordings of me on guitar singing all my songs in his apartment long before I ever recorded for a recording company. I never found out what happened to the tapes.

But Eddie and me, we used to go to lunch together because I used to like to watch Eddie eat. He'd eat for hours. And he was just a little skinny guy then, and you'd wonder where the food was.

Eddie said, "Why don't we write a song together?" And I said, "Jeez, I've never written with anybody. But I guess we could try."

So we went over to his apartment, and I said, "What do you want to write about?" And he said, "I really like that song you wrote about old people. Let's write another song about old people."

I said, [*laughs*] "I can't, Eddie. I said everything I wanted to in 'Hello in There.' I can't do it."

So I thought for a while and said, "How 'bout a song about a middle-aged woman who feels older than she is?"

And Eddie goes, "Naw." [*Much laughter*]

But the idea stuck with me, and when I went home I started "Angel from Montgomery" that night. With the words "I am an old woman named after my mother." I had this *really* vivid picture of this woman standing over the dishwater with soap in her hands and just walking away from it all. So I just kept that whole idea image in mind when I was writing the song, and I just let it pour out of that character's heart.

That song was like a lesson for so many of us songwriters about how to write in character. I can remember hearing the song the first time with that opening, "I am an old woman," and thinking what an extraordinary way to start a song, especially written by a man.

Again, I didn't realize all this at the time, but if you come up with a strong enough character, you can get a really vivid insight into the character that you've invented. You let the character write the song. You just dictate from then on. You stick to it, and whatever the character is saying, you have to figure out how to keep that in the song, you know? That's how I do it. I almost go into a trance. Once I've got an outline, a sketch in my mind, of who the person was, then I figure I'd better let them speak for themselves. Rather than me saying, "Hey, so here's a middle-aged woman. She feels she's much older." It wouldn't have been nearly as effective.

I got asked years later lots of times how I felt I could get away with writing a woman's song first-person. And that never *occurred* to me because I already considered myself a writer. And writers are any gender you want. You write from the character, and how can you go wrong?

But there aren't a lot of songwriters, outside of Broadway, who write effectively in character. You do it, and Randy Newman does—

I love the way Randy does it. The character stuff, so determined that they believe what they're saying. I got to tour with Randy a lot early on. We did a lot of shows together, just him on piano and me on guitar.

You're similar not only that you're great at character songs but also can be funny in songs, which isn't easy. You're both very serious and very funny.

Yeah. For me, I find humor in just about every situation. Even the most serious situations. And I find if you use it right, it allows the listener not to feel so uncomfortable. Or to even empathize with that character.

With "Angel from Montgomery" do you remember where the title came from or why you placed it in Montgomery?

No, I can only guess like other people. I'm so far away from myself. I'm removed when I'm writing.

Eddie always kidded around and told people, "Yeah, I wrote half of that, and John just bought me lunch." [*Laughter*]

Eddie thinks I got it from the angel down on Michigan Boulevard [in Chicago]. There was evidently a gargoyle that came out from the Montgomery Ward building. But I'm prone to think that it's because I was a huge Hank Williams Sr. fan and I knew he was from Montgomery. And I think that's where I thought the woman was from in this image that I had, this woman with the soapsuds on her hand. She lived in Montgomery, Alabama, and she wanted to get out of there. She wanted to get out of her house and her marriage and everything. She just wanted an angel to come to take her away from all this. And her memory of this cowboy she had once—or whether she had him or not—it doesn't matter now.

Yeah, you're not only in her real life, but in her dreams, in what she's yearning for.

Yeah. Man, they did a book of the famous poster people here in Nashville, the ones who did those giant posters of Hank Williams and the Grand Ole Opry and everything. They're still going today with the original presses. It's a great place to go. It's not far from the Ryman Auditorium. They put a book out of their famous posters. And the poster on the cover is a poster of a rodeo, a guy with a bucking bronco, and it's got the words to the beginning of "Angel from Montgomery" on it. And it's a really good-looking poster. I asked them to give me a copy of it. It looked very much like whatever I had in mind when I wrote it.

I remember as a kid listening to that song and learning so much about how you set the mood—instead of saying she's bored, you say, "There's flies in the kitchen / I can hear 'em there buzzin' / And I ain't done nothin' since I woke up today . . ."

I think the more the listener can contribute to the song, the better. The more they become part of the song and they fill in the blanks. Rather than *tell* them everything, you save your details for things that exist. Like what color the ashtray is. How far away the doorway was. So when you're talking about intangible things, like emotions, the listener can fill in the blanks and you just draw the foundation. I still tend to believe that's the way to tackle it today.

Whenever I cowrite with people—and it's very difficult to dodge co-writing in Nashville [*laughs*]—I tell people I'm just trying to write with myself right now, and it's very difficult to jump back and forth between the two. Because I enjoy cowriting when it's with the right person. I can go into a different head with a cowriter. Let them take the song on, and I'm just helping them with their idea. But if I'm gonna write my idea, I want to stick with it myself. I usually won't be the one to initiate a cowrite.

The old cliché for writers is "write what you know." Yet you seem to reach beyond your own personal experience often. A song like "Sam Stone," about a man who comes back from Vietnam a junkie—is that someone you knew?

Well, I had just gotten out of the service myself. I got drafted with about six of my best friends, and some of them got sent to Vietnam. Everyone I knew, they got back, they came back. I knew two kids I went to school with who didn't come back from Vietnam. In fact, they didn't last a week there. But my own personal friends, they all came back. But there were big changes in their lives. And there are still to this day.

I remember when they first came back, whenever it seemed appropriate, I would question them about how it was there. I pretty much got the same story from everybody, that it was pretty much a wait-and-see situation over there. You could be in a place in Vietnam where there seemingly wasn't much action; you weren't anywhere near the front. But it soon became evident that there was no front. There was always a front as far as if we made an invasion or they did and there was a battle going on, there was that. But the whole place was the front. You could be walking over to the officer's club for a drink some night and step on a mine. Or nothing would happen for six months, there wouldn't be a sound, and all of sudden you'd be walking around and they'd come over and bomb. And that kept you on edge, I guess, all the time.

I always thought one of the great mistakes they made in the service, I don't know if they even tried to correct it with the guys coming back from the Middle East, but if they spent half the time that they do getting you ready and the intensity that they put you through in basic training for combat, if they spent half that time bringing you down and teaching you how to be a civilian, it would make a big difference. I would liken it to a person who has done prison time. They all speak of, especially if they've been in for a very long time, of how difficult it is to be back on the street. And how difficult it is to accept freedom once you get used to living incarcerated. So all my friends that were over there were affected, like I said. I wasn't writing about anybody specific. I made up the character of Sam Stone, obviously, just 'cause he rhymed with "home."

But I remember a story in the papers about some soldiers coming home from Vietnam, in San Francisco they landed. And some people at the airport—I don't know if they were protesters or hippies or what—but they were spitting on them. Saying they shouldn't be over there killing babies and stuff. And I was totally repulsed by that. And here, mainly, I was against the war, and I was for all the hippies and didn't mind burning the flag and stuff, you know? [*Laughs*] I mean, to blame a soldier—maybe because I was one—I felt like, "Gee, you don't know what you're talking about. To blame the guys who are going over there. Because they didn't run to Canada and say they're not gonna fight for their country." But that just seemed really awkward and stupid to me.

So I wanted to explain through a fictional character what it might be like to come home. Not to be there, because I was never in Vietnam. I was stationed in Germany. And I was drafted at a time when most people were being sent to Vietnam, and I thought I was going there for sure. But when the day came that they gave me orders to go overseas, I was thankful for it. Whereas other guys who got sent to Germany, as soon as they got there, they put in for Vietnam. They didn't want to be in Germany; they wanted to be in combat. And I'd just say, [*laughs*] "You guys are *nuts.*" [*Laughs*] It's not John Wayne time.

I had my guitar over there, though I didn't do much writing. I was about three bunks down from a guy who sang beautiful Lefty Frizell songs. He could sing just like Lefty. And he and I became fast friends. I sang Hank Williams songs and he sang Lefty songs. I think "Aw Heck" might have been the only song I wrote while I was over there.

Songs like "Sam Stone" and "Angel from Montgomery" are such mature, sophisticated songs for a beginning songwriter to write. Any idea how you were able to write at that level so early on?

No, I don't. I was very nervous about singing the songs in public for the first time. Because I thought that they would come across as too detailed, too amateurish. Because I hadn't heard anybody being that detailed. And I thought there must be a reason for that. I must not be doing it the right way, whatever the right way is. But I knew the songs were very effective to me. And they reached me. And I was very satisfied with the songs. But I didn't know how they would relate to other people because I didn't consider myself a normal person. [*Laughter*]

Did audiences take to them right away?

Right away. They were very effective. The first crowd just sat there. They didn't even applaud, they just *looked* at me. I thought, "Uh-oh." [*Laughs*] I thought, "This is pretty bad." I started shuffling my feet and looking around. And then they started applauding, and it was a really great feeling. It was like I found out all of a sudden that I could communicate. That I could communicate really deep feelings and emotions. And to find that out all at once was amazing. Whereas it would have been different if I would have written a novel or something and waited two years for somebody to write me back and said, "I think we're gonna take a chance and publish it." That must be a whole different feeling. But mine was *immediate*. It was there before other people. Nobody knew me from Adam.

Do you remember the first song you wrote?

Yeah. I think I wrote two at the same time. I had a girlfriend whose father was a janitor. And the reason I'm telling you that is because he had access to a tape recorder, and nobody else I knew had one. They were really rare. A reel-to-reel. He got it from the language department. It was broken, and he fixed it and had it at home. And I sat down and taped three songs for this girl and her sister. And the three songs were "Frying Pan," "Sour Grapes," and "Twist and Shout." And I know I didn't write "Twist and Shout." [*Laughter*] Those were the three, and I made her a present of them.

Years later I ended up marrying that girl. She was my first wife. She found the tape. It was after I had made the first album, so I put two of those songs on *Diamonds in the Rough*. And those were the first songs I remember writing.

You said you wrote "Sam Stone" and "Hello in There" when you were working as a mailman—

Yeah. That was only six months before I first got up and sang, and six months after that I got a record contract.

When you started writing those songs was your intention to become a professional musician?

No, because I didn't think that kind of thing happened to people like me. [*Laughs*] I thought that people that you heard records by were from a whole 'nother world. No matter what their biography says, they're either French or from Britain or had rich relatives. [*Laughter*] And therefore I wrote the songs more for myself.

I was surprised that the songs connected as well as they did when I first sang them for an audience. I think I was more surprised than the audience. I just got the nerve up behind a couple beers one night to stand up onstage—'cause it was an open mic—and the competition, the bar, was very low.

Which club was it?

The Fifth Peg, which was across the street from the Old Town School when it used to be on West Armitage. Before that it was on North Avenue. And there was always a club that the people from the Old Town School frequented. When they were on North Avenue it used to be the Saddle Club. Which was a couple of blocks from the Earl. And when they moved over to Armitage, this club, the Fifth Peg, opened up across the street and featured folk music, and that would be the club where the people would gather after the classes. But the link was always the Old Town School.

So becoming a performer was not something you had considered—

Right. I was writing these songs totally myself not thinking that anybody was going to hear them. And I went from that to being a very nervous public performer. Who had no voice whatsoever. I would kind of speak the words. Very fast or very slow, depending on how the melody went. And I'd hold certain notes [*laughs*] to let people know I was going to the next idea. And that's about how limited it was. It was very painful for me to stand up in front of people and sing.

Meanwhile I enjoyed singing. I would sit for hours just by myself and just bellow out and beat on the guitar. I loved the actual act of singing. But to listen to myself on tape or to sing for other people was really painful. And the first time people heard me, [*laughs*] evidently they felt the same.

Steve Goodman was such an astounding performer—

He certainly was. I think Steve had arrived, except for timing. He really worked hard, and he was entertaining. He and another friend who played piano for me had an act before Steve was a single act. It was almost like Chad Mitchell Trio stuff. Steve did everybody else's songs before he ever wrote "City of New Orleans." I read the entire Clay Eals book [*Steve Goodman: Facing the Music*], so I should know.

I did as well. Clay's a good guy, and that's a wonderful book.

No kidding, man. The amount of people he interviewed for that book was amazing.

Yeah. He did Steve justice.

He sure did.

Did you learn much about performing from watching Steve play?

[*Pause*] Jeez, the way he handled an audience, you couldn't help but pick up things. I might not have thought about it like that at the time. I developed my own thing from my own mistakes. What I considered my mistakes. My own nervousness. I made it an asset. That's how I started talking between songs. And I found out that people liked the stories I was telling—they were just totally out of pure nervousness: I was trying to kill time till I had to start singing [*laughs*] those painful notes again. I put the two together—the talking and the singing—and noticed that worked.

You just find out things from your own shortcomings. It's easy to say in hindsight, of course, and I never would have said this at the time, I didn't think so, but that's what I did—I gathered all my shortcomings and made them into the stronger points, you know, the points I could stretch 'cause they worked. You find out real fast when you stand just in front of twelve people what's working or not. Sometimes it's just the way you present it that makes it not work. It's got nothing to do with the material.

Do you generally have an idea in mind before you start writing a song?

Yes. Because otherwise I don't see any reason in sitting down [*laughs*] to do it. A lot of time I'll have the song written, and I only write it down so I don't forget it. I could write behind a steel mill. But it's easier to get behind a guitar.

You said that sometimes when writing it feels like a trance. Do you have experience of lines just coming to you, almost from beyond?

Yes. Sometimes they come so easily that you check yourself, you know? And the more you travel, the more I've been around music—like when you've been around forty years around other songwriters' music constantly. I go down to the grocery store and people drop CDs in my pocket. And so when I do get something, I got to check and make sure I didn't hear that somewhere. And when I'm sure, I proceed, and I take whatever the image or the line is, I take that and I don't try to fix it. I check it like a diving board, you know? And it's like I'm gonna go swimming in their pool today.

Is it easy for you to get to that place where songs start coming?

No. It's very elusive. Patience. You gotta learn patience. I know that I'm basically a very lazy person. At everything, including writing. As much as I enjoy writing, I would rather do anything in the world but sit down and write. But once I get into it, I'm into it. I mean, if you said, "Let's go get a hot dog first," I would always go for the hot dog. I wouldn't go, "No, let's finish this song." [*Laughter*] I'd say, "Sure!" [*Laughter*] And I know that about myself. So I have to balance out my patience waiting for the right thing to come along with my laziness, knowing I'm trying to avoid working.

So you never force yourself to write—

No. [*Laughs*] No. Unfortunately a lot of your best first-person songs come from a person's relationship, from something awful happening, like in your life, to someone you love very much. So you wouldn't want to force those things. Not for the purpose of a good song. Some guys I've met, I wouldn't put anything past them. [*Laughs*] Some people, for a good song, might go through all kinds of changes to get to that.

Your songs seem to suggest you are having fun writing them, with the rhymes and the rhythms—

Once I get into it. And I almost need, not someone standing over me—I do need some prodding. I have to realize, "Jeez, okay, it's been long enough without a record." Because I can afford just to go play my songs for big crowds. I play in some of the nicest places in this country. And they got nice dressing rooms. I've moved up to where the dressing rooms actually don't have rats running around in them. It'd be very easy to just keep doing that. But every once in a while I've got to write and get myself into a fresh state of mind. And I have to look forward, 'cause I know it's gonna take a couple of years to process.

I don't write ten songs in two weeks and go into the studio. I just don't do that. I'll write three songs and love them, and I'll go sing them for a year and then write the next three. I just know how I am. Like I say, there's nobody standing over me. I've got my own record company, my own publishing. I try and make a place for myself to write that I want to go to.

Having written such amazing songs right from the start, was there a sense after your first album that you had a lot to live up to?

Only after so many people told me that so many times. [*Laughter*] And then I got to remember that the gift I have, I only owe it to myself to honor that gift. I don't have to compete against myself. Because that's crazy. Why try to write a better song about old people or a better song about a veteran coming home? Why try to update "Sam Stone"? There's no reason to. So I try and stay true to wherever the writing comes from. And it comes from the deepest well of emotion. Whether it's something political, something humorous, something that might break your heart—if that's what's down in the well, that's what I'll come up with.

You said you write songs in your car. Do you mean that you write music too, or just words when you're away from the guitar?

To me the melody usually comes along hand in hand with the words. It's very rare that I'll get a little piece of music that I keep playing over and over, like something I'll do at a sound check that I can't get rid of. And in order to get rid of it, I'll write a song to it. But usually they start with the idea or the image, and I want to say one thing. Just one sentence. And I'll figure out who would say that and how can I build a song on that.

Do you collect titles and think of titles before writing?

No, but funny enough, when I first started cowriting, at first I only wrote with really close friends who also happened to be songwriters. Just because I knew I liked spending time with that person, so I didn't really care if I came out with a song or not. As long as we had a good time together.

One of the first people that I wrote with when I first moved to Nashville was somebody I didn't know but I just wrote with because of all the great songs that they'd written, Bobby Braddock. He wrote "We're Not the Jet Set" and "He Stopped Loving Her Today."

So when Bobby and I got ready to write, we wrote "Unwed Fathers." The night before we got together I said, "Do you like to start any particular way, Bobby?"

And he goes, "You know, if you feel like it, bring a little list of song titles. Just as a way to get started. We can go, 'Naaaah . . .' [*Laughs*] And that must mean we got a better idea."

I was watching the Super Bowl and I wrote down twenty titles. And I used five of those titles in the song. I used the title "Children Having Children." And I pulled different ones I liked to go with that subject that I liked of "Unwed Fathers." Sometimes there's not titles; they're just random thoughts you can associate with something else. I don't like to waste paper. [*Laughter*] I don't like to write and throw it away. I don't like starting over. Usually I write because it's already kind of written in my mind. I may not know the words, I may not know the character's name, I may not know any of that, but like I say, I get the picture. It's a matter of me transferring it to paper.

You said it almost feels like it's dictated to you from somewhere else? Any idea where that is?

No. None. I don't know what the rules are. I don't know if I ever cheated at the game. I don't like to get so close to it. Every once in a while it's safer to go for a hot dog. [*Laughs*]

Some of the songs come so fully, it's like they're prepackaged. There have been a couple that came in the middle of the night. And I thought, "Jeez, I'll never forget *that*" and went back to sleep and it was gone. You'll hear something years later that another songwriter that you respect writes, and you go, "Jeez, I think that was the remnants of that song that got sent to me."

Your songs seem so distinctive to you. Do you think someone else could pick up one of your songs?

Just the basic part. Like I'm saying, I get the picture and the emotion. And if you don't grab that and pull it down and start drawing your drawing so you can show it to somebody else to see if they can recognize it, you can lose it. That's why I say it's like taking dictation. But like I say, where it comes from, I don't know and I don't care. [*Laughs*] I don't care.

Many songwriters feel that songwriting is more a sense of following a song than leading it—

Exactly. Because if you approach it the other way, it seems that you are outguessing it. Like people who are trying to write hit songs are guessing what the public wants. Or, worse, what the record executive wants.

One of your most beautiful and poignant songs is "Souvenirs."

I wrote that in my car. A '65 Chevelle. Driving to the Fifth Peg. Like the fifth or sixth time playing there. I used to play there just Thursdays after they hired me. They hired me from that open stage the very first time I sang for the crowd. They invited me back a week later, and I did it again for an open stage. And that night the owner asked me if I wanted to sing once a week. I didn't know I was auditioning. I didn't know what to do, how long you're supposed to sing or anything. So I went home and wrote a bunch of songs to fill in the time. They told me to do three sets of forty-five minutes. So about the fifth time I was driving down there I thought, "God, the same people are gonna be sitting there. I better have a new song." So I wrote "Souvenirs" in the car on the way down. And then I thought I'd come up with a melody. And I thought I had come up with a pretty sophisticated melody in my head, and I was surprised to find out it had the same three chords that all my other songs have. [*Laughter*] Really surprised. I thought I had written a jazz melody.

You've written several songs like that one, really poignant songs about time passing and what we lose in time—

Yeah. Where any of that song came from, I have no idea what the start was.

Was there someone in mind you wrote it to?

I have three brothers—two older, one younger. And one of them was asking me about "Souvenirs" once. He was five years older than me, and I remember once we were at a carnival and we were very small, and he got lost for a while, and I got very, very scared that I would never see my brother. I remember that. It was a different kind of scared than I had ever experienced before in my life, like being scared by ghosts or creepy stuff. And I kept that emotion buried somewhere, and it came out in "Souvenirs." How, I don't know.

I told him, "I remember you standing there holding a little plastic horse that you either won or somebody gave you. I put it all together in a picture, and that's what came out."

Is it true that "Bruised Orange" is a title you had long before you wrote the song? You also named your publishing company that.

Yes. When I was still a mailman I had about eight songs, and somebody told me if I wanted to sing them in public, I should think about copyrighting them. And another fella told me that if I just copyrighted them all under one title, as a musical, then I could do it all for five dollars instead of five dollars per song.

So I found this music professor from Northwestern, and he would make the sheet music for a couple bucks per song. He'd write it out in music, and I'd include a cassette and lyric sheet and mail it to myself, get it postmarked, and that was considered a legal copyright. I put it all under the name "Bruised Orange." [*Laughs*] Which I used many years later. That's what I called the imaginary musical. They were all songs like "Sam Stone," "Blow Up Your TV," "Paradise." I had them all under one title. I found it not too long ago, the envelope. I finally opened it. I had to. [*Laughs*] I figured it was safe to do now. [*Laughter*].

I thought, "Jeez, I'm supposed to come up with a title for my musical." And I thought, "I'll just pretend." 'Cause I knew I could put all the songs under one name. Later somebody explained to me that all they do is give you a number. You could write "White Christmas," and they just give you a number. I thought when you sent in a song to the government to be copyrighted that there'd be a thousand guys with a thousand pianos in a warehouse [*laughs*] and they'd play about eight notes of your song and go, "Sorry, man. That's 'Your Cheatin' Heart'" [*Laughter*] and then stamp it "reject." But when I found out you could put them all as a musical, and [Bruised Orange] was just a name I came up with off the top of my head.

I listened to the song "Bruised Orange" last night and realized that someone might normally call it "Chain of Sorrow," as that's the most prevalent line. How come you chose that title for that song?

I liked the title and the image, and I wanted to do something with that image without saying anything about an orange or a bruise in the song.

It was based upon something that actually happened. I was an altar boy, and the Northwestern train tracks were not far from the church that I went to. I was going down there one day, and there was this big ruckus going on at the train tracks. I had to go shovel the snow off the church steps before Mass. Because they'd sue the church if people fell and broke their legs.

So I was going down there to get the snow and ice off. I went over to the train tracks. A kid who had also been an altar boy at the Catholic Church, I found out later, was walking down the train tracks. And evidently the commuter train came up behind him. They were taking him away in bushel baskets—there was nothing left of him. There were a bunch of mothers standing around, trying to figure out—'cause it was Sunday morning and all their kids were gone and they didn't know—they all hadn't located their children yet, and they didn't know who it was.

I told that story on TV once—I was asked about that song when it first came out. And the family of that son lived near Madison, Wisconsin, years and years later—twenty years later—just wrote me the nicest letter and told me they recognized the subject. They gave me the date of when it happened and that would have been around the time when it happened. And so it was just a vivid memory that I had, and I put it together with how I felt about my job as an altar boy. I was supposed to be the maintenance man at church, and they were short an altar boy. They baptized me and confirmed me on a Saturday, and Sunday I was wearing a robe, lighting a candle. Then I had to go early and shovel the snow as a maintenance man or cut the lawn in the summertime. And that's when I bought my first guitar.

Listening to your songs, including great early ones like "Sabu Visits the Twin Cities," it's evident that you can write about anything in songs, using content nobody else ever has. Was that something you felt?

[*Softly*] Yeah. [*Laughs*] Definitely. [*Laughs*] If I could get away with the song about the veteran coming home and a chorus like "there's a hole in Daddy's arm where all the money goes," even as powerful as it turned out to be, that I could write anything. But when I wrote it, it was very *odd*. When I'd sing that chorus, I'd be nervous, and by the second time around there'd be dead silence. And I just figured, "Yeah, you can

write about anything. Anything at all." As a matter of fact, the less familiar, the better.

**Many songwriters feel you have to write about yourself. Yet you've
shown that isn't the case—unless you feel you're writing about yourself
all the time?**

There's a certain amount of yourself in it, I'm sure. But as a writer
you don't need to be writing about yourself all the time. Maybe you're not
that interesting, really. Without an outside thing.

**Was there ever content or an idea for a song you couldn't get into a
song, that wouldn't work?**

Yeah, definitely. More often than not I can't jump into a song too
quick. Because there's always the danger of painting yourself into a corner. There's no tougher corners to get out of than the ones that you paint.
Because you can't change the rules if you made up the rules. And then
you get to the third verse that needs to be there, and you can't define that
line where you can just repeat the first verse. You can't get out of it that
way—so how are you going to get out of it? Especially if it's a story song.
You'd better be going somewhere. [*Laughs*] I think that's what the listeners are always thinking, that "Hey, this is precious time I'm giving you,
so you'd better be going somewhere. [*Laughs*] This joke better be funny."

Do you generally write more and then cut stuff out?

No. I edit as I go. Especially when I go to commit it to paper. I prefer
a typewriter even to a computer. I don't like it—there's no noise on the
computer. I like a typewriter because I am such a slow typist, I edit as I am
committing it to paper. I like to see the words before me, and I go, "Yeah,
that's it." They appear before me, and they fit, you know, and I can see that
the line fits with the previous line and the line after it. I can see the inside
of the song as well, not just rhyming the last word so that the song sounds
right. I pretty much do that as I go. I don't usually take large parts out. If
I get stuck early in a song, I would take it as a sign that I might be writing
the chorus and don't know it. Sometimes you're writing the first verse or
second verse and you're actually writing what you want to repeat. And you
gotta step back a little bit and take a look at what you're doing.

Do you write a song from beginning to end?

I guess now I do. I'm not sure if I always did that. Sometimes I feel it
from the middle out. Where I realize that perhaps I wasn't starting at the
beginning. I just start with a character and I have to develop it more, so I
have to go back and write a first verse or an introduction.

You said that in "Hello in There" you used all the chords you knew at the time. Have you ever done that with other songs?

Yeah, I still haven't used that many. I think when I wrote "Storm Windows" somebody had just taught me the Elvis Presley song "That's When Heartaches Begin." And it had a C minor chord. And I really wanted to learn the song, so I learned a C minor. And I know how that chord feels. It's the one chord that with a G, I know how it feels, what the emotions are there. So I felt I wanted to write a song that goes there and gets out of it, and that was "Storm Windows."

When you're at the typewriter working, do you use your guitar?

Sometimes. And sometimes when the melody is so apparent I can just sit with just the words.

Do you remember where the idea of writing "Sabu," a song about the famous elephant boy, where that came from?

I know it was from somewhere else. Because it took me several weeks before I would play it for anybody. And the whole song came at once, just like it is, fully written. [*Laughs*] I didn't know whether to show it to anybody or what, whether it was an ugly baby or what.

Being from Chicago, I always loved that line about "the land of the wind chill factor."

[*Laughs*] Me too. I know what gets me and I know what I like, and usually in the end I've got to go with that.

We were talking about funny songs, and there aren't really that many funny songs that work over many years. The joke wears out. But your funny ones are still funny. Is that hard to do?

I never know until the years pass. [*Laughs*] I'm surprised as anybody. I pulled the song "Your Flag Decal Won't Get You into Heaven Anymore" out of mothballs. I stopped singing that when most of the thing with Vietnam was over. People asked me about it after we were in Iraq. I thought that if George Bush kept tinkering so much about patriotism, that if you talked out against that war, you definitely were a Lefty. When he started with that bullshit, it really got under my skin. So I thought one night I would pull that song back out and start singing it again. I had no idea if it would work as well. And it felt really good too.

I have a lot of songs I haven't touched in years. I need to be prodded to bring them out. I only have to play them once or twice to see if they work. It's not even so much the crowd reaction; it's more how I feel when

I'm singing the song. I can just tell if I stopped singing that for a reason. Maybe I'll feel that I didn't get everything right in that or everything I could have. 'Cause I'll never go back and change a song. I just feel that would violate it. But I've had an amazing track record of my stuff working—at least for me. Not only do I not get sick of it, but still for a large part I appreciate it.

We were talking about "Souvenirs," and you said Steve Goodman used to play on that song and—

Yeah, I can still hear him playing it. He played a back melody so that you could *barely* hear the difference of who was playing. On tape or when we did it live. And I realized a large part of what he was doing was making it sound like I was playing the good part. [*Laughs*] And that's basically the kind of guy he was. The kind of guy who wouldn't need to shine the light on him, even though he could ham it up with the best of them.

He produced your *Bruised Orange* album. What was that like to have him produce?

He was definitely doing me a favor. I had made the record already, but I didn't have it. I worked with Cowboy Jack Clement, who was a huge mentor to me and the reason why I moved to Nashville. I moved there, and we worked for three to four months, solid. And through all kinds of outside forces and things that shouldn't have been going on in the studio, we didn't get the record that we were playing every day. We really enjoyed making the record, but we didn't get it on tape the way we were hearing it in the studio.

This was the first one I was doing for Asylum Records, and they kept spending money on it. And Jack was on Asylum as well, and his record was about two years late. [*Laughs*] So these were both of our first records on this label, and here we were working on mine. And we were having a great time. And listening to music too. It was a very musical summer we spent.

Then I got involved with somebody, and it got to be a very sticky affair. What I'm saying is that I had a record that I put my heart and soul into with the songs and gone ahead and made the record, and I didn't have anything to show for it. I had to walk away from the whole thing.

So I went out to LA, and I talked to, Christ, twenty different producers, really great guys, great producers. Big-time producers. And I just didn't want to do it. I just didn't have the heart to do the record again. And Goodman said he would do it. And I said, "Well, just don't look to me to approve or disapprove. I'm just totally . . . *numb*." I said I'd come in and do anything—you just tell me what songs to do today and I'll do it, and if you say it's done right, I'll believe you. I totally put it in his hands.

And he handed me back a beautiful record. So that's the way that one went down. It was no fun for Steve, I'm sure. I was not a fun guy to be around. [*Pause*] Anyway that's the name of that tune. [*Laughter*]

Funny how things turn out. Steve, he was a tough producer to work with.

How so?

Very stubborn. I think because he knew me so well. If someone doesn't know me, they kind of keep at a distance. Which is fine with me. [*Laughs*] But he knew me. So he would push me. Some nights at the studio I'd say, "Steve, get off my back, man." But he knew what he was going for.

Do you remember the first time you met him?

Yeah, I met him briefly the first time with Fred and Ed [Holstein]. He came to check me out. He didn't stay long enough to say hello after. They just kind of ducked in and ducked out and went back over to the Earl. And I started going over to the Earl to check it out on the nights I wasn't playing at the Peg.

Goodman came up to me one night, walked up to me—this is the first conversation we ever had at any length—they were already playing a tape on *The Midnight Special* [a beloved Chicago folk music radio show on WFMT], a cassette of Steve singing "City of New Orleans." From that night I had Goodman pictured in my mind as a tall, skinny banjo-playin' guy with a little beard. [*Laughs*] That's who I thought was playing "City of New Orleans." He was actually about all of five foot one. He'd poke you in the chest when you talked to him like Edgar G. Robinson. [*Laughter*]

As a kid I used to play the open mics at his club, Somebody Else's Troubles, and he'd walk in and just barely clear the bar—

Right. But onstage he was ten feet tall.

He could be a tough critic too. Once he heard one of my songs and he said, "That's good, but I could've written the whole thing in two lines."

[*Laughs*] Yeah.

Would he criticize your songs?

Yeah. The first time Kristofferson introduced Bob Dylan to Steve and me—this was back in the Village in Carly Simon's apartment, 1971—my first record wasn't coming out for a week. And Kristofferson said, "Come on over" and gave us Carly's address. Carly was opening for Kristofferson at the Bitter End. He said, "I got a surprise for you guys." So we come over and we're sitting in Carly's place, and there's a knock on the door, and in walks Bob Dylan. At this time Bob Dylan was not doing any shows—yet. It was after the motorcycle accident, years after, in the early seventies. He had just written "George Jackson." You familiar with that song? "Lord, Lord, they cut George Jackson down / Lord, Lord, they laid him in the ground."

So we're passing the guitar around. Kris sings one. I sing one. Bob takes the guitar and says he'd like to play something he just wrote, so he sings that. Goodman looks at him [*laughs*] and says, "That's great, Bob. It's no 'Masters of War,' though." [*Much laughter*] Man, I'll tell you. "It's no 'Masters of War.'" [*Laughs*]

And I sang "Far from Me," and Dylan sang with me. He had an advance copy of my record that Jerry Wexler had sent him. And he already knew a couple of the songs. So he showed up at the Bitter End and played harmonica behind me on "Donald and Lydia" and "Far from Me." It was like a dream.

So, yeah, that's Goodman criticizing. It wasn't just your song.

Another great song you wrote with previously untouched content is "Jesus the Missing Years."

I wrote that in a total state of inebriation. I was afraid to look at it for about a week. I knew I had written it, and I was totally surprised that it was as together as it was. I didn't change too much at all. I think I've still got the original transcript, if you wanna call it that. With arrows here and there moving lines around.

On the original record I went all around town trying to find the best recording of a lightning bolt. So I could start to sing with a big clap of thunder. I bought nature albums [*laughter*] with the sounds of rain and hurricane, till I finally found a clap of thunder. Put a bunch of echo on the voice just for the title where it goes "Jesus the Missing Years." Then I play, boom-boom-boom, and go into this talking thing. I think it was mostly about Hank Williams's "Luke the Drifter." I was just trying to emulate that, though I knew Hank Williams would never talk about Jesus that way.

You and Steve Goodman wrote the song "The Twentieth Century Is Almost Over" together—

Stevie actually had that. I thought it was a complete song. He just didn't have enough verses. I wrote a couple of verses. In other words, it was his baby, and he wanted to cut me in on it. He wanted me to help him with it, and I said, "Here" and came up with some fresh ideas. And next thing I know he's in the studio and he's got Pete Seeger singing. And it was the first time I had ever met Pete. He's really something, man.

I agree. Another unusual collaboration you did was with Phil Spector on "If You Don't Want My Love."

Right. The writer for the *LA Times*, Robert Hilburn, was trying to get together a book on Spector. He was interviewing him at length over a period of time. I came to town, and Hilburn was a big fan [of mine], and he would mention my name at the drop of a hat. I mean, if he was doing a Led Zeppelin review, he'd somehow fit my name into it, you know? I was amazed at how much press he'd give me.

I ran into him—I think it was when I was out there interviewing all those producers I told you about for *Bruised Orange* before I settled on Goodman. And I wasn't talking to Spector about producing, but Hilburn told me he was going out to his house a lot and said, "Would you like to come over? He likes your songs a lot, you know." I said, "Yeah." He said, "He's a big fan of 'Donald and Lydia'" and mentioned a couple of others. I said, "Yeah, I'd love to meet him."

Yeah, and you know, *wow*! He is *out* there. Met him a couple of times since then. And now this whole deal went down [Spector's trials for the death of Lana Clarkson], and I don't know, I'm surprised but I'm not.

Did you see the gun?

Oh yeah. He had the gun. He always had it. You'd always see it before the end of the evening.

How did you write a song together?

It happened on the way out the door. We'd been there for seven hours, jokin', drinkin'. And by the way, when you go in the house, he's got two bodyguards on his shoulder. It was just craziness, you know. This chick came down to say good night and he goes, "Who is the king of rock and roll?" And she said, "You are, Daddy, you are!" [*Laughs*] I'll never forget that.

So I was leaving around four in the morning, and all of a sudden Phil sits down at the piano as I was getting my jacket on and he hands me an electric guitar unplugged. And I sit down on the bench next to him. I played him "That's the Way the World Goes Round," and he really liked it.

He said, "Let's do this," and he played the beginning notes of "If You Don't Want My Love." And we came up with the first couple lines, and he insisted that we repeat them. Over and over. He said it would be very effective. And we took "That's the Way the World Goes Round" and took the melody and turned it inside out and used that as the basis of "If You Don't Want My Love." And he played it on piano, and I just strummed back on the guitar, and we just wrote the thing in less than an hour. And that was on my way out the door. And as soon as he sat down and had a musical instrument, he was normal.

That's the way he was. He was just a plain old genius. He'd just finished the Leonard Cohen album [*Death of a Ladies' Man*], and it hadn't been released yet. He played it for me in his billiard room and turned the speakers up so high that the balls vibrated across the table. And this is the Leonard Cohen album! [*Laughs*]

And I went back playing the song. Didn't know I would do it for the record, but I played it for Goodman, and he said, "You oughtta do that for the record. That's great." And I said, "But I don't know if it's done." He said, "It's done. Believe me. I'd tell ya if it wasn't."

So I cut it for *Bruised Orange*. Went back to his house after I cut the record to play it for him. Said he liked it. Said he would've produced it differently, but he liked it. [*Laughs*] I said, "You can take that up with Goodman sometime." [*Laughs*]

Do you remember where "The Late John Garfield Blues" came from?

It was originally called, on paper, "The Late Sunday Evening Early Monday Morning Blues." There was a sort of movie that you'd see on Sunday night that you would not see the rest of the nights of the week. And I believe it was on WGN. They'd show these old black-and-white flicks. And a lot of my favorite ones were John Garfield movies. I put the two together—the image of him and that kind of odd Sunday time, the Sunday funnies would be laying around and *Parade* magazine. Probably had a big dinner at some point. Your typical Sunday, which was not a typical day at all. It was always different. Lonelier than the other days. And there was the feeling that you had to go to school the next day or to work.

So late Sunday night would always be a different time to me. I wanted to try to pinpoint that, so I chose a John Garfield movie, and I didn't mention the movie at all, I just called it "The Late John Garfield Blues." There's an old Jimmie Rodgers melody-wise song that I was using. Just the chord change. "Treasures Untold." It's a really pretty ballad that he wrote. I learned that song early on, and I always wanted to use that G to the B7.

Do you have a favorite key?

G.

Yeah, you play a lot in G.

I can fingerpick really good in G. [*Laughs*] I can pick "The Star-Spangled Banner" in G. I can pick out just about anything I want in the key of G.

I've seen you play a lot in G but with a capo on.

I use the capo up and down the neck and play in G quite a bit. I only get out of it out of sheer boredom.

Do you use the capo while writing the song, or does that come later?

Usually later. No. When it's more comfortable to sing in a higher or lower key.

Do you feel different keys have different colors or moods?

Yeah. Definitely. It makes a big difference. After I had my throat surgery I had to drop the key on a lot of my older songs. And I was still singing them in the same key I wrote them in. My voice had changed anyway before the surgery. My voice was very nasal; my nose was a more comfortable place to sing out of than my throat. [*Laughter*] But my voice dropped quite a bit, and some of my songs, to me, just blossomed in the new key, and I got to actually enjoy them as if they were brand new. Which was a really amazing thing. I had no idea changing the key would make such a big difference.

Your song "Donald and Lydia" is your only one I know of which is really about two characters with separate stories who you then bring together. Did that come together naturally, or did you plot it out?

Well, like I say, my guide for the song was "Lonesome Death of Hattie Caroll." Just in terms of the character and what the character's doing. And then the chorus could be a moral for the whole thing. I had the characters in my mind, but I brought them together. Somewhere in boot camp I'd seen the character Donald. And in an Army town where I was stationed, I think Louisiana, I'd seen Lydia. And mostly they just formed together in my mind.

You're a writer who has written about loneliness effectively—

Yeah. And the more I sing about it, the more I realize I'm not the only one. [*Pause*] I think it's great therapy to sing about the stuff that's goin' on inside you. And other people say, "Gee, I didn't think anybody would ever write about that particular emotion." And they tell you that you nailed it right on the head. That's a really great feeling.

I think of your song "Speed of the Sound of Loneliness," which is kind of a later version of the same theme.

Yeah, that came out all at once. From a broken relationship I was in. I could not understand what went wrong, and I had to explain to myself, and I did it through this song. The next day I thought, "Jesus, that's beautiful." I didn't recognize it at the time—it was just pouring out of me.

Very cool title.

Yeah. Yeah, I really liked it. I guess it must have been a play on the words of "The Loneliness of the Long-Distance Runner." Probably. I'm guessing. [*Laughs*] When it was all said and done I don't know where it came from, but I'm thinking that's maybe that's where I got the idea to use "loneliness" like that. 'Cause it was a long title and kind of abstract, and I guess I'm attracted to stuff like that.

You've written a lot of songs out of heartbreak and turmoil. Can you write songs as well when you're happy and things are going well?

Yeah, but usually when you're happy you don't have time to write a song. 'Cause you're enjoying your life. But when you're not happy, you have *all the time in the world* to go and write a song.

◆◆◆

Michael Smith
Tulips Beneath the Snow

Chicago, Illinois 1992; Alta Dena, California 2013

When Amsterdam is golden in the morning
Margaret brings him breakfast
She believes him
He thinks the tulips bloom beneath the snow
He's mad as he can be but Margaret only sees that sometimes
Sometimes she sees her unborn children in his eyes

From "The Dutchman," Michael Smith

Hearing the songs of Michael Smith in this day and age is like reading a novel by Fitzgerald or Hemingway after a lifetime only of comic books. It's a realization that songs can hold a lot more than they're usually expected to hold, that they can possess a genuine sense of place and time as evocative and magical as the finest literature. He not only paints beautifully detailed images in his songs; he also suggests the emotions underneath that imagery—the tulips beneath the snow, the unborn children in the Dutchman's eyes. His songs are so resonant with layers of myth and magic and so perfectly enhanced by the genuine beauty of his melodies and instrumental arrangements that you can listen to a single one over and over for a whole day and feel happy. Each line and nuance of each of his songs is so completely realized and rendered that a day spent with only "Demon Lover," for example, would be a day well spent. As I know well.

In Chicago, where I'm from, Michael Smith has been a local hero for many years, ever since the late great Steve Goodman made him famous by recording—and beautifully interpreting—many of his songs. "The Dutchman" was the first one, the opening cut on Goodman's now-legendary second album, *Somebody Else's Troubles*.

Michael Smith's songs entranced Goodman the first time he heard them in a Miami club and began regularly attending his shows. Steve quickly memorized many of Michael's songs—though never perfectly, a characteristic we discuss in the following—and started adding them to his own repertoire and making them his own.

Besides "The Dutchman," he also recorded Michael's beautiful "Spoon River," inspired by the anthology of stories by Edgar Lee Masters. Also "The Ballad of Dan Moody," which unfolds like one of John Ford's great Westerns.

Goodman was one of the most emotionally committed performers ever to sing on stage. When he sang funny songs, as he often did, he was hilarious. When he played rock and roll, he was as exultant as Buddy Holly. And when he played one of Michael Smith's beautiful ballads, he would tear your heart out. I'll admit I idolized the guy. To this day he remains the greatest solo acoustic performer I have ever seen. And it was through Goodman that I came to Michael Smith.

"Spoon River," for example, opens a window into America just past the Civil War that is so real, it is haunting. His use of tender but historic details combined with melodies of great grace and beauty have led to successive masterpieces. To this day few other songwriters have reached the places he reached—and surpassed—in his songs.

All of the riverboat gamblers are losing their shirts
All of the brave Union soldier boys sleep in the dirt
But you know and I know there never was reason to hurt
When all of our lives were entwined to begin with
Here in Spoon River
("Spoon River," Michael Smith)

I started doing "Spoon River" myself in shows when I was a kid and have done it so many times for so many years, it feels as if I wrote it. And I wish I did. It is a perfect song. But many of his songs have that feeling—that they are so seamlessly conceived, so poignant and yet unforced, that there's just no doubt they are things of providence. Songs meant to be, without which the world would be a lesser place. John Prine's "Hello in There" is such a song, as is James Taylor's "Fire and Rain." "Spoon River" and "The Dutchman," along with many of Smith's songs, belong in this category.

Michael Smith was born and raised in South Orange, New Jersey, and went to high school in Little Falls, where the local references from "Demon Lover" originate. His first song was written in 1956, when he was fifteen. It was an imitation of the Everly Brothers and Harry Belafonte, he remembered, and was called "The Lonely One." "There wasn't too much to it, musically," he said. "It was basically C, A minor, F, G."

Two years later, when Smith was seventeen, his father committed suicide. Having to contain this tragedy while only a teen instilled a darkness in his psyche that might explain the emotional depth of his songs. "I've had some unsettling things happen to me in my life," he said, "so when it comes time to make art, I come at it from a strange angle. It's kind of like the oyster with the pearl."

He's lived in many places, from Florida to California, and presently resides in a Chicago apartment with his wife, the singer Barbara Barrow. He and Barbara were a team for many years and recorded albums together. On his own he's recorded several albums for Chicago's Flying Fish label. One of my favorite treasures is a combination of two of his albums, *Michael Smith* and *Love Stories*, which collects so many of these masterpieces, including "Panther in Michigan," a vivid and vital account of real darkness in the Midwest; "Three Monkeys," an excursion into the Tropic of Capricorn in which unmentioned evil is everywhere; "Loretta of the Rivers," a love song set on the line drawn between two worlds; and "Sister Clarissa," an evocation of a child's world embodied in the character of a nun we first see from the perspective of the child: "Sister Clarissa is eleven feet tall / Her rosary hangs and it clatters and it clangs . . ."

Another miraculous song that he wrote from the perspective of a child is "Crazy Mary," which Goodman often performed but didn't record but was beautifully recorded by Chicago legend Bonnie Koloc. Like "Sister Clarissa," it's about a real character from his past, which gives the song haunting resonance. It's also about the way we remember our lives.

This conversation combines two talks, the first from his home in Chicago, and the second in Alta Dena, California, where he came out to perform at the Coffee Gallery Backstage.

Was "The Dutchman" a story you thought about before writing it?

Michael Smith: No, it started with the first line: "The Dutchman's not the kind of man who keeps his thumb jammed in the dam that holds his dreams in." Those lines sounded so of a mood that it was a challenge to figure out where you would go to make it work. So then it was a question of making a second line and then sailing out into this story. I was in the middle of the song, not knowing what the ending would be. And I was conscious of trying to make a verse for the morning, a verse for the afternoon, and a verse for the evening.

Do you have any idea where the idea for the first line originated?

In school I had a friend who was Dutch. He lived down the street from me. I was sort of conscious of Dutchness. Other inspiration for it came from stories like "The Boy Who Held His Finger in the Dike." It was a traditional story from Holland. And when I started this song about my friend, I realized it was about that story. And I used my sister's name, Margaret. And when I worked on that part I realized it didn't sound like someone you went to high school with; it sounded like someone who is old and actually lives in Holland. So then I had to pursue it down that path.

So any song where you're winging it, if you start off a story interestingly, you have to justify it by finishing that story. And I read a lot of books by Jan de Hartog who wrote about Dutch tugboat captains during World War II. So I used things I remembered from his books, verbal pictures.

It's interesting that you can point to the source of so much of your work, whereas other songwriters say that their songs come from someplace that is beyond them.

The thing I think is beyond is the mood. The yearning to make "Loretta of the Rivers" or "The Dutchman" or "Spoon River" into something that would voice what I was feeling. It's feeling very dissatisfied that I haven't justified my visions well enough, so I have to make something that will work better than the ones before.

The mood is something I can't control. It's just nature. Human nature. God is expressing himself in my nature. Thank goodness I don't have control over that. Because I try, you know. It's a good thing that you can't give away your hearing because there are people who would be imploring you to do so. We don't have any say in how our natures are.

So we must trust that our nature is in line with what God has in mind. And I think the one that God loves, who is not conscious of himself, is the one who makes up the songs. And the one that's here and talking to you and being a conscious human, he only arranges for it. He gets determined about writing a song, but in truth, he's not doing anything. So clearly it's not up to you.

How conscious are you, while writing a song, of where you want it to go?

I'd say it's not where I want it to go at all; it's more a question of me coping with writing this line and where do I go now? In the interview you did with Dylan, he talked about getting himself into a puzzle and having to work his way out. You write one line. And that line forbids you from having anything but a certain second line.

Finally, say you've done four lines, you say to the song, "Can I go here?" And the song says yes or no. Though in truth it's you saying yes or no. It seems as if you take your cue from the song. It really is, with the songs that work, almost inevitable. If someone else was writing "Loretta of the Rivers" and the first line was "Living on the borderline," what is he going to do next? At that point he would diverge and go off into his own thing.

Like Dylan, you show a lot of respect for the craft of songwriting in that you use real rhymes and often intricate rhyme schemes.

I'm glad you picked up on that. I like doing that because I like discovering it in other people. And I do. Certainly with Dylan, he's always showing me things.

I think of it as an opportunity to show craft. Or an opportunity to jar people. One or the other. For me I prefer to show them the craft. People will consciously realize that it's wrapped up kind of neatly. If you didn't do it, they wouldn't get that. The great guys, the great ones, will do it with a flair.

It's like you're skipping across a stream on little rocks and it has to do with how you skip and what rocks you land on.

With "Loretta" I wanted to make a picture that was very moody, and I didn't want to put in anything that would not contribute to that mood.

"Demon Lover" is an amazing song. It succeeds in being completely real while being mythic at the same time, and the music is heartbreaking.

"The Demon Lover" legend is a traditional legend from the Middle Ages. There are old ballads called "Ballad of the Demon Lover." And there's one ballad called "The House Carpenter" that Joan Baez recorded. The premise is that a woman is engaged, her lover goes off to sea, and he's gone for seven years. By this time she's married and has three children, and a guy looking just like him returns. And her husband's away, and he says, "Will you forsake your children to come with me?" And she says, "Yes, I will."

He takes her out to his golden boat. And she notices getting on the boat that his feet are cloven hooves. And it's too late. He's got her and takes her down to hell in this boat. That's the "House Carpenter Ballad" because she was married to a house carpenter.

Then I read this wonderful book by Shirley Jackson called *Adventures of the Demon Lover*. I read this when I was about eighteen. And I wanted to do this ancient story in a modern setting. So I used things that were common to my New Jersey upbringing and used the name of a girl I knew in grade school, Agnes Hines. She was the first girl I knew whose father had died. I thought of her as being a tragic figure when I was about ten.

I worked on "Demon Lover" for a long, long time. I had the idea for a couple of years.

With that song, did you finish the words before writing the music?

I liked the idea of making the tune almost like jazz. I was trying to make something that sounded like Mel Torme. I figured that if I could make this tune that has major seventh chords in it that is talking about demons and people disappearing in the middle of the day, there will be a mood.

There's a reason why myths last for centuries. They give us a skeleton that we're not even aware of but is full of strength in its structure. Like fairy tales do that. Like the song "Down in the Willow Garden." "I put my sabre through her . . ." I would never think of anything like that. I am a suburban white guy in the twentieth century.

It's powerful to have an ancient story not only linked up to modern images but especially linked to that beautiful melody, which is modern but also haunting.

I realized I could do others that way. In a sense Dylan did that, specifically with the song "Seven Curses," which is an old story that he told in a new way.

"Demon Lover" is such a rich narrative that if you miss a single line, you miss out on the story. It's a rare example of a song that causes people to hang on every line.

That's wonderful. I love that. Because for me, that was my interest in folk music. Because you'd hear a song like "Bells of Rhymney" and you'd want to know what those lines meant. You could think about those lines.

The song leaves unanswered the question: Is the kid who returns and sweeps her off her feet the real kid or a demon disguised as the kid?

Here's what I think is going on in that tune: she wants him back so bad that she gave over the power in her life to some creation that only responded to desire. In a sense it was him, and in a sense it was a solidification of her dissatisfaction.

Have you done a lot of reading of myths in general?

Yeah, I read like a crazy person.

Do you read poetry?

Yes. I love Wallace Stevens. I like Yeats. And I think the verbal pictures in folk music are beautiful and powerful. You hear them and you can't help but be struck by their power and beauty so much that you want to write a song like that. "Loretta of the Rivers" was my attempt to write something that sounds like the beautiful Mexican mariachi tunes.

Also, I happened to meet someone whose name was Loretta Del Los Rios.

That's a gorgeous song. Was it one that you worked on for a long time?

I would say what was most of the work part was finding the guitar riff. And the words occurred to me to match the music. It was done without thinking. If I can persuade myself that this is just a little abstract project that I'm working on and not some song that had better be real good, then I'm better off.

For me the pleasure of writing a song is getting to hear it back. Not playing it. I love being an audience to my own songs.

I love the structure of the song, how the choruses connect with the verses.

Yeah, I think if you write songs a lot, there will be times when you're really possessed and you don't have any doubts. It becomes more like this is what I do and I'm doing it now, and I'm not a hero and I'm not a fool. I think "Loretta" is like that, and that's when they come out best.

It's funny to me that you mentioned thinking of the work as an abstract project like that. I know with my own songwriting that if I trick myself by thinking this is a song just for fun and not to be played for anybody that the best things can often come that way. I've written many songs that way, and I always fall for the trick.

[*Laughs*] Absolutely. Because there's a child inside you. And that child has to be very, very reassured before it can come out. And the world doesn't want the child to come out. The world wants you to pay the bills. That's what the world wants. I know that I'm so aware of money that it drives me crazy sometimes. The only problem with being poor is that you have to think about it so much. So for me, the child hides when the bill collector comes to the door. The child says, "You have to go out and get a job and feed me. Don't worry about getting any songs." And my life is a process of reassuring the child that it's okay to come out.

If you're very successful at an early age and make a lot of money, you can exist in that child's world. Michael Jackson did it. John Lennon did it. Elvis did it. He made that world for himself where he didn't have to be an adult.

When I'm writing a song I'm really vulnerable. I'm not being aggressive at all. I'm just having a good time. And the older I get, the harder it is.

Through the years have you found any ways to let that child get out?

I get high. I get high all the time. I'm just like The Beatles. [*Laughs*] And I drink more lately. I know it's the fashion these days to say I don't do drugs. But I can't see how a person can live in the modern world and not do drugs and be an artist. The world is saying to me, "What you're doing is trivial and not important. Get a job." And the world will say that to me as long as I'm not a Beatle or John Denver. That's the way the world is toward artists. If you're an artist, who needs you?

I was raised in a very rigid and accomplishment-oriented environment. I don't mean my family. I mean being Catholic and white and in America in the fifties, when everybody had crew cuts. I think you have to get past that somehow.

Throughout the centuries people have been very upset about artists seeking to escape the world through whatever means. But for me, at least, what I see is that Edgar Allan Poe got it, The Beatles did it—that's enough for me. And I know how music was for me before I got high. I used to be nervous about reality shifting. And my whole approach to music was a whole lot less sensual because I didn't stop to smell the roses. And it was The Beatles saying to stop and smell the roses that made me shift my consciousness and become a hippie. And for me to become a hippie was a big shift. It was like Wally Cox turns into Marlon Brando.

Marijuana is not a big shift in consciousness. If there is underlying fear, it shows. If there is underlying peace, it shows. If I get a poetic image when I'm high, it seems much more beautiful, and I look at it and I become an audience. And when I become an audience, that gives me enthusiasm to finish the project.

Under the influence of some drugs certain things can seem more beautiful than they are. But in your songs the beauty and the depth is a real part of the work.

I think that has to do with your perception of what simplicity is. I would say that with Dylan, for example, he will send you a message, and you'll get more than he meant. That's a talent. And Dylan had that talent before he ever smoked dope. So if you're not a good songwriter to begin with, you can smoke all the dope you want and it's not going to help. At the same time, I think it will maximize your sensual appreciation.

Your song "Vampire" is also mythic and so genuine, it made me wonder about you.

That's interesting. I think "Vampire" is highly sexual. It really is a sex song but with imagery that stands in the way. I was simply trying to write a song of seduction, and it seemed interesting to do that with imagery that is not sexual but sensual. Also I had read a lot of Stephen King and Anne Rice's books. She was the first person to ever make me think being a vampire could be a glamorous thing. People had attempted to do that. So she turned my head around for sure.

It also had a lot to do with an E minor 9 chord. [E-G-B-F sharp]. E minor 9 chords sound like horror films to me. There is this guitarist named Tony Mottola who was the staff guitarist on the TV show *Danger*, and he used to play this chord that went from the bass note up, E-B-F sharp-C-D-E. Try that some time. It's a wonderful chord.

Do you generally write more than you need and then edit out lines?

I write lines that I take out. But it's not like I have two pages and only use one. I wish I was more like that. Stevie Goodman was like that. Bob Gibson is like that when he writes songs. He'll set an alarm clock for ten minutes and just write like crazy for ten minutes. That's too free for me. I'm much more careful than that. I write line by line.

For "The Dutchman," for example, did you write any other verses than the ones we know?

No. I had a couple of lines that didn't go anywhere, so I took them out.

Your song "Three Monkeys" concerns Central America. Did a trip there trigger the song?

No. No. The first line was a lift from Zane Grey, I believe, in one of his Western novels: "It gets so hot here, the natives say, that the wind has forgotten how to blow." That was the line. I lifted it, and then it was like "The Dutchman," having a first line and saying, "Where do I go with this?" I wanted to create something that had a feeling that was like a spy movie, like Graham Greene or Somerset Maugham.

Where were you when you wrote that song?

I was in Chicago. It was probably the middle of the winter. Like a lot of people in folk music, I get my culture secondhand. John Stewart [see page 194] used to say that he makes imitation folk songs, and that's what I do too. "Loretta" is a lot like a John Stewart song. I can hear him doing it. He does a thing to me that I do, which is the use of a lot of imagery of a specific nature. I imitate him in some ways. I think he's really talented.

Do you recall where the title for "Three Monkeys" came from?

That started out when I watched a TV show about people being "love addicts." I liked that phrase and wanted to use it. It seemed very heavy metal to me. I started working on it, and I thought of what imagery I connect with "addict" and one of them is "monkey on your back." I was thinking about that and I thought about the three monkeys that you see in old Sydney Greenstreet movies: see no evil, hear no evil, speak no evil. And that imagery to me was a lot more exciting than love addicts or monkey on your back. There was a mood there. It was clear, right away, that if you have a song called "Three Monkeys" that it takes place in the tropics. Having that title was such a mood.

"Spoon River," to this day, is to me one of the most beautiful songs ever written, both lyrically and musically. Was it inspired by the anthology by Edgar Lee Masters?

Yes. I love that book. I was seventeen, and it was just the right time to read that sort of thing. They did a Broadway version of it that I really hated.

For a long time I had this imagery of someone taking someone for a carriage ride. I had that image for about two years and when I thought of placing it in "Spoon River," it seemed like the perfect emotional climate for it.

I so love the use of the rich time-specific imagery, such as all of the calico dresses, the gingham and lace. It is so beautiful visually and verbally both.

Songs are more personal now and more concerned with the emotion. For me, even Randy Newman is more personal and concerned with emotions than me, though sometimes he will tell stories. That's an old way of doing things. "Eleanor Rigby" is an old song. Though for me, if I could write songs like "Eleanor Rigby" for the rest of my life, I'd be a happy man.

Your songs share that richly detailed quality and a real sense of character and place—

I like songs that delight in giving you a picture. I don't get that much anymore. I don't get it from U2. What I'm getting is youth, and youth seems more fragmented to a person who has grown old.

I love the description of Sister Clarissa being eleven feet tall. It really makes you feel like a kid looking up at this mammoth figure.

That was the first line I thought of, as a matter of fact. I was doing a show with Bob Gibson called The Women in My Life. It was his idea to separately write songs about the women in our lives. The first song I wrote was "Sister Clarissa." And I had that first line about her being eleven feet tall, and Gibson said, "You know, I think that should be the second verse." And it was just like tumblers falling into place. Of course. Of course, I'm grateful to him for that because it never would have occurred to me in a million years to shift the first verse and the second verse.

I also love the line about getting a star for "spelling Connecticut right."

Yeah. That's essentially true. Working out the rhythms of that song was fun. It was like I was trying to make it like a Jacques Brel tune.

I was wondering if Brel was an influence because your songs to me are as resonant and beautiful as a Brel song. You and Brel—and few others—are in the same league.

Well, thank you. I love Brel. He's the one that makes me cry the most. And that's true because he's sentimental but also because you really hear his worldview. At the time of "The Dutchman" I was particularly focused on Brel, Piaf, and Leonard Cohen. I always thought that "The Dutchman" sounded like a Leonard Cohen song.

Yeah, it's definitely in that area. As is "Crazy Mary," another one of my favorite Michael Smith songs. Is that one fictional?

No. That's true. I made up her motivations. When I was a kid on the way to school every day there was an old lady on the street corner who had a lot of warts, and she was Italian, and she stood at the street corner and essentially screeched and hollered and talked to no one in particular. If any children came near her, she would do things like give you gum out of her mouth or give you candy with maggots crawling in it. Or she'd want to give you a big kiss. And it was awful, and it was scary. And when you're ten you don't know how to cope with someone saying, "Come here!"

When I wrote that song it never occurred to me that there wasn't one of those in every neighborhood. Now I see it's a specialized memory. But as a kid I thought it was part of the neighborhood. There was the butcher, the baker, and the crazy lady. So in that song I was trying to make something of her, trying to give her something back, I guess.

Do you write songs all the time?

I'm always trying to do something. I'm always thinking about something. Sometimes just a guitar riff. But to physically sit down and do it, I'd say I luck out to do it three times a week. That's a lot for me.

Today I was watching *Let It Be*, and they were singing "Don't Let Me Down" [by Lennon] up on the rooftop, and I thought, I have to go, "The Dutchman's not the kind of man to keep his thumb jammed in the dam that holds his dreams in." It takes me all this time to get out this poetic imagery to people, and they do "Don't Let Me Down," and suddenly you're *there*. And I saw that there's a freedom and a subtlety and a lightheartedness in making good pop music that people who are writing folk songs are trying to approach but are not getting. It's like I'm doing Norman Rockwell and The Beatles are Picasso.

Well, some of those Norman Rockwell paintings tell such poignant American stories, as do your songs. They are not cubist songs; they're more traditionally structured. But that is perfect for the song. "Spoon River" touches me so deeply because it's so much about America and our unique history.

Also The Beatles had many songs, such as "Across the Universe," also by Lennon, with long poetic openings like "Words are flowing out like endless rain into a paper cup . . ."

Yes, that's very true. Lennon did get rattling along at times. I think I've got a big hero-worship with them that maybe does not serve me well.

Part of the premise of pop music is to reach out to people. Not people you love or people you trust, but just people. And I think because of that, it gives the music an impersonal, frantic quality that ethnic or folk music doesn't have.

When I hear people perpetrating those really dramatic stances with the slamming drums and the electric guitars, it doesn't work for me. It has to do with the franticness with which they are pursuing the approval of the masses. It shows in every fiber of the music. I'm not saying they're not talented people—they're just too uptight. They're so anxious for approval that they make fools of themselves.

There's a big gulf in people's hearts, and people are so fragmented because they don't have an Elvis and they don't have a Beatles. And they don't have a Kingston Trio. Those artists consolidated us and brought us somewhere new. Now it's like a vast wasteland in a certain way. So when I say Beatles, it's a way of saying to keep your light burning in the middle of a lot of bullshit. Their music was never forced. It had a succinctness and a subtlety to it that was real.

I noticed when listening to the song Steve Goodman did that he often changed your words. And usually the originals were better.

Stevie was a real approximator in certain ways. And it gave him his lightheartedness. And you could even call him on it and say, "Hey, you didn't learn this right." And he'd say, "Yeah . . . It's just my way." It was part of his charm.

In truth I think that's what a great artist does. That's what Ella [Fitzgerald] does. You put a song in her machine, and it's going to come out different because she's Ella. Same with Billie Holiday.

In general I think it was Stevie not learning it right and militantly not giving a shit. And that was part of his picture of himself. I do think that "The Ballad of Dan Moody" would have been better if he would've gotten all the words right.

What started you writing the kind of songs that you write?

I've had unsettling things happen to me—not tragic, necessarily. But when it comes time to make art I come at it from a strange angle. Also, I think I tend to think too much for my own good, and I think that gives what I do an aura of tension. It's like an oyster with a pearl—maybe there's a certain amount of oddity about my life and that creates a tension in trying to make it acceptable in art.

I don't know where the songs lie. If I could get a handle on it, I could make more. It's almost as if each time I do it, it's a different path.

◆ ◆ ◆

Dave Stewart

Eurythmics and Beyond

Hollywood, California 2015

Meeting with Dave Stewart at his Hollywood dream factory is a dizzying experience, not unlike what one imagines visiting Warhol's Factory was like in the day, except minus the zombies and cocaine. There's a whole lot of people in a unified space doing a whole lot of art all the time. To Dave, it's more Wonka than Warhol, "except instead of candy we make ideas."

A lot of ideas. The Dave engine, which sprawls over two stories above Hollywood and Vine, goes 24/7, sparking always in many directions at once: besides his myriad musical projects as artist, songwriter, and/or producer—including, at the time of this talk, a glorious recent solo album, *The Blackbird Diaries*, and the phenomenon of his most recent supergroup, SuperHeavy, which includes Mick Jagger, Joss Stone, A. R. Rahman, and Damian Marley—there are films (he films everything always), books, TV shows, photographs, and always more. Dave's staff is forever editing and mixing and working away to his instructions, though they're remarkably agile when it comes to showing a visitor a film of

Dave and Shakira dancing in a barn or soloing Stevie Wonder's miraculous harmonica solo on The Eurythmics' "There Must Be an Angel."

He's the great collaborator. Most famous of course for The Eurythmics, his collaboration with Annie Lennox, his genius is for humbly standing behind the singer, whether it's Annie or Mick or Tom Petty (they concocted "Don't Come Around Here No More") or any of the other stars with whom he's written songs—such as Bono, Dylan, Bryan Ferry, Stevie Nicks, and Sinead O'Connor—and making them shine. "There's only two kinds of people," his mother told him. "There are drains and radiators. People who drag you down and people who spark you up." Without a doubt Dave Stewart is a radiator. He brings out what is essential and best about an artist, whether it's Dylan, Petty, or Jagger.

In Eurythmics he and Annie Lennox cowrote every song, but Dave was the producer. Always, from the very start. The song—and the sonics surrounding the song—were always part of his vision and always was attained by experiments, by combining acoustic and electronic textures in brand-new ways.

In signature fedora and dark shades and nursing a freshly brewed cappuccino, Dave opened up about his years working with Annie Lennox in The Eurythmics and what came after. "We never did break up," he said of The Eurythmics. "We just stopped. We have paused. But nothing is over."

Where did you meet Annie Lennox?

Dave Stewart: I met her in London. She was a waitress at a health food café in Hampstead High Street. My friend knew her, and I went with him. I remembered she looked a bit sort of quirky and odd, wearing Kellogg's Frosted Flakes' Tony the Tiger sunglasses and had cropped spiky hair. But she got off work and came with us; we went back to her tiny bedsit room in Camden Town. Just a little room with a little bed and her old wooden harmonium. We started talking and didn't stop talking for the next twenty years.

She already wrote songs and played me some, singing and playing harmonium. One was "Tower of Capricorn," and the other was "Song for Matt," about a boyfriend who had died. I was utterly *knocked out*.

By the songs? The singing? Or everything?

Everything. Everything about her. The singing, the chords she was playing, her delicate words, and her haunting beauty. Her music reminded me somewhat of Joni Mitchell. Sad and beautiful both.

What was the first song you and Annie wrote?

The first song wasn't a song, really; it was an instrumental we composed during our time in The Tourists, before Eurythmics. A sound collage, really, called "From the Middle Room." It was an experimental track, electronic and weird. We did it whilst recording a Tourists album, but nobody was in the studio—no Peet, no producer, just me and Annie and the engineer. I said, "Let's just experiment," and we got the guy to record our sonic doodling. And that's where it all started. We recorded the crickets outside and brought in this weird psychedelic harpsichord sound. It was pure experimentation.

Then you set up your own studio?

Yes. Eight-track. A friend helped me determine what gear we needed, and we got space in a picture-framing factory and put together a very small, basic, but workable studio.

I learned that anything is possible if you ignore the rules. If I wanted to distort the drum machine, no one could stop me. If I wanted to mix the sound of the street with the guitar, that was fine too.

Once I had this freedom, I would go into the studio on my own for hours. I'd work twenty hours in a row, easy. Annie would be back in her little flat. She'd come in and I would play this stuff that was just insane, bonkers stuff, very weird and totally experimental. There would be monks chanting against drum loops, and I would be playing weird instruments I'd bought in Camden Market, like Thai stringed instruments or Moroccan percussion.

But she was always great about it, always interested, because she loved being experimental too. I'd get other kids in from the street of all nationalities to shout or make noises to record. It was very important for me to experiment to the point of extreme madness. And then reel it all back into the *Sweet Dreams* album.

The drum machine was quite complicated to operate. It had analog and synthesized drum sounds and a tiny visual monitor. We were recording on an eight-track tape recorder, and one of the tracks had to be used to record time code to synch up to the drum machine. On the first beat I'd tuned one of the tom-tom drums down so low, it sounded like a slave drum. It was deafening and blasting on the first beat of every bar, but I couldn't get it to stop. It was like driving an out-of-control steam engine.

The sound of these drums woke Annie up out of her depression. She went straight to the keyboard and landed on this great riff with a string sound on the Kurzweil, and it locked in with my weird drum pattern. I grabbed our Roland SH-101 synthesizer and started playing a pattern with her. These three sounds together—the keyboard, the drum, and the synthesizer—were the only tracks happening, yet they created this monstrous feeling. We were *very excited*!

She immediately started to get some ideas for lyrics and went down to this little empty room below the studio. Shortly after, she came out with "Sweet dreams are made of this"! *Incredible!* And could there be a more appropriate title?

Very quickly the song was getting constructed, and then we realized it was just doing the same thing all the time, so I suggested there had to be another bit, and that bit should be positive. So in the middle we added these chord changes rising upward with "Hold your head up, moving on. Keep your head up, moving on."

When Annie was really excited about something a lightbulb would go off in her head, and the race to the end was always incredible. She was singing, "Some of them want to use you. Some of them want to get used by you. Some of them want to abuse you." All great lines that she was coming up with off the top of her head. In the space of twenty minutes Annie changed from being down on the floor to leaping about the room.

To us it was a major breakthrough, but I remember later some publishers said they didn't get it at all. They just kept saying, "I don't understand this song. It doesn't have a chorus." But the whole song is a chorus! There is not one note in the whole song that is not a hook.

And after that you kept writing songs in the same way?

Yeah. Having the studio to create in every day, Annie and I started to become amazing creative songwriting partners, true collaborators, and we began to write all our songs together. When we were together sparks would fly. We played different roles and didn't step on each other's toes. I was always experimenting at the desk or on an instrument, and Annie would sit behind with a notepad, thinking or writing furiously.

It's a kind of alchemy that occurs, a magical process of making something out of nothing. One minute a song doesn't exist, and twenty minutes later it does. We always knew within ten or twenty minutes if it was worth pursuing an idea, and very rarely disagreed. Once or twice I would fight for something but usually we were on the same page.

And you were essentially writing the songs and making the records at the same time. There was no division between songwriting and production?

Yes. By default I had become the record producer. Along with Annie, we could do *anything*. We could play all the instruments between us, record ourselves, make mistakes, and not care—just laugh about it. Freedom at last. Sometimes I would have programmed the drums, played the bass on synth or real bass, played the guitars and other keyboard parts, engineered myself recording the sounds and Annie's vocals and keyboard parts, and then mixed it all in a few hours—a magic feeling, as for once we were in full control!

Usually there was no one in the room while we were writing, as whoever was working with us would tactfully make an exit when they felt something was brewing. Then when we recorded there would be one engineer. Someone we trusted not to break the spell. We didn't use expensive studios or expensive equipment. We were always about keeping it close or DIY.

One of my favorite Eurythmics songs is "There Must Be an Angel."

Annie started that one. Sometimes she'd have the whole idea for a song, like a melody and lyric both, and she had both words and music for "There Must Be an Angel." When she wrote it she said, "This could be great for Stevie Wonder." I heard it and said, "It would be great for us too, but why don't we get Stevie to play harmonica on it?" So we sent the song to Stevie's people, and we didn't hear anything and figured, "Okay, he isn't interested." Turned out that he did like the song, and one night, very late after we went home from the studio, Stevie showed up! So we got out of bed and went back. And there's Stevie, in all his glory. And he played that extraordinary solo. One take. To this day I play that track—Stevie Wonder playing a harmonica solo on our song—and it is breathtaking.

How did "Would I Lie to You?" come together?

We were in Paris. I was having breakfast in my kitchen. Eating a bowl of cereal, my acoustic guitar on my knee as always. I wanted to come up with a killer R&B riff, and that's where I came up with that riff for "Would I Lie to You." I was belting it out in my boxer shorts till I had the whole guitar part for the song mapped out in my head.

I couldn't wait to play it to Annie. At first she wasn't too sure about it, as it sounded too removed from what we were doing. But the great thing about Annie is, even if she's not sure at first, she will let the experiment develop, whereas some people are too afraid and shut down before even trying.

When we started putting it down, the song had a lot of energy and inspired Annie to come up with the great lyric "Would I lie to you?" She also came up with the melody on these very odd answering harmonies, "Now, would I say something that wasn't true?" These harmonies are unusual, and she's a genius at working them out very quickly in her head.

It became a fusion between Stax-type R&B and Eurythmics. We soon realized this could be a monster track. Annie's lead vocal was fantastic and a killer to record.

Were there any times you had to struggle for songs or had a dry spell?

Not really, no. It was always immediate. People would witness us doing this and would go, "What? Hang on. Did you just make that up?"

And we're going, "Yeah. We're busy making it up now." And they would be amazed. We never ever did spend days working on a song. Probably the longest time we ever spent writing one must have been an hour. And we wrote maybe 140 songs. When we were together we knew within minutes where we were going. We knew each other so well that I would play a chord and she'd go, "No, not that chord." I'd play another chord. No. Then she would sing, and I would say no.

It was like we were honing in on a very precise thing. That was the essence of us. It was like being a surfer catching a wave. You wait, and you say, "No, not this wave. Not this wave." We both knew when it was the one.

And if you don't catch the wave at the right time, you lose it.

Yes, absolutely. You lose the spark of the thing. People are so used to taking forever on every project. I like to make an album in a week. Annie and I [in Eurythmics] used to take ten days or two weeks, *tops*. I was amazed when I found out people would take a whole year. I do it like they did it at Motown—two or three records in a day.

You wrote "Worth the Waiting For" with Bob Dylan—

We wrote so many songs together. We have songs we never finished. I remember working on that one with him. It was midnight, and we were both drinking tequila. We were in my kitchen in London. Dylan was wearing a big Mexican hat. We'd been that day jamming in my church, and we were playing it back on a cassette recorder and then recording that on another cassette recorder. We had Joni Mitchell playing the drums. Like fifty people in the church, all playing the instruments they don't play. *Huge* burners of frankincense burning. That night we sat in my kitchen and wrote the words.

Besides Dylan, you've worked a lot with great songwriters who rarely collaborate, or if they do it's with one person only, as with Mick Jagger,

who usually writes with Keith Richards. You've written many songs with Mick—

I'd say we've written about *fifty*! Mick only makes a solo album once every ten years or so. But as writers, we never stop writing. [*plays tape of "Time Drags On" with Mick singing—an unreleased gem*].

I love the duet with Colbie Caillat, "Bulletproof Vest." A very beautiful song.

I like melancholia, especially in a girl's voice. I like raw blues soul power or melancholy. And usually the best singers can do both. Like Etta James—

And Annie Lennox—

Well, yeah. That was like our whole thing, this melancholy thing that suddenly went very powerful.

I think there is great strength and power in things people think are sad. Acceptance of death gives you great strength to live the day. I love a garden when it's all sort of overgrown and the roses are blood red, not the bright, tight spring buds. I love the tangled disarray where it seems like it's falling apart. And I'm trying to put that into music and words.

How do you do that? How do you translate something so abstract into a song?

Ultimately it's about discovery, about being receptive to the magic soul of a song. It's like following Tinker Bell. I'm always looking to discover what is the magic thing. The magic thing in it might come from something you weren't expecting. It might be a mistake or a word that just pops into your head. And what I've got the ability to do is just scrap the rest and go for the magic.

So much of the genius of Eurythmics and of your other collaborations with great writers is that you have a great gift for bringing the best out of creative people. Even Dylan said that: you recognize the genius in someone and let them express it without manipulating them.

That is true. These people with whom I have written songs are so talented, it is a matter of how to channel their energies. Annie is a genius songwriter in her own right. I was a kind of a catalyst in a way, a trigger to explore and explode a wealth of songs and styles. But Annie, like many songwriters, can become prone to writer's block, which, if you dwell on it, can be torturous. When we wrote together I think I could break that spell because it's a collaborative effort, and you can spark off each other and use what I would call "breaking the plane," which could be anything from taking a walk to standing on your head. It doesn't matter what it is, as long as it changes the train of thought.

Annie has within her the talent and instincts to write some of the greatest songs ever and already has. But she might not necessarily feel like doing it all the time, which I understand, as there are many other things in life that overwhelm us all, particularly if you have become a mother and a known figure.

But I will say I always saw Annie as a writer from the beginning. That's what I realized about her when we first met. Those songs she played on that harmonium were astounding.

But it's really in the collaboration with you that greatness emerged. Something about your joyful approach to life fused with her melancholy—

Yeah, with me and Annie, on any Eurythmics tracks, we always hit the nail on the head with this dynamic of despair and hope at the same time. It would be really dark, and then *boom*, it would transform musically and lyrically and in every way. And those two things together made a magic vibe.

You wrote "Don't Come Around Here No More" with Tom Petty.

Yeah. It was after a show in my hotel room, using my little four-track Portastudio, I started to create a track with a drum machine, a tiny synthesizer, and this Coral Sitar guitar, which has sympathetic strings that make it sound like a real sitar. I came up with this whole track but without any words, and then the line came to me. I was singing it with the track and it fit well: "Don't come around here no more, don't come around here no more . . ." I had that with the music, but no other lyrics.

Tom listened to it and went in the studio, and he was trying some stuff. He was singing, "Don't come around here no more"—he got the chorus I had written. He goes, "Okay, that fits this."

We ended up finishing it in his garage studio. He was making a Heartbreakers album, and the band wasn't on the song. So we decided to go into a sort of double-time groove at the end and have the band come in. The guys in the Heartbreakers really didn't seem to like the song because it was different and he made it without them. It was the start of Tom doing a lot of solo projects. But he never broke up the band—he does both.

After that double-time part there's an almost impossible-to-reach high note. We had a singer there, and I got that note when I shocked her by leaping naked into the studio. That worked! After that note the whole band comes crashing in. Everybody played great, and the whole experience was a trip.

Did you and Annie write "Here Comes the Rain Again" in New York?

Yes. We used to stay at the Mayflower Hotel, and we had a corner room overlooking Central Park. We used to like to stay in this hotel because of the windows looking onto the park. I'd been out on 46th Street and bought a tiny little keyboard, a really tiny little thing. It was an overcast day. Annie was sitting in my room, and I was playing some little riff on the keyboard, sitting on the window ledge, and Annie was saying, "Oh, let me have a go at that keyboard." But I had just bought it and, a bit like a kid, I said, "*I'm* playing with it now." So we had this fight over the keyboard, like two seven-year-olds. I was playing chords I knew would get to her, especially on a rainy day, these little melancholy A minor second chords, an A minor with a B natural in it. I kept on playing this riff while Annie looked out the window at the slate-gray sky above the New York skyline, and she just started singing spontaneously, "Here comes the rain again . . ."

And that was all we needed. Like with a lot of our songs, you only need to start with that one line, that one atmosphere, that one note, or that intro melody. And the rest of it became a puzzle with missing pieces we filled in.

And you finished the puzzle then and there.

We did. No need to wait. We had it.

You love the process of writing and recording, which inspires others. Whereas for so many people it's torturous—both the writing and the recording.

Yes. One of the secrets to my ability to collaborate with so many other talents is that I take all the pressure away. As Mick [Jagger] said, there's no angst. It's done out of joy. Stevie Nicks was very happy when she realized this and said, "Oh, hang on. We can just have fun and not worry?"

And I said, "Yeah. You know why? Because if we don't like it, nobody will ever hear it."

People have gotten used to the pattern of having to make a new album at the same time they're touring, and the record company is waiting for it, so there is a lot of pressure. Suddenly they have a handful of weeks to write and record twelve new songs. The pressure is remarkable and not conducive at all to writing good songs.

So when I come along and say, "Well, you know, it doesn't really matter if you don't like it—nobody will ever hear it. We'll just throw it away. We'll *burn* it! It doesn't make a difference," suddenly it's a whole new world. There is no pressure, and you're allowed to make mistakes, and you know everything is fine. You don't have to think everything is precious.

And that freedom opens up artists to doing great work.

When you're relaxed great things happen and you can capture something truly amazing. And this creates a momentum because you use that energy, and it leads to more ideas and inspiration. People get excited, and it becomes fun. And when you're having fun making music, it's infectious, for yourself and everyone around you. And it's also much nicer for your family when you eventually get home. When you say nothing matters and we can burn it, often your collaborator will say, "Oh, but I really like that! Let's keep it," or "Let's put it on the track." It's a kind of reverse psychology.

It is a psychological experiment, writing a song with someone else. And an intimate one.

Writing songs with other people is like falling in love over and over again. It's a fast track into somebody's soul—you can feel their heart beating against yours. When I play guitar and they start to sing, even when we are just improvising, there's something else that starts to happen that no one can explain. We try to follow whatever that something is and understand what it is telling us to do.

It's like when you were a child and you got to run through a wooded glade with a friend, and you came across a hidden stream where you could bathe or quench your thirst—except this race is in your mind, and when words start to fall out of the improvisation they are like fireflies lighting the way: they guide us back through the woods till we see the village in the distance. We are soon inside a safe place where our minds meld in the warm glow of creativity.

◆ ◆ ◆

Joan Armatrading

Walking Under Ladders

Hollywood, California 2000

It's late afternoon in Los Angeles, and at the House of Blues on the Sunset Strip Joan Armatrading's band is in the midst of a sound check. Folk art fills the walls in a rainbow of colors as the smell of fried catfish, chicken wings, and other soul food delights waft in from the kitchen. Onstage the band is cooking on a funky instrumental, their leader nowhere in sight. After a few moments a small woman sidles onto the stage with her back to the empty house, an electric guitar slung around her neck. She easily joins the jam, strumming a chunky rhythm before laying down a tasty and slinky solo. When she turns around it's surprising to realize that this is Joan herself— seeming much smaller in the flesh than the mighty figure suggested by her powerful voice and the robust vigor of her music. "People often feel I'm tiny when they meet me," she says later. "I guess it's because I'm much bigger in my songs then I am in the world."

Unlike so many songwriters who are pushed by their parents down musical pathways, Joan Armatrading was pushed in the opposite direction. Though her father owned a guitar, he prohibited her from playing it. "My father had a nice guitar," she recalled, "but he would never let me near it. We had a cellar behind this big bank-vault door, and he would keep the guitar in there. And not only that, but he used to hide it on the topmost shelf in that room, so even if you could get into the room, you couldn't get to that guitar."

This forced separation from the instrument of her choice created a kind of Romeo and Juliet complex between Joan and her guitar, resulting in a profound hunger on her part to make music. Eventually she broke down her mother's resistance and persuaded her to pawn two dilapidated baby carriages in exchange for an old acoustic guitar. Though it had "strings about a foot from the neck," this condition didn't stop her from diligently teaching herself to develop the distinctively rich, muscular guitar style she has retained ever since.

"I didn't know what I was doing," she said. "I just played my own stuff, and so I invented my own way of playing. I wanted to hear bass and drums and rhythm and lead and everything, and so I tried to play all those things at once."

Born in the rural splendor of the West Indian island of Saint Kitts, she moved with her family in 1958 to the urban confines of Birmingham, England, where she was raised. Unlike almost all songwriters whose first songs are imitations of what they hear on records or the radio, her first songs were inspired by no one other than herself. "When I started writing," she said, "the only person I was listening to was me."

It was while acting in a 1971 production of *Hair* that she met Pam Nestor, with whom she wrote songs for *Whatever's for Us*, her 1972 debut. When the partnership dissolved, Joan continued to write songs on her own, and in 1975 she made *Back to the Night*. Her next album, *Joan Armatrading*, propelled her into the UK Top Twenty and produced her first and only Top Ten single, the amazing "Love and Affection."

It was the unexpected strength and beauty of this song that introduced her unique voice and style to America. Here was a love song as rich and sensuously jubilant as love itself, rendered by a singer with an undeniable abundance of soul. Its immense international popularity led to the success of follow-up albums *Me Myself I*, *The Key*, and *Walk Under Ladders*, the latter of which began with the exultant and anthemic "I'm Lucky."

Instead of taking the familiar path of focusing on personal vulnerability, she opted instead to project faith, the pursuit of personal happiness, and the strength to sidestep superstition and fear. Of course, when she did write about vulnerability, as in her powerful "The Weakness in

Me," few people could do it better, coming as she was from this position of strength and positivity. It's the reason why so many female songwriters, including Melissa Etheridge, Jewel, Joan Osborne, and others point to Armatrading as an idol, as a woman who proved early on that both strength and weakness could be genuinely projected in the song if the underlying emotion is real.

Of the many that emerged in her wake, the first and most notable was Tracy Chapman, whose acoustic guitar and vocal style owed an unmistakable debt to Joan. It's been a source of some frustration for her; although Chapman and Etheridge covered both "Love and Affection" and "The Weakness in Me," Joan felt burnt and bewildered by journalists who omit her name when discussing rock's most influential women. "It has been frustrating to an extent," she said. "But I can't spend a lot of time worrying about it. I know that I am lucky just to be able to do what I do, and that's where I have to keep my focus."

Following the sound check, she sits down to do this interview but requests that we refrain from digging too deeply into the origins of her songs. "I'll be happy to talk about songs," she says, softly perched on a wooden bar stool as miscellaneous roadies and soundmen loudly haul equipment and tables around the club. "I just don't want to talk about *my* songs." When informed that this was a little problematic, as there are few songs I'd rather discuss with her than her own, she smiles softly and says, "Well, I'll do my best, but I'm not sure how much I can give you. I know people always want me to give more. But you know, in my songs and my shows I really feel as if I have already given enough. But you just go ahead and do your job. And I'll do my best to give you what I can."

When starting a song do you have a clear idea of what you want the song to say?

Joan Armatrading: I have a clear idea of what I want to say, but I don't have a clear idea of how I want to say it, [*laughs*] which are two very different things. The trick is to find the words that will say the thing you were trying to say.

How do you do that?

I can't tell you. I know that when I am writing I am trying to have the words make sense. I want them to have a beginning, a middle, and an end. Whenever somebody asks me how to write a song, that's all I can say. [*Softly*] But how do you find the words, I don't know. [*Pause*] Do you know?

No. Sometimes it seems that the music tells me what the word should be—

Yes. Songs can be written as words and music together. As if you're singing the song. Sometimes the words come first, and sometimes the music comes first. There is no pattern.

After all these years of writing songs? Do you find that anything helps the writing process—

No. [*Laughs*] Whatever that is, whatever response you want, the song itself will just dictate how it is supposed to be. Some songs come from somewhat of a nonprocess; they just come like that. [*Snaps fingers*] With some songs the chorus will come easy, and all the rest of it will be hard. None of that changes. I wish there was some formula that I could find that would make it all easy. But there is none. [*Laughs*] Yet I still keep looking.

In a way that is one of the great things about songwriting, that there is no formula—

Yes. I agree. The mystery remains.

Does it feel to you more a sense of following where the song needs to go as opposed to leading it?

When I am writing a song—say, a blues song—it's not up to me to try to make it a reggae song. Because the song tells you, "I am a blues song. I am not a reggae song." Maybe when it's finished and it's in its pure form somebody else could take it and change it and then it will work. Because it has already become what it was meant to be.

But writing a bad song and saying, "Well, it's bad because it's not reggae, or it's not blues, or it's not a ballad," that doesn't make much sense. Because a song is what it is. It also sets its own tempo. It tells you what pace it should be taken at. And it also sets its own key.

Really?

Yes. That's what I find. The song is in a particular key, and I just follow it.

A lot of guitar players will play in keys that fit easily on guitar, such as E or G. But your songs are often in keys that are tough for the guitar, such as E flat.

Yes, that's because I'm just writing the song. I'm not thinking about guitar. The song said that's the key it's meant to be in. I have even written songs in keys that are not particularly right for me to sing. But the song is in that key.

So even when a key isn't great for your voice, you go with that key?

Yes. You must let it tell you. If you impose something on top of it before you begin, that can overpower it. So you have to back off a little bit and find out where it wants to be rather than making up your mind about it before you even begin. However it goes. Whatever instrument there is, that is what I will use to push the music along.

Is that instrument usually a guitar?

Guitar or piano. Piano songs tend to be the more melodic ones, such as "The Weakness in Me." More rhythmic things, like "Steppin' Out" or "Kissin' and Huggin'," those are guitar songs. You can tell the difference because you can hear how heavily dominated by the instrument it is.

Do song ideas sometimes just pop into your head?

Rarely. Usually something has to trigger an idea for me. It's very unusual that I would just be walking along and a song out of nowhere would come to me. More often they come out of something that happens from watching life. The song "All a Woman Needs" came out of a friend telling me about somebody that we both know. A man who was in love with a woman. And he would shower her with presents. Whatever she wanted. But he never said, "I love you," which is all she really wanted. When she told me that, I was able to think of a song, and I connected with it well because of knowing how he was. So it's usually something real that will trigger a song.

Does using true details give songs more emotional resonance?

Yes, and it's much easier than just making something up. I have done that. The song "At the Hop" is just made up, but it's a good song, but it's just made up. The song "The Shouting Stage" is about people I know who have gotten to that point. Where they have gone through all this nice loving stuff and are now at this horrible place. When you think of how they used to be, you wonder, "How is it possible?" Here are two people who were one, blinded by the same light, and suddenly it's all gone.

Is writing an enjoyable process for you?

Oh yes. That's what I do. What I do is write songs. So I had better enjoy it. I like the process. It's good. That's the part that gets you the song. The part I don't particularly like is the writing out chords and lead sheets.

Do you write often lots of lyrics without any music?

I used to do that more than I do now. I still do a little bit, but not as much as I used to. The other thing that I do is that when I write, whatever I am writing, good or bad, I finish it. I can't leave a song unfinished.

Why?

Well, I don't know what it is. Maybe I feel if I don't finish it, I will never be able to finish *any* song, or something like that. If I am writing a song that I'm thinking is just a bad song—because you can hear it right off the top—I have to just keep at it. I'll finish it and then I'll just chuck it. Some, if they're not so bad but they're just not that good, I'll keep.

Do you find that judging it while writing can make the writing tough?

Well, it can be tough, but sometimes you just have to be honest with yourself. If you're writing it and it's sounding horrible, maybe you just have to know that it's horrible. If not at that point, what better point is there? [*Laughs*]

But can you sometimes take something that is horrible and turn it into something that's good—

No. I have written some horrible songs. They just have to go. And if they're that horrible, they get erased.

Do you mean lyrically horrible or musically—

Everything. Everything is bad. The music's bad, the lyrics are bad, the rhythm's bad, the key is awful. I mean, it happens.

Do you have many of those?

No. [*Laughs*]

"Love and Affection" is the first song of yours that many of us heard, and it was such a powerful and individual statement. Do you remember what led you to the writing of that one?

Yes, I do. Remember me saying I don't usually talk about why I wrote my songs? Some songs I am quite happy to talk about, and others I'm not.

Do you not want to discuss the songs because there's something too personal attached to them?

Yes. Exactly.

But apart from the personal connection to your own life, "Love and Affection" is such a powerful song. Were you surprised when it came through you?

Absolutely. In fact I said to the record company that I would like this to be the single. And they said, "Well, remember you are the one who wanted this." [*Laughs*] I just thought it would be a very big hit. I really did. And I think they weren't so sure of it. So they reminded me that if it didn't work, it was my fault.

And you were right.

Yes. It was a hit over the whole world. It was great. I loved getting the whole arrangement to that right, all the voices and all. I knew exactly what I wanted with that. I wanted the bass to be melodic. I knew all those things and I did all the arranging. I tend to arrange all the songs anyways. I like to think of that—once I have written a song, the most important part is how the arrangement should go. To me it's part of the song. It's part of my songs, anyway.

Your song "I'm Lucky" has the great line "I can walk under ladders." That happy defiance of silly superstitions was so great, and it became our theme song all that year—

[*Laughs*] I can talk about that one. That's me. I just feel like I am a very lucky person. I say in the song that I'm so lucky that I'm as lucky as me, [*laughs*] because I do feel very lucky. There are a lot of people who are talented who never have a break and can never make anything of their work. I have been so lucky to make this life where I'm able to do my work and have people enjoy it.

I started that one with the big riff on the synthesizer.

You play less guitar on *Walk Under Ladders* than on your other albums.

Yes. Because that's what I heard in my head then. I don't always want to play on my albums. But then on some things I think I want to play on everything. I play all the guitars. Sometimes I have to be talked into playing. It goes back to what I was saying about how the song dictates everything.

Is "Me Myself I" about you?

Yes. [*Laughs*] That's definitely about me. That one came reasonably quick. I don't remember it being very agonizing. There's a song called "Body to Dust" that took forever. It took so long. Normally a song that takes that long, by the time I get to the end of it, it's not worth it. But that one, even though it took so long, it still came up pretty good.

How about the song "Drop the Pilot"?

That one was pretty quick. I wrote that to be a single. I sat down and said, "I am going to write a single." And it worked. [*Laughs*]

Is that something you don't normally do?

Right.

Some songwriters believe if you intentionally try to write a hit, it can screw you up—

Yes, that's right. It really can. I didn't do that again for that reason.

Were there any other songs that were attempts at radio singles?

No . . . name one.

"(I Love It When You) Call Me Names."

No. I'll tell you how I wrote that song. I wrote that in Santa Barbara because there were two chaps in my band. One was quite tall and one was little, and they were always at it, always fighting, always calling each other names and winding each other up. And it was like this love affair. [*Laughs*] I like that song.

How hard is it to remain inventive and inspired in your work within this industry, which has such a short memory and often forgets where the inspiration for so much of today's music originated?

[*Laughs*] I know where you're going, and I'm not sure I want to go there. I still just do what I do. I'm not trying to follow the trends. I've no idea whether it's good or bad. It's what I do—I write songs and I enjoy singing them. I write all kinds of music, music that is bluesy or jazzy or folky. I have lots of things I can change while I still remain me. Whatever I do, it always remains me. I'm not trying to please anybody. So that does it for me.

Will you keep doing it?

There's no reason not to. Even if I write a song and nobody hears it, that's okay. When I started to write songs nobody heard them, and that didn't stop me. I was just writing because it was something that's in me. Still is. [*Laughs*] I don't see that changing. There's no reason for me not to write, even if nobody listens. [*Laughs*]

It's a nice thing. I am very lucky to be able to do what I do. I'm very lucky to be able to write songs that are meaningful for people and help other people to express their feelings. It's quite a special thing.

◆◆◆

Chris Difford and Glenn Tilbrook

Being Squeeze

Burbank, California 1999

"Well, it's 'cause I already know what he's about to say," said Glenn Tilbrook about his tendency to tune out while his partner speaks, "so there's really no need to *monitor*." Asked the same question about his similar tendency, Chris Difford said, "See, the thing about *that* is I prefer not to listen, in case he says something wrong, which will just lead to a debate. And no one wants that."

So, unlike other collaborators who finish each other's thoughts and team up on every sentence, Glenn and Chris sat at opposite ends of the table, paying attention only while talking and tuning out completely while the other spoke. It made the setting of our second talk, a tennis court, the perfect place for such a meeting, as I was compelled to constantly turn from one to the other, as if watching tennis.

It's a style indicative of their entire artistic relationship: these guys don't sit face-to-face and write songs à la the early Beatles but create completely separately, lyrics and music conceived individually, an approach closest to that of their compatriots Elton John and Bernie Taupin. Like

493

that writing duo, Difford and Tilbrook have established themselves as writers of infectious and sophisticated pop rock, songs like Elton and Bernie's that have everything going for them: great grooves; powerful, chromatic melodies; and a perpetually poetic and dynamic use of language.

Glenn Tilbrook, the composer, was eleven when he wrote both the words and music to his first song. Though he never felt himself to be particularly gifted with words, the music always came easy to him, and he decided at that early age to become a songwriter, but one in search of a lyricist. He met one when he answered an advertisement looking for a guitarist, and though the meeting of Difford and Tilbrook was initially the meeting of a guitarist and a bassist, they soon discovered that their potential was limitless as a songwriting team.

They wrote songs together for a few years, waiting until 1974 to form a band. They called it UK Squeeze at first to distinguish it from an American band called Squeeze. They released an independent EP produced by John Cale, who also produced their first eponymously titled album. The song "Take Me I'm Yours" was a hit for the band, the first of many hits Difford and Tilbrook would write in the coming years. Although the lineup of the band shifted a few times, the high quality of the songwriting was constant, and subsequent albums featured countless soulful pop-rock gems, such as "Tempted," "Pulling Mussels (From the Shell)," "Annie Get Your Gun," "Black Coffee in Bed," and more. All had the Squeeze signature of powerful, sophisticated, but seductive music and ironic, slightly skewed, finely detailed lyrics.

They opened for Elvis Costello, a major admirer of Squeeze's songs, and he produced their marvelous *East Side Story* album. Though the band essentially broke up in 1982, playing a farewell concert for the Jamaica World Music Festival, fortunately the core of Difford and Tilbrook remained together and, as a duo, released the 1984 album *Difford & Tilbrook*, which was produced by Tony Visconti.

In 1985 Squeeze re-formed again to play a benefit concert in England, and because the energy within the band seemed better than ever, they decided to keep Squeeze alive and have released five albums since then, including *Babylon and On* and *Frank*.

The great *Play* was produced by Tony Berg soon thereafter, and it was in 1989 that this interview was conducted. They then broke up again in 1999 and returned in 2010 with *Spot the Difference*. In October of 2015 came a whole album of new songs, *Cradle to the Grave*.

Quick personal aside: One always remembers the impact of great music, and never will I forget the sound of Squeeze—that brilliant, shiny, and beautiful sound—emanating from great speakers back when

I first came to Hollywood in 1981. I had a job as a third engineer in a recording studio, a job of many mundane morning chores that were enlivened by constant Squeeze. Nothing was more exultant or electric then. The perfect fusion of traditionally great songwriting—dynamic melodicism, brilliant word play, and romance, all lit boldly by a brightly modern sound, abundant soul, and delicious vocals. To this day that sound brings me back. As I know it does for Squeeze fans the world over.

I met up with Difford and Tilbrook twice, both in LA on mornings after concerts, meaning that Glenn Tilbrook, the lead singer of the band, was weary of voice, leaving Chris Difford—who does provide all the words for the songs, after all—to do the majority of the talking. This is a combination of those two interviews.

Did you guys write songs together before Squeeze was formed?

Chris Difford: Yes, we wrote for about two or three years without playing too many shows at all. We used to write pretty much solidly the whole year round. Which was a good apprenticeship, spending that time growing and writing different types of things.

How did you first meet?

Difford: I put an advert in a local shop window, and I was looking for a guitarist to join our band and get a record deal and go on tour and all the rest of it. I didn't have an album deal or a touring deal or any of those things. It was a complete bluff. I was just lonely, looking for a friend. [*Laughs*]

Glenn Tilbrook: And he found me.

Difford: And I found Glenn. I had just tasted being in a couple of groups, and I thought it was a good living, that it could be a good living, better than a job. And I didn't want to put an ad in *Melody Maker* because it was too serious.

So you were looking for a band more than a songwriting partner?

Difford: I can't look back at it now and say how it actually happened. It just happened that way.

Tilbrook: I saw the sign in the window. I was interested by the influences Chris had put down there: Kinks, Glenn Miller, Lou Reed. I thought, "That's interesting." I replied and got together with Chris, and he was very vague about the band. Then went on holiday for two weeks, and then when he got back we got together and sat down and played together. At that point what we did was play our own songs for each other. And within about a month or two we tried writing one together, and it so happened that without even talking about it, our strengths became apparent: Chris's as a lyricist and mine more as a tunes-man.

Do you remember the first song that you wrote?

Tilbrook: I remember it well. It's not at all . . . distinguished. [*Laughs*] We didn't record it. But it was sufficiently encouraging for us to look at that and see that it was probably better than what we had been doing individually, and from that point onward carry on writing together rather than separately.

What was the title of the first song?

Tilbrook: "Hotel Woman" it was called.

Difford: The titles haven't gotten any better, have they?

How did hearing Dylan affect you as a writer?

Difford: I didn't get hooked on Dylan until *Blood on the Tracks*, and at that point I went back and bought all the early albums and started really listening to them. I just loved the way he could create an imaginary story that would be right there in your mind as you're listening to the song. "Lily, Rosemary and the Jack of Hearts," for me, is the most fantastic lyric for that particular scene within your mind. Where you can play the track and you can see the film running by. And I thought I'd like to be able to do that sort of thing, to be able to create a minifilm in someone's head.

I can see Dylan's influence lyrically on you. Was he a musical influence as well?

Tilbrook: Interestingly enough, "Up the Junction" was very Dylan-influenced musically, although it didn't sound at all like it. I sort of had in mind, when we were recording it, I was saying that we should try to sound like The Band, and it should be seamless and flowing and not particularly making any differential between the verses and middle bits. Just try to create an atmosphere, which I think The Band did excellently.

Dylan wasn't really that much of an influence on me. I was more interested and drawn to melodic things—a lot of sixties stuff. I was madly into pop radio, and it was a great time to be exposed to all those things when I was growing up, and I think a sense of that time has stayed with me ever since then. Further on, toward the time that we first got Squeeze, I was very influenced by Jimi Hendrix, who I thought was a great songwriter. His songs are incredible; there's such a vast imagination, besides being the best guitarist there ever was. He was a big influence on me melodically.

Unlike most songwriting teams I've talked to, you sit on opposite sides of the table and only speak separately. Is this indicative of your writing relationship, that you work separately?

Difford: Yeah. It's very individual in that respect. It's more like Bernie Taupin and Elton John in that respect. And when we do interviews, because we've done so many together, I instinctively know what Glenn's going to say. So I just sit back and relax. And probably likewise. I know what you mean. Sometimes the interviewer feels like somebody in the middle of a tennis match.

When you began writing together you instantly knew that Glenn should do the music and Chris should do the words?

Difford: It just happened that one day I was writing a lyric, and I passed it to Glenn, and it seemed to take shape right there and then. Glenn asked me to write some more lyrics and give them to him, so I did, and it kind of snowballed from there. We wrote a hell of a lot of stuff in that first summer we were together. For a time we lived in a house together. I lived in a room downstairs. And we literally wrote as much as possible, which was good. It was an exciting, transitional time.

So that is the usual process, you write the lyric first?

Difford: Yeah. And now it's become the case that I'll write a bunch of lyrics, and Glenn will write a bunch of tunes, and then we'll have sort of an open-house affair with the lyric at a later stage, when it's going to the vocal stages of the album.

When you write a lyric, Chris, do you write it to a melody in your head?

Difford: Occasionally I get a sort of feel for some kind of flow, yeah. But mostly not. Mostly you're just trying to build a story that's going to rhyme.

Do you signify the different sections—what is the chorus, the verse, etcetera?

Difford: Not anymore, no. I think the verses always pretty much speak for themselves, and the choruses and the middle eight sort of speak for themselves. Quite often I'll give a whole lyric to Glenn, and Glenn will find his own middle eight and his own interpretation of that. I don't think there's any rule at all. Sometimes it's very obvious. Other times it's a complete open book.

Are you the kind of writer who jots down notes constantly, or do you only write when writing?

Difford: More and more, sadly, it's just when you know you have the time to sit down and write. I sort of miss, in a way, the regimented way I used to work, which was quite frequently. On our last tour with Fleetwood Mac there was such a lot of time to kill that I did do a lot of writing, though I was out on the road. I got a portable Macintosh, and I found that quite inspiring to work with. Occasionally a notebook.

For this album [*Play*] a lot of lyrical ideas came from one of those little portable tape recorders. Because I lived in the country and driving into town, you can waste a whole hour just sitting there, looking at the road, listening to the radio. And quite a few ideas actually came to me, so I went and bought a little Olympus minicassette thing and just spoke into it. Or go for walks and speak into it. If I'm riding in a car or walking across a field, it's usually just a dribble that you have to sort of create a lake of when you get home. You get home and put it on the computer and say, "That's a good idea. Where can it go from here, logically speaking?" Then you take it a stage further.

Do you usually write more than you need to and then cut it back?

Difford: Glenn mainly does the editing in that respect, because I am one for rambling. Again, going back to songs like "Lily, Rosemary and the Jack of Hearts" [by Dylan], if I could write thirty-six verses to a song, I would. And it's fun because you can ever expand the characters. But I know it would be difficult to fit that kind of thing onto an album. The last time that lyrically that succeeded with me was a song called "Melody Motel." The lyric kind of flowed and told a story, and it all sounded like a good, old-fashioned song.

When you set a lyric to music, do you try many musical approaches before settling on one?

Tilbrook: Good question. I think I try to settle on one approach from the beginning, but sometimes I'll get so far down the road with something and realize that it's not working. I try to always finish off every idea that I've had. I would rather finish it up and leave it and figure it's no good or be able to come back to it. Very rarely, but sometimes I will completely abandon what I'm doing and start anew. Sometimes I have the tendency to write these horrendous tunes and not be able to see it.

Is "The Truth" a true song?

Difford: Yes. It's very autobiographical. For a long time I had a lot of trouble with the truth. I think most men do. It's very easy to paint yourself into a corner sometimes, and the only way out of it is to lie. It's an awful sin, but everybody does it. I was very clever for a long time, juggling the truth with lies. And then I got to a point where I didn't know which was real.

So this song is about me turning round to all the men in the world and saying, "Face up to it. We're all liars. This is the truth." Lots of men come up to me and say, "I understand 'The Truth.' It makes perfect sense." It's the most masculine of lyrics on the album.

How did "Walk a Straight Line" originate?

Difford: It was a story about somebody who is crippled by alcohol and the kind of abuses that come with that. It's really about a character trying to find some reformation in himself. Looking for a reason to believe, I suppose. Tony Berg, our producer, brought up a good point. He thought the two characters were trying to get sober, to walk a straight line together to get married in a church. So they could walk a straight line to the altar to get married. I think that's really a good observation.

Had you looked at it that way yourself?

Difford: To be honest, I hadn't.

It's about time you were honest!

Difford: At long last. [*Laughs*]

Your collaboration is similar to that of Elton and Bernie Taupin, except for the fact that, unlike Bernie, you also sing and play in the band.

Difford: Yeah, unfortunately. I like being in the band, but I am a lyricist-songwriter. That is my trade. If I were a carpenter, somebody who was building furniture, that is what you would do. But I'm a songwriter and somebody who goes on the road. And when I go on the road I can't usually do any songwriting. One negates the other.

So you can't always concentrate your whole time on one particular aspect of your life. You have to keep swinging from one to the other. It's great to be in a band, but as one gets older you tend to wonder where your loyalties really lie. Are you a writer or are you in a band? And then the catch is that one doesn't really exist without the other anyway. So it's an interesting twist.

Being a musician yourself, do you have musical input to the songs when you write a lyric? Do you have melodic ideas that accompany lyrical passages?

Difford: Sometimes I do, yeah. Sometimes I can sing a lyric into a tape recorder, write the lyric down, and give it to Glenn, and he will never know where the melody has come from. For the most part I write mainly from the first word on. From the first idea. Without melody. It's an interesting phenomenon, which I still don't understand. How can you sit in front of a computer and create a lyric like "Satisfied," which took maybe three minutes to write lyrically? How that came about without any melody in my head? I'm not really sure.

You mentioned the lyric for "Satisfied" took only three minutes. When writing something like that, do you write it in meter so that it's easily set to music?

Difford: Glenn approached me once and said, "Your metering isn't as good as it could be." He was finding it hard to put music to some of the lyrics. And ever since that event I've been very careful to make sure the metering is as close as it could be to a mathematical equation. I labored over it for a long time, but now it just comes naturally.

Do you usually start with a title, or do you create the title later in the process?

Difford: I'm not terribly good with titles. That's probably my weakest aspect, I think. Glenn always seems a little shocked by the audacity of my titles. I used to steal a lot from book titles and film titles. I thought I came up with one the other day that was not from a book or a film. It's more of a pun, and for the week or so I've been conjuring up the image of what this particular title and song could be.

Can you divulge that title?

Difford: It's a thing called "Third Person Removed." I thought of the title, and now I've got to fit lyrics into the title.

Songs often share titles with other songs or with movies or books. Yet in songs you are able to present a fresh twist on a title.

Difford: Indeed. It's not like plagiarism. It's an interesting way of drawing people's attention to the song.

As in your song "'Annie Get Your Gun," which is a wonderful usage of that title.

Difford: Indeed. Annie was not a real person. It was a jumble of ideas, really. Kind of a melting pot of images more than anything else. I had written, a lot earlier in my life, songs about Annie Oakley. I don't know whether that had anything to do with that, but it probably did.

Do you recall writing "I've Returned?"

Difford: Yes. For the most part that whole album, *Sweets from a Stranger*, was sort of soaked in alcohol. There are a lot of alcoholic images in the context of that album, that song being one of them. A drunken character returning. Abruptly. Onto the scene, as it were. The way alcoholics do.

Yet it seems a triumphant return.

Difford: Yeah, it's almost like a fanfare. You expect trumpets to come blaring out.

One of your most intriguing titles is "Pulling Mussels (From the Shell)."

Difford: That song was influenced really by The Small Faces. I used to adore the way they would write about English situations. Very British picture-postcard situations, really. I wanted to write about the experience that a lot of working-class English people do of going to the seaside and what a day out for them would be. And then taking it a step further by talking of old people, young people, and family people at the seaside.

The result is a cross-section in each verse, virtually, of how I saw seaside villages. So you have the old people looking round the shops, and then in the chorus you have the young people who are trying to have sex with strangers behind the chalet on the beach. A lot of working-class people in Britain go on holiday in England. That's as far as they ever go, you know. I suppose it's the same here in the States. People only go to the end of their garden for a holiday, and they come back and they're satisfied with that— that's their life. I find that really intriguing. I think it's island mentality.

I don't like to travel. If I wasn't in a group, I wouldn't go anywhere. It must be something steeped way back in your past, hundreds of years ago.

Could you be as good of a writer without traveling? Some say you can sit in your room and do it, that you don't have to go all over the globe.

Difford: I'd like to think that you could sit in your room and imagine. The traveling that we do, you don't really experience anything. You're on a bus, a plane, in a hotel. It's not like we're going to the Museum of Modern Art every day or exploring my environment.

One day I'd like to come to America and hire a Winnebago and drive around and see it for real. There are influences, of course. You turn on the TV in America and you can see the absurdities of Richard Simmons and the church ladies and that sort of thing. But you're really only scratching the surface.

What was the inspiration for your song "Piccadilly?"

Difford: It was basically about a couple that used to drink in a pub where I used to work in London, and I just happened to be observing them one night. They seemed to have reached a pinnacle in their relationship at the bar. And they'd been out somewhere, to the theater or something. They looked as if they didn't have anywhere to go, as if their evening had ended. And I took their situation a step further and put them back at her house, where her mother was, and he wasn't supposed to spend the night, the age-old situation.

I've been through it myself when I was younger. You go back to their house, and they say, "You can't really stay, but if you're quiet, we can sneak up to my room." You've spent all evening trying to impress upon this girl what a great guy you are by taking her to the theater and taking her for an Indian meal. And then you get found out.

How about "I Think I'm Go Go"?

Difford: Yes. Now that was influenced by touring. I felt like I was going go-go last night after doing two shows. I felt like this is murder. The lyrics speak about different continents. And the middle verse that I sing is obviously about America. It's about a state of mind one can get in as a young musician on the road for the first time. Abusing one's self to the nth degree.

Was the ascending chord progression and melody in the chorus on "Go-go-go-go" part of your original conception?

Difford: No, Glenn did that. I don't know what enhanced him to do that, but it made perfect sense. He's fantastic at weaving a chord sequence, there's no doubt about that. It mesmerizes me how he gets that together. He creates some really fascinating tapestries with what he does.

Tilbrook: Why, thank you.

Glenn, how do you go about setting a lyric to music? Do you work on an instrument?

Tilbrook: Yeah, almost always. I've done it various different ways. I think the way I like best is to look at a lyric when I'm at a piano or guitar, to see if I feel—this is very difficult to articulate—see if I feel something that would suggest a tune. If I'm lucky enough to get started that way, then I'll alternate between guitar and keyboard all the time, just for the change of perspective that it will give me. Things look different if you play them on guitar than if you play them on keyboard. So I'll sort of learn it on both and switch about every half hour and switch back and forth. Other times I will stick to one instrument.

Other times, very rarely, I'll just sing a tune with a drum machine and see what chords fit behind that. That's unusual for me, but it's a nice way to work. It leaves your imagination free to go in other places. I like just running a tape and improvising and then figuring out the bits that are good and trying to fashion that in some way.

Or you can work the other way, which is also valid, which is to actually slave away on a tune for ages and keep coming back to it. I used to think that that would be overanalytical, but in fact, going back as far as "Tempted," that took me a week to actually get it right and get the changes right. And I know that you can get back to things that can have a spark all the time as long as you use your sense of judgement and are willing to say at some point that that's enough.

Are your piano songs more harmonically complex than guitar songs?

Tilbrook: Almost always. There's a greater opportunity with my playing to expand on keyboard than there is on guitar. But then, that's not always the case. There's a song called "House of Love," which is quite complex musically, and that was all written on guitar.

Was "Tempted" a piano song?

Tilbrook: Yes, it was written on piano. Which is the way I'm playing it tonight, in a fashion. [*Laughter*]

You invariably come up with chord progressions that are unexpected but so great. I'm always dying to figure out how you do those.

Tilbrook: [*Laughs*] Me too. I don't always know. Sometimes you just land on something and you're lucky.

Difford: In "Satisfied," for example, going from a B flat to a G in the chorus is such a magic moment for me. It's such a strange selection. On "House of Love," when you played me that on acoustic guitar, I thought I'd been hit by a machine gun—there were so many chords in it. For that reason it really complements the lyric. The lyric is very bizarre, and the chords are very bizarre, so it all makes for a bizarre picture.

Where did you get the idea for "If I Didn't Love You?"

Difford: Again it came from one particular line: "Singles remind me of kisses, albums remind me of plans." That line I wrote first because I was going out with a Swedish girl at the time, and I was finding it very difficult to make love with her. I found it very hard going, if you'll excuse the pun. So I put on a Todd Rundgren album, *Something/Anything?*, that had a very long side to it, twenty-eight minutes, I think it is. I used to play that because I knew I had twenty-eight minutes to get it on with this girl. And that led me to write that line. And the rest of it followed on from there.

Do you ever feel restricted by having to be at the screen when writing?

Difford: When I write I go and turn the computer on in the morning, come to the front page of what I'm writing, and then generally leave the room immediately as the lyric appears. I go and have some tea or do whatever I have to do, and then come back to it later. There's a mystical element of having the lyric sort of churning away in the computer. It's very odd. I'm sure it's just my imagination.

Do you enjoy the use of a computer for writing lyrics?

Difford: Yeah. It's good. I think the fascination came from being brought up on TV when you're a kid. Now I see my own lyrics on a TV screen, and I'm impressed. It's like watching *Wagon Train*.

◆ ◆ ◆

Aimee Mann
On Memory Lane

Aspen, Colorado 2005

So that's today's memory lane
With all the pathos and pain
Another chapter in a book where the chapters are
    endless
And they're always the same
A verse, then a verse, and refrain

From "4th of July," Aimee Mann

Aimee Mann is in Aspen. The altitude is getting to her, and driving around the towering mountains and rolling Colorado canyons to arrive here has made her a little queasy on top of the exhaustion from being in the midst of an ongoing tour that brought her to the majestic Red Rocks

Amphitheatre outside of Denver on the previous night. So happiness is not the headline on her front page at this moment.

On this night we are to appear together onstage at the glorious Belly Up club in the heart of Aspen—she is the guest of the Aspen Writers' Foundation's ongoing Lyrically Speaking program, in which I have the fortunate mission of interviewing great songwriters, a discussion punctuated by intimate performances. It's a great gig for many reasons, not the least of which is that it allows me to come frequently to Aspen, also known as heaven on earth. People I knew from Los Angeles who were consistently dour and miserable in the vast urbanity of LA are completely different people in Aspen—they ride bikes, they smile frequently, they are as peaceful as Buddhist monks.

Aimee is performing on this night with a stripped-down band—just her on acoustic guitar and a bass player and keyboard player, the latter of which requested an old Wurlitzer, which was a challenge to find anywhere in Colorado, but was eventually located and transported to the club. On this early afternoon the chore is to do a sound check and to configure the stage: where we will sit, if she will stand or sit, should the mics be on stands or handheld—those kinds of logistics. The stuff that can be painfully dull when feeling healthy and simply painful when you're not. And she wasn't feeling healthy.

So after much discussion among musicians and managers and soundmen, we settled on a stage structure that seemed to make sense, and there was Aimee, unsmiling, discontent, evidently unhappy to be there or maybe anywhere at this moment. We sat on tall stools with twin wireless microphones. Sound-check time had arrived, and my role was to pose a question or two, just to check the mics and also to maybe establish some kind of rapport. I'd interviewed her in the past on the phone, but we'd done very little in the way of in-person interaction. My instinct, as always, was to loosen things up, inject a little levity, if possible, into the proceedings, and let the artist know that although a serious discussion is intended, that it's not impossible to also have some fun. So I asked her about her boxing.

Yes, Aimee Mann boxes. She is in great shape, and among other physical activities, she loves boxing. Real boxing—in the ring, gloves, punching, the attempted KOs, the whole thing. It seemed like the logical topic from which to launch our inaugural discussion. "How would you like to box Bob Dylan?" I asked, unsure as to how she might respond. Silence from all gathered. Then a slow smile spread over her face, and she caught the ball and ran with it.

"I'd *love* to box Bob Dylan," she said with relish. "And he does box. I think he'd probably be pretty good in the ring. But I think I could take him." This made us all happy and relieved: not only was she willing to entertain absurdity—always a good sign—but she did it with easy panache. Soon a discussion ensued about other songwriters she'd like to box—Neil Diamond, Neil Sedaka, Paul Simon—during which time sonic dynamics were balanced and tweaked.

She's an astounding songwriter. One of the best. Like Jules Shear, Paul Simon, Joni Mitchell, and very few others, she's equally gifted and focused on being inventive and innovative with both music and lyrics. Her melodies are consistently as engaging as her lyrics. And like her potential boxing mate Dylan, she embraces traditional song forms while breaking new ground within them—Krishnamurti's mantra that "limitation creates possibilities" in action. She uses real rhymes almost exclusively, lending her songs a powerful inner matrix that many listeners might never consciously register but certainly sense. She employs often intricate rhyme schemes to great effect and understands, as Dylan put it, that phrasing is everything. The flowing river rhythms of her words is as alluring as her rhymes and imagery. Her songs don't fall apart like cheap watches on the street, to paraphrase Van Dyke Parks. They are sturdy. They are poetic and colloquial both, ideally balanced and beautifully rendered.

She said once that she likes songs to be conversational. Confronted with some rather enriched poetic language found in her verses, she laughed and said, "Well, maybe I just have a larger vocabulary than a lot of people do." Indeed she does. She has a keen intelligence and a gentle and humorous knowingness, and she is unafraid of instilling it into her songs. Unlike the majority of songwriters who created their best work in their twenties, she has surpassed her early work and has gone on to craft one great album after the next.

She is a fan of other songwriters: she loves her husband Michael Penn's work, of course—they are married after all. But she is also a big fan of former beau Jules Shear as well as Dylan, Bacharach, and Elvis Costello. It was Elvis who said that truly great songwriters show a lot of attention to detail. She does that: her use of telling details is measured and inspired. She consciously creates a rich sense of place, of time, and of character in her songs, and always with genuine passion.

Much of that richness can be found in her most recent album, a remarkable song-cycle called *The Forgotten Arm*. It's the story of two lovers, John and Caroline, a musical fable painted with dimensional cinematic scenes, poignant poetry, and classic melodicism. She knows about the essence of singability; regardless of any other concerns, the words always flow flawlessly on the current of music. Her songs, even the morose ones—and there are many of those—are imbued with genuine joy: the joy of making music.

Born on September 8, 1960, in Richmond, Virginia, she studied music at Berklee in Boston, and joined her first band, Young Snakes, there in that historic city. In 1983 she formed 'Til Tuesday with her boyfriend Michael Hausman, an amiable man and agile drummer who is now her manager, and they struck gold in 1985 with their hit single "Voices Carry," which she wrote. Unlike many songs of that era, it wasn't a mindless confection; it bore her signature of a powerful melody with provocative words and sounds as good in this twenty-first century—she caved to repeated demands and performed it onstage in Aspen—as it did in the previous epoch.

The band recorded several albums, and multi-instrumentalist Jon Brion, who went on to become an influential producer, joined them. The pressures of operating within the industry started to rattle her in every way, as such pressures will, and she broke up the band in 1990 to go solo.

Her next illustrious companion was the songwriter Jules Shear—for whom she wrote the song "J for Jules." (When I asked her about putting his name into a song and thus stating her private truth so bluntly, she laughed and said she did it only because she liked rhyming "Jules" with "fools," and had his name been Byron or Henry it wouldn't have gotten in.)

Her first solo outing was *Whatever*, the first of many albums to establish her, outside of the band, as one of the most talented songwriters and performers on the scene. Jon Brion produced two of her albums as well as the soundtrack for the movie *Magnolia*, which director-writer Paul Thomas Anderson constructed around her songs. It earned her an Oscar nomination for Best Song and launched the beautiful "Save Me" into the culture.

These days she's much happier than she was during her long winter of discontent entrenched in the corporate confines of Geffen Records (where *Bluerailroad* columnist Peter Case also dwelled). She made the superb solo album *Bachelor No. 2* while still under contract to Geffen, but it was roundly rejected by the company, who objected to both its artistic direction and content. They insisted it be radically rehauled, she refused, and a long season of legal skirmishes ensued. Her ultimate victory allowed her to release *Bachelor* on SuperEgo, and it has generated a spirit of liberation that has led in turn to the deeply brilliant and beautiful cycle of songs that became *Lost in Space* and all of her subsequent albums. These days she's a little weary when it comes to discussing such history but brightens considerably when discussing her new music, and she expounds with understated exuberance on the diverse and delicate considerations necessary to coax a song into being.

Music always comes first. Her primary songwriting process is to find a provocative musical idea and allow it to define the direction of the melody and the content of the lyric. Her most recent work, *The Forgotten Arm*, is produced by Joe Henry (see page 624) and captures the energy of live performance by having been recorded mostly live in the studio; it's another compelling chapter in the musical tome she's been writing now for decades. As Jon Brion said, "She's certainly one of my all-time favorite intelligent, emotional pop songwriters. She is by far one of the best lyricists, I mean, by a long shot. And the fact that she also happens to be gifted melodically just really puts it over the top. I still don't think the world at large even fully understands how good she is. I just think she's nothing short of remarkable."

That expresses the essence of what is at the core of this admittedly expansive introduction: that the world at large might not even get it yet. It's true of many of our greatest artists—painters, poets, and musicians. What they are doing is so good and is at such a level that it takes a while for people to catch up with it. But those in the know certainly know, and they know there are few better than Aimee Mann. Though she said in Aspen that she writes her best songs when she's bored, there is nothing boring about her work—quite the opposite. And just as it elevates the artist herself from the everyday doldrums of life as lived, so do these songs enhance our lives with a sweet and solemn confederation of sound and soul and thought.

When you work on a song, do you always keep at it till it's finished?

Aimee Mann: It really depends. I think I'm pretty good at recognizing when I'm getting to the flogging-a-dead-horse space. And then you've just got to let it go. And those kind of songs, it might be years later that I pick it up, and it seems like a totally new song, so I can work on it more. I think for me it's when a song needs a different section, and you don't know where to go, and that often requires a certain perspective. Like a bridge, for example, you need a section that has a lift to it or a different kind of cadence, and sometimes I can get too caught up in the vibe of the verse that it's difficult to go to a different place, and the bridge turns out to be just like the verse, sort of rewritten, and it get a little stale. That was the case with "Invisible Ink," where I needed a lot of time to see it differently and to discover a new place to go with it.

Musically and lyrically?

Both. I started writing "Invisible Ink" with a friend in Boston *years* ago and never finished it. I remembered it and was able to reconnect with it and write a new section that made it complete. It has lyrics that I rewrote, but what it really lacked was a bridge. I could never write a bridge to it, and then twelve years later I sat down and wrote a bridge to it. That song is different from the rest musically because the music was mostly written by a songwriter friend of mine in Boston. So it goes to different places.

You wrote many of your early songs in Boston. Does it affect the song where you are when you write it?

No. I think what matters more is that I have some quiet time, without interruption.

When you start a song, do you start with words or music?

I start with music mostly. I'll have a couple of lyric lines, and I'll fool around with them on guitar and try to find some kind of melody that works.

Do you start with an idea that you are trying to express, or does that come while working on the song?

Both. I think they come together. Usually I'm playing the guitar and humming the melody, and usually they will form themselves into words, and I'll think about what it sounds like and follow that. Music definitely leads me into lyrical themes. I'll find some music and then see what it sounds like it's about. So the music is more of a driving force in forming the song and what the song is about.

Do you have one guitar you use?

Yes, an acoustic 1954 Gibson J-160 that I use. It's my main guitar. It's the best for everything. I record with it, I write with it, and I take it on the road and perform with it. It's really beat up. It was beat up when I got it. And then I was in a car accident and it got thrown from the car. It got shredded, and I got a guy in Ann Arbor who rebuilt it for me. And he did a pretty great job. It looks pretty beat up, but it essentially sounds great.

Do you write with a capo?

Oh yeah, frequently. I do a lot of capo action. Usually if something is not in my key. Sometimes it's helpful because it puts me in a new place I'm not overly familiar with, which can lead to new musical ideas. But I do often end up playing the same chord changes anyway. I think, "Oh look, this is a different progression," and then realize it's the same chord progression I've used before, only with a capo putting it in a different position. You know, I sing a lot of stuff in B—B major and B minor—so I put the capo on the second fret and play in A or A minor.

So you don't strive to come up with new progressions you haven't used before?

No, I *do*. Sometimes I *deliberately* try to come up with chords that are put together in a different way. But sometimes I'm just writing and I have a chord progression that works, and I just let myself go ahead and finish the song, even though I know the progression might be similar to something I've written before.

"This Is How It Goes" is in A flat, which is not a common guitar key.

Yeah, there you go. That was capoed on the sixth fret. Starting on a B minor shape.

Your songs are often very ingeniously structured with great bridges. Is song structure something you enjoy working with?

Yeah, I really like the kind of traditional pop song structure. You know, verse-chorus-verse-chorus-bridge-chorus. I rely on that heavily.

Sometimes I find I like songs that have simpler structures, and these are probably songs that are built in the studio. I kind of like it to sound like it's a complete song before I get to the studio. I don't want to have to rely on the studio to complete the song. I work hard to make sure both the melody and words are strong before thinking about recording or production.

Your songs are always wonderfully melodic. Have you always been a fan of strong melodies?

Yeah. I think that the artists I like the most are artists who have a really strong melodic sense. Like The Beatles and Elton John.

"Pavlov's Bell" has a great structure, the way it builds up to the chorus, which then explodes.

That was a conscious choice. You try to build the momentum into the writing so that kind of prechorus section is a little sort of floaty and then tightens up to the chorus. So that was done intentionally.

When you are working on a song are you concerned with the guitar part or just strumming chords?

Just strumming chords. I can't really play anything. I'll have an *occasional* arpeggio.

"Humpty Dumpty" is a powerful song, with that great line "All the perfect drugs and superheroes wouldn't be enough to bring me up to zero."

That's how I felt. Sometimes you feel bad, and you can't imagine anything that would make you feel better. That's in A minor. There's a lot of A minor to E minor in these songs. I also like to contrast major and minor—that one is in A minor for the verses but goes to F major in the chorus, which gives you that contrast. I think there's some irony and a feeling of an almost anthemic quality to having this very depressed lyric; it's like having defeat and triumph all in one.

In a song like that are you leading where you want the song to go, or following?

With that song it came from the music I was working on, and then there was a sense of building in the prechorus that kind of hinted what the chorus chords were going to be, and then I ended the chorus, which kind of built up to a certain thing harmonically. Then I play that music and think, "What does this sound like to me?" and that's what it sounded like. To me the music dictates a certain area, but then I try to picture it and translate that picture into words.

Do you finish the music first usually and then work on lyrics?

Sometimes. Probably I always end up playing catch-up with lyrics. That's always the last thing that has to be done. I very rarely have lyrics written out completely before finishing the melody. It's much harder for me to fit music to lyrics than to find lyrics that fit the music.

Do you always work on these lyrics with guitar?

Sometimes I'll keep it in my head—while I'm doing chores or driving somewhere. I find it helps sometimes to think of it as somebody else's song and then decide what I would do with it or where else I could go with it. If you're playing it on guitar, you can get caught up in the chords, or your hands will automatically go to familiar chord changes that you've heard a million times. So it's good to sort of hear it first and then figure out what it is. So you have to put the guitar down and just focus on the melody and later figure out the chords that will fit that. This happens only when the melody and the meter of the song is already there so that I can get away from the guitar and think about the lyrics. The mind keeps working on the songs when there's something there worthwhile.

Mentioning meter, the phrasing to so many of your songs is so nice, even without the music, such as "Baby kiss me like a drug, like a respirator . . ." Using those multisyllabic words that fall into the music so well.

I work on that as much as anything. I also try to get the best rhyme scheme I can. There's a lot of stuff I throw out because I don't think it fits the meter or it doesn't sound right within the meter.

Your rhymes are also great, such as in "It's Not," the rhyme that holds together the title with "astronaut" and "afterthought" is so pleasant. Traditional aspects such as rhyme and meter are elements you are concerned with?

Yeah. If it's not a perfect rhyme, it's either because I either got so sick of working on it or because I just couldn't find any other way to phrase it. I do spend a *lot* of time trying to get a perfect rhyme. That is important to me because I think that helps a lot in communicating certain ideas to a listener. I think it makes a nice little surprise that helps you connect with a song. Even if the listener doesn't realize it, subconsciously they feel it. I don't always have perfect rhymes, but I work hard to get them.

Is rhyming fun for you?

Yeah. I feel as a songwriter, that's your job. There's not only the *thing* that you are saying, but there's the best way to say it. It's your job to find out the best way to say it, to make sure the meter is good, and that it sounds very conversational. "Baby, kiss me like a drug . . . ," that's kind of the cadence of how you would actually say a line like that. It's your job to try to make it be as good as it can be, and these are my standards for good.

You have a great mixture of conversational language with infused poetic language.

I try to keep it conversational. That's always my goal. Maybe I have a vocabulary that other people don't have, I don't know.

A line like "Let me fall into the dream of the astronaut" is a poetic thought.

True. But it also says exactly what I want to say. That was the image. It was very *2001*, kind of that image of the astronaut floating away. On the one hand, it's very peaceful and dreamlike, but it's also *very* bereft and alien. Those things are all there in that picture.

And it's a picture, which is something you give us a lot in songs.

That helps me write. If I have a picture or image in mind, I can describe what the image is, and that makes my job easier.

"It's Not" is a haunting song, and it's cool that way you use the title, in that it has a different meaning each time.

I try to do that. That's definitely something I like to incorporate into my songwriting, that the title can mean something a little different every time you land on it. It's got a nice string arrangement, which really adds a whole different layer to it.

With that one I wanted to have the first few verses to be broad and sort of this vague, like a kind of mental exhaustion, and then you find out in the final verse, you realize where it's all directed, and it suddenly becomes more personal, and the words are directing you. It all ends with "and I believed it was you who could make it better, but it's not." Well, [*laughs*] that's kind of the way it goes.

That song has the line "lost in space," which is also the title song of the album. Which came first?

Actually I had the title for the album first before either song. I knew that was what I wanted to call it. The song "Lost in Space" didn't have that line in it at first. But as I was working on the song I felt it just wasn't good enough, and I had to take it apart and keep working on it to rewrite the lyric. And I ended up using it as my first line, and it became the title line. And once that was there, when I was working on "It's Not," which was the last song I wrote for the record and the song I knew would be last on the record, I wanted to tie them together. I felt that would be perfect.

Do you find that using true details from your own life adds resonance to songs?

Yeah, you always have to connect it to yourself or it becomes just an exercise in writing. I would feel like it's cheating, in a sense, if I don't have some real emotional involvement with the song. Plus, it's just harder to write—if you have no emotional involvement, what's the point? Some writers, like McCartney, have written little story songs, like "Maxwell's Silver Hammer," that have nothing to do with him. Maybe if I had more talent, I could write outside of myself, and I might do that. But I'm just not that interested, if a song does not directly relate to me in some way, to work on it.

Are lyrics and melodies equally important?

I think it's a balance. It's all part of the same thing in songwriting. Songs are interesting because it's always the music that gets to you first. It is for me because music has feeling in it too. The music does have a story in it itself. It sets up an emotional tone which then, as you listen more closely, you find out more details. With songs, if you listen more closely, if you realize it's just kind of thrown together, it's a letdown. It's the difference between seeing someone who looks really interesting and then getting to talk to them and find out they're a moron—it's a real letdown. Certain celebrities are that way. They look so cool, but when you hear them speak, it's really disappointing.

"This Is How It Goes" is interesting in that regard, in that it has an upbeat chorus, yet the lyrics contrast that feel with "It's all about drugs, it's all about shame . . ."

It doesn't seem like a contrast to me because those words and music came at the same time.

You've written frequently about drugs and addictions and battles with those kinds of demons.

I think that's true. That's a theme that comes up a lot in many of these songs. Sometimes when I write about drugs, that's a shorthand to describe certain kinds of compulsive behavior. And then some of the other songs are connected to a certain kind of emotional disassociation and depression.

"Humpty Dumpty" starts with the idea of being split into fragments.

That started with the music. That's one of my favorite songs.

"Lost in Space" is great, with the lines "By just pretending to care / Like I'm not even there / Gone, but I don't know where . . ."

That's another song, like "Humpty Dumpty," which is about disassociation and trying to have a face that interacts with other people, but you feel it's not really you. I think a lot of people feel that way. They feel that there's a false front, where they feel that they have to interact with people in a certain way, but they feel really divorced from the people they are with.

"Pavlov's Bell" is kind of a road song.

It's also a song that uses a kind of fear of flying as sort of a natural thing and what people do to try to mask certain fears and certain phobias.

When you're working on a song, even if you don't think it's a great one, do you allow that critical voice to be heard, or do you try to keep that outside?

For me what defines "great" or not is just if I am interested in it and connected to it emotionally. I can think something is really good and just not be connected to it, and that's the end of that song. I stop working on it. There are a lot of songs I just drop along the way. And then I might try to pick them up at a later time. And then there are definitely songs I've tried over and over again to finish or work on and I fail or succeed. I tape myself while working, so I can preserve any melodic ideas I think might be good at the time.

"The Moth" takes the idea of "a moth to a flame" and bends it in new ways.

Yeah, I love that. I like to do that—to take a cliché or an idiom in the language and examine them. And the moth in a flame is perfect. It is obviously the perfect kind of addiction reference. And having a kind of discussion about how the moth feels about the flame and how the flame feels about the moth.

I love your version of "One" written by Nilsson, which was featured on the great album *For the Love of Harry* and was also on the *Magnolia* soundtrack.

That was almost a note-for-note remake of his original demo version. It was just so great. If you listen to his demo version, we just copied those.

You've had well-publicized battles with record companies. Did those battles ever cause you to be creatively derailed?

Well, I think there were definitely times that I felt having to deal with the record companies added a real inhibitory factor. It's very difficult to feel really good about writing a song when you know that there are people who are going to give it thumbs up or thumbs down before anybody else has a chance to hear it. And more likely than not, it's going to be thumbs down. I don't think they ever understood what kind of an artist I am. I think they had this weird perception of me, where people kept looking at me as if I'm this real commercial artist who suddenly, out of nowhere, is doing this other thing. And I guess that comes from being in 'Til Tuesday, I'm not really sure. But there is this perception, and it did hinder my work during one period to the point where I couldn't write at all. It was very difficult. I couldn't write and I couldn't sing. I just kind of shut down. It lasted a while. It was while I was making *Bachelor No. 2*. It was a real struggle to circumvent writer's block.

How did you get beyond that?

Therapy. I went to therapy and tried to figure out what was behind it.

You've since shown us that it is possible to do it on your own without a major label. Is that liberating for you?

Oh, completely. Because I can just think about the music. I can just write songs that are great. You know what? Some people won't like it. But at least the people who *do* like it will have the chance to hear it before it's thrown into the trash. But I think the corporate big labels will collapse of their own weight. Any minute now.

◆ ◆ ◆

James Taylor

The Secret o' Songwriting

Massachusetts 2007

To get to his home you drive down a winding country road in the verdant heart of Massachusetts, under sun-dappled arches of ancient oaks and elms, over railroad tracks, and past a graveyard of tombstones so old they look like dominoes frozen in midfall. A long and winding road leads through the trees, past a big red barn, and, just beyond it, the house. Though it's not quite October, there's already a little pumpkin by the front door.

With a gentle smile, JT strides through the kitchen to greet me and introduces me warmly to his wife, Kim. Their living room is washed with sunlight and punctuated by a long, carpeted wooden beam that connects the high-ceilinged first floor with the second and on which Ray, their cat, can swiftly ascend, which James and Kim happily encourage him to do. Built with the same kind of economical ingenuity James brings to his work, this skyward ramp is sturdy, functional, and elegant.

We sit on a porch in the back and talk over lunch. He speaks with the same blend of wisdom, awareness, and curiosity that he brings to his songs—from explaining the unshakable fidelity of Bostonians for the Red Sox to the characteristics of a hog-nosed snake (it plays dead). "You have to learn to grow fonder of your burdens," he says, underscoring a trajectory both zealous and Zen-like, wise enough to flow with the current but unafraid to dip in his own paddle. Like the harmonic structures of his songs, there's more depth and complexity there than what's on the surface. Asked if he considers songwriting to be a conscious or unconscious act, he expounds expansively on the nature of consciousness and the physics of music.

More than anything, he's humble. He questions the premise of anyone truly owning a song and generally deflects and diffuses any praise about his work, though he does receive and even harbor criticism. When told many songwriters, such as Randy Newman, admire his harmonic virtuosity, he worries whether his songs are "too chordy" and in need of simplification. Complimented on the profusion of genuine soul in his singing, he laments the exploitation of black musicians. Questioned about the philosophy of acceptance expressed in "Secret o' Life" ("the secret of life is enjoying the passage of time"), he minimizes its message as facile and presumptuous. When asked about the intimate clarity of his work, he disparages it for being "too self-referential."

He's been both lauded and lambasted for being the ultimate representative of the confessional school of songwriting. But it's not the whole truth. Although he's famously written about private and personal explorations of the heart, he's also always been a remarkable narrative songwriter, spinning mythical musical yarns, from "Mud Slide Slim" to "Millworker" to "The Frozen Man." Indeed, his intention in songs has sometimes been misread—the best example being "Sweet Baby James"—which many interpreted as self-referential and perhaps even self-indulgent when, in fact, it was written as a lullaby for his newborn nephew, who was named in his honor.

Which isn't to say he hasn't written songs that could be considered confessional. But he's always done it in a way that springs not from a bleeding heart as much as from an empathetic soul. The very declaration "I've seen fire and I've seen rain" echoes biblical verse, and the song resounds with a measure of mythical grace much more so than any kind of self-pity. Even the direct allusion to Flying Machine, the dissolved band of his youth, doesn't speak of narcissism as much as it does wistful resignation: "Sweet dreams and flying machines in pieces on the ground."

There's an authenticity there in his songs, a human connection that's undeniable. It's there in the earthy resonance of his voice, the gentle focus of his guitar playing, the ripe and soulful splendor of his melodies, and in the lucid dynamism of his lyrics. His songs have long provided a sense of tranquility in the midst of turbulence, an unflustered alternative to the fleeting frenzy of modern times. And though his work has long impacted the very culture from which it springs, he's existed outside of the marketplace, outside of any desire to bend to the whims of fashion, and for this reason his work remains timeless. Sting, who has declared on more than one occasion that James is the modern musician he most admires, said, "His singing and his sound are always contemporary and yet timeless, totally immune to mere fashion."

He was born on March 12, 1948, in Belmont, Massachusetts, and raised in North Carolina. His first instrument was cello, which, from ages eight to thirteen, he played "badly, reluctantly." His older brother Alex had a profound influence on his musical sensibilities, as did his friends the guitarist Danny "Kootch" Kortchmar and the drummer Joel O'Brien, with whom he formed his first band, Flying Machine.

It was Kootch who delivered a demo of his early songs to Peter Asher who, galvanized by Paul McCartney and George Harrison's enthusiasm, made James Taylor the first non-Beatle act signed to Apple Records. JT recorded his debut album in between Beatles sessions for what became *The White Album* and wrote one of his most classic songs then, "Carolina in My Mind," on which McCartney played bass and also sang harmony with George Harrison. When Apple ultimately collapsed, JT moved back to the States and signed with Warner, where he recorded the album that forever cemented his reputation, *Sweet Baby James*. Containing a chain of breathtaking originals, such as the poignantly pastoral "Blossom," "Country Road," and "Anywhere Like Heaven," he presented an organic alternative to the urban school of songwriting, culminating in an unprecedented masterpiece of personal songwriting: "Fire and Rain." And from that moment on, James Taylor became a beloved and venerated artist, as deeply ingrained into the cherished fabric of American culture as Stephen Foster, Woody Guthrie, or Hank Williams.

Perhaps more than any other single quality to be found in his musical persona is an unassailable affability: the powerful sense that this singer is your friend. And not just any friend—an *old* friend. Someone who's been there when you needed him. His reedy baritone resonates with rustic warmth and empathy. It's the reason why he so thoroughly inhabits "You've Got a Friend," even though Carole King wrote it. When he sings it, you believe it. A sense of spiritual generosity, of Lincolnesque honesty, radiates from his singing, adding an extra dimension of sincerity no one else could summon. It's the reason why Randy Newman, when he wrote "You've Got a Friend in Me" for *Toy Story*, wanted James to sing it. (Because of scheduling, however, that didn't happen, but he did sing and play Randy's wistfully glorious "Our Town" from last 2006's *Cars*.)

At the televised MusiCares tribute to him, in which Simon, Sting, and Springsteen were all present to honor him and perform his songs, Carole King closed the show by saying, simply, "Everyone has been telling these great James Taylor stories, and nothing for me says it better than this song." With that, she launched into "You've Got a Friend." At the conclusion of the evening James, the antithesis of someone who enjoys basking in self-glory, said, "It's strange to be at an event like this and still be alive. It's very moving, very terrifying, and very wonderful."

When we met, he was just finishing up a CD-DVD set entitled *One Man Band*, derived from his recent almost-solo concert tour, supported only by keyboardist Larry Goldings and a pickup-truck-sized drum machine of JT's invention. He was on the very verge of completing it, working the previous night with an engineer and editor till dawn. During our interview he led me up to a loft above his barn to show me a clip from the film of the band performing "My Traveling Star," a song that, like so many of his, touches on his own wanderlust and that which led his own father away from his family for so many years. And there is James, the family man, sitting quietly beside me as I listen. And there is James Taylor on the screen in performance mode. And there, beyond this monitor, is a window that looks out on the verdant New England hills of his home, where his twin sons, then six years old, are swinging on swings and tumbling down the hill. And here is an equation that works: a man whose songs are everywhere at once, enriching the lives of millions, as he succeeds in being a man of the family and a man of the world at once.

Your songs, from the start, have always been poetic but clear. They made sense. Was that intentional?

James Taylor: No, that's the way it comes out. It's a cliché, but that's because it's true to say I don't have any real conscious control over what comes out. I just don't direct it. I wish I could say, "Oh, that would be great to write a song about . . ." But what I am doing is assembling and *minimally* directing what is sort of unconsciously coming out. It's not something I can direct or control. I just end up being the first person to hear these songs. That's what it feels like, that I don't feel as though I write them.

Many feel songwriting is more a sense of following than leading—

I know you're a songwriter. Is that your experience too?

Yes. I find it's both. I'll think of a subject and I'll lead it, but the best lines are those which just occur. And then I might consciously think of a set-up rhyme. So it's both conscious and unconscious at the same time.

Yes, that's right. And I think there's a *phase* that's unconscious. And then there's a phase where you kind of have to button it up and finish it and pull it into a form that's presentable. Make it five minutes long. I don't know why songs are five minutes long, but they are. Three, four, and five minutes long. That's a conscious process, when you're trying to finish off a song and find a third verse that's gonna complete the first two or complements them somehow, or a bridge that's gonna make a general statement about the whole thing, or look at it from afar and then come back down into it again.

There are stages in it that are very conscious. But it all starts with a lightning strike of some sort, an unconscious emergence. And to me it happens most when I'm sitting down and playing the guitar. That's when these things will iterate.

Words and music at the same time?

Yeah, usually. A melody will suggest itself in the context of whatever I'm playing. And then the rhythm of that melody, the cadence of it, will suggest words. And those words and the rhythm of them I don't think comes from a conscious place. Often, for instance, if I'm stuck on a song, I'll lie down and close my eyes. Take a nap. Fifteen minutes or so, and when I wake up often it will be solved. There will be a solution, and I think it happens when you're asleep.

It's somewhat surprising to hear you say that, that the words come unconsciously, because some of your songs are so specific. "Copperline," for example, presents a theme and explores it and is so well crafted.

When I wrote it, though, the first idea was that I had a version of an old song called "A Dog Named Blue": "I had an old dog and his name was Blue / Bet you five dollars he's a good dog too." I played that with Jerry Douglas and Mark O'Connor on an album of Mark's. And so I was playing the changes that I had come up with on that song. And then the line "down on Copperline" came up. I don't know where it came from or what it means. I've since interpreted it as being a place about a mile and a half away from where my home is. There was a creek that flowed by at the bottom of a hill by my house. Morgan Creek. And down there, there was a stone quarry, and that's what I think about when I think about "Copperline," and I'm the person who can decide what the song is about. [*Laughs*]

I assumed that was what people called that region.

But the first verse is about "even the old folks never knew why they called it like they do . . ." They call it Copperline. So it starts by saying I don't know why this song is called "Copperline." It makes some suggestions: copperhead, copper beech, copper kettle.

And then it says, "Half a mile down to Morgan Creek / Only living till the end of the week." "Only living till the end of the week," that has to do with how people will ask me, "Could you have foreseen, when you were eighteen years old in New York City, writing 'Rainy Day Man,' could you have thought of yourself at the age of sixty still doing this?" And my answer is always, "When I was eighteen years old I could never think beyond maybe a week in the future." I just never planned for anything, I never planned for anything. And I didn't think I would be alive at fifty-nine. I just didn't anticipate it at all. And so that thing about only living till the end of the week refers to not being able to think ahead.

"Hercules and a hog-nosed snake." A hog-nosed snake is a strange kind of a creature. It's a snake that pretends to be dead. But even if you go over and poke it with a stick and tread on it, it won't move. It will act like it's dead. And my dog Hercules killed snakes, and there were lots of snakes where we lived. I tell people sometimes when I perform the song, "Hercules—not the god, the dog." [*Laughs*] Anyway, he would kill snakes. But he wouldn't kill a hog-nosed snake because it was already dead. But it wasn't—you would walk away and come back later, and it would have slithered off. It survived by pretending not to be. And that, to me, playing possum, as a survival skill, as a way of getting out of a particularly dangerous situation, playing dead—that's what I was talking about.

But that verse in which you explore all those different copper elements—copperhead, copper beech, copper kettle—that seems consciously crafted. Was it?

You sit down and those things come to your mind. It's hard to say whether that is conscious. Sometimes I open a rhyming dictionary just to remind myself of what words might fit the bill. But it's what those words mean and if one of them will catch.

The other day I sang with Tony Bennett—we sang at Radio City Music Hall—we sang "Put on a Happy Face" from *Bye Bye Birdie*. It has that line, "Take off that gloomy mask of tragedy, it's not your style / You look so good that you'll be glad you decided to smile." So "tragedy" and "glad you de-cided," that kind of word game is delightful. Those things are great. I love that kind of lyric. That's very self-conscious and very on purpose, premeditated.

I've written a few songs that were real Chinese puzzles of rhyming schemes. "Sweet Baby James" has about three rhyming schemes in each verse.

Yeah, it's got "horse and his cattle" with "sits in the saddle," and "companion" with "canyon."

Right. "Lives on the range" and then, four lines later, "his pastures to change." It is. That's right. There are a number of rhymes in it.

Was that one that emerged or you consciously crafted?

Another place I write a lot is I'm either sitting down playing the guitar, I'm walking, or I'm driving. Those are the three things I'm apt to be doing when I write. I was driving down Route 95 to North Carolina after I picked up my car in Elizabeth, New Jersey, a car that I bought in England in 1968. And I was driving it down to see my brother Alex and his wife, Brent, who had given birth to little James. First child born to my generation in my family. And they had named a kid after me, and I was gonna go down and see the little baby. And I was driving down there thinking of a cowboy lullaby, what to sing to little James. Rock-a-bye, sweet baby James.

I was very excited that they had a kid, and very moved that they named it after me, and I was behind the wheel for twenty hours or so, straight, maybe fifteen hours, driving straight down. And that song just assembled itself as I was driving down there. My memory was good enough in those days that I remembered it all. As soon as I got home I wrote it down.

The music came to you too when you were driving?

Yeah. I already had been working on the music to it. That arrived intact, that song. So did "Millworker." I was asleep on Martha's Vineyard in my bed, and I woke up with the song entirely in my mind. I walked down, it was a moonlit night, I walked down and turned on the light on the desk that was in this library space in the house. And wrote down the song, went back upstairs, and fell back to sleep. In the morning I *really* didn't know if the song was down there. I came down and there it was. It was amazing.

You write on guitar, but unlike some guitarists who write simple, diatonic songs, your songs are often harmonically complex. A song like "There We Are" or "Secret o' Life" have some adult chords.

[*Laughs*] Yeah, yeah. I write as a guitarist. I write on guitar, though the song "There You Are" was written on piano. But a song like "Mean Old Man" has some changes. It's just a series of descending scales.

It sounds like a standard.

You know I got a great compliment from my mentor and the guy who gave me my break, Paul McCartney. He bought a bunch of those albums to give to his friends, and he said the reason he did was because when he heard "Mean Old Man" he thought it was a Porter tune. And he thought it had to be a standard and looked to see who wrote it and was surprised that it was mine.

I looked too. And was surprised. Lyrically, too, it has that style.

Yes, it's an old-fashioned style. And McCartney, of course, does that too. "When I'm 64," "Honey Pie," "Maxwell's Silver Hammer"—

"Your Mother Should Know."

That's right. He writes from that music hall experience. Which you could call old-fashioned. It was superseded by rhythm and blues and Elvis and stuff. But my personal feeling is that the Broadway musical, that was the apex, the epitome of American popular song. The lyrics and the changes and the melodies. The sophistication of it. It's high art. It's a very high form. And what's happened since with rhythm and blues and a return to folk music is a simplification of that.

Though I think people have a clichéd idea of folk music when I say I am a folk musician. I just mean somebody who has basically learned music without studying it in any formal way. I basically just absorbed what I learned.

I agree that the work of the Gershwins, Porter, etc., was high art. Though their songs were primarily about melody—and great melodies. But it was those from your generation—you, Dylan, Simon, The Beatles—who, in writing songs for yourself, brought a new intimacy and depth and poetry to lyrics of popular song. A song like "Fire and Rain," for example, is not a song Ira Gershwin would have written—

No, that's right—

Or "Copperline" or "Frozen Man." You brought songwriting to a new place, which is also high art.

It is very self-referred and very personal. And often I feel uncomfortable about that, and I regret that is the case because often I feel it's a little bit self-obsessed. Sometimes. But basically I've just accepted that that's the way I write, and I'm not surprised if and when people get fed up with it. In other words, I don't think it's for all audiences all the time. But occasionally I'll stumble on something that resonates with people as much as it resonates with me, and then I've got something I can work on or work behind.

You're known for being one of the great "confessional songwriters," yet from the start you wrote story songs as well. You wrote "Mud Slide Slim," and you went on to write "Millworker" and "The Frozen Man," which are not songs about you—

That's true. But "Frozen Man" is about my father. So is "Walking Man." It's not about him, but it's informed by him—

Were you consciously thinking of your father when you wrote "Frozen Man," or was that a later revelation?

Somewhat when I wrote it. There are a lot of those can't-quite-get-home kind of songs, or highway songs, or songs that romanticize the call of the road or the inability to settle down, the inability to find peace. And a lot of those wandering songs are about my dad.

When you would write a song—say, "Copperline," which I love—that has a verse about your father, did you intend to include that, or does that come during the writing?

In the process. It's sort of like an area. A song will be open for a while. I typically will work on a lyric in a three-ring binder. And on the right side I'll write the lyric, and on the left side I put in alternate things and things that might be alternates or improvements. And I'll turn the page and I'll do it again. And I'll turn the page and do it again or incorporate the improvements. Eventually I end up with some material, and often it needs to be ordered.

I remember when writing "Copperline" that Reynolds Price and I had some late-night discussions about what order to put the verses in and where to break it for the bridge. So it is. In the liner notes to *One Man Band* I wrote that a strange thing about the modern version of the popular song is that the first time a song is heard is the first time that it's performed. You set it in stone in its first performance. You might even finish it in the studio on the day you record it. You don't very often write a song and play it. It takes, like, twenty times of playing it in front of an audience before it kind of completes itself. But often it's going straight from your head into wax, and that's the final version of the song that goes out. But it's only after you've played it on the road twenty or thirty times that it becomes really finished and polished and you really realize what it *means* and you get the phrasing right. One would wish you could write an album, tour with it for a year, and then record it. It never happens that way, though. It's always straight out of the box and then set it cast in stone.

So it is sort of odd that I write for my own recordings. I think one of the points you made early on is that as a singer and a recording artist and a touring performer, I'm writing material for my own show, my own albums. And I don't often get the chance to sort of do a commissioned work—write something about *this*. That's what "Millworker" was and "Brother Trucker" and a couple of songs that were in that show *Working*. That was a rare opportunity to write stuff that was commissioned, where I was asked to be a songwriter and apply my capacity to a task.

And you met that challenge. "Millworker" is a classic song.

Did you hear Springsteen's version of that? It was great. He sort of boiled it down a bit.

One of the things about writing for guitar and voice is that I think I tend to be a bit more chordy than I need to. I throw in more changes just to interest myself than is often good for the song. I consciously try now to limit, to be spare, with my changes so I'm not having a chord change every second. The problem really is that I don't write chord changes; I write melodic lines that basically organize themselves into these little wheels that turn themselves over and over again. They're not really chord changes. You can write changes that follow them, and you can see them as a succession of changes that go from one harmonic center to another. But really what they are is more horizontal than vertical. And then a melody suggests itself that works in the context of one of these little wheels. And you can make one turn away or go into another one or come back into it, and that's really what I end up doing.

By that do you mean you think of the melody first, apart from changes? Or do you generate the melody based on the changes?

There are different kinds of ways of dealing with it. Sometimes there are changes first and you find a melody that goes through it. Sometimes it's a melody and you find chords. Like the final line in "Mean Old Man," at the end of each verse is [*whistles descending line*]. It's just a long, chromatic fall. And in order to find changes that bring you back to the letter A, the changes that are jammed in there, there's only one melody line that goes through them. If you tried to find another workable melody line to get through those changes, you would end up with something that is disjointed.

You once said that the sign of a good song is that it can stand without any accompaniment, just pure melody. So you have written songs melody first?

Yes. I did write "Mean Old Man" melody first. But that is an exception. Usually I am playing the guitar. I will have three lines that are happening at once. Usually a bass line, an internal line, a top line, and a melody line that I am thinking of at the same time. Sting writes in this way too, and he and I have that in common. I'll write a melody, and the chords will shift under it. And then it will mean something else because of the chord underneath it. My song "4th of July" is the same melody over and over again. But the changes continue to shift, so the melody means something harmonically different 'cause the context changes.

And that's a great sound, when the harmonic foundation shifts under a repeating melodic phrase.

Yes, when it works. "One Note Samba" is like that. Jobim does that a lot too.

You said once that Paul Simon had showed you some diminished chords, which surprised me, 'cause I felt you already knew diminished chords—

Calling it a diminished [chord] is really too simple. Paul has this way of kind of escaping from a melody or from a harmonic sort of context and jumping into another one. Like the bridge to "Still Crazy." He was trying to explain it to me, and I tried to pay attention.

He said he was trying to use every note in the twelve-tone scale which he hadn't used in the verse—

That's a very mathematical game.

Yeah. But it worked.

Oh *God*, it worked.

I learned a lot of chords from playing your songs. You use augmented chords or chords with alternate bass notes. Not the straight-ahead diatonic chords that a lot of rockers or folk musicians use.

As soon as I found those chords, I used them. I was talking to Paul McCartney, and we were amazed that there was, like, this F 13 chord in "Michelle." I love all of McCartney's music. And Paul said that was the only jazz chord [he and John] knew. They used to go down to a record store in Liverpool, and there was somebody there who played guitar, and he showed Paul and John this thirteenth chord. So the second chord in "Michelle," under "ma belle," that second chord is a very unlikely chord—it's a thirteenth. And you wouldn't expect to see it.

McCartney's chords are surprisingly simple when you take them apart. But, boy, the way he bounces one onto another. It's really very much like cubism, to listen to McCartney's stuff. Because it represents so much in just a simple line. He's really brilliant.

Even in the earliest stuff, like "I Want to Hold Your Hand," the bridge goes to the minor V instead of major.

That's right. Which is a great sound. He did that in a few songs.

It's interesting that your career started pretty much because of Paul Mc-Cartney. You made your first album for Apple while The Beatles were recording *The White Album*. What was that like?

It was great. It was *unbelievable*. I was a huge Beatles fan. I listened to them—as did millions—with absolute utter focus and attention to every note and every word. And just devoured everything that they came out with and parsed it and learned it and reinterpreted it. So when it turned out that I got the opportunity, when the song "Carolina" says "the holy host of others standing around me," that's what it refers to. Just the fact that I was in this *pantheon*, really being present in Trident Studios in Soho, Leicester Square, where they were recording *The White Album*. It was just amazing.

I was at a session for "Revolution," a recut of it that was done at Abbey Road, and some of *The White Album* was cut at Abbey Road, but most of it was cut at Trident. The reason for that is that it had the only eight-track board in England. They had been working with eight-track at Abbey Road, but the engineers there were distrustful of the eight-track machines that were on the market. They trusted four-tracks, so they synched them up, and that was as close to multitracking as Abbey Road would come. So they went to Trident, and we just took the interstices; anytime they weren't tracking, we would go in.

You mentioned the line from "Carolina" that refers to The Beatles. So you wrote that song after you got your deal? It wasn't on your demo?

No. What was on the demo was "Something in the Way She Moves," "Rainy Day Man," and "Circle Round the Sun."

McCartney played on "Carolina"—

Yes, he did. He played bass. Paul sat in on that one, and he and George sang on that one too. I think the song that was the strongest on that demo was "Something in the Way She Moves," and I think that's the thing that got me signed.

Did Paul lay down the bass with the band, or was that an overdub?

He laid down the bass with the band. A guy named Don Shinn played piano, I played guitar, and I think Joel O'Brien played drums.

You're known to be pretty specific with your bass lines. But did you allow McCartney to come up with his own?

The song had its own bass line when it was written. As you say, I am pretty specific about those lines. I wrote out a simple chart, a Bible-Belt chart with chord symbols. I think he probably just learned it.

That song was started on this little island in the Mediterranean. We took a break 'cause The Beatles stopped recording for a break and the studio closed down. So I went out of town with a friend of mine. A very affable, friendly, beautiful, flower-child hippie scene going on down there on this primitive Mediterranean island. The houses all made of stone and mortar and whitewashed. And beautiful landscape, and this amazing brilliant Mediterranean and the sun all the time. It was just an amazing place and beautiful. I had a bit of a drug habit, I'm afraid, and I wasn't terribly comfortable. And I kept moving. And I wrote "Carolina" there. I started writing "Carolina" thinking about my home, thinking about what was going on with me. But I couldn't shake this idea that I needed to get home.

I've written maybe 150 songs. But really what I've done is written 25 songs ten times. That's what I do. I write different versions of the same thing. There are themes I will write about.

I was just noticing how similar "Country Road," one of your earliest songs, is to "My Traveling Star," and one of your most recent ones, "Another Highway Song."

Yeah. And I have a song called "Highway Song" and "Nothing Like a Hundred Miles." That's another one. That's a song that Ray Charles covered, one of my favorite covers that I ever got. There's a beautiful version that he and B. B. King did. For me, he was the man, Ray Charles.

Ray Charles used to say he was like a radio and songs came through him. Lennon said the same kind of thing, that songwriters are receivers, picking up songs like a radio picks up radio waves. Does it seem that way ever?

Yes. Some songs seem to come from outside. "Gaia" seemed to come from outside and sort of pass through, be filtered through. "Secret o'

Life." I mean, to call a song "Secret o' Life" is preposterous. That's why the title is "Secret o' Life"—it's meant to be a Life Savers flavor.

Do those kind of experiences cause you to have any notion what the source of those songs is?

I think it's largely unconscious and out of my control. Like language itself. When kids begin to speak they say gobbledygook that takes the form of sentences and syllables and has the form that sounds like a question or sounds like a statement or an expletive or whatever. The cadence is already there, and it comes out as language. They start to plug language into it as they hear it more and more. I speak French and a little bit of German, and I'm constantly, in the back of my brain, translating things into those two languages. It's just a little game that I'm constantly playing to see if I know how to do that. And somehow songwriting is like that. It's always making little attempts.

And as I said before, I find that now I'm revisiting topics over and over again that I'm compelled to write about. Loss or celebration. Or a kind of mystical statement. Trying to give consciousness the slip. And relax back into the context that we come from.

I think that human beings are an experiment in consciousness, and we are individuated and ego based, and we re-create the world with these conscious minds we have, and that allows us to be isolated. We live in these conscious re-creations of the world. And what that does, it predicts the world. It predicts behavior; it predicts reality so that we can basically stay out of trouble. That's the essential job of consciousness, to look for and avoid trouble. And secondarily you want food and third you want sex. So I think that this individuated consciousness that we are an experiment in allows us to be isolated and it also allows us to get things wrong, to get lost.

So we're always doing two things almost constantly: one is that we're comparing our worldview, our reality, with other people's to make sure we're not getting it wrong. Because otherwise maybe the tree *will* fall on your tent or whatever. And the other thing that we're constantly doing is trying to somehow get back to give that whole mechanism the slip. Because it is an illusion. Everybody says it's an illusion, and that's because it is. Consciousness is an illusion. It's hopelessly subjective, and it is not the truth. Because it is too tainted by individual and human priorities.

So you're constantly trying to give that individuated consciousness the slip and trust falling back into the context out of which we emerge. Which is, basically, to my mind, the skin of life that's on the planet

Earth. The thing that has, for some reason, produced us. And maybe the reason we're here is to burn fossil fuels, I don't know. But we're here for some unknown reason.

So that's one of the things I write about. Finding a way to relax. Just put your mind aside and be in the moment. Be without judgment, be without examination, analysis, and question. And just accept for an unknown reason—and it must stay unknown, or else you're kidding yourself—for some unknown reason we are here. It's very unlikely, but for some reason we are.

So it's basically agnostic spiritualism that I engage in repeatedly. That's one of the kinds of songs I write. "Gaia" is that song, "Upper May" is that song, "Migration" is that song, "Country Road" is that song. And the last verse of "Sweet Baby James"—"there's a song that they sing when they take to the highway, there's a song that they sing when they take to the sea . . ."—that's also a statement about that kind of surrender and surrendering control and human consciousness. To go back to the well. It's just a long, hard, lonely slog being *constantly* human and having the responsibility of having to reinvent the world every second. It is a lonesome road. So that's a type of song I write too.

But is it always individual? Is that consciousness connected? Are you tapping into consciousness beyond your own when you write songs?

[*Pause*] It's an act of consciousness to write a song. But the most compelling thing about music is that we manipulate it and arrange it, but it obeys laws and represents laws about the physical universe—an octave is an octave because it's twice as fast as the octave below it. A fifth is a mathematical reality; it's not just something we decided on. People say there's a real cultural bias to what people consider musical and what emotional states they relate to what harmonic equivalence. And people say major is happy and minor is sad, or a diminished chord has a certain amount of tension and wariness to it, or a thirteenth chord is apprehensive, and when you have an augmented fifth and you let it fall into a chord a fourth above it, anyone feels that as home. If you play an E augmented fifth and then go to an A, no matter *who* hears that, they will feel there has been tension and resolution. So I feel that music exists outside of human consciousness. So to practice music at all is to give human consciousness the slip. That's why it's so associated with spirituality. Because to listen to it is to experience another type of reality. And one that must be true, because it's mathematically true. It is physics. Music is physics.

Do you feel that each musical key has its own nature, its own color?

People really do. I feel rather that modes have their own nature. With me the key is only relevant in terms of where it will be relative to my vocal range. And I don't feel that E has some kind of an emotional feeling. I mean, when you're playing guitar, E feels a certain way.

Yeah. It feels like home.

[*Laughs*] Yeah, it feels like home. And D has a certain feeling because of the way the other chords constellate around it. But for me, I never have noticed that thing of C major being a certain emotional state—

Or a color.

I never have thought about it. That might be the case. Or it might also be just completely random. I mean, what color would you say the key of D was?

Light blue.

See, I would have said sort of an ultraviolet. Also I play with a capo. So to me, the key of E is really like the key of D, because half the time that I play in E, I'm playing D fingering on the second fret.

I was wondering about that, because often I can hear those sounds of the D major chord—and the pull-offs and hammer-ons you do on it that so many of us learned from your playing. But I realized these are often in other keys, such as E. So you use the capo a lot?

Yes, I do. I usually capo on the first, second, and third fret. Very seldom on the fourth. And sometimes I'm open. And I don't stray up the neck much. I don't play many inversions up the neck. I stay pretty close to under the fourth fret usually.

Do you use capos while you write songs?

Yes. When I sit down and play the guitar, I often have the capo on it. I like to sing in E, but I like to play in D. So it's natural for me to put a capo on the second fret.

Do you recall writing "Steamroller?"

Yes. "Steamroller" isn't a serious blues; it's a takeoff on an eighteen-year-old white kid's idea of the blues, like I was coming to New York City with Mom and Dad's money and the family station wagon and buying these electric guitars and amplifiers at Manny's Music on 48ᵗʰ Street and then going back to their garage and pretending I'm Muddy Waters or Howlin' Wolf or Bo Diddley. "I'm a man, I'm a rolling stone, I'm a hoochie coochie man, I'm smokestack lightning . . ." Yeah, you want to tap into that thing. You want to emulate it. It's pathetic, though.

Funny you saw it that way, because it was one of the first places I learned the blues, playing that song, long before I heard Muddy or Bo or Howlin' Wolf.

I was the same way. I learned from listening to John Hammond play and listening to Ry Cooder. I also listened to Don Covay and to James Brown and Lightnin' Hopkins. And Sonny Terry and Brownie McGhee.

With a song like "Gaia" that comes through you, does anything affect or enable that to happen?

I used drugs for a long time. I think that sometimes a number of these things were facilitated—they weren't generated by it—but a state of artificially induced bliss. You take what you can get. In other cases I find that the song itself *creates* that state and that actually *singing the song* takes me back to that place again, and actually the song and the music can be relied upon to reiterate an emotional state, a place where I was at a certain time. And that's remarkable to get that.

I play these songs often. I never stop touring, basically. I just always tour. And have been. I made some early bad mistakes on record contracts and such, and I just never made any money on records. The Warner catalog was a big bust for me—

But you had big hits. I thought if you had hits, you would make money—

Well, you don't if you sign away the rights to them. When I was eighteen I signed a publishing contract with April-Blackwood. Chip Taylor and Al Gorgoni were their names. They promised the band a recording contract, but I would have to sign a publishing contract. We were desperate to get recorded. So I signed it, and they own half of "Fire and Rain" and "Something in the Way She Moves" and "Don't Let Me Be Lonely Tonight," and it was just a mistake I made one afternoon.

Speaking of "Something in the Way She Moves," George Harrison based his famous song "Something" on it. How did that strike you, that he used your line?

It was actually a couple of weeks after I turned in the demo of the same song. [*Laughs*] I never thought for a second that George intended to do that. I don't think he intentionally ripped anything off, and all music is borrowed from other music. So I just completely let it pass. I raised an eyebrow here and there, but when people would make the presumption that I had stolen my song from his, I can't sit still for that. Actually, you know that song, [*sings*] "She's in love with me and I feel fine . . ."— "I Feel Fine." The end of "Something in the Way She Moves" is "I feel fine." "She's around me now almost all the time and I feel fine." That was taken directly from a Beatles song too.

I believe George acknowledged that his song came from your song.

I wish I'd known that. I always regretted the prospect that he might have felt uncomfortable about that. But I never gave it a second thought. I have stolen things much more blatantly than that. A *lot* of stuff. And I also steal from myself and just rework different things into songs.

You once said that you felt your music, since always written for your own style, seemed "inbred." Yet I've found that throughout your career you've attempted to go to new places musically and not repeat yourself.

It has to be compelling. I can't finish a song because I have a deadline. I write songs because they mean something to me, because it gives me a feeling.

Aside from the great Broadway songwriters, I like Lennon and McCartney, I like Jimmy Webb, I like Paul Simon, Randy Newman and Carole King and Joni Mitchell. Of my contemporaries those are the ones.

Was Bob Dylan an important influence for you?

Yes. Dylan was a revelation. There's nothing like the effect of hearing Bob Dylan with a guitar and singing "Bob Dylan's 114th Dream" or whatever it was, "419th Dream." [*Laughs*] Dylan was a real revelation. I guess he would say he was listening to Cisco Houston and Eric Von Schmidt and Woody Guthrie. But he really turned the world on its ear and opened the door for a lot of us. He and The Beatles were the biggest influences on my lyrics. And then musically the thing I was most thrilled by was to hear Ray Charles. Sam Cooke was also great. And Marvin Gaye—and Marvin was also a writer, and it's just *so* beautiful, his stuff. And Stevie [Wonder], of course.

When someone like you or Dylan or Simon performs a song you wrote yourself, one feels a closeness to the material, an intimacy—

Yes, and sings it themselves with the guitar that they're playing. Yes, there's definitely a direct connection. That's sort of a combination of songwriting and performance art and self-expression that can really be meaningful, can really offer people an emotional path. It can be a container for their own emotion. It can help them organize and deal with their own emotions, because someone like Dylan has shown them a way of handling it, of laughing at it. "If for one moment you could stand in my shoes, you'd know what a drag it is to see you . . ." [*Laughs*] That's *useful*, that's really useful. It allows you to take that feeling and say, "Yeah, that says it all for me." It allows you to process something or to handle it. Someone walks a path, and you can follow that.

When you hear Ray Charles—though he didn't necessarily write it—sing, "He came home with a watch / Said it came from Uncle Joe / I looked at the inscription, it said, 'Love from Daddy-o.' I got news for you, somehow your story don't ring true, and I got news for you." You know: somebody's cuckolding him. She's coming home, she says, "Before the day we met you said your life was tame / I took you to a nightclub and the whole band knew your name." [*Laughter*] You listen to that song later, and you say, "Yeah, I took her out."

Or to hear Mose Allison write something like "Long ago a young man was a strong man, and all the people would stand back when a young man walked by / Nowadays the old men got all the money and a young man ain't nothing in the world these days." So you just say, "Yeah."

Songs are useful. They're like myths. Myths are useful because they allow you to cast yourself and your life and your own experience. And for some people "Fire and Rain" speaks to them in that way. Dustin Hoffman came to me once and said, "'Fire and Rain' allowed me to go from one side of an experience that I didn't think I could ever get out of to the other side of it." I met Bob Dylan, and he told me he liked "Frozen Man." That's all I need. Miles Davis even once gave me a compliment, so I can remember that even when reviews are not favorable. I once read a *Rolling Stone* review of me that said I was derivative—and it was true—but after that I never read past my name in print again. It's like a blowtorch on a flower. It's a drag.

What did Miles tell you?

Miles said, "You own the key of D." All right.

It's interesting that the subject of your father comes up in so many songs. You've said "Walking Man" and "The Frozen Man" are about him, but he also comes up in songs not about him, such as "Copperline" and "Traveling Star"—

He's a part of me. My dad, his wanderlust, his conflict between being a good father and a man. If you're a family man, you're almost a man in a woman's world. You have to learn as a man to live in that world. You feel it as a traveling performer. If you want to stay home and be with your family, you have to somehow deal with these instincts to go out and sail around the world. My father had that in spades. He wanted to go to the South Pole and live under the ice. He wanted to sail a boat single-handed around the world. This is what he really was interested in. He was itching.

One of your most famous songs is "You've Got a Friend," which Carole King wrote. How did you come to do it?

She encouraged me to do it. I thought it was amazingly generous of her to offer me this song when she was about to go into the studio herself. I was just trying then to complete a second album of songs myself. I was impressed. But the fact is that she was a Brill Building writer and had always been trying to place songs. She and Gerry [Goffin] wrote sequels. So it was the most natural thing for her to try and place a song on someone else's album.

She was one of the first to make that transition from a hit songwriter for others to becoming a performer herself.

That's right. It was a very conscious effort.

It's funny, when I started writing songs, because it was the folk music era and people were doing it all the time, it wasn't like you had to be a studied musician. Anyone could basically write a song. So you pretended that you could, and maybe it would turn out that you were right if you acted as if you could write a song. It was a very kind way to get into it. Folk music and the folk scene was, above all, accessible to everybody. It allowed you to write songs, even if they were really primitive. If my first song had to be on the level of a Broadway tune, I could have never have gotten off the ground. But you could write a song like "Something in the Way She Moves" and get started.

Yet very early on, you brought a sophistication and depth to your songs. "Fire and Rain," which came early, is a masterpiece of songwriting.

I started young. I wrote my first song at the age of fourteen. I started playing when I was fifteen in front of people. I dropped out of school and started playing with a band at eighteen. I signed away my publishing at the age of eighteen. I had put in, by the time that The Beatles picked me up, five years. Carole, too, was writing some of those amazing hits with Gerry when she was only fifteen years old. She was just a kid.

"Fire and Rain" is such a direct, authentic statement from your soul.

It is sort of almost *uncomfortably* close. Almost confessional. The reason I could write a song like that at that point and probably couldn't now is that I didn't have any sense that anyone would hear it. I started writing the song while I was in London, toward the end of the time I was working on the first album. But I still hadn't had anything out and I was totally unknown, and I didn't have any idea or experience of an audience who would listen to these things. So I assumed they would never be heard, so I could just write or say anything I wanted. Now I'm very aware, and I have to make a deal about my stage fright and my anxiety about a lot of people examining what I do or judging it. The idea that people will pass judgment on it, that's not a useful thought; that's only gonna inhibit me. So I try not to think about that, obviously. I try to sit with the music and enjoy it.

Right now I have about seven starts on tunes. They're music and a scrap of lyric and a direction that the song is going. I have a couple of notebooks that I carry with me, and in them are little pieces of lyric. Lots and lots of little pieces of lyric that belong with one or the other of these musical ideas that I have. They are beginning to organize themselves into another set of songs.

It's a strange thing to think in terms of ten or eleven songs or twelve songs being a batch. If you're a recording singer-songwriter, you learn to produce in batches of ten to twelve, like a baker's dozen. I'm still trained that way. If I were writing for motion pictures, I would write them one at a time. If I was writing for musicals, that would be a different paradigm, a different dynamic.

You always work on many songs at once?
   Yeah, I usually work on three or four.

Many of your songs touch on the subject of time, of trying to recapture the past, of moving into the future. "Copperline" is like a cubist painting showing many times at once: the present propels you into a memory of your father, which links him to his past. And then you see it in the present, but you say it doesn't change the past: "it can't touch my memory." And of course "Secret o' Life" says "time isn't really real."
   Right. Of course, "Secret o' Life" is one of those songs which came intact in an afternoon a few years ago. Yes, trying to get back is often an element in these songs. Comparing times or remembering old times. "Long Ago and Far Away" is that.

Did all of "Secret o' Life" come at once, even the Einstein reference?
   Yes. All of it came in short order on a Sunday afternoon.

The philosophy in it—to enjoy the passing of time—has rarely been expressed like that in a song.

Well, it's actually a glib thing to say. It's one thing to enjoy the passage of time; it's another to do it on chemotherapy. It's an easy lyric. I was aware in putting it out that it was a glib thing to say. A sort of facile thing to say. But I still like the tune, and a lot of people tell me that they really like it, that it's one of their favorites. The idea is *hackneyed*. To be in the present moment, to actually be able to tolerate being here now as opposed to being obsessed with what's about to happen or reliving something that's happened in the past over and over again. They say that the future doesn't exist and the past is unchangeable, so the present moment is really all we've got. And that's the simple message of that song.

It seems your work, and especially your performances in recent years, reflect that kind of calm acceptance of life.

Acceptance, that's right. Acceptance and surrender. That and gratitude are the basic appropriate attitudes. So says the platitude. There's nothing new under the sun. It's a restatement of things that have been said before but that bear repeating.

What's new are the songs you've written—nobody else wrote them. And you went through intense addictions which a lot of people didn't survive, and you became a healthy, centered, and happy person.

Yes, it just took me a long, long time to integrate. At least to the extent that I have now. It was a dangerous passage. It well could have killed me. At six or seven specific points in my life I could have easily died. I made it through. It just took a *long* time. I wouldn't *suggest* it as a method for anyone to emulate. It was a lot of wasted time; I'm lucky I didn't do more damage than I did. But I supposed it's what I had to go through to get here. I'm grateful that I'm here, and I try to remember that I'm lucky and remember to be grateful. It's the right attitude.

You wrote many songs out of deep pain. And so many songwriters complain about the process of writing. Randy Newman has frequently spoken about how much he hates it. Yet in your work there seems to be a joy. Do you enjoy it?

Because of "Fire and Rain," mostly, and "Don't Let Me Be Lonely Tonight," I was sort of cast as somebody who was troubled or hurting. But it's not really the case. My instinct is to humor and to ecstasy and to bliss.

You once said your songs came out of melancholy.

Well, that is a place that a lot of them come from. But not all of them. Some of them are celebratory. And there's a political tune or two in there too. "Slap Leather" is one and "Let It All Fall Down" is another. "Gaia" in a way is political.

It's very rare that songwriters, with the exception of Stevie Wonder, can write genuinely happy songs. You've done it, though: "Your Smiling Face" is a great example. It's truly happy without being corny or going over that line—

I wouldn't say that it's not corny. I would say that it is, and well over the line. Again, I take what I get. You know, sure, "Your Smiling Face" is just a relentlessly cheerful and almost saccharine song. But I do, I have a number of pretty happy songs. But some of them have a wistful aspect to them. "Secret o' Life" is a positive song, for sure, but it also has the element of "since we're on our way down, we might as well enjoy the ride . . ." The way down that that refers to is actually entropy in the universe, but that's not a very useful concept for people, so I don't think people think of it as, well, I don't know *how* actually people think of it. If you thought about the song—

Which I have—

Well, what do you think of when you hear "We're on our way down"?

That our lifetimes do end, but while we're in them, to enjoy them, to enjoy that ride. That's the message—to enjoy it, as opposed to a song like "Slip Slidin' Away" which is basically just about going down. Though I feel that's a good song—

Oh, it's a great song.

Yes. But "Secret o' Life" has a more positive message about how to deal with the progression of time.

Right. And the inevitable loss. And the fact that it ends, which is also unacceptable. But that's the conundrum of human consciousness. Not that I have credentials to speak in such terms. But when individuated consciousness comes up against the idea of individual death, something's got to give. That's why people invent afterlives and versions of the afterlife, which there is absolutely no evidence for whatsoever. [*Laughs*]

You feel that's a human invention?

Oh yeah. I think God is the name of a question. God is not an existing thing. That's what we've named an unknown. It's a known as well. It's not a matter of whether or not God exists. The need for God to exist is an almost inevitable human trait. So that's still an open question. My father was an atheist, as distinguished from an agnostic. He felt that anyone who suggested that they represented God was to be deeply distrusted. That anyone who opened his mouth saying that he represented anything divine was a charlatan. And furthermore that the world could ill afford that kind of defended worldview, that kind of defensive tribalism, which is essentially what it is. He felt it was the enemy of civilization.

Do you share that feeling?

You know, I was raised with that idea. He was a Southerner and a scientist. The way in which religion presented itself to him was unpalatable. Sure, that's what I was given as a set of beliefs from my father.

Yet your songs represent something transcendent. They will exist after your linear lifetime is over—

Yes, but so will our children.

But the songs don't age. They exist outside of time.

I think the question comes up how much you can sort of say that you own a song and that it's your creation. I do—and it's really a way of dodging the question—I do feel they are unconscious occurrences, and I'm lucky enough to just be the first person to hear the songs that I write. That's essentially what it is.

It's striking to me that you're reluctant to accept ownership of your songs when they are praised, but when they are criticized, you do accept that.

That kind of defensiveness, the epitome of that is the idea that if I turn myself in, people will go easy on me. [*Laughs*] I'll get a lighter sentence if I turn myself in. So I'm sort of prejudging myself, trying to anticipate people's criticism of it. I just shouldn't be going there at all. I shouldn't worry about what people's judgments might be on my songs. It does nothing but slow me down. But that's one of the things that happens over time: You start with the expectation that nobody will ever *hear* anything that you write so you can create anything that you want. You're just doing it for yourself and some girl you're trying to impress. And then the next thing you know, you've had a couple of dodgy reviews and you're always worried about how people will take this lyric or that lyric and you'll worry about whether they'll think you're derivative or whether they'll think you're self-centered or sappy.

I should try to dispense with those anxieties as efficiently as I can. They're not of any help to me at all. And if I'm here to do anything, it's to write and perform songs and record them. That's what I'm supposed to do. The rest of it is really unimportant.

The other day—I don't know how it came up—my kids were asking me what jobs are important. I said that parent is probably the most important job, and after that teacher, and then after that maybe farmer and then maybe carpenter and then doctor, and policeman. But those are things that contribute in the present to the quality of other people's lives. Those are jobs that do service. Then there are pastimes. For some reason in this country, we've come to glorify greed and raise it to the level of patriotism. And that's a neat trick, an Ayn Rand sort of trick.

But you don't feel artists enrich our lives—

I think they can. I think it's possible. But it was interesting to me to go down that list of what I think are important jobs. I don't know where art comes into it.

That says a lot about who you are, that you wouldn't put musician or songwriter up near the top.

Well, you need a *meal* before you need a song.

But certainly in your own life, apart from the music you've created yourself, music has enriched your life. Music enriches our lives; it brings meaning, joy. We wouldn't die without it, but it's profound what it can do.

No, I think you're entirely right. Sure, it's true. I love doing this. That's the main thing. And it's just an amazing stroke of good fortune that I'm able to make a living at it. Because I really have no *clue* what alternative I might have. I have weathered some really dodgy times, and I'm in a period in my life with Kim here in Western Massachusetts, our home and our work are sort of here in this place that we've made for ourselves. It's a good time. Everybody's healthy; everybody's well. We worry about things in our immediate field of view. But mostly because, as I said before, human consciousness evolved to look for trouble. I just would hope that I could enjoy this period, because I've really come up smelling like a rose. I've come up in a good place.

It does seem like a wonderful environment here.

It is. It would be nice to try to communicate some of that too. It would be nice to try to write more joy, to write more celebratory stuff. If there's any such thing—although I've denied it for the past four hours [*laughs*]—if there's any such thing as a conscious effort in songwriting, I'll try to steer it in that direction. But who knows? As I heard myself say in a performance recently, in my way of introducing "Traveling Star," here's another traveling song, and after a while you're gonna get a lot of those. If you spend your life traveling on the bus on tour, after a while you just get a lot of traveling songs. And that's a time-honored theme.

That one, "Traveling Star," is so beautiful. It brings in your father, and there's so much heart there. It's more than just another highway song.

It's a song about being a man and trying to also live civilized. One of the central issues of modern life is what to do with male energy in a civilized context. And how a man's energy cannot be too destructive. Because the instincts that men have—to conquer, to hunt, to procreate—eventually they start to hurt the earth. The tribal warrior, that's the dynamic that's sort of directly opposed to civilization. If we collapse into anything, we collapse into tribalism. The world can't afford it anymore. It's one thing when you're throwing a stone; it's another when it's an atomic weapon. So what does a man do in this world? How can you be a man and live with the sheets and the blankets and babies and all?

Well, a lot of us grew up with you as a role model. That you could have this powerful male energy but also embrace and create something tender and beautiful. That a man could reach that kind of tenderness—in a song like "Anywhere Like Heaven," for example—was an important model to emulate.

Yes, that's right. It's a difficult thing. We get so much macho crap. And we are paying a huge price for the macho fantasies of people who have bought into—dare I say it—the Bush administration. That's what they've been selling, this macho crap. It just immediately shows how useless it is. It's like trying to fix a watch with a hammer. It takes sensitivity, it takes skills of people, it takes understanding, and it takes patience. It takes embracing them. We're supposed to embrace instead some tribal tough-guy stance? We're gonna smoke then out; we're gonna hit them hard? We're paying a high price for their fantasy. We're also paying, in this country, a high price for this fantasy of people who want to own guns. Something that does absolutely nothing which is positive. At least a cigarette makes you feel good. What does a gun do except kill, except punch a hole in a man? And we have one for every man, woman, and child in this country. There are 300 million of them. Maybe 500 million. It's crazy. So we're paying a big price for their fantasies.

I suppose you could say that one of the themes of my music is how to become a man.

Someone once asked you if you were ever embarrassed by any of your songs, and the only one you mentioned was "Blossom," which you said was too floral, too cute. But I've always loved that song.

No, "Blossom" is fine. It's not that I am so much ashamed of any songs; I do get a little squirmy about some of them. It's not so much that they are confessional but they are so relentlessly self-referred. Again, I accept that that's the way I write. But it is pretty self-absorbed. And that's the thing that makes me uncomfortable. But again, it's what I seem to have done. I don't know, I might have another batch of songs or two in me. Irving Berlin continued to write into his nineties. And he wrote a lot of good stuff in his seventies.

It's more common for songwriters to do their best work in their twenties. But you and Simon and few others continue to do it—

Randy Newman continues to write great stuff too. "I Miss You" or "Every Time It Rains." Great stuff. It's amazing.

Randy, like you, is extremely down on himself. He doesn't take praise—

No, he doesn't at all. He's extremely down on himself. Maybe it's the thing of "If I turn myself in, they'll go easy on me."

And he seems to judge himself by the marketplace, how many hits he's had compared to other songwriters.

I know.

And you once said the only thing that really gets between you and your music is the industry itself.

You hire people to advise you and sort of help you. And they end up thinking that their priorities are the important ones. If you hire a business manager, he thinks that you should be thinking about business all the time. And the same thing is true with someone whose job is in publicity and promotion: they think that's what your job is—to publicize yourself. But in fact that just gets in the way. You just want as much publicity as can bring people's attention to what your project is, and then let it go. Because that one will kick back at you. And if you spend so much time with that hat on so that your job is actually being a celebrity, then you're standing on *real* thin ice. That's been shown over and over again.

Do you judge your work on how popular it is, on album sales?

Yeah, you can't help but do that. You can't help it. The tendency in capitalism is to put a dollar value on everything. That people don't feel comfortable trying to figure things out until they know what the dollar value of it is. So that's our way of evaluating people, and we end up doing it to ourselves, saying "I have this much worth, this bank account."

Does that mean you feel the songs that were hits are better than the others?

"Only a Dream in Rio" wasn't a hit. Neither was "It's Enough to Be on Your Way." Or "Caroline I See You." But I do think that's some of my best stuff. Or "Carry Me on My Way." I know whether a song is good or not relatively. The thing that shows me is how often they show up in a set. And sometimes a song is in a set because an audience likes it. And there's nothing like giving an audience something they like. That's very compelling. But the other reason I like songs is because they're easy to perform and you connect emotionally with them when you play them.

I liked that once, when somebody asked you if you got tired of performing "Fire and Rain," you said no. They wanted to hear that it had lost its power for you, and you said it hadn't.

Sometimes something can get a little stale and you have to rotate it out for a while. There is a performance mentality. A sort of personality type that wants to perform and is *very* interested in the reaction of an audience. And I'm not saying it's terribly *evolved*. To be *stuck* in this place where I constantly need that kind of affirmation. But it does compel me. I'm very interested in having a performance go well and having the audience pleased by it and getting them. Putting something across. It's what I do. For better or for worse, it's the thing that really motivates me.

Does it bring you some sense of joy or contentment that your songs live on, that they have their own life?

Without a doubt. The idea that they might.

They are. Presently.

Yes. It's hugely validating. And it does, it makes you feel great. The epitome of that for me was that I hit a low point in '84, '85. I bottomed out, and I went through a year of awful withdrawal from the drugs I'd been addicted to. And I came out the other end really trashed. And a marriage had gone down, and I really just felt awful. And I went to Brazil and walked out onstage in this soccer stadium there. And there were three hundred thousand people who knew the words to "Fire and Rain," to "Blossom," to "Sunny Skies." And I didn't even know this audience existed. And not only that, it was Brazil, so they were all singing on key and in time. [*Laughter*] You know, a kid on the street there has better time than half the studio percussionists that you run into in Los Angeles and New York. It was a huge thrill for me to discover that, completely unbeknownst to me, there were this million or so people in this country far away for whom I was a part of their life. And in this very highly, *richly* musical place. And it really *picked* me up and turned me around. It also happened to be the moment when this country *shook* off this twenty-year junta that had been ruling them, and it was the night of the first elections in twenty years. And the whole place was *absolutely electrified*. I doubt I'll ever experience anything like it.

The wall coming down was equivalent to it. Being in Berlin when the wall came down. So it really put me back on my feet. So that was the very epitome of the things which you mentioned, having your songs mean something to people.

And of course, they are very personal expressions. So often when I meet people and they feel as though they know me, they're actually not too far off. They probably have as good of a take on me as you could expect a stranger to have. Much more than you'd expect a stranger to have.

Well, I think you should put songwriter higher on that list. Because it is a lonesome road, as you have written, and songs like your songs unite us, and they bring a lot of beauty and resonance to our lives.

There's no question about it. And you can have a song that says "onward, Christian soldiers" or "fight, fight . . ." But "there are ties between us, all men and women living on the earth, ties of hope and love, of sister and brotherhood." That's the direction I think we need to go in. As corny as it seems, it's a fact. So again, I'm gonna sidestep responsibility and credit to a certain extent. I feel when I'm playing a concert, I have a common experience with the audience that's there. I'm making the kind of music I know how to make, but we're both basically having the same experience. Me and my band are making the music, but we're also listening to it. And listening to music is *very* much like making music. It's like 90 percent the same experience.

And when songs have so much genuine heart in it, people feel that. "My Traveling Star" has that.

Yes, "My Traveling Star" is as good a song as I've written recently.

I look forward to the next ones.

Me too. I don't know when I'll get around to it. But as I say, there are a lot of seedlings.

◆ ◆ ◆

Randy Newman

The World Isn't Fair

Los Angeles, California 2007

He's at the piano. It's one place that he always seems the most comfortable. Like many musicians, his thoughts are musical as often as they are
verbal. When we talk about his songs, he frequently starts playing and
singing to make a point. And his playing is always quite astounding—
intricate, sometimes thundering, complex arrangements set against
beautiful melodies. (Although he often jokes that he isn't much a melodist, in fact he's one of the best.)

Today we're sharing the stage at the annual ASCAP Songwriters
Expo, where it's my fortuitous mission to interview Randy onstage for a
vast audience of fans and songwriters. He's onstage, doing a sound check.
We're at the Hollywood Renaissance hotel, now ritzy but once a funky
Holiday Inn where this writer was known to pool-crash on occasion
back in the day. Later, during the event, I am introduced to the crowd,
and then I, in turn, introduce Randy as the crowd spontaneously erupts
into a standing ovation. We talk—Randy is in showbiz mode, making

lots of jokes to great gusts of laughter—and he bursts frequently into song: "Political Science," "Sail Away," "Marie," "I'm Dead (But I Don't Know It)," "The World Isn't Fair," "Great Nations of Europe," "Davy the Fat Boy," "Simon Smith and the Amazing Dancing Bear," "I Love L.A.," and others are all performed for the spellbound crowd.

How does one introduce Randy Newman? It's not easy, 'cause there's a lot to say and it's easy to get overblown. But unafraid as always of unchained hyperbole, I said something quite close to this: Some human beings are way more talented than most. It's true. You think of someone like Michelangelo, for example. He was not only a pretty great sculptor but also a great painter and a poet. George Gershwin was a great songwriter, composer, and pianist but also an accomplished photographer. And Randy is one of these people.

"He's one of the most important American songwriters now or ever. He's defined an entire school of songwriting—so often in the press we see songs referred to as "like a Randy Newman song"—because his work is really on a level all its own. He's defined the art of writing songs in character. Musically and lyrically he has created a world no one else exists in. Some try, but nobody else does it like he does. Randy's songs are sophisticated, brilliant, often hilarious, often historical, timeless—and endlessly relevant. And musically they are compelling and beautiful. If he was only a melodist, a composer, he would be one of the best. But he's also one of the greatest living lyricists there is, despite Sondheim's problem with Randy's inclination to rhyme "girl" with "world." Sondheim never wrote "Louisiana 1927" or "The World Isn't Fair."

But there's more: since Randy's heartbreakingly beautiful score for Milos Forman's *Ragtime* in 1981, he's become one of the world's foremost film composers. Other songwriters have written scores—and other film scorers have written songs—but never in the history of the cinema has there been a serious songwriter who is also such an accomplished and experienced and great film composer. Usually people are good at one or the other—but not both. Randy is a seriously great film scorer—as the scores to *Ragtime*, *The Natural*, *Toy Story*, *Monsters, Inc.*, *Cars*, *Meet the Fokkers*, *Avalon*, and so many others attest. And unlike others in the field—he isn't a "hummer"—he writes and conducts full orchestral scores that stand up to repeated listenings, as I know well, having a seven-year-old who loves nothing more than to watch *Monsters, Inc.*, for example, thousands and thousands of times.

That was pretty much all of my introduction before I brought Randy to the stage. And I don't know if he heard it, but I know if he did, he'd bristle at the comparisons to Gershwin or Michelangelo. He's extremely self-critical. When told, for example, of the exceeding genius exhibited in a song like "Great Nations of Europe," which miraculously condenses the brutality of sixteenth-century European history into a single hilarious and pointed song, he remarks on the one line in it he felt wasn't perfect.

Yet it's this yearning for perfection that makes him the artist he is. It's the "divine dissatisfaction" that Martha Graham spoke of years ago, that quality in all great artists that is never satisfied because art is always human, never perfect, and yet they strive for the absolute. And it's that drive that compels him to always expand his range and his expression musically and lyrically and results in a new album every few years or so that is as great or greater than his previous masterpieces. Unlike so many of his peers who peaked decades ago, Randy Newman is still at it, still writing songs in his sixties that match the level of the masterpieces he wrote in his twenties.

> Broken windows and empty hallways,
> A pale dead moon in a sky streaked with gray.
> Human kindness is overflowing,
> And I think it's going to rain today.
> **"I Think It's Going to Rain Today,"** Randy Newman

When asked about his ability to maintain quality throughout all these years, on more than one occasion he's answered that it's because songwriting has always been a matter of "life or death" for him. Which is not to say he enjoys the process of writing songs—he doesn't. (Maybe because he's created such a formidable creative challenge in his life: matching the level of previous Randy Newman songs—no easy feat.) But he thinks about this, this pattern of popular songwriters peaking early in life. He received many laughs at the expo by saying that although most pop songwriters did their best work in their twenties, none of them have retired. He then sent the crowd into hysterics with a song he wrote, featured on *Bad Love*, about this very subject, continuing to do it when you have nothing left to do, called "I'm Dead, (But I Don't Know It)." ["I have nothing left to say / But I'm gonna say it anyway."]

He's capable of writing songs on subjects other songwriters don't even dream of approaching. He's written about racism in America, small-mindedness, and prejudice better than any other songwriter ever. Though slavery in America and the genocide of Native Americans are momentous chapters of not-so-distant American history, our greatest songwriters have rarely broached either topics. Yes, Dylan does refer to the "ghosts of slavery ships" in "Blind Willie McTell," but that's about it. Whereas Randy wrote one of the most poignant and telling songs ever about slavery, "Sail Away" (written in the character of a slave trader luring young black men to his boat), and on his album, *Bad Love*, he succeeded in entailing the twisted history of Columbus and his effect on this land and others in "Great Nations of Europe."

His songs contain solid content. Whereas so many songs we hear are sadly devoid of any details at all, any richness, any human texture, Randy's are always about something—a person, a place, an event, or a bit of history. His use of history—which he started years prior to the Google-era of instantly accessed history—is widespread throughout his work, from the landmark "Louisiana 1927" about the great flood that decimated the state (and was the most poignant of all songs sung after the horrors of Katrina) to "Sail Away" to "Kingfish," written about Huey "Every Man a King" Long, who was elected governor of Louisiana in 1928, to the masterful "Great Nations of Europe." And in the remarkable "The World Isn't Fair" from *Bad Love* he somehow succeeds in connecting the history of Karl Marx to the modern tale of rich "froggish" men with young beautiful wives to crystallize the inequality in the world. It's a song only Randy could write, and he did.

Many years ago, when *Saturday Night Live* was still new, Paul Simon was the host, and to introduce his friend Randy Newman, he played the first verse of Randy's beautiful love song "Marie." Of all of Simon's appearances on the show, it's the only time he performed a song he didn't write, with the exception of his duet on "Here Comes the Sun" with George Harrison. His performance of "Marie," which is perhaps the ultimate love song, was momentous. Here was one of the world's greatest songwriters letting us in on what was still somewhat of a secret back then in 1974: Randy Newman was among us. "Marie" remains remarkable in Randy's work not only because it is heartbreakingly beautiful but because it's such a straight-ahead love song, something Randy has always said he wished he could write but rarely did because his voice wasn't made for outright declarations of ardor. But to get around that problem, he put the song in character and employed an unprecedented technique: having the narrator get drunk enough to spill out emotions he'd never be able to express sober.

Simon, of course, isn't the only famous songwriter to sing Randy's praises. When I interviewed Dylan in 1993 he spoke of the greatness of legendary songwriters Hank Williams and Woody Guthrie. And when I asked him to cite a living songwriter who was great, the first who came to his mind was Randy. "There aren't many songwriters in Randy's league," he said. "He knows music. A song like 'Louisiana' or 'Cross Charleston Bay' ['Sail Away'], it just doesn't get any better than that."

The chief distinguishing characteristic of your work is your uncanny ability to write in character. How did that start?

Randy Newman: What I did for years was I tried to be Carole King. It was at Metric Music, in Hollywood. Jackie DeShannon and Leon Russell were there. When I started at sixteen Carole King was just the *greatest*, I thought. And I still do. And so when Gene McDaniels would need a follow-up, or the Chiffons, she would always beat us. Occasionally Jackie got a record.

The first song I wrote I was writing for Frank Sinatra Jr., who, in combination with his father, makes a very good Harry Connick Jr. [*Laughter*] So I was writing a song, and I couldn't take it. So I wrote this [*plays "Simon Smith and the Amazing Dancing Bear"*]. I think that was the first one. And then I justified it since by saying why shouldn't songwriters have the latitude that a short-story writer, like John Updike, has when he writes a short story or a novel—it doesn't have to be he who is the protagonist.

What was the reaction of people to that kind of song? Did anyone say, Randy, this is not what you should do?

They already said that to me when I thought I had a great follow-up for Bobby Vee. Carole had "Take Good Care of My Baby," and I'd come in with this [*plays a slow shuffle*]. That's not *bad*. [*Sings*] "I know someday I'll find a boy who'll softly say, little girl, can I take you away . . ." Oops, I just modulated without meaning to. [*Laughter*] I wrote that when I was very young. For The Ventures. That was called "Take Me Away." I don't know if anyone ever recorded it.

"Davy the Fat Boy" was among your first character songs—

Yeah. Originally it was totally different. Using the orchestra was *so* important to me, coming from the family I did, that I would tear up songs just so I could use the orchestra and get the place right. It was one of the first things I ever conducted. And when you conduct a whole orchestra, it's like this *weight*. They slow you down unless you do certain tricks that I don't know. [*Laughter*] So it's like building a mountain that you can't climb. [*Sings dramatic intro at a very slow tempo*] So I did arrangements for myself that I couldn't sing. And you'd see, it was right in the mainstream of what pop was doing at that time. [*Laughter*]

"Davy the Fat Boy," like so many of your songs, is still just as relevant as it was—

And the income hasn't increased. I think that made four cents, that song. Some of my songs with a good deal more shittiness to them earned a lot more. Like this one [*sings "I'll Be Home"*]. "I'll be home / I'll be home / When your nights are troubled / And you're all alone / When you're feeling down / And need some sympathy / There's no one else around / To keep you company / Remember baby, you can always count on me / I'll be home / I'll be home / I'll be home." That song earns more than others. Wrote it for Mary Hopkin. But, I mean, it's songs like that, that if I'd gone down that road, I'd be oil painting in Kauai today. [*Laughs*] I've been very lucky, considering the type of writing I've done. People who are fans of mine. I think their favorite songs of mine are the ballads, the ones that are when I'm closer to the mainstream than, say, "Davy the Fat Boy."

"Davy" really fits today's climate of *American Idol* and other shows people love, which ridicule people.

The song is about the narrator, who is so callous he tells Davy's mother and father that he's gonna be a pal to Davy and then he puts him in the circus. I find that funny for that reason. That degree of meanness. It's not like a cautionary tale or anything. None of us are that bad, or if we are, we don't admit it. I've written songs about people who are worse.

Leonard Cohen told me, "If I knew where the good songs came from, I would go there more often."

Yeah, I'm so tired. I'm even tired of hearing myself say that. I'm tired of hearing myself whine about it. So I'm stuck now with saying nothing. But it's true. It's not easy. I talked to [Don] Henley, and he said, "I haven't written anything in five years." But he was fighting that war.

You've been writing songs now for decades. Do you find it ever gets easier?

It's always easy for me when I have an assignment, a movie assignment. Everything I've ever written for a movie has come relatively easy. And once you get started on something, for yourself, sometimes that will go quickly. But starting can be difficult. I haven't *learned* anything that I didn't know before. The real secret to that, like so much else, is stamina. Hanging in there. And showing up every day.

With a movie deadline, you have no choice. And what it does is, for motion picture composers, a lot of them, when you don't *have* to do anything, after having to do something *every day, every day, every day*— James Newton Howard just did *King Kong* in four weeks—so when you don't *have* to do anything, you don't want to do *anything*. I mean, there ain't nothing I want to do. Not much past brushing your teeth. At least, that's the way I feel about it. It's not healthy.

So you haven't been working on any songs for yourself?

I got a few. But it's coming funny. Usually I write a really simple kind of country song to start with, and I have done that. Pretty much so, yeah. But I'm leaving them. I'm not a good *finisher* anymore. I'm not finishing off the three or four that I have. I'm *hoping* that I'll have a better idea.

When you say you need stamina, some songwriters have said their best ideas come all at once, words and music. Does that happen to you?

Sometimes, yeah.

But it takes stamina to stick with it?

It takes stamina to go in there and sit and work at it unless you're optimistic about a final result. Which I haven't learned. I'll start, and it will sound *terrible* to me, absolutely *terrible*. I never think I'm gonna get anywhere with what I'm playing, where things are taking me. No plan. So it makes you want to quit and do something else. Particularly when you don't exactly *have* to do it. The world isn't waiting for the next Randy Newman record, like, you've *got* to have this record. Those days are gone for the whole record business.

I saw Paul Simon play at some special memorial kind of thing, and I also heard James Taylor—on the last picture I did, he sang a song ["Our Town," from *Cars*]—and both those guys were great. Simon did "Bridge Over Troubled Water," but he was playing different kinds of chords with it. When I get a song I don't mess with it; I leave it alone.

But I admire both those guys for looking for chords other than I-IV-V-I. It's not easy. They're trying to find something *better*, not just taking what comes. Sometimes you just take what comes, and that's the best thing to do. Not revise.

Both of them are great at using guitar to come up with some wonderfully complex chord progressions with great melodies—

Yeah, Simon, and Taylor too. That's pretty fancy, that stuff—

James uses augmented chords sometimes—

Sting will too. But it's slightly different. It's jazz oriented.

Do you find the use of the guitar in songwriting has diminished the harmonic range of popular songs?

Well, in rock and roll itself, from 1953 or 1954, the beat itself did a lot to diminish harmonic invention and to narrow the harmonic vocabulary and make it small. When something is beating behind you, I-IV-V just sounds great. "Louie, Louie"—I like it. And I love a lot of that stuff. Carole King, early on, knew the repertory. It's obvious she knew Irving Berlin, Rodgers, and all that stuff, and there'll be some of that stuff in her work.

But it really did do that, and you can see why the old dinosaurs—they're too good to be called dinosaurs, actually—but *arrangers* who did the big-band stuff and people who knew that music and loved it, they would just *hate* rock and roll. They just would never get over it, how really simple and primitive it would sound to them. And their attempts at it were terrible. You would see sometimes in movies when some composer had to do a rock and roll thing, it would be just *embarrassingly* bad. They just had no feel for it. It's not often that people can do both.

Do you think the piano is inherently a better instrument for writing inventive harmonic music?

Well, I can't think of too many major composers, except Berlioz, who played guitar. But he got places. If you're a tremendous musician, it doesn't matter much.

Such as The Beatles—

Yeah. And they get the piano, easily. When I tried to play guitar I never got past the F chord. It hurt my fingers. I didn't have the stamina for that. But no, not necessarily. And it's hard for me to say. I haven't listened close to what's going on, but in rap sometimes it's harmonically fancy. Or heavy metal. I remember hearing Megadeth, and they sometimes go to odd places. Maybe it's just things bumping into each other, but it sounds like they're trying to do something. It's not simple. Jimmy Page, it wasn't *simple* what he did, and that's guitar.

What with layering now and synthesizers, you can get to those places. And there's nothing wrong with a straight diatonic approach in a pop song. I've done it most of the time.

Simon, like you, is a rare example of someone whose words are as inspired and inventive as the music. There aren't many songwriters— even Tin Pan Alley writers—whose words were as good as their music.

No. It's the rarest commodity in pop music. Because it's not really wanted that much. And the beat, the groove, is an overpowering thing. [*Sings part of "Staying Alive," by The Bee Gees*] Like I say, these are ancient references, because I haven't paid attention to [*laughs*] anything current. It's the music that does it.

When I first started hearing rap, it was straight rap. There was no melody. I knew in general they would *have* to get some hooks in there. The public is never gonna put up with something they can't sing along with. I knew at some point that would change. And now some of those guys like 50 Cent are singing the fifth. And Eminem is too. And they're getting music in the middle of things.

Do either words or music come more easily to you than the other?

[*Pause*] I think words that interest me are a little more difficult. I'm not so sure that I wouldn't have been more comfortable in a world of words. If I hadn't had music in my family and all, I'm not so sure that I would have been a musician. If I wasn't pushed in that direction, if I didn't just have to make music. But words I may have had a gift for. I probably *don't* anymore. When I try to write a letter I can't find the right words to use.

When you approach songs, do you finish a melody before you finish a lyric?

Sometimes. Never the obverse. Or I'll finish the *form* of it and know where it's got to go.

Do you ever come up with ideas for songs when you're not working at the piano?

Very rarely. More so recently. I've started carrying a notebook around because I have gotten ideas apart from the piano. I got one the other day that I liked. But usually it was always when I was sitting there. It always was when I was *compelled* to, when I had to. When I didn't, I didn't think about it.

"That would make a good song" hasn't occurred to me too much. Sometimes when I've read something or seen something on television, I might get an idea. There was more of that in the last record, I think, than there has been.

What was that topic you came up with?

I'd like to see if I could write about the big change in Europe and America, where—it's not news—that we're drifting apart and that it's to our detriment that they're doing a little better than we are in terms of education, in terms of higher taxes and getting the programs that are really better, better phone reception, better roads, less poverty. And they want to pull away. Naturally, the mass culture is still McDonald's and the [American] movies and Starbucks and things like that. That's our big hit everywhere. But in general they don't want to be like us. They always protested that they didn't want to be like us, but they did. And now they really don't. And we should emulate them in some ways. That's a change, and it's a good one. But it's not very singable. But I can do it, probably.

You've taken so many subjects that might not seem ostensibly singable, but you've pulled it off—
Yeah, that's true.

Has there ever been a subject you couldn't make into a song?
No. Oh yeah, there have been a bunch of things I couldn't do for whatever reason, but I can't think of anything that you couldn't deal with. Music isn't great for transmitting a lot of information. You can tell a lot about character by what you have him say. I sometimes forget that that's what I like *best* about some of the stuff that I've written, that it reveals more about the narrator than he knows about himself.

On the last record I made, which was too long ago, was *Bad Love*, and I did want to see if I could legitimately do pop music at the age of fifty-five or whatever age I was then and write from that perspective. And not an old croc perspective, necessarily, but where you could legitimately do it and still be doing that kind of music. All that talk about "we're not doing this when we're thirty," or "we're not doing this when we're forty," there's some validity to it, and everyone forgot about it, you know, because they just went on. You know, "Here we are—we're still doing it." But some of the stuff doesn't work anymore because they're too old.

But I'm satisfied that I succeeded in doing that, and those songs, as a bunch of songs, aren't inferior to what I've been doing. I think they're just as good as any batch of songs that I've written for any record. But I don't want to write from that perspective all the time. I don't always want to be an old guy chasing a young girl and that kind of thing. I don't want to have to do that. I don't want to have to *be* in my songs. I never have.

Occasionally you are in your songs yourself, as in "I Miss You" or "Dixie Flyer."
Yeah, but it's not exactly true. They're about me, yeah. In fact, they're all about me—as I've said to you before, you can guess more about what I'm like and what I think from my stuff than you could about people who are ostensibly self-revelatory in what they're doing. If you had to *guess* what I think about this, that, or the other, you'd probably be right.

***Bad Love* certainly isn't inferior to your past work. Which is unusual: most songwriters wrote their best work in their twenties—**
Ninety percent of them.

And there are few who haven't.
Have you ever written about that?

Yeah. I spoke to Simon about that.
What does he think? He's done it. Neil Young has—

He said, "I can do it because I'm still as interested in it as ever."
And *really* focused.

How do you explain your ability to do it?
Well, it's always been life or death to me, like it is to him. And also I think doing the movies has kept me in shape. Able to do it. I care a lot about it, but that's not to say other people don't.

The thing about it is, that's interesting to me, is *why. Why* during that period of time did Lennon and McCartney, Carole King—and why not later? And I think some of it, some of it is focus, but some of it is competitive. When Lennon was *with* McCartney, and they were writing not with but against each other, [*laughs*] in a way, when you're in the middle of it, when you're in Aldon Music or you're in a group and there's other people writing all around you, that's when people did that great work. The great songwriters of the period right before it, they stayed, they were doing it for thirty years, forty years. They were writing for other people; they weren't up there themselves, performing and making tons of money and being warped by fame and fortune.

I once talked to Chrissie Hynde [see page 406]. I had never met her, and I saw her at a recording studio a couple of years ago. And I said, "Geez, I'm *really* a fan of your writing. I think you're one of the best writers ever in pop music." And it was like she didn't know what I was talking about. She thought I was kidding her or something. It's like she didn't feel that way about herself.

But it isn't like classical music, in which people get better and better. People do their best work before they're twenty-seven quite often in rock and roll. Much more often than not.

Many songwriters I've spoken to, like Simon or Petty, seem to really enjoy the process—
I don't. I hate it.

And yet you continue to grow in your work.
I don't know whether Simon enjoys the process. He never told me he enjoys it. Petty might. It *certainly* is a saner way to go about things, to look forward to it, to love writing. Stevie Nicks used to *love* writing.

She would write hundreds of songs. But Henley and I always hated it. [*Laughs*] But you know the old saying: "Only a fool would write for anything other than money." That's one of the sayings. Another one is "Writing can be very difficult, but having written something is great."

Yeah, you've said in the past that when you get something going, then you enjoy it.

Yeah, when something's working. The first flush is good. You might get down on it the next day or something. But that first thing is the reason for going through hours of dead time.

When you are working on something that is going well, do you always finish it?

I've had things lately that I've put aside, but I used to finish them. I might be faking. I'll think, "Oh, I'm happy enough with that" and go watch television. It's like I'm getting lazy or something. And also it's all pretty simple harmonically. It's bothering me. Blues-oriented stuff. I get better and better over the years at writing for my voice. And it's limiting. If I'm writing for assignment, like "When She Loved Me" for Sarah Mc-Lachlan, or a different song for James Taylor, which I just wrote for *Cars*, I write differently. It's like if I'm writing for an oboe or a bassoon.

Did you ever think you would be a songwriter for other people?

I thought I was gonna be a movie composer. But then Lenny Waronker suggested that I try to write some songs. And like Mickey Rooney and Judy Garland, he went around pushing me. So I remember playing for Lou Adler. And I would play the melody along with myself. (Later he called me "Lenny's Robot.") I was seventeen. And he said, "You know, Carole King, she plays something different when she sings." And I thought she was the greatest at the time. And I was right. So I did.

And then we went to see Leiber and Stoller out in New York. And Leiber said I should move out there. He said, "You'd be one of the top people in five years." I was real young, real young.

And that didn't appeal to you, the idea of moving to New York?

No, I was still going to school, I think. But Leiber is *certainly* one of the best pop lyricists of the century, in my opinion. He's right up there with anybody. Those lyrics he wrote, a ton of those things, are really great. It's funny stuff. It's remarkable.

Was it at age seventeen that you wrote your first song?

Sixteen. The very first song was called "Don't Tell on Me." [*Sings plodding melody*] And the next one was "They Tell Me It's Summer," which was recorded by The Fleetwoods.

Was it writing for yourself that shaped your songwriting approach?

Yes. If I'd had a voice like Simon or Sting or a voice that I saw as seductive in some kind of way, or like a romantic hero, maybe I'd have written that kind of thing. Though I'll tell you, I'm not sure it would have interested me. I remember I changed before I started recording. I changed with "Simon Smith and the Amazing Dancing Bear" in '65. That was the one. Because I couldn't stand it, what I was doing. Maybe I couldn't do it as well as Goffin and King or Mann and Weil. But there are millions of ways of saying "I love you" or "I don't love you," and that's what 95 percent of the repertory is. But I just didn't want to do it. And I was writing for Frank Sinatra Jr. about some girl named Susie. [*Sings simple tune*] But I just said, "Jesus Christ." I just wasn't interested. I didn't care what I rhymed with what. So I changed.

Was it a conscious choice to start writing from a character's point of view?

No. Not conscious. But once I did it, I liked it. The song being slightly oblique. The song is about some guy who has some kind of gimmick and uses it and is kind of cynical. It isn't as if a lot of people followed me down that road or that there's been a lot of people before me doing it. I can think of almost no one. There isn't much of it. Because the medium is made to be more direct so people can put themselves in it. They're not used to hearing irony. More so with rap, when people are characters more often. But you're not used to it on the radio.

Yeah, but maybe because people can't do it. There are people who have tried but haven't been able to pull it off like you have.

That may be. You have to get the diction right. You have to have the vocabulary that the person you're writing about would have. And you have to have it not be you. But I mean, if I could write "I Love You Just the Way You Are," I'd have been happy to have done it. But I would have written the whole thing, and at the end I'd have gone, "I love you just the way you are, you stupid bitch" and blown my chances.

There are songwriters like Sondheim who have pulled it off, but he has the context of theater.

Yeah, he's writing for shows. He said that if he didn't have an assignment or some reason to write a song, he doesn't know how he'd do it. He did a good job writing that song for Madonna ["Sooner or Later" from *Dick Tracy*].

One of the best pieces of advice you gave me about songwriting is "Don't let the critic become bigger than the creator."

Yeah, it'll kill you. But I'm not able to do it. Not always. It'll shut you down. Sometimes I just won't let it go. Like I say, now all this stuff I'm writing is so blues oriented, so simple, that I'm a little dissatisfied in a sense. But I could be wrong, and I may end up finishing these songs.

This reminds me of the first time I met Leiber. I talked to him about songwriting, and I was writing all these songs with straight eighth-note accompaniment. I was doing that before The Beatles did it. I did it really early for some reason. And I complained to him about the fact that that was what I was doing, and he said, "If that happens, you just write yourself out of it. You let yourself do it, and eventually you'll get tired of it and think of something else." And that's *very* good advice, and I've thought of it often. You make yourself just finish them off, and do it, and you *will* move on. It may be even more likely when I was twenty than now, but I am pretty sure that that's the case.

You've always written both bluesy songs, such as "Lucinda," as well as harmonically complex ones. What affects which kind you do?

Sometimes my songs become a little bit more complex when I have to think about the chords and write them down and move the voices around. The Kurt Weill harmonic vocabulary is something I could sing to. But it is something that I think about. In fact, I'm thinking about it too much. You know, you can find substitutes for the blues. When I say bluesy, I mean this: [*goes to piano and plays a cavalcade of moving chords, far beyond a standard blues*]. I mean, I'm including that kind of shuffling around.

You've been playing for so many years—do your hands go to the same patterns?

Yeah. [*Laughs*] They go to shuffles. I have to not do that. Rock and roll players are really used to straight time. And I like shuffles too. That's what I love. I have to force myself not to do it.

Do you consciously experiment with chords you've never played before?

Yeah, all the time. In movies, for sure. And in songs, yeah. You can do it to the *detriment* of what you're working on. I've torn songs apart, just so I can do something with the orchestra. But I've stopped doing it because I thought I was hurting the song, slowing it down.

Do you generate your melodies from chords, or do you think of melody lines separate from chords?

I'll sing it against what I'm playing. Though I'll tell you, what movies do and have done to me, in part, when you write for an orchestra, you've sort of got to move the right ways. The rules of harmony apply; it sounds better if you follow these stupid basic things. Like contrary motion, and no parallel fifths, and things like that. And it just sounds better to me, and it works better, voicings and stuff. So then when I'm playing songs when I'm not even thinking about it, I'll do things that I wouldn't ordinarily do. My hands will go to the right place, but it's the wrong place for the song.

And then when you have to write a melody down, to dodge it, when you do an arrangement, it changes things. Some of the things I sing, when my ear's in shape, they sound *out* to me. They didn't bother me when I did them, and they don't bother me, ultimately. But I probably could have done it differently. It's a different kind of writing.

You said your film work keeps you in shape for songwriting—

I would think so, because you're doing creative work every day, and you're forced to do it, and it's harmonically, certainly, more complicated than songs. The harmonic vocabulary is bigger than what it is in a song.

It was interesting to me that you said you didn't want to go to the Hal Wilner tribute to your music because you didn't want to hear people do your songs wrong.

It wasn't exactly that. I just didn't want to be like a gray cloud, where I'm listening and it's not what I want to hear. I've had that experience before where I can't fake it too much if it's my music. Maybe it was fine.

As a songwriter, don't you want people to interpret your songs in different ways, or do you want them to stay exactly—

Not exactly. But I want it not to be embarrassing. Not to be *enormously* emotive, like versions I've heard of "I Think It's Going to Rain," and running the gamut of the emotions. Or getting things *wrong*, like happy "Sail Away"s. Or just really making it their own. What are you going to do? I generally had a specific intent. If someone sings their own notes . . . I mean, I heard a version of "Vincent" [by Don McLean] where a guy changed notes and took liberties with it and made it his own. That's put together too good. To screw with a song like that, I *hated* it.

Garfunkel was criticized for being too schmaltzy with your song "Old Man."

I was too schmaltzy with it too. I should have been colder even than it is, with the strings. I haven't heard it for a while.

Did you like his version?

Yes. I thought it worked. He is a very great singer. In my version I should have just put a lid on the strings a little more than I did. But maybe not. I haven't heard it in so long.

"The World Isn't Fair" is such a remarkable song. There's a lot going on in that one—it's both one of your deepest and funniest.

I'm proud of that one. I had the idea first on that one. It came fairly easily for a while. And I wrestled around with the fact that it's like one long verse. It doesn't *get* to a tonic or something. It never stops.

Yeah, but it's such a good melody with those words that it works.

I thought that "The Great Nations of Europe" would be one of the best songs I ever wrote. But for *some* reason, and I know what it is, I don't think it is. It's a little didactic. It's a little like a guy pointing to a board, and it doesn't have a *character* for a narrator. The guy in "The World Isn't Fair" is interesting as a character. He's glad. It's me. I'm glad the world isn't fair. I'm glad that Marx was wrong. In a way, you know. I've been very lucky. And yet I'm not *that* happy about it. [*Laughs*]

So many people I know still feel that "I Think It's Going to Rain Today" is their favorite Randy Newman song.

It's amazing. I was a baby when I wrote it. And they pick that, and they pick "Marie." And those things are atypical of my work. You *can't* win if you're looking at numbers, if you're looking at how much money you're making or how much money someone is making. I told my boys that people who think that way are *never* happy. The Buddhists are really right about material things. Absolutely, for sure. And you can't win if you go out listening to what people say about you, even when they praise you. They say, "God, I love 'Think It's Going to Rain,'" you can't help thinking, "Geez, you like something I wrote when I was twenty-one—what about the last forty years?" [*Laughs*] Even Springsteen, people like that, if you let the nature of the compliments bother you, the *quality* of them, you get stung all the time. Paul [Simon] doesn't want people saying, "God, I *love* 'Bridge Over Troubled Water'" with Artie singing the lead. [*Laughs*]

Yeah, it bothers him still.

Sure it does. And it's like Salieri in *Amadeus*. I saw [Simon & Garfunkel] at Shea Stadium years ago, and Paul's written everything, all this *fancy* music, great music, and the crowd's reacting great. But Artie comes on and does "Bridge Over Troubled Water" and the *lid comes off!* There's this curly-headed handsome guy, and I just *know* Paul's dying. But you can't get into it.

When I interviewed Dylan he singled you out as a great songwriter.

That's very nice, coming from him.

Yeah, he's pretty good.

Yeah, he is. Or was—or is. It's hard to say.

He mentioned "Louisiana" as one of your greatest songs. And I heard you do it—and also Aaron Neville do it—at Katrina benefits. And it was more moving than any other song sung. Is it surprising to you at all when past songs apply so powerfully to modern times?

Yeah, it is surprising. That one, of course. It's surprising how they've held up in a way. Same's true with Donovan, however. If you listen to those old Donovan records, [*laughs*] and I didn't notice them then for being great records or anything, but they hold up.

Yeah, they're good. But a handful of his songs, not all of them. Whereas you've never done a weak album.

No. *Born Again* is odd. But not weak, I don't think. And *that's* what I try to think of myself as hoping I can keep doing. If I ever think I'm getting appreciably worse, I won't do it. But I haven't felt it. And as I say in the song "I'm Dead," you wouldn't know, maybe. I think my early stuff earns more money in royalties every year than stuff of the nineties or even the eighties, except for "I Love L.A." But it's that stuff, the stuff on *Sail Away* and *Good Old Boys* and *Little Criminals* to *some* degree, that is what people know me for. So, I mean, in a way you could say that *I* had this window, like Neil Young from '71 through '75, where you write everything people love. He stayed good, but the bulk of his estate was written then. And mine too, maybe.

Yet you've written so many great songs since then, like "The World Isn't Fair" or "I Want You to Hurt Like I Do"—

Yeah, but they're not comparable in what they generate. But yeah, the new songs are improvements to me. "The World Isn't Fair" is real good. But the reality is that they're not as popular pop songs [*laughs*] as the early stuff.

You've often put yourself down, because you say you haven't written many hits—

But it's a fact. I sometimes wonder about Bacharach. My Uncle Lionel [Newman] was a musician, and he said about Bacharach: "You know, all his tunes sound like third oboe parts." [*Laughter*] But I went to this tribute to Bacharach, and those tunes are *very* impressive. I mean, he wanders all over the place, but when he gets to the hook, he knows that he's there.

Bacharach has defined a sound in popular music. A Bacharach song is distinctive. And you have done that as well, not only musically but lyrically too. Is there some satisfaction in the fact that you've created something unique in popular song?

There's some satisfaction, yeah. There is. And there's some satisfaction that I'm still *around*. And functioning almost at the same level I was. Maybe 65 percent, 73 percent. I thought that the *Bad Love* stuff was as good a bunch of songs as I've written since *Sail Away*. So I was happy. Because if I think I'm getting appreciably worse, I wouldn't do it.

You are so busy writing film scores, and I know a lot of the fans of your songwriting worry that it takes you away from songwriting. Does it, or does it inspire new songs?

It inspires them. I'm usually glad to get back to it. And harmonically it opens things for me because you go places you wouldn't go. And I take it very seriously, writing for the orchestra. So I don't look at it as time taken away [from songwriting]. But certainly, when I'm gone, what I'll be remembered for are the songs.

◆ ◆ ◆

Alice Cooper
Inventing Alice
Phoenix, Arizona 2009

Long before Tom Waits was playing a street urchin, before Bowie became Ziggy Stardust, and before KISS became KISS, a little man named Vince created a rock and roll legend named Alice Cooper. And he became him. He was the first to fully embrace the theatric aspects of rock spectacle, understanding that a character who gets beheaded onstage and rises to sing about it could be compelling stuff.

And he was right. He led the way toward a whole new concept in rock and roll, but always with the power of song firmly under his belt. He knew the best way to define Alice Cooper was with words and melodies, and from the start—and usually by collaborating—he was a serious songwriter. Yet whenever you talk songwriters with him he points to the one he loves the best: Laura Nyro. About whom much is said in the following.

He's known to be a nice guy. Always generous with song credits, he even impressed his manager, who told me that Alice is the opposite of

"that guy who will only give you four percent of a song. Alice is generous, and we work with other people who are generous."

He was born Vincent Furnier in Detroit, Michigan, in 1948. Alice
Cooper was originally the name of the band he formed in Phoenix in the
late sixties, breaking through in 1971 with "I'm Eighteen." The following
year brought "School's Out." He left the band to be Alice Cooper himself
and established himself with his musical manifesto *Welcome to My Nightmare* in 1975.

At the end of the interview I divulged the truth—that my son Joshua,
who was ten at the time, was a great fan as well. In fact, Alice was one of
the few artists we both loved equally. "That's good parenting," Alice said.

**When you invented the character of Alice Cooper did you intend for it
to become what it did?**

Alice Cooper: No, not at all. When I created Alice he was such an intense character, and, of course, I had to be him. And I really didn't know
where I ended and where Alice started. I would be out drinking and partying with Jim Morrison and Jimi Hendrix and Keith Moon—you know,
they're like my big brothers. And I'm doing, well, I guess I got to be Alice
all the time. And I *tried* that. And I drank more. And it was really hard
to be this character all the time. To the point that when I quit drinking I
became very clear on one thing: Alice is an institutional character. He's a
character like Captain Hook. Or any of these ubiquitous characters. And
that's what makes Alice fun to play. He's somebody who's totally opposite
of me. I didn't see that when I was drinking because I was a little foggy.

But I realized when I'm writing songs I have to write songs for Alice,
not for me. So that's a tricky thing. When you're a lyricist, if I was going
to write a song for Green Day, I wouldn't write it with Alice's attitude; I
would write it to their attitude. Or if it was for Lady Gaga, I would write
it for her attitude. But when I write for Alice, I know he has a certain
sense of humor. He would say things I wouldn't say. I know his humor. I
know his style.

You know, people write songs, and every once in a while they hand
them to me and say, "Here, this is a great Alice Cooper song." And I
read it and think, "Alice would never say that." They go, "What do you
mean?" I say, "I know Alice, and he would never say that."

**A lot of people know you as the character and not as the songwriter
behind the character.**

I know. Being a songwriter is something I absolutely love more than anything else. It's fun to play the character. But being a songwriter is greater. I saw Ray Davies the other night. I said to Ray, "When I started writing lyrics I realized I wanted to tell a story in three minutes. You are the expert at that." The only other guy who is really good at that is Chuck Berry. If Chuck Berry wanted to tell the story of Nadine or May-bellene, he could do it in three minutes and make it really funny and make you get the whole story in three minutes. And Ray Davies could do that with "Lola" and with a lot of songs. So I think I even made him blush because I told him that I fashion a lot of my songwriting after Ray Davies. I talk to young bands all the time. They give me their tape, and I listen to it and I say, "Okay, I get it, you're angry. But I'm not hearing a song here!"

You know Bob Ezrin was my George Martin. And he told me, "If you can't sing the verse, the bridge, the prechorus and the chorus, if you can't sit down at the piano and sing all of those parts, it's not a song. It's a riff with some lyrics to it." So I learned how to write songs from him. Bob Ezrin took what I wrote and turned it into a song, and he turned me into a songwriter.

I didn't know he took that role. I knew you wrote many songs together—

And for every one we used, we wrote eight songs and threw seven of them away. But you have to get your hands dirty. You have to get in there and actually throw a lot of songs away. [*Laughs*]

When you started writing songs, did you start with songs for this character? Or did that come later?

At first I was just writing for me. I wrote "Eighteen": "I'm eighteen and I like it." The songwriting was developing as Alice was too. They were working hand in hand. "School's Out," "Billion Dollar Babies"—those were just me writing, and then Alice was evolving out of those songs.

But it's funny: when I listen to who I think are great songwriters, it's not who you might think. When I tell bands who they should listen to if they want to be great songwriters, I tell them to listen to Paul McCart-ney. I want you to listen to Burt Bacharach, Laura Nyro.

Yes, I know we both share a great passion for Laura.

Yes. Listen to her "Eli's Comin'" album. That is amazing songwriting. Laura Nyro is my favorite female songwriter of all time. I've worn out all of her albums. And with all the people who cover her songs, nobody does it better than her. And I don't know how she does it, but she comes up with some of the most unique lyric lines that I have ever heard in my life. And it's almost *Porgy and Bess*. It's got this strange quality. Nobody writes like her. I appreciate other writers, but nobody was ever in the league that Laura Nyro was in. I listen to her.

Is it true Laura Nyro is your favorite songwriter?

Absolutely. I was hoping she'd be in the Rock and Roll Hall of Fame class that I was in. I would have asked if I could induct her. Because the guys that I know in the business who are Laura Nyro fans are the guys who are the real songwriters. I appreciate Burt Bacharach and Laura Nyro, and I appreciate people like Arthur Lee, Brian Wilson, Paul Simon—those are the great songwriters. And McCartney and Lennon, of course.

The very first time I heard one of her songs—I think it was "Wedding Bell Blues" or "Eli's Comin'"—I thought *Porgy and Bess*. It reminded me of that. It has that Gershwin-esque thing to it. And her lyrics were so unique. I listen to her lyrics now, and it's just astounding to me. Sometimes I don't know what she is saying. It's pure Laura Nyro.

Some of her stuff like "Timer" I love so much. I learned later it was about her cat.

So interesting she's the one you point to, yet your own songs are so different than the kind of thing she would write.

Totally different from hers. Even though I have been focusing on ballads. Even Burt Bacharach has shown me so much about how a song is put together. When you listen to something like "Always Something There to Remind Me" or "Say a Little Prayer" or any of those Bacharach songs and listen to how they're constructed, and then we take a hard-rock song and construct it just like that, it's just a different style of music. It *still* has a verse and a B section, a bridge, a chorus, back to the bridge, guitar break, double chorus. There's a formula to it that works.

And great melodies—

Well, [producer] Bob Ezrin would never let us put a song on the album that you couldn't sit down at the piano and sing. He said, "We don't scream songs. We don't use germ songs. We don't do riff songs." He said, "It's great to have a great riff, but your melody line has got to be able to be sung. And it has to have a melody to it. I don't care how crazy it is." "I Love the Dead" or any of those songs, we were able to sit and play them. And I think the songwriting was what Bob really emphasized with us. You can't give up the songwriting: it is the most important thing. And I believe that.

The show's the show, but if you don't have the song, it won't work. If you don't have the cake, you can't have the icing.

And your shows resound with the greatness of the songs, one after the next, like an opera.

I think people, when they look back and realize when you start the song, they know the melody! And that lyric is married to that melody line, and you can't have it any other way. It's like a Beatles song. When you hear any Beatles song you know that lyric is really perfect for that song structure.

And like their songs, yours have been around for decades and still sound great.

And are being covered. I love the fact that I hear covers of our songs. I just heard a girl do a version of "You and Me." So good. And I heard Tina Turner do "Only Women Bleed." *Geez*. I mean, it'll rip your heart out.

I also listen to Burt Bacharach. I tell bands: if you can write a song like Laura Nyro or like Burt Bacharach, you're a great writer. That might found funny talking to a heavy metal band. But if you listen to how the song is constructed and take that in—then write me an angry song! But make it so I can sing the verse and sing the B section. Make it as angry as you want it to be, but it doesn't have to be one note. Right now you have a riff, and all you're doing is yelling at me. That might work on one song, but you can't do an *album* of it because it's not a song.

Yes. Which is why I am happy to have this discussion with you. Because at the heart of all the theater and the image of this iconic character are really strong songs. "Poison," "School's Out," "I'm Eighteen"—these are anthems, and they are sturdy and melodic.

I would write a lot with Dick Wagner. And Dick and I would write the ballads. And to me, when we listen to our ballads, those are the best song songs. I always said that "Good Vibrations" is a great record, but "Yesterday" is a great song. With me, "Only Women Bleed," "Might as Well Be on Mars," "I Never Cry"—those were the songs that will stand up as great songs. "School's Out" is a great record.

Not a great song?

Well, it is a song that you can sing all the way through. It's a good song, and it's a great record. If I was going to say what my best song was,

I would say one of the ballads. "Only Women Bleed" was recorded by eleven or twelve different women. And each gave it their own interpretation because they could all sing the B section and the chorus. It can be interpreted in different ways. To me that is what makes a great song. When you can do it your way. Frank Sinatra did our song "You and Me." And he did a version I would never do. He made it into a Rat Pack kind of jazz, drunk-in-the-bar version.

Where do you start usually when you write a song? Do you write lyrics first?

I think there's a magic thing that songwriters do, and that's when you can marry a lyric with a certain chord and melody line that breaks your heart, that's when you know you've got something. If you can hit one line that is *exactly* in tune with that chord, maybe that chord is a minor chord, or it does something that twists your heart a little bit, and the lyric does the same thing—nothing's better. I play my songs for my daughters and my wife, and if I feel that that one line broke their heart, I sing it. [*Laughs*] Or if it makes her sigh, then I know I've got it. If you hit that romantic chord, you know you got it if women go, "Yeah, you've just nailed me." You've just found the core of what makes women work, what makes women sigh. That's when you have a hit.

So to write a song, do you sit there with your collaborator and work together?

Yes. Well, a lot of times you write in tandem with. But sometimes the lyric will write the melody like "Only Women Bleed." To me, that wrote itself. It was the rhythm of that lyric that wrote that melody line. I write most of the melody lines, though I don't sit down at the piano. I go to Bob Ezrin, and I'll go sing a line, then he sings the next line. So we're kind of a throwback to the old Broadway writers. Like Lerner and Loewe.

I came up with that title "Only Women Bleed." And he had been noodling around on the piano and had these little noodle things he was working with. And all of a sudden he hit that one, [*sings vamp*] and I went, "Whoa, whoa, whoa! That is *exactly* the right feel for this." You know it. He could play twenty different things, but that was the one. That was the one that made me go, "Stop. That is exactly the feel for this."

I don't think you can explain feel. It's something that you know or you don't know. I worked with Alan Menken on some stuff. We were writing a ballad for a project called "Alice's Deadly Seven" about the Seven Deadly Sins. And we got to this ballad, and I said I wanted to write a love song, but I wanted it to be about food. About gluttony. The guy is singing, and you think he's singing to a girl, but he's singing to food. And it was the *prettiest* song. It was just a heartbreaker. And then you realize he's singing to this table of food. And I went, "That is brilliant." That works on both ends. It works as a love song, or it can be a song about gluttony. So it was one of those moments.

Working with Alan Menken was great. Every time he would play something I would go, "Wait—yeah, yeah!" and he'd say, "No, how about this?" And I would say, "Yeah—wait!" He was so tuned into writing chords that make you go "Stop!" but then he would play one that is better. I could have written twenty songs with him that day, all ballads.

So when you say chords, you mean he would play changes, but you would sing melodies over those chords?

Yes. A lot of times lead singers write the melodies. Lead singers will even write better lead guitar parts than a lead guitarist player. Because he's more in tune with the melody line. If I come up to my guitar player and tell him I want it to go like this, and sing him a melody, he'd go, "I never would have played it that way, but I see exactly what you're doing there." So I do write a lot of the melody lines. I don't write chords. But if I have a title, like "Every Woman Has a Name," I will think of a tune that goes with that. And then he'll start chording it. And he'll say, "Okay, to get to the next section, let's go down to this chord, and it will fall right into this next section." So we work pretty close, hand in hand. I really want the songwriter in me to hear where that song is going. My mind will write something, and I'll think it sounds forced. Where does it want to go? If you put water on a green—if you want to see which way it's gonna break—you put water on a green and watch where it wants to go. It's the same for a song. You get to the B section and ask, "Where does this want to go? How does it want to release? That part we just wrote, it sounds like we're forcing that part in there. Let's figure out where it wants to go." And then he might say, "I think it wants to go to B minor." And he hits it and I say, "Yes! That is where we want to go!"

So when you're a lead singer and a lyricist, you are also writing the melody because you're gonna be singing it. I have people bring me songs, and I tell them, "You know, I just can't sing this song. Steven Tyler could kill this song. But it's not an Alice song."

"Poison" has such a compelling melody.

I wrote that with Desmond Child. When you're working with him, you're working with another guy who is full of music. You know all that background singing on that? We did that in three days. And he was doing things that I couldn't even hear. He would say, "No, it has to have this vocal right here." So once we got the lead vocal done I just let him go on the background vocals. Because he had this insane idea, and it worked.

In addition to you and Desmond Child, John McCurry is also credited on "Poison."

He wrote that great hook guitar line. [*Sings the guitar part*]

You are generous with credits. Not everyone would give him credit for a guitar part.

Yeah, when it's something that is that important to the song, I think you should. That was as much of a hook as anything else in that song.

How was "I'm Eighteen" born?

"Eighteen" started off as a jam. It was something that we used to warm up with. And we didn't even know that it was a song until Bob Ezrin said, "You know that thing that you guys always warm up with? That is really powerful." I said, "What is powerful about it?"

He said, "What we have to do is take that song and work on it." So we wrote words for it. And every time we would play it for him, he would say, "Nope. Dumb it down." And we'd say, "Wait a minute!" And he'd say, "Take those chords out. It needs to be dumber. It's about a guy who is eighteen. And he's eighteen, and he's kind of not a boy, not a man. It can't be sophisticated." He kept saying, "Dumb it down, dumb it down." Till finally we had this basic, kind of dumb song. And we let the lyrics sell the song. To us, we would have kept writing and putting chords in there and making it complicated. We needed somebody like Bob to come along and say, "No! Take things out."

It's hard to be simple sometimes.

The Beatles. The Beatles are the best at that. Everybody wants to write a Beatles song. And the trick that The Beatles had was that there was never anything in the way of the melody line. There was never in their record anything that was fighting the melody line. That is so hard to do.

"School's Out" has five names on it: you, along with Glen Buxton, Michael Bruce, Dennis Dunaway, and Neal Smith.

That's a band song. We all did parts of it. Glen Buxton did the guitar pattern. I wrote the lyrics. Somebody else wrote the B section. I said, "You know, if this is gonna be the song that represents us forever, it should have everybody in the band's name in there."

That is generous of you.

Yeah, well. I am old school. If the bass player comes in and plays a part that is the whole part that the song is based on, I put his name on it. And it might be just 15 percent. But that is 15 percent of a hit. And it's because that part really worked. When guys get so greedy about how much they wrote and how much the other guy wrote, it's not fun anymore. When it comes down to that, I always usually go, "What do you think is fair?" I let them come to me. But I might be the one who goes, "Hey, remember when that guy played that little guitar thing that we built the whole bridge on? We got to give him ten points on that." I really believe everybody gets a piece.

I saw you in concert with Rob Zombie, which was an amazing night.

Yeah, Rob Zombie is like my little brother. We got a chance to tour together, and it was so much fun. You put both of our shows together, and they're entirely two different kinds of shows. My show is much more *Phantom of the Opera* scary. His show is more media blitz, you know? His energy is every bit as high as my energy onstage. We'll do more of that.

Some of your songs are so famous—do they overshadow the others? A song like "I Might as Well Be on Mars" is so great and as strong as any.

Oh yeah. Some of the best songs that I ever wrote were not the hits. "I Might as Well Be on Mars" was one of the best songs I ever wrote. And there's a new one called "I Am Made of You" and another called "Something to Remember Me By," which I wrote with Dick Wagner thirty years ago. We wrote it the same time we wrote "I Never Cry." But I wasn't as good of a vocalist then and I couldn't sing the song. And it took me thirty years to be able to put that song up and know I could sing that song. I think it's one of my best songs.

Alice Cooper is, of course, a character you play. When you write songs, are you writing in character always?

You know, a lot of it, to be honest with you, a lot of sentimentality I have to invent for Alice. Because Alice is a stone-cold villain. But every once in a while I let you in on the fact that he's got a soft side. And it's an extremely romantic side. It's an Errol Flynn against his normal Basil Rathbone. There's a surprisingly good ballad there. But I allow that. For every song that is really gut-wrenching and scary, there's a ballad. There's one song my wife says, "All of your ballads break my heart." I said that's the best compliment I've ever got. Because if it's gonna be a hit, it's got to break the girl's heart. [*Laughs*]

After all these years of writing songs, does it ever get any easier?

For me it's as easy as it's ever been. I always told people that I'm one of these guys who if you came to me and said, "Alice, I need a song about a giraffe and a rhinoceros that are gonna get married on the Empire State Building," I would ask you, "Do you want it to be funny? Do you want it to be fast? Do you want it to be pop? Do you want it to be heavy? You tell me what you want and we'll write it." I'm one of those guys who is sort of a utility songwriter.

But every now and then a lyric will just hit you. Just the other day I was thinking of this idea for a song. And I knew this song was not a song Alice would put on his album. But I would love to write this song with Burt Bacharach. It's that type of song that Hal David used to write with him. And the lyric is so there. And now I've got to write these lyrics and send them to Bacharach and write, "Pretend that you've never heard of Alice Cooper. Just listen to these lyrics and tell me this isn't a song that you should write." [*Laughs*]

◆ ◆ ◆

Donald Fagen

Being Steely Dan

New York, New York 2012

He's famously a curmudgeon. Cloaked usually in some combination of regret, worry, and weary suspicion, he's also one of the world's most creative songwriters. He is Fagen, one half of the Fagen-Becker juggernaut at the core of Steely Dan.

Growing up when I did, born in 1958, I still remember the impact of hearing The Beatles on the radio for the first time. And I remember their rapid evolution, from "I Want to Hold Your Hand" in '64 to expansive masterpieces like "Strawberry Fields Forever" and "A Day in the Life" only three years later. I was hyperaware of the expansion in terms of lyrical content and expression as well as musical sophistication. So I presumed that the song would continue to evolve as rapidly and profoundly as it did between these few years.

Of course, I was wrong. There have been spurts of new song avenues, but mostly the evolution of the popular song, as Dylan stated to me

573

in *SOS I* on this issue, "is like a snake with its tail in its mouth." It goes round and round in infinity. It begins where it ends and begins again.

I asked David Crosby about this. His life—and all his ideas—he said, were shifted forever by The Beatles. Asked if there was anything ever that profound in their aftermath, he said, "Yes. Steely Dan."

And it's true. Steely Dan did take the song to a new place. They combined the harmonic sophistication of jazz with the essence of soul and the fire of rock and roll. With lyrics often comic, complex, darkly sardonic, and dimensional, they concocted a soundtrack that forever expanded the chordal vocabulary of rock and roll.

I had the privilege of interviewing both Becker and Fagen for *SOS I*, but it was, admittedly, a challenge to speak to both at once, as Becker is the more gregarious by far and Fagen a tad reticent to say too much. So I was thrilled in 2012, upon the release of Fagen's fourth solo album, *Sunken Condos*, that I had the opportunity to talk to Donald solo.

You and Becker are among the few songwriters to extend the vocabulary of chords—

Donald Fagen: It used to be, in the forties and the fifties, back in the days when they wrote standards, especially moving into the end of the fifties and into the sixties, a lot of the composers were using more jazz progressions, like Harold Arlen or Burton Lane. And jazz composers who wrote songs were into interesting changes. These days it's because it's now all guitar-based music. You do hear it on guitar occasionally with guitar tunings and such. But that's a different thing.

Speaking of Arlen, not only were his chords adventurous, but he wrote such beautiful melodies over those changes, like you do—

Thank you. Harold Arlen is one of my favorites. He was very influenced by jazz, going back to the twenties.

What do you think makes a melody work?

[*Laughs*] That's a tough one. Melodies can be good depending on the context. You can have a very simple melody, and if the harmony behind it is interesting, it can make a very simple melody really different depending on the harmonic context. And then again you can have a complex melody also. But the more complex it is, the harder it is to sing, and then sometimes it can sound contrived. In other words, you could write a melody that would be fine on a saxophone, but sometimes, if you give it to a singer, it can sound a little bit raunchy.

Which is another hallmark of your work, that although some of the melodies are quite sophisticated, they are always eminently singable. And soulful.

Thanks. Well, I think I am as influenced by instrumental players as by vocalists. So I listen to a lot of saxophone playing.

I love your song "True Companion," which wasn't included on any of your official albums.

Thanks a lot. Yeah, I like that song. That was written for a film called *Heavy Metal*. It was an animation in the seventies and had a lot of different people who wrote for it. I said to them, "What scene is this for?" And they said, "It doesn't matter. Just write a science-fiction song." [*Laughs*] So I did.

You've written several songs about history, such as "Parker's Band" and "The Royal Scam"

Walter and I used to like to make history songs. We even did a pre-history song, "The Caves of Altamira," which is prehistory.

Is it your feeling that a song, lyrically, can contain anything?

Yeah, for sure. You'd hear about events in folk music, and when we were growing up folk music was popular, especially Bob Dylan. He opened up popular music so you could write about anything. He started using surrealism in his songs and all kinds of songs that showed the interior mind at work. Nothing like that existed before he started doing it, and we were big Bob Dylan fans.

And like him you have reflected that embrace of content in your songs, where you could write a song about content we've never heard about.

Right, right. He was the first person to open that up. People forget that. But he was the man.

Was there ever content you tried to get into a song and just couldn't pull it off?

[*Laughs*] Yeah, we failed many times. We started songs that we didn't finish. We once tried to write a song about the Congress of Vienna, [*laughter*] which divided Europe after the War of 1812, I think it was. And we never pulled that one off. [*Laughs*] Yeah, we gave up on a few tunes.

Back in the days of Dylan and The Beatles there was a real sense of pop music evolving quickly, and we felt that it would continue to evolve. And it really didn't. Which I mentioned when interviewing David Crosby, and he said, "Yeah, except for Steely Dan. Steely Dan brought it to a new place."

Oh, that's nice of him to say so. I know he's a fan; he came backstage a couple times at shows. Very nice dude. You know, I did hear a song the other day by Martha Wainwright. Her mother, Kate McGarrigle, died a couple years ago. They used to write songs about all different things. They were great songwriters. And apparently the last song was "Proserpina," about a mythological woman. It was great, and Martha did a magnificent vocal on it. And that song certainly expands. It shows what you can do with unusual content.

You're obviously an expert on all kinds of songwriting—R&B, classic rock, standards. Are you at all surprised that songwriting hasn't evolved more, and does it have somewhere new to go?

As I say, I have a new record that just came out. So there's still a chance for things to happen, but it just happens less than it did because the sixties was an era where the artistic imagination was going through a period where it was really intense and society was changing. It was just one of those times. I think now we're still in the downward turn from those days. But it's just another time. But once in a while you'll hear something that's interesting.

Your work has expanded both the harmonic and lyrical content of songs, but the form of popular songs, the structures, haven't changed much. Do you think there's still something new to be done?

Absolutely. You know, I think it's just that there's not a lot you can do about people's tastes. People don't buy records.. Though I think that might change now because the record companies are dying. With the Internet you have a whole new independent music society, really. The problem is, I think, the masses of people haven't been exposed to good music in many decades. So it's gonna be a minority of people who come up with good stuff.

You've written songs now for over forty years. Does songwriting get easier over the years?

No, it gets harder every year. It takes longer. I think when you get older your mind kind of slows down and you don't have a lot of energy, and you've used up a lot of your ideas. You've really got to work to do it.

Do you enjoy that work?

I do, but it's just exhausting. [*Laughs*] You think just sitting in a room and thinking things would be easy, but it's not. I throw out so much stuff, that to get a few bars or a few good lines, I throw out so much stuff that it takes a long time.

Do you have any method for getting the ball rolling?

Go for a walk. I live in New York, so it's great to go for a walk and see other people on the street. Go to a movie. For some reason, when I come out of a movie, even if it's a bad movie, the whole thing of seeing these giant faces and hearing loud music gives me ideas, I don't know why.

So ideas for songs come to you when you're not writing?

Yeah, I usually get the ideas separate. I don't usually get ideas when I go to a room with a piano and sit down to write. I have a list of ideas I got at random times. The ideas usually come after dinner.

Are you good about preserving those ideas?

I wish I was better. I've lost a lot of stuff because I didn't write it down. But I do write [*laughs*] enough of them down that I end up with some songs, yeah.

I love the song "Slinky Thing" on the new record. Last time we spoke about the feelings of keys, and that has a classic A minor mood.

Yeah, well, my vocal range tends to move well with A minor, B minor, G flat minor. I don't have a big range, and those keys tends to be my best keys.

I love the title "Planet D'Rhonda"—do you remember where that came from?

I just started writing that song from the top of it, and when I got to that place, that phrase came into my mind.

Do you collect titles?

Yeah, I do. I keep a list of titles. But that one just came to me when writing the song.

Do you have any kind of regular habit or routine that surrounds your songwriting?

I mainly have three modes: writing mode, recording mode, and touring mode. When I'm in the writing mode, I keep a regular schedule. I get up about ten and write till about seven or so.

That's a long day.

Yeah.

Do you tape yourself while working?

Yeah, I have a little boombox with cassettes. I still use cassettes. I have boxes filled with labeled cassettes.

Do you try to finish everything you begin?

No. I have all these fragments on cassettes. Sometimes I'll listen to a few of them and see if there's anything there that's good.

There's old demos of you and Becker online, and I fell in love with the song "Stone Piano."

I vaguely remember that one. That was very early on.

Back then, on those demos, it was always the two of you singing, not just you, right?

Yeah, when we first started we were going to be the white Sam and Dave. [*Laughs*] I took the high part. I think I was Dave and he was Sam. [*Laughter*]

When you write songs alone for solo projects, do you play them for Walter?

No. Unless it's something we're gonna work on together. If I think it's a good tune for Steely Dan, I'll show him what I got and we'll work on it together. No, I never show him anything and he never shows me anything. [*Laughs*]

Do you remember writing "FM"?

Yes, I do. Wrote that in California. There was a film called *FM*, and we were asked to do the title song. And I said, "Does it have to have any specific words?" And they said, "No, it just has to be about FM radio." We wrote that very quickly, I remember, in one or two days. And we also recorded it very quickly too.

What a great chorus.

Johnny Mandel came in and did the string chart. It was fun to meet Johnny Mandel.

Is that unusual, for you to write something good fast?

Well, it was a simple tune. But yes, it is unusual for us to write something quickly.

You have made so many classic albums, but as you know, some people say albums are over. Will you always make albums?

Yes. I think in albums. I'm just used to it. And I think it's a good length. I think fifty minutes or so is a good length. It's not too long, but it's long enough to be satisfying. I don't know if anyone listens to albums anymore.

Well, your fans do. Listening to your new album has been a joy.

Thanks. I like it. For someone who enjoys sitting there listening to music, it's a good length. It may be a dead art form, though. I think songwriters like listening to whole albums.

Last time we spoke about musical keys, and you said how different keys to you almost have a different smell. Do they have different colors? Do you visualize keys?

No, but my wife sees numbers in different colors.

Do you have a favorite song that someone else wrote?

That depends on the genre.

Do you have a preference for major keys or minor keys? I think you have written more in minor keys, but I could be wrong.

I think you could be right about that. I do think that minor keys have more opportunities for richness. But maybe just because I am a depressive person. [*Laughs*]

◆ ◆ ◆

Jorge Calderon
On Writing with Zevon
West Hollywood, California 2014

The first thing that Zevon loved about him was that he was great at breaking into any house or apartment. It was a useful talent, especially on those nights when one comes home drunken and keyless. First time it happened, Jorge disappeared into the dark behind Zevon's apartment building, and in an instant, it seemed, the lights in Warren's windows were on, and two friends bonded forever.

Zevon also found in Jorge a lifetime collaborator. Zevon was a genius songwriter, perhaps more capable than most humans ever of writing a song all by himself. Not only was he a brilliant, sardonically romantic wordsmith, he was an exceptional composer, one of those rare songwriters, along with Randy Newman and Van Dyke Parks, who not only write songs but can arrange, orchestrate, and even conduct them.

So he didn't need a cowriter. He was also a tremendously genial man, a musician most in love with music and his fellow musicians, and a famously faithful and devoted friend. In interviews Zevon would often jokingly refer to himself as a lazy songwriter who had to devise easy methods of writing songs. And one of the best was to invite great friends to write songs with him. Sure, he'd steer, but he'd welcome all the power they could bring. Zevon journeyed into song with many famous non-songwriters, such as the writers Mitch Albom and Hunter Thompson. They'd say, "But, Warren, I don't even know how to rhyme!" And he'd say, "No sweat. I'll make it all rhyme—leave that to me." In other words: "I got the craft nailed. You just bring me some content. And I'll expand on what you bring and you expand on that till we get somewhere."

But with Jorge Calderon it was different. He wasn't there just for words. Like Warren, he's a serious and soulful musician and so could craft the thing as solidly as Warren and could balance both words and music adeptly. Unlike those authors with whom Zevon collaborated, Jorge was in the ring with him, returning every punch. He would match him chord for chord, groove for groove, symbol for symbol. He'd be in on the metaphor but also the modulation.

They also shared the same dark sense of humor, which informed all their songs, and love of the beautiful physical detail, so delicate and dynamic in songs, so that when Jorge showed Warren a photo from Elvis Presley's TV room at Graceland of one very fragile, ornate porcelain monkey, they both knew that was the key to the kingdom in terms of writing an Elvis song. And "Porcelain Monkey" was born.

Jorge was also there for Warren during those nonwriting times, which is most of life—when you are charging the batteries and passing all the time at hand. Together they'd endure the long LA days by meeting in the valley for afternoon movie matinees—always the worst science-fiction and horror films they could find, which they both loved.

They'd also go out and eat a lot, so it only seemed right, that if I was going to meet up with him and to talk about all things Zevon, that we meet at Warren's favorite hang, Hugo's, in West Hollywood. And Warren's spirit was ever present as we discussed the long list of miracle songs they wrote together as well as touching on some of Warren's infamous life and times.

I'll admit my love of Zevon has been steadily expanding for some time now. During his lifetime I admired the work I knew and listened often to certain albums, such as *Sentimental Hygiene*. But during these last past years it's been an ongoing revelation for me to discover, one after the other, countless brilliant songs he wrote that I had never heard. There's not a weak one in the bunch. His lyrics were always brilliant—erudite, unique, sardonic—and enriched with a great love of language, both poetic and colloquial. And his music was always just right. Pianistic but soulful and with a visceral command of song structure to always bring home the chorus—or the title—in a way both traditional and very modern, and always right.

Having a conversation with Jorge was heady and fun, as it was from conversation that all the songs he and Warren wrote together were born. And I could tell why Warren loved him so. He's smart, funny, talented—and nothing throws him. He has calm in the midst of the Hollywood storm.

There's also the undeniable mixture of sorrow and joy. The joy stemmed from the expansive spirit of their friendship and collaboration, their love of songwriting bringing them closer, as that closeness enabled many astounding songs to be written. Often Jorge's eyes would flash with exultant wonder describing Zevon's passion for songwriting and his celebration and elevation of the process. "This is high art, what we are doing," Zevon would say, and that flame still burns in Jorge's aspect.

But there's also the vast sorrow for this connection severed and for an absent friend who is absent now forever, especially one who so often laughed at death. Forever that light and darkness are intertwined.

And their songs remain.

Born in San Juan, Puerto Rico, he's a gifted guitarist who also plays keyboards, percussion, and more. He became part of Stevie Nicks and Lindsey Buckingham's pre-Fleetwood duo, Buckingham Nicks, as their touring percussionist and also worked with Fleetwood Mac, cowriting their song "Kiss and Run."

He was with Warren through the good times, and he was also there with him—more than anyone, really—through the dark times, especially Zevon's final chapter, when he was diagnosed with terminal cancer. Zevon had avoided going to the doctor for decades, a decision he later darkly remarked to David Letterman was maybe "a bad strategy." But rather than float away on a cloud of morphine mixed with misery, Zevon elected to make one more album. It was *The Wind*. It was songwriter as real hero, making one final masterpiece for the world before moving on and letting the kids take over.

And Jorge was assigned and accepted the impossible mission of making it happen. Not only did he cowrite the songs with Zevon—beautiful, deeply sad, but shining songs like "Keep Me in Your Heart"—he also produced the recording sessions, inviting in famous friends to pay a musical tribute, including Bruce Springsteen, Jackson Browne, Ry Cooder, Tom Petty, Emmylou Harris, Billy Bob Thornton, and others. If ever a songwriter had a true friend, his name was Jorge Calderon.

"Veracruz" was the first song you wrote together?

Jorge Calderon: The first one that was recorded. The first song we did was a thing called "Shy Girl." It started out like all the other ones: in conversation. I forget what I said, but he liked something I said, and it went back and forth. It was never finished, you see. But he always thought that was the first song we wrote.

After he passed away Crystal sent me a page where he had written the lyrics for "Shy Girl," the verse and the chorus. Typed by him on his typewriter. Old-school typewriter. It said "Music and Lyrics, Jorge Calderon and Warren Zevon." He put my name first! [*Laughs*]

And I like it. Maybe one day I'll try to finish it.

Was that unusual, that you would write one that you didn't finish?

It was just one that we started, and he'd always bring it back, sometimes, to me. He'd say something about the song.

Things started rolling along for him. And all of a sudden we were doing *Excitable Boy*, and that's when he asked me to help him with "Veracruz."

Is it true you met him on the night he got out of jail?

[*Laughs*] Yeah. Yeah, I used to live here in Hollywood, around Norton, up from Santa Monica Boulevard. And Crystal called me real late at night. Or maybe two or three in the morning. Woke me up. And she said, "Can you do me a favor? My boyfriend, I've got to pick him up. He was in the drunk tank in jail. And he doesn't have a ride, and I don't have a car . . ." Just a mess. So I picked her up, and I drove her to get him. Then we drove to an apartment building, and she couldn't find the keys to get into the house. So that is how I met Warren. Because I said, "Don't worry—I'm Puerto Rican. I can get into anybody's house." He loved that.

So I went to the back and found some kind of window that was half opened, and I got in and did my thing. And he loved that. He didn't say much, 'cause he was still coming down from being straight in the drunk tank. But he had a smile on his face. And from then on, he kept wanting to get together. He'd say, "Hey, man, you want to come over to my chili party?" He was making chili all the time.

Had you heard his music before you started working with him?

No. I met him that night, and then I became familiar with what he did.

Did you have any estimation, when you started working with him, of what kind of songwriter he was?

Well, by the time I worked on "Veracruz," I sort of knew what he was doing. I heard all the songs that he had. Demos of "Werewolves of London" and early songs like "Carmelita."

He'd made studio demos?

He'd made some demos with somebody before he got the deal with Elektra through Jackson [Browne]. That's when I met Jackson. Warren asked me to come. He said, "I've got a deal. I'm gonna make this record. Some guys are gonna produce me . . ." So he called me one day to sing on "I'll Sleep When I'm Dead." So when I went to the studio I met Jackson.

What did you think when you heard songs like that or "Carmelita"?

I thought he was great. He was grittier than other guys from the West Coast that I heard, like Jackson or Henley. He got deeper into the trench with his songs. He was deeper. One thing that attracted our relationship is that we were both big fans of hard-boiled books like Raymond Chandler and Ross Macdonald. We were always constantly quoting books like that. And then I heard his music; I heard that grittiness. He'd go for the underbelly of hurt and despair, and all those things those books and noir movies have. The despair, the place where you really get to the bottom of things, instead of being flowery, which a lot of songwriters here [*laughs*] were doing.

And such a beautiful use of language—

Exactly. Well, yeah, that's the thing. Why he is the most unique and greatest of all those guys, from here or anywhere else—it was a love of language. He had a command of language, and he loved language. And also the musicality. His piano playing and his ideas about harmony and all, were different. And on top of that he had the blues, and the whole thing. He loved Bo Diddley; he loved Muddy Waters—so all of that combined.

He could play classical, right?

Oh yeah, he was great. You know that song "Accidentally Like a Martyr" with that passage of music? That was always amazing to me, and later on, when we were doing *The Wind*, he showed me that and said some classical piano player showed him that pattern and how to use it in every key. He said, "Every little piece of thing I learn in my life, I try to use it in a song. Yeah, that's all we do."

The language, that's the thing that attracted us. Both big readers. And he liked that English was my second language; he would laugh at the way I would say things sometimes. Because I was translating from a different language to say something. Or I would come up with phrases that were different, and he'd never heard them before. That is what attracted him to want to write with me. Because he was always looking for a way to say something different in a song. That's how we clicked a lot.

And that comes across. The songs are fresh—to this day. They are not the same as other songs.

Exactly.

And he was capable of writing beautiful melodies but also great rock songs. Something like "Porcelain Monkey" is a great groove around a good riff. Did you discuss the musical setting ever before doing the song?

With that one, "Porcelain Monkey," we wrote the words first, no idea what the music would be.

The whole lyric?

Yeah. That was 1999. He was doing *Life'll Kill Ya*. He called me and said, "I'm working on this album, and I need two more songs. I want you to be involved. I need help here. I ran out of ideas."

So I said, "Okay, let's give it a try." I went to his house. And for freak circumstances I brought a notebook I had. Because I was the guy, if we had any idea, who would write them down.

He wouldn't do that himself?

No. He'd keep it in his mind. And if it was really good, he'd sit down and write it. Or let me write it.

I had been on the road with David Lindley for about a year. And we went to Graceland. And I went across the street and was buying postcards of Graceland. One of them had that room they called the TV Room. It had three TVs, a lounge area, and a table with this big porcelain monkey. A white monkey with big dark eyes. You can Google it. I pasted this thing to the cover. I had it for years. When I brought it out he said, "What's that?" I said, "That's a porcelain monkey." He took out a magic marker and in big letters wrote "Porcelain Monkey" and said, "That's what we're gonna write today."

So I gave him the whole story about Elvis and that monkey and how Elvis would go in this TV room, and the three TVs, and then we started writing that song.

But he liked that title before knowing the story?

Yes. He loved to get titles first. When he chose that title I don't think either of us knew where it was going. But he knew that it had to do with Graceland.

He had the first line. "He was an accident waiting to happen." We wrote that down and kept going and going and going. We wrote a little piece of it, a part of it, and I phoned him back and said something about "Hip-shakin' shoutin' in gold lame / That's how he earned his regal sobriquet." As soon as I said that to him, he said, "Oh, we just opened the garage door and parked the limo inside." Meaning, now we got something.

And that was pure lyrics, with no music?

Yes, just thinking of lyrics. Without thinking of where the song should go. Because once you got the lyrics, then when you read them, you get some kind of beat to it, where you can grab onto something.

Yeah, and I told him about Elvis and velveteen. And the great thing, where he started at a "shotgun shack singing Pentecostal hymns / Through the wrought-iron gates to the TV room / He had a little world, it was smaller than your hand / It's a rockabilly ride from the glitter to the gloom."

Wow.

That's one of my favorite verses.

I love that too. Often his rhymes are not perfect rhymes, but that one does have perfect rhymes.

That's one thing I learned from working with him. His big thing was not to ruin the context for rhyme. It doesn't have to be a perfect rhyme; it has to be a close rhyme, and you get the message clearer.

Sometimes I am surprised that they are not perfect rhymes, 'cause they work so perfectly.

Yeah. A lot of Dylan songs were like that. At first he was rhyming, rhyming, rhyming, but after a while he was rhyming less perfect rhymes, and it's wonderful. I remember when Warren and I wrote "Fistful of Rain." He said, "You've got to write the hard verse." And I said, "In a heart there are windows and doors / You can let the light in / You can hear the wind blow." And "doors" and "blow" don't rhyme. So I asked him, should it be "let the wind soar" or "let the wind roar"? He said no. And I said, "You're right." It passes by—it's perfect and it's not perfect.

And it comes across that this wasn't contrived to be a rhyme; these are the words that matter.

Exactly. He liked to do the thing that *hit* you. It wasn't intellectually great, trying to say, oh, he's a great writer 'cause he rhymed this with this. No, it's got to be gut level. His music would bring you to a place people live, where you can walk the streets.

Seems like Warren really enjoyed writing songs, especially with you. Was it fun?

It was always so much fun to be with him, writing or not. We had so much fun. We'd be drinking Turkish coffee from Noura and get *really* lit up. And he'd say, "I have this song called 'Mr. Bad Example,' and I have one or two verses . . ." So I gave him a verse for that one, and he put it as the first verse. The one about "I was the altar boy working at church . . . I took it from a box labeled children's fund . . . cummerbund . . ." We were having so much fun, and we already had so many verses, so I said, "Let's keep going! Let's do it like 'Bob Dylan's Hundredth Dream' about Captain Arab when he goes on and on and on . . ." [*Laughs*] So Warren said, "Yeah!" So we wrote all these verses, and at one point we were on the floor laughing. And I finally said, "I don't think we can keep going."

That is a long one, very expansive. So he had the title to start that one?

Yeah. He said he was on the road in Australia, and he was getting ready for a gig and talking to some Aussies. And out of this conversation "Mr. Bad Example" came out. So he wanted to do it. He had the verse about the seven deadly sins and the verse about "I worked in hair replacement." So he had all these ideas, and we kept finishing verses. With his idea, my idea. It was always a give-and-take like that. He would say something and I would finish it, or I would say something and he would finish it. That is the great thing about songwriting. You're writing with somebody on your wavelength, and you're at the same place.

You guys were on a unique wavelength. Not many people at that wavelength!

[*Laughs*] Yeah, well, that's good. We hadn't written for years before we wrote "Fistful of Rain" and "Porcelain Monkey," and I told him, "Man, you know, it's amazing, this one," and he said, "I know! It's high art! It doesn't sell for shit, but, you know, we're doing it, man. You and I are doing it."

And I said, "When I get together with you it's like playing basketball with Michael Jordan. Your game goes up when you're playing with somebody like that." He said to me, "It's the same for me, Jorge." So that was the best compliment ever. We had this thing. It was unique, and it would elevate to this point. And that helped us with *The Wind*.

Of all people to do this with, Warren Zevon. Such an amazing talent. Clearly your game had to be pretty high to even go there.

Totally. I understand that.

Musically and lyrically.

Totally. Let me tell you, man, I used to be a guy, and I still am sometimes, who would get very insecure and would think that I would have nothing. I would think, "I have *nothing*. I have to write something that is good," while I would be putting aside things that are really good. And he used to tell me, "Jorge, what are you *doing*? This is great!" He was like a cheerleader for me. He would say, "Man, you think this is nothing. But this is something. This is great!" Kind of opened my eyes to things I was doing, that I was knocking it down myself. He would chase me around in the beginning because I would say something funny and he would crack up. He'd say, "You are like the Puerto Rican James Joyce. [*Laughs*] Because you say these things that are jokes, but your jokes are on a level that I love." And that is what started a lot of those gag songs, about laughing about something.

And funny about those gag songs, they are all serious. All his funny songs are serious.

Yeah. I call those songs Chauncey Gardiner songs. Chauncey Gardiner was the character in *Being There* who says nothing but it means a lot to a lot of people. Mundane things, and you go, "I know what you are saying!" And they connect with something bigger. [*Laughs*] That is what I call that. You are passing the time, but somebody sees more in the song than you actually intended.

Yet your songs are so rich in terms of detail that they don't require the listener to bring a whole world to them. They are there. As opposed to so many songs that are opaque, and you can bring a whole thing to it. It was interesting to me that Warren loved Dylan so much, though Warren's songs were never abstract the way many of Dylan's are. It was more descriptive, story songs.

Yeah, he loved to get to the point. He loved to—and I've said this before many times—he loved less is more. He loved the economy of words. He loved language, but he loved the economy of words. There was a great quote that Jackson [Browne] said about Warren. It was about the song "Studebaker," about one line that says so much. He brings all these feelings from the beginning of the line to the middle to the end, with at least three different images and feelings inside about this line. And that was what Warren was great at too. Economize: less is more.

That is a great song. And he never officially recorded "Studebaker," did he?

No, but his son [Jordan Zevon] did.

That's such a great song—why didn't Warren record it?

It's a great song. Well, you know, Jordan did a good thing because he combined two early versions of that song into one and got the best out of two. I think they had a couple of lines differently, and he made it be the best of the two. I listen to that once in a while because that is a great song. I've been thinking about doing it, 'cause it's a great song to do live.

I wanted to ask you about his song "Tule's Blues." There is a beautiful demo version of it, piano and voice, that is slow and great. And then he did a faster version of it on the album Jackson produced. But I know he wanted to include it on *Excitable Boy*, and Waddy Wachtel and others talked him out of it 'cause it was a ballad. I wondered what you think of that one.

I think it's great. I always loved "Tule's Blues." I love Waddy. He's a producer, and he's producing the album. And a different producer might have included it. Maybe Jackson wanted that song on the album and Waddy talked him out of it. I don't know. You go, "Oh no, we need another fast song and not a slow song here." That kind of mentality. If it was me, I would have left it there. [*Laughs*]

My understanding is it was because Waddy wanted Warren to be thought of as a rocker and not a balladeer.

I don't know. It happened on a later album that Waddy was producing. Warren and I wrote this song called "I Volunteered." And it's all about looking back at your life and all the things that you did. The end was "I don't blame you, I volunteered." Meaning that I did all this shit, and I'm not blaming anybody.

A great title.

We refined it, at the end, for *The Wind*. But then "Keep Me in Your Heart" came out and we forgot about these other things.

So it wasn't recorded ever?

No. I will do it at some point. I haven't wanted to do it live because I would like to record it first. Warren and I wanted to do that song on the *Mr. Bad Example* album. Waddy heard it and said, "No, not for this album." So that was the end of that song then. Then it lived all those years until *The Wind*, and I brought it back, looking for songs. I said to Warren, "Here we are, and you're looking at your last album." So we looked at it, but it had gotten washed away. Just like *The Wind*.

Were there other songs that didn't get recorded?

Yes, there are a few. There's one, "Give Me Back My Heart," about a horrible breakup. He was always breaking up with girls, and it was a heartache all the time. He used to live on Barham Boulevard at the Oakwood Apartments. He used to call them Gorky Park. I went to see him, and my wife and I, though we have been married a long time, had this horrible argument.

I knocked on the door, and he knew we were gonna write something. He opened the door and said, "What do you have?" I said, "Give me back my heart." He said, "Great, come in." And we started writing that song. It was that—getting a title about some situation and writing a song about it.

I actually recorded it already, but I haven't put it out. He wrote the music for it. Sort of an organ thing, and we worked on the chorus together.

Like on "Porcelain Monkey," we wrote the words, and then I would let him come up with the music. Because it was his album. His career. If I'm writing a song, mainly I would let him do his music because I trusted him a thousand percent musically.

I always had a guitar with me. But we worked mostly on words, words, words. He would ask me about music, but mostly he'd do it. It changed later on with *The Wind*, when I had more to do. Because when he went home he didn't do much. "Mr. Bad Example," he asked me where to go with the chorus. But usually I let him do the music because I loved what he did with music.

Sometimes he'd call me his lyricist. And I would think to myself, [*laughs*] Warren Zevon is calling me his lyricist. A better lyricist than him would be hard to find.

Yet your lyrics—like the "windows and doors" line from "Fistful of Rain"—match his words and style so well.

You got it, man. His girlfriends used to say that all the time. Women can read right through it. I was working on the phone with him on a lot of stuff on *The Wind*. His girlfriends would say, "I read what you wrote and what he wrote, and it's seamless. It seems like one person is writing it." Which is the best compliment there is.

That's what you're looking for. When you're collaborating with somebody that has a career and a persona, it has to be tailor-made for him.

During the making of *The Wind* they prescribed him all these drugs. One time he called me on his cell phone and said, "I'm on the corner of Crescent Heights. I just came out of a drugstore and I'm numb as a statue. And I'm gonna beg, borrow, or steal some feelings from you so I can have some feelings too." He was telling *me* that. He wasn't giving me the line for a song; he was telling me that to make me laugh. I hung up and started writing a verse. When I called him back he said, "Yeah, that's good, that good." We had a lot of fun with that song.

So some of your songs came out of your own conversations with each other?

Yes. And when he told me that, I made it more romantic, 'cause he was seeing a lot of girls at the time. And he was having the time of his life, doing as much as he could in his last days. I gave him "I don't care if it's superficial / . . . Just bring enough for the ritual / Get here before I fall asleep." He was with all of these girls but was so out of it and sick.

When we wrote "Keep Me in Your Heart," I said the lines, "Hold me in your thoughts / Take me in your dreams / Touch me as I fall into view / When the winter comes / Keep the fires lit / And I will be right next to you." There was silence, and then he said, "I don't know, Jorge. I don't know." I still have that page, and I scratched it with an X. If it didn't work for him, it was out.

A couple of months went by, and he asked if I had written any more. So when we went to do it, he said, "Everything is great." I put it back. The point I am trying to make is that if he didn't like it, even if I felt it was a great line, if it doesn't work for him, fine. Because you know why? Because sometimes you slash something and get to something even better.

But at first he didn't like it 'cause it was just too sad?
Yes. It was too heartbreaking for him.

The vocal sounds like he was sad. Was that hard for him to do?
Yeah. It was very hard for him, very hard.

I was so moved by the lines about "when you're doing simple things around the house / . . . I'm tied to you like the buttons on your blouse." It's so intimate.
Let me tell you about that. He wrote the first verse, and I had to write everything else. The only thing he helped me with there were the simple things around the house line. I was saying something about when you are doing things around the house, like watering the plants, and he said, "How about 'simple things'?" And then when I told him about the buttons of the blouse, he wasn't sure. He gave me a hard time about that too. I went, "Okay, fine, if you don't like it."

Then he called me and said, "I changed my mind. It's good. It's great." He said his girlfriend really liked that line.

So there was a back and forth of him accepting things, more on this song than any.

And of all the songs you wrote together, it's so personal and close to the bone. And he had problems with that but as a songwriter could see the strength in it.
You know, he was going through so much. Knowing he was gonna die. Going through all of this physical stuff. He started drinking again. I

was being a good friend, a good brother. Anything he was going through, I would let it be. My job with him, aside from loving him dearly, was to accomplish what he asked me to do. He said, "I want you to do this last album. I want to leave my kids something that will help them. And finish my career with something great."

Was he sure it was the best thing to do, as opposed to taking time off from work—

I tried to tell him that. I tried to say, "Maybe you should just take off with your kids and get treatment." And he said, "No, I don't want treatment. I want to do the album. You've got to help me do it. You've got to do it." So I jumped in.

As a songwriter, it was a heroic choice to make. I have one last thing to do on Earth, and it's to write more songs.

It was funny. I did say that, that it was heroic. But very painful. Because at first we had a lot of fun, then Christmas came, 2002. He went home. And he never came out. He just went into this deep depression. And the big thing about this album that people don't understand is that it almost didn't get done. Because he went home. I did the tracks in the studio for three or four songs. Got the lyrics and everything. We had the songs, but he wouldn't sing them. He said he couldn't. He said, "You sing them."

I said, "Are you crazy? This is your fucking album."

It was like that. And I was also worried that he just might die one day. So finally, at some point, three months after going back and forth, his kids, I think, Ariel and Jordan, went there with a doctor and told him he had to get up from this depression. The doctor might have given him some antidepressant medication or something. He had to stop drinking for a while. Cool it down, and bring yourself up to finish this thing that you really want.

So we came to him. Brought all the equipment to his home. And he sang the songs. He sang "El Amor de Mi Vida," "Keep Me in Your Heart," "Rub Me Raw." But people don't know: that almost did not get completed. And that was the beauty of it, that it did.

Hard to imagine, knowing your life is about to end, that he could summon up the energy to do any writing, let alone great writing. "El Amor de Mi Vida" has such a beautiful melody.

When we wrote the words of it, he said, "You try something musically for it, and I will try something musically, and we'll see what happens." So I put it into this Southwestern thing that was good. He listened to mine and really loved it. And then he did what he did with his music, which is what it became. So when the Spanish comes, you don't expect it. He was a big fan of Richard Rodgers and all that Broadway stuff, and he said, "I channeled Richard Rodgers and this is what I got."

So it was his music totally. I loved it. It was gorgeous and wonderful.

And that Spanish section, with that melody, is so beautiful. You did that in "Veracruz" too, in which you wrote a Spanish section.

Yeah. With "Veracruz" he gave me a tape with the section ending with "Guernavaca." And I came up with it.

Did he understand Spanish, or did you translate for him?

I translated for him. What happened is that he told me he wanted these lyrics to be in Spanish, the chorus. I said, "Okay, what do you want to say?" He said, "You're the love of my life. I've been looking for you and can't find you." He gave me the thought. So I translated it. And then I wrote a few things in English: "I close my eyes, you reappear." Then he said, "I carry it inside, in here." We went like that, line by line, and got the whole song.

Were there ever any times when you really couldn't agree about a song?

With him it was like we had a brotherly thing, where if it wasn't gonna work, I would know he didn't like it. We didn't need to get into an argument. He'd give some kind of facial thing that I would know. And vice versa. He'd say, "Oh, you don't like that?" We made it work. We never went over the fence into where it wouldn't work.

Was he someone who liked to always finish a song, or were there things that he'd discard?

No. Everything we worked on, except for "Shy Girl," got finished. It was his main excitement in life, writing. During *The Wind* the creativity of writing these songs kept him alive longer than the doctors told him. He was so energetic, so thrilled. I have messages from him that he would leave me on my machine. "Oh man, you don't know how great this collaboration is. These songs are great." His manager, Brigette, who was constantly in the car with him, taking him to doctor appointments, said, "Jorge, what you two are doing is so great. He's so excited about working with you and how immediate everything is. You're keeping him in a place where he's not thinking about anything except writing." He felt very high about it for a while, until after Christmas he got depressed and that spiral went down, and it became hard to finish the album.

In this song cycle of so many intimate songs, you have "Prison Grove." Where did that come from?

When we were doing *Life'll Kill Ya* we used to joke around a lot with prison stuff. And they all started with my joke. I was singing this unbearably high harmony on one of his songs. And he said, "What—you can't reach it? What's your problem?" And I said, "Hey, I'm not your boy in prison." And he stopped and cracked up. And after that, everything was about being your boy in prison and prison love. So I think at one point he said, "Prison Grove." He insisted I said it, but I think he said it.

He went to go see Letterman do his final show. I was working on *The Wind*. I wanted to keep moving forward, so I suggested "Prison Grove." But this time I would make it serious, not a joke. So I started with a guitar riff. When I was done, I had three verses. I played it for him, and he went, "Oh man, Jorge, this is fantastic. This is the cornerstone of the record and expresses what this album is." But I wanted to write it together. I had several verses, and he said, "You almost wrote the whole song." But I told him we needed him to write more verses, and we had to write the chorus. I went to his house, and he came out with the last verse, about the "wacky wack." And we wrote together the chorus. He wanted to write something about "the light shines" or "shine the light" and asked, "But shine the light on what?" And I said, "These broken lives." And he liked that. And we wrote the chorus with this gold pen. Got a hammer and a nail, and he nailed the paper to the wall and said, "We nailed it!" And that's how "Prison Grove" happened.

I love that on that last Letterman show he played his brilliant song "Genius," and with a remarkable string arrangement he wrote, which was just pure genius.

He was a genius. From the beginning. You know that old joke, "I'm a genius, and I don't use that word lightly"? But he was. He was amazing. He was a big Dylan fan, and Dylan has this song "Silvio." Warren loved that so much; he showed me. He wrote every part of the arrangement of the song and showed it to me. "This is what the drums are doing. This is what the girls are doing . . ." If I ever meet Dylan, I will tell him that.

Would Warren transcribe his own songs like that?

Yeah. He wrote out the whole thing. Once he gave me one, and I couldn't read it. I told him, "Warren, I need a chord sheet!"

He loved writing stuff out. All of it. There was nothing more pleasurable to him than writing a song.

◆ ◆ ◆

Don McLean
American Pie and Beyond
New York, New York 2010

Most songwriters don't try to do anything new. They're busy enough just trying to write a good song. Stretching the form itself—that is something rarely tried. Mostly it's about working within the form and discovering something new within the limitations given.

Which is only one reason why Don McLean's "American Pie" remains such a remarkable song. Sure, Bob Dylan had written multiverse songs that blew our minds with epic verses of expansive lyrics before this. But except for him, few artists had ever done something quite so bold as describe the rise and fall of American rock and roll in an infectious and expansive pop song. Till Don McLean did it.

He coined the term "the day the music died" to paint the scene—and its aftermath—of the triple death of Buddy Holly, Ritchie Valens, and J. P. Richardson (the Big Bopper) on February 3, 1959. It's his magnum opus, still in constant radio play, and it was covered a few years back by Madonna, who took it up the charts again.

Had he written only "American Pie," he would matter forever, of course. But the same can be said about another miracle song, "Vincent." Which remains one of the most quintessentially poignant bio songs ever. To write an effective song about a historical personage is never easy and always prey to maudlin sentimentalism. But then we got "Vincent," with its brilliant descriptions of the artist's art, heart, and mind and the great culminating wisdom "this world wasn't meant for someone as beautiful as you." Perfect lyric wed to the ideal tune, the essence of a standard. But a new kind of standard, and one for the ages.

When I asked Randy Newman a few years back for an example of a great song, he said, "I like a song like 'Vincent' by Don McLean. I mean, there it is—it's a beautiful goddamn song."

But he's also written every kind of song under the sun, always with elegant, unique lyrics and rich melodics. From his beautiful reflection on homelessness, "Homeless Brother" (a duet with the great Pete Seeger), to the classic melodicism of "And I Love You So" (which not only became an unlikely number-one hit for Perry Como but was also the last song ever recorded by Elvis), his songs wed folk narratives with contours of standards, rock, and country and the ineffable colors of human joy and sorrow.

> *And I watch the river flow and I know I must let go*
> *But it's oh so hard*
> *For the waves are all around my small canoe*
> *I had always hoped this boat would carry two*
> **"Oh My What a Shame," Don McLean**

Don played that song "Oh My What a Shame" for me several decades before this interview took place. I was in college then at Boston University, 1978, and discovered that Don, one of my heroes, was performing an outdoor concert on campus that night. I bicycled quickly to the concert site, where he was finishing up his sound check. Even then—long before I commenced this journey of interviewing songwriters—I knew that few things flatter songwriters more than recognition of one of their lesser-known but great songs.

So I told him of my enduring love for "Oh My What a Shame." He smiled, picked up his Martin guitar, and played it for me solo. And he sang it beautifully. It was stunning, a moment I will always cherish.

It's true that the song "Killing Me Softly With His Song" by Norman Gimbel and Charles Fox was written about one of Don McLean's performances. The singer Lori Lieberman, who was working with the songwriting team, heard McLean in a 1971 concert and was so knocked out by the experience, she described it as McLean killing her softly with his songs. They wrote the song to that title and idea, which she first recorded, before it became a major hit for Roberta Flack. To this day most people don't realize it, but the one killing us softly with his song all these years was Don.

Born Donald McLean III in New Rochelle, New York, on October 2, 1945, he suffered from asthma as a kid and had long bouts away from school. It was a time he used to concentrate on that which moved him the most: music. "The whole time I was growing up I was dogged with a lot of sickness," he said. "I was home from school a lot. And basically the record player and the television became my best friends. I didn't have any brothers or sisters who were my age. I had a very much older sister who left the house when I was very little. So I spent that time absorbing an *enormous* amount of music. Just because I loved the stuff."

By sixteen he bought his first guitar, a sunburst Harmony archtop. Eventually he fell in with Erik Darling and Fred Hellerman, both members of the legendary band The Weavers, along with Pete Seeger, Lee Hays, and Ronnie Gilbert. Through them he connected with their manager, Harold Leventhal [who shared an office with Marjorie Guthrie, as related on page 15], and launched a career as a folk musician. A gifted singer and guitarist, he was a great interpreter of folk songs. But like Dylan and others who emerged from that very world, he was more excited about writing his own. And also like Dylan, Don could write all kinds of songs. But he never gave up his folk roots, often joining Pete Seeger and others on the sloop *Clearwater*, the boat built to promote the cleanup of the Hudson River.

"American Pie" is an iconic epic, a remarkable song and record. And unlike anything you had written at the time. Where did it come from?

Don McLean: I was trying to create a dream. So there were lines in there that were dreamlike, almost, in order to connect other concepts that I had that were semi-real, but it was a dream, and the idea came from the idea that politics and music flow parallel to one and other.

I wanted to write a song that summed up everything I felt about America and music, and I did it, and it turned out beyond my wildest dreams. It didn't take a long time to write. The body of the song was written pretty quickly once I got the gist of where I was going. The first part, the opening part and the chorus, I had for a few months. I couldn't quite figure out where to go with it. Then I decided to speed it up and change it. So I found a way to do it. The [Buddy Holly plane crash] is the start of it. But then it moves into a whole other realm.

It was a well-written song, and I felt it was a really good idea. But when I first played it people yawned. They didn't know what I was talking about. It was way too long. It was just verse-chorus-verse-chorus, but we broke that up by having a slow beginning and a slow end. Ed Freeman, who produced the record, deserves a lot of credit for making a record out of it that was very, very special. And which was commercial. I also deserve a lot of credit, because I made the band play it until it was right. I had to fight on so many things with people who were my allies. Ed Freeman and I damn near killed each other a few times over some of this stuff. I said, "This is not right."

Finally we got a guy named Paul Griffin, a black piano player. He came in, and he just jumped all over that song. He understood exactly how to play that song, and he played the living hell out of it. And I drove that guitar right up his ass, in his earphones, my acoustic, and that's what made him jump all over it, and that's how it happened. And then I said, "Now you're talking. Now we've got the track." This stuff isn't easy. If I'd have given in, we would have had a lousy track and you'd have never heard the song.

You have to have great music in your head. Cole Porter, Gershwin. You've got to put good stuff in to get good stuff out if you want to write songs. You've got to go back to the Irving Berlins and The Beatles and the good stuff from the 1950s.

Randy Newman, in describing what he considers a great song, named "Vincent." And I agree. It's one of those miracle songs, musically and lyrically. How was it born?

I read a book about [Van Gogh] and decided to write a song. But how will I write a song about him that doesn't sound stupid? And I figured the way to do that was to look at the *Starry Night* picture. And I came up with this idea to use him, to use all these images I see and tell the story with a verbal or poetic representation of the colors and energy [of his work]. That was the plan, and it just clicked.

The miracle line is "This world was never meant for one as beautiful as you." That line does so much and in such simple and poignant language.

That line came while I was writing. A lot of people feel that way about themselves. It's one of those lines that people take to heart. They think, "Well, it is hard to be in the world, and maybe I'm not right for the world." A lot of us feel that way.

So you were writing about yourself in this song?

Of course. About being an artist in this world.

I was completely devoted to music making in those days. I was in love with the record business, and I was in love with making records, and I was in love with the studio. It's all gone now. I don't like what they replaced it with. It used to be about creating something beautiful, something that would last. Now it's computer music, and it's nasty, mean, and negative. It's music that doesn't help anyone.

Your first songs were quite sophisticated. How did you learn to be such a good songwriter?

I didn't come from a musical family. And my parents were not the type of people to encourage me. All these songs came out of my life.

You asked me when I wrote my first song. There was nothing in my background that would give me an indication that I could be *arrogant* enough to think I could write a song, do you know what I'm saying? My family were very quiet people; they didn't want to be noticed. There were just really your run-of-the-mill American family. My father and mother were older than the other parents. I was born when they were in their forties. So basically they were quiet people.

The first thing I did—what got me going was when all this music I had absorbed my whole life started to get focused. First on rock and roll: Elvis Presley, Buddy Holly, Eddie Cochran, doo-wop music. I'd heard James Brown, stuff like that. And then—because there was no fashion element attached to music, you just liked what you liked—next thing I knew there was this folk thing going on. And you could play guitar and sing by yourself. You didn't have to be in a group. And I wasn't very good at getting along with people and being a group member. I wanted to do it all myself. And so I started down that path, and the simple folk songs that I heard started me thinking maybe I could write a verse and a chorus, a verse and a chorus. That's what made me think I could possibly do something like that.

Prior to that, I was interested in just being a singer and a guitar player. Singing songs. But as an amateur, everything I wanted to sing had already been sung. So I had to start looking around for songs that nobody sang. And that was the first thing I started to do. I slowly began to find a song here or there. Or I would adapt a song that nobody else would do. Like I used to do a version of "Angel Eyes," the Matt Dennis song, when I was fifteen. And I'd also sing "Hard Travelin'" or "This Little Light of Mine." So I was already mixing these things up and really drawing on the multitudinous big mixture of things that was on the charts that I grew up hearing on the radio. I liked "Summer Place" a lot. I thought that was a *beautiful* thing. I still get chill when I hear that wonderful song. "A pretty face . . ." I loved that.

There was nobody there like *Rolling Stone* to say this isn't good and this is. It was a magic time because music made it somehow—it was a mystery. Nobody really knew how these songs managed to find their way from Philadelphia or Memphis or New York or wherever. Record companies were really artistic institutions. They were like impresarios. They had their Sol Hurok, their Goddard Lieberson at Columbia. They put out *The Student Prince* or whatever. Then they would have folk music and all these different things. They thought of themselves as being institutions of culture. And not bottom-line, what's-the-next-hit kind of thing.

Those were the days I grew up. That was the environment that was around. I chose folk music because it was what I could do solo. I wasn't sophisticated enough on the guitar to really do a groove.

Then by the midsixties I was trying to write a song and write about ideas that meant something to me. I really made an effort never to repeat myself stylistically. If I wrote "Castles in the Air," I would turn around and do something entirely different.

I loved your album *Homeless Brother*, which you made with the producer Joel Dorn. It was a beautiful collection of songs and so lovingly produced.

Thank you. I read some Kerouac and decided that I had a bunch of ideas, and they started to come together. I saw the homeless brother idea. It was a complete package. My brother-in-law was a genius Spanish painter, and I gave him a photograph of a woodcutter in the Ozarks and the other was a picture of my little white dog. And I asked him to make these elements in a boxcar, and he created those paintings. Those paintings are much more important than the album, I can assure you.

I went to visit Lee Hays of the Weavers toward the end of his life. I read about this hobo who lost his legs, and he was taken in, mummified, put in a tuxedo, and billed as the Amazing Petrified Man and taken around. And that led to the song "The Legend of Andrew McCrew," which is also on that album.

The song "Wonderful Baby" is wonderful—very odd—and such a great-sounding record.

Joel Dorn made that record like a cartoon orchestra. I had spent the summer listening to Fred Astaire records. I didn't realize that maybe a third of all the great popular songs were all written for Fred Astaire. I didn't know that. And I studied his movies, like *Swing Time*. When he and Ginger would do this dance and jump over the railing at the end, I almost would want to cry when I would see that. Something so beautiful about being a human being. And I felt this is what music and art are supposed to make people feel. Now so much of what we see is ugly and negative and nasty and mean, and it doesn't help people.

Do you recall writing "The Grave"? It is one of the most haunting of all songs. It seems ancient.

That was a dream I had. It was a vivid dream that I had that here was a soldier digging in the ground to save his life; he was actually burying himself. I woke up and ran right to the guitar and sang it into the tape recorder. I just went with a chord that felt right for my voice and started working off that from there.

Your song "And I Love You So" is a modern standard and was a hit as recorded by Perry Como.

That came out of all the great music I'd absorbed. "And I Love You So" was the last song Elvis ever recorded. His people called up and said Elvis wants to do this song, and he wants the publishing. And we said, "Sorry, we can't give up the publishing." So he did it anyway. You can't deny a good melody.

◆ ◆ ◆

Richard Thompson

Inside the Beeswing

Santa Monica, California 2009

It's a crystal-blue morning in Santa Monica, a few blocks from the Pacific, and Richard Thompson is waiting at a table in a little coffee shop. Around him there's a tranquility and a warmth, and although this legendary British songwriter lives in this vast city during much of the year, he seems untouched by the volume and vagaries of an Angeleno existence.

When I first interviewed him about a decade ago, he answered my first query into his songwriting methodology with "Hey, there's a lot of competition. I'm not about to give away my *secrets*." Reminded of that response, he laughed and said, "The competition must have thinned out." In fact, he's right—so many contenders have fallen by the wayside, while Richard Thompson, somewhat miraculously, continues to write astounding songs. Not only is he one of this world's most distinctively gifted songwriters—as inventive and inspired with words as with music—he's also one of the most prolific. As a teenager he founded the folk-rock supergroup Fairport Convention, with whom he wrote a profusion of amazing early songs before branching out into a stellar solo career—and sometimes duo with his wife, Linda Thompson.

He also happens to be one of the world's greatest and most distinctive guitarists, and as an instrumentalist alone he could easily have a distinguished career—if not for the fact that he's one of this world's most gifted songwriters. He also happens to be one of the most brightest and most eloquent songwriters alive, which is why sitting down with him over coffee to talk songs is a privilege not to be taken lightly.

Born in London in 1949, he absorbed all the music his family had to offer—first his father's jazz collection and next his sister's rock and roll—so that his leap from Django Reinhardt to Buddy Holly, a fusion forever instilled in his own work, was natural. As was his early love of folk ballads both Scottish and Irish, books of which he pored over for years. It all came together in his own work—richly detailed narratives that reel like timeless ballads, propelled by the rock in his veins and the jazz at his fingers.

Now in a world where the entire concept of making albums is increasingly arcane and much of the music-buying public is downloading single songs, he's determinedly swimming against the current, writing both a song cycle and a folk opera. "Songs like to be together," he says with a wry grin.

Your songs stay alive over many years. Is that something you work at?

Richard Thompson: I don't think it's something you can consciously think about. But I studied the old ballads—that's the music I grew up with. In the house there were these books of Scottish and Irish ballads. And I liked to read the stuff when I was a kid.

You'd read them as opposed to listening?

Yes, it was my only source. I didn't have anywhere I could listen to the stuff, and I didn't really get into records until later. When people like Dylan came along—the first Dylan album, my sister's boyfriend had it—it was very much the same school. That's what he learned as well, Scottish and Irish ballads. When he started to write those longer songs he was very schooled in those traditions. So it was a familiar thing when Dylan came along; it didn't seem that strange.

But that's a great place to learn songwriting.

Other British songwriters and people outside of America listened to Dylan and American blues and their music seems very American. Whereas yours does not. The Scottish, Irish, and Celtic influence is very much a part of your work musically as well as lyrically—

Yeah. I think it's a good thing to write from where you come from. To express something of your own culture. That can be influenced by other cultures, but if you have a kind of roots that is yours, then the music is going to be stronger. It's got that firm foundation, and it expresses something of the time and place of where you come from. It's more individualistic, I think. I always felt with British blues and R&B acts, people like The Kinks wrote more from home. When Ray Davies was expressing more of a British musical tradition, then the music was more interesting. When The Yardbirds were writing their own songs when they were writing "The Shapes of Things" and "For Your Love," these things mixed blues with things that came from home, and this was more interesting music. The Yardbirds playing "I'm a Man" compared to the Muddy Waters version, it's trivial. If you were going to judge The Yardbirds by that, you'd say, "Well, there's no comparison."

Muddy Waters grew up in the blues tradition. He embodied the spirit of Mississippi and the spirit of Chicago. This is as good as it gets, Muddy Waters singing a blues song. The Yardbirds were imitators. They'd only heard him on records. They'd never been to America, let alone Chicago or Mississippi. It's like a Japanese bluegrass band or a Swedish jazz band. It can be very good and accomplished, but it will never be as good as the original.

So I've always been concerned to put something of the culture I come from into the music. It can always be a blend. It always is a blend. There's always a bit of rock and roll in there and other traditions that get in there. But I like the strongest element to be British.

It's interesting to me also that your guitar solos, that they don't seem as bluesy as electric guitar solos we hear, even by British players. Your solos never seem to use riffs and scales we hear in other people's solos.

I think consciously at some point I said, "No blues." When I was a teenager, when I was in school I'd be playing Chuck Berry riffs; I'd be playing B. B. King riffs. Otis Rush. So I could do all that stuff, but I really didn't want to be a secondhand musician. I really wanted to express something different. And at a time when everybody and his brothers were guitar players, to be individualistic and have your own style seemed to be almost the most important thing. So it was a conscious decision to really turn away from the blues, and if I used bent notes on guitar to make them more Celtic than blues, to bend notes on the guitar.

How do you bend a note to make it more Celtic than bluesy?

There are overlaps. You're bending different intervals sometimes. You're bending up from the tonic rather than up to the tonic.

Are you using different scales too?

Yes. I am probably using more of that scale that doesn't have a third in it. Like a Scottish scale, where if you're in D, it's like D, E, G, A, C, D. It's more of a pentatonic scale, a real Scottish bagpipe scale, or using the third in a passing sense rather than stating the scale. But I do use a lot of that. It's a lot more ambiguous, and the music floats a little bit more.

It's a great sound—and uniquely yours—both on electric and acoustic.

Yeah. Well, on acoustic guitar, well, one of the things you want to achieve is size. If you're gonna strum, strum, strum, strum, that gives you a certain size of accompaniment, but it's quite small. If you use finger-style and a tuning, as many songwriters do, that gives you more orchestral possibilities on guitar: you can play bass sometimes, you can play the chords, you can play lead. You can widen the whole thing out. And if you're using open tunings, you can have more notes that ring out. So this gives the illusion of size, of a bigger accompaniment.

That's something I've heard in your playing—

Excellent. [*Laughter*]

I just watched a video of you playing "1952 Vincent Black Lightning" solo acoustic, and you're playing it so effortlessly, but it really sounds like two guitars because you're playing bass notes, a high lead part, and there's rhythm. Actually maybe it sounds like three guitars—

Okay, three. I was hoping for five. [*Laughter*]

And it looks so effortless—

Well, it *looks* effortless. That's a good showbiz trick, to look effortless. I think some of the things that we think of a pianist doing—having two hands and being able to separate rhythmically the hands, you can do some of that on guitar. People like Blind Blake and Chet Atkins. You're playing the bass and the rhythm and the tune over the top. These are possibilities as songwriters and accompanists that we should look at because they make the experience broader.

It's interesting that you said to me last time that when you work on a song you really don't want to bring it to the guitar too soon. You want to work on the music in your head before you lock it down on the guitar. Is that generally true?

I think that before you pin music down, while it's still floating a bit in your head, it always sounds fabulous. It's never that good again. It's almost *celestial* when you haven't quite figured out what it is yet. It's kind of still floating around, and you haven't quite grabbed it and defined it. It's almost like music of the heavens. But at some point you have to bring it to earth, and I suppose at that point you pick up an instrument. And you decide actually it's in A and there's three other chords. And it becomes a little more mundane, more of this world, and it's a little bit of a sad time, but it's rewarding that you capture it. It's a bit like there's a butterfly floating in the air, this beautiful butterfly, and you really enjoy watching it and you think, "I've got to have it." So you get your butterfly net and your grab it and you're really excited to see what it looks like when you take it out of the net, and you find the colors have all faded and it's become this kind of gray thing, and the colors have all faded, but you can still see the suggestion of where the color was. It's become this sort of slightly less interesting object.

It's interesting to hear you say that, because as you know, most song-writers use a piano or guitar as a tool to reach that butterfly, and find it within chords—

Well, I must say I do that as well. But sometimes if I have a chord sequence I like and I am looking for a tune, I find I can sit and play for a while, but I find it's good to leave the guitar alone and go out for a walk and stop *thinking* about chords. Because things are looser in your mind. They're not so defined. Your fingers fall into habits. If you think about guitar playing rather than actually playing it, it's a looser thing. You can imagine your fingers going places. You can see your fingers making chord shapes. But somehow it's not so defined. There's a slightly more ambiguous element in there that can be created, that can take you other places.

It would seem to me, because of your skill on guitar, that it wouldn't be mundane when moving it to guitar—

Sometimes that does happen, absolutely. But sometimes it doesn't. Especially if you're stuck and you can't find the way forward in a song. If halfway through it you can't see where it will go, it's helpful to get away from the instrument. I do some rhythmic activity like walking or surfing.

Do you surf?

No. [*Laughs*]

You said that when you bring it to a guitar you'll decide on a key, like A. Do you choose that key because it fits the melody or for the specific color or mood of that key?

That's a very good question. I suppose ultimately you have to pick a key that will suit your voice if you're a singer-songwriter. But sometimes your voice is flexible enough that you have a few possibilities of key.

Do you find in your experience that keys have different colors or moods?

Absolutely they do. It can really change the way that you perceive a song. Suddenly a song will sound right in a certain key. Sound better. You might choose a key because when you move up to the IV chord you get a low E or a low D-tuned D that suddenly gives the song a lift at that point. There's desirable things about different keys. And it's only through experimenting that you realize what the possibilities are. And it's different with every song. Depending on the range and the emotion that you're trying to express with the song.

Do those natures of each key exist for you separate from the guitar?

I think it's really how they sound on each instrument. Some things sound particularly good on a guitar that don't sound that good on a keyboard, and vice versa. Something will sound fabulous on piano and puny on guitar. Or perhaps the best a song ever sounds is accompanied by solo mandolin, for whatever reason. Sometimes you say, "This song is better without chords underpinning it. So I'll play this song just with penny-whistle playing the tune along with voice." Because then the tune floats, it's ambiguous, and people can fill in the chords with their own minds. But I don't want to pin it down.

When you do have a melody in your head, separate from a guitar, how do you preserve it? Do you tape it?

I write tunes down in notation because I don't trust cassettes. And I don't trust digits as a way of preserving things. Because I lose things, especially electronic things. I have to be very careful, and I back things up forever. I don't trust the recording process just because I'm frightened of losing. So I write down tunes in notation, and I write down the lyrics.

And then is it pretty clear to you what chords will go with that melody, or do you try different things?

I think it's usually clear. Sometimes it changes, but it doesn't usually change very much. That's interesting—it's something I've never really considered before. Usually the first way you hear it is the harmony you end up using. Sometimes the revelatory moment of writing the song can be when you do change the melody. Just that one little twist somewhere. You think, "Whoa, that's it!" I'm thinking of, like, Buddy Holly writing "Peggy Sue," and he gets into the studio and says, "How about third time through we go to an F chord?" You know, it's in A. Singing the same note over an F chord. It's the big moment of the song, the defining moment, which otherwise is a twelve-bar blues. So things like that. You find a harmonic opening that you weren't expecting. Certainly in the musical component of a song that can be a big lift as a writer, an exciting thing.

Do you think anything affects the melodies that come to you? Like if you're in LA or London do circumstances affect what you come up with?

I don't think so. I kind of think you carry a culture in your head. For me Los Angeles is a blank canvas. It's not as if someone has already painted The Beach Boys and Jan and Dean up there that you have to pay attention to. To me it's culturally blank. You can be who you want in this town. If I lived in New Orleans, it would be different. The local music is so strong a characteristic that you would have to absorb it, and you would want to absorb it.

Yet it's a mostly sunny place, pretty warm all year round so that you can go outside and feel happy. Does that affect things?

Yeah, but creatively, internally, it's a bleak Brontë-esque moorland.

Is it?

Yes. Always. I can't write sunny songs. I could be lying on a beach in the Caribbean, but what I write is still grim and Dickensian. I don't know why that is. But I'm glad it's that way. If I was a painter, it probably wouldn't be that way because you paint what you see. But perhaps I'd paint what I feel. Perhaps it would come out like Francis Bacon as opposed to a pretty Matisse.

You talked about the influence of folk ballads on your work, which is about storytelling, and you've always been very good at telling a story in songs, which is not something every songwriter can do. Did that come naturally to you?

Well, I enjoy doing it. I think every song really tells a story. Some are more fleshed out than others. Some are more linear than others. But most pop songs, apart from pretty basic dance music, is telling some kind of a story. Usually a love story, sometimes a political story.

But often not a narrative—

No, not a narrative. But I think in modern songwriting there is a lot of cinematic technique, where you jump in in the middle of the action. And you might be writing in first person through the eyes of the protagonist. And you jump out before the end of the story. It's just this little cinematic scene, and you do these hard cuts through the song. And some more is left to the imagination. And I do a lot of that in addition to the narrative songs. And I enjoy doing both kinds. And I'm probably surprised by how popular the ballads are, the story songs. So in a sense I'm reacting to what the audience would like.

Why does it surprise you that the audience likes those?

Well, you wouldn't think that that would be a way that people still enjoy receiving a story. In the old days of ballads, in the sixteenth century, eighteenth century, before the gramophone and the cinema, the way people heard news was not from newspapers; it was from ballads. You'd hear about the local murder, and it would be a ballad. A song like "Tom Dooley." It was a local murder in Appalachia, I think, in the twentieth century. And that's how that local murder was defined and delineated.

It's interesting to me how much people hunger for stories about other people. There's nothing people are more interested in, through the ages, than stories about other people's lives.

Yeah, it's extraordinary. And I'm surprised people have the attention span to sit through a five- or six-minute song that's telling a story. I'm glad they do. I'm very rewarded to know that this process, which goes back thousands of years, still works—in the age of so many distractions and so many different ways of mediating information.

There are some songwriters, like Lennon, who felt writing about one's self was more important and put down McCartney for writing story songs. Do you feel one kind of songwriting is more powerful than others?

I don't think there's a difference, really. When McCartney's writing a story song, it's still about *him*. It expresses McCartney's worldview; it expresses McCartney's morality. It's McCartney with a different hat on. So you can be dazzled by the hat for a while, but it's still McCartney. When Lennon's writing about some of his own life, sometimes it becomes very surreal and abstract.

Like "Strawberry Fields"—

Yeah. "I Am the Walrus." Which, in my personal interpretation of that, the "I" is not Lennon. It's probably Brian Epstein. But I have my own theory about that song. So we won't get too esoteric here.

So you start off writing about yourself, and you end up with some universality. Because we are all humans. So Joni Mitchell writes very confessionally about her own life, and we like it because we recognize her dynamics in our own lives. But she's one of the few. She and Loudon Wainwright are the two great confessional songwriters, the ones I can stand to listen to. Because of their honesty. There's a lot of kind of whiny singer-songwriters who write confessionally about their lives and it's of no interest whatsoever. There's too much self-pity there. There's too much of looking for a reaction. Unless you're scrupulous about that process, you flirt with failure. I tend to avoid that area because I'm not sure I can pull it off. It takes real discipline.

So it's a process where you start out writing a personal song and it becomes universal, and you write a song about other people and it ends up ultimately being about you. So it's almost a different process, arriving at the same midpoint. And if it's a good song and the song is honest and you tell the truth about the human condition, through self-examination and examination about other people, then you kind of arrive at the same thing.

When you write a story song do you give any thought to the moral of the story or what people will take away from it?

I suppose you shouldn't think about those things because they're a distraction. But I'm sure they go through our mind from time to time. You do think of what will people think of this. I suppose the part you should be concerned with is communication. You want your song to communicate. And you want to speak to people in a language they understand. But that's about it. In terms of whatever morality you're expressing, that shouldn't be your concern. Your morality will be expressed.

Is being too conscious about your intention, while writing, something to avoid?

Yeah, I think so. Yeah. 'Cause I think it can stop you in your tracks. If you think, "Oh, here I am being creative again—isn't this great?" Because you can outmaneuver your own subconscious. You want to get to the point where it's almost a semiconscious or unconscious act of writing. And if you're looking at yourself the whole time, you'll never get to that point. You know, Picasso said, "I never question my own work. I don't question the morality of my work—that's the critic's job. People think I make these sexist pictures. That's not my business. I just create and I put it out there." I think that's basically correct. As an artist, you are your own first critic. But you apply that to certain things and not other things.

Are you able to keep that critic out of it?

I think it's unconscious. I think sometimes you can't express or bring to the front of your mind what's good about something or what's bad about something. But I think after doing it for a few years your instincts become hardened. And you might say, "I don't know what's good about this song, but I trust in this song. I believe this to be a good song, but I don't know why. I don't know what it's about. And I'm going to sing it anyway." And maybe a few years down the road you think, "Oh, I see. Now I get it. This is really about my mother, or my cat. But I couldn't see it at the time." The process was so unconscious. And I trust my unconscious. I trust my instincts.

It is involving the unconscious, yet consciously so, using rhymes, guiding it. Is part of the process conscious?

Yes. I think making music, either creating it or playing it, is sort of a handshake between the two sides of the brain. I forget which side is which. The intuitive part of the brain is kind of flying, and the logical part of the brain interjects occasionally and says, "Four bars left," or says, "Key change," or says, "F chord coming up," or says, "What rhymes with 'bush'?"

Do you sometimes put up a rhyme and then work backward from it?

Yeah, absolutely. Totally. I think sometimes you can write a song totally backward. You get this killer line that ends the song and you think about how you get back from there. Or you start from a title or an idea. Something that sounds cool, an oxymoronic title or something. And you build from that. You can hear it in writing by Dylan, when he has some line he wants to use and he writes backward from there. And occasionally, I'm happy to say, you hear the oddly laid line in a Dylan song. Where he doesn't really care; he just wants to get to the good line. Which means he's human after all.

And the real brilliance comes when the setup line is as perfect as the rhyming line.

Yeah. Alexander Pope, which is all rhyming couplets, his skill at the setup line is just incredible.

Dylan, like you—and Byron—often uses intertwining rhyme schemes, ABAB, where every line is rhymed. And he does it quite well.

Yeah, so does Byron. Obviously, that's harder to do. But with certain songs you can do it, or you'll have internal rhymes that run through a song, and it doesn't distract; it just fits right in.

Is it a fun process for you? Is it enjoyable?

The whole process is enjoyable. I think that's what gets you writing in the morning. The whole thing is fun. You might put it off and feed the cat or empty the dishwasher. But actually once you sit down to it, it's an enjoyable process. I really like it. Even the darkest possible theme is actually fun to write about.

That comes across in the writing and is probably one of the reasons your work hasn't diminished over the years, that you enjoy the process. Whereas other songwriters don't like it at all.

Yes, that's true. Some people can only write when they're in pain. Some can only write when they're young.

That's pretty common.

Yeah. There are different curves. Everybody has their own curve.

In terms of the lines that are good that you set up, do you have any idea where they come from or how to reach them?

I don't know. We're getting into a difficult area where it's hard to talk about. There are all kinds of things which start your mind rolling. You might overhear someone say, "Don't step on my blue suede shoes," and you might think there's a song there. Or you might just think that's a good line. Sometimes I wake up in the morning and there's a rhythm or a rhythmical phrase in my mind. And I don't know where that comes from, if it's from dreaming about it or when you're half-awake. Probably when you're half-awake. Or you wake up with some solution to a problem that you've been thinking about. When your mind's in a relaxed enough state, you can almost dream of the solution. Sometimes if I'm writing during the day and I take a nap, a ten-minute nap, and I wake up, everything seems clearer. Sometimes solutions seem to have been located. I don't know why. It's hard to say.

Interesting that you talk about seeing or overhearing a phrase. I think of "Beeswing." Isn't that a word you saw?

Yes. It is the name of a village.

It's such a great word for something very delicate. Interesting that you found it and also recognized how to use it in a song. Also "Wall of Death" is another title you found in the world.

I suppose these are just symbols that you latch onto or pick up.

Seems part of it is always being open to the possibilities.

Yes, that's absolutely true. The more that you're awake to possibilities, the more success you have with writing. If you're basically on twenty-four hours a day, the more awake you are, the more stuff seems to come in. It can be exhausting as well—to be on all the time. I think sometimes you switch the TV on and watch *Wheel of Fortune* just to stop the process for an hour or so. [*Laughter*]

I can't imagine you watching that for very long—

Well, yeah, culture is interesting. I wouldn't watch it every day. I have watched it at least once. [*Laughter*] Because it's interesting what people do and what the media says to people, how TV culture impinges on people's lives.

Yes. In a huge way.

Yes, it's huge. It's a huge component of culture. In some countries—I won't mention which—it's a dull culture. And it's hardly giving you anything.

Do you find you're almost always in the place where you can connect with ideas, or are there periods when there's nothing?

Well, when I'm touring or performing I don't tend to write much. I almost have a performing brain that's different from a writing brain. Where I'm having to remember stuff I've already written. I'm remembering forty, fifty sets of lyrics. And I find that's a distraction from writing. So when I'm on the road I'm still open to ideas and looking for ideas, but it's more taking notes than getting anything finished. I can't get any serious writing done on the road. I know other people really do very well, writing in a hotel room. I find that quite difficult. So I jot stuff down. But when I get home or somewhere where I am for a few days anyway, where I can really get stuff worked out.

When you are in writing mode do you have any schedule or find that any time of day is best?

I find I get more done the earlier I start. I get up early these days—it's an old person's thing. I'm up at six. Sometimes I can work before I take my son to school. Otherwise I'll start when I get back. I'll plan to do the morning—six to twelve or eight to one. And then if it's going well, I'll keep going into the afternoon. But normally I look to be writing about six hours a day. But then it could be sixteen hours if it's going well. Especially if I have a project coming up, like an album or something. Then I'll be writing most of the time, like fourteen, sixteen hours a day.

Do you find you can perfect a song, or do you have to settle sometimes?

It's got to be right. It has to be as good as you can get it. There is no perfect, but you do it as well as you can. Then you say, "Right, finished, done it." But then a year later or five years later you might think, "That's a bad verse, I don't know what I was thinking."

Will you rewrite a song after you've recorded it?

That depends. Particularly with older stuff, I think you want to write some changes. A song like "Meet on the Ledge," which I wrote when I was nineteen, is an immature song. And it's very hippie-dippie sixties in that it's elusive. And rather ill-defined, and the imagery doesn't always work. It's a song I'd like to change. But that song is sort of owned by the audience at this point. It's become anthemic to the point where I couldn't really change the lyrics, so I have to forgive myself for being immature and say, "Well, that's that." And I'll find whatever I can in it when I play the song. So it has some meaning when I perform it. In that sense the elusiveness in it is a good thing because I can say, "Well, I take this to mean this. When I was a kid, I probably meant it to be this, but I now see it as this." So I can interpret it in a different way. I can't change it, but I can live with it.

You spoke about your surprise that people's attention spans can take in a six- or seven-minute song. Have you ever wanted to do a longer piece, something extended far beyond a typical song, like Dylan's "Sad-Eyed Lady of the Lowlands"?

Sometimes. Mostly I edit things down to a digestible chunk for the audience. "Sad-Eyed Lady of the Lowlands" is probably not a song Dylan performs a lot, if ever. I don't know. Again, it's quite a personal song, I would think, so maybe he's not comfortable doing it. But I'd like to think I could do a ten-minute song or a fifteen-minute song and people could listen all the way through. But then you have the other burden that if people absolutely love it and are screaming for it every night, then you have to play it every night. It becomes "Alice's Restaurant," which Arlo refuses to play anymore. He's sick of doing it. So if you create a monster, then you have to live with that monster.

Some songwriters, like Dylan, will change a song drastically in concert, while others present them pretty much as they were recorded. Do you ever feel that urge to reinvent a song?

Only occasionally. With other artists I like to hear the song more or less; it doesn't have to be the same song exactly. I like to recognize the tune and the words.

Do you think songwriting will continue to evolve, and are there new places to go with songs?

I have to believe that's true, otherwise I would not see the future as very interesting. I think it's absolutely possible to write a song and in the process to go somewhere where no one's been before. You come up with an idea, a tune, and it's uncharted territory. And I think as a writer, that's what excites you. I think the other great thing is to write a song that has three chords, like a Hank Williams song, but it's emotionally naked and honest. But to write a song like that which has a couple of tweaks in it that makes it an original song but an instant classic is one of the great things to aim for. And I think the other thing to aim for on the other extreme is a song that's charting new territory. I think I try to do that. On records, often the failures—the ones I consider failures—are often ones that are trying to be something different, that are trying to go somewhere no one's ever been before. And you can't always succeed at that.

You seem more ambitious than most songwriters in doing that, especially in terms of content you get into songs that nobody's previously used.

I try to. But in terms of content, I see limitations where there should be none. I know there are things I wouldn't write about. But that shouldn't be the case. You should be able to make a song out of anything, out of any situation. But I'll think it's just too ridiculous. Or it can't be done. It's too mundane; it's too something. But that's a lack of imagination. That's a lack of my being able to put a spin on whatever that is.

Edward Elgar's wife said [to him], "You think you can write about anything, don't you?" And he said, "Oh, absolutely. Anything is an inspiration." So she said, "Why don't you write about your friends?" And he went away and wrote *The Enigma Variations*, which is probably his greatest, most recognizable piece of music. Each piece is about a friend, but it's also cryptic. But it's a fantastic piece of music. But it's Elgar seeing the possibilities in everything but having to be reminded of it by his wife. But then taking that step to write about something he wouldn't think of writing about.

Is it harder to write about something closer to you, like your son or your wife?

No. Well, if it's too close to home you turn it into a story. You change the names to protect the innocent. I certainly do a lot of that.

You're very good with dialogue. Not many songwriters do that, yet you'll sometimes start right in with dialogue, such as "Said Red Molly" [from "1952 Vincent Black Lightning"].

Well, again, that's the folk tradition. That's the old ballads, you know. "Where can I get me a skeely skipper to serve this mighty boat of mine?" That's powerful language, but it's just speech, just spoken word. And the one I just quoted would not go down well with the modern listener. But the trick is to make speech in a song sound natural, to make it sound like it is someone you overheard on the bus just talking as naturally as possible.

You're a songwriter who seems unafraid of filling your songs with details and speech that is outside the American realm of culture, which is nice to hear. And it works. It challenges the listener to move beyond his own little world.

Well, I think so. For a long time American folk music really dominated the West. The blues is so universally popular. You go to Italy and everyone wants to hear the blues, which is very strange. You know, it's exciting music, and America taught the world to improvise. So it's deservedly the most popular culture in the world. People around the world love American culture. They hate American politics, but they love American culture. Especially the culture of the underclass. We've all been subjected to "got my mojo working." What the hell's a mojo? No one knows, but they sing along. Or Little John the Conqueror or whatever. All these kinds of obscure things. And place names that we don't really know where they are, or train names we don't know. But it all comes as part of this exciting musical package. So you go along with the lyrics. And so I feel it's America's turn to be slightly baffled and bamboozled by other cultures. Just as Americans don't get the references in Jamaican music. They might get some of them, but they don't really understand the culture; they don't understand Rastafarianism, which is all over Jamaican music. But again, it's got a good beat, and they'll go along with the package. So really I'm just doing the same thing. I'm expressing my culture and hopefully enough that people do understand and it pulls them along and glosses over the bits they don't understand. And if they're real fans, they might research and find out what stuff is. I mean, The Beatles were singing "fish and finger pies"—

Yellow lorry slow—

Yeah, obscene or obscure references.

And we loved those because they were exotic to us—

Because it's different. Well, I'm very willing to be exotic. I'm very happy to be exotic.

Your songs also have specific details with concrete nouns, which many don't have. Do you feel the more specific you are, the more universal a song can be?

Yes. Though it depends. It depends on the song. What you're trying to do with something is hit the nail on the head—emotionally and in terms of telling the truth about the human condition. And sometimes that means being very specific. If there's a rule about it, it's only there to be broken.

I think very visually about songs. I always run little movies in my songs. And I like to be sensual. I want to express taste, touch, sound, smell in a song. Because I feel that really puts you in the moment. You want to put the listener right there, and that does require the songwriter to be specific.

Always there are gonna be bits that the listener fills in with his mind. That's true of any song. You're not writing a novel.

Do you appreciate the fact that songs are short? Is that a pleasing form to work within?

Well, it's less work. It's easier than writing a damn novel or something. Much easier.

But because it's such a short form, every line has to really count.

Well, it should count. But it should be succinct. If you look at Scottish ballads as the ultimate pared-down succinct language, not a word wasted, not an image wasted, everything is relevant, everything is beautiful. And it pulls you forward to the next verse. It's a neat place to go to school, I think.

Another great aspect of your work is the phrasing of your lines. There's a great rhythmic propulsion there. Dylan said that phrasing matters more than anything.

Singability is crucial. A couple of times I sat in on a songwriter panel—that's the big difference between amateur and professional songwriting. Singability. Sometimes a singer is so good, such as Joni Mitchell, that she makes her songs in situations where no one else could sing them. She can get words out really quick, like Lambert, Hendricks, and Ross. But if you want somebody else to sing your songs, singability it crucial. There's a lot of other factors in singability. Assonance, alliteration, internal rhymes, open-sounding, closed-sounding words—all of that matters. And I don't think about these things, but you get instincts for what works. It's one of the reasons Hank Williams is good. For the singability. And the words are good too. I can remember every word of every Buddy Holly song perhaps more than any other writer. He was so good at the sounds of words. Just making all that flow and the words blending into each, it's just beautiful.

◆ ◆ ◆

Rob Zombie
Doing the Impossible
Los Angeles, California 2013

"Doing anything interesting seemed *impossible*," he said with a smile about his formative years. Sure, he loved the idea of making music and making movies. But it didn't seem real. "I was just a little kid dreaming of things."

Now he's a big kid dreaming of things. Things of horror, often, and things that rock. And where those two come together. He followed in the cherished footsteps of his friend and hero Alice Cooper (see page 563) to not only make his own kind of horror rock but to invent his own kind of horror rock star. To become a song and then to sing it. And Rob Zombie was born.

Before that happened, though, he was born Robert Bartleh Cummings on January 12, 1965, on the banks of the Merrimack River in Haverhill, Massachusetts. It's from Haverhill that many of the accused witches of nearby Salem came. It's a haunted place, no doubt forever darkly coloring his imagination.

He formed his band White Zombie in the mid-1980s, and they released their first album, *Soul-Crusher*, in 1987. In 1993 came *La Sexorcisto: Devil Music, Vol. 1*, with the greatly loved single "Thunder Kiss '65."

In 1998 he went solo and made *Hellbilly Deluxe*, which included some of his biggest and most beloved songs: "Living Dead Girl," "Dragula," and "Superbeast." He's since done five albums, including *Educated Horses* (2006), *Hellbilly Deluxe 2* (2010), and, most recently, *Venomous Rat Regeneration Vendor* (2013).

The man contains multitudes—it's no secret. He's created a creative empire, from which not only music springs but also movies. He also has a monumental parallel career as a director, writer, and producer of films in the horror genre, including *House of 1000 Corpses* (2003), *The Devil's Rejects* (2005), *Halloween* (2007), and *The Lords of Salem* (2013).

In concert he puts on a ferocious show, ferocious in every way—sonically, visually, and even texturally. He's assembled one of the great live bands currently touring around, starring the astounding John 5 on guitar as well as Piggy D. on bass and Ginger Fish on drums. Just weeks ago I saw him and the group at the Roxy, an intimate venue on the Sunset Strip in Hollywood that is, as Zombie told the audience, smaller than their rehearsal space. They were there as a valentine to their lucky fans and to launch their summer arena tour.

Seeing them there at the Roxy was not unlike seeing a jumbo jet rev up and take off in a Starbucks. To behold that much sheer power in such a small space was staggering. Yet it was exhilarating and great, and Rob and the gang seemed to enjoy it as much as the audience. Mr. Zombie was on fire all night, spinning like a dervish with the dark gravity of an ancient prophet wearing war paint. He delivered the crowd-pleasing Zombie anthems with deep passion, none so resonant as "Living Dead Girl," to which the entire audience bounced vertically in beat, singing the refrain. "Dragula" burst out of that gate propelled by a deep, killer groove as Ginger and Piggy laid down a rhythmic bed so solid that both Rob and John could rocket off of it and yet return where they started. It's a rock and roll lesson in abandon and restraint, as Rob and the electric guitar seemed ready to career off into orbit while the drums and bass, like gravity, kept them tethered to the earth.

I'll admit, having known him only from that roaring incendiary character he plays onstage, a character always cloaked in darkness and blood scarlet, I was a tad apprehensive about interviewing him. The man does horror rock, after all, and horror movies, so there's a real horror vibe around him. But like Alice Cooper, he proved to be anything but scary in person. As usually happens, when he recognized he was talking to a fellow musician and that we spoke the same language, we had a great conversation.

I so love the grooves of your music. When you do "Living Dead Girl" live, for example, the groove is amazing.

Rob Zombie: Yeah, I like grooves. All the music I grew up with grooves. Like Led Zeppelin is like the fucking grooviest band in the world. Somehow groove left hard rock after a while. But in the seventies all that shit really grooved, and it stuck with me.

I was wondering if you liked Zeppelin. Asked about your influences, you once said it was only Alice Cooper. But I knew there had to be others.

It's everything from the seventies. I loved Elton John, Alice Cooper, KISS, Zeppelin, Black Sabbath—everything. That was when I was pretty young. And as I became a teenager I started discovering The Ramones and the Dead Kennedys. So it's always been a mixture of arena rock and punk rock, in a way.

You also once mentioned your other heroes growing up, and you named Steven Spielberg, Bela Lugosi, and Stan Lee. Back then were you thinking of this kind of career, as both a musician and a filmmaker?

No, I wasn't thinking about anything. I was more like a little kid dreaming about stuff. I never had a plan. None of it ever seemed possible, growing up where I did. Doing anything interesting seemed *impossible*, so I didn't think about it. I say that now kind of flippantly. But it was kind of this thing where I loved movies, I loved comic books, I loved TV—I *knew* I wanted to be part of that. But being part of it seemed absolutely impossible and seemed a million miles away. So the fact that I eventually got there, on some level, is still a mystery to me. That's how it happened!

Was making music and making movies all part of the same dream? Or was music more of the aim?

None of it seemed real. Truthfully, until punk rock really came along, it didn't seem like you could be in a band. If you looked at Queen or Led Zeppelin, they just seemed larger than life. Like you had to be a complete virtuoso in every way to think about being in a band. So it seemed beyond. You didn't look at Alice Cooper and KISS and think, "Oh yeah, I'm one of those guys." It was like they were from another world.

But when I got into punk rock and it had the look and feel, I could see that happening. I always say The Ramones launched a million bands.

Even though they were, of course, brilliant songwriters, there was an element that you could see yourself in them to some degree.

As a kid, were movies and music equally compelling for you?

Kind of hand in hand. I loved them both. That was my whole life, 24/7. I didn't care about sports; I didn't care about hanging out with other kids or anything. I'd watch TV, watch movies on TV, and listen to music. That is all I wanted to do, every day.

When did you start writing your own songs? Was that after hearing The Ramones?

Yeah. I was never in a cover band or anything like that. In high school me and a couple friends bought some instruments and tried to play, but somehow it petered out after two days. It wasn't until I moved to New York City to go to college, to art school, that White Zombie came together, which was the only band I ever had. And that was a great time. It was 1984, New York City, so there were still a lot of the remnants of what I thought New York City was from before. So that was a good time.

So the very first songs you ever wrote were ones for White Zombie?

Yes. The very first songs ever written went on the record. I am not saying they should have gone on a record. [*Laughs*]

You wrote those first songs with Scott Humphrey. How did that collaboration work?

Well, he never wrote lyrics at all. Nobody ever has but me. And then we would collaborate on music. Basically the first record I made was just me and Scott. I didn't have a band yet. White Zombie fell apart. I was just with a producer I really didn't know at all. And we just started working, and slowly it came together. And as we were working, different musicians would come in to play. Like Tommy Lee, who had been with me in the studio at the time. That's how it came together. Now, 3 million copies later, it seems like a great idea. But at the time nobody really wanted to work on it because it was a typical, "Oh God, this is a solo album. It's gonna be a huge failure." Nobody really wanted to be a part of it. It had disaster written all over it. [*Laughs*]

Back then would you write the lyric first before working on music?

Usually what we would do is find a drum beat or something to set the tone. I could usually write lyrics to that. Sometimes we'd write a section, like a chorus or a verse. I'd sing over it. And I might even remove the music, and when we had the vocals, put some other music behind it.

It was always a very cut-and-paste process. It wasn't a very specific man-ner of working by any means.

I read that you once said you liked titles, and titles would come to you. Do you often get titles first for your songs and write to the title?

Sometimes. I don't really have a method. It's pretty haphazard. Some-times I'll just hear a groove idea or a guitar idea that might work. I might have a vague notion of the kind of song I want it to be and relate it to whoever is gonna play. Now I have a band and it's solid. But back then it was very haphazard.

It's hard, musically, to figure out your songs. Like "Living Dead Girl," it seems it's mostly on one chord but hard to figure out what that chord is.

Sometimes when we do that we'd almost find a piece of noise and loop it, and it would sound like a guitar. We did this with "Dragula." We had found this messy guitar loop that wasn't from anything. And when we turned it into the song we thought we would replace that with real guitar. And when we did that, we thought, "Now the songs suck." There was some magic in just the mystery of "What is that?" It's like that with a lot of things. There are a lot of bands I *love*, and their records sound *ter-rible*. And they'd go back and rerecord and remaster it. And now it *sucks*! There is *magic* in that chaos you created, which is all missing in your attempt to make it perfect. Which is why, especially now, I don't worry about the records being perfect. That was what I tried to return to on the last record. If there's mistakes or feedback or noise, *leave it*. That's where the beauty lies sometimes. It's too easy to sit there with Pro Tools. You can make everything absolutely perfect all day long. But it's a bore.

And then it doesn't sound like real music—

No, it's boring. It's like all pop music. We're one step away from where all music sounds like it comes from robots. [*Laughs*]

Those sounds in your music match the mystery in the lyric.

Yeah, I am trying to make each song have its own vibe, if possi-ble. Make them different from each other but with an overall vibe. Make them pretty dense as possible. Sometimes I'll go back and listen to old records and I will hear stuff that I forgot I did, all these layers.

Recently you said you don't finish songs before going into the studio. Is that accurate?

Yeah, that's the way I've pretty much always done it. A long, long time ago with White Zombie we'd go into the rehearsal space and jam, and record everything, and *jam*, and record everything. And I felt, "This sucks." It would feel like we'd been jamming for hours and get nothing.

But now we just go into the studio with nothing and just start. There are days with every record when you walk into the studio in the morning with no idea, and by the end of the day it's a completely mixed song that is done that we never touch again.

You've got to have good musicians. That is one of the great things about working with John 5. He's such a phenomenal guitar player that no matter what I say to him, he can do it. He never says, "Oh, let me think about it and go home and work on it." Because he knows I'm not gonna want to do that. So he can just do whatever I want on the spot: Play banjo here. Or make it sound like a Spanish guitar. He can just do it—he's just so talented. It's a luxury having him in the band. It's not always like that, you know. It used to be a big struggle.

I just saw your show in Pomona, and it was such a great night. And as always I was just amazed by John 5's playing. It is extraordinary.

Yeah, he's so great. We've been playing together now for almost nine years now. It's a really good match; I'm so glad we hooked up. It is a luxury to have *all* these guys in the band. For me it's the best, perfect lineup I've ever had to work with. After all these years. Which I think is why things are going so well at this point.

Where did "Living Dead Girl" come from?

I don't recall where it came from. But I know we wrote it and threw it away as we were putting the record together. And I found a cassette and played it, and that song was on it. And I thought, "This song is great— why did we throw this song away?" So that almost didn't make the record. It was literally something we wrote and thought sucked, [*laughs*] for some reason, never finished it, and then I just happened to find it on a cassette. That's what happens when you record sometimes and are just writing and writing and writing. You don't hear it at the time. And I thought, "Why did we hate that song? That is pretty good!"

That song, like others you have done, shows us you don't need a lot of chords to make a great song. It has, I think, two chords. And it is such a compelling song.

No, I think that's a mistake that people think. I see a lot of young bands, and people will overplay so much. That doesn't mean it's a good *song*. And you ask them what their favorite band is and they say, "AC/ DC!" Yes, the epitome of not overplaying. [*Laughs*]

◆ ◆ ◆

Joe Henry
With Blood from Stars
Burbank, California 2015

It all started with a black Bakelite AM radio beside his bed growing up. From that source emanated music mysterious, grand, and even terrifying. And it changed his life.

"My first and most visceral memory," he said, "was hearing Ray Charles on the radio, and he wasn't singing 'What'd I Say.' He sang 'Yesterday.' And it absolutely scared the piss out of me. It *terrified* me. Hearing that song from a twenty-two-year-old Paul McCartney, it sounds like lost love. But even as a boy of not quite seven, I feel like I understood in no uncertain terms that what he was talking about was *mortality*, the fact that we were going to die, and that there were more yesterdays on the books than there would be tomorrows. And it got under my skin."

Born in 1960 in North Carolina, he moved to Atlanta at five and then grew up near Detroit. After Brother Ray's rendition of "Yesterday" other songs soon entered his consciousness: "When I was seven and eight I heard 'Rain' [by The Beatles], I heard Glen Campbell doing these great

Jimmy Webb songs, and I heard Dusty Springfield do 'Son of a Preacher Man.' I can practically remember where I was standing when I heard those things the first time. They were movies that played in back of my eyes."

But there was one songwriter, above all the rest, who changed his life. "Like so many songwriters of my generation," he said, "my life was changed by Dylan. I heard him when I was eleven, and I do remember where I was standing when I heard it, and I didn't know why it mattered to me, but I absolutely knew in the most fundamental way that my life was different. I felt like somebody with really poor eyesight who didn't know they had poor eyesight until somebody put a lens in front of me. It changed everything."

He went to high school with Madonna and eventually married her sister, Melanie Ciccone. But he knew Madonna first. They both acted in a twelfth-grade play, *The Night Thoreau Spent in Jail*. "She played the wife of Ralph Waldo Emerson," he said, "and I played their son." Slight pause. "I don't like picturing that now," he said.

He was my esteemed guest on *Songwriters on Songwriting Live* at the Songwriting School of Los Angeles on June 25, 2015. This talk is from that interview, conducted in front of a live audience of songwriting students and lovers of music. We spoke, and he also sang some of his remarkable songs, such as "Odetta"

The list of all his albums plus all those he has produced adds up to a voluminous profusion of work. The Joe Henry albums begin in 1986 and include *Talk of Heaven, Murder of Crows, Shuffletown, Short Man's Room, Kindness of the World, Trampoline, Fuse, Scar, Tiny Voices, Blood from Stars, Reverie,* and *Invisible Hour*. All were self-produced except for two, *Shuffletown*, produced by Joe's mentor, T Bone Burnett, and *Fuse*, produced by Daniel Lanois.

His productions include ones for Mose Allison, Solomon Burke, Elvis Costello, Aimee Mann, Meshell Ndegeocello, Loudon Wainwright, Rodney Crowell, Aaron Neville, Bonnie Raitt, Billy Bragg, and more.

I read all these names and more in what was a very lengthy introduction, for which I apologized. "Didn't bore me," he said with a laugh.

There's a lot there in your intro. As you know, in music, people have a hard time if you do more than one thing. It confuses them. And being such an accomplished songwriter and an accomplished producer, do people have a hard time with that, or can they accept that you can do both?

Joe Henry: I don't have any trouble walking up the street, if that's what you're talking about. [*Laughs*] But from the very beginning, because I've never aligned myself with a particular genre of music, it has worked out for me. I think that those labels—I'm not being coy—I just don't think they serve us very well. And people who grew up in my generation, we had access to everything, and we were authentically influenced by everything. So of course, we start writing songs, and they don't adhere to one particular discipline as people understand that.

People didn't know what to call what I did, and in the beginning every interview sort of started that way. After there was a couple of records that didn't sound like each other, people would say, "Well, what do you call what you do?"

And I said, "Well, I don't call it anything. That's *your* job." [*Laughs*] They say, "Don't play hard to get. You go in a record store—what section do I look under?" "You look under the Joe Henry section. I don't know what else to tell you." [*Laughter*] But I did have a problem. I still have a problem with it in some regard, because people are brushed back on what they don't know how to identify. If they can't name it, if it's elusive in that way, then they think you're not being faithful to their expectation.

Some people love that. I came up in an age where the artists that I most admired, all you knew about their next record was it wouldn't sound like the one that you just heard. And I thought that was part of the bargain, part of the job description.

You got to make a different movie, you know? Scorsese makes a gangster movie, then he wants to make a Western. We should have that same autonomy as artists and songwriters to say, "Well, you know, I *did* that. I don't need to wear that uniform anymore." I didn't join the Boy Scouts. I don't have to wear that uniform every day. That embodied a certain sonic landscape because that served that batch of songs. And far from wanting to be trapped by that after it's happened, I felt liberated by it. There's an idea I don't have to babysit anymore, it has its own life, and now I'm free to do something else.

The industry knows it's easier to market people when you put them in separate bins. But musicians have always known that we're all connected. Pete Seeger said, "All songwriters are links in a chain," which is the guiding principle for this book. But even when I was first trying to get it published, people said to me, "You know, you can't have Mose Allison and Pete Seeger and R.E.M. in the same book—they're all different. You can't mix that up." But it is all songwriting, and songwriters understand that. We're doing the same thing. It's words and music.

I think we've grown to have a very limited idea in our culture about what's acceptable, what's musical. We all know people who, for instance, will tell you a story that they grew up in Catholic school, and they said, "Well, I had to go to choir every morning, but the nun told me not to sing because I couldn't sing." You know, we have a very limited idea about who we decide can sing. They say about some artists, "Oh, that person, they can't really sing."

Just because it doesn't speak to *you*, maybe, for you to decide that that is not a valid human expression is really unwarranted. There's all kind of ways. It's a very human impulse to want to give voice, to sing out. It's instinctive. And I think we do ourselves a great disservice to limit who we allow to do that and who we keep behind the velvet rope.

And that concept of who is a singer has shifted so much in our lifetime.
Sure.

Especially since Bob Dylan came along and changed it. But still to this day you have people going, "Oh, Bob Dylan. He can't sing." Actually, he is an amazing singer—
I think he's the greatest singer of his generation, actually, of the rock age. I think he's a tremendously great singer because what he does is make the song vivid, and to me that's the whole job.

Yes.
I love singers that people refer to as classically great singers. I'm a great fan of Édith Piaf. I'm also a great fan of Mississippi John Hurt, and he probably had a five-note range, but don't tell me that I wasn't moved by it. I was. I am. I just don't think that serves our humanity, to limit people to a very particular sort of expression as being: "This has value. This does not."

The industry is telling artists, "Stay within your own confines if you want to get airplay." Especially now, with niche radio and all the Internet radio, if you're going to do a folky thing, keep it really folky if you want to get airplay. Otherwise you're not going to be understood. It encourages people to stay in narrow confines.
We're always invited into what's familiar. It comforts people if they think they know what's coming. That's as old as time. But for people like me, when the record industry really collapsed as we understood it, I found it as liberating as it was disheartening because I came up in a time where even though nothing I did really was going to get any airplay. There was always the label insisting that there had to be something on the record that they felt they could, in one way or another, take to radio and beg them, pay them, whatever they had to do to get them to pay a moment's attention to it.

At the moment when I realized—and a lot of us did—that the industry as we had all been seduced to imagine it had sort of vanished, I said, "That's fantastic. We don't have to talk about a song being under four minutes. We don't have to talk about it working a certain way." They were never going to pay attention to us anyway.

We were still forced to genuflect to the idea, even though we were not going to be led into the sanctuary. We still had to stand outside and be on our knees to that idea, that it still has to be tailored to somebody else's idea of what is acceptable and what is engaging.

I personally believe that most of us have a much wider palate of musical experience than the industry has ever wanted to acknowledge. I think most people do. Not everybody obsesses over records and digs them out and goes searching for it. But plenty of people are enriched by song, and I think that if we went tomorrow and we all took over KROQ—I don't know if there is such a thing still [laughter]—we could take over KROQ at drive time tomorrow and put on Édith Piaf, and there would be a certain number of people who would pull over to the side of the road and say, "I don't know what this is, but my life is different now."

But, you know, we're so busy telling people that "This shouldn't matter to you. This music's too old for you" or "You're too young to accept this" or "You're too old to participate in this kind of music." That doesn't serve any of us, and I pay it no mind.

I know Dylan changed your life.

He did. I was really coming out of a folk tradition, and I did what so many of us did: I started peeling back the onion. I went deep into whatever Bob was doing, and when I wanted to know, "Well, what did he come out of?" I went back to Robert Johnson and Woody and Leadbelly and Lightnin' Hopkins and Blind Willie McTell—who's still really heavy for me—Skip James, but also Hank Williams, Jimmy Reed. I just followed the trail. And it's a deep and a rich mine. It's still a mine that's producing. That's all still a living organism.

It's nice how Dylan connected so many of us to those traditions and those people. I remember Woody Guthrie had a lot of impact on me because I knew he was Dylan's hero.

I probably wrote the first song when I was either fourteen or fifteen. I don't remember what it was called. I sort of just have a vague memory of its tonality. It probably sounded a lot like "Boots of Spanish Leather," something like that.

But at that time I was also following the trail of other very singular American songwriters: John Prine and Randy Newman, very particularly. I heard Randy when I was, I think, not quite thirteen. It was right when *Good Old Boys* came out, because on the encouragement of my older brother, I bought a vinyl copy of *Good Old Boys* right when it came out. And it was sort of like my epiphany courtesy of Bob Dylan. I felt like I understood in some instinctive way that it was a theatrical statement, that he was writing in character.

So even though this was 1974, I think, and the very earnest singer-songwriter movement was well in place, I rejected the idea that a good song was your diary set to music, that the truer you were being within the context of the song, the better song it was. I heard Randy and I knew that he was not from Birmingham, and I didn't think he was married to a woman named Marie. [*Laughter*] I didn't think he had a dog named Dan. I knew that I was being put on, and I was completely seduced by it.

I think that informed my whole landscape, that I entered that picture believing fully that in my job I was completely free just to make up a lot of shit. [*Laughter*] I look at my life, and I still don't think that my life as I live it is in and of itself interesting enough to be the focus of song. I do recognize after the fact, when I recognize elements of my own life that I see, it's like taking an X-ray. It's like, "Oh, there's the spot." I know where it is when I hear it later. But I can count on one hand how many times I ever wrote a song and I was consciously in any way trying to articulate some particular personal experience of my own. That's just not what's interesting to me as a songwriter.

Randy had a similar effect on me too, and Tom Waits too—that you can write about a character. And when I talked to Dylan I asked him who he thought was great, and he pointed to Randy Newman.

Yeah.

He said something like, "'Sail Away' or 'Louisiana'—it doesn't get better than that."

It really doesn't.

Yet any song a songwriter writes is about the songwriter, about their choices. From Randy Newman's songs you get a lot of idea who he is. All the songs are about him, are they not?

It's impossible not to write about yourself ultimately. But I think, at least for me, I'm not interested in being self-conscious. I write to get liberated. I've said before that it's really my ethos. I'm not big on writing as self-expression. I write for discovery. I write to find out what I'm writing about.

There are many great songwriters who—my dear friend and some-time collaborator Loudon Wainwright, he mines his own life in a way that very few people, in my opinion, do successfully. And I believe that when he sets out to write a song, he has a very fully formed subject in mind. He might not know for sure how the arc gets drawn in the course of the writing of the song, but he knows what he's after as far as what story he needs to tell. He knows it in advance. And I promise you, I've never known in advance, ever, what I was writing about.

Is that right?

Pretty sure that's true.

You never come to a song with an idea of what it will be about?

Not as a subject. Honestly, I don't think I've ever approached a song and thought, "Oh, I'd like to write a song about this particular thing." I just start writing, and I discover as I'm writing. It just sort of gets revealed.

And I work really hard to keep myself off-balance that way. I think it's a really particular and important balance, as writers, to marry our hearts and minds, but we can't let one ever overtake the other. And when I say that, I'm talking about your intellect and your instinct.

I think it's a really interesting thing as a songwriter to keep your-self as off-balance, in some ways, as possible. I will get a song going and sort of know that there's something alive on the line there, and I will just begin the next verse in the most random way that I might. It's an image that strikes me; it's a tonality; it's a particular rhythm that feels good to me but is not necessarily, in a linear way, connected by thought to what's just come before it. So I tend to just write a line, and then I employ my intellect to try to find my way through that dark room that I've just opened the door to. [*Laughs*] You know, I just start and then say, "Okay, now I have to make sense out of what I've just begun, and when I get to the other side of this, I'll know whether it's of any use to me." As opposed to saying, "Here's an idea that I already have—how do I put it in a very clever way in four verses that rhyme, four lines that rhyme, so that people can carry it away easily?" That's just not how it works for me.

So the process becomes more about following, though you are also leading.

Well, you try in that really particular balance—I think that's when you know that. We engage a song in process, and we know that something there is beckoning us forward. We know that there's a living thing there in the midst, in a way. And you walk toward it with a bit of good faith and courage. But I think it's really important not to be too sure about what you think the outcome should be, to stay out of the results business as much as possible.

I've cowritten with people who think really, really differently. [*Laughter*] And when it's worked, I think that's probably why it's worked. But I've had awkward moments trying to write with people. And I don't do it a whole lot. I mean, over the course of many years I've written with Madonna, I've written with Meshell Ndegeocello, I've written with Mose Allison, I wrote with Billy Bragg, with Loudon, with Rosanne Cash.

Some good ones. [*Laughter*]

Jakob Dylan. People I'm forgetting. But I've almost never been in the same room with somebody when I was doing it, because to sit there and have to account for what I might just have written after sitting with somebody and they go, "Why would we start the next verse there?" I'd say, "Well, I have no idea, and I don't want to know. [*Laughs*] And keep your voice down." [*Laughs*] And you know, the whole thing. A song is inherently mysterious, and I promise you—I've said it before—that it's not about *dispelling* mystery; it's about *abiding* mystery. It's about staying with it and letting it move around you like weather. Again, back to the idea of not letting your intellect drive everything. Your intellect is the problem solver, but you want to somehow create a problem first because when you're thinking your way out of a dark room, it's frequently where a song comes from.

Yeah, and embracing the mystery and enjoying the mysterious aspects of it is a big part of it.

Yeah.

A lot of people feel that the song almost is—they're discovering it, but they're uncovering something that's perfect in form almost. Is that how you're looking at it, or are you looking at it like you want to keep it more random?

It's probably a little distracting to talk about it as random, though I believe in the way that the random occurrence alters our field all the time as we're working. You know, John Cage said that we have to be really careful not to confuse the creative mind with the analytical mind because if you're writing something and you're already thinking in real time about how it works and if it's working and whether it's going to be of any use to you or whether anybody might like it, you've already stepped out of the living stream. You're already standing on the bank, evaluating. You've just ended the séance.

Yes.

So I work really hard, when I talk about staying off-balance, to not let the editorial mind come into it at any part of the stage where you're just spooling off raw fabric. If you catch a good wave as a writer, I would think of it as just creating raw fabric. It's really easy to go back later and tailor that into a pair of slacks you can walk around in. But what you really need to do is create that fabric. You can't be trying to cut an inseam while you're creating that bolt of cloth.

Randy Newman said a similar thing: don't let the critic become bigger than the creator while you're doing it because then you can squash the creator. Rickie Lee Jones said too, it's like a living spirit and it's very delicate—you can destroy it. But some people say they don't want that analytical, intellectual mind in there at all while they're doing it. But you seem open to both.

Well, I think at a certain point, for it to be a piece at the end of the day that has its own integrity, you have to have applied your intellect to it. You have to bring yourself to it, and the great jazz pianist Brad Mehldau—who I've worked with on a number of occasions both on record and in performance—he's got an incredible mind, and he talks about Beethoven the same way he talks about Shakespeare, the same way he talks about Bird. He says, "You have to meet it halfway. You've got to bring your intellect to it." You can't just lay back with your arms folded as a listener and expect it to wash over you and hand it all the responsibility to move you. You have to bring yourself to that place where you are available to be moved. You're willing and anxious to be, and I think as a writer we can't let the intellect overpower everything because almost nobody's smart enough to make something that is timelessly evocative.

Depending on how spiritual you want to be in your language. Quincy Jones said, "As a record maker, you always have to leave room for God to enter the room. You have to leave a door open." And I think in whatever language you use to talk about that thing outside of us that is this spiritual weather moving us all the time, I think any kind of great art is an active engagement with that mysterious other. Your intellect has to be aware of that. Your intellect has to be the thing that is the crossing guard that says, "Stay back and let it go through." You have to be awake, but it's a mistake, I think, to try to steer it. Because it's like trying to go to sleep at night and trying to dictate in advance what you're going to dream. You will not be successful in anything, and I think the day we step away from it, it still feels like a living thing.

To me, as a writer and as a record maker, that's the entire game. I don't care anything about genre distinction, really. Nothing. My job as a writer and my job as a producer is to make something meaningful come out of a pair of speakers, something that stands alone, walks away from us, and exists without us. And then you're free to go to the next thing.

So when you're creating that fabric, does that mean you write a lot and you put a lot more down on paper than you're going to use?

Oh, sure. I'll write until the Ouija board goes cold. [*Laughs*] Because you can always get rid of stuff. I just try to stay as active in that process as I possibly can and keep my analytical mind, my judgmental mind, as far away. Because if I start thinking about how it works and whether anybody's going to like it—me, my wife, anybody who's paid attention to anything that I've ever done—I know that I have to stop working because I've taken myself out of the real game.

And that's an odd process for most people to consider, that it's more of a discovery than something you're going to invent. Normally when you're making something you just build it. But to discover something is a whole other thing.

Yes. Having an idea can be like you've got a compass that says, "Walk in this direction." The compass is not telling you what you're going to find when you get there. It's not going to tell you what obstacle you may encounter. But it sets you off in motion, and that's what I look for—anything that will put me, as a writer, in motion. It might be a phrase, an image, just a certain rhythmic tonality, but I find that any time I'm set into motion, I can make something out of it.

So do you work on music and words at the same time, or sometimes is it just words?

It happens every different way. I'm not the first to say that the best songs, the ones that live with us longest, are the ones that seem to just show up fully intact. That happens once in a while. But I do feel like I have more control over what I'm doing as a lyric writer than I do as a musical articulator. I love playing guitar, although I don't think I'm a great guitar player. So I'll have pieces of music going, and I'll have hunks of fragments of lyrics going, and I try to keep them all floating off the floor just enough. I don't want to nail down anything as far as a lyric. I don't want to nail down meter. I don't want to get too boxed into a form until I have to. But I'll have some fragment of music going, and then I'll start to see how they might start pairing off and influencing each other.

If the melody's strong enough, I'll wrestle the lyric into that service. But if the lyric seems to be the really dominant character in what's happening, then I will try to leave the melodic idea as open as I can so that it might be in service to wherever that lyric might be trying to go.

Speaking of mysteries we embrace, melodies are mysterious. Some have said we have moved beyond the age of melody. Do you think melodies always matter? And what makes a melody strong?

Oh, it's a good question. It's like saying, "What makes blood good?" [*Laughs*] Because it moves through me and animates me.

Melody is the delivery system for so much, and I find for somebody who's as lyric oriented as I tend to be—and I really did come into it, not exclusively, being lyric obsessed, though the songs that I most gravitated to, I knew that there was something about the story, about the narrative that was riveting to me—but the delivery system of the music had everything to do with how that was able to penetrate. I think great melodies are timeless, and they cross every genre, every culture.

I've had amazing experiences in my working life recognizing connections between music from different parts of the world and how people respond to so much of the same thing. And I don't know why that is, but there's a default base human response to melody.

And again, to quote John Cage, who created random operations so that he could make music that was free of his ego, he said, "I'm not trying to write what I think is pretty. I want to work like nature works." He said, "I want to set up a system where music happens, and then I want to hear, 'What does that sound like?'" It's not about whether it would play well over dinner in the distance.

He talked about that idea that anything becomes melodic if you repeat it long enough. The most random-sounding thing becomes melodic. The most random noise becomes rhythmic if you hear it enough times that you start identifying a pattern, because patterns have integrity and they don't come out of nowhere, and they are not just immediately recognizable to us. That's why a lot of music works on us and gets through to us in ways that we don't know how to guard against. You can be somewhere and be really unprepared for some piece of music that drifts by and brings you to your knees, literally or spiritually, psychically. And you're going to be unprepared for it. Music is incredibly stealth that way.

Filmmaker Ingmar Bergman said that every art form desires to work the way that music works, and I think that music is only music when it is in the air. Vinyl, CD, my iPod, a piece of sheet music—it's just a road map, but it's not the road. Music is only music in that real-time moment that it is in the air, and we're defenseless against that when we encounter it.

Yeah, it's about very simple things, like a I to a VI chord can be so powerful. You mentioned Jimmy Webb, and like a lot of great musicians, he probably knows almost every chord there is, and yet I asked him about writing music, and he said he just throws himself in new places, puts his hands in new places. So it's a process where you've been doing this and you're an expert for years, and yet you're just trying new things, putting yourself in a whole new area where you've never even been before. When you're writing music, is that what the process is like for you? How do you get to the melodies?

Oh, very much so. I play almost exclusively in open tunings now, and I have for years, and I got there because I needed to get out of a very rudimentary way that I approached guitar. I wanted it to be more orchestral; I didn't want to know so much about what I was going to habitually do.

So I started playing in open tunings, and even the most basic changes, once I found out how to articulate them within this new tuning—because I'd been working like a blind man in a dark room. It makes no sense, [*laughs*] you know what I mean? That in the process of blindly trying to find in this new tuning—you know, "Where is a IV chord?"

I hear a new voicing in the way that I've approached it. In fumbling to find it, I've found something else that I don't know how to make. All the time when we're recording I work with really great musicians who can read and write. I'm an illiterate. I learned how to play music like people learn to speak a language on the street. You might learn to speak; you might even learn to speak really well and be grammatically correct. But you don't know, consciously, the rules that are underlying what you do.

I learned from sitting in front of a record player, putting on a record, and trying to play, in some way, everything that went by. And you learn some very basic things, and you start recognizing the ways in which they keep reoccurring in our Western idea of how music is shaped, how a song is shaped. And it's like being on the street in Spain, and you don't speak the language, and over a few days you learn how to ask for a very few things. "Can I have another coffee?" "Where's the library?" "Does she have a sister?" [*Laughs*]

And pretty soon your vocabulary expands out of necessity. And I found out as a writer that playing music—I started recognizing things that I was doing because they were the threads that kept connecting everything that moved me. But at a certain point, because I wasn't schooled as a player, I find that I write in open tunings because I do a lot of things by accident that come out really well. And I'm forever being in the studio with people and they're saying, "What chord is that?" And I say, "It's this one." [*Laughs*] And they say, "Play a string at a time." Okay.

I know, because today I was trying to figure out some of your chords, and I couldn't figure them out. But there's a lot in G—are you in a G open tuning?

I live in open G. [*Laughs*] I mean, I don't always stay there. Irving Berlin, he only played in C.

Actually F sharp.

Was that F sharp?

Yes, but he had a transposing piano. So he could play in any key but still stay on those black notes.

Yeah, I play in G a lot. It's really funny, because I had been playing for a really long time. I was already probably forty before I really had that happen to me, and it completely changed my relationship to the guitar.

My friend, who is a very significant guitar player named Doyle Bramhall, he and his family were at the house for dinner one night. I can't watch what he does—he plays left-handed and upside down, and even when he's playing straight chords, they're not recognizable to my eye. But he left a guitar of mine in open G tuning, and he said over his shoulder as he was leaving, "There's a whole folk score in that tuning." [*Laughs*] And then left the house. And for whatever reason I understand myself in that tuning like somebody sitting at a keyboard. I can visualize where I am, and I reach for things that I do not know how to do in a standard tuning. I can take some of that back with me to a standard tuning if I need to, but I really had a completely different relationship with the instrument once I started to treat that as my default place from which to work.

That's another concept a normal civilian might not understand, that to really get someplace new you have to put yourself in kind of an unknown area. Because we're so used to playing the same patterns, and you get in the same routines. To get out of that, you want to consciously break out of the stuff you normally do.

Well, in every aspect of life, not just your creative life, you have to stay vulnerable in every possible way. I mean, I'm not the first to say that; I didn't make that up. It just happens to be one of those truths. If you're going to be a great spouse, a great parent, a great artist, you have to be vulnerable. And that's, again, what I was talking about when I said,

"Keep your intellect in check" because as soon as you think you know what's going to happen, you start consciously or unconsciously trying to steer things there, either in your personal life or in your creative life.

I don't want to be limited by my own experience only. And I don't want to be limited by my own imagination. Same way when I'm producing a record: I don't want to tell anybody what to play. I'd never tell anybody what to play. You don't invite people into the room just because of the instrument they play; you're inviting them in because they're bringing a lifetime of experience.

Another musical mystery—earworms, when a melody gets stuck in your head. And I have listened to so many of your songs, but the one that haunts me the most is "Odetta." It is an extraordinary song.

Thank you. People have asked me, "Is that song about Odetta?" Well, I only know one Odetta, and so do you. It's not her story, but the character in the song, I really think is just calling upon her countenance for good courage. And the character's in some kind of struggle, and he's—like a lot of us—looking for some kind of affirmation, and in this case, he's looking to her, who's not on this earth anymore.

It's a wonderful song. It's almost like a prayer to Odetta.

That's how it felt to me.

And Odetta, like Woody and Pete, has kind of a holy quality to her. These are our saints.

People tended to talk about her, even when she was still alive, that she was an ethereal, spiritual rock.

Yeah, you hear that in her voice, the soul in her singing. In your song I so loved the second chord in the chorus, on her name. Which is an A major. The song is in G, and you go to the A, which would normally be minor but here it is major, which is such a great sound. When you come up with something like that, are you thinking in terms of the chords, or is it just pure sound?

As much as possible, again, I try to be thinking about the sound. Again, playing in open tunings has allowed me to be a lot freer. For whatever reason I can reach for what I hear a lot more easily than when I'm in a standard tuning and thinking I need to know the name of the next chord I'm going to land on.

You were saying you don't think of songs beforehand; you discover them. You had no concept of writing a song about Odetta or with that title?

One day I woke up and I just heard her name, and then I thought that that would be a really good name to sing. I have a number of songs that have in their title a reference to some cultural figure or songs that reference culturally known people. I have a song called "Curt Flood."

Yeah.

A sixties baseball player, African American baseball player who took a stand against the baseball owners. And I have a song called "Edgar Bergen," and I wrote a song very important to me called "Richard Pryor Addresses a Tearful Nation." So that day Odetta's name was in my mind, and I just thought, "Oh, I need to create something that allows me to sing her name out." I don't know whether chickens came. [*Laughs*]

Did you write a book as well, about Richard Pryor, with that title?

I did. It was not called that; it was called *Furious Cool*. My brother David and I wrote a book. It's not a traditional biography of Richard Pryor; it's as much a cultural study trying to look at the world that he came out of.

Did the song come first, before the book?

The song came first. The quickest way I can tell the story is that I wrote the song "Richard Pryor Addresses a Tearful Nation" when I was listening to a lot of Sinatra. I listen to a lot of Sinatra, all the time.

Really?

All the time. And I was trying to write something that was going to be orchestral and like this languid blues, but not a rocking blues. I wanted to do an orchestral, sort of Ellington blues piece. And that worked, at least initially, with the vocabulary of the standard. I've written a lot of songs that I think began in the mode of what we think of as standards. I wrote this song, and very quickly I was into it. I was singing in the first person, as I almost always do, but for whatever reason I realized really early on—I was driving in a car and hearing this first verse unspool and realizing that I thought the "I" in the song was Richard Pryor, and that he was lamenting something and that what he was really at odds with was his place with this country, desiring its acceptance but also being completely at odds with its culture.

I wasn't intellectual about it; I'm just thinking this was an instinctive thought. And I went deeper into it, thinking, "Okay, if it's going to be about a character as volatile as Richard, and it's going to be this languid, orchestral blues, I need some musician, some musical voice to sit in the middle of this and represent the magnitude of Richard's importance and the chaos at the heart of his life."

And just as a bookmark, to identify the idea, I thought, "You know, I need an Ornette Coleman to be a soloist against this orchestra." The next day, just serendipitously, I had an in to Ornette Coleman. So I created the song around this moment of Ornette playing, still, to my ear, the most raw blues I ever heard in my life.

I was on a label owned by Disney, and they wanted nothing to do with me using Richard Pryor's name without his permission because they were so afraid of him as a volatile character, even though I had a song on the same album called "Edgar Bergen." Ain't no problem with that. [*Laughs*] But what they did was they forced me to find Richard, and I became friendly with Richard, and he gave me his permission to use his name in the song.

Even writing a song about Richard Pryor or Curt Flood is different than how it was. As you know, back in the days when Sinatra was young, almost all songs were about love, except Broadway musicals. Then along came Dylan and other people who showed you could write a song about anything, really. It changed it. You're known for writing about really adventurous content and content that hasn't been in songs before. Can a song contain any content?

I've never encountered an idea that couldn't be musical, I don't think. There are some words that just aren't musical. If I'm writing a poem, I understand that it's something different than a song, that sometimes I can take something that began as a poem and then find a way to mutate it into a song, rob its bones and make a song out of it. Because I know what to do with a song; I don't always know what to do with a poem. But they show up as different animals.

So there's words sometimes. I would think, "If this was a poem, that would be the right word. If this is a song, it's not the right word." That's not a musical word coming off my tongue. It's not rhythmically what this phrase needs. A different dynamic at play.

Often songwriters are called poets. Even you have been.

Well, usually that's a little bit of a backhanded compliment, I think. When people say, "You know, you're not just a songwriter, you're a poet," what they're really saying is, "That's really pretty, and I don't know what you're talking about." [*Laughs*]

Yes. And there's the idea that a poet is a more elevated job than a songwriter.

Yes. I think a great song is as great and as powerful as any great poem. So the idea that you get elevated to the top of the totem pole by being a poet—I think there's no higher place for me than songwriter.

I'm with you.

As long as it's a powerful song.

Absolutely.

But people have a tendency, because they have such a skittish relationship with poetry, so many people do—then they sort of elevate it just to keep it away from them [*laughs*] and protect themselves from it, like power lines. Keep them way up there so you won't get hurt. [*Laughs*]

Back to that idea of if there's a subject that's not approachable, I think there's nothing that's not approachable in song. Buckminster Fuller was an amazing mind, a poet, architect, inventor, philosopher, every such thing. And I always remember him saying, you walk out on the beach, you get lost out on the beach—he takes a stick and he draws a circle in the sand. He knows he's drawing a small circle. He doesn't realize he's also drawing a big one. And everything in the circle. And you also just described everything outside of the circle. So I think with song, you can imply a lot. I really believe in specificity, being really detailed.

I remember when I was producing a record for the great Irish songwriter Lisa Hannigan, who I just think the world of, and she was writing a song, and a question she had of the opening line of the song, if it should be "in the winter" or "in December." I said, "Oh, absolutely in December." Put them in a very particular place, not a vague notion. If you're in doubt, details are what hooks people in because it's more intimate to say what something actually is than to allude to a vague abstraction. Keith Richards wrote "Angie"—you attach a name. You don't have to know who Angie is. There's an intimacy to calling out her name, and that detail is the great hook.

Yes. And that's one reason I love your songs so much, because they're so rich with detail. You can create a song that has a sense of time and place just like a novel. There's no limit to what you can do. There are so many songs that almost don't even have nouns in them, songs such as "Emotions." Or "Feelings." As in "I'm feeling feelings."

Yeah. It's very vague.

But some people think if you're too specific, you're likely going to lose the audience.

I think there's a difference between leaving things open and being vague. Nobody's seduced by vague, and every song needs to seduce in some way. I don't only mean in a romantic way. But if you make people believe that the story you're telling is a real story, not a conceit, they're much more inclined to listen.

You mentioned the novel. I happen to think that for anybody learning to be a songwriter out in the world as a practicing songwriter, I think it's really limiting to only talk about songwriting in terms of other songwriters. I will say in all honesty that when I was twenty-two, Gabriel García Márquez did to me what Bob Dylan did to me when I was eleven. And it was just as real, and it impacted my musicality absolutely as powerfully. It remains with me as powerfully as Bob's turning the key for me in whatever way his work did. I find sometimes that when we're talking about songwriting it's almost too on-the-nose to talk only about other songs. When I'm in the studio making a record, if we need to reference something, I almost never reference another record while I'm trying to make a record.

Is that right?

It's just too on-the-nose. You're not offering any new perspective. I reference film all the time.

Do you think there are still new places for songs to evolve to and new kinds of songs and new places to go with songs?

Oh, I have to believe it. But also, I don't think in terms of "new" as means we must invent a new form or a new language. Think of the ways in which a song is a delivery system. You could be a genius and create an entire new language of your own, and nobody would understand you. But the idea of using language that we share to then say whatever you want, and the thought is what expands—that's what takes us into someplace we haven't been before, not coming up with a radically new musical form.

For instance, the blues form has held up. It's durable like a haiku or a sonnet is durable. We understand that form itself has authority. The blues form of two pairs—a couplet that repeats and then another couplet that puts paid to it or puts a new light on it or puts it on its ear in some way. That is a really powerful form, and we keep going back to that in some way. So I don't really think it's about that we've stopped inventing; I just think we might have got a little bit bogged down in focusing our inventive energies on the new technology of how music gets recorded and passed around.

I read you said once that your wife, Melanie, had really good instincts, and she heard your song "Stop" and she said, "This might be a song for my sister to sing." And her sister happens to be Madonna.

Yes, she did. I've always had a great relationship with [Madonna], and for many years I believed that the reason I had a great relationship with her is I never asked her for anything. If she ever saw me coming, I didn't have my hand out. I considered my sister-in-law's and mine to be completely different lines of work. And it was tricky, because when I got married, Madonna was the only professional musician her father knew, so he looked at me and thought, "You're trying to do that, and you're failing miserably." [*Laughs*]

I'd say, "You know, that's not where I'm going." But anyway years went by, and I never tried to pitch a song to her over the Thanksgiving table or anything. But when I wrote the song "Stop"—and it's one of those things that happened in about twenty minutes—we had just moved house and I had set up a new studio in our little guest house in South Pasadena, and I needed something to record. I'd set up the room, and I thought, "Well, the only way to find out whether everything's working is to just start recording something and see where I hit a snag. See where a line is not connecting." I could have done a cover of something, but I just thought, "Well, I'd better just write something up, and then I will just record it." And it happened really fast. I invited Melanie to come out and hear it, and I remember I thought it was so trivial that I was blushing. I was embarrassed by it.

Madonna was in London working on a new record at the time, and Melanie said, "You know, I don't know why—I really think that she could do this song." And I said, "Well, if I was going to pitch something to her, I have some things I would pitch, but it wouldn't be this." She goes, "Well, will you burn me a copy of it?" I said, "Sure."

So she FedExed it to her sister, and thirty-six hours later I get a call from Madonna. "What are you doing with this song?" "I'm not doing anything with it. It's on a pile." You know, songs go on a pile until I need them. And she said, "Can I do something with it?" And of course I said, "Knock yourself out, sister." [*Laughs*]

And I never heard any more about it. She's just that way. A month went by, and then Christmas Eve I got an e-mail from her wishing us Merry Christmas, and she said, "P.S. I recorded your song. I hope you'll like it." I did. [*Laughs*]

It's funny how many people asked me about it later—because it's so radically different from my version of it—how many people are so willing to assume that you'd be offended that somebody did something with your song other than what you would do with your song. People said, "Oh, so what did you think of that?" I said, "What do you think I thought of it?" It's like the sound of my children's teeth being straightened. [*Laughs*] It's the greatest thing I've ever heard.

It's interesting: she changed it around and she made a part into the chorus that wasn't the chorus and gave it a different title.

Yeah. But every word of it was from my original. I wrote it like a tango, and when I recorded it on the album *Scar*—that has the "Richard Pryor" song on it—we recorded it and put orchestration on, and it's played like a tango. But she went somewhere else with it entirely, as I hoped that she would. And it was a great lesson for me. I didn't hear where there was a chorus; there's no chorus in my version of the song. But she took a pair of lines and repeated them like a chorus, and that became her thing. I didn't hear that.

She's in [Volume I] of *Songwriters on Songwriting*. People don't know that she's a songwriter, but she's quite a talented songwriter and good at taking elements like that and putting stuff together.

She's an alchemist, you know? She's not only a fine songwriter; it's not all that she is. In the way that she constructs songs, she's supernaturally gifted in some ways. I hesitate to compare her to Bob Dylan, and I certainly don't, as far as their intention, not as far as their writing, I don't. She's better. [*Laughs*] When *Highway 61* happened, you can still go back to that and understand; you can hear all the pieces. You can hear Jimmy Reed and you can hear Hank Williams and you can hear the beat poets. He just put them in a cocktail shaker in a way that nobody had and shook it up and poured it out, and we all drank from it. He didn't invent any of those elements, those varying elements. It's like salt—it's a mineral that was around in the earth—those reference points.

And Madonna, in a similar creative way, is really great at, "This person who is doing this with rhythm and this person is doing this with lyric and this person is doing this coming out of hip-hop music." She's really gifted at taking those elements and reassembling them in ways that become new because we've never had that perspective of those elements before.

I've written at this point four songs with her that she has recorded. And we've never sat in a room passing the guitar around. We did it in front of a fire once in England; I was playing old folk songs or something. I don't know, but she was just into that. But as far as writing something, we have never been in a room trying to do it. I've sent her something that I had known that she thought was interesting. I would say, "Here. This might interest you," and she'll run away with it, because that's how our collaborations have happened.

I used to have a ritual, because every time I heard that playing in a department store, I bought a pair of shoes. [*Laughs*]

So you've got a lot of shoes now?

I've got a few shoes.

♦♦♦

Sia

On a Chandelier

Hollywood, California 2014

It was hearing Sia sing "Chandelier" over and over in a sound check that introduced this song into my head and my heart. I was outside in Hollywood, behind the former Masonic Temple on Hollywood Boulevard, now the home of *Jimmy Kimmel Live*, the nightly ABC late-night talk show. Musical artists performing on the show often film their segment on a big outdoor stage set up between their building and Hollywood High School.

The song had yet to become the cultural phenomenon it became, and it was the first time I heard it. From the start I was entranced. Her great vocal leap to the start of each chorus, to "I'm gonna swing on a chandelier . . ." is one of the most dramatic melodic ascensions since Tom Petty's "Free Fallin'," which does the same thing, leaping a full octave in range to lift that chorus—and the song—into a whole other realm, one of anthemic passion. It's a beautifully and classically structured melodic hurtle, both triumphant and anthemic. Hearing her sing it over and over only affirmed what I felt from the start: this is a remarkable song here, performed by a powerfully soulful singer.

But what I didn't understand is why she stood toward the back of the stage, facing away from the audience as she performed. And why, in her stead, a young female sprite of a dancer took center stage.

I also didn't understand that this chandelier-swinging song worked on two levels at once. That although it resounded like a perfect party anthem, it was deceptive. And as I came to discover, with delight, it's an antiparty anthem, that it's not about the joy of swinging on chandeliers but about the darkness of addiction, the false sense of bravado that drinking can create. It's about drowning out the world and all surrounding concerns to live instead for this one night "like tomorrow doesn't exist."

She was born Sia Kate Isobelle Furler in Adelaide, Australia, in 1975. Her first band was the Australian acid jazz ensemble called Crisp. From there she did some solo work and the duo Zero 7. She went solo again and released several solo albums, including *Some People Have Real Problems* (2008), *We Are Born* (2010), and *1000 Forms of Fear* (2014), from which came "Chandelier."

That such a song could become a monster hit is a good sign for this music business, which often enables unworthy contenders to reach the top of the charts. There are weak songs that are tremendously catchy records and catch fire all the time. But to have a song like "Chandelier," not unlike "Umbrella" by Terius "Dream" Nash, performed by Rihanna, soar to these heights shows us that people still love a powerfully constructed melody wed to a compellingly dark lyric. This is Randy Newman territory, as the narrator of "Chandelier" is untrustworthy yet delivering her message with music as beautifully seductive as the music in "Sail Away," Randy's beautiful invitation to America sing to potential slaves by a slave trader. It's a marriage of opposites, which is often more powerful in song than a marriage of words and music that match in every way.

Sia, though, the world has come to learn, is not comfortable facing the camera and emoting while singing her heart out, as she does in this song. It's one of the reasons she resisted being the singer of her own songs for so long, preferring to write them and have Rihanna or another popular artist do the singing. And she wrote "Chandelier" with Rihanna in mind, but when she heard the sound of her own voice on the demo she recorded, she realized, as she explains in the following discussion, that this was a song for her to sing herself.

To answer the questions everyone asked about why she didn't want to do what is the dream of so many—to face the camera, to accept fame—she wrote an "Anti-Fame Manifesto" for *Billboard* in 2013, in which she explained why she didn't want to be a famous person. "Imagine the stereotypical highly opinionated, completely uninformed mother-in-law character and apply it to every teenager with a computer in the entire world," she wrote. "Then add in all bored people, as well as people whose job it is to report on celebrities. Then, picture that creature, that force, criticizing you for an hour straight once a day, every day, day after day. That's what it's like, even the smallest bit of it. Of course, that's if you even allow yourself to stay in touch with the world using public media. If I were famous, I wouldn't."

She added, "I've worked with a lot of famous people, and I've seen a lot of their mothers-in-law. And I can tell from what I've seen that I don't want one of my own. I've worked with a lot of artists who have mothers-in-law, and on occasion I've inherited their family. Even that is not something I'm interested in. I have a family I love. They tend to say, 'Great job!' Or 'You work really hard! Good for you!' Or 'You look nice today!' Or 'Don't be ridiculous—order the fries!' Or 'You are hilarious.' That's all the family I need. So me and fame will never be married."

But how do you get around the need to perform on TV? Every show wanted her when the song became a hit, including *Saturday Night Live*, *Jimmy Kimmel Live*, *The Ellen DeGeneres Show*, and others. She said yes to each but with the unprecedented requirement that she not be forced to face the camera. Instead, she proposed, she would have the eleven-year-old dancer Maddie Ziegler (discovered at the age of eight on the TV show *Dance Moms*) perform an interpretive dance to the song, while she, Sia, sang toward the back of the stage, facing backward. This was how she performed on each of these shows, linking to the music video of the song, which also stars Maddie. So striking and unusual was this approach that it was quickly mocked on TV—Jim Carrey did his version of the dance on *SNL*, as did others. And on the 2014 Grammys, for which the song was nominated for Best Song of the Year, the song was performed again in this style, but this time Maddie was joined by Kristen Wiig.

This led many to conclude that it was all a gimmick, that Sia turned away not out of any genuine need to do so but simply to garner attention. Which isn't the case. People often assume the worst of those in the public eye, especially in showbiz, but what this was in fact was a brilliant solution to the stage fright that has crippled so many great artists. Whoever knew that facing away was even an option? Well, Miles Davis did, often performing with his back to the audience. But Miles, though a genius, was also considered crazy. But Sia did what she did so she could reach those stratospheric notes in the chorus without being self-conscious of what she looked like while doing it and bringing us this song of triumph and vulnerability with purity. After all, it's not an easy song to sing. Yet on each of these performances, as Maddie danced up a little storm, Sia sang stunningly and brought it home each time.

But she enjoys facing journalists as much as facing the camera and resisted doing this talk. Eventually a solution was found—we would do the interview by e-mail. I sent my questions to her publicist, suggesting she skip any she didn't want to answer, and waited. Two days later the e-mail came back, and she'd answered every one.

How was "Chandelier" born?

Sia: I was playing around on the piano in Greg [Kurstin]'s studio when Jesse [Shatkin] came in and started playing on the marimba. I recorded it on my phone and sent it to Jesse, who built the track over a few days. He sent it back to me and I wrote the lyrics, thinking it'd be good for Rihanna. I recorded the lead vocal on it for the demo. But once I had recorded the vocals, however, and we heard the sound of it, I realized I had accidentally written a pop song for myself. I felt I couldn't give it away.

Where did the title come from? Did you have it before starting the song?

Yes. Often if I find or see a word or object that I think could make a strong title or concept, I add it to my "song ideas" list in my notes. That was one I had in there.

Jesse is credited as cowriter. You said he made the track. But did he also write the song?

I think I wrote the chords, but Jesse brought *so* much to the table with production. So I gave him 25 percent of the songwriting credit for his mad genius.

It is such an amazing chorus. Truly one of the most beautiful and triumphant choruses in pop music.

Thank you! It really just fell out of me that way.

At first it sounds like a song of triumph, of pure celebration. But then we realize there's more there—it's a song of escaping. Was that part of the original idea?

Well, when I saw a chandelier, I remember thinking that I could write a song about swinging from the chandelier. A party anthem of some sort. But as I was writing it, it turned into a song about my battles with addiction, inadvertently. And so that is where I took it.

You have sung vocals on other demos of songs you wrote and then gave away to Rihanna or other singers. What was it about this one that made you want to do it yourself?

I sat down with the intention to write for Rihanna, but as the song took shape I realized it was personal and that I was attached to it somehow. My intuition told me to sing it myself.

Is it true you'd rather write songs than perform?

Yes, that is true. Performing takes so much time and energy, and I would rather devote that time to writing songs and making records and putting out my music into the world.

◆ ◆ ◆

Matisyahu
Darkness into Light
New York, New York 2012

He radiates an ecstatic, timeless spirit, a connection to ancient, beautiful wisdom, both in his music and his performances. His is a courage of creative proportions unlike really any songwriter before him or since, a bridge to a whole world in song almost universally untouched, emerged whole from a miracle wedding at the intersection of what's most modern with that which is ancient.

He was clothed at first in the Hasidic garb of a rabbi but wrapped deeply by the music of his soul, a delicately dynamic union of reggae and hip-hop with melodics informed by both the jukebox and the shul. Out came beautiful exhortations of Jewish wisdom, reflecting on modern times and subjects rarely broached in popular song, even by legions of Jewish songwriters—the Jewish experience itself.

So the assumption that he is more holy prophet than earthbound human is an easy one to make. In fact, he's both. He is human—and a very funny, brilliant, and exultant one. He is also deeply religious and in love with the infinite and always unfolding wisdom that he first discovered as a teenager and has inspired and informed his life ever since. He's all this and more. He is Matisyahu. Friends call him Matis. His is a story and a career utterly unlike any in the annals of American popular song.

None of which would matter if the songs themselves weren't imbued with greatness. But they are. And have been since the start. Passionate, triumphant invitations to open new doors abounded at the electric intersection of techno-reggae tinged with hip-hop, deliciously deep-pocket beatboxing, and the romantic, ecstatic wisdom of a devoted student of life and lover of wisdom both brand new and ancient.

> *Givin' myself to you now from the essence of my being*
> *And I sing to my God, songs of love and healing*
> *I want Moshiach now, time it starts revealing*
> **("King Without a Crown," Matisyahu)**

After all, the chief mantra for Jews who emigrated here from Eastern Europe at the dawn of the twentieth century was *assimilation*. To gently melt in the big melting pot. To blend in. If you've got a yarmulke, wear it in temple on Shabbos (the Sabbath), but not on the street. And if you're a songwriter, such as George or Ira Gershwin, Harold Arlen, Yip Harburg, or Irving Berlin, don't focus on temple music; write songs for the masses. For America. And so Berlin famously, in "White Christmas," took Christ out of Christmas and made it about snow. All the other Jewish songwriters wrote great Christmas songs, such as Livingston and Evans (interviewed in *SOS I*), who wrote "Silver Bells." Berlin also famously wrote a beautiful love song to America in which he invoked the creator, bringing religion and state together forever: "God Bless America."

Such has been the tradition of Jews writing songs in America: submerging the Jewish identity. Even among the next generation of Jewish songwriters, such as Bob Dylan, Paul Simon, Randy Newman, Leonard Cohen, and others, rarely is Judaism directly mentioned. In "Ring Them Bells," Dylan offers, "Ring them bells so the world will know that God is one." But that's about the extent of it, whereas he also devoted several albums of songs to Christ.

Matis, though, from the start has proudly and bravely examined the Jewish journey and the meaning of this ancient identity in songs of stunning courage and deep passion. Whereas many Jewish scholars and writers would condemn any reference to the Holocaust in secular song, Matis shed arcane chains to shine a light even into this darkest, most forbidden place:

Rebuild the temple and the crown of glory
Years gone by, about sixty
Burn in the oven in this century
And the gas tried to choke but it couldn't choke me
("Jerusalem," Matisyahu)

His courage transcends the art. By recently shedding his iconic beard and stepping away from the Brooklyn sect to which he long belonged, he has angered those who feel he's abandoned Judaism itself. Which he hasn't. (Nor has he committed to being beardless. "The world has not seen the last of my facial hair," he said.)

Asked why he walked away, knowing many would interpret it as abandoning Judaism itself, he said, "I used to think that being devout meant following a lot of rules. And that if you simply followed all the rules, you would reach the goal. But now I know it isn't about rules. And it isn't easy. People will believe what they believe. I haven't abandoned my faith, and those who understand me know that."

Born Matthew Miller in West Chester, Pennsylvania, in 1979, he grew up in White Plains, New York. He became a Phishhead, following Phish around the country, and became Matisyahu in 2004. Clothed in the garb of a Hasidic rabbi, he created stunning streams of spiritual exhortation in remarkable songs such as "Jerusalem," King Without a Crown," and others.

Opening for Phish in 2004, he was introduced to a world that had never before experienced anything remotely like him. Many presumed he was a novelty act until they witnessed the heartfelt authenticity of his work.

On *Light*, he brought astounding epics like "Darkness into Light" as well as one of the most beautiful songs about peace ever written, "One Day," which resides along side Lennon's "Imagine" as a classic song of peace. Adopted as the official song of peace for the 2010 Olympics, it's a song that proves there's nothing this man can't do.

Akeda is his most recent album, a collection of expansive and remarkable spiritual journeys such as "Reservoir," which explodes the song form into many directions at once, unified by soul and spirit focus.

He's one with whom any conversation seems incomplete. So what follows is by no means the ultimate dialogue with Matis. But it is a start. On a cold winter night in New York we began.

You've spoken about being conscious in your work. How conscious was your decision to go in the music direction in which you've gone?
Matisyahu: It was a natural, organic outgrowth of my life.

I know you were a big Phish fan. Was there other music you loved growing up?

I was always very passionate about music from being a kid listening to Michael Jackson and listening to my parent's records, like Paul Simon's *Graceland* and some really classic music. And then a lot of pop music in the eighties. I always loved music. Phish, I guess, was really a life-changing musical experience I had when I was about sixteen. I got introduced to their music and really connected with it and realized that's what I wanted to do in my life, to make my own music.

How did you make that happen?

I guess I started out—I didn't know exactly what I wanted to do—I started writing poetry and lyrics, and I started singing songs that I liked, Bob Marley songs, and then I started beatboxing. That was a big thing for me. At a certain point I got really into the beatboxing and realized I could create music just with my voice and without an instrument. I started to really get into that and practicing beats and melodies. And then I started performing with different people, friends, and putting little bands together, little acoustic shows.

How did you get so good at beatboxing?

I started doing it in high school, in party settings with friends who were rapping. And I was beatboxing, and I really enjoyed it and got really into it. And when I started listening to Phish I found myself when I was alone or walking I started writing songs through beatboxing. And I'd record them. I spent a bunch of time just trying to create music through the beatboxing.

Your songs have a very spiritual message. Was that what you did from the start?

It was always a spiritual message or some kind of spiritual consciousness, even before the time I was religious. Growing up in a relatively secular household, as a teenager I got into spirituality, and then I wrote from that place. Also, my mentor, my hero for songwriting, was Bob Marley. Those were the kinds of songs I wanted to write, that had meaning, wisdom, consciousness, and, those days, listening to Bob Marley, a lot of quotations from the Bible. Even though I didn't have that much knowledge, I had some understanding of Judaism, and I started to incorporate my Jewish identity and Jewish imagery, just like Rastafarian imagery, into my lyrics.

What brought you to Marley's music, and what about it spoke to you?

I don't know how I got introduced to it. I must have been in high school and an older kid played me some of his music. I don't remember how exactly I got into it; I remember at some point I really felt really passionate about it. I am sure there were a lot of reasons why his music spoke to me, but the biggest reason is when you hear something that resonates inside of you in such a powerful way, it's just truth, and the words, they come out.

What is your writing process?

It depends. "King Without a Crown" came from a certain melody that occurred when I was singing. I went into the studio and I sang the melody, and we played it out, put chords to it. I beatboxed the beat into the microphone, and we copied the beat with programmed drums. Then we added a few parts, and once we had a basic track, we looped it, and then I started writing stream of consciousness for about thirty minutes. And then I went into the booth and just kind of spit it all out without constructing it too much. And that was the first recording of "King Without a Crown," which developed when I had my first trio. We kind of created more parts, a solo section, and different parts. And that developed into something else.

My process has been really different for different songs. On the last record there was a song that came out on the *Shattered* EP called "Two Child One Drop" a year ago. On that, my guitar player came over, and we'd record these jam sessions where we'd play for forty-five minutes straight, an hour—

You're singing and he's playing?

Yeah. He'll play guitar with his pedals and a lot of different sounds. And then I'll sing and beatbox. And when I beatbox, it's bass line; it's drums and other melodic parts. And then we'd listen back to it and we'd find one part we really liked, which was a very simple bass line with a beat—the thing I was singing. So we'd loop that, and then a friend of mine who was a producer with this group The Glitch Mob came out, and we sort of programmed glitch sounds and drums to that. And then I brought in a bass player to play a bass line. I bring in people who I know their taste and who have a certain style or feel they want on a record. So I reach out to different people depending on what that is. Then we went in and I wrote lyrics.

The lyrics were based on a process for me, sort of a two-year process, a study of a certain story and a sort of Kabbalistic, mystical Hasidic philosophical ideas behind that, and then creating an actual story. So I put in lyrics and brought in the producer, and we had Sly and Robbie lay down real drums and bass. And in the track we combined beatboxing with programmed real drums.

A lot of the *Shattered* record was made that way, bringing in different sounds and styles mixed together. So my point is that my process can run the gamut from something that comes together from a stream of consciousness, real free-flowing, to being a real process where a song, the whole process, can take two years.

So generally, when we see other names on your songs, those are people who bring in different musical elements, but you write the words yourself?

It happens all ways. I have a cowriter for the words. A teacher, Ephraim Rosenstein. We study together, and before a record we'll study and have a certain focus. On the last record we spent two years developing the concepts behind it. And then I will elaborate those concepts into song lyrics. But a lot of the original words that were used in our teachings I will sometimes use, and then I will credit him as a cowriter.

Are these teachings from the Torah?

From the Torah and also not. We look at mainly ideas about existentialism and God. Our starting point is usually within the Jewish canon, the first rabbis, philosophers, writers, mystics, sages. Then we try to cut away and get to the core of what it is they are saying about the world and about God. And then we spend time in meditation, really delving deeply into ideas and trying to write songs about it.

So many great songwriters are Jews, from Irving Berlin and the Gershwins through Dylan, Simon, Leonard Cohen, and beyond. Yet they rarely if ever wrote songs that mentioned being Jewish. Yet you started at this place they have mostly avoided.

Yes. When I was a teenager and I started to write songs I was writing about spiritual ideas. And when I came across classic texts, whether it was Hasidic texts from hundreds of years ago or whether it was line quotations from psalms or from the Torah, I would find certain lines that could really be sparkplugs for me. And I would develop songs around them. So most of my writing was inspired by the texts and the ideas, and then in terms of the *style* now, that I was writing in, that was initially informed mainly by reggae music—you know, Bob Marley or a lot of conscious reggae artists that are out there and were the ones who were able to bring those ideas out in the most authentic way.

And that music adds such a grace and beauty to the message you are delivering.

Thank you.

As everyone knows, reggae music stems from Rastafarianism and the smoking of weed. You wrote, "I don't need no sensimilla," and you've taken on reggae music but not that aspect of it. Does that dynamic confuse people who love reggae?

I guess, you know, what's happened is music in general and ideas and inspiration have become pretty generic over the years. There are reggae artists who have their song about smoking weed and their song about Jah and their song about natural living. I think that the original Bob Marley, in his canon of lyrics and words and ideas, it's so much deeper and more authentic than that. That is what I was looking toward. If there were certain ideas I didn't jive with, I didn't feel I needed to dwell on them just to make authentic reggae music. It wasn't about that for me.

Your closeness to Marley is powerful. Your record of his "Redemption Song" is beautiful, and it sounds like it's your song.

Thank you. I think that's how it is, how I always felt: when you have a music connection or a soul connection to a certain piece of music, then you totally immerse yourself in it. You kind of go through what that artist was going through when they were writing or singing that song.

Your song "One Day" is so beautiful. How did that come together?

My record was pretty much finished, and I went back into the studio to work with some guys who had produced a song that I really, really loved by an artist called K'naan called "Wavin' Flag." And I really liked the style of that song, and I felt, since the time I had started, I wanted to make a song like that. A very accessible and basic song about hope. With a big beat and a nice chord change. Simple. So I went into the studio specifically to create that type of song. The guys I worked with were really good at doing that.

It has a beautiful simplicity in its music and message. Reminds me of "Imagine." Was Lennon or The Beatles an influence on you?

It really wasn't, actually. It wasn't until a little later that I got into The Beatles a bit.

How about Bob Dylan?

Yeah, I did. I loved a lot of his earlier, classic works. It wasn't that big of an influence for me.

Did the words to "One Day" come quickly?

Yes. Very quickly.

Is that how it usually happens—the words come quickly?

Yeah. There's the back-end development of construction and a whole educational process behind the songs. So it depends. At that point I had kind of exhausted my journey and my studying for the record, so this was a summation. Going for a very basic idea.

When words come quickly like that, do you have any thought as to where that comes from and how to control the process?

A big part of it is the music. I think when it's one of those things when you turn on the track or the music, the words sort of write themselves, and it comes very easily. And certain ideas make themselves known. And when something comes quickly like that, the music is really the source of inspiration for it.

Your lyrics, unlike the lyrics of many songs, seem quite intentional. They are poetically energized, but your message is clear. Do you bring a lot of conscious intention to the words when writing, or do you get out of the way of that kind of thought?

I try to get out of the way when it's that type of situation. Then it's just about what's the easiest way to let it flow. Whereas other times it's more about calculating and really trying to get down to the core of the idea with very calculated words. The way it works is that I sort of, after studying this story, this process I went through for a couple years, I got together with my teacher and outlined the core ideas that we've explored. And maybe it was twenty-five ideas. And for each of those ideas we had hours and pages of discussion about. We would then try to write it in very intuitive and very primal language. To express each of those ideas in maybe four sentences. Maybe one of those ideas was, for example, Rosh Hashanah. That was the idea, and the question was: What is the philosophical and mystical and spiritual meaning behind Rosh Hashanah? And what was it for this Rebbe, or what was it for this Kabbalist, and how did they differ in terms of their vision of Rosh Hashanah and the creation of the world, the birthday of the world, and God's place in it? And maybe one of them is more connected to the idea of wildness or madness in God creating this world, or tragedy in God, and maybe one is more connected to the idea of a spiritual, scientific-almost outline of how God created the world.

So I pare down these ideas into very primal language, and I was walking around with this packet of ideas, each one maybe a paragraph long. And then when I would go in and write the music and get a basic track together or a rough sketch of the music, I would turn that music on, listen to it to get the inspiration, and then go through my packet and I would say, "Well, the music really lends itself to this specific idea emotionally. It's connecting to this idea." And then I would take that paragraph of intuitive language and I would develop a stream of consciousness, a flow, almost like a rapper would write, based on that idea and those words.

That's a fascinating process because it's a conscious mixture of the conscious deliberate message and the unconscious inspiration, which is always the challenge of songwriting—to put across an idea but with language that is both simple and inspired.

Yes. It's always about trying to get to the core language, the intuitive language. It's not how many words or how big of a vocabulary you have. To me it's really about what's the most basic line that just says it all. Just like poetry.

And I love the freedom in your lyrics, that it's almost free-verse poetry at times. It's so musical but not restricted by conventional song structures or rhyme schemes. Was that a natural progression, to move away from that?

I think it was pretty natural for me.

It's always been interesting to me how many of America's greatest songwriters have been Jews. Do you have any idea why that is?

It's a great question. There's another question too, which is how such a small group of people in numbers have excelled in so many various subjects. There's so many subjects where the Jewish community has excelled: business, the music industry, in psychology. I don't have the answer to that. But I do think that music in general, and things of a spiritual nature, I think there is some kind of link to Judaism in some kind of removed way. I think it's part of our DNA or part of our history of searching and knowing through our spirituality.

◆ ◆ ◆

About the Author

Paul Zollo is a singer-songwriter, author, photographer, and music journalist. Currently the senior editor of *American Songwriter* magazine, he's the author of several books, including *Songwriters on Songwriting* (the first volume), *Conversations with Tom Petty*, *Hollywood Remembered: An Oral History of Its Golden Age*, *The Beginning Songwriter's Answer Book*, and *Schirmer's Complete Rhyming Dictionary*. He's released two CDs as a solo artist of all original material, *Orange Avenue* (which features Art Garfunkel on the song "Being in This World") and *Universal Cure*. He's collaborated with many songwriters, including the late Steve Allen ("Blue Stars"), Severin Browne, Bob Malone, Steve Schalchlin, James Coberly Smith, and Jeff Gold. With Darryl Purpose he's written many songs, including all eleven on Darryl's most recent album, the critically acclaimed *Still the Birds*. He's recently finished his first novel as well as a book of photo essays and is beginning work on a book with Matisyahu. A Chicago native, he lives in Hollywood with his wife, son, and several cats.